SYSTEMS
ANALYSIS and DESIGN
Third Edition

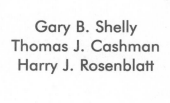

Gary B. Shelly
Thomas J. Cashman
Harry J. Rosenblatt

SHELLY
CASHMAN
SERIES®

COURSE TECHNOLOGY

ONE MAIN STREET

CAMBRIDGE MA 02142

an International Thomson Publishing company   I(T)P®

CAMBRIDGE · ALBANY · BONN · CINCINNATI · LONDON · MADRID · MELBOURNE

MEXICO CITY · NEW YORK · PARIS · SAN FRANCISCO · TOKYO · TORONTO · WASHINGTON

COURSE
TECHNOLOGY

© 1998 by Course Technology — I(T)P®

Printed in the United States of America

For more information, contact:

Course Technology
One Main Street
Cambridge, Massachusetts 02142, USA

International Thomson Editores
Saneca, 53
Colonia Polanco
11560 Mexico D.F. Mexico

ITP Europe
Berkshire House
168-173 High Holborn
London, WC1V 7AA, United Kingdom

ITP GmbH
Konigswinterer Strasse 418
53227 Bonn, Germany

ITP Australia
102 Dodds Street
South Melbourne
Victoria 3205 Australia

ITP Asia
60 Albert Street, #15-01
Albert Complex
Singapore 189969

ITP Nelson Canada
1120 Birchmount Road
Scarborough, Ontario
Canada M1K 5G4

ITP Japan
Hirakawa-cho Kyowa Building, 3F
2-2-1 Hirakawa-cho, Chiyoda-ku
Tokyo 102, Japan

TRADEMARKS

DISCLAIMER

PHOTO CREDITS

Chapter 1: *Figure 1-1* Courtesy of NASA; *Figure 1-6* Tony Freeman/PhotoEdit; *Figure 1-8* Courtesy of Motorola Corporation; *Figure 1-10* David Young-Wolff/PhotoEdit; Chapter 2: *Figure 2-4* David Falconer/Folio; *Figure 2-7* Eric Bazin/Gamma Liaison; *Figure 2-9* John Lund/Tony Stone Images; *Figure 2-14* Bruce Ayres/Tony Stone Images; Bob Schartz/Liaison International, drop; Chapter 3: *Figure 3-3* Tom McCarthy Photos/Folio; *Figure 3-6* Richard Pasley/Stock Boston; *Figure 3-11* Mark Richards/PhotoEdit; Chapter 4: *Figure 4-1* Paul Avis/Liaison International; *Figure 4-15* Courtesy of Land's End; *Figure 4-22* Hank Morgan/Photo Researchers, Inc.; *Figure 4-37* Amy C. Etra/PhotoEdit; Chapter 5: *Figure 5-1* Crandall/The Image Works; *Figure 5-3* B. Bachman/The Image Works; *Figure 5-8* David Young-Wolff/PhotoEdit; *Figure 5-23* The Image Works; Chapter 6: *Figure 6-4* David Young-Wolff/PhotoEdit; *Figure 6-6* Tony Freeman/PhotoEdit; *Figure 6-12* HMS Images/The Image Bank; Chapter 7: *Figure 7-2* Al Cook/Stock Boston; *Figure 7-14* Ermakoff/The Image Works; *Figure 7-15* J. McDermott/Tony Stone Images; *Figure 7-31* B. Daemmrich/The Image Works; Chapter 8: *Figure 8-11* Michael Newman/PhotoEdit; *Figure 8-16* David Weintraub/Stock Boston; *Figure 8-23* David Young-Wolff/PhotoEdit; *Figure 8-41* Richard Pasley/Stock Boston; Chapter 9: *Figure 9-1* Bob Thomas/Tony Stone Images; *Figure 9-4* W. Hill/The Image Works; *Figure 9-13* Tony Freeman/PhotoEdit; *Figure 9-14* Courtesy of The Maytag Corporation; Chapter 10: *Figure 10-1* Kay Chernush/The Image Bank; *Figure 10-9* Frank Herholdt/Tony Stone Images; *Figure 10-10* Ted Kawalerski/The Image Bank; *Figure 10-11* Pedrick/The Image Works; Chapter 11: *Figure 11-1* Gary Gladstone/The Image Bank; *Figure 11-3* HMS Images/The Image Bank; *Figure 11-5* Charlie Westerman/Liaison International; *Figure 11-12* Jeff Smith/The Image Bank; Chapter 12: *Figure 12-1* Michael Grecco/Stock Boston; *Figure 12-2* B. Busco/The Image Bank; *Figure 12-3* Dean Abramson/Stock Boston; *Figure 12-9* D. Brody/Stock Boston.

ISBN 0-7895-4266-8 (Textbook)
ISBN 0-7895-4313-3 (Textbook with Visible Analyst — Student Edition)

4 5 6 7 8 9 10   BC   02 01 00 99 98

CONTENTS

Systems Analysis and Design
Third Edition

Phase 1
Systems Planning

CHAPTER 2
Preliminary Investigation

Phase 2
Systems Analysis

CHAPTER 3
Determining Requirements

CHAPTER 4
Analyzing Requirements

CHAPTER 5
Evaluating Alternatives and Strategies

Phase 3
Systems Design

CHAPTER 6
Output Design

The Systems Analyst's Toolkit

PART 1
Communications Tools

PART 2
Feasibility and Cost Analysis Tools

PART 3
Project Management Tools

PREFACE

Systems Analysis and Design
Third Edition

The Shelly Cashman Series® offers the finest textbooks in computer education. *Systems Analysis and Design, Third Edition* continues with the innovation, quality, and reliability that you have come to expect from this series. We are proud that our previous editions were best sellers, and we are confident that this edition will join its predecessors.

This textbook emphasizes a practical approach to learning systems analysis and design. In it, you will find an educationally sound and easy-to-follow pedagogy that artfully combines full-color pictures, drawings, and text to produce a visually appealing and straightforward presentation of systems analysis and design. The popular Tradeoffs and case studies in each chapter, which encourage critical thinking, have been enhanced significantly. The World Wide Web has been integrated into the textbook to offer students current information and links to Web-based resources. These and other features of the book promise to make your systems analysis and design class exciting and dynamic — one that your students will remember as one of their better educational experiences.

OBJECTIVES OF THIS TEXTBOOK

Systems Analysis and Design, Third Edition is intended for a three-unit introductory Systems Analysis and Design course. The objectives of this book are to:

- Present a practical approach to systems analysis and design using a blend of traditional development with current technologies

- Define and describe in detail the five phases of the systems development life cycle (SDLC): systems planning; systems analysis; systems design; systems implementation; and systems operation and support

- Present the material in a visually appealing, full-color format and an exciting, easy-to-read style that invites students to learn

- Provide students with a comprehensive Systems Analysis Toolkit that highlights the importance of communications, economic analysis, and project planning skills across all phases of the SDLC

- Give students an in-depth understanding of how information systems support business requirements in today's intensely competitive environment
- Make use of the World Wide Web as an online information resource
- Teach real-world systems analysis and design skills in the context of solving realistic problems and present practical guidelines and tips for career success
- Provide a clear picture of how systems analysts interact with users, management, and other information systems professionals in a typical business organization
- Offer interesting case studies and exercises that promote critical-thinking skills and encourage student participation

DETAILED COVERAGE OF FUNDAMENTAL TOPICS

While providing broad coverage of the five phases in the system development life cycle, this book also presents fundamental systems analysis and design topics that should be covered in any introductory systems analysis and design course. Such topics include business information systems concepts; mission statements; strategic planning; feasibility studies; fact-finding techniques; data flow diagrams; structured English; decision tables; decision trees; enterprise computing; make or buy decisions; employee empowerment; prototyping; CASE tools; system flowcharts; the use of codes; report, document, and screen design; reducing input errors; data security; automated design tools; entity-relationship diagrams; cardinality; normalization; database design and management; traditional file organization; online versus batch processing; centralized versus distributed processing; LANs and WANs; client/server systems; software engineering; unit, link, and system testing; documentation; training; system changeover; post-implementation evaluation; support activities; maintenance activities; capacity planning; communications tools; feasibility and cost analysis tools; and project management tools. Each of these topics is covered in detail and is clearly linked to the appropriate phase or phases of the SDLC, so that students understand where they fit within the larger systems development life cycle.

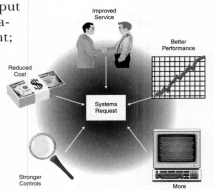

DISTINGUISHING FEATURES

Systems Analysis and Design, Third Edition includes the following distinguishing features.

A Proven Book

This book has evolved over the past fifteen years and is based on our previous best-selling books on systems analysis and design. More than one-half million students have learned about systems analysis and design using the previous editions.

A Blend of Traditional Development with Current Technologies

This book does not present a theoretical view of the systems development life cycle. Every effort has been made to use the tools and techniques that are used by systems analysts in today's dynamic business world.

Numerous realistic examples support all definitions, concepts, and techniques, and examples and case studies are drawn from actual systems projects. This enables students to learn in the context of solving realistic problems. In this textbook, students learn what works in the real world of information technology, and they receive many specific tips for on-the-job success.

This textbook allows students to do systems analysis and design right from the start. They begin their case study work in Chapter 1 and continue to perform systems analysis and design tasks in every chapter that follows.

Visually Appealing

A great deal of effort was expended to combine pictures, drawings, and text into a visually appealing, easy-to-read, full-color textbook. Throughout the book, figures are used to reinforce important points, and the illustrations reflect the latest trends in systems analysis and design. The many color photos are a valuable addition that allows students to see examples of actual people, activities, and other subjects described in the book. The state-of-the-art drawings are geared towards simplifying the more complex concepts. The book's combination of pictures, drawings, text, and a full-color design sets a new standard for systems analysis and design textbooks.

Nontechnical Presentation of Systems Analysis and Design

The text is written to assume no previous systems analysis and design experience and requires no mathematics beyond the high school level. This offers the continuity, simplicity, and practicality that students need and appreciate. Numerous insights, based on the authors' many years of experience in teaching, consulting, management, and writing, are included throughout the book.

Relevant New Case Studies

The case studies at the end of each chapter have been updated and enhanced significantly. The primary objective was to promote active student participation and show how systems analysis and design skills are applied in realistic situations. A continuing case study — SoftWear, Limited — gives students an opportunity to work as a member of a systems development team and perform Your Turn assignments in each chapter. Another continuing case study at the end of each chapter allows students to apply their knowledge and skills to act as a systems analyst and develop an information system for New Century Health Clinic. Many additional cases are provided to illustrate key points and concepts throughout the textbook.

Expanded Coverage of Client/Server Systems

Client/server systems are becoming more prevalent today, and this edition emphasizes their use. As early as Chapter 1, students learn that, in IBM's words, *Knowledge Management Calls for a New Way of Thinking*. This theme is repeated throughout the text, with many examples of how corporations are reengineering their businesses to meet the challenge of global competition. The text describes client/server systems that can allow a company to share data and processing across the organization and provide more efficient, powerful data management.

Integration of the World Wide Web

Each of the previous editions introduced sound educational innovations that separated them from the rest of the market. *Systems Analysis and Design, Third Edition* continues this tradition of innovation with its integration of the World Wide Web. The purpose is to (1) provide examples of Web-based resources that relate to key subjects in the text; (2) link students to up-to-date information on the Web and suggest Internet sites for additional exploration; and, (3) underscore the importance of the World Wide Web as a basic tool that can be used by information systems professionals in all facets of their work. The World Wide Web is integrated into the book in two major ways:

- Throughout the text, marginal annotations provide suggestions on how to obtain additional information via the Web on an important topic covered on the page.
- ON THE NET assignments in each chapter provide an opportunity to search the Web for information and report back the findings.

Latest Analysis and Design Trends

The terms and technologies your students see in this book are those they will encounter when they begin working in the field. New topics and terms include JAD (joint application development), RAD (rapid application development), object-oriented application development, e-commerce, DDBMSs (distributed database management systems), data mining, Web-centric design, enterprise-based computing, data encryption, and natural language queries, among others.

Systems Analyst's Toolkit

The Systems Analyst's Toolkit, which follows Chapter 12, presents communications skills, economic analysis tools, and project planning skills that can be used across the five phases of the SDLC. Topics include guidelines to successful communications, feasibility and cost analysis methodologies, and project management tools. Throughout the twelve chapters, students are reminded to use the Systems Analyst's Toolkit to enhance their understanding of how a task in a particular phase might be completed.

Tradeoffs and Key Questions

In Tradeoff discussions in each chapter, students focus on a key topic that analysts must deal with. Each Tradeoff presents an issue or problem with various alternatives and discusses the advantages and disadvantages of each solution. To reinforce this knowledge, each Tradeoff is followed by a Key Question, usually in the form of a minicase study, which requires students to apply the Tradeoff concepts and select the best approach in a specific fact situation.

Visible Analyst – Student Edition Available with This Book

You can bundle Visible Analyst – Student Edition with the textbook so students can have their own copy to work with in the lab, at home, or in a distance education environment. A review copy of Visible Analyst – Student Edition is available for preview with the Instructor's Resource Kit. Additional information on this powerful CASE tool can be found later in this preface.

ORGANIZATION OF THIS TEXTBOOK

ystems Analysis and Design, Third Edition is organized so students will know clearly where they are and how their progress relates to the systems development process.

Chapter 1 presents the basic organization of the book — a five-phase systems development life cycle approach to conducting a systems project. The chapter also explains how companies use various types of information systems and the role of the systems analyst in typical organizations.

Chapter 2 covers the first phase in the systems development life cycle: systems planning. Students learn about the initiation of systems projects and how to investigate a system and perform a feasibility study.

Chapter 3 focuses on requirements determination and fact-finding tools and techniques, including interviews, questionnaires, document review, observation, sampling, and research.

Chapter 4 features structured analysis, including data flow diagrams, data dictionaries, structured English, decision tables, and decision trees.

Chapter 5 concentrates on evaluating various systems development alternatives, including in-house development versus purchase of a software package. The chapter also discusses the use of prototyping and computer-aided software engineering (CASE) tools.

Chapters 6 and 7 provide a practical, balanced treatment of output and input design. Text-based and graphical user interfaces are covered equally.

Chapter 8 is dedicated to file and database design, including normalization, entity-relationship diagrams, and cardinality.

Chapter 9 covers system architecture, including client/server systems and various processing methods and functions. The chapter also describes the major types of network configurations and design.

Chapter 10 and 11 describe the systems implementation phase. Chapter 10 covers application development and testing, including the role of systems analysts and programmers; Chapter 11 explains the installation and evaluation process and covers training, changeover methods, and post-implementation evaluation.

Chapter 12 is dedicated to the systems operation and support phase of the SDLC and includes topics on various types of system maintenance and support.

Finally, the Systems Analyst's Toolkit is presented following Chapter 12 as a cross-phase resource that will support students as they progress through the textbook. The Toolkit includes guidelines for successful communication, economic analysis, and project management.

VISIBLE ANALYST — STUDENT EDITION

A commercial-grade CASE tool, Visible Analyst – Student Edition, can be bundled with this textbook so each student has a personal copy. The package includes a tutorial manual and software to provide students with an easy-to-use and affordable CASE tool. The ISBN for the textbook and CASE tool bundled together is 0-7895-4313-3.

Visible Analyst — Student Edition includes an Integrated Data, Process, and Object Modeling ToolKit to support the planning, analysis, and design phases of the SDLC and has a fully functional and accessible Repository with extensive reporting capabilities. It includes various cross model analysis, reports, and matrices. Diagram types supported include functional decomposition diagrams, data flow diagrams, entity-relationship diagrams, and structure charts. Model techniques include Yourdon, DeMarco, Constantine, Page-Jones, Gane and Sarson, Chen, Martin, and Bachman. It also allows multiple models to be used for different phases of the SDLC, and system outputs can be included easily in a word processing or desktop publishing package. Because the Visible Analyst — Student Edition also is one of the easiest tools on the market to use, it is perfect for an introductory systems analysis and design course. Visible Analyst — Student Edition includes all the operational and functional capabilities of the professional versions, with the following constraints:

- One Project (running on the single-user system at a time)
- Project is limited to 10 diagrams per type supported
- No import, export, or code-generation capabilities

Adopting schools that bundle Visible Analyst – Student Edition with this textbook can receive up to two free copies from Visible Systems Corporation (800-684-7425, ext. 312), one for each 25 copies sold to the bookstore. Schools also can purchase additional copies (single-user or multiuser configurations) for their laboratory facilities at a minimal price from Visible Systems Corporation whether or not they bundle Visible Analyst — Student Edition with this textbook. For more information, visit www.visible.com or contact your Course Technology representative.

INSTRUCTOR'S RESOURCE KIT

A comprehensive Instructor's Resource Kit (IRK) accompanies this textbook in the form of a CD-ROM. The CD-ROM includes an Electronic Instructor's Manual (called *ElecMan*) and teaching and testing aids. The CD-ROM (ISBN 0-7895-4267-6) is available through your Course Technology representative or by calling one of the following telephone numbers: Colleges and Universities, 1-800-648-7450; High Schools, 1-800-824-5179; and Career Colleges, 1-800-477-3692. The contents of the CD-ROM are listed below.

- **ElecMan (*Electronic Instructor's Manual*)** ElecMan is made up of Microsoft Word 6 files. The files include lecture notes, answers to exercises, and a large test bank of more than 1,300 questions. The files allow you to modify the lecture notes or generate quizzes and exams from the test bank using your own word processor. ElecMan includes the following for each chapter: chapter objectives; chapter overview; detailed lesson plans with page number references; teacher notes and activities; answers to the end-of-chapter exercises and case study questions; test bank of 110 questions for every chapter (50 true/false, 25 multiple-choice, and 35 fill-in-the-blank) with page number references; and transparency references. The transparencies are available through the Figures on CD-ROM described below. The test bank questions are numbered the same as in Course Test Manager. Thus, you can print out a copy of the chapter test bank and use the printout to select your questions in Course Test Manager.

- **Figures on CD-ROM**   Illustrations for every figure in the textbook are available. Use this ancillary to create a slide show from the illustrations for lecture or to print transparencies for use in lecture with an overhead projector.
- **Course Test Manager**   Course Test Manager is a powerful testing and assessment package that enables instructors to create and print tests from the large test bank. In addition, instructors with access to a networked computer lab (LAN) can administer, grade, and track tests online. Students also can take online practice tests, which generate customized study guides that indicate where in the textbook students can find more information for each question.
- **Visible Analyst – Student Edition**   A copy of this powerful CASE tool is available on the IRK for instructor preview. This preview copy runs only from the IRK CD-ROM. For more information on Visible Analyst – Student Edition, see the discussion earlier in this preface.

SHELLY CASHMAN ONLINE

 helly Cashman Online is a World Wide Web service available to instructors and students of computer education. Visit Shelly Cashman Online at www.scseries.com. Shelly Cashman Online is divided into four areas:

- **Series Information**   Information on the Shelly Cashman Series products.
- **The Community**   Opportunities to discuss your course and your ideas with instructors in your field and with the Shelly Cashman Series team.
- **Teaching Resources**   This area includes password-protected instructor materials.
- **Student Center**   Dedicated to students learning about computers with Shelly Cashman Series textbooks and software.

ACKNOWLEDGMENTS

The Shelly Cashman Series would not be the leading computer education series without the contributions of outstanding publishing professionals. First, and foremost, among them is Becky Herrington, director of production and designer. She is the heart and soul of the Shelly Cashman Series, and it is only through her leadership, dedication, and tireless efforts that superior products are made possible.

Under Becky's direction, the following individuals made significant contributions to this book: Peter Schiller, production manager; Ginny Harvey, series specialist and copy editor; Mike Bodnar and Stephanie Nance, graphic artists; Mark Norton, interior illustrations and cover designer; Betty Hopkins interior designer and typographer; Nancy Lamm, proofreader; Sarah Evertson of Image Quest, photo researcher; and Cristina Haley, indexer.

Special thanks go to Jim Quasney, our dedicated series editor; Lisa Strite, senior product manager; Jessica Evans, developmental editor; Lora Wade, associate product manager; Scott MacDonald and Tonia Grafakos, editorial assistants; Jonathan Langdale, online developer; and Sarah McLean, marketing director.

Special thanks go to the reviewers of this book: Sherry Green, Purdue University Calumet; Misty Vermaat, Purdue University Calumet, Clayton Frye, College of the Albemarle; David Collopy, Ohio University–Lancaster; Jeff Hedrington; Carol Jones, Isothermal Community College; and Robert Saldarini, Bergen Community College.

We hope you will find using this book an enriching and rewarding experience.

Gary B. Shelly
Thomas J. Cashman
Harry J. Rosenblatt

SHELLY CASHMAN SERIES — TRADITIONALLY BOUND TEXTBOOKS

T he Shelly Cashman Series presents the following computer subjects in a variety of traditionally bound textbooks. For more information, see your Course Technology representative or call one of the following telephone numbers: Colleges and Universities, 1-800-648-7450; High Schools, 1-800-824-5179; and Career Colleges, 1-800-477-3692.

COMPUTERS

Computers	Discovering Computers: A Link to the Future, World Wide Web Enhanced
	Discovering Computers: A Link to the Future, World Wide Web Enhanced Brief Edition
	Using Computers: A Gateway to Information, World Wide Web Edition
	Using Computers: A Gateway to Information, World Wide Web Brief Edition
	Exploring Computers: A Record of Discovery 2e with CD-ROM
	A Record of Discovery for Exploring Computers 2e
	Study Guide for Discovering Computers: A Link to the Future, World Wide Web Enhanced
	Study Guide for Using Computers: A Gateway to Information, World Wide Web Edition
	Brief Introduction to Computers 2e (32-page)

WINDOWS APPLICATIONS

Integrated Packages	Microsoft Office 97: Introductory Concepts and Techniques, Brief Edition (6 projects)
	Microsoft Office 97: Introductory Concepts and Techniques, Essentials Edition (10 projects)
	Microsoft Office 97: Introductory Concepts and Techniques (15 projects)
	Microsoft Office 97: Introductory Concepts and Techniques Workbook
	Microsoft Office 97: Advanced Concepts and Techniques
	Microsoft Office 95: Introductory Concepts and Techniques (15 projects)
	Microsoft Office 95: Advanced Concepts and Techniques
	Microsoft Office 4.3 running under Windows 95: Introductory Concepts and Techniques
	Microsoft Office for Windows 3.1 Introductory Concepts and Techniques Enhanced Edition
	Microsoft Office: Advanced Concepts and Techniques
	Microsoft Works 4* • Microsoft Works 3.0*
Windows	Introduction to Microsoft Windows NT Workstation 4
	Microsoft Windows 95: Introductory Concepts and Techniques (96-page)
	Introduction to Microsoft Windows 95 (224-page)
	Microsoft Windows 95: Complete Concepts and Techniques
	Microsoft Windows 3.1 Introductory Concepts and Techniques
	Microsoft Windows 3.1 Complete Concepts and Techniques
Word Processing	Microsoft Word 97* • Microsoft Word 7* • Microsoft Word 6* • Microsoft Word 2.0
	Corel WordPerfect 8 • Corel WordPerfect 7 • WordPerfect 6.1* • WordPerfect 6* • WordPerfect 5.2
Spreadsheets	Microsoft Excel 97* • Microsoft Excel 7* • Microsoft Excel 5* • Microsoft Excel 4
	Lotus 1-2-3 97* • Lotus 1-2-3 Release 5* • Lotus 1-2-3 Release 4* • Quattro Pro 6
Database Management	Microsoft Access 97* • Microsoft Access 7* • Microsoft Access 2
	Paradox 5 • Paradox 4.5 • Paradox 1.0 • Visual dBASE 5/5.5
Presentation Graphics	Microsoft PowerPoint 97* • Microsoft PowerPoint 7* • Microsoft PowerPoint 4*

DOS APPLICATIONS

Operating Systems	DOS 6 Introductory Concepts and Techniques
	DOS 6 and Microsoft Windows 3.1 Introductory Concepts and Techniques
Word Processing	WordPerfect 6.1 • WordPerfect 6.0 • WordPerfect 5.1
Spreadsheets	Lotus 1-2-3 Release 4 • Lotus 1-2-3 Release 2.4 • Lotus 1-2-3 Release 2.3
Database Management	dBASE 5 • dBASE IV Version 1.1 • dBASE III PLUS • Paradox 4.5

PROGRAMMING AND NETWORKING

Programming	Microsoft Visual Basic 5*
	Microsoft Visual Basic 4 for Windows 95* (available with Student version software)
	Microsoft Visual Basic 3.0 for Windows*
	QBasic • QBasic: An Introduction to Programming • Microsoft BASIC
	Structured COBOL Programming (Micro Focus COBOL also available)
Networking	Novell NetWare for Users
	Business Data Communications: Introductory Concepts and Techniques, Second Edition
Internet	The Internet: Introductory Concepts and Techniques (UNIX)
	Netscape Navigator 4: An Introduction
	Netscape Navigator 3: An Introduction • Netscape Navigator 2 running under Windows 3.1
	Netscape Navigator: An Introduction (Version 1.1)
	Netscape Composer
	Microsoft Internet Explorer 4: An Introduction
	Microsoft Internet Explorer 3: An Introduction

SYSTEMS ANALYSIS

Systems Analysis	Systems Analysis and Design, Third Edition (available with Visible Analyst — Student Edition)

*Also available as a Double Diamond Edition, which is a shortened version of the complete book

SHELLY CASHMAN SERIES — CUSTOM EDITION® PROGRAM

I f you do not find a Shelly Cashman Series traditionally bound textbook to fit your needs, the Shelly Cashman Series unique **Custom Edition** program allows you to choose from a number of options and create a textbook perfectly suited to your course. Features of the **Custom Edition** program are:

- Textbooks that match the content of your course
- Windows- and DOS-based materials for the latest versions of personal computer applications software
- Shelly Cashman Series quality, with the same full-color materials and Shelly Cashman Series pedagogy found in the traditionally bound books
- Affordable pricing so your students receive the **Custom Edition** at a cost similar to that of traditionally bound books

The table on the right summarizes the available materials.

For more information, see your Course Technology representative or call one of the following telephone numbers: Colleges and Universities, 1-800-648-7450; High Schools, 1-800-824-5179; and Career Colleges, 1-800-477-3692.

For Shelly Cashman Series information, visit Shelly Cashman Online at **www.scseries.com**

COMPUTERS	
Computers	Discovering Computers: A Link to the Future, World Wide Web Enhanced
	Discovering Computers: A Link to the Future, World Wide Web Enhanced Brief Edition
	Using Computers: A Gateway to Information, World Wide Web Edition
	Using Computers: A Gateway to Information, World Wide Web Brief Edition
	A Record of Discovery for Exploring Computers 2e (available with CD-ROM)
	Study Guide for Discovering Computers: A Link to the Future, World Wide Web Enhanced
	Study Guide for Using Computers: A Gateway to Information, World Wide Web Edition
	Introduction to Computers (32-page)

OPERATING SYSTEMS	
Windows	Microsoft Windows 95: Introductory Concepts and Techniques (96-page)
	Introduction to Microsoft Windows NT Workstation 4
	Introduction to Microsoft Windows 95 (224-page)
	Microsoft Windows 95: Complete Concepts and Techniques
	Microsoft Windows 3.1 Introductory Concepts and Techniques
	Microsoft Windows 3.1 Complete Concepts and Techniques
DOS	Introduction to DOS 6 (using DOS prompt)
	Introduction to DOS 5.0 or earlier (using DOS prompt)

WINDOWS APPLICATIONS	
Integrated Packages	Microsoft Works 4*
	Microsoft Works 3.0*
Microsoft Office	Using Microsoft Office 97 (16-page)
	Using Microsoft Office 95 (16-page)
	Microsoft Office 97:Introductory Concepts and Techniques, Brief Edition (396-page)
	Microsoft Office 97: Introductory Concepts and Techniques, Essentials Edition (672-page)
	Object Linking and Embedding (OLE) (32-page)
	Microsoft Outlook 97 • Microsoft Schedule+ 7
	Introduction to Integrating Office 97 Applications (48-page)
	Introduction to Integrating Office 95 Applications (80-page)
Word Processing	Microsoft Word 97* • Microsoft Word 7* • Microsoft Word 6* • Microsoft Word 2.0
	Corel WordPerfect 8 • Corel WordPerfect 7 • WordPerfect 6.1*
	WordPerfect 6* • WordPerfect 5.2
Spreadsheets	Microsoft Excel 97* • Microsoft Excel 7* • Microsoft Excel 5* • Microsoft Excel 4
	Lotus 1-2-3 97* • Lotus 1-2-3 Release 5* • Lotus 1-2-3 Release 4*
	Quattro Pro 6
Database Management	Microsoft Access 97* • Microsoft Access 7* • Microsoft Access 2*
	Paradox 5 • Paradox 4.5 • Paradox 1.0 • Visual dBASE 5/5.5
Presentation Graphics	Microsoft PowerPoint 97* • Microsoft PowerPoint 7* • Microsoft PowerPoint 4*

DOS APPLICATIONS	
Word Processing	WordPerfect 6.1 • WordPerfect 6.0 • WordPerfect 5.1
Spreadsheets	Lotus 1-2-3 Release 4 • Lotus 1-2-3 Release 2.4 • Lotus 1-2-3 Release 2.3
	Quattro Pro 3.0 • Quattro with 1-2-3 Menus
Database Management	dBASE 5 • dBASE IV Version 1.1 • dBASE III PLUS
	Paradox 4.5 • Paradox 3.5

PROGRAMMING AND NETWORKING	
Programming	Microsoft Visual Basic 4 for Windows 95* (available with Student version software) • Microsoft Visual Basic 3.0 for Windows*
	Microsoft BASIC • QBasic
Networking	Novell NetWare for Users
Internet	The Internet: Introductory Concepts and Techniques (UNIX)
	Netscape Navigator 4: An Introduction
	Netscape Navigator 3: An Introduction
	Netscape Navigator 2 running under Windows 3.1
	Netscape Navigator: An Introduction (Version 1.1)
	Netscape Composer
	Microsoft Internet Explorer 4: An Introduction
	Microsoft Internet Explorer 3: An Introduction

*Also available as a mini-module

CHAPTER 1

SDLC PHASES

Phase 1
Systems Planning

Phase 2
Systems Analysis

Phase 3
Systems Design

Phase 4
Systems Implementation

Phase 5
Systems Operation & Support

Introduction to Information Systems

Chapter 1 introduces you to information systems and their components. You will learn how companies use various types of information systems and about the information systems department, including the role of the systems analysts who work there. This chapter also describes the major phases and objectives of the systems development life cycle (SDLC).

OBJECTIVES

When you finish this chapter, you will be able to:

- Describe an information system and explain its components and characteristics
- Identify six common types of business information systems and describe their primary features
- Explain how different levels of a business organization use and handle information
- Describe the phases and objectives of the systems development life cycle
- Explain the use of software tools in the development of information systems
- List the major functions performed by the information systems department
- Discuss a systems analyst's responsibilities, skills, and opportunities

INTRODUCTION

ave you seen headlines like these?

- Enormous Internet Growth Opens Worldwide Markets for U.S. Firms
- The Best of Both Worlds: Client/Server Architecture Meets the World Wide Web
- Even Small Businesses Can Cruise on the Information Highway
- Companies Swap Stories About How They Handled Year 2000 Software Challenges
- Corporate PC Sales Leap as Companies Continue to Empower Lower-Level Employees
- Have Your Computer Call My Computer — New Relationships between Customers and Suppliers
- Powerful Networks Make It Easy for International Partners to Communicate
- Many Firms Hail ISO 9000 Quality Standards as a Global Model for New Software
- Portable Technology Allows Corporate "Road Warriors" to Stay in Touch
- New Security Technology Boosts Confidence in Internet Credit Card Transactions

As these headlines suggest, businesses depend more than ever on computers. In the face of global competition and intense pressure for quality, information technology actually can mean the difference between survival and failure. Having the right computer hardware and software is not enough. What it really takes is a team of talented, motivated people who use information technology to achieve business goals. In its Business Solutions Web site shown in Figure 1-1, IBM summed it up this way: *Knowledge Calls for a New Way of Thinking*.

For more information on **Knowledge Management**, visit Systems Analysis and Design Chapter 1 More on the Web.

www.scsite.com/ sad3e/ch01/

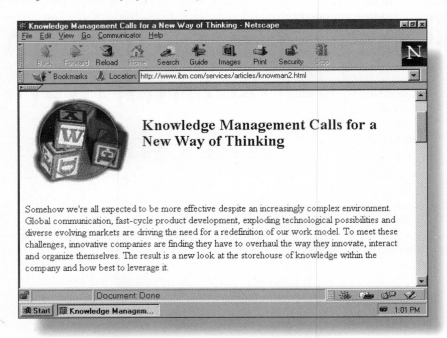

Figure 1-1   IBM's statement highlights the impact of information technology on business success.

In a recent study, IBM asked more than 3,000 North American and European organizations to identify their most important business objectives and how technology supports these goals. More than 90 percent of the respondents said they wanted to use technology to serve their customers better, provide more access to information, be more flexible in responding to business changes, and increase employee productivity. The study also indicated that most firms are developing an information technology strategy that can handle rapid, dynamic change. Acquisitions, leveraged buyouts, total quality control, downsizing, rightsizing, and layoffs are all part of today's corporate landscape. Successful companies adapt to the new environment by redefining their businesses and rethinking their approach to information management.

The IBM study cited four basic rules for success in the new marketplace. First, the customer is always right. Acquiring new customers or replacing old ones is more difficult than ever. Second, it takes skilled employees to create satisfied customers. Many firms are doing more training, providing employees with more powerful technology, and helping employees improve their productivity. Third, the organization and its information systems must be aligned with customer expectations and business needs — not the other way around. Finally, information technology will be the *essential* factor in determining a company's success.

With these principles in mind, how does an organization develop a successful strategy? The IBM study suggested a simple answer: Information systems professionals need to work closely with managers and users to create a shared business model that reflects the new environment. These teams must develop systems that meet the needs of customers and suppliers, as well as managers and users within the company.

This chapter introduces you to concepts, processes, methods, and tools that you can use to develop powerful and reliable information systems that will meet these goals.

SYSTEMS AND PROCEDURES

T he operation of a company requires many separate activities such as filling customer orders, delivering the right product on time, and preparing payroll checks. These tasks all require **procedures** that specify how the work must be done. A **system** is a group of related procedures for a particular business function such as inventory, production control, or payroll. Even the most complex system, such as a NASA launch system, must contain procedures for reaching the final goal of liftoff, as shown in Figure 1-2. Whether building rocket engines or handling credit union deductions, every system is built on a series of individual procedures. For example, a payroll system must check the hours worked, verify the pay rate, calculate gross pay, handle all deductions, and print the checks.

Figure 1-2   Systems can be simple or complex. Imagine the systems used to launch the space shuttle into orbit and return it to Earth safely.

For more information on **Systems**, visit Systems Analysis and Design Chapter 1 More on the Web.

www.scsite.com/ sad3e/ch01/

In the payroll example, hours worked, pay rate, and deductions are called data. **Data** consists of basic facts that are the system's raw material. The finished product is called **information,** which is data that has been processed into a useful form of output, such as a paycheck. The objective of **processing** is to transform input into accurate, meaningful information that businesses require.

In the example shown in Figure 1-3 on the next page, an employee provides *input* by completing a deduction form. A human resources representative submits the completed form to the payroll department, which enters the deduction. The system performs *processing* and produces *output*, including a paycheck deduction, a report to the employee on the check stub, and a credit to the employee's account. As shown in Figure 1-4 on the next page, all systems take input and process it into useful output. Large information systems that operate across a business enterprise can have hundreds of input items and information outputs.

Procedure 1: An Employee fills out a deduction form for the savings plan.

Procedure 2: The employee submits her completed form to the human resources department for approval.

Procedure 3: After approving the form, the human resources representative gives it to the payroll department for processing.

Procedure 4: The payroll department enters and processes the deduction.

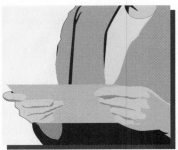

Procedure 5: The employee receives her paycheck with the savings plan deduction.

Figure 1-3   Example of a payroll system with five procedures that handle employee savings plan deductions.

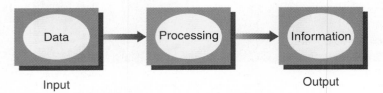

Figure 1-4   Model of a simple system.

INFORMATION SYSTEM COMPONENTS

Figure 1-5 expands the model shown in Figure 1-4 to include all the components of an information system. Notice that data input and information output still exist, but the processing step now has five key elements. An **information system** (**IS**) is the effective use of hardware, software, data, procedures, and people to achieve specific results that support the company's business objectives. An information system also can be called a **system** or an **application**.

Hardware

Hardware refers to the physical layer of the information system. This component includes computers, networks, communications equipment, scanners, printers, digital capture devices, global positioning satellite (GPS) equipment, and other technology-based infrastructure.

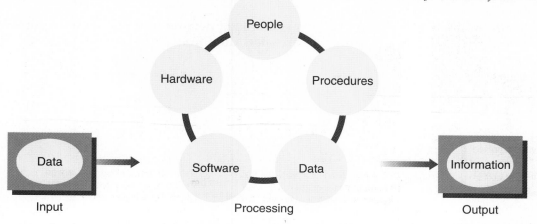

Figure 1-5 Components of an information system.

Software

Software consists of system software and application software. **System software** controls the hardware and software environment and includes the operating system, communications software, and utility programs that handle common functions such as sorting data, converting files into a different format, and making backups. Either the hardware manufacturer supplies the system software, or a company purchases it from a vendor. Systems software also allows users to access local or wide area networks, a company intranet, or the Internet.

Application software consists of programs that process data to produce information needed by users. As shown in Figure 1-6, many types of application software exist, such as spreadsheets, word processors, database management systems, and payroll, order entry, and accounts receivable programs. In some companies, when the information systems department develops systems, they are called **in-house applications**. An alternative to in-house development is to purchase a system from an outside vendor that develops and sells software packages. A **software package** is a basic system that can be adapted for use in many companies.

Figure 1-6 Software is used for many personal and business decisions.

Companies typically use a combination of in-house developed software and software packages. A new system often must interface with older systems, or **legacy systems**. For example, a new human resources system might need to exchange data with an existing payroll application.

Data

Data stored in files and databases is a vital component of every system. As shown in Figure 1-7 on the next page, all information either is produced directly or derived from data. For example, hours worked and pay rate are stored in files

> For more information on **Legacy Systems**, visit Systems Analysis and Design Chapter 1 More on the Web.
>
> www.scsite.com/ sad3e/ch01/

and used to calculate gross pay. Another example of derived information is an employee's net pay after deductions and taxes are subtracted from gross pay.

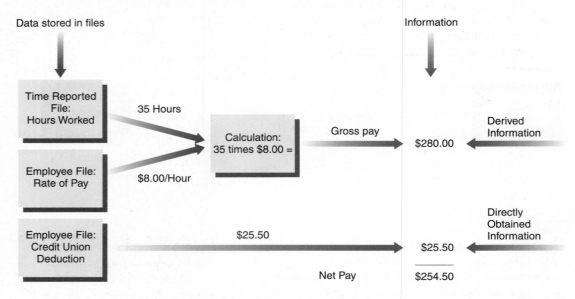

Figure 1-7   Information can be obtained directly from a file or derived from data stored in one or more files.

Procedures

Procedures define the tasks that must be performed by people who work with the system, including users, managers, and information systems staff. Procedures typically are described in written documentation manuals and online reference material.

People

The primary purpose of an information system is to provide valuable information to managers and users both within and outside of the company. **Users**, who are sometimes called **end users**, include employees, customers, vendors, or others who directly interact with the system. For example, users include Federal Express customers who track their packages using the Internet, General Motors suppliers who access GM's production system to plan their manufacturing schedules, and college students who use a Web-based class registration system.

Successful information systems also require the efforts of skilled professionals, such as systems analysts, programmers, and IS managers.

Above all, information systems must fulfill business needs and support company objectives. The success or failure of a system depends on whether users are satisfied with the system's output and operations.

BUSINESS INFORMATION SYSTEMS

I n addition to having its own goals, methods, and information systems requirements, every firm also has an underlying culture. A **corporate culture** is the set of beliefs, rules, traditions, values, and attitudes that define a company's personality and influence its way of doing business. To be successful, a systems analyst must understand the corporate culture and how it affects the way information is managed. Companies sometimes include statements about corporate culture in their mission statements, which are explained in Chapter 2.

Although many types of business organizations exist, companies are classified based on their main activities, as follows:

- **Production-oriented (industrial) companies** — primarily manufacture and sell goods, such as the cellular telephones shown in Figure 1-8. Motorola, Intel, U.S. Robotics, and Compaq are examples of companies that offer high technology products.

- **Service companies** — mainly offer information, services, or sell goods produced by others. Examples in this category include consultants, publishers, package delivery services, telecommunications companies, mail-order sales firms, and companies such as Microsoft and Netscape Communications Corporation.

- **Combined industrial and service companies** — manufacture products, act as value-added resellers of goods produced by others, or offer a flexible combination of services, information, and technical assistance to customers. For example, in a recent financial statement, IBM reported that over 52 percent of its total revenue was derived from the sale of software, services, and maintenance, compared to just 48 percent for hardware.

Figure 1-8 Motorola is an example of a production-oriented company that manufactures and sells products, such as cellular telephones.

In the past, industrial companies had more complex information requirements than service companies, but this no longer is true. The services sector has expanded tremendously, and information technology has fueled much of the growth. The technology explosion includes the enormous growth of the Internet, more online financial services, and the emergence of powerful tools for telecommuting and mobile computing. These forces have created new industries that are reshaping the global economy.

Today, facing intense competition, many companies offer a variety of products *and* services to an increasingly diverse group of customers. For example, a manufacturer might use the Internet to advertise products worldwide, offer online customer and technical support, and maintain an electronic mailing list to notify customers when new products are released. In addition to selling its products, the company also might launch an international consulting division, a leasing unit, and a financial services branch.

Another type of organization is the government, including city, county, state, and federal levels. **Governmental organizations** are similar to service companies because they provide a wide range of services.

The total business information system of a company normally consists of a series of **subsystems**. In small companies, all subsystems might be handled by a single person. In larger companies, a department might be responsible for only one subsystem. Figure 1-9 on page 1.9 shows common business systems and subsystems in an industrial organization.

Each of the subsystems shown in Figure 1-9 is actually a smaller information system that processes data to produce information. A purchasing system manages the purchasing of goods and services and control payment for these purchases. A production system manages the manufacturing process in production-oriented organizations. A finance system manages the company's financial requirements. A human resources system handles personnel information. A receivables system manages customer billing and payments. A marketing system supports promotion and sales of the company's products and services.

A breakdown in any one of these systems can affect a company's operations drastically, and the larger the company, the more severe the consequences. For example, telecommunications and Internet service providers experience major service disruptions when a system fails to function properly.

Characteristics of Business Information Systems

Business information systems have four main characteristics that affect their complexity:

1. *Relationships with other systems* — Information systems often are **interdependent**. For example, output information from the purchasing system becomes data input to the production and finance systems. The arrows shown in Figure 1-9 illustrate the flow of data between information systems. Thus, what is information to people responsible for the purchasing system is data to those in charge of the other two groups of systems. The finance system is central to a company's information processing because all other systems feed monetary data to it.

For more information on **EDI**, visit Systems Analysis and Design Chapter 1 More on the Web.

www.scsite.com/ sad3e/ch01/

   One company's information systems also can interface with systems operated by other firms. An example is the input of a payment from one company's accounts payable system to another company's accounts receivable system when an invoice is paid. Another example occurs when one business orders something from another business. Here, the input is an order from the customer's purchasing system to the vendor's order entry system. Many companies use computers to handle this transfer of data with other companies in a process called electronic data interchange. **Electronic data interchange** (**EDI**) is the computer-to-computer transfer of data between companies. EDI has expanded rapidly as companies form closer working relationships with their suppliers and customers. In the past, EDI was used mainly for processing transactions between two companies, such as purchasing or payments. Today, EDI can help a firm plan its production, adjust inventory levels, or stock up on raw materials, all based on data that comes from another company's computer. For example, using EDI, millions of Social Security payments are transferred directly to bank computers that apply them to individual bank accounts. EDI also has affected the way people pay their taxes — the Internal Revenue Service now permits computerized filing and direct deposit of refunds. As security and reliability improve, the Internet will become a major channel for marketing goods and services on a global scale.

2. *Boundaries* — A **boundary** between two systems indicates where one system ends and the other system begins. The boundary between two systems is not always clear-cut. For example, when are customer payments part of the accounts receivable system, and when are they included in the finance system? If customer payments need to be adjusted, must these adjustments take place in both systems? Who makes the adjustments? What procedures and files are involved? If you change the way adjustments are handled, what hardware, software, and other information system components are affected? Clearly, it takes coordination and proper system definition to set these boundaries correctly.

3. *Specialized business needs* — In addition to the typical business information systems, many **specialized information systems** are in use. At a school, specialized information systems handle class registration, classroom scheduling, student grading, student loans, and transcript processing. At a hospital, specialized systems manage patient admissions, room scheduling, and insurance billing. Many industries such as banking, insurance, airlines, and telecommunications require specialized information systems to run their businesses effectively.

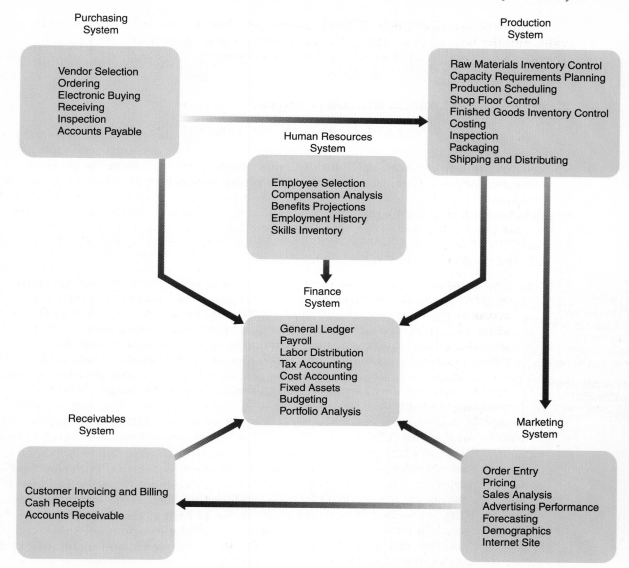

Figure 1-9   These are typical business information systems and subsystems in an industrial company. Arrows show the flow of data and information from one system to another.

4. *Size of the company* — Large and small companies in the same industry have very different information systems requirements. For example, banks can range in size from a local operation with a main office and one or two branches to a multinational bank with branches in many states and foreign countries. Both banks handle loan processing, savings and checking accounts, and funds management. The multinational bank, however, has a much higher volume of customers, transactions, and accounts. The large bank's processing is more complicated because it operates internationally and must consolidate information from banking centers around the world. The multinational bank also needs to deal with foreign currencies and must offer a tremendous variety of banking products and services to a diverse group of customers.

TYPES OF INFORMATION SYSTEMS

I nformation systems fall into six broad categories: operational systems, management information systems, decision support systems, executive information systems, expert systems, and office systems.

Operational Systems

An **operational system** processes data generated by the day-to-day business transactions of a company. Examples of operational systems are the accounts receivable, order entry, and production scheduling systems shown in Figure 1-9 on the previous page. Operational systems also are called **transaction processing systems**.

Management Information Systems

Most early business computer systems were operational systems that performed electronic data processing (EDP). Usually, the purpose was to computerize an existing manual system for faster processing, reduced clerical costs, and improved customer service. Managers soon realized, however, that computer systems could be used for more than just day-to-day transaction processing. The computer's capability of performing rapid calculations and comparing data also could produce meaningful information for managers. This vision led to the concept of management information systems.

A **management information system** (**MIS**) is a computer-based system that generates timely and accurate information for top, middle, and lower managers. For example, to process a sales order, the operational system records a sale, updates the customer's balance, and then makes a deduction from inventory. A related management information system, however, also could produce valuable information. For example, MIS reports could highlight slow- or fast-moving items, customers with past due balances, and inventory items that need reordering. With this kind of information, better management decisions can be made. Large retail chains, such as Wal-Mart and Sears, use hand-held scanners such as the one shown in Figure 1-10 to manage sales information, spot trends quickly, identify *hot* product items, and maintain a competitive edge. In a management information system, the focus is on information that management needs to do its job. MIS systems, however, also can be used by operational employees who need specific information and feedback to make on-the-job decisions, adjust a production process, or troubleshoot a problem.

Figure 1-10   Scanners are used to input data into the system. They offer the advantages of portability, accuracy, and processing speed.

Decision Support Systems

Frequently, management needs information that is not provided routinely by operational and management information systems. For example, a vice president of finance might want to know the effect on company profits if sales increase by 10 percent and costs go up by 5 percent This type of information, sometimes called **what-if analysis**, usually is not provided by operational or management information systems. Decision support systems were developed to provide this information.

A **decision support system** (**DSS**) is designed to help make business decisions by analyzing internal or external data. Internal data comes from an organization's own files, such as sales, manufacturing, or financial records. Data from external sources might include information on interest rates, population trends, or new housing construction. Decision support systems often include query languages, statistical analysis capabilities, spreadsheets, and graphics to help the user evaluate the input data. More advanced decision support systems also allow users to create a model of the factors affecting a decision. A simple model for determining the product price would forecast the expected sales volume at each price level. With a model, users can ask *what-if* questions by changing one or more of the variables and viewing the projected result.

For more information on **DSS,** visit Systems Analysis and Design Chapter 1 More on the Web.

www.scsite.com/ sad3e/ch01/

Executive Information Systems

Many management decisions are periodic and predictable. For example, companies regularly make decisions regarding minimum inventory levels or customers with past due accounts. The information required for these decisions can be predefined and alternative actions can be specified in advance. These decisions are called **structured decisions**, because they occur regularly, have predefined information requirements, and result in predetermined actions.

At the other extreme are **unstructured decisions**, which cannot be predicted and whose information needs cannot be predefined. Unstructured decision making is very common for top managers, where complex issues of corporate strategy and policy are involved. For example, corporate researchers often try to predict consumer tastes and spending patterns for the next five to ten years. Some managers believe that unstructured decision-making is based on intuition and judgment and does not lend itself to systematic analysis. Others feel that unstructured problems are just more complex, with more variables and are resistant to analysis because they do not understand the problem fully — not because an answer is nonexistent.

Somewhere between these two decision types is a third category of decisions known as semistructured decisions. **Semistructured decision**s are not as predictable and definable as structured decisions. An example of a semistructured decision might involve the impact of inflation on production costs. At some point, management needs to make a decision about whether to increase prices in response to rising costs, but a set of predefined inputs and outputs does not exist.

An **executive information system** (**EIS**) or **executive support system** (**ESS**) supports the information requirements of top-level managers and their need to make unstructured decisions. An executive information system combines the features and capabilities of both management information systems and decision support systems, but with more flexibility and better support for unstructured decision-making.

For more information on **EIS,** visit Systems Analysis and Design Chapter 1 More on the Web.

www.scsite.com/ sad3e/ch01/

Expert Systems

Expert systems simulate human reasoning and decision-making by combining the subject knowledge of human experts, called the **knowledge base**, and **inference rules** that determine how the knowledge is used to reach decisions. Although they might appear to think, current expert systems actually operate within preprogrammed limits and cannot make decisions based on common sense or intuition. Many expert systems use a multivalued approach called **fuzzy logic** that allows logical inferences to be drawn from imprecise relationships. Using fuzzy logic, values need not be black and white, like binary logic, but can be many shades of gray. This type of expert system is used to control elevator behavior in a busy office building, regulate an automobile fuel injection system, and decide the best place to drill for oil. Fuzzy logic systems are examples of **artificial intelligence** (**AI**), which is the application of human intelligence to computer systems.

Office Systems

In the past, an office system often was called an **office automation system** (**OAS**) because management expected the system to reduce the number of people employed as office staff. Although repetitive clerical work has decreased greatly, office employment actually has increased as office systems have empowered employees and made them more productive.

Today, most companies have powerful **office systems** that include local and wide area networking, electronic mail, voice mail, fax, video conferencing, word processing, automated calendars, electronic filing, database management, spreadsheets, desktop publishing, presentation graphics, company intranets, and Internet access throughout the company. Office systems often are designed with client/server architecture that permits users to share corporate data across the entire business enterprise.

Office systems are used by a new class of knowledge workers, who need constant access to information. This group has grown rapidly as companies assign more responsibility to lower organizational levels. Relatively inexpensive PC hardware, corporate downsizing, and a move toward employee empowerment also have contributed to this trend.

Integrating Information Systems

With today's sophisticated software, it is sometimes difficult to classify a system into one of the traditional categories. For example, many current systems combine operational power, MIS capabilities, and decision support features. As users demand more support for their business functions, system developers respond by building more capability into a single information system.

ORGANIZATIONAL LEVELS

I nformation is a vital asset, along with people, equipment, and financial resources. Companies must make this asset available throughout the organization to employees with a wide range of information requirements.

Most companies organize as shown in Figure 1-11, with operational personnel reporting to lower managers, who report to middle managers, who report to top managers. In a corporate structure, top managers report to the board of directors who are elected by the shareholders. Figure 1-12 describes the responsibilities, decision-making styles, and information systems requirements of each level.

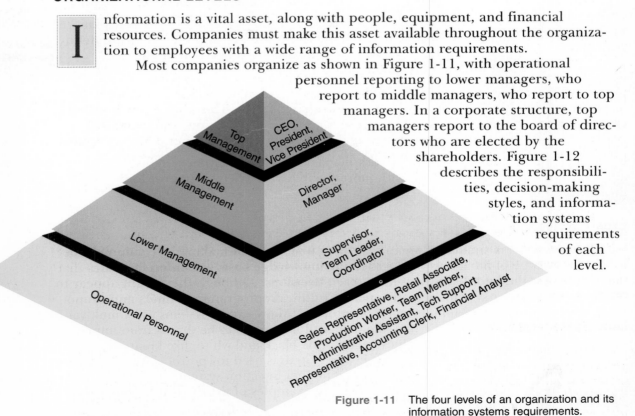

Figure 1-11   The four levels of an organization and its information systems requirements.

Organizational Level	Responsibility	Decision Making	Information Systems Requirements
Top Management	Develop long-range goals, plans, and strategies	Unstructured	Executive information systems MIS summaries Decision support systems Office systems
Middle Management	Develop short-range goals, plans, and tactics	Semistructured	MIS summaries and exceptions Decision support systems Office systems
Lower Management	Develop day-to-day plans and supervise operational personnel	Structured	Operational systems details Some MIS summaries and exceptions Office systems
Operational Personnel	Perform routine functions	Structured	Operational systems details Expert systems Office systems

Figure 1-12 The four organizational levels and their responsibilities, decision-making styles, and information systems requirements.

For more information on **Empowerment**, visit Systems Analysis and Design Chapter 1 More on the Web.

www.scsite.com/ sad3e/ch01/

Operational Personnel

Operational personnel spend most of their time performing repetitive, day-to-day functions that follow well-defined procedures. Production-line workers, clerks, sales representatives, and auditors are examples of operational personnel.

Operational employees usually interact with information systems at a detailed level, although the use of decision support systems by operational personnel is growing, enabling them to handle tasks and make decisions that were assigned previously to people at higher organizational levels. This philosophy is called **empowerment** and results in faster response time, better motivation, and increased customer satisfaction. Some manufacturing ventures, such as the General Motors Saturn plant in Tennessee, are excellent examples of companies that stress empowerment. Saturn advertises itself as a new kind of company, and its Web site shown in Figure 1-13 on the next page emphasizes a democratic management style and the importance of Saturn's people.

Operational employees use information systems to enter and receive data they need to perform their jobs. For example, warehouse clerks use orders to select products, sales representatives use sales reports to contact customers, and the accounting staff uses bank statements to determine which checks have cleared the bank. Data entered by operational personnel is the basis for the information produced for all levels of the organization.

Lower Management

Lower managers, or supervisors or team leaders, supervise operational employees and carry out day-to-day plans. They direct operations, ensure that the right tools, materials, and training are available, make necessary decisions, and take corrective actions. Most lower-manager decisions are highly structured. Just as with operational personnel, however, the trend in many firms is toward transferring more responsibility to lower organizational levels.

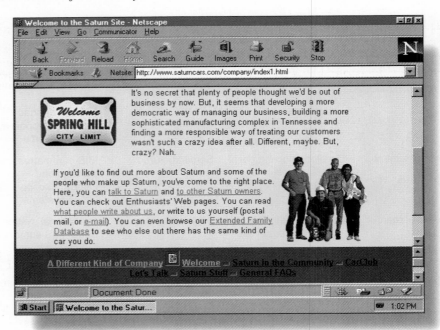

Figure 1-13   The Saturn Corporation uses a democratic management style that stresses empowerment.

First-line supervisors often need detailed operational information and some exception or summary information. **Exception reports** identify variances from set targets and help managers identify situations that require action. Examples of exception reports might be a list of customers who are late in making payments or a list of inventory items that must be reordered. A supervisor's information needs usually are narrow, because he or she only requires information in one area of responsibility. Lower managers primarily use office systems, operational systems, and management information systems.

Middle Management

Middle managers focus on a somewhat longer period, usually ranging from one month to one year. They develop plans and allocate company resources to achieve organizational objectives in a process called **tactical planning**. Middle managers delegate authority and responsibility to first-line supervisors and work closely with them to provide direction, necessary resources, and feedback on performance. Most middle management decisions are semistructured and occur in routine patterns. Middle managers, however, face a more complex set of problems and need good judgment and analytical skills to make sound decisions.

Compared to first-line supervisors, middle managers need less detail and more exception and summary information. For example, a middle manager might need a summary of salaries by department or a recap of sales by geographic region. A middle manager's information needs are broader than those of a first-line supervisor, because the manager might be responsible for several activities and departments. Middle managers use management information systems, decision support systems, and office systems.

➡ For more information on **Strategic Planning**, visit Systems Analysis and Design Chapter 1 More on the Web.

www.scsite.com/ sad3e/ch01/

Top Management

Top managers are responsible for long-range planning, and they establish the overall company mission, policies, and goals, including future products and services. This type of planning is called **strategic planning**, which ensures that the company will survive and grow in the future.

Because top managers are concerned with the entire company, they need information from a variety of systems. They need summary information, such as total company salaries and sales, which comes from management information systems. Because many top management decisions are unstructured, however, top managers also need *what-if* information from decision support systems, plus the overview of an executive information system. Top managers, just as with other organizational levels, also use office systems. Finally, top management needs information from outside the company to address issues involving economic trends, technology, competition, governmental agencies, and shareholders.

Systems Analyst's Toolkit Ahead

The **Systems Analyst's Toolkit** appears at the end of this text. All professionals need a set of tools, and systems analysts are no exception. Here are some questions and answers about your Toolkit:

Q: What is the Systems Analyst's Toolkit?

A: A successful systems analyst needs to learn many skills, which are included in the chapters and case studies in this book. Some skills, however, cut across the entire systems analysis and design process, and can be used anywhere in the book. These basic skills are so important that they are called *power tools*, and they are included in the Systems Analyst's Toolkit.

Q: What is included in the Systems Analyst's Toolkit?

A: Three main types of power tools are provided: communications tools, cost-benefit analysis tools, and project management tools.
Communications tools help you write an effective report, design and deliver a powerful presentation, and conduct a productive meeting. **Cost-benefit analysis tools** provide valuable information about project feasibility and financial impact. These are measuring tools that can be used throughout the process of information systems development and use. **Project management tools** help you organize, plan, estimate, execute, and monitor IS projects of various levels of complexity.

Q: How do I use the Toolkit?

A: The tools are flexible, and your instructor might want to use them in several ways. At this point in the text, before starting the study of the systems development life cycle, you could review the communications tools and some of the cost-benefit concepts to prepare for the systems planning phase of the SDLC. Or, you can wait until the tools are required for a specific case study or assignment, and then select the tools you will need at that time. Either way, learn all the tools before the end of the course, because they are important to your success as a systems analyst.

SYSTEMS DEVELOPMENT LIFE CYCLE

I nformation requirements change as a company grows, matures, and reacts to internal and external forces. This is especially true in today's dynamic business environment, where constant change is the norm. To be successful, a company needs information systems that can handle a continuous stream of new demands. First, however, the information system must be constructed.

The **systems development life cycle** (**SDLC**) is a series of steps that companies use to build an information system. Although it is the most common development strategy, alternatives exist to the structured SDLC approach. Several other development methods are discussed in later chapters.

The systems development life cycle consists of five phases:

1. Systems planning
2. Systems analysis
3. Systems design
4. Systems implementation
5. Systems operation and support

The SDLC can be pictured in several ways. Figure 1-14 shows the overall development cycle and the interaction of the five major phases. Figure 1-15 shows a waterfall model, where each phase appears in a box, and arrows connect the inputs and outputs. As you can see, the results of each phase flow down into the next phase. Because information systems are not static, however, constant change is to be expected. It is common to return to an earlier phase to perform additional analysis or review new information that has been discovered. The rest of this section discusses each SDLC phase in detail, with an overview followed by a discussion of specific issues regarding that phase.

For more information on **SDLC**, visit Systems Analysis and Design Chapter 1 More on the Web.

www.scsite.com/ sad3e/ch01/

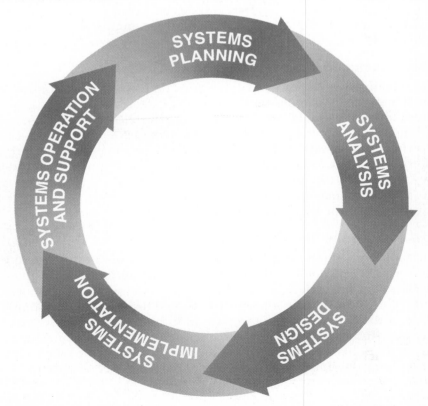

Figure 1-14   The systems development life cycle has five major phases.

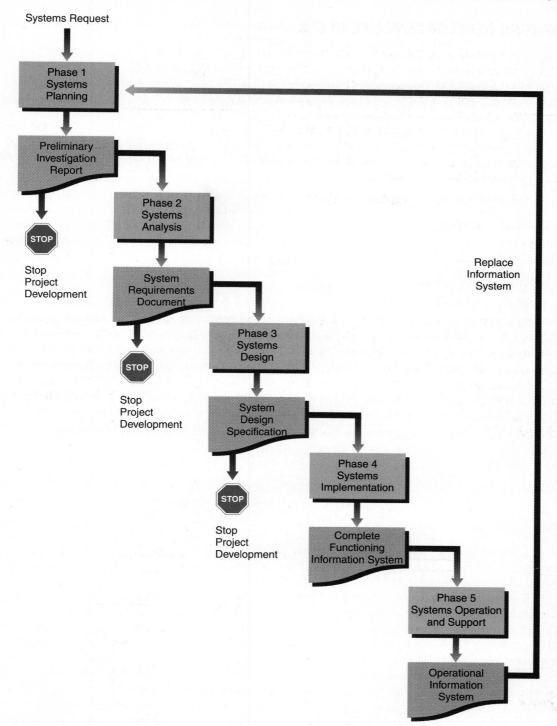

Figure 1-15   The five phases of the systems development life cycle and their end products.

Phase 1: Systems Planning

The systems development life cycle usually starts with a written request, called a **systems request**, that identifies the information system and describes the desired changes or improvements. The request can be very significant or relatively minor. A major request might involve the creation of an entire information system to meet a new business need or the replacement of an existing system that can no longer handle current requirements. In contrast, a minor request might ask for a new report or a change to an existing calculation. Major systems requests can require many months or years of effort, while some minor requests can be handled in just a few hours.

The purpose of the **planning phase** is to identify clearly the nature and scope of the problem. This requires a **preliminary investigation**, which is a critical step, because the outcome will affect the entire development process. The end product, or deliverable, of this phase is called a **preliminary investigation report**.

As a systems analyst, suppose you receive a request for changes or improvements to a system. Your first step is to identify the problem. Perhaps the system functions well, but the users need more training. You need to determine whether it makes sense to launch a preliminary investigation at all. If you decide to proceed further, you will have to make several choices. If the request is relatively simple, you might complete a preliminary investigation and prepare your recommendation. If the proposal involves major changes, however, you would start a preliminary investigation that might continue during the systems analysis phase. Your goal is to reach a sound decision without getting into unnecessary detail at this early stage, and it often is hard to steer a middle course. Each situation is different, with no clear guidelines.

The preliminary investigation often is called a **feasibility study**. Based on economic, technical, and operational factors, you recommend whether the proposal should be pursued further. This study is an initial determination, and the project's feasibility will be reviewed constantly during the SDLC. If management decides to proceed, the next step after the preliminary investigation is the systems analysis phase.

The Systems Analyst's Toolkit at the end of this book has tools to help you assess project feasibility.

Phase 2: Systems Analysis

The purpose of the **systems analysis phase** is to learn exactly how the current system operates, to determine and document what the system should do, and to recommend alternative solutions.

Through the process of **fact-finding**, or **requirements determination**, you define all the functions performed by the current information system and determine what improvements are needed. After gathering the facts, you analyze them carefully and develop a specific plan to solve problems in the current system. This process is called **requirements analysis**.

The end product, or deliverable, for this phase is the **system requirements document**, which describes all management and user requirements, alternative plans and costs, and your recommendation. If management decides to continue development on the project, several possibilities exist. The company might decide to develop a system in-house, purchase a commercial package, or modify an existing system. Even if development work continues, management might terminate the project later because of high costs, changing priorities, failure to meet objectives, or other reasons.

The Systems Analyst's Toolkit has communications tools that can help you present your recommendations to management.

Phase 3: Systems Design

The purpose of the **systems design phase** is to develop an information system design that satisfies all documented requirements, whether the system is being developed in-house or purchased as a package. During systems design, you make a logical determination of *what* the system must do, not *how* it will be done. You must identify all necessary outputs, inputs, files, application programs, and manual procedures. In addition, you must design internal and external controls, including computer-based and manual features to guarantee that the system will be reliable, accurate, maintainable, and secure. The design is documented in the **system design specification** and presented to management and users for their review and approval. Management and user involvement is critical to avoid any misunderstanding about what the new system will do, how it will do it, and what it will cost. After completing all design steps, you begin the next phase — systems implementation.

Phase 4: Systems Implementation

During **systems implementation**, the information system is constructed and put in place. In this phase, application programs are written, tested, and documented; operational documentation and procedures are completed; and approval is obtained from users and management. If the system was purchased as a package, any necessary modifications and configuration are performed. The objective of the implementation phase is to deliver a completely functioning and documented information system that has been reviewed and approved.

At the conclusion of this phase, the system is ready for use. Final preparations include converting data to the new system's files, training users, and performing the actual transition from the old system to the new one. At this point, users begin to operate the new system. The systems implementation phase also includes an assessment, called a **post-implementation systems evaluation**, to determine whether the system operates properly and if costs and benefits are within expectations.

Phase 5: Systems Operation and Support

Following implementation, a company uses the system to operate its business. During **systems operation and support**, maintenance and enhancements sometimes are requested to resolve problems identified by users. **Maintenance changes** are made to correct errors or to conform to government or other requirements. **Enhancements** are modifications that increase capability, such as providing new information in an existing report or adding a new report.

Some information systems have been in use for many years. Most businesses experience extensive changes, however, and find that their information systems need to be replaced after several years of operation. The replacement of a system constitutes the end of its overall life cycle.

General Considerations

You should keep the following suggestions in mind as you build an information system.

COMPLETE THE PHASES IN SEQUENCE • The successful development of an information system requires that you follow the SDLC phases in order by completing one phase before you start the next phase. When phases are bypassed or rushed, you can expect problems with the developed information system. If you first understand all the requirements, you will create a better design, and a good design helps avoid problems in later phases. In addition, it is cost effective to complete one phase before moving to the next phase. Suppose you complete the systems design phase, but then discover that you overlooked certain requirements. You now must rework both the system requirements document and the system design specification.

Completing the phases in sequence, however, does not mean that you must restrict all your thoughts to just the current phase. As you work on a particular phase, you also should consider the impact of your decisions on later phases. If you plan carefully, tasks from later phases sometimes can begin before the completion of the prior phase. The ability to overlap phases is especially important when you are working on a system that must be developed rapidly. Powerful project management tools and techniques are available to help you manage multiple tasks. These techniques are discussed in the Systems Analyst's Toolkit.

Even after you complete a phase, you might have to review your work. For example, you might be implementing the system when changes in company requirements or new hardware or software force you to reconsider your design and go back to the systems analysis phase.

FOCUS ON END PRODUCTS • Always concentrate on end products, or deliverables. Figure 1-15 on page 1.17 shows the end products, or deliverables, for each phase of the SDLC. Each **end product** or **deliverable** represents a milestone or checkpoint in the system's development and marks the completion of a specific phase.

Management uses these checkpoints to assess the status of the project and decide what should happen next. Possible choices are to proceed to the next phase, redo portions of the work just completed, return to an earlier phase, or terminate the project entirely. One major factor in management's decision is the quality of the end product. Because the end product from each SDLC phase is highly visible, you should strive for strong content and high quality.

ESTIMATE REQUIRED RESOURCES • Cost-effective information systems are vital to the success of every organization, and management needs to know what it will cost to develop and operate the system. At the start of each phase, you must provide specific cost estimates for that phase, for all succeeding phases, and for the operation of the information system.

During early phases, projected costs usually are given as a range. For example, at the start of the systems analysis phase, you might estimate a cost of $11,500 for the current phase and between $30,000 and $50,000 for the design and implementation phases. By the end of the systems analysis phase, you will be expected to provide a more specific estimate. Sound business decisions require accurate cost projections, so your figures must be reliable.

Automated Tools for Systems Development

The systems development life cycle helps you organize and structure the complex task of developing an information system. You also can use **software tools** that help you perform many of the required development activities. These tools increase your productivity and result in better quality applications.

Software tools include general-purpose applications, such as word processing for preparing memos and documents, spreadsheet programs for calculating net present value and return on investment, and graphics packages for drawing company organization charts and designing presentations. Other tools are more specialized, including data dictionaries, report writers, screen generators, program generators, fourth-generation languages, and graphical tools that can create data flow diagrams, systems flowcharts, and entity-relationship diagrams. You will learn more about these software tools in later chapters.

When you define a system's requirements during the analysis phase, you can use software tools to develop a prototype of the information system. A **prototype** is an early working version of the information system. The prototype can serve as a model of user requirements or as the initial version of an information system. Either way, prototyping can speed up the SDLC process significantly.

Computer-aided software engineering (**CASE**) uses powerful software tools to help develop and maintain information systems. A **CASE** tool is a software product that automates a specific systems life cycle task and eliminates much of the manual effort. Many CASE tools are integrated and can handle multiple activities or SDLC phases.

The number of phases in the systems development life cycle is not fixed. The purpose of the SDLC is to provide a specific process for information system development; the exact number of phases is not important. What matters is that a company follows a series of logical steps. As shown in Figure 1-14 on page 1.16, the SDLC must include the major activities: systems planning, systems analysis, systems design, systems implementation, and systems operation and support. Companies that have more than these five phases have subdivided the phases into several parts.

Is it better to have more or fewer phases? More phases require more checkpoints, more end products, and more work, which results in greater cost and more development time. More phases also means that checkpoints occur more frequently. With a major development effort, the extra phases and additional checkpoints can be useful to ensure that the project remains on target. With smaller projects, however, the extra phases might be burdensome.

Successful development has nothing to do with the number of phases in the SDLC. The SDLC is simply a framework for development, similar to blueprints used in designing and building a house. Success really depends on the skills and motivation of the people on the development team.

A KEY QUESTION

Suppose you worked in the IS department of Global Hotels, a large multinational hotel company. Your company just acquired Momma's, a small chain of 12 bed and breakfast inns. Momma's currently has its own IS operation. Should Momma's adopt your SDLC process? Why or why not?

INFORMATION SYSTEMS DEPARTMENT

The **information systems** (**IS**) department develops, maintains, and operates a company's information systems. The structure of the information systems department varies among companies, as does the name and its placement within the organization. In a small firm, one person might be able to handle all computer support and services, while a large multinational corporation would need hundreds of people with specialized skills to provide information systems support. Figure 1-16 shows a typical IS organization in a company that uses a combination of networked PCs and centralized multiuser computers. Four common functional areas within the information systems department are operations, technical support, applications, and the information center.

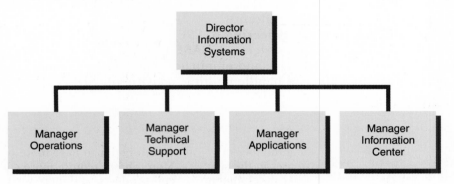

Figure 1-16   Typical organization of an information systems department.

The **operations group** is in charge of the centralized computers, communications links, high-volume printers, and system backup. This group also schedules execution of batch jobs, distributes printed output, and performs centralized data entry.

The **technical support group** installs and supports systems software, such as operating systems, data communication software, application development tools, and centralized database management systems. This group also serves in an advisory and support capacity to other groups in the IS department.

The **applications group** analyzes, designs, programs, tests, installs, and maintains the company's information systems. If the company uses software packages, the applications group installs, upgrades, and maintains these programs. Members of this group work with users throughout the company.

The **information center** (**IC**) provides users with technical resources, information, and support. The IC staff trains users and managers on hardware and software, including typical application software such as word processors, spreadsheets, and graphics packages. The IC also provides training and support for single-user information systems, cross-platform network applications, and the exchange of data between PCs and a centralized computer environment.

THE SYSTEMS ANALYST POSITION

Most companies assign systems analysts to the IS department, but analysts also can report to a specific user area such as marketing, sales, or production. As a member of a functional team, an analyst can understand the needs of that group better and how computer technology might be applied to reach departmental goals. Other companies hire outside consultants to perform systems analysis work on an as-needed basis.

Responsibilities

The systems analyst investigates, analyzes, designs, develops, installs, evaluates, and maintains a company's information systems. On large projects, the analyst works as a member of an IS department team; on smaller assignments, he or she might work alone. Whether working as a team member or alone, the systems analyst constantly interacts with users, managers, and others.

The systems analyst is responsible for a wide range of activities involving the systems development life cycle. Some tasks are technical in nature, such as selecting hardware and software packages, designing computer files, and training users. Other work supports the company's business operations, such as recommending improvements to business procedures or building a new Web site.

The systems analyst must plan projects, develop schedules, and estimate costs. To keep managers and users informed of progress, the analyst must conduct meetings, deliver presentations, and write memos, reports, and documentation. The Systems Analyst's Toolkit at the end of this text includes tools to help you with each of these important skills.

For more information on **Systems Analyst**, visit Systems Analysis and Design Chapter 1 More on the Web.

www.scsite.com/ sad3e/ch01/

Required Skills and Background

A systems analyst must have strong technical skills and broad knowledge of information management concepts, tools, and techniques. In addition, a systems analyst needs a solid understanding of the company's operations and of business in general.

A systems analyst interacts with people at all levels, from operational staff to senior executives, and also deals with people from outside the company, including software and hardware vendors, customers, and government officials. The analyst needs strong people skills to work well with others.

Above all, a systems analyst must have the capability to communicate effectively. Being a good communicator requires strong oral and written skills and the capability to interpret written feedback and be a good listener. Often, an analyst must lead an IS development team. When functioning as a team leader, the analyst needs strong leadership skills to plan, estimate, and control the project and to coach and motivate others. A systems analyst must be comfortable dealing with complex problems that might involve ambiguity and uncertainty. The analyst must use creativity and analytical skills to deal with these situations successfully.

State-of-the-art knowledge is the mark of a professional systems analyst. As a systems analyst, you must work hard to keep up with a rapidly changing business and technical environment. You can maintain your skills by attending training courses, seminars, workshops, and by reading current journals, periodicals, and books. Networking with colleagues is another way to keep up with new developments and trends, and membership in professional associations also is important. The systems analyst, like any other professional, needs to manage his or her own career by developing the knowledge and skills that are valuable in the marketplace.

Companies today require that newly hired systems analysts have at least a two- or four-year degree in information systems, computer science, business, or a closely related field. Experience as a programmer often is required. Figure 1-17 on the next page shows a typical ad for a systems analyst position.

Entry-Level Systems Analyst

Formal Education
Two- or four-year degree in computer information systems, computer science, business, or a closely related field.

Skill Prerequisites
Works well with people at all organizational levels.

Communicates effectively orally and in writing.

Understands business information systems and their impact on the organization.

Exercises mature judgment and can make independent decisions.

Understands computer hardware and software technologies and their applications to business information systems.

Functions well in team leadership and project management positions.

Experience
Minimum of three years experience as a programmer.

Figure 1-17   Sample ad for a systems analyst at a typical company.

ON THE NET

Use the Internet to explore the many job postings for systems analyst positions. Search the Web sites of companies that employ systems analysts, such as IBM, Boeing, or Hewlett Packard, or search with a search engine such as Yahoo! or AltaVista using the keywords, systems analyst, and job posting (written as "systems analyst" + "job posting"), to list sites that include these keywords. Print at least three job postings for systems analysts.

Career Opportunities

The demand for systems analysts is expected to remain strong well into the twenty-first century. Computer technology will continue to change rapidly, and companies will need people with strong analytical skills to help them apply this technology. The systems analyst position is an extremely challenging and rewarding career path that can lead to senior positions in information systems, including management responsibility.

Because talented systems analysts are knowledgeable in both technical and business areas, career opportunities also are available in user departments. Many companies have named presidents and senior managers who started in IS departments as systems analysts. With the right skills, and ambition, prospects as a systems analyst are unlimited.

The responsibilities of a systems analyst at a small firm are different from those at a large corporation. Would you be better off at a small or large company? Where will you find the best opportunity to gain valuable experience and continue your professional growth? What about the corporate culture discussed earlier in this chapter? Will you *like* working there? Each person looks for different rewards in a job. What will be important to *you*?

First, do not rely on job titles alone. Some positions are called systems analysts, but involve only programming or computer operations. In other cases, systems analyst responsibilities are found in positions titled computer specialist, programmer, programmer/analyst, systems designer, software engineer, and various others. Be sure the responsibilities of the job are stated clearly when you consider a position.

Also, find out all you can about the company and where the IS department fits in the organization chart. Where are IS functions performed, and by whom? The firm might have a central headquarters, but systems development might be decentralized. This sometimes occurs in large conglomerates, where the parent company consolidates information that actually is developed and managed at the subsidiary level. Where would *you* rather work?

In small companies, a systems analyst usually does a little of everything, including systems development, maintenance, and operation. In larger companies, an analyst often concentrates on a particular area and becomes a specialist. Between these extremes, a medium-sized company might allow a degree of specialization within several areas.

If you like more variety, then a smaller firm might suit you best. If you want to specialize, however, then consider a larger company with state-of-the-art systems. Although you might have more responsibility in a smaller company, the promotional opportunities and financial rewards often are greater in larger companies. You also might want to consider working as an independent consultant, either on your own or with others. Many consulting firms have been successful in offering their services to smaller business enterprises that do not have the expertise to handle systems development on their own.

Finally, consider salary, location, and the company's prospects for future growth and success. Think about your impressions of the company and the people you met during your interviews. You should consider your short- and long-term goals carefully before deciding which position is best for you.

A KEY QUESTION

Lisa Jameson has to choose between two job offers. The first offer is from Pembroke Boats, a small builder of sailboats that employs 125 people in a small town in Ohio. Pembroke does not have an IS department and wants her to create one. The job position is information coordinator, but she would be the only IS person. The second offer, which pays about $7,500 more annually, is from Albemarle Express, a nationwide trucking and warehousing firm located in Detroit. There, Lisa would be a programmer/analyst, working mainly on maintenance programming, with the promise that if she does well, she eventually will move into a systems analyst position and work on development of major new systems. In addition, some talk of Albemarle Express being acquired by another company has circulated, but this rumor has occurred before, and nothing ever happened. What should Lisa do, and why?

SOFTWEAR, LIMITED

SoftWear, Limited (SWL) is a continuing case study that illustrates the process of information systems development in a practical setting.

SoftWear, Limited manufactures and sells casual and recreational clothing for men and women. SWL was formed in 1991 when a national apparel firm sold the division during a corporate downsizing. A group of managers obtained financing and became owners of the company. With clever marketing, competitive pricing, and efficient production, SWL has grown to 450 employees, including the corporate headquarters and manufacturing plants. By 1997, SWL had annual sales of $250 million.

SoftWear, Limited's headquarters are in Raleigh, North Carolina, where the company employs 125 people, including officers, managers, and support staff. Another 35 salaried and 250 hourly people are employed at production facilities in Haskell, California and Florence, Texas. The company also is in the process of building a new factory in Mexico.

SWL maintains a site on the Internet with information about its products. SWL's Web site features text, graphics, and audio, and allows customers to send e-mail, order products from the SoftWear catalog, and request special promotional items including beach umbrellas, hats, and T-shirts customized with the purchaser's logo. SWL also is studying other ways to use the Internet to boost product sales and expand its marketing efforts, including a special European promotion designed to increase awareness of SWL's Web site.

The headquarters includes the following departments: Executive, Operations, Marketing, Finance, and Human Resources. The organization chart of top-level management is shown in Figure 1-18. Four vice presidents report to SWL's president, Robert Lansing.

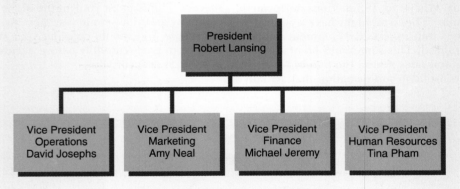

Figure 1-18 Organization chart of SoftWear, Limited.

Figure 1-19 shows a more detailed organization chart of the management positions within SWL. Notice that the director of information systems, Ann Hon, reports to Michael Jeremy, vice president of finance. The director of the payroll department, Amy Calico also reports to Mr. Jeremy.

The management structure of the information systems department includes the director, Ann Hon; an applications manager, Jane Rossman; a technical support manager, Kerry Krauss; and an operations manager, Gene Talkington. Figure 1-20 shows the organization of the IS department. The systems analysts, programmer/analysts, and programmers report to Jane Rossman, the manager of applications. The primary functions of the systems analysts are to analyze and design information systems, while the programmer/analysts spend their time both analyzing and designing systems and writing application programs. The programmers' primary work is to write programs.

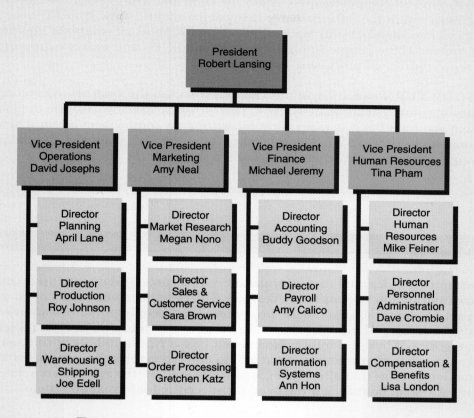

Figure 1-19   Detailed organization chart of SoftWear, Limited.

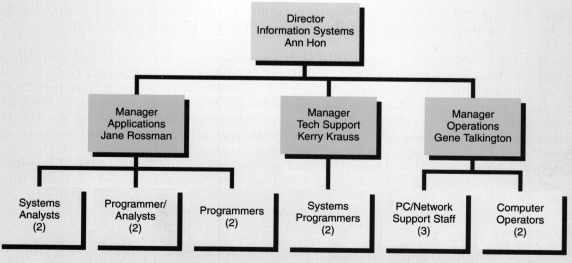

Figure 1-20   Organization chart of the information systems department of SoftWear, Limited.

The technical support manager and the systems programmers are responsible for the systems software on all computers used within the company. They also advise and support the other two groups within the information systems department.

The operations manager and her staff install and support all computer equipment at SoftWear, Limited. Three people within this group handle PC and network support; three others focus on centralized processing functions.

 YOUR TURN — Earlier in this chapter, you used the Internet to explore job postings for systems analysts. Now, Jane Rossman asked you to use the job postings that you found as a starting point for writing an employment ad for a new systems analyst position at SWL. Consider the size of the SWL company and the job requirements described in the case when you write the ad.

CHAPTER SUMMARY

In this chapter, you learned that information systems process data into useful information and how information systems are developed. The essential components of an information system are hardware, software, data, procedures, and people. An information system can be created and developed in-house or purchased as a commercial software package.

The six categories of business information systems for a typical industrial company are finance, human resources, purchasing, production, marketing, and receivables. Four special characteristics of business information systems that affect their complexity are how the systems are related to each other, the clarity of system boundaries, the need for specialized information systems, and the company's size.

The six types of information systems are operational systems, management information systems, decision support systems, executive information systems, expert systems, and office systems. How various information systems are used depends mainly on an employee's position and organizational level. These levels consist of operational personnel, lower management, middle management, and top management. Each organizational level has different responsibilities and different information needs.

The systems development life cycle (SDLC) is a structured approach that companies use to develop an information system. The SDLC consists of five phases: systems planning, systems analysis, systems design, systems implementation, and systems operation and support. Software tools are used during systems development for productivity, cost, and quality reasons. Many of these software tools support prototyping and computer-aided software engineering (CASE). After an information system is developed, a company uses the system to achieve its business goals during the systems operation and support phase of the systems development life cycle.

The IS department develops, maintains, and operates a company's information systems. The systems analyst investigates, analyzes, designs, develops, installs, evaluates, and maintains information systems.

Review Questions

1. What is a procedure? How are procedures related to systems?
2. What other names are used for input to or output from an information system?
3. Describe the components of an information system.
4. What is derivable information?
5. Define an information system.
6. List the six categories of common business information systems.

7. Define EDI and give an example of its application.
8. Does the Saturn Web site describe the company's corporate culture? How?
9. What are the four factors that affect the complexity of a business information system?
10. What are the six types of information systems and what are their characteristics?
11. Name the four organizational levels and explain the information requirements for each level.
12. What is the systems development life cycle (SDLC)?
13. List and briefly explain the five phases of the systems development life cycle.
14. What is a systems request? What is its importance to the SDLC?
15. What are two types of changes that can be made to a system during systems operation?
16. Name the end products created at the end of each phase of the SDLC.
17. Explain the use of a prototype in the systems development life cycle.
18. What is computer-aided software engineering (CASE)?
19. What are common subdivisions of the information systems department?
20. What does a systems analyst do? What are the skills that a systems analyst should have?

Discussion Questions

1. Do you agree with IBM's statement that *Knowledge Management Calls for a New Way of Thinking?* Is IBM referring to a new way of thinking, or a new way of doing business? Explain your views.
2. Present an argument for and against the following proposition: The heart of a company is the information systems operation. Because members of information systems management are knowledgeable in all phases of the business, a company should fill vacancies in top-level management positions by promoting IS managers.
3. Discuss the advantages and disadvantages of having the information systems director report to the chief financial officer of the company such as the vice president of finance.
4. Schedule a visit to the information systems department of your school or a nearby company. Prepare a diagram similar to Figure 1-9 on page 1.9 that shows the information systems your school or the company uses. If possible, classify whether each information system is an operational, MIS, DSS, EIS, expert, or office system.
5. Schedule a visit to the information systems department of your school or a nearby company. Does the department use the SDLC to develop its information systems? If it does use the SDLC, how many phases does it have, and how do these phases differ from those presented in this chapter? If it does not use the SDLC, what methodology does it use and why? Does it use CASE tools? Which ones?
6. Schedule a visit to the information systems department of your school or a nearby company. Prepare a complete organization chart of the department and describe the functions carried out by each unit in the department.

CASE STUDIES

 ase studies offer an opportunity for you to practice specific skills and knowledge learned in the chapter. New Century Health Clinic is a continuing case study that provides practical experience for you as the systems analyst in the development of information systems. Other case studies are revisited in later chapters so you can apply new concepts and techniques to a familiar fact situation.

NEW CENTURY HEALTH CLINIC

Early in 1994, cardiologists Timothy Jones, M.D., and Dolores Garcia, M.D., decided to combine their individual practices in Fullerton, California, to form the New Century Health Clinic. They wanted to concentrate on preventive medicine by helping patients maintain health and fitness, along with providing traditional medical care. Chris Bean, M.D., a nutritionist, later joined the practice. In 1997, a physical therapist, Misty Creswell, M.D., joined the group, which then moved to its current location near a new shopping mall in a busy section of the city.

At the present time, the New Century's staff includes the four doctors, three registered nurses, four physical therapists, and six office staff workers.

New Century Health Clinic currently has a patient base of 3,500 patients. Its patients are employed by 275 different employers, many of which provide insurance coverage for employee wellness and health maintenance. Currently, New Century must deal with 34 different insurance companies.

Anita Davenport, who has been with New Century since its inception, is the office manager. She supervises the staff, including Fred Brown, who handles office payroll, tax reporting, and profit distribution among the associates. Susan Gifford is responsible for maintenance of all the patient records. Most of the paperwork concerning insurance reporting and accounting is handled by Tom Capaletti. Lisa Sung has the primary responsibility for the appointment book, and her duties include making reminder calls to patients and preparing daily appointment lists. Carla Herrara primarily is concerned with ordering and organizing office and clinic supplies.

Each of the six office staff people has one or more primary responsibilities; however, all members of the staff help out whenever necessary with patient records, insurance processing, and appointment processing. In addition to their regular responsibilities, all six office workers are involved in the preparation of patient statements at the end of each month.

Assignments

1. Prepare an organization chart of the office staff at New Century Health Clinic.

2. New Century Health Clinic currently is not computerized in any way. Do you think the clinic should computerize all or part of their office procedures? Explain the reasons for your answer.

3. What types of information systems might help New Century be more efficient and effective? For each type of information system listed, provide a specific example of how the system might be used.

4. Based on your recommendations, New Century has decided to begin computerizing some office procedures. As a systems analyst, which operations would you computerize first? Why?

GREEN PASTURES, INC.

Kirby Ellington graduated with a two-year degree in computer programming and worked as a programmer for three years at a large insurance company in Hartford, Connecticut. Kirby was responsible for maintenance programming on several older systems. He was competent in carrying out his duties, but he wanted to advance to a systems analyst position and did not feel this opportunity was forthcoming at the insurance company.

Kirby answered an ad he saw in a computer periodical for a systems analyst position at Green Pastures, a solid waste recycling company located in Millwood, New York. Kirby decided to add to his resume that he had more than two years experience as a systems analyst and had been the lead systems analyst for two major projects at the insurance company. When Green Pastures reviewed Kirby's resume, the company was impressed with his systems analyst and leadership experience and flew him in for an interview.

During the interview Kirby communicated well and appeared to be knowledgeable about programming, personal computer software packages, such as spreadsheets and word processors, and all the latest personal computers on the market. This knowledge fit well with Green Pastures' needs, because it started using computers six months ago, when three PCs were installed in the company's office headquarters. Because Green Pastures had no one with programming experience on its staff, it felt a systems analyst would be able to develop the specialized information systems it needed. Green Pastures offered Kirby a job as a systems analyst, and he accepted the offer.

Kirby initially did a great job at Green Pastures. He was able to help everyone with his or her spreadsheet and word processing problems, and he advised Green Pastures management on the purchase of a database management system. Next, Kirby started developing a billing information system. He really enjoyed using the C++ programming language when he was in school and decided to use this language for the billing system.

After four months of work, Kirby finished the billing system. The clerks at Green Pastures began using the system and encountered immediate problems. The clerks had difficulty understanding what they should do and when they should do it. Although no documentation or written directions for the system were prepared, Kirby always was available to help users. The clerks spent one week entering data and making corrections to the data until all the input was entered correctly, and the time came to print the billing statements. The printing went well, and the statements were mailed to customers.

Two days later, Green Pastures began receiving calls from customers complaining about the errors in the billing statements they had just received. After a thorough review, they discovered that all the statements were incorrect and would have to be redone manually.

Assignments

1. Identify the components of the new billing information system. What key component(s) is/are missing from the information system?

2. Identify two or three things that contributed to the problems with the billing system. Who is at fault for these problems? Why?

3. What could have been done to avoid these problems? If you were a systems analyst working with Kirby, what suggestions might you offer?

4. Six types of information systems are defined in the chapter. What type of information system did Kirby develop for Green Pastures?

RIDGEWAY COMPANY

R idgeway Company specializes in the purchase and development of recreational land. The company currently manages several major operations, with revenues of about $75 million last year.

Ridgeway's senior management includes George Ridgeway, president; Helen Hill, executive vice president; and three vice presidents who report directly to Ms. Hill: Luis Sanchez, vice president, finance; Trinh Lu, vice president, administration, research, and development; and Thomas McGee, vice president, operations. Bob Logan reports directly to the president in a staff capacity as the company's land development consultant.

Ridgeway Company recently acquired a large recreational complex containing both a tennis club and a golf course. Now named the Ridgeway Country Club, the facilities include twenty lighted tennis courts, an eighteen-hole golf course, a pro shop that sells tennis and golfing supplies and related items, a clubhouse containing a restaurant and bar, and other recreational facilities, including a swimming pool and exercise room. Thomas McGee is the general manager of the Ridgeway Country Club.

Ridgeway recently acquired a minicomputer system to handle its information management requirements.

Linda Usher, as director, heads the information systems department and reports directly to the vice president of finance. Reporting directly to Ms. Usher are a manager of systems development, a manager of operations, and a manager of systems support.

Linda Usher recently met Bob Logan for lunch. Linda was surprised at the invitation, and Bob's secretary had given her no reason for this informal meeting. After some small talk, the discussion went like this:

BOB: I really need your help, Linda. Several months ago, I bought a personal computer for my office. Believe me, I wasn't trying to get around your department. It's just that I know you folks are very busy, and I thought this was something I could do without bothering you.

LINDA: You're not bothering me. What's on your mind?

BOB: All I needed was a program to help me keep track of how many members use each of the Ridgeway Country Club's facilities. I figured it would help me predict future usage, spot trends, and point out potential problems of over-demand for certain facilities. For example, I'm sure we will need to build several additional tennis courts someday soon. I didn't think it would be a big deal to get a computer program to help me figure out how soon we'll need them.

LINDA: What did you do next?

BOB: Well, the store where I bought the personal computer recommended a spreadsheet package that can handle statistics. They said it was very popular and would do exactly what I wanted. But it isn't working out. I had originally planned to keep track of weekly usage, but now I realize that in some cases I need daily or even hourly figures. But the package can't handle that many different numbers. And I can't get it to do the seasonal analyses I need. So now what should I do?

LINDA: Bob, this is a common story. It happens all the time. People think that if you simply turn on a computer and start a program, anything is possible. But it doesn't work that way. Computers and programs are just tools. You still have to figure out exactly what you want to do before you can determine what tools you need to do it.

BOB: I see that now, Linda, but what I want to know is how I can salvage what I've already done. Do you have a few minutes this afternoon to look at what I've got on the computer and tell me how I can make it do what I want?

LINDA: It isn't going to be that easy. I can't come up with answers that quickly. We need to look at exactly what you want to do, what kinds of information you need from the system, and what data you have available. Then we'll be able to determine what kind of computer system you need. Maybe there's a personal computer package that can do the job. Or maybe we'll need a specialized information system. That system might be able to run on your computer, or maybe it will have to be written for Ridgeway's minicomputer. But frankly, Bob, this will all take time. There are no magic shortcuts.

Assignments

1. What mistakes did Bob make?
2. Do you think Linda's assessment is correct? Do personal computer systems need the same kind of systems development life cycle as mainframe systems?
3. Prepare an organization chart of the top-level management of Ridgeway Company.
4. Add the organizational structure of the information systems (IS) department to the top-level organizational chart.

Phase 1
Systems Planning

Preliminary Investigation

Phase 1
Systems Planning

Phase 2
Systems Analysis

Phase 3
Systems Design

Phase 4
Systems Implementation

Phase 5
Operation & Support

SDLC PHASES

Systems planning is the first of five phases in the systems development life cycle (SDLC). In this chapter, you will learn how projects get started and how they are evaluated initially.

CHAPTER 2

SDLC PHASES

Phase 1
Systems Planning

Phase 2
Systems Analysis

Phase 3
Systems Design

Phase 4
Systems Implementation

Phase 5
Systems Operation/Support

Preliminary Investigation

Chapter 2 begins the study of the systems development life cycle (SDLC). The first phase in the SDLC is called **systems planning**. *In the systems planning phase, you learn how projects get started, how they are evaluated initially, and what takes place during systems investigation.*

OBJECTIVES

When you finish this chapter, you will be able to:

- Describe the strategic planning process, and why it is important to IS managers
- Explain the purpose of a mission statement
- Explain why and how systems projects are initiated
- Explain how systems projects are evaluated
- List the objectives of the preliminary investigation
- Describe what activities occur during the preliminary investigation
- Carry out fact-finding procedures to evaluate the systems request
- Describe what takes place at the completion of the preliminary investigation

INTRODUCTION

In this chapter, you will learn about systems planning, which is the first phase of the systems development life cycle. During the systems planning phase, the information systems department examines the systems request and conducts a preliminary investigation to determine whether further development is justified.

First, you will look at why and how requests for systems projects originate and then you will examine the criteria that are used to evaluate systems projects. Next, you will study the objectives of the preliminary investigation and factors that can affect the scope of the investigation. You will learn about the major fact-finding tasks that begin in this phase and continue in more detail in later SDLC phases. Finally, you will look at activities that complete the systems planning phase.

THE STRATEGIC PLANNING PROCESS

Every organization has a reason for existing and a plan for the future. To describe its overall strategy and vision, a company writes a mission statement for its stakeholders. A **mission statement** describes the company's overall purpose and direction and usually mentions the company's main products, services, and values. **Stakeholders** are people who are affected by the company's performance, including customers, employees, suppliers, stockholders, members of the community, and others. Figure 2-1 contains examples of mission statements from several well-known companies.

To view additional examples of **Mission Statements**, visit Systems Analysis and Design Chapter 2 More on the Web.

www.scsite.com/ sad3e/ch02/

Federal Express

Federal Express is committed to our PEOPLE-SERVICE-PROFIT philosophy. We will produce outstanding financial returns by providing totally reliable, competitively superior global air-ground transportation of high priority goods and documents that require rapid, time-certain delivery. Equally important, positive control of each package will be maintained utilizing real-time electronic tracking and tracing systems. A complete record of each shipment and delivery will be presented with our request for payment. We will be helpful, courteous, and professional to each other and the public. We will strive to have a completely satisfied customer at the end of each transaction.

Toshiba International Corporation

Toshiba International Corporation is a customer driven team that takes pride in providing 100% customer satisfaction through the dedicated participation and initiative of every single employee.
Our Goal: To supply customers worldwide with a variety of high quality products and services that meet and exceed their requirements.
Our Vision: To be constantly growing and continuously improving ourselves and our product.
Our Conduct: Fundamental to achieving our goals and supporting our culture.

Keyport Life Insurance Company

Keyport Life Insurance Company is a customer-focused, premier provider of innovative annuity and life insurance products which enable customers, in selected market segments, to reach their long-term financial goals. We provide outstanding product value and quality service to our customers and a rewarding environment for all employees, while optimizing shareholder value.

Figure 2-1 Examples of company mission statements.

A mission statement is the starting point in the strategic planning process. After developing a mission statement, the company identifies a set of goals that will accomplish the mission. These goals usually are stated broadly and are accomplished over several years. For example, the company might set one-year, three-year, and five-year goals for expanding its market share, developing new technology, and increasing shareholder value.

ON THE NET

Companies often publish their mission statements on the Internet so customers, employees, suppliers, and others can learn about the company's objectives. When you log on to a company's Web site, you might see a menu selection that provides information about the firm. Explore the Internet, and see if you can locate information technology companies that publish mission statements. What companies can you find, and what are their missions?

Next, the company develops a list of objectives to achieve these goals. **Objectives** are specific tasks that must be performed within a certain time frame. Each major goal usually requires the completion of several essential objectives. For example, if the goal is to increase Web-based customer orders by 30 percent next year, a company might need to achieve three specific objectives, each with a definite timetable and target dates. These objectives might include creating an exciting new Web site with animation and audio, designing a set of promotional materials on disk and CD-ROM, and training a special customer support group to respond to e-mail inquiries.

The process of creating a mission statement and developing organizational goals is called strategic planning. **Strategic planning** requires a company to make decisions about long-range goals and how to get there, as shown in Figure 2-2.

Companies support their strategic plans with vital resources, including business information systems, and IS managers are key players in the strategic planning process.

The Impact of Technology

Successful companies must offer quality products and services that customers want to buy, from cars to PCs. Today, another major factor exists: the rapid expansion of information technology that is creating entirely new

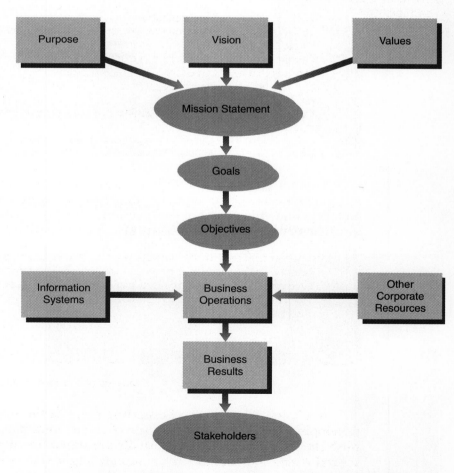

Figure 2-2   Overview of the strategic planning process that leads to a mission statement, goals, objectives, and business results that affect the company's stakeholders.

industries and new ground rules. In the future, the winners will be the companies that get out front with new concepts, new technology, and new markets.

Perhaps the best example of technology-driven business is the Internet itself. The Internet has become a powerful communications tool that affects the way the world does business. Web-based transactions are called **e-commerce**, and hundreds of firms are racing to gain a competitive advantage by offering technology and expertise in this area. Figure 2-3 shows the Web site of CyberCash, a firm that provides secure financial transactions on the Internet and credit card authentication based on digital signatures.

For an overview of **E-commerce**, visit Systems Analysis and Design Chapter 2 More on the Web.

www.scsite.com/ sad3e/ch02/

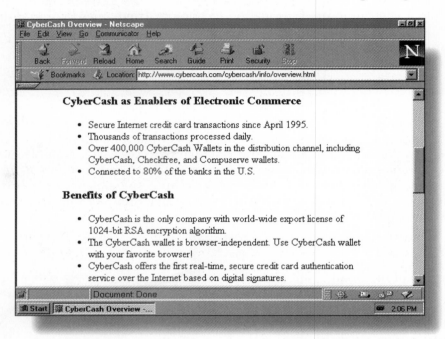

Figure 2-3   CyberCash is a firm that provides security technology for Internet financial transactions.

Another growth area is online stock trading, which allows a customer to buy and sell stocks at the click of a mouse. As shown in Figure 2-4, online trading allows anyone, including individuals in home offices, to use a personal computer to conduct and monitor their financial business. Firms such as E*TRADE, whose Web site is shown in Figure 2-5, market these online accounts aggressively, prompting traditional brokers to battle back by creating their own Internet trading sites.

New industries, services, and products will need powerful information systems. Top managers will expect IS departments to provide the hardware, software, and systems support that the company needs to survive and grow. To some firms, intense change will be threatening; to others, it will represent an opportunity.

In the mid-1980s, Tom Peters wrote a popular book called *Thriving on Chaos* that became a standard guidebook for many corporations during the 1990s. Peters

Figure 2-4   This individual can trade online from his home office.

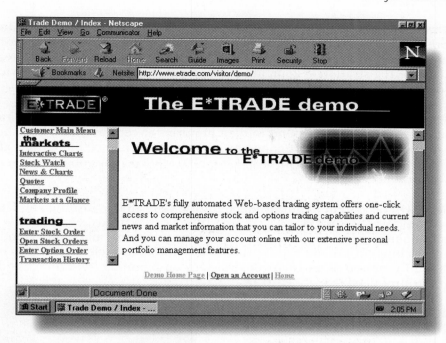

Figure 2-5   E*TRADE is an example of an online brokerage services firm.

said that change would be constant and successful companies must reinvent their businesses and learn how to thrive on change. He accurately predicted global competition, rapidly changing markets, and the explosive growth of information technology. Today, top managers know they need powerful information systems to handle new problems and opportunities.

For more information on **Systems Requests**, visit Systems Analysis and Design Chapter 2 More on the Web.

www.scsite.com/ sad3e/ch02/

INFORMATION SYSTEMS PROJECTS

This section discusses the main reasons for systems projects, the typical sources of systems projects, and systems request forms and procedures.

Reasons for Systems Projects

The starting point for modifying an information system is called a **systems request**, which is a formal way of asking for assistance from the IS department. A systems request might propose enhancements for an existing system, the correction of problems, or the development of an entirely new information system.

As Figure 2-6 shows, the main reasons for systems requests are improved service to customers, better performance, more information for making decisions, stronger controls, and reduced cost.

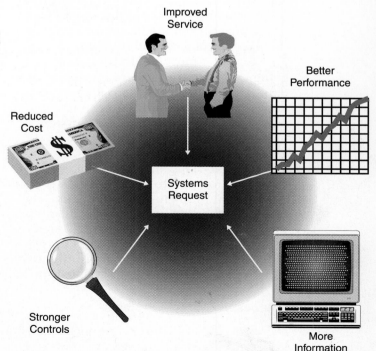

Figure 2-6   Five common reasons for systems requests.

IMPROVED SERVICE • Systems requests often are aimed at improving service to customers or users within the company. Allowing mutual fund investors to check their account balances on a Web site, storing data on rental car customer preferences, or creating an online college registration system, are examples that provide valuable service and increased customer satisfaction.

BETTER PERFORMANCE • The current system might not meet performance requirements. For example, it might be slow to respond to data inquiries at certain times, have limited flexibility, or be unable to support company growth. Performance limitations also result when a system that was designed for a specific platform becomes obsolete when new hardware is introduced.

MORE INFORMATION • The system might produce information that is insufficient, incomplete, or unable to support the company's changing information needs. For example, a system that tracks customer orders might not be capable of analyzing marketing trends. In the face of intense competition and rapid product development cycles, managers need the best possible information to make major decisions on planning, designing, and marketing new products.

> To learn more about **Reasons for Systems Projects**, visit Systems Analysis and Design Chapter 2 More on the Web.
>
> www.scsite.com/ sad3e/ch02/

STRONGER CONTROLS • A system must have effective controls to ensure that data is accurate and secure. Some common controls include passwords, various levels of user access, and **encryption**, or coding of data, so it cannot be read easily. Sophisticated controls can include devices that scan a person's retina to use it as a fingerprint, as shown in Figure 2-7. Weak controls can allow data entry errors or unauthorized access. For example, if an invalid customer number is entered, the order system should reject the entry immediately and prompt the user to enter a valid number.

Controls must be effective without being excessive. If a system requires redundant data input or takes too long to verify every data item, internal users and customers might complain that the system is not user-friendly.

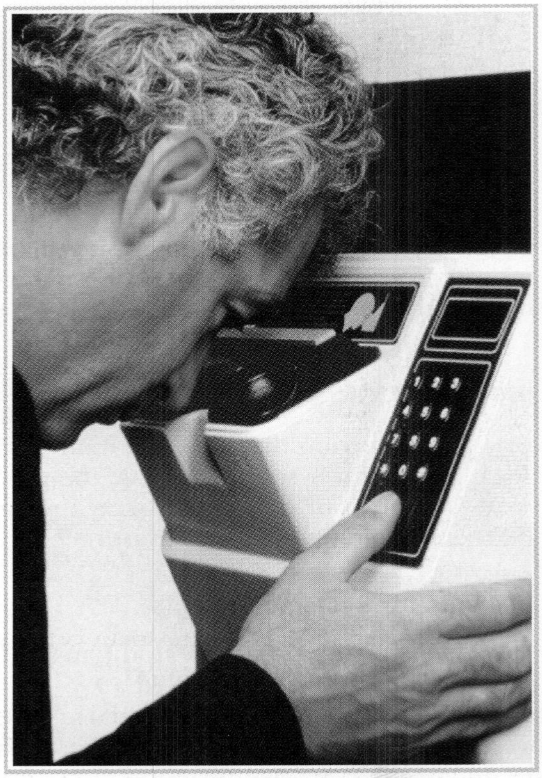

Figure 2-7   This retina scanning device ensures effective controls.

REDUCED COST • The current system could be expensive to operate or maintain as a result of technical problems, design weaknesses, or the changing demands of the business. It might be possible to adapt the system to newer technology or upgrade it. On the other hand, cost-benefit analysis might show that a new system would be more cost effective and provide better support for long-term objectives.

Sources of Systems Projects

Who initiates systems projects? One way to answer this question is to analyze who generates systems requests, as shown in Figure 2-8. Notice that both internal and external factors are involved.

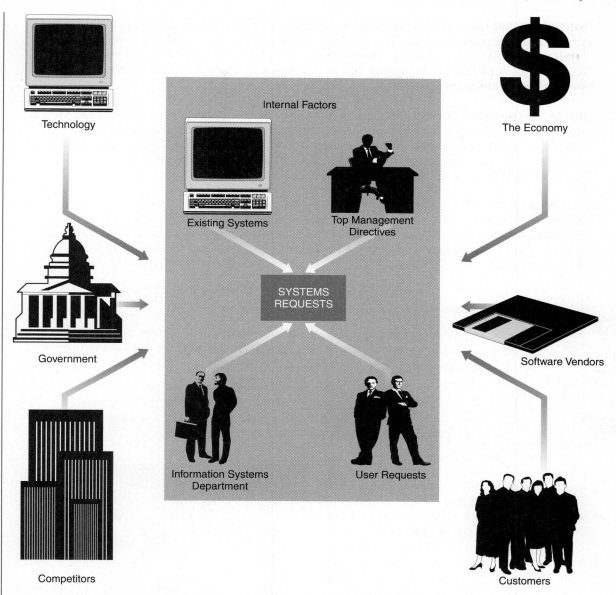

Figure 2-8   Systems requests are the result of internal and external factors.

USER REQUESTS • As users gain experience with an information system, they are likely to make more systems requests for services. For example, users might request a new Web site to market company products, a more powerful sales analysis report, a network to link all production locations, or an online system that allows customers to obtain the status of their orders instantly. Users might not be satisfied with the current system because it is difficult to learn or lacks flexibility. They might want information systems support for business requirements that did not even exist when the system was developed.

TOP-MANAGEMENT DIRECTIVES • Directives from top managers are a second source of systems projects. These directives could result from new company objectives, a need for better information for decision making, or additional support required to meet strategic business goals.

EXISTING SYSTEMS • Errors or problems in existing systems can trigger requests for systems projects. System errors must be corrected, but analysts often spend too much time reacting to day-to-day problems without looking at underlying causes. This approach can turn an information system into a patchwork of corrections and changes that cannot support the company's overall business needs.

INFORMATION SYSTEMS DEPARTMENT • Systems projects also come from the information system (IS) department's own suggestions. If IS staff members clearly understand company operations and needs, they can recommend useful, efficient systems. IS departments sometimes overestimate user needs, however, and design systems that are more sophisticated and complex than necessary. The risk is that a system might never be implemented successfully, even after enormous effort. When this happens, management becomes wary of large projects proposed by information systems people.

EXTERNAL FACTORS • External or outside forces also cause changes to existing systems or require the creation of new systems. Examples of external forces as a source of systems projects include:

- Changes in government tax regulations and reporting requirements.

- New releases or versions of software packages.

- Competitors offering new products or services that the company also must provide. Examples might include online banking or a Web site to help customers obtain technical support and product information.

- Industrial and organizational relationships. For example, an automobile company might require that suppliers code their parts in a certain manner to match the auto company's inventory control system. As shown in Figure 2-9, Gateway 2000 uses *smart* forklifts that read the numbers as their corresponding parts are picked.

- Advances in technology. For example, the success of scanner technology in supermarket checkout lanes resulted in universal bar coding that affects virtually all products.

Request Form and Procedure

Many organizations use a special form for systems requests. Figure 2-10 shows a sample request for information systems services, or systems request, form. A properly designed form streamlines the process and ensures consistency. The form must be easy to understand and use and include clear instructions. The form should contain enough space for all required information and should indicate what supporting documents are needed. Some companies have designed online systems request forms that can be filled in and submitted via e-mail.

Figure 2-9   Gateway 2000 uses *smart* forklifts that read bar codes of part numbers.

SWL **REQUEST FOR INFORMATION SYSTEMS SERVICES**

Date: _____
Submitted by: _____ Title: _____
Department: _____ Location: _____
Phone: _____ e-mail: _____

REQUEST FOR:

[ ] Correction of system error
[ ] System enhancement
[ ] New system

URGENCY:

[ ] Immediate attention needed
[ ] Handle in normal priority sequence
[ ] Defer until new system is developed

DESCRIPTION OF REQUESTED SYSTEMS SERVICES:
(ATTACH ADDITIONAL DOCUMENTS AS NECESSARY)

(To be completed by the Information Systems Department)

[ ] Approved   Assigned to IS contact person: _____
                  User: _____
                  Urgency code (1 low to 5 high): _____

[ ] Modified (see attached notes)
[ ] Rejected (see attached statement)

Date _____   Action: _____

> For more information on **Systems Request Forms**, visit Systems Analysis and Design Chapter 2 More on the Web.
>
> www.scsite.com/ sad3e/ch02/

Figure 2-10   Sample systems request form.

When a systems request form is received, a systems analyst or IS manager examines it to determine what resources are required for the preliminary investigation. A designated manager or a committee then decides whether to proceed with a preliminary investigation.

In some cases, however, a system failure requires immediate attention and there is no time for a formal request or a normal investigation. In these situations, an IS maintenance team attempts to restore operations immediately. When the system is back to normal, the team conducts a thorough review and prepares a systems request to cover the work that was performed.

➤ For more information on **Steering Committees**, visit Systems Analysis and Design Chapter 2 More on the Web.

www.scsite.com/ sad3e/ch02/

EVALUATION OF SYSTEMS REQUESTS

Many organizations assign responsibility for evaluating systems requests to a group of key managers and users, who form a **systems review committee**, which also is called a **steering committee, computer resources committee**, or a **computer policy committee**. The objective is to use the combined judgment and experience of several managers to evaluate systems projects.

Instead of a committee, in some companies, one person is responsible for systems development and maintenance decisions; this often is the case in smaller companies, or firms where only one individual has information technology skills. In this situation, the systems person must consult closely with users and managers throughout the company to ensure that business and operational needs are considered carefully.

Instead of relying on a single individual, a systems review committee provides a variety of experience and knowledge. A typical committee consists of the IS director and several managers from other departments. Even where there is a committee, the IS department has the responsibility for successful development of the system and the IS director must act as a technical consultant to the committee to be sure that members are aware of crucial issues, problems, and opportunities. With a broader viewpoint, a committee can establish priorities more effectively than an individual, and decisions are less likely to be affected by one person's bias.

On the other hand, action on requests must wait until the committee meets. To avoid delay, committee members can communicate through memos, e-mail, and teleconferencing. Another disadvantage of a committee is that members sometimes favor projects requested by their own departments, and internal political differences can delay important decisions. If a systems review committee is having difficulty working as a team, top management usually responds with corrective action to resolve the problem.

A KEY QUESTION

You are the IS director at Attaway Airlines, a small regional air carrier. You serve as the chair of the company's systems review committee and you currently are dealing with strong disagreement about two significant projects. Dan Esposito, the marketing manager, says it is vital to have a new computerized reservation system that can provide better customer service and reduce operational costs. Molly Kinnon, vice president of finance, is just as adamant that the new accounting system is needed immediately, because it can no longer provide accurate and timely financial information. Molly outranks Dan, and she is your boss. The next meeting, which promises to be a real showdown, is set for 9:00 A.M. tomorrow. How will you prepare for the meeting? What questions and issues should be discussed?

Evaluation of Projects

In most organizations, the IS department receives more systems requests than it can handle, and the systems review committee must evaluate the requests and set priorities. Suppose the committee receives four requests: a request from the marketing group to analyze current customer spending habits and forecast future trends, a request from the technical support group for a cellular link so service representatives can download technical data instantly, a request from the accounting department to redesign customer statements and allow them to be accessed via the Internet, and a request from the production staff for an inventory control system that can exchange data with major suppliers directly.

With a limited staff, which of these projects should be considered for further study? What criteria should be applied? How should the committee decide the priorities? To answer these questions, the committee must assess the feasibility of each systems request.

Overview of Feasibility

A systems request must meet several tests to see whether it is worth-while to proceed further. This series of tests is called a **feasibility study** and is a vital part of every systems project. A feasibility study uses three major yardsticks to measure or predict a system's success. These tests are **operational feasibility**, **technical feasibility**, and **economic feasibility**, as shown in Figure 2-11.

Sometimes the initial study is quite simple and can be done in a few hours. If the request involves a new system or a major change, however, the feasibility study will require more time and will not be completed during the systems planning phase.

Every systems request must pass an initial review to decide whether it deserves further study. How much effort

To learn more about a **Feasibility Study**, visit Systems Analysis and Design Chapter 2 More on the Web.

www.scsite.com/ sad3e/ch02/

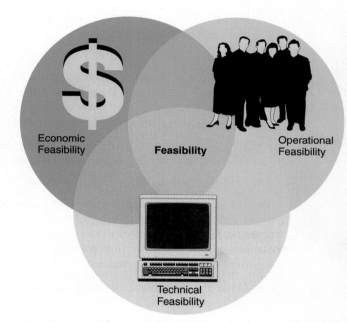

Figure 2-11   A feasibility study includes tests for operational, technical, and economic success.

needs to go into that decision? That depends on the request. For example, if a department asks that an existing report be sorted in a different order, the analyst can decide quickly whether the request is feasible. On the other hand, if the marketing department proposes a new Web site or a market research system to predict sales trends, more effort will be required. In both cases, the systems analyst asks three important questions:

- Is the proposal desirable in an operational sense? Is it a practical approach that will solve a problem or take advantage of an opportunity to achieve company goals?

- Is the proposal technically feasible? Are the necessary technical resources and people available for this project?

- Is the proposal economically desirable? What are the projected savings and costs? Are there other intangible factors, such as customer satisfaction or company image? Is the problem worth solving, and will the request result in a sound business investment?

Later in this chapter, you will learn some techniques that can be used in the fact-finding process, including the examination of company documents and organization charts, interviews with managers and users, and a review of current system documentation. If the systems request appears feasible and the project is substantial, these tasks will begin now and then continue in the initial part of the next SDLC phase — systems analysis.

OPERATIONAL FEASIBILITY • An operationally feasible system is one that will be used effectively after it has been developed. If users have difficulty with a new system, it will not produce the expected benefits. Operational feasibility depends on several vital issues. For example, consider the following questions:

- Does management support the project? Do users support the project? Is the current system well liked and effectively used? Do users see the need for change?

- Will the new system require training for users? If so, is the company prepared to provide the necessary resources for training current employees?

- Will the current system result in a workforce reduction? If so, what will happen to affected employees?

- Will users be involved in planning the new system right from the start?

- Will the new system place any new demands on users or require any operating changes? For example, will any information be less accessible or produced less frequently? Will performance decline in any way? If so, will an overall gain to the organization outweigh these individual losses?

- Will customers be affected adversely in any way, either temporarily or permanently? Will any risk to the company's image or goodwill result?

- Is the schedule for development of the system reasonable?

- Do any legal or ethical issues need to be considered?

TECHNICAL FEASIBILITY • A systems request is technically feasible if the organization has the resources to develop or purchase, install, and operate the system. When assessing technical feasibility, an analyst must consider the following points:

- Does the organization have the equipment necessary for the system? If not, can it be acquired without difficulty?

- Does the organization have the needed technical expertise? If not, can it be acquired?

- Does the proposed equipment have enough capacity for future needs? If not, can it be expanded?

- Will the hardware and software platform be reliable? Will it integrate with other company information systems, both now and in the future? Will it interface properly with external systems operated by customers and suppliers?

- Will the combination of hardware and software supply adequate performance? Are there clear expectations and performance specifications?

- Will the system be able to handle the projected growth of the organization in the future?

To learn more about **Technical Feasibility**, visit Systems Analysis and Design Chapter 2 More on the Web.

www.scsite.com/ sad3e/ch02/

The Systems Analyst's Toolkit has tools to help you assess economic feasibility.

ECONOMIC FEASIBILITY • A systems request is economically feasible if the projected benefits of the proposed system outweigh the estimated costs involved in developing or purchasing, installing, and operating it. Costs can be one-time or continuing and can be incurred at various times during project development and use. To determine economic feasibility, the analyst needs to estimate costs in each of the following areas:

- People, including IS staff and users
- Hardware and equipment
- Software, including in-house development as well as purchases from vendors
- Formal and informal training
- Licenses and fees
- Consulting expenses
- Facility costs
- Other required costs

> For more information on **Economic Feasibility**, visit Systems Analysis and Design Chapter 2 More on the Web.
>
> www.scsite.com/ sad3e/ch02/

Costs must be identified as initial development costs that are incurred only once or as continuing expenses that must be paid monthly or annually during system operation. In addition to costs, you need to assess tangible and intangible benefits to the company. **Tangible benefits** are those benefits that will produce dollar savings or reduce existing expenses. **Intangible benefits** cannot be measured specifically, but also are important.

You also must consider the timetable for completing the project, because some benefits might be realized as soon as the system is operational, but others might not occur until later. Finally, you should consider the estimated cost of *not* developing the system at all or postponing the project.

Determining Feasibility

The first step in the evaluation of a systems request is to make an initial **determination of feasibility**. Any request that is not feasible should be identified as soon as possible. For example, a request might require hardware or software that the company already has rejected for other reasons. If so, the request will not fit the company's technical environment and should not be pursued further.

Even if the request is technically feasible, it might not be the best solution. For example, a request for a new report that is needed only once could require considerable design and programming effort. A better alternative might be to download the data to a personal computer-based software package, and have users produce their own reports. In that case, it would be a better investment to train users instead of producing the reports for them.

You should keep in mind that systems requests that are not currently feasible can be resubmitted as new hardware, software, or expertise becomes available. Development costs might decrease, or the value of benefits might increase enough that a systems request eventually becomes feasible.

Conversely, an initially feasible project can be rejected later. As the project progresses through the SDLC, conditions often change. Economic conditions might shift, and costs might turn out to be higher than anticipated. In addition, managers and users sometimes lose confidence in a project. For all these reasons, feasibility analysis is an ongoing process that must be performed during all phases of the SDLC.

Criteria Used to Evaluate Systems Requests

After rejecting systems requests that are not feasible, the systems review committee must establish priorities for the remaining items. Most companies give priority to projects that provide the greatest benefit at the lowest cost in the shortest period of time. Many factors, however, influence a decision on the selection and scheduling of systems projects. The questions on the next page might be asked during the project evaluation process:

- Will the proposed system or changes in the current system reduce costs? Where? When? How? How much?

- Will the system increase revenue for the company? Where? When? How? How much?

- Will the systems project result in more information or produce better results? How? Are the results measurable?

- Will the system serve customers better?

- Will the system serve the organization better?

- Can the project be implemented in a reasonable time period? How long will the results last?

- Are the necessary resources (i.e., money, people, and equipment) available to proceed?

- Is the project absolutely necessary? Projects where management has a choice are called discretionary projects. Projects where no choice exists are called nondiscretionary projects. Creating a new report for a user is an example of a discretionary project, while adding a report required by a new federal law is an example of a nondiscretionary project.

Very few projects will score high in all areas. Some proposed systems might not reduce costs but will provide more timely management reports. Other systems might reduce operating costs substantially but require the purchase or lease of additional hardware. Some systems might be very desirable, but require several years of development before producing significant benefits.

Whenever possible, the analyst should evaluate a project based on tangible factors. A **tangible factor** can be assigned an actual or approximate dollar value. A reduction of $8,000 in network maintenance is an example of a tangible factor.

Often, the project evaluation decision also involves consideration of intangible factors. An **intangible factor** is a factor for which it is difficult to assign a dollar value. Enhancing the organization's image and improving customer service are examples of intangible factors. In many cases, such intangible factors weigh heavily in the decision for or against a systems project.

If a particular project is not discretionary, is it really necessary for the systems review committee to evaluate it? Because the project must be done, the committee must approve it. Some people argue that it is pointless to bother the committee with nondiscretionary systems requests. Besides, waiting for committee approval can delay critical nondiscretionary projects unnecessarily.

Others argue that by submitting all systems requests to the systems review committee, the committee is kept aware of all projects that con-

sume the resources of the IS department. As a result, the committee can assess the priority of discretionary projects better and schedule them more realistically. Additionally, the committee might need to prioritize nondiscretionary projects when funds or staff are limited.

Many nondiscretionary projects are predictable. Examples might include annual updates to payroll tax percentages or quarterly changes in reporting requirements for an insurance processing system. By planning ahead for predictable projects, the IS department can manage its resources better and keep the systems review committee fully informed without needing prior approval in every case.

A KEY QUESTION

Back at Attaway Airlines, the morning meeting ended with no agreement between Dan Esposito and Molly Kinnon. In fact, a new issue came up. Molly now says that the new accounting system is entitled to the highest priority because the federal government soon will require the reporting of certain types of company-paid health insurance premiums. Because the current system will not handle this report, she insists that the entire accounting system is a nondiscretionary project. As you might expect, Dan is upset. Can part of a project be nondiscretionary? What issues need to be discussed? The committee meets again tomorrow, and in your position as the IS director, the members will look to you for guidance.

PRELIMINARY INVESTIGATION OBJECTIVES

I f a systems project appears feasible and has a high enough priority, a preliminary investigation begins. A **preliminary investigation** involves one or more systems analysts investigating a systems request to determine the true nature and scope of the problem and recommend whether it is worthwhile to continue the project. Suppose, for example, that a request for systems services involved complaints that the payroll system was not functioning properly. As a systems analyst, you would perform a preliminary investigation into the complaints. If your preliminary investigation reveals problems, you would submit a report to management recommending a systems analysis of the payroll system.

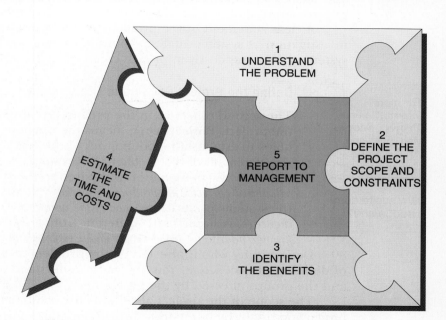

Figure 2-12   The five interlocking objectives in a preliminary investigation.

The purpose of a preliminary investigation is to gather enough information to determine whether it is worthwhile to continue the SDLC. A preliminary investigation is not a comprehensive data-gathering activity. You are not expected to define all the problems and you should not attempt to propose all possible solutions. Instead, as Figure 2-12 shows, you should meet these five related objectives:

1. Understand the true nature of the problem.

2. Define the scope and constraints of the proposed systems project.

3. Identify the benefits that are likely to occur if the proposed systems project is completed.

4. Specify time and money estimates for the next SDLC project phase, systems analysis, and for subsequent developmental phases.

5. Present a report to management describing the problem and detailing recommendations relative to the desirability of conducting a systems analysis of the current system.

Understand the Problem

The first objective in the preliminary investigation is to understand the true nature of the problem and the reason for the systems request. In many cases, the stated problem in the systems request is not the real problem, but only a symptom. For example, a request for additional hardware to speed up processing actually could be the result of weak systems design or improper scheduling. Similarly, a request for analysis of customer complaints might suggest a quality control problem in the manufacturing plant.

When interacting with users, you should be careful in your use of the word *problem*, because generally it has a negative meaning. When you ask users about *problems*, some will stress current system limitations rather than desirable new features or enhancements. Instead of focusing on difficulties, you should question users about additional capability they would like to have. Remember, every problem is also an opportunity. Using this approach, you highlight ways to improve the user's job, you get a better understanding of operations, and you build better, more positive relationships with users.

A clear statement of the problem also helps define the scope of the preliminary investigation. A systems analyst should not recommend a complete study of the entire system when a less costly approach could be just as effective in solving the problem.

Define the Project Scope and Constraints

For more information on **Project Scope**, visit Systems Analysis and Design Chapter 2 More on the Web.

www.scsite.com/ sad3e/ch02/

The second objective in the preliminary investigation is to define the scope of the project. **Project scope** means the range or extent of the project. Project scope helps to establish the boundaries of the systems request, because it requires a precise statement of the problem. For example, a statement, *payroll is not being produced accurately*, is very general, compared to the statement, *overtime pay is not being calculated correctly for production workers*. Similarly, a statement that the scope of the systems project is, *to modify the accounts receivable system to allow online customer inquiries*, is significantly different from a statement that the project scope is, *to provide additional information about customer account balances*.

Determining who is affected by the problem and the solution is an important part of defining project scope. You first must understand all the business functions involved, and the groups affected by the problem.

The scope of the project also limits the solutions that you can impose. If you set no limits, you might be tempted to investigate unrelated systems, and a project scheduled for completion in several weeks could take months or even years to complete.

Along with defining the scope of the project, you need to identify any constraints on the system. A **constraint** is a condition, restriction, or requirement that the system must satisfy. A constraint can involve hardware, software, time, policy, law, or cost. System constraints also define project scope. For example, if the system must operate with existing hardware, this is a constraint that affects potential solutions. Other examples of constraints are: *the order entry system must accept input from 15 remote sites, the human resources information system must produce statistics on hiring practices, and the new Web site must be operational by March 1*.

When evaluating constraints, you should identify their characteristics as follows:

1. *Present vs. future.* Is the constraint something that must be met as soon as the system is developed or modified? Or is the constraint necessary at some future time?

2. *Internal vs. external.* Is the constraint due to a requirement within the organization or is it imposed by some external force, such as government regulations?

3. *Mandatory vs. desirable.* Is the constraint mandatory? Is it absolutely essential that the constraint be met or is it merely desirable? If desirable, how important is the constraint?

One common mistake is to list all constraints as mandatory, which results in increased development time and costs. Present, external, and mandatory constraints usually are fixed and must be met by the system when it is developed or modified. Constraints that are future, internal, or desirable often can be postponed. Regardless of the type, all constraints should be identified as early as possible to avoid future problems and surprises.

You must clearly define the project's scope and constraints to avoid misunderstandings that can happen when a manager assumes that the system will contain a certain feature and supports the project, but later finds that the feature is not included. A clear definition of project scope and constraints reduces this problem.

Identify the Benefits

The third objective of the preliminary investigation is to identify the tangible and intangible benefits that are expected to result from the systems request. These benefits, along with the cost estimates you provide, will be used by management in deciding whether to pursue the project beyond the preliminary investigation phase.

Tangible benefits are those that can be stated in terms of dollars. Tangible benefits result from a decrease in expenses, an increase in revenues, or both. Examples of tangible benefits include a new scheduling system that reduces overtime, an online package tracking system that improves service and decreases the need for clerical staff, and a sophisticated inventory control system that cuts excess inventory and eliminates production delays.

Intangible benefits are difficult to measure in dollars, but also should be identified. Several examples are a proposed system that eliminates repetitive clerical tasks and improves employee job satisfaction, a system improvement that supplies more information for marketing decisions, and a new design for customer statements that enhances the company's image.

Estimate the Time and Costs

The fourth objective of the preliminary investigation is to develop specific time and cost estimates for the next phase of the SDLC, which is the systems analysis phase. In making your estimates, you should consider the following issues:

1. What information must you obtain, and how much information will you need to gather and analyze?

2. What sources of information will you use, and what difficulties will you encounter in obtaining the information?

3. Will you conduct interviews? How many people will you interview, and how much time will you need to meet with the people and summarize their responses?

4. Will you conduct a survey? Who will be involved? How much time will it take people to complete it? How much time will it take to prepare it and tabulate the results?

5. How much will it cost to analyze the information gathered and to prepare a report with findings and alternative solutions?

The Systems Analyst's Toolkit has tools to help you calculate the present value of costs that will not be incurred until a future time.

In addition to accurate estimates for the systems analysis phase, you also should provide ballpark estimates of the money and time required for all subsequent project phases. These estimates can be stated in broad ranges, such as $35,000 to $50,000, or 10 to 12 months. Management needs an overview of the entire project to make a decision based on total costs and benefits.

Report to Management

The final task in the preliminary investigation is to prepare a report to management. The report includes an evaluation of the systems request, an estimate of costs and benefits, and your recommendation. The Systems Analyst's Toolkit can help you achieve effective written and oral communications.

PRELIMINARY INVESTIGATION STEPS

To conduct a successful preliminary investigation, you should perform the five steps described in this section and shown in Figure 2-13. These steps apply regardless of the size of the project.

Step 1: Obtain Authorization to Proceed

A systems project often produces significant changes in company operations. Employees may be curious, concerned, or actually opposed to these changes. It is not surprising to encounter some user resistance during a preliminary investigation.

Employee attitudes and reactions are important and must be considered. In addition, a preliminary investigation often involves managers who are not direct users of the system. As a systems analyst, you will have to explain the potential benefits of the study to them and seek their cooperation and support.

Before beginning the preliminary investigation, you should obtain clear authorization from management. The authorization could be a memo or an e-mail message to all affected departments. The main thing is to let people know about your involvement and role. Often, a good first step is to arrange an initial meeting with key managers and IS personnel to explain the project, describe your responsibilities, and invite questions, comments, and suggestions. This starts an important dialog with users that will continue throughout the entire SDLC.

Step 2: Identify the Necessary Information

You should prepare a list of the specific information you want to obtain during the preliminary investigation. To identify what you need, you should go back to the five key objectives for a preliminary investigation as shown in Figure 2-12 on page 2.17. For example, what information do you need to:

1. understand the problem
2. define the project scope and constraints
3. identify the benefits
4. estimate the time and costs
5. report to management

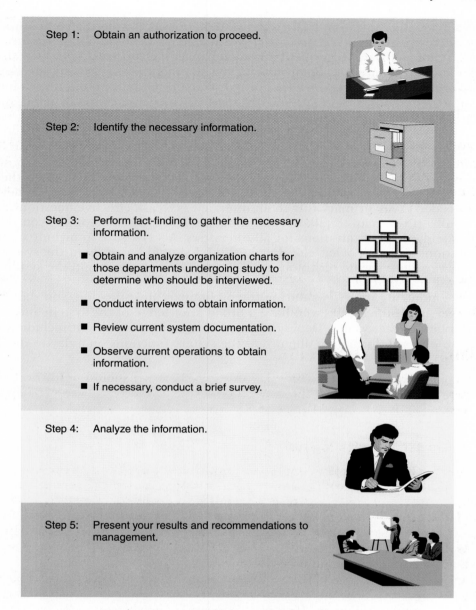

Step 1:   Obtain an authorization to proceed.

Step 2:   Identify the necessary information.

Step 3:   Perform fact-finding to gather the necessary information.

- Obtain and analyze organization charts for those departments undergoing study to determine who should be interviewed.

- Conduct interviews to obtain information.

- Review current system documentation.

- Observe current operations to obtain information.

- If necessary, conduct a brief survey.

Step 4:   Analyze the information.

Step 5:   Present your results and recommendations to management.

Figure 2-13   Preliminary investigation activities.

With this list of requirements, you can prepare a schedule of your activities during the preliminary investigation phase.

Step 3: Perform Fact-Finding to Gather the Required Information

Depending on the project, this step can involve just one of the following techniques or all of them. Fact-finding might take an hour or as long as a month —whatever you need to get the job done. Some major techniques that you can use during fact finding are analyzing organization charts, conducting interviews, reviewing current system documentation, observing current operations, and conducting user surveys.

ANALYZE ORGANIZATION CHARTS • In many instances you will not know the organizational structure of the departments involved in the study. You should obtain organization charts to understand how the department functions and identify individuals you might want to interview. Organization charts often can be obtained from the company's human resources department. If such charts are not available, you should obtain the necessary information directly from department personnel and then construct your own charts.

When organization charts are available, you should verify their accuracy. Keep in mind that organization charts show the formal structure of a group but not its informal alignment, which also is important. You can draw organization charts by hand, or you can use a software package to create them.

CONDUCT INTERVIEWS • The primary method of obtaining information during the preliminary investigation is the interview, as shown in Figure 2-14. Remember that the purpose of the interview, and of the preliminary investigation itself, is to uncover facts about the existing system. The purpose of the interview is not to convince others that a new system is needed. Your primary role in an interview is to ask effective questions and listen carefully. If you plan to talk to several people about the same topic, you should prepare a standard set of questions for all interviews. Also be sure to include open-ended questions such as, "What else do you think I should know about the system?" You will learn other interviewing techniques in Chapter 3, when you begin the systems analysis phase of the SDLC.

When conducting interviews during the preliminary investigation, you should inter-view managers and supervisors who have a broad knowledge of the system and can give you an overview of the system. Depending on the situation, you might include other personnel to obtain information about how the system functions on a day-to-day basis.

Figure 2-14   The interview is the primary method of obtaining information.

REVIEW CURRENT DOCUMENTATION • Although interviews are an extremely important method of obtaining information, you also may want to investigate the current system documenta-tion. The documentation might not be up to date, so you should check with users to confirm that you are receiving accurate and complete information.

OBSERVE CURRENT OPERATIONS TO OBTAIN INFORMATION • Another fact-finding method is to observe the current system in operation. You might see how workers carry out typical tasks. You might choose to trace or follow the actual paths taken by input source documents or output reports. In addition to observing operations, you might want to sample the inputs or outputs of the system. Using simple statistical techniques, you can obtain valuable information about the nature and frequency of the problem.

CONDUCT A BRIEF SURVEY OF PEOPLE WHO USE THE SYSTEM • Interviews can be time-consuming. Sometimes you need a small amount of information, but you need it from a larger group. In this case, you should consider a brief survey that people can complete quickly and return to you.

Step 4: Analyze the Information

After gathering the data that you listed in Step 2, you are ready to analyze the information, identify alternatives with costs and benefits, and recommend a course of action. At this stage, you have several alternatives. You might find that no further action is necessary, or that some other solution, such as additional training, is needed. If the problem and its solution are both minor, you might recommend proceeding directly to the systems implementation phase. Most often, however, your recommendation will be to proceed to the next phase of the SDLC, which is systems analysis.

Step 5: Present Your Results and Recommendations to Management

After conducting a preliminary investigation, you must submit a report to a systems review committee or top management. The report should include what you found concerning the operation of the system, the problems that you observed, and your recommendations for future action. Your report will be presented in written form, and you also might be asked to give an oral presentation. The format of the preliminary investigation report varies from one company to another, and an example is shown in Figure 2-15 on the next page. A typical report includes the following seven sections:

1. *Introduction*. The first section is an overview of the report. The introduction contains a brief description of the system, the name of the person or group who performed the investigation, and the name of the person or group who initiated the investigation.

2. *Systems request summary*. The summary describes the basis of the systems request.

3. *Findings*. The findings section contains the results of your preliminary investigation, including a description of the scope of the proposed project and the main conclusions you reached.

4. *Recommendations*. Next, the report contains the recommendations for further action by the IS department. Members of management make the final decisions on future action, and they do not always follow the recommendations of the information systems department. In most cases, however, those recommendations are important factors.

5. *Time & cost estimates*. One factor that will influence management's decision is the cost of the information systems department's involvement. You must include an estimate of time and cost if you recommend further action. Your goal is to make management aware of all costs whenever any systems activity takes place.

6. *Expected benefits*. The next section contains the anticipated tangible and intangible benefits of implementing the recommendations. Whenever asked to spend money and commit resources, management must be informed of the results it can expect from the expenditures.

7. *Appendix*. The report should include an appendix if you need to attach supporting information. For example, you might list the interviews you conducted, the documentation you reviewed, and other sources of information you obtained. You do not need detailed reports of the interviews or other lengthy documentation. It is critical, however, that you retain these documents to support your findings and to serve as sources for future reference.

Figure 2-15   Sample organization of a preliminary investigation report.

If you give an oral presentation, you need to explain the current situation, describe the problems, and present your recommendations. Chapter 3 and the Systems Analyst's Toolkit contain some suggestions about delivering presentations.

SOFTWEAR, LIMITED

hen SoftWear, Limited (SWL) was created in 1991, the management decided to use an outside company, called a service bureau, to handle payroll processing and other standard accounting functions such as payables and general ledger. The service bureau, called Business Information Systems (BIS), uses its own hardware and software to perform information processing for SWL and dozens of other companies. A contractual agreement between BIS and its customers identifies the specific services that BIS will provide, with a schedule of prices.

SWL grew rapidly, and by 1995, the management decided that SWL should purchase its own central computer to handle manufacturing operations, marketing, and customer order entry systems. The company felt that this would save money and provide better support for SWL's long-range plans. To accomplish this goal, the company created an information systems department that reports to the vice president of finance.

As time went on, SWL continued to upgrade its hardware and software. In addition to the mainframe, the company currently has personal computers in most offices and many shop floor locations and has started to install local and wide area networks. Even though it could handle its own payroll processing, SWL has continued to use BIS for payroll services, because BIS seems to be doing a good job at a reasonable cost and it relieves SWL of this responsibility. Recently, however, problems with the system have developed, and payroll department employees have worked overtime to correct errors involving employee deductions.

SWL employees can make two types of voluntary payroll deductions. Starting in 1993, employees could contribute to the newly formed SWL credit union. To enroll or make changes, an employee completes a deduction form. Then, in 1995, the company gave employees an opportunity to purchase SWL company stock through payroll deductions. Employees enroll in the stock purchase plan or change their deductions by visiting the human resources department, which then sends a weekly list of transactions to the payroll department.

In addition to the credit union and stock purchase deductions, SWL employees soon may have other savings and investment choices. SWL's top management, with strong support from the vice president of human resources, is considering a new Employee Savings Investment Plan (ESIP) that will allow employees to purchase mutual funds, stocks, and other investments through regular payroll deductions. Under this 401(k) plan, tax-sheltered deductions will be managed by an outside investment firm, Court Street Securities, which will service the individual accounts. Employees will have direct control over their investments via a 24-hour, toll-free number, and receive information via monthly statements. Management expects to make a final decision about the new ESIP in several months.

The Request for Information Systems Services

Tina Pham, vice president of human resources, learned that a number of SWL employees had complained about improper paycheck deductions, and she became concerned about employee morale. She decided to discuss the subject with Michael Jeremy, vice president of finance. At their meeting, he listened carefully and promised to look into the matter further.

That afternoon, Mr. Jeremy met with Amy Calico, director of payroll, to ask her about the problem and a recent increase in overtime pay in her group. Amy stated that the overtime was necessary, because payroll operations had required more effort and her budget did not allow her to hire any additional people. She did not have any specific explanation about the payroll deduction errors.

Mr. Jeremy then decided to ask the IS department to investigate the payroll system. He prepared a Request for Information Systems Services, as shown in Figure 2-16, and forwarded it to the IS department for action. In the request, he mentioned problems with the payroll system and requested help but did not identify the causes of the problems or propose a solution.

S⚡L **REQUEST FOR INFORMATION SYSTEMS SERVICES**

Date: _____September 15, 1998_____
Submitted by: ____Michael Jeremy____ Title: _Vice President - Finance_____
Department: ____Finance____ Location: _Raleigh_____
Phone: _____Ext. 239_____ e-mail: _mjeremy@swl.hq.fin.org_

REQUEST FOR:

[X] Correction of system error
[ ] System enhancement
[ ] New system

URGENCY:

[ ] Immediate attention needed
[X] Handle in normal priority sequence
[ ] Defer until new system is developed

DESCRIPTION OF REQUESTED SYSTEMS SERVICES:
(ATTACH ADDITIONAL DOCUMENTS AS NECESSARY)

I recently had several reports about incorrect deductions in employee paychecks. Also, I am concerned about overtime in the payroll department.

Amy Calico, director of payroll, tells me that the payroll system still requires a great deal of manual effort and that she needs more people to handle the workload properly.

I think there may be more to it than that, and I would like you to look into the situation. The purpose of using BIS, the outside service bureau, was to save money, not to incur additional expense. Also, I wonder where the errors are coming from. I thought we sent all the source data to BIS and they did the processing for us.

I would like you to find out what we need to do to eliminate the deduction errors and the payroll department overtime.

(To be completed by the Information Systems Department)

[ ] Approved   Assigned to IS contact person: _____
                 User: _____
                 Urgency code (1 low to 5 high): _____

[ ] Modified (see attached notes)
[ ] Rejected (see attached statement)

Date _____   Action: _____

Figure 2-16   Michael Jeremy's request for information systems services.

Jane Rossman, manager of applications, normally receives systems requests and does an initial review to see whether a preliminary investigation is warranted. After a quick look at Mr. Jeremy's request, Jane decided to contact her boss, Ann Hon, director of information systems. Because SWL does not have a formal systems review committee, Ann normally makes the initial decision on most systems requests. She always consults with other managers, however, if the proposal is significant or could affect their areas. After discussing the proposal with Jane, Ann decided that a preliminary investigation should start right away. It seemed likely that they would find some problems in the current payroll system that was developed in 1991 without a major update.

Jane assigned Rick Williams, a systems analyst, to conduct a preliminary investigation of the payroll system. Ann sent the e-mail message shown in Figure 2-17 to Mr. Jeremy so he would know that Rick would start the preliminary investigation the following week.

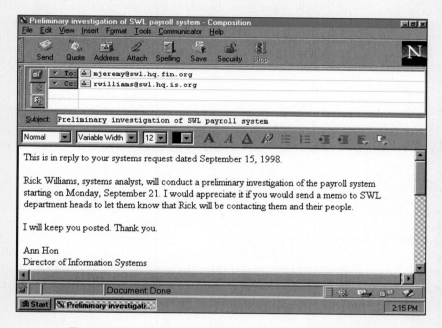

Figure 2-17   Ann Hon's e-mail message to Michael Jeremy.

Because the information systems department reports to him, Mr. Jeremy sent the memo shown in Figure 2-18 on the next page to all SWL departments. Although the memo gives few details, it alerts employees that Rick Williams has been authorized to conduct a preliminary investigation and requests their full cooperation.

MEMORANDUM

Date: September 18, 1998
To: SWL Department Heads and Managers
From: Michael Jeremy, Vice President, Finance
Subject: Payroll System Investigation

This is to advise you that Rick Williams from the information systems department will be investigating the payroll system, starting next week. The objective is to learn more about processing so we can improve operations.

Rick may be contacting you or people in your department to arrange for interviews or other assistance. Please give him your full cooperation.

Thank you.

Figure 2-18   Michael Jeremy's memo announcing the start of the payroll system investigation.

Organization Charts

   To begin his investigation, Rick met with Tina Pham, vice president of human resources. She gave Rick copies of job descriptions for all payroll department positions but did not have a current organization chart for that group.
   After reviewing the descriptions, Rick visited Amy Calico, director of payroll, who explained how the department was organized. She did not have a formal chart either, so Rick used a feature on his word processing program to draw the chart shown in Figure 2-19.

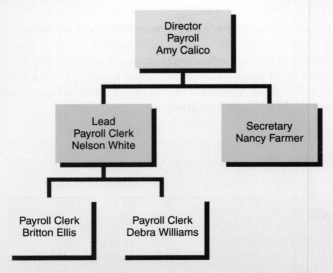

Figure 2-19 The organization chart of the payroll department
at SoftWear, Limited.

Interviews

Rick next decided to interview Michael Jeremy, Amy Calico, and Mike Feiner, director of human resources.

Mr. Jeremy provided an overview of the recent problems within the payroll system, including the costs of the current system. He had no specific data, but he believed that the majority of the errors involve stock purchases, rather than credit union deductions.

Later that day, in his meeting with Mike Feiner, Rick found out more about the reported deduction errors. He learned that stock purchase enrollments and changes are handled differently from credit union deductions. For legal reasons, Mike explained, employees must complete a special form for stock purchase plan transactions. When enrolling or making changes, an employee visits the human resources department for a brochure and an information package called a *prospectus*, which includes the sign-up form. At the end of each week, the human resources department prepares a summary of deduction requests and sends it to the payroll department. Payroll clerks then file the changes with the employee's master record.

The next morning, Rick met with Amy Calico, the payroll director. In the interview, Amy told Rick that some problems with deductions existed, but she did not feel that the payroll clerks were at fault. She suggested that he look elsewhere for the source of the problem. Amy stated that the payroll process generally works well, although a substantial amount of manual effort is required. She said that if she could hire two additional clerks, any remaining problems would be resolved. After the meeting, Rick decided that her opinion might be somewhat biased. As payroll director, Amy might not want to call attention to problems within her department, and Rick guessed other issues might be involved.

Review Current Documentation

After completing the three interviews, Rick reviewed his notes and decided to find out more about the actual sequence of operations in the current system. He studied the documentation and found that step-by-step procedures were followed for preparing the payroll. When he asked the payroll clerks about these procedures, however, he learned that some procedures were outdated. The actual sequence of events is shown in Figure 2-20 on the next page.

Rick also discovered that the payroll department had never seen a copy of the form that an employee fills out in the human resources department when joining the stock purchase plan or changing deductions. Rick obtained copies of several forms that are used in the current payroll system and put them in a file for later review. The forms included employee master sheets, employee time sheets, credit union deduction forms, and SWL stock purchase forms.

During the preliminary investigation, Rick was not concerned with the detailed information on each form. He would review this information only after management authorized the IS department to continue with the systems analysis phase.

Step 1: A new SWL employee completes an employee master sheet and a W-4 form. The human resources department then enters the employee's status and pay rate. Copies of these forms are sent to the payroll department. The payroll department updates the employee master sheet whenever changes are received from the employee or the human resources department. Updates are made with various forms, including forms for credit union and employee stock purchase plan enrollment and changes.

Step 2: On the last day of a weekly pay period, the payroll department prepares and distributes time sheets to all SWL departments. The time sheets list each employee, with codes for various status items such as regular pay, overtime, sick leave, vacation, jury duty, and personal leave.

Step 3: Department heads complete the time sheets on the first business day after the end of a pay period. The sheets then go to the payroll department, where they are reviewed. A payroll clerk enters pay rates and deduction information and forwards the time sheets to the BIS service bureau.

Step 4: The BIS service bureau enters and processes the time sheet data, prints SWL paychecks, and prepares a payroll register.

Step 5: The checks, time sheets, and payroll register are returned to SWL. The payroll department distributes checks to each department, creates reports for credit union and stock purchase plan deductions, and then transfers necessary funds.

Figure 2-20 Sequence of events in payroll processing at SoftWear, Limited.

Presentation of Findings and Management Decisions

After Rick finished his investigation, he analyzed his findings, prepared a preliminary investigation report, and met with Jane to plan the presentation to management. Jane sent the report to Mr. Jeremy with a cover memo that announced the time and location of the presentation, as shown in Figure 2-21.

SWL   **MEMORANDUM**

Date: October 5, 1998
To: Michael Jeremy, Vice President, Finance
From: Jane Rossman, Manager, Applications
Subject: Payroll System Preliminary Investigation Report

The information systems department has completed a preliminary investigation of the payroll system, as required. A report with the findings and recommendations is attached.

We have scheduled a presentation in Conference Room A on Monday, October 12 at 10:30 a.m.

If you have any questions, please let me know.

Figure 2-21   Cover memo for the SWL preliminary investigation report.

Figure 2-22 on pages 2.32 and 2.33 shows the preliminary investigation report that Rick prepared. Following the presentation to several of SWL's top managers, a question and answer session took place. The management group discussed the findings and recommendations and decided that the payroll system should be analyzed. Several members also asked whether the new Employee Saving and Investment Plan (ESIP) could be handled by the current arrangement with the BIS service bureau. Ann replied that no clear answer could be given, and everyone agreed that the scope of the systems analysis phase should be broadened to include that question.

 YOUR TURN — Do you think the absence of a systems review committee at SoftWear, Limited contributed in any way to the difficulties they now are experiencing with the payroll system? Do you think the lack of a systems review committee adversely affects the resolution of problems?

PRELIMINARY INVESTIGATION REPORT
Subject: SWL Payroll System
October 12, 1998

INTRODUCTION
The information systems department has completed a preliminary investigation of the payroll system. This investigation was the result of a systems request from Michael Jeremy, vice president of finance, on September 15, 1998.

SYSTEMS REQUEST SUMMARY
Two problems were mentioned in the request for information systems services: incorrect deductions from employee paychecks and payroll department overtime to perform manual processing tasks and make corrections.

PRELIMINARY INVESTIGATION FINDINGS
The following problems were found during the investigation:
1. Employee stock purchase deductions are reported to the payroll department in the form of a summary list from the human resources department. Data entry errors may be occurring during this process.

2. The payroll processing arrangement with Business Information Systems (BIS) requires a considerable amount of manual effort on SWL's part. The BIS system does not provide summary reports required for verification, reporting, and application of total credit union and stock purchase plan deductions. These tasks are handled manually by payroll department staff at the end of each pay period.

3. Payroll overtime has been running about six hours per week, plus an additional eight hours at the end of every month when stock purchase deductions are applied. At an average base rate of $10.00, this means about 408 overtime hours, at a cost of $6,120 per year.

The following factors are contributing to the payroll system problems:
1. The current payroll procedures were developed in 1991, when the company consisted of 75 employees, and have not changed significantly since then. Today, more than 450 SWL people are covered by the payroll system, and various new options such as the credit union and SWL stock purchase plan have been added.

2. Several years ago, payroll clerks only had to copy pay rates from the employees master sheets to the weekly time sheets. Now, in addition to the pay rate, a clerk must handle employee deduction information.

Figure 2-22 The SoftWear, Limited preliminary investigation report.

PRELIMINARY INVESTIGATION REPORT
October 12, 1998
Page 2

RECOMMENDATIONS
The problems identified in this preliminary investigation will increase as SWL continues to grow. Also, it is unclear whether the current system can be modified to handle tasks that are now done manually, or whether the system could handle the requirements of the proposed Employee Savings and Investment Plan (ESIP).

Accordingly, the information systems department recommends that a systems analysis project be performed. The analysis would include the following areas:
- Manual processing done at SoftWear, Limited
- Computer processing done by BIS service bureau
- Determination of whether the current system can meet SWL's current and future needs

TIME AND COST ESTIMATES
We estimate that two weeks will be required for an analyst to perform the recommended systems analysis. Also, we will need to conduct approximately 20 hours of interviewing and discussion with people outside the information systems department. The following is an estimate of costs for performing the systems analysis:

4.0 weeks	Systems Analyst	@ $900/week	$3,600
0.5 weeks	Other SWL people	@ $700/week (average)	350
		Total	$3,950

If the systems development work continues on this project, total cost will depend on what approach is taken. If the current system can be modified, we estimate a total project effort of $15,000 to $20,000 over a three- to four-month period. If modification is not feasible, a revised cost estimate will be submitted for review.

EXPECTED BENEFITS
At the end of the systems analysis phase, the IS department will define in detail the problems that exist in the payroll system and assess the future capability of the current system. We will propose alternative solutions that will eliminate overtime costs, sharply reduce deduction processing errors, and provide more flexibility for future SWL employee deduction options.

Figure 2-22   The SoftWear, Limited preliminary investigation report (continued).

CHAPTER SUMMARY

 ystems planning is the first phase of the systems development life cycle. Systems projects are initiated to improve performance, provide more information, reduce costs, strengthen controls, or provide better service.

Effective information systems help an organization reach its objectives, support its goals and carry out its mission. Sources of systems projects include user requests, top management directives, existing system errors and inefficiencies, and the IS department itself.

The systems analyst must evaluate the feasibility of the systems request. If the analyst initially determines that the request is not operationally, technically, or economically feasible, the request can be rejected with a minimum of cost and effort. Analysts evaluate systems requests on the basis of their expected costs and benefits, both tangible and intangible. Requests that are approved are scheduled for a preliminary investigation.

The purpose of the preliminary investigation is to gather enough information for management to decide whether it makes sense to proceed further. The five basic objectives of the preliminary investigation are to determine and understand the true nature of the problem, define the scope and constraints of the systems request, identify the benefits of resolving the problem, estimate costs for subsequent project development phases, and prepare a report and presentation to management covering the information identified in the preliminary investigation phase, with a recommendation for further action. The report must include an estimate of time, staffing requirements, costs, benefits, and expected results for the next phase of the SDLC.

Review Questions

1. What is a goal? What is an objective? How are they different? How are they related?
2. What possible types of desired improvement can cause the initiation of a systems request?
3. By what other names might the systems review committee be known?
4. What is the role of the systems review committee?
5. Is systems review always done by a committee of people, or can it be done by an individual? What are some advantages and disadvantages of a committee approach?
6. What is feasibility? List and briefly discuss three kinds of feasibility. At what points in the systems development life cycle could a systems request or a proposed solution be determined not feasible?
7. What is a discretionary project? What is a nondiscretionary project?
8. What is scope?
9. What is a constraint? In what three ways are constraints classified?
10. List and briefly describe the seven basic sections of the preliminary investigation report.
11. What is the purpose of the preliminary investigation?   ✓ 2.19 ˙˙
12. How do tangible benefits differ from intangible benefits?

Discussion Questions

1. One source of new systems projects is a directive from top management. In your position as director of information systems, the vice president of marketing tells you to write a program to create 500 computer mailing labels for a one-time advertising promotion. You know that the labels can be prepared more efficiently by simply using a word processing mail merge feature on a PC workstation in the marketing department. How would you handle this situation?
2. The vice president of accounting says to you, the director of information systems, "This systems development life cycle stuff takes too much time and money." She tells you that her people know what they are doing and that all systems requests coming from her department are necessary and important to the organization. She suggests that the information systems department bypass the initial steps for any accounting department request and immediately work on the solution. What would you say to her?
3. What would you do as a systems analyst if a vice president insisted that a system be computerized, but you knew that the system's cost could not be justified?

CASE STUDIES

NEW CENTURY HEALTH CLINIC

New Century Health Clinic's office manager, Anita Davenport, recently asked permission to hire an additional office clerk because she feels the current staff can no longer handle the growing workload. The associates discussed Anita's request during a recent meeting. They were not surprised that the office staff was feeling overwhelmed by the constantly growing workload. Because the Clinic was busier and more profitable than ever, they all agreed that New Century could certainly afford to hire another office worker. Dr. Jones then came up with another idea. He suggested that they investigate the possibility of computerizing New Century's office systems. Dr. Jones said that a computerized system could keep track of patients, appointments, charges, insurance claim processing, and reduce paperwork. All the associates were enthusiastic about the possibilities and voted to follow up on the suggestion. Dr. Jones agreed to direct the project.

Because no member of the staff had computer experience, Dr. Jones decided to hire a consultant to study the current office systems and recommend a course of action. Several friends recommended you as a person who has considerable experience with computerized business applications.

Assignments

1. Dr. Jones arranges an introductory meeting between the associates of New Century Health Clinic and you to determine if mutual interest exists in pursuing the project. What should the associates try to learn about you? What should you try to learn in this meeting?

2. What kind of questions would you ask to assess the initial feasibility of this project? Based on the information above, does the project seem feasible?

3. New Century Health Clinic management decided to contract for your services to perform a preliminary investigation. What would be your plan of action?

4. You begin the preliminary investigation. What information is needed? From whom would you obtain it? What techniques would you use in your fact-finding?

PEMBROKE IMPORTS

Four months ago, David Jackson was hired away from an advertising agency to become the director of marketing for Pembroke Imports. Jackson recently submitted a systems request to redesign Pembroke's customer billing statements. Hannah Holt, the systems analyst assigned to do the preliminary investigation, interviewed Jackson to determine the reasons for the request. David explained that the current statements are much too unattractive and dull. "Pembroke needs to update its image," he said. "We have to show our customers that Pembroke Imports has contemporary ideas and tastes. The best place to start is with the monthly statements we send them. We need something more eye-catching, more artistic, more upbeat!"

Hannah next interviewed the director of accounting, Karen Alexander, who oversees the accounts receivable (A/R) system, which produces the monthly customer statements. Karen told Hannah that no problems with the A/R system have been reported, and no complaints from the customers about the statements have ever been received. She assured Hannah that the current forms were clear and easy to understand.

Confused, Hannah decided she should talk with Cecil Collier, the manager of customer relations. Cecil assured Hannah that Pembroke was having no problems with its customers. She even showed Hannah the latest annual report, which clearly showed that Pembroke Import's annual sales were increasing at a healthy pace.

Assignments

1. The chapter identifies five major reasons for systems projects. Had David made his systems request for one or more of these five reasons? If so, which one(s) and why? If not, why not?

2. Do you think this is a feasible project? Why or why not?

3. Of the three tests of feasibility — operational, technical, or economic — which would you perform first to measure the system project's feasibility? Why?

4. What should Hannah do next?

RIDGEWAY COMPANY

A t Ridgeway Company, senior vice president Helen Hill, vice president of finance Luis Sanchez, and director of information systems Linda Usher, form the permanent steering committee that approves and schedules all systems projects.

Thomas McGee, vice president of operations, recently talked to Hill about the committee's work. "It just isn't fair," McGee began, "for the committee to be able to turn down projects that one of my facility managers thinks is worthwhile. After all, Ridgeway runs all the facilities as separate profit centers. The Country Club pro shop, the golf course, the restaurant and bar, and the tennis club have separate budgets. When the information systems department does a project for one of them, the facility is charged for all development costs. My pro shop manager, Chris Connely, is planning to submit a request for a computerized inventory system for the pro shop. We have the figures to prove that the system will save the shop and the company money in the long run. The pro shop has the funds to pay for the system development, but what's so frustrating is that after all our planning, the committee might say no. I can see why the committee has to have the power to set priorities and schedules, but if we are willing to pay for a system, and if we believe the system is worthwhile, why should the committee be able to veto it?"

Assignments

1. Chris has asked you to help him with the systems request form. What are the reasons for the systems request? How would you describe the benefits of the new system? (Describe both tangible and intangible benefits.)

2. Review the criteria used to evaluate systems requests (page 2.15). Based on these criteria, does the computerized inventory system seem feasible? Explain the reasons for your answer.

3. Is a project that is good for the pro shop necessarily good for the company? For what valid reasons might the steering committee turn down this project request?

4. How should Hill respond to McGee's complaint?

G. H. AMES & COMPANY

K elly Tompkins, a systems analyst at G. H. Ames & Company, often is assigned responsibility for maintenance changes to the company's sales analysis system. She recently noticed that the frequency of requests for fixes and additions to that system was increasing. Kelly mentioned this to her manager, Chris Lyle, who asked if the marketing department had made any specific complaints about the system. When Kelly admitted that she was unaware of any such complaints, Chris said, "Then don't worry about it."

Assignments

1. If the frequency of fixes and enhancements on the sales analysis system is increasing, what are some possible causes?

2. Do you agree with Chris' decision? Why or why not? How else could Chris have responded to Kelly's concerns?

3. After further conversations with Kelly and a review of the systems requests, Chris agrees that it might be time for a major system upgrade. Who/what were the sources of this systems project?

4. Upon review, Chris assigns Kelly to be systems analyst on the project. What should be her next step?

Phase 2
Systems Analysis

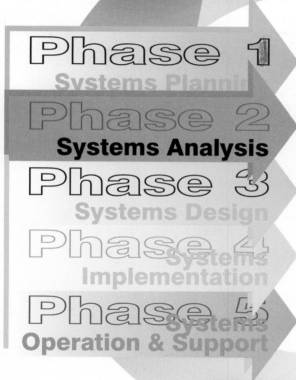

Phase 1
Systems Planning

Phase 2
Systems Analysis

Phase 3
Systems Design

Phase 4
Systems Implementation

Phase 5
Operation & Support

Determining Requirements

Analyzing Requirements

Evaluating Alternatives and Strategies

SDLC PHASES

Systems analysis is the second phase in the systems development life cycle (SDLC). In the systems planning phase, you conducted a preliminary investigation to learn about the systems problem or opportunity that led to the systems request and to determine if it is necessary to proceed to the next phase. Now, in the systems analysis phase, your objective is to learn exactly how the current system works, to determine and document fully how the system could work better to support business needs, to develop a logical, business-related model of the proposed system, and to make recommendations to management.

CHAPTER 3

SDLC PHASES

Phase 1
Systems Planning

Phase 2
Systems Analysis

Phase 3
Systems

Phase 4
Systems
Implementation

Phase 5
Systems
Operation & Support

Determining Requirements

OBJECTIVES

When you finish this chapter, you will be able to:

- Explain how systems analysis relates to business needs, problems, and opportunities

- List and describe the types of system requirements that must be identified during systems analysis

- Describe how to conduct a successful interview

- Explain when and how to use fact-finding techniques, including interviews, documentation review, observation, questionnaires, sampling, and research

- Set up effective documentation methods to use during systems development

- Describe alternative systems development approaches, including joint application development (JAD) and rapid application development (RAD)

- Explain object-oriented systems development and how this approach differs from structured analysis and design

Determining requirements is the first of three chapters in the systems analysis phase. Chapter 3 emphasizes the process of gathering facts about the current system and proposed changes.

INTRODUCTION

This chapter begins with an overview of the systems analysis phase and then discusses fact-finding techniques, including interviewing, documentation review, observation, questionnaires, sampling, and research. It also describes methods used to record the results. The chapter includes a description of other systems development techniques and closes with an overview of requirements analysis, which is the next step in the systems analysis phase.

OVERVIEW OF THE SYSTEMS ANALYSIS PHASE

During the systems analysis phase, your main task is to gather and record facts about the current system — whether it is manual or computer-based — and what is required to support business needs. To obtain this information, you must ask the right questions, such as, What business functions are supported by the current system? What current or future business functions must be supported by the system? What procedures and documents are being used currently? Who is involved in each operation? What transactions does the system process? What information does the system generate and use? What information do users and managers need from the system? What are the strengths and weaknesses of the current system? What procedures in the current system could be eliminated? The answers to these questions will help you determine the current condition of the existing system and where improvements are needed.

The fact-finding process helps systems analysts and managers make informed decisions about changes to the system. Many approaches to decision making exist, but managers usually use a simple three-step method:

1. Determine the facts.
2. Analyze the facts.
3. Make a decision.

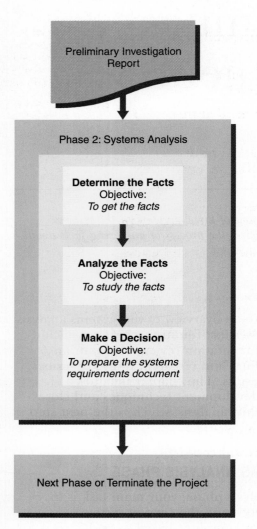

Figure 3-1   The systems analysis phase includes the three steps in

The first step in the systems analysis phase is to determine the facts. This process is called **requirements determination** or **fact-finding** and is the subject of this chapter. In the second step, you analyze the facts. This task, called **requirements analysis**, is explained in Chapters 4 and 5. After you determine and analyze the facts, the third step is to reach conclusions and present your recommendations to management. This three-step approach shown in Figure 3-1 is a sound method for identifying alternatives throughout the SDLC.

During the systems analysis phase, you apply many of the same techniques you used during the systems planning phase, but in more depth. In the preliminary investigation, you did an overview to see whether to proceed further. Now you must investigate the system in more detail.

Although software is available to assist you in analyzing facts and data, no program actually performs fact-finding for you. In this chapter, you will find many suggestions and ideas to help you determine the system requirements.

THE CHALLENGE OF SYSTEMS ANALYSIS

The systems analysis phase of the SDLC can be especially challenging when a large system is involved. The main objective of systems analysis is to understand the dynamics of an information system and the company's information needs. Business systems are never static — they must change rapidly to meet the organization's needs. If revisions have been made to a system, it might not resemble the original systems design at all. In some cases, the systems analyst must perform **reverse engineering** to find out how the original system functioned before it was modified. It is possible that several layers of changes were made at various times because of enhancements and maintenance. Large systems projects that involve a team of analysts will require additional effort to coordinate the tasks, people, and project details.

To be successful during systems analysis, you must have both critical-thinking and interpersonal skills. **Critical-thinking skills** enable you to recognize the problem, analyze the elements, and communicate the results effectively. **Interpersonal skills** are especially important for a systems analyst because you must work with people at all organizational levels and balance the needs of users with conflicting objectives. The systems analysis phase is extremely important because it becomes the foundation for building a system solution.

Systems analysis requires clear answers to the five questions *who, what, when, where,* and *how.* For each of these questions you also must ask another, very important question: *why.* Some examples of these questions are:

1. *Who?* Who performs each of the procedures within the system? Why? Are the correct people performing the activity? Could other people perform the tasks more effectively?

2. *What?* What is being done? What procedures are being followed? Why is this process necessary? (Often, procedures have been followed for many years and no one knows why. You should question why a procedure is being followed at all.)

To learn more about **Critical Thinking**, visit Systems Analysis and Design Chapter 3 More on the Web.

www.scsite.com/ sad3e/ch03/

3. *Where?* Where are operations being performed? Why? Where could they be performed? Could they be performed more efficiently elsewhere?

4. *When?* When is a procedure performed? Why is it being performed at this time? Is this the best time?

5. *How?* How is a procedure performed? Why is it performed in this manner? Could it be performed better, more efficiently, or less expensively in some other manner?

There is an important difference between asking what *is* being done and what *could* or *should* be done. The sequence of these questions is very important, especially at this point in the SDLC. The systems analyst first must know what the current situation *is.* Only then can he or she tackle the question of what *should* be done. To illustrate this, Figure 3-2 lists the questions and when they should be asked.

Requirements Determination		Requirements Analysis
What is done?	Why is it done?	What *should* be done?
Where is it done?	Why is it done there?	Where *should* it be done?
When is it done?	Why is it done then?	When *should* it be done?
Who does it?	Why does this person do it?	Who *should* do it?
How is it done?	Why is it done this way?	How *should* it be done?

Figure 3-2   Sample questions in the two stages of systems analysis.

SYSTEMS REQUIREMENTS

A **system requirement** is a characteristic or feature that must be included in an information system to satisfy business requirements and be acceptable to users. Identifying the system requirements is essential because they will define the characteristics of the new system. These requirements also will serve as benchmarks to measure the acceptability of the finished system.

System requirements fall into five categories: *outputs, inputs, processes, timings,* and *controls.* Some examples of typical system requirements for each category are listed next.

Outputs

- The inventory system must produce a daily report showing the part number, description, quantity on hand, quantity allocated, quantity available, and unit cost of all parts, sorted by part number.
- The sales tracking system must produce a daily *hot item* report, listing all products that exceed the forecasted sales volume, grouped by style, color, size, and reorder status.
- The customer analysis system must produce a quarterly report that identifies changes in ordering patterns or trends, with statistical comparisons to the previous four quarters.

Inputs

- Manufacturing employees swipe their ID cards into online data collection terminals that record labor costs and calculate production efficiency.
- Student grades are entered using machine-scannable forms prepared by the instructor. Each form has course and section codes, and includes student numbers, names, and grades.
- A staff person at a doctor's office inputs patient services into a billing system, and a claim is sent to the patient's insurance company.

Processes

- The student records system allows access by either the student name or the student number.
- As the final step in year-end processing, the payroll system updates employee salaries, bonuses, and benefits and produces a personalized compensation report for each employee.
- The warehouse distribution system analyzes daily orders and creates a routing pattern for delivery trucks that maximizes efficiency and reduces unnecessary mileage.

Timing

- The accounts receivable system prepares customer statements by the third business day of the following month.
- The student records system produces class lists within five hours after the end of registration.
- The online inventory control system reports all low-stock items as soon as the quantity falls below a predetermined minimum.

Controls

- An employee record may be added, changed, or deleted only by a member of the human resources department.
- The manager of the sales department must approve orders that exceed a customer's credit limit.
- Before a data entry operator can enter an order, the customer must have a valid ID number.

Volumes, Sizes, and Frequencies

To identify specific requirements, you need information about current and future volumes, sizes, and frequencies for all outputs, inputs, and processes. For example, to create a Web site for customer orders, you need to know the estimated number of online customers, the periods of peak online activity, the number and types of data items required for each transaction, and the method of accessing and updating customer files.

Even to print customer statements, you need to know the number of active accounts and a forecast for one, two, or five years, because the information will affect future hardware decisions. In addition, with realistic volume projections, you can provide reliable cost estimates for related expenses such as paper, postage, and online charges.

You must ask similar kinds of questions about all system outputs, including screen displays and data files, as well as all inputs and processes. For example, in a motel chain, you could determine the frequency of online queries about room availability, the time required for each query, and the average response time. With that information, you could estimate the amount of time that the server is busy with such requests.

Or, you might learn that a transaction file must be retained for five years. If the information is stored on tape cartridges, and you calculate that two cartridges are needed for each month's data, then you would determine that the company will need 120 cartridges (2 cartridges per month x 12 months x 5 years). Transaction volume also can affect hardware needs, file activity, system response times, processing schedules, and related costs.

Volume can change dramatically if a company expands or goes into a new line of business. For example, a new Web marketing effort might require an additional server and 24-hour technical support.

INTERVIEWS

So far, this chapter has discussed the five categories of system requirements and the questions you must ask to determine these requirements. The next step is to begin collecting information. This task is called **fact-finding** and it involves a variety of techniques, including interviews, documentation review, observation, questionnaires, sampling, and research.

As previously noted, systems analysts spend a great deal of time talking with people, both inside and outside the information systems department. Much of this time is spent conducting interviews, which is one of the more important fact-finding tools. An **interview** is a planned meeting during which you obtain information from another person. You must have the skills needed to plan, conduct, and document interviews successfully. The process of interviewing consists of these six steps:

1. Determine the people to interview.
2. Establish objectives for the interview.
3. Prepare for the interview.
4. Conduct the interview.
5. Document the interview.
6. Evaluate the interview.

For more information on **Interviews**, visit Systems Analysis and Design Chapter 3 More on the Web.

www.scsite.com/ sad3e/ch03/

Determine the People to Interview

To get an accurate picture of the system, you must select the right people to interview and ask them the right questions. During the preliminary investigation, you mainly with middle managers or department heads. Now, during the systems analysis phase, you should interview people from all levels of the organization. While you can select your interview candidates from the formal organization charts that you reviewed earlier, you also must consider any informal structures that exist in the organization. **Informal**

structures usually are based on interpersonal relationships and can develop from previous work assignments, physical proximity, unofficial procedures, or personal relationships such as the informal gathering shown in Figure 3-3. In an informal structure, some people have more influence or knowledge than appears on an organization chart. Your knowledge of the company's formal and informal structures will help you determine the people to interview during the systems analysis phase.

▷ For more
**Interview
Guidelines**, visit
Systems Analysis
and Design
Chapter 3 More on
the Web.

www.scsite.com/
sad3e/ch03/

Figure 3-3   An analyst must consider informal structures in the organization when selecting interview candidates.

Establish Objectives for the Interview

After deciding on the people to interview, you must establish objectives for the session. First, you should determine the general areas to be discussed, and then list the facts you want to gather. In addition, you must plan to solicit ideas, suggestions, and opinions during the interview.

The objectives of an interview depend on the role of the person being interviewed. Upper-level managers can provide the big picture and help you to understand the system as a whole. Specific details about processes are best learned from people who actually work with the system on a daily basis.

In the early stages of systems analysis, interviews usually are general. As the fact-finding process continues, however, the interviews should begin to focus on topics that are more specific. Interview objectives also vary at different stages of the investigation. By setting specific objectives, you create a framework that helps you decide what questions to ask and how to phrase the questions. If you interview several people about the same topic, try to keep your questions consistent so you can analyze their responses objectively.

Prepare for the Interview

After setting the objectives and developing your questions, you must prepare for the interview. Careful preparation is essential because this is an important meeting and not just a casual chat. Schedule a specific day and time for the meeting and place a reminder call to confirm the meeting. Remember that the interview is an interruption of the other person's routine. Business pressures might force a postponement of the meeting; when this occurs, you should schedule another appointment as soon as it is convenient for both of you. Remember to keep department managers informed of your meetings with their staff members. Sending a memo to each department manager listing your planned appointments is a good way to keep them informed. Figure 3-4 is an example of such a memo.

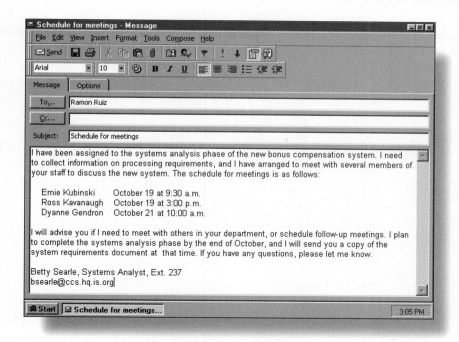

Figure 3-4   Sample memo to a department head about interviews with people in his group.

Creating a list of interview questions will help keep you on track and avoid unnecessary tangents. Also, if you interview several people who perform the same job, the question list allows you to compare their answers based on the same criteria. Although you have a list of specific questions, you might decide to depart from it because an answer to one question leads to another topic that you want to pursue.

The interview should consist of several different kinds of questions: open-ended, closed-ended, or questions with a range of responses. **Open-ended questions** encourage spontaneous and unstructured responses. Open-ended questions are useful when you want to understand a larger process or draw out the interviewee's opinions, attitudes, or suggestions. Some examples of open-ended questions are: Is the system operating properly? How is this task performed? Why do you perform the task this way? How are the checks reconciled? What added features would you like to have in the new billing system?

Closed-ended questions limit or restrict the response. You use closed-ended questions when you want information that is more specific or need to verify facts. Examples of closed-ended questions are: How many personal computers do you have in this department? Do you review the reports before they are sent out? How many hours of training does a clerk receive? Is the calculation procedure described in the manual? How many customers ordered products from the Web site last month?

The third type of question — called a **range of responses question** — is a specific type of closed-ended question that involves asking the person to evaluate something by providing limited answers to specific responses or on a numeric scale. This method makes it easier to tabulate the answers and interpret the results. Some examples of range of responses questions are: On a scale of one to ten, with one being the lowest and ten being the highest, how effective was your training? How would you rate the severity of the problem: low, medium, or high? Is the system shutdown something that occurs never, sometimes, often, usually, or always?

When concluding the interview, ask a final open-ended question that encourages the interviewee to offer general feedback, such as, Do you think I should know anything else about the system to help me understand it better?

You should send a list of essential questions to an interviewee several days before the meeting, especially when detailed information is needed, so the person can prepare for the interview and minimize the need for a follow-up meeting. Figure 3-5 shows a sample memo that confirms the date, time, location, and purpose of the interview.

 MEMORANDUM

Date: October 12, 1998
To: Ross Kavanaugh, Compensation Manager
From: Betty Searle, Systems Analyst
Subject: Bonus Compensation System Meetings

I would like to confirm our meeting on October 19 at 3:00 p.m. in your office. As part of my information gathering for the new bonus compensation system, I need to know all details about the steps you and your staff perform in processing bonus compensation. I plan to ask the following questions:

1. What portion of bonus compensation processing is handled within your department?

2. What other areas of the company are responsible for different aspects of bonus compensation? How do these other areas interact with your department?

3. What procedures do you handle and what specific steps are involved?

4. What improvements would you like to see in the bonus compensation processing when we implement this system on the computer?

5. Are portions of bonus compensation processing confidential? What special security requirements are needed?

If you have written procedures, standard forms, or special calculations for the bonus compensation system, please have them available for me to review during our meeting. I will need my own copies of some of this material, but we can decide which material should be copied during our meeting.

Please contact me if something comes up and we have to reschedule our meeting.

Figure 3-5 Sample memo to interviewee to confirm a planned meeting.

If you have questions about documents, ask the interviewee to have samples available at the meeting. Your advance memo should include a list of the documents you want to discuss, if you know what they are. Otherwise, you can make a general request for documents, as the analyst did in her memo shown in Figure 3-5.

Conduct the Interview

After determining the people to interview, setting your objectives, and preparing the questions, you should develop a specific plan for the meeting. When conducting an interview, you should begin by introducing yourself, describing the project and explaining your interview objectives. During the interview, ask questions in the order in which you prepared them, and give the interviewee sufficient time to provide thoughtful answers. When you finish asking your questions, summarize the main points covered in the interview and explain the next course of action. For example, mention that you will send a follow-up memo or that the interviewee should get back to you with certain information. When you are ready to conclude the interview, thank the person and encourage him or her to contact you with any questions or additional comments.

Establishing a good rapport with the interviewee is important, especially if this is your first meeting. If the other person feels comfortable and at ease, you probably will receive more complete and candid answers. Your primary responsibility during an interview is to *listen carefully* to the answers. Analysts sometimes hear only what they expect to hear. You must concentrate on what is being said and notice any nonverbal communication that takes place. This process is called **engaged listening**.

After asking a question, allow the person enough time to think about the question and arrive at an answer. Studies have shown that the maximum pause during a conversation is usually three to five seconds. After this interval, one person will begin talking. You will need to be patient and practice your skills in many actual interview situations to be successful.

At the end of an interview, you should summarize the session and seek a confirmation from the other person. By stating your understanding of the discussion, the interviewee can respond and correct you, if necessary. One good approach is to rephrase the interviewee's answers by saying, "If I understand you correctly, you are saying that ..."

Two schools of thought exist about the best location for an interview. Some analysts believe that interviews should take place in the interviewee's office, while other analysts feel that a neutral location such as a conference room is better.

Supporters of interviews in the interviewee's office believe that the interviewee's own office is the best location because it makes the interviewee feel comfortable during the meeting. A second argument in favor of the interviewee's office is because that is where he or she has the easiest access to supporting material that might be needed during the discussion. If you provide a complete list of topics in advance, however, the interviewee can bring the necessary items to a conference room or other location.

Supporters of neutral locations stress the importance of keeping interruptions to a minimum so both people can concentrate fully. In addition, an interview that is free of interruptions takes less time. If the meeting does take place in the interviewee's office, you should suggest tactfully that all calls be held until the conclusion of the interview.

A KEY QUESTION

How much does the organizational level of the person being interviewed affect the interview process?

FastPak, the nation's fourth largest overnight package service carrier, is headquartered in Fullerton, California. Jesse Evans is a systems analyst on an IS team that is studying ways to update FastPak's package tracking system. Jesse prepared well for her interview with Jason Tanya, FastPak's executive vice president. Mr. Tanya did not ask his assistant to hold his calls and visitors during the meeting, however. After several interruptions, Jesse tactfully suggested that she could come back another time, or perhaps that Mr. Tanya might ask his assistant to hold his calls. "No way," he replied. "I'm a very busy man and we'll just have to fit this in as we can, even if it takes all day." Jesse was unprepared for his response. What are her options? Is an analyst always in control of this kind of situation? Why or why not?

Document the Interview

Although there are pros and cons to taking notes during an interview, the accepted view is that note taking should be kept to a minimum. While you should write down a few notes to jog your memory after the interview, you should avoid writing everything that is said. Too much writing distracts the other person and makes it harder to establish a good rapport.

After conducting the interview, you must record the information quickly. You should set aside time right after the meeting to record the facts and evaluate the information. For this reason, try not to schedule back-to-back interviews. Studies have shown that 50 percent of a conversation is forgotten within 30 minutes. Therefore, you should use your notes to record the facts immediately so you will not forget them. You can summarize the facts by preparing a narrative describing what took place or by recording the answers you received next to each question on your prepared question list.

After the interview, send a memo to the interviewee expressing your appreciation for his or her time and cooperation. In the memo, you should note the date, time, location, purpose of the interview, and the main points you discussed so the interviewee has a written summary and can offer additions or corrections.

Evaluate the Interview

In addition to recording the facts obtained in an interview, try to identify any possible biases. For example, an interviewee who tries to protect his or her own area or function might give incomplete answers or refrain from volunteering information. Or, an interviewee with strong opinions about the current or future system might distort the facts. Some interviewees might answer your questions in an attempt to be helpful although they do not have the necessary experience to provide accurate information.

Tape recorders can be effective tools during an interview. Many people, however, feel threatened by the presence of recorders. Even careful use of tape recorders can make some people uncomfortable. Before using a recorder, you should discuss its use with the interviewee. Assure the interviewee that you will erase the tape after you transcribe your notes and that you will stop and rewind the tape at any time during the interview at his or her request. If you ask sensitive questions, or the interviewee wants to answer a question without being recorded, explain that you will turn off the tape for a period of time during the interview.

Disadvantages to using a recorder do exist. For example, you could tend to rely too much on the recorder and forget to listen carefully to the interviewee's responses so you can ask good follow-up questions. If this happens, you may have to return for a second interview to ask the questions you missed the first time. When discussing personalities or sensitive information, you should not record the discussion, so the interviewee feels comfortable discussing important issues. Finally, remember that each recorded interview is twice the normal length, because you must listen to or view the recorded meeting again after conducting the interview itself.

A KEY QUESTION

Should you interview several people at the same time? What problems can occur? Is the organizational level of the interviewee still a primary factor?

As she continued to work on the package tracking system at FastPak, Jesse ran into another unusual situation. She needed to interview Carole Scott and Tony Lorenzo, the two regional operations managers who report to Jason Tanya. To save time, she decided to meet with them together. She also thought it would be useful to ask about the interaction between the two regional operations. Jesse encountered a problem right away when she asked if she could use a tape recorder so she could transcribe her notes later. Tony had no problem with this, but Carole objected and said it made her uncomfortable.

Jesse said that her handwritten notes would be sufficient, so she went ahead with her questions. As the interview proceeded, she wondered if the joint meeting was a mistake. Carole dominated the conversation, even when the questions were addressed specifically to Tony. Jesse did the best she could and completed the interview. Later, she asked her supervisor, Sharon Fairchild, what she should have done. If you were Sharon, what advice would you give Jesse?

Unsuccessful Interviews

No matter how well you prepare for interviews, some are not successful. One of the main reasons could be that you and the interviewee did not get along well. This situation can be caused by several factors. For example, a misunderstanding or personality conflict could affect the interview negatively, or the interviewee might be afraid that the new system will eliminate or change his or her job.

In other cases, the interviewee might give only short or incomplete responses to your open-ended questions. If so, you should try using close-ended questions or questions with a range of responses. If that still does not help, you should find a tactful way to conclude the meeting.

Continuing an unproductive interview is difficult. The interviewee could be more cooperative later, or you might find the information you seek elsewhere. If failure to obtain specific information will jeopardize the success of the project, inform your supervisor, who can help you decide what action to take. Your supervisor might contact the interviewee's supervisor, ask another systems analyst to interview the person, or find some other way to get the needed information.

OTHER FACT-FINDING TECHNIQUES

Document Review

During the requirements determination or fact-finding process, you should review the existing system documentation to understand how the system is supposed to work. Remember that system documentation is sometimes out of date. Forms can change or be discontinued; documented procedures often are modified or eliminated. You should obtain copies of actual forms and operating documents currently in use. You also should review blank copies of forms, as well as samples of actual completed forms. You usually can obtain document samples during interviews with the people who perform that procedure. If the system uses a software package, you should review the documentation for that software.

For additional details on **Fact-Finding**, visit Systems Analysis and Design Chapter 3 More on the Web.

www.scsite.com/ sad3e/ch03/

Observation

For more information on **Observation**, visit Systems Analysis and Design Chapter 3 More on the Web.

www.scsite.com/ sad3e/ch03/

The **observation** of current operating procedures is another fact-finding technique. Sometimes, you can understand a system better by observing it in operation. Seeing the system in action gives you additional perspective and a better understanding of the system and its procedures. Personal observation also allows you to verify statements made in interviews and determine whether procedures really operate as they are described. Through observation, you might discover that neither the system documentation nor the interview statements are accurate.

Personal observation also can provide important advantages in later SDLC phases. For example, recommendations often are better accepted when they are based on personal observation of actual operations. Observation also can provide the knowledge needed to test or install future changes and can help build relationships with the operating staff who will be using the new or modified system.

Plan your observations in advance by preparing a checklist of specific tasks you want to observe and questions you want to ask. Consider the following issues when you prepare your list.

1. Ask sufficient questions to ensure that you have a complete understanding of the present system operation. A primary goal is to identify the methods of handling situations that are *not* covered by standard operating procedures. For example, what happens in a payroll system if an employee loses a time card? What is the procedure if an employee starts a shift five minutes late but then works ten minutes overtime? Often, the rules for exceptions such as these are not written or formalized. Therefore, you must try to document any procedures for handling exceptions.

2. Observe all the steps in a processing cycle and note the output from each procedural step.

3. Examine each pertinent form, record, and report. Determine the purpose each item of information serves.

4. Consider each person who works with the system and the following questions: What information is received from other people? What information is generated by this person's work? What tools are used in the process? To whom is the information passed? What questions do the people ask each other? How quickly must each step be completed? How much concentration does each step require? How often do interruptions occur? How often must a worker take a break from a concentrated activity?

5. Talk to the people who receive current reports to see whether the reports are complete, timely, accurate, and in a useful form. Ask whether information can be eliminated or improved and whether people would like to receive additional information.

For more background on the **Hawthorne Effect**, visit Systems Analysis and Design Chapter 3 More on the Web.

www.scsite.com/ sad3e/ch03/

As you observe people at work, as shown in Figure 3-6, remain aware of a factor called the **Hawthorne Effect**. The name comes from a study performed in the Hawthorne plant of the Western Electric Company in the 1920s. The purpose of the study was to determine how various changes in the work environment affect employee productivity. The surprising result was that productivity improved during observation whether the conditions were made *better* or *worse*. The conclusion was that productivity seemed to improve whenever the workers knew they were being observed.

Thus, as you observe workers, remember that normal operations might not always run as smoothly as your observations indicate. Operations also might run less smoothly because workers might be nervous during the observation. If possible, meet with workers and their supervisors to discuss your plans and objectives to help establish a good working relationship. In some situations, you might even be able to participate in the work yourself to gain a personal understanding of the task or the environment.

Figure 3-6   The result of the Hawthorne study is that worker productivity improves during observation. Always consider the Hawthorne Effect when observing the operation of an existing system.

Questionnaires

In systems development projects where it is desirable to obtain input from a large number of people, the questionnaire can be a valuable tool. A **questionnaire** is a document containing a number of standard questions that can be sent to many individuals. Questionnaires can be used to obtain information about workloads, reports received, volumes of transactions handled, types of job duties, difficulties, and opinions of how the job could be performed better or more efficiently. Figure 3-7 on the next page shows a sample questionnaire that includes several different question and response formats. A typical questionnaire starts with a heading, which includes a title, a brief statement of purpose, the name and telephone number of the contact person, the deadline date for completion, and how and where to return the form. The heading usually is followed by general instructions that provide clear guidance on how to answer the questions. Headings also are used to introduce each main section or portion of the survey, and include instructions when the type of question or response changes. A long questionnaire might end with a conclusion that thanks the participants and reminds them how to return the form.

What about the issue of anonymity? Should people be asked to sign the questionnaire, or is it better to allow anonymous responses? The answer depends on two questions. First, does an analyst really need to know who the respondents are in order to match or correlate information? For example, it might be important to know what percentage of users need a certain software feature, but specific user names might not be relevant. Second, does the questionnaire include any sensitive or controversial topics? Many people do not want to be identified when answering a question such as, How well has your supervisor explained the system to you? In these cases, anonymous responses might provide better information.

When designing a questionnaire, the most important rule of all is to make sure that your questions collect the right data in a form that you can use to further your fact-finding. Here are some additional ideas to keep in mind when designing your questionnaire.

- Keep the questionnaire brief and user-friendly.
- Provide clear instructions that will answer all anticipated questions.
- Arrange the questions in a logical order, going from easy to more complex topics.

For tips on preparing **Questionnaires**, visit Systems Analysis and Design Chapter 3 More on the Web.

www.scsite.com/ sad3e/ch03/

PURCHASE REQUISITION QUESTIONNAIRE

Pat Kline, Vice President, Finance, has asked us to investigate the purchase requisition process to see if it can be improved. Your input concerning this requisition process will be very valuable. We would greatly appreciate it if you could complete the following questionnaire and return it by March 9 to Dana Juarez in information systems. If you have any questions, please call Dana at x2561.

A.   YOUR OBSERVATIONS
Please answer each question by checking one box.

1. How many purchase requisitions did you process in the past five working days? _____

2. What percentage of your time is spent processing requisitions?
    [ ] under 20%   [ ] 60-79%
    [ ] 21-39%   [ ] 80% or more
    [ ] 40-59%

3. Do you believe too many errors exist on requisitions?
    [ ] yes
    [ ] no

4. Out of every 100 requisitions you process, how many contain errors?
    [ ] fewer than 5   [ ] 20 to 29
    [ ] 5 to 9   [ ] 30 to 39
    [ ] 10 to 14   [ ] 40 to 49
    [ ] 15 to 19   [ ] 50 or more

5. What errors do you see most often on requisitions? (Place a 1 next to the most common error, place a 2 next to the second, etc.)
    [ ] Incorrect charge number   [ ] Missing authorization
    [ ] Missing charge information   [ ] Other (Please explain) _____
    [ ] Arithmetic errors
    [ ] Incorrect discount percent used

B.   YOUR SUGGESTIONS
Please be specific, and give examples if possible.

1. If the currently used purchase requisition form were to be redesigned, what changes to the form would you recommend?

    _____
    _____
    _____
    _____
    _____
    _____

    (Please attach another sheet if necessary)

2. Would you be interested in meeting with an information systems representative to discuss your ideas further? If so, please complete the following information:

    Name _____   Department _____

    Telephone _____   E-mail address _____

Figure 3-7   Sample questionnaire.

- Phrase questions to avoid misunderstandings; use simple terms and wording.
- Try not to lead the response or use questions that give clues to expected answers.
- Limit the use of open-ended questions that will be difficult to tabulate.
- Limit the use of questions that can raise concerns about job security or other negative issues.
- Include a section at the end of the questionnaire for general comments.
- Test the questionnaire whenever possible on a small test group before finalizing it.

Sampling Work and Work Products

When studying an information system, you should collect examples of actual documents using a process called **sampling**. The samples might include records, reports, operational logs, data entry documents, complaint summaries, work requests, and various types of forms.

Several sampling techniques are systematic sampling, stratified sampling, and random sampling. Suppose you have a list of 200 customers who complained about errors in their statements. A **systematic sample** selects every tenth customer file for review. If you wanted to be sure that the sample is balanced geographically, however, you could use a **stratified sample** to select five customers from each of four ZIP Codes. Another example of stratified sampling might be to select a certain percentage of transactions from each work shift, rather than a fixed number. Finally, a **random sample** selects any 20 customers.

The main objective of any sample is to ensure that it represents the overall population accurately. If you are analyzing inventory transactions, for example, you should select a sample of transactions that are typical of actual inventory operations, and do not include unusual or unrelated examples. For instance, if a company performs special processing on the last business day of the month, that day would not be a good time to sample *typical* daily operations.

Graphics

The systems analyst might want to display the results of fact-finding in a **graphical format**. This approach often is used in quality control analysis because it highlights problems and their possible causes, and is effective when presenting results to management. One common tool for showing the distribution of questionnaire or sampling results, for example, is a vertical bar chart called a **histogram.**

Most spreadsheet programs can create histograms and other charts, as shown in the Help window in Figure 3-8 on the next page. Figure 3-9 on the next page displays a typical histogram that might have resulted from the questionnaire shown in Figure 3-7.

Research

Research is another important fact-finding technique. Your research can include reviewing journals, periodicals, and books to obtain background information, technical material, and news about industry trends and developments.

The Internet is an extremely valuable research tool. Most major hardware and software vendors maintain sites on the Web where you can obtain information about products and services offered by the company and send e-mail with specific questions to company representatives.

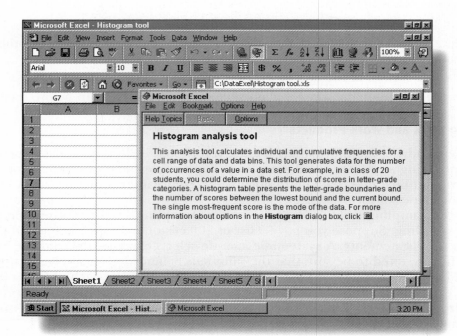

Figure 3-8 Microsoft Excel Help describes how to use the Histogram analysis tool.

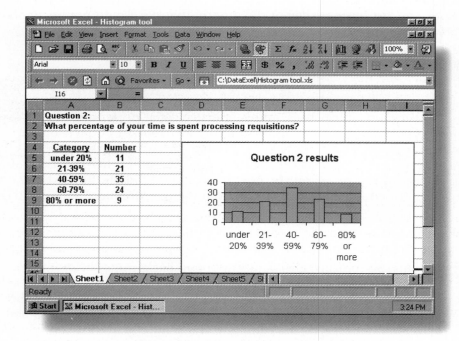

Figure 3-9 A histogram using Microsoft Excel displays results from the sample questionnaire shown in Figure 3-7 on page 3.16.

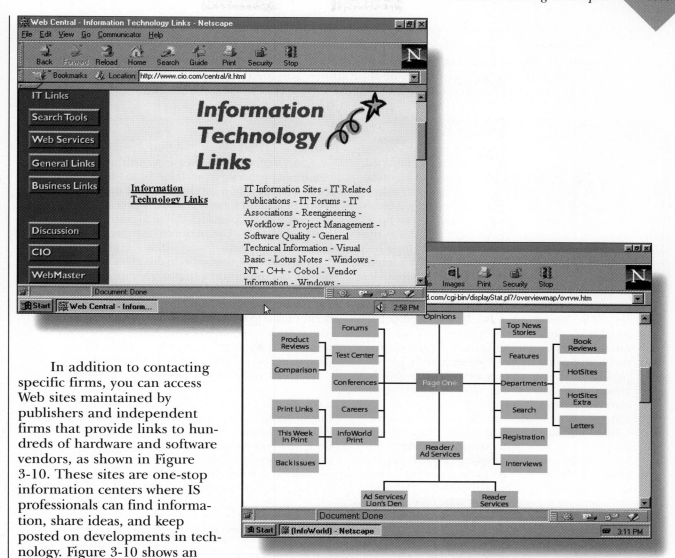

Figure 3-10 Examples of Web sites maintained by CIO magazine and InfoWorld with various features for information technology professionals.

In addition to contacting specific firms, you can access Web sites maintained by publishers and independent firms that provide links to hundreds of hardware and software vendors, as shown in Figure 3-10. These sites are one-stop information centers where IS professionals can find information, share ideas, and keep posted on developments in technology. Figure 3-10 shows an example of a powerful search engine that you can use to request information and track developments in information technology. Using the Internet, you also can access information from federal and state governments, as well as from publishers, universities, and libraries around the world. Finally, **newsgroups** are good resources for exchanging information with other professionals, seeking answers to questions, and monitoring discussions that are of interest to you.

In addition to electronic research, you can attend professional meetings, seminars, and discussions with other IS professionals, which can be very helpful in problem solving.

Research also can involve **site visits**, where the objective is to observe a system in use at another location. If you are studying your firm's human resources information system, for example, you might want to see how another company's system works. Site visits also are important when considering the purchase of a software package. The software vendor usually will suggest possible sites to visit where the software is in use. A vendor is likely to suggest only satisfied customers, however, so be aware that such sites may constitute a biased sample. A single site visit seldom gives you a true pictures, so you should try to visit more than one installation.

Before a site visit, prepare just as you would for an interview. Contact the appropriate manager and explain the purpose of your visit. Decide what questions you will ask and what processes you will observe. During your visit, observe how the system works and note any problems or limitations. You also will want to learn about the support provided by the vendor, the quality of the system documentation, and so on.

When you must ask a series of identical questions to many individuals, a questionnaire can be very useful. On the other hand, if you require information from only a few people, then you probably should interview each person individually. Is it better to interview or use a questionnaire? What about situations that do not fall neatly into either category?

The interview is more familiar and personal than a questionnaire. People who are unwilling to put critical or controversial comments in writing might talk more freely in person. Moreover, during a face-to-face interview, you can react immediately to anything the interviewee says. If surprising or confusing statements are made, you can pursue the topic with additional questions. In addition, during a personal interview, you can watch for clues to help you determine if responses are knowledgeable and unbiased. Participation in an interview can be an important human relations factor as well, because people who are asked for their opinions often view the project more favorably.

An interview, however, is a costly and time-consuming process. In addition to the meeting itself, both people must prepare, and the interviewer has to do follow-up work. When a number of interviews are planned, the total cost can be quite substantial. The personal interview usually is the most expensive fact-finding technique.

In contrast, a questionnaire gives many people the opportunity to provide input and suggestions. Questionnaire recipients can answer the questions at their convenience and do not have to set aside a block of time for an interview. If the questionnaire allows anonymous responses, people might be more candid than they would be in an interview.

Preparing a good questionnaire, however, like a good interview, requires skill and time. If a question is misinterpreted, you cannot clarify the meaning as you can in a face-to-face interview. Furthermore, unless questionnaires are designed well, recipients might view them as intrusive, time-consuming, and impersonal. As an analyst, you should select the technique that will work best in a particular situation.

A KEY QUESTION

Should you conduct interviews or send out questionnaires? Pros and cons exist to both methods. No matter which fact-finding technique you select, you must decide who will participate. This process often involves choosing a sample, especially when you are investigating the cause of a problem. To be useful, a sample must reflect the overall population. What kind of sample will give the most accurate picture? What factors should you consider?

Ann Ellis is a systems analyst at Cyberstuff, a large company that sells computer hardware and software via telephone, mail order, and the Internet. Cyberstuff processes several thousand transactions per week on a three-shift operation, and employs 50 full-time and 125 part-time employees. Lately, the billing department has experienced an increase in the number of customer complaints about incorrect bills. During the preliminary investigation, Ann learned that some Cyberstuff representatives were not following established order entry procedures. She feels that with more information, she might find a pattern and identify a solution for the problem.

Ann is not sure about how to proceed. She came to you, her supervisor, with two separate questions. First, is a questionnaire the best approach, or would interviews be better? Second, whether she uses interviews, a questionnaire, or both techniques, should she select the participants at random, include an equal number of people from each shift, or use some other approach? As Ann's supervisor, what would you suggest, and why?

RECORDING THE FACTS

The Need for Recording the Facts

 eeping accurate records of interviews, facts, ideas, and observations is essential to successful systems development. The ability to manage facts is the mark of a successful IS professional and probably is the most important skill that systems analysts can learn.

As you gather information, the importance of a single item can be overlooked or complex system details can be forgotten. The basic rule is to *write it down*. You should document your work according to the following principles: record information as soon as you obtain it, use the simplest recording method possible, record your findings in such a way that they can be understood by someone else, and organize your documentation so related material can be located easily.

Often, systems analysts use special forms for describing a system, recording interviews, and summarizing documents. One type of documentation is a **narrative list** with simple statements about what is occurring, apparent problems, and suggestions for improvement. Other forms of documentation that are described in Chapter 4 include data flow diagrams, flowcharts, sample forms, and screen captures.

Software Tools

Many programs are available to help you record and document information. These programs are described in the next section.

WORD PROCESSING • Using the features of a powerful **word processing program**, such as Microsoft Word or Corel WordPerfect, you can create reports, summaries, tables, and forms. In addition to standard document preparation, the program can help you organize a presentation with templates, bookmarks, annotations, revision control, and an index. You can consult the program's Help system for more information about these and other features.

SPREADSHEETS • A **spreadsheet program**, such as Microsoft Excel or Lotus 1-2-3, can help you track and manage numerical data or financial information. You also can generate graphs and charts that can help you and others understand the data and possible patterns. You can use the statistical tools in a spreadsheet to tabulate and analyze data from questionnaires.

DATABASE • A **database program** allows you to manage information about events, observations, and samples. You could use a database package, such as Microsoft Access or Borland Paradox to manage the details of a complex project, create queries to retrieve specific information, and generate reports.

PRESENTATION GRAPHICS • A **presentation graphics** package, such as Microsoft PowerPoint or Corel Presentations, is a powerful tool for organizing and developing your formal presentation. Presentation graphics programs enable you to create organization charts that can be used in a preliminary investigation and later during requirements determination. These high-quality charts also can be included in written reports and management presentations.

PERSONAL OR DESKTOP INFORMATION MANAGERS • A busy analyst needs to keep track of meetings, interviews, appointments, and deadlines that are weeks or months in the future. A personal or desktop information manager, such as Microsoft Outlook or Lotus Organizer, can help manage these tasks and provide a personal calendar and a To-Do list, with priorities and the capability to check off completed items.

OTHER SYSTEMS DEVELOPMENT TECHNIQUES

Introduction

Although structured analysis and design is still the most common method of systems development, many companies use other techniques to develop information systems, such as joint application development (JAD) and rapid application development (RAD), which are team-based approaches, or object-oriented (O-O) systems development, which defines a system in terms of objects, rather than traditional data and processes. These methods are not mutually exclusive. Instead, they are important techniques and strategies that are available to the systems analyst.

Figure 3-11   A JAD development team is a task force of primary users, managers, and IS professionals that works together to develop a new system.

Joint Application Development (JAD)

Joint application development (JAD) is a popular systems development technique developed by IBM. As you learned at the beginning of this chapter, in a traditional structured analysis process the IS staff collects information from many users and managers, and then develops the requirements for a new system. In contrast, using the JAD approach shown in Figure 3-11, the company creates a task force of users, managers, and IS professionals that works together to gather information, discuss business needs, and define the new system requirements.

The JAD team usually meets over a period of days or weeks, in a special conference room or at an off-site location. The objective is to analyze the existing system, work on potential solutions, and agree on requirements for the new system. The group usually has a project leader and one or more members who document and record the results and decisions. The JAD process involves intensive effort by all team members. Because of the wide range of input and constant interaction among the participants, many companies believe that a JAD group produces the best possible definition of the new system.

Compared to traditional methods, JAD is more expensive and can be cumbersome if the group is too large compared to the size of the project. Many companies find, however, that JAD allows key users to participate effectively in the requirements determination process. When successfully used, JAD can result in a more accurate statement of system requirements, a better understanding of common goals, and a stronger commitment to the success of the new system.

Rapid Application Development (RAD)

Rapid application development (RAD) is a technique that reduces the time needed to design new information systems. Like JAD, RAD also uses a team approach, but goes further. While JAD typically focuses on the task of requirements determination, RAD involves a mini-SDLC that parallels the traditional SDLC phases. The creator of RAD, James Martin, proposed four RAD phases: requirements planning, user design, construction, and cutover. The objective of the RAD approach is to save development time and expense by using a project group to perform a wide range of systems development tasks.

To be successful, RAD requires an IS development team that works closely and interactively with a small group of important users and managers, who actively participate. RAD also involves systems development tools that you will learn in Chapters 4 and 5, including prototyping and computer-aided software engineering (CASE) tools.

When successfully implemented, the RAD process results in a more continuous design process, rather than clearly segmented SDLC phases. The development team can make any necessary modifications quickly, as the design evolves. Like JAD, rapid application development combines the knowledge and skills of users, managers, and IS professionals. Unlike JAD, the RAD process does not stop at requirements determination, but continues through system design and implementation. Many companies feel that RAD techniques can reduce new system costs substantially because the development team has the resources, skills, and management support needed to handle the project in a compressed time frame.

The RAD method has advantages and disadvantages compared to the traditional SDLC. The primary advantage is that systems can be developed more quickly with significant cost savings. A disadvantage is that RAD stresses the mechanics of the system itself, and does not place enough emphasis on the company's strategic business needs. The risk is that a system might work well in the short term, but the corporate and long-term objectives for the system might not be met. In addition, another potential disadvantage is that the accelerated time cycle might allow less time to develop quality, consistency, and design standards. RAD can be an attractive alternative, however, if an organization understands these possible risks.

Object-Oriented Systems Development

While structured analysis and design is based on data and processes that affect data, object-oriented (O-O) systems development is based on objects. To understand this approach, you need a basic understanding of objected-oriented concepts.

The basic idea of **objected-oriented (O-O) systems development** is to build a system model based on objects and their interaction, rather than on processes and data flows. Using this approach, the focus on objects starts with systems planning and continues during system analysis and systems design. Finally, during systems implementation, object-oriented programming techniques produce modular code that can be reused by many programs, which is an important advantage.

For an explanation of **JAD**, visit *Systems Analysis and Design* Chapter 3 More on the Web.

www.scsite.com/ sad3e/ch03/

For more information on **RAD**, visit *Systems Analysis and Design* Chapter 3 More on the Web.

www.scsite.com/ sad3e/ch03/

An **object** is an abstract entity that the system recognizes and interacts with. Objects have specific characteristics, or **attributes**, and behaviors. For example, a delivery truck is an object, with attributes that include a fleet ID number, a vehicle identification number, and physical specifications such as weight and capacity. Attributes also can indicate whether a truck is in service or its current cargo contents.

A **class** is a group of objects with similar attributes. Classes also can have **subclasses**. An object in the subclass inherits all the attributes of the parent and might have additional attributes and behaviors. For example, the TRUCKS class might have a subclass consisting of RENTAL UNITS, with additional attributes, such as lease agreement numbers and monthly payment amounts. Objects interact by exchanging information and messages or by processes that change the attributes or behavior of another object. For example, a DRIVER (object 1) can designate a TRUCK (object 2) to be IN SERVICE (message 1) and LOAD it (process 1).

For a basic overview of **OO Concepts**, visit Systems Analysis and Design Chapter 3 More on the Web.

www.scsite.com/ sad3e/ch03/

Because O-O is an entirely different approach to systems development, some factors must be considered. One concern is that an object-oriented approach does not focus on the big picture from a business point of view. Some IS managers feel that object-oriented systems development is less effective in resolving major business problems, because it requires so much emphasis on the design process, and views data totally apart from the processes that affect it. Supporters believe, however, that the new approach allows several systems to use the same objects, which provides more flexibility and better information management in a dynamic business environment.

Although structured analysis and design, in various forms, is still the leading development technique, you might use an object-oriented approach in some situations. You will learn more about object-oriented techniques in Chapter 8, where file and database concepts are discussed.

PREVIEW OF THE REQUIREMENTS ANALYSIS STAGE

Requirements analysis — the second major stage of the systems analysis phase — is described in Chapter 4. During requirements analysis, you will organize the facts you obtained during the requirements determination stage. Your objective will be to develop a logical design of the information system, using the methods and tools that are covered in Chapters 4 and 5.

Two important tasks conclude the systems analysis phase. The first task is the creation of a formal report called the **system requirements document** that describes what you have learned about the information system and summarizes your conclusions. This formal report will serve as the starting point for systems design, which is the next phase in the SDLC.

The final task of the systems analysis phase is the formal presentation of your findings. Although the audience has received your written report, the oral presentation gives you an important opportunity for interactive discussion and to answer questions about the project.

The Systems Analyst's Toolkit has tools to help you learn the elements of a good presentation and to develop successful presentations.

SOFTWEAR, LIMITED

I n Chapter 2, you learned that SWL's vice president of finance, Michael Jeremy, submitted a request for information systems services to investigate problems with the company's payroll system. Jane Rossman, the manager of applications, assigned systems analyst Rick Williams to conduct a preliminary investigation to study the payroll system's problems.

Rick's investigation revealed several problems, including input errors and a need for manual preparation of various reports. The payroll department is working overtime to correct the errors and produce the reports.

The information systems department recommended conducting an analysis to investigate these problem areas in the payroll system, and Mr. Jeremy approved the study. Thus, the second phase of the systems project, the systems analysis phase, is underway.

Human Resources Department Interview

During the preliminary investigation phase, Rick prepared the organization chart of the payroll department shown in Figure 3-12. He also prepared the organization chart of the human resources department shown in Figure 3-13.

Rick learned that some errors occurred in employee stock purchase deductions, so he decided to study this process. He knew that the human resources department initiates stock purchase deductions. He reviewed the organization chart and

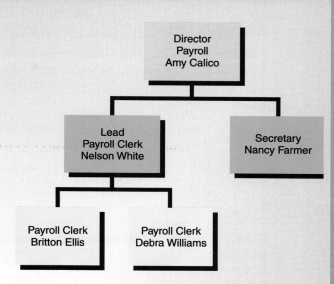

Figure 3-12   Payroll department organization chart.

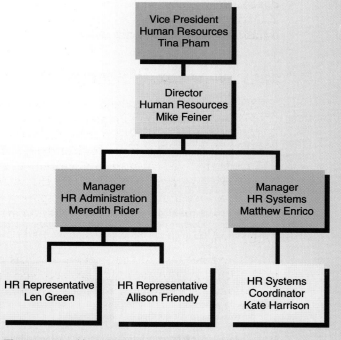

Figure 3-13   Human resources department organization chart.

decided to interview Meredith Rider, manager of human resources administration. Meredith is responsible for completing the personnel records of newly hired employees and sending the forms to the payroll department.

Before arranging any interviews, Rick sent the memo shown in Figure 3-14 to the human resources director, Mike Feiner, to keep him posted. Then Rick called Meredith to make an appointment and sent her the confirmation memo shown in Figure 3-15 that describes the topics and requested copies of related forms.

SWL   **MEMORANDUM**

Date: October 15, 1998
To: Mike Feiner, Director of Human Resources
From: Rick Williams, Systems Analyst
Subject: Payroll System Investigation

The information systems department currently is investigating improvements to the payroll system. We are interested especially in problems relating to the employee stock purchase plan.

I plan to meet with Meredith Rider to discuss this topic. I also may need to meet with other people in your department, and I will keep you informed.

Thank you for your assistance.

Figure 3-14 Rick Williams's memo announcing the start of the payroll system investigation.

SWL   **MEMORANDUM**

Date: October 16, 1998
To: Meredith Rider, Manager of Human Resources Administration
From: Rick Williams, Systems Analyst
Subject: Payroll System Investigation

Confirming our telephone conversation this morning, I will plan to meet you on Wednesday, October 21 at 10:00 a.m. in your office.

I would like to discuss the procedures you follow for handling employee payroll information, including voluntary deductions for the credit union and the SWL stock purchase plan. I would like to discuss the following specific questions with you when we meet:

1. How is the payroll department notified of a new employee's pay rate and status, and what forms are involved in the process?

2. What is the procedure for handling changes in the initial information and how is the payroll department notified of these changes?

3. Do employees use a standard enrollment form to sign up for the SWL stock purchase plan?

4. What is the procedure for submitting stock purchase deduction information to the payroll department, and what forms are involved in the process?

When we meet, I would like to have blank copies of any standard forms that are used and samples of the forms filled in with typical data. Thank you for your assistance. I'll look forward to meeting you next Wednesday.

Figure 3-15 Rick Williams's memo to Meredith Rider regarding preparation for the interview.

In the interview, Meredith explained that when employees are hired, they complete a Payroll Master Record Form (Form: PR-1) that includes personal data and other required information. The human resources department completes the form by adding pay rate and other data, and then sends a copy of the PR-1 form to the payroll department. Meredith gave Rick a blank copy of a PR-1 form shown in Figure 3-16. She explained that because payroll and personnel information is confidential, she could not give Rick a completed form.

When an employee's pay rate or status changes, the human resources department completes the Payroll Status Change Form

Figure 3-16 Sample employee Payroll Master Record Form (Form: PR-1).

Figure 3-17 Payroll Status Change Form (Form: PR-2).

(Form: PR-2) shown in Figure 3-17, and sends a copy to the payroll department. The payroll department files these forms with the employee's PR-1 Payroll Master Record Form.

Meredith also explained that after completing a 90-day probationary period, employees are allowed to participate in the SWL Credit Union, using the Payroll Deduction

Change Form (Form: PR-3) shown in Figure 3-18. An employee submits the form to the human resources department, and from there, it is forwarded it to the payroll department.

SWL also has an Employee Stock Purchase Plan. An individual must be employed for 180 days to be eligible for this plan. The employee receives a brochure and prospectus, and then completes the Employee Stock Purchase Plan Form (Form: PR-4) shown in Figure 3-19 to enroll. The human resources department completes the weekly report of all stock plan enrollments and changes on a PR-5 form shown in Figure 3-20 and then sends a copy to the payroll department. The payroll department records this information on a card that is filed with the employee's master record.

After the interview with Meredith, Rick sent the follow-up memo shown in Figure 3-21 and attached a copy of the interview documentation shown in Figure 3-22 on page 3.30.

SWL PAYROLL DEDUCTION CHANGE FORM

Please print clearly

Social Security number _____ Date _____

Name _____
                last   first   middle

W4 exemption change ☐ Old _____ New _____

Credit Union change ☐ Old _____ New _____

Employee signature _____ Date _____

_____
(FOR HUMAN RESOURCES DEPARTMENT USE ONLY)

Effective date of change _____

                               By: Human Resources Department

(Form: PR-3)

Figure 3-18 Payroll Deduction Change Form (Form: PR-3).

SWL EMPLOYEE STOCK PURCHASE PLAN
Enrollment and Change Form

To be completed by Employee
(Please print clearly)

I, _____ , hereby acknowledge that I have received a brochure and prospectus on the common stock of SoftWear, Limited (SWL) and that I understand the terms and conditions by which SWL stock is offered to employees.

I understand that an account will be established in my name, and stock will be purchased through payroll deductions. I also understand that my ownership rights in SWL stock purchased for this account are subject to the provisions of the Stock Ownership Plan (the Plan) and I agree to the terms thereof.

I understand that I may change or discontinue my contributions at any time, and that I am entitled to a return of my contributions with thirty days written notice.

I wish to contribute a total of $ _____ per week to the Plan. I understand that deductions will be invested monthly on a pro rata basis pursuant to the SWL systems and procedures manual.

_____ SSN _____ Date _____
    (Employee signature)

(Form: PR-4)

Figure 3-19 Employee Stock Purchase Plan Enrollment and Change Form (Form: PR-4).

SWL

**EMPLOYEE STOCK PURCHASE PLAN
WEEKLY DEDUCTION SUMMARY REPORT**

Week ending _____   (Form: PR-5)

Code: N = New C = Change	SSN	Employee Name	Deduction Amount

Figure 3-20   Employee Stock Purchase Plan Weekly Deduction Summary Report (Form: PR-5).

SWL   **MEMORANDUM**

Date: October 23, 1998
To: Meredith Rider
From: Rick Williams
Subject: Payroll System Investigation

Thank you for meeting with me on October 21 and explaining the procedures involved in preparing and submitting employee information for the payroll system.

I have attached a summary of the interview and my observations about the information flow in the current system.

Please examine the interview summary and give me your comments, including any additions or corrections. We will be submitting a final recommendation in two weeks, so I would like to have your input by October 30.

I appreciate the time you spent with me. If you have any other questions, please let me know.

Attachment: Interview Summary

Figure 3-21   Follow-up memo from Rick Williams to Meredith Rider and request for her comments on the interview summary.

INTERVIEW DOCUMENTATION

Name of System: Payroll   **Page** 1 of 1
Date: October 21, 1998
Prepared by: Rick Williams
Title: Systems Analyst
Purpose: Interview Summary: Meredith Rider, Manager of Human Resources Administration
Location: Raleigh

Five basic forms are used by the human resources department that relate to the payroll system:
1. Payroll Master Record Form (Form: PR-1)
2. Payroll Status Change Form (Form: PR-2)
3. Payroll Deduction Change Form (Form: PR-3)
4. Employee Stock Purchase Enrollment and Change Form (Form: PR-4)
5. Employee Stock Purchase Plan Weekly Deduction Summary Report (Form: PR-5)

When an employee is hired, the following takes place:
1. The human resources department prepares a Payroll Master Record Form (Form: PR-1), with employee data, including Social Security number, name, address, telephone, emergency contact, and information about the position, title, and initial pay rate.
2. A copy of this form is sent to the payroll department, where it is filed and maintained.
3. Subsequent pay rate or status changes are submitted by the human resources department to the payroll department on a Payroll Status Change Form (Form: PR-2). Payroll then files these change forms with the employee's PR-1 form.

After 90 days of employment, the employee is eligible to join the SWL Credit Union.
1. To enroll, or to make changes in existing deductions, the employee goes to the human resources department and completes a Payroll Deduction Change Form (Form: PR-3). The human resources department sends the form to payroll, where it is filed with the employee's Payroll Master Record Form (Form: PR-1).

After 180 days of employment, the employee is eligible to enroll in the SWL Stock Purchase Plan.
1. To enroll, an employee completes an Employee Stock Purchase Plan Enrollment and Change Form (Form: PR-4).
2. The human resources department prepares an Employee Stock Purchase Plan Weekly Deduction Summary Report (Form: PR-5) and sends it to the payroll department, with copies of the PR-4 forms, which then are filed with the employee's PR-1 form.

Changes in employee status that affect payroll involve the following forms:
1. Pay rate   PR-2
2. Status (exempt vs. non-exempt)   PR-2
3. Federal tax exemptions   PR-3
4. Credit Union deductions   PR-3
5. Employee Stock Purchase Plan deductions   PR-3

When an employee changes Credit Union deductions or federal tax exemptions:
1. The employee completes a Payroll Deduction Change Form (Form: PR-3).
2. The form is forwarded to the payroll department.
3. The form is filed with the employee's PR-1 form.

I have identified several problems with the current procedures:
1. Data errors can occur when the human resources staff prepares the weekly summary of employee stock purchase deductions, and no system verification takes place until incorrect deductions are reported.
2. The system performs no verification of employment dates, and it is possible that the 90- and 180-day eligibility periods are applied incorrectly.
3. The filing of the PR-2, PR-3, and PR-4 forms with the Payroll Master Record Forms in the payroll department could lead to problems. If any of the forms are lost or misfiled, incorrect data is entered into the system.

Figure 3-22   Documentation of the interview with Meredith Rider.

Payroll Department Interview

Rick's next interview was with the lead payroll clerk, Nelson White. During the interview, Nelson confirmed that when an employee is hired, a PR-1 form is completed in the human resources department. This form then is forwarded to payroll, where it is filed. He explained that each week the payroll department sends a time sheet to every SWL department manager. The time sheet lists each employee, with space to record regular hours, vacation, sick leave, jury duty, and other codes for accounting purposes.

After each pay period, SWL managers complete their departmental time sheets and return them to the payroll department. Payroll then enters the pay rate and deduction information and delivers the sheets to Business Information Systems (BIS), the service bureau that prepares SWL's payroll.

After the payroll is run, a BIS employee returns the time sheets, paychecks, and the payroll register to SWL. The director of payroll, Amy Calico, sends the paychecks to SWL department heads for distribution to employees.

Nelson uses the weekly payroll register to prepare a report of credit union deductions and a check to the credit union for the total amount deducted. Stock purchases, on the other hand, are processed monthly, based on the stock's closing price on the last business day of the month. Using the weekly payroll registers, Nelson manually prepares a monthly report of employee stock purchases and forwards a copy of the report and a funds transfer authorization to Carolina National Bank, which is SWL's stock transfer agent.

Rick asked Nelson why BIS did not produce a report on employee stock purchase deductions. Nelson replied that although the payroll is run weekly, the stock deductions are invested only once a month. Because the two cycles do not match, the BIS system could not handle the task.

Nelson then referred Rick to the *SWL Systems and Procedures Manual* page that describes how monthly Employee Stock Purchase Plan investment amounts are calculated, as shown in Figure 3-23. After blanking out the employee's name and Social Security number, Nelson also gave Rick a sample of three monthly deduction registers, as shown in Figure 3-24 on the next page. Rick began to see why it was taking so much effort to prepare the reports. The process that Nelson described provided much more detail than the general description that Rick had received during the preliminary investigation from Amy Calico, payroll director.

SoftWear, Limited   Payroll
Systems and Procedures Manual   Page 29

VII.   Employee Stock Purchase Plan

The human resources department will notify the payroll department of the weekly deduction that the employee has specified on the Employee Stock Purchase Plan Enrollment and Change Form and send a copy of the Employee Stock Purchase Plan Enrollment and Change Form (Form: PR-4) and the Employee Stock Purchase Plan Weekly Deduction Summary Report (Form: PR-5) to the payroll department.

Deduction will be made weekly and then invested on a monthly basis. The payroll department will calculate the proper monthly investment amount on a pro rata basis, as follows:

A.   A nominal per diem deduction rate will be established by dividing the weekly deduction by 7, rounded to 3 decimal places.

B.   The monthly Plan investment will be the number of calendar days in the month times the nominal per diem rate, rounded to 2 decimal places. For example:

Weekly deduction: \$20.00 / 7 = 2.8571 = \$2.857 per diem
Month of January = 31 times 2.857 = 88.567 = \$88.57

C.   At the end of each month, the payroll department will prepare a monthly deduction register (Form: PR-6) that shows individual employee deductions by week, and a monthly total.

Figure 3-23   Sample page from SWL Systems and Procedures Manual.

SWL

EMPLOYEE STOCK PURCHASE PLAN
MONTHLY DEDUCTION REGISTER

(Form: PR-6)   Period: ___July 1998___

Name	SSN	Week Ending Date	Weekly Deduction	Monthly Investment
		7/3/98	23.00	
		7/10/98	23.00	
		7/17/98	23.00	
		7/24/98	23.00	

SWL

EMPLOYEE STOCK PURCHASE PLAN
MONTHLY DEDUCTION REGISTER

(Form: PR-6)   Period: ___August 1998___

Name	SSN	Week Ending Date	Weekly Deduction	Monthly Investment
		8/7/98	23.00	
		8/14/98	23.00	
		8/21/98	23.00	
		8/28/98	23.00	101.87

SWL

EMPLOYEE STOCK PURCHASE PLAN
MONTHLY DEDUCTION REGISTER

(Form: PR-6)   Period: ___September 1998___

Name	SSN	Week Ending Date	Weekly Deduction	Monthly Investment
		9/4/98	23.00	
		9/11/98	23.00	
		9/18/98	23.00	
		9/25/98	23.00	98.58

Figure 3-24   Sample of the Monthly Deduction Register for the Employee Stock Purchase Plan for July, August, and September 1998, showing the weekly deduction and monthly investment amounts.

Business Information Services Interview

Rick decided that he should talk with someone at the BIS service bureau to find out more about its operations. He learned from Nelson that Linda DeMarco was BIS's customer relations manager, so he scheduled an appointment with her.

When Rick arrived at BIS, Linda greeted him warmly. She explained that she had planned to meet with members of SWL's payroll department within the next month or two to discuss the latest developments. Because Rick was now working on SWL's payroll system, however, this meeting would save her a trip. Rick temporarily abandoned his interview plan and asked Linda what she had in mind.

"The payroll system that your company is using, which we call GAPP, for Generalized Automated Payroll Program, was originally developed here at BIS in 1991," Linda began. "In fact, SoftWear, Limited was one of our very first customers. We've worked together for a long time, and we are very committed to your firm. As you know, GAPP has been modified and updated many times since 1991. But let's face it, even with the patches, GAPP is an antique! Anyway, I have some exciting news. A few months ago, our company decided to develop a new, state-of-the-art payroll system. We are going to call it CHIPS, for Comprehensive High-powered Interactive Payroll System. I am really looking forward to working with your company when you switch over to CHIPS," Linda said.

Rick took a few moments to consider this surprising development. He then asked what would happen with GAPP. Linda stated that GAPP would be available to customers for another year or two, but that BIS would make no further enhancements to that system. Using BIS resources to maintain an obsolete system would not make sense, she explained.

Rick had been hoping that the manual deduction reporting problems could be solved with some changes to the BIS payroll system. He now realized that was impossible, so he decided to learn more about CHIPS.

Rick described the problem with the mismatched deduction cycles and asked if CHIPS would handle that. Linda said that she already had looked into the matter. She pointed out that SWL was their only customer with more than one deduction application cycle. From BIS's point of view, programming CHIPS to handle multiple cycle reports did not make sense. Linda suggested that perhaps a special add-on module could be written, once CHIPS was up and running. BIS could do that kind of job on a contract basis, she added.

Rick then asked when the new system would be available and what the cost would be. Linda stated that current plans were to begin offering CHIPS sometime in the following year. She explained that the system was still in development, and she could not be more specific about timetables and costs. She was sure, however, that the monthly fee for CHIPS would not be more than 30 percent above the current GAPP charges.

As Rick was preparing to leave, Linda urged him to keep in touch. In the next few months, she explained, plans for CHIPS would become more specific, and she would be able to answer all his questions.

New Plans and Developments

When Rick returned from his meeting with Linda, he immediately went to his manager, Jane Rossman. After he described his visit to BIS, Jane telephoned Ann Hon, director of information systems. Within the hour, Jane and Rick were meeting with Ann in her office. Rick repeated the details of his visit, and Ann asked for his opinion on how the developments at BIS would affect SWL's current systems analysis.

Rick explained that one of the problems — possible input errors when transferring data from the human resources summary list — might be solved easily by developing a new form or procedure. Nevertheless, he admitted that he saw no obvious solutions for the stock purchase deduction problems, except to change the scope of the payroll project.

Jane, Rick, and Ann then analyzed the situation. They all agreed that because of the upcoming changes at BIS, the current payroll system project would produce very limited results and should be expanded in scope. They totaled the costs of the SWL project to that point and prepared estimates for a detailed investigation of the entire payroll system in order to meet SWL's current and future needs.

Later that week, Ann met with Michael Jeremy, vice president of finance, to discuss the situation and present her proposal to go forward with an expanded analysis. Before she even started, however, Mr. Jeremy filled her in on the latest announcement from SWL's top management: the company had decided to move forward with the new Employee Savings and

Investment Plan (ESIP) that had been under consideration. He said that in December, Robert Lansing, SWL's president, would announce a target date of April 1, 1999 for the new ESIP plan. Mr. Jeremy explained that the new plan would be a 401(k) plan with tax advantages for employees. Facing these new constraints on top of the existing payroll system problems, it looked like SWL would need a new payroll system after all.

The Revised Project

Jane Rossman assigned Carla Moore, a programmer/analyst, to work with Rick Williams on the revised system project. Because they now had to determine the requirements for the complete payroll system, Rick and Carla conducted follow-up interviews with Nelson White and Meredith Rider, as well as Allison Friendly, a human resources representative, and both payroll clerks, Britton Ellis and Debra Williams. During the payroll department interviews, the payroll staff prepared samples of all the existing payroll reports.

The Payroll Register report is shown in Figure 3-25. On this report, each employee is listed on a separate line, along with his or her earnings, deductions, and net pay. BIS creates three copies of this report each week. One copy is sent to Michael Jeremy, and one copy goes to Amy Calico. The third copy is used by the payroll department for determining SWL's obligation for tax withholding and FICA payments, and for applying credit union and stock purchase plan deductions. BIS also prints three copies of the Employee Compensation Record shown in Figure 3-26, which shows year-to-date payroll information for each employee.

SWL   **PAYROLL REGISTER**

Week Ending _____   *Page 1*

Employee Data		Earnings			Deductions					Net Pay	
Name	SSN	Regular Pay	Overtime Pay	Total Pay	Federal Tax	State Tax	FICA	Credit Union	Stock Plan	Net Amount	Check Number

Figure 3-25   Sample page of SWL Payroll Register report.

SWL   **EMPLOYEE COMPENSATION RECORD**

Name _____   SSN _____

	Weekly Payroll									Year to Date								
	Earnings			Deductions					Net Pay		Earnings			Deductions					Net Pay
Week Ending	Reg. Pay	OT Pay	Total Pay	Fed. Tax	State Tax	FICA	Credit Union	Stock Plan	Net Pay	Check No.	Reg. Pay	OT Pay	Total Pay	Fed. Tax	State Tax	FICA	Credit Union	Stock Plan	Net Amount
8/7/98	352.00		352.00	45.00	7.40	22.40	10.00	9.20	258.00	01675	11,264.00		11,264.00	1,440.00	236.80	716.80	320.00	294.40	8,256.00
8/14/98	352.00		352.00	45.00	7.40	22.40	10.00	9.20	258.00	02342	11,616.00		11,616.00	1,485.00	244.20	739.20	330.00	303.60	8,514.00
8/21/98	352.00		352.00	45.00	7.40	22.40	10.00	9.20	258.00	03919	11,698.00		11,698.00	1,530.00	251.60	761.60	340.00	312.80	8,772.00
8/28/98	352.00		352.00	45.00	7.40	22.40	10.00	9.20	258.00	04313	12,320.00		12,320.00	1,575.00	259.00	784.00	350.00	322.00	9,030.00

Figure 3-26   Sample page of SWL Employee Compensation Record report.

Mr. Jeremy receives a weekly overtime report from BIS that lists every employee who worked overtime that week. When Carla asked him about this report, he stated that he consulted it occasionally but admitted that he did not need the report every week. He also receives an accounting report, but he routinely forwards it to the accounting department. He mentioned that an overall financial summary would be more valuable to him.

Another key output of the payroll system is the payroll check shown in Figure 3-27 that is distributed weekly to employees. In addition to the check itself, a stub lists hours worked, gross pay, all deductions from gross pay, net pay, and year-to-date totals.

SWL

SOFTWEAR, LIMITED
999 Technology Plaza
Raleigh, NC 29991

55-555/5555
1234567

No. _____

Date _____

Pay to the Order of _____ $ _____

_____ Dollars

(Not Negotiable)

Carolina Bank
999 Ninth Street
Raleigh, NC 29999

_____
1234>>567>>8888

Week Ending _____	This Period	Year to Date Totals
EARNINGS		
Regular pay		
Overtime pay		
Total pay		
DEDUCTIONS		
Federal tax		
State tax		
FICA		
Credit Union		
Stock Plan		
Net pay		

Figure 3-27   Sample SWL employee paycheck and stub.

YOUR TURN

1. When Rick Williams met with Meredith Rider, he asked for copies of actual reports and completed forms that contain confidential information. When developing a new system, can a systems analyst be trusted with confidential information? What are the pros and cons of giving an analyst simulated copies of forms and reports that contain fictitious data?

2. When Rick met with Linda DeMarco of the BIS service bureau, he abandoned his planned list of questions after she started to explain the developments at BIS. What questions do you suppose were on his original list?

3. Assume that you were with Rick at the meeting with Linda. Draft a follow-up letter to her that describes the interview.

ON THE NET

Rick wants to learn more about CASE tools and techniques. He has asked you to help him do some research on the Web, using a search engine such as Yahoo! or AltaVista. He wants to identify at least three firms that offer CASE tools so he can obtain more detailed information. When your research is done, write a brief summary memo to Rick about your findings.

CHAPTER SUMMARY

The systems analysis phase consists of obtaining answers to the questions who, what, where, when, how, and why. The systems analysis phase is the second step in the systems development life cycle and consists of two stages: requirements determination and requirements analysis. During requirements determination, you identify the business-related requirements for the new information system, including outputs, inputs, processes, timings, and controls. You also collect quantitative information about volumes, sizes, and frequencies for all outputs, inputs, and processes.

Specific techniques are used in requirements determination, which is the first stage in the systems analysis phase. The same techniques can be applied throughout the systems development life cycle. Interviewing is a detailed process. You must decide on the people to interview, how to set interview objectives, and how to prepare for, conduct, and analyze interviews. Then, you examine other fact-finding techniques, including document review, observation, questionnaires, sampling, and research. The analyst also can use software tools during fact-finding. This topic ended with a discussion of why and how to record the collected information.

Joint application development (JAD) and rapid application development (RAD) are systems development techniques that involve a team effort by an interactive group of users, managers, and IS professionals. The JAD approach can result in an accurate definition of system requirements based on input and participation by team members, who develop a greater commitment to the project and to their common goals. RAD goes even further than JAD and involves a mini-SDLC, with users, managers, and IS staff working together in a concentrated effort to produce a better system in a shorter time frame and at less cost.

Object-oriented (O-O) systems development focuses on system objects instead of on data elements and procedures. A system is a collection of objects and the relationships between them. Each object is a data unit, along with the actions that can affect that unit. Objects are defined from specific to general and a subclass inherits all the characteristics of the parent object upon which it is based. An advantage of object-oriented techniques is that object definitions can be accessed and used by other systems.

The chapter concluded by mentioning the importance of presentations and listing the elements for successful presentations. More information is provided in the Systems Analyst's Toolkit at the end of the text.

Review Questions

1. The systems analysis phase is divided into what two stages? *3.4*

2. What is an informal organizational structure? Why is it important?

3. Systems analysis consists of obtaining answers to what five questions? What additional question is asked in the process of answering each of those five questions? *3.5*

4. What is a system requirement? Into what categories can system requirements be classified? *3.5-3.6*

5. What are the three different types of questions? How do these different questions affect the answers given? *3.9*

6. Why might an interview be unsuccessful? If an interviewee is not answering your questions satisfactorily, what should you do? *- change another person - . 3.13*

7. Should you take notes during an interview? Should you use a tape recorder? Why? *3.12*

8. What are three types of sampling, and why would you use them? *3.17*

9. What software tools are available to the analyst during the systems analysis stage and how can they be used?

10. What is the Hawthorne Effect? Why is it significant? *3.14*

11. What is JAD and how does it differ from traditional methods used to determine the requirements of the new system? *3.22*

12. What is RAD? What characteristics does it have in common with JAD and how is it different? *3.23*

13. What are some major advantages and potential disadvantages of using JAD and RAD?

14. What is object-oriented systems development, and how does it differ from traditional approaches to structured analysis? *3.26*

15. In object-oriented systems development, what is the definition of an object, a class, and a subclass? *3.29* *Reusable* *big picture - not specific -*

16. What are some major advantages and potential disadvantages of object-oriented systems development?

    Answer the following questions after you complete the presentations section of the Systems Analyst's Toolkit.

17. To what three different audiences might you have to give a presentation? How would the presentation differ for each? If only one presentation is given with all interested parties in attendance, to whom should the presentation primarily be addressed?

18. How should you react if your hands shake while you are giving a presentation, or if you are nervous when people are looking at you?

Discussion Questions

1. A group meeting sometimes is suggested as a useful compromise between interviews and questionnaires. In such a group meeting, one systems analyst meets with and asks questions of a number of users at one time. Discuss the advantages and disadvantages of such a group meeting.

2. Some authorities feel that during the presentation, the job of the systems analyst is to sell to management the one solution that the information systems department believes will offer the greatest benefit to the company. Others argue that the job of the systems analyst is to present all alternative solutions objectively and have management assume responsibility for the decision. Which position do you support and why?

3. Suppose you were a systems analyst assigned to a JAD team working on a new Web-based technical support site for your company, a leading manufacturer of modems. At the first meeting, you are asked to give an overview of the JAD process and why the team is using it for this project. What would you say?

4. Both JAD and RAD require strong interpersonal and communication skills on the part of the systems analyst. Are these skills different from the ones that an analyst needs when conducting one-to-one interviews? Explain your answer.

Answer the following questions after you complete the presentations section of the Systems Analyst's Toolkit.

5. Review magazines or textbooks to find examples of each of the following types of visual aids: bar chart, pie chart, line chart, table, diagram, and bulleted list of key points. How effective do you think each aid is? Find at least one example that you feel could be improved. Describe its shortcomings and prepare an improved version of it.

6. Attend a speech or presentation and analyze its effectiveness. Consider the speaker's delivery and how he or she organized the material, used visual aids, and handled audience questions. Describe specifically how the speech or presentation was most effective, as well as how it could have been improved.

CASE STUDIES

NEW CENTURY HEALTH CLINIC — DETERMINING REQUIREMENTS

New Century Health Clinic has decided to computerize its office systems. The associates hired you, a local computer consultant, to perform a preliminary investigation. You had several meetings with Dr. Tim Jones to discuss the various office records and accounting systems. Anita Davenport, New Century's office manager, participated in these meetings.

In a report to the associates at the end of your investigation, you recommended conducting a detailed analysis of the patient record system, the patient and insurance billing systems, and the patient scheduling system. You believe that New Century would benefit most from implementing these three systems. Although the systems could be developed independently, you recommended analyzing all three systems together because of the significant interaction among them.

You presented your findings and recommendations at a late afternoon meeting of the associates. After answering several questions, you left the meeting so they could discuss the matter privately. Dr. Jones began the discussion by stating that he was impressed with your knowledge and professionalism, as well as your report and presentation.

Dr. Jones recommended accepting your proposal and hiring you immediately to conduct the systems analysis phase. Dr. Garcia, however, was not as enthusiastic and pointed out that such a study would certainly disrupt office procedures. The staff already had more work than they could handle, she argued, and taking time to answer your questions would only make the situation worse. Dr. Jones countered that the office workload was going to increase in any event, and that it was important to find a long-term solution to the problem. After some additional discussion, Dr. Garcia finally agreed with Dr. Jones's assessment. The next morning, Dr. Jones called you and asked you to go ahead with the systems analysis phase of the project.

Assignments

1. Review the office organization chart you prepared in Chapter 1 for New Century.
2. List the individuals you would like to interview during the systems analysis phase.
3. Prepare a list of objectives for each of the interviews you will conduct.
4. Prepare a list of specific questions for each individual you will interview.
5. Conduct the interviews (if requested by your instructor).
6. Prepare a written summary of the information gained from each of the interviews.
7. Suppose you wanted to send a questionnaire to a sample of New Century patients to see whether they were satisfied with current insurance and scheduling procedures. Design a questionnaire that follows the suggestions in this chapter, and decide what sample of patients should receive it.

BAXTER COMMUNITY COLLEGE — PART ONE

Baxter Community College is a two-year school in New Hampshire. Twice a year, the records office at Baxter mails requests for donations to the alumni. The staff uses a word processing merge file to create personalized letters, but the data on past contributions and other alumni information is stored manually. The registrar, Mary Louise, recently submitted a systems request asking the college's information services department to develop a computerized alumni information system. Baxter Community College does not have a formal systems review committee, and each department head has an individual budget for routine information services.

Todd Wagner, a systems analyst, was assigned to perform a preliminary investigation. After reading his report, Mary asked him to proceed with the systems analysis phase, saying that a formal presentation was unnecessary. Todd has scheduled an interview tomorrow with her, and he asked you to help him prepare for the meeting.

Assignments

1. Make a list of the topics that you think Todd should cover during the interview.
2. Prepare a list of specific questions that Todd should ask. Include open-ended, close-ended, and range of response questions.
3. Conduct interviews in class, with half the students assuming Todd's role and the other half playing the registrar.
4. Document the information covered during the interviews.

BAXTER COMMUNITY COLLEGE — PART TWO

Todd Wagner completed the systems analysis work and prepared a recommendation for a new alumni system with online update and query features. He discussed his ideas with Penny Binns, the IS department head, and several coworkers. They all felt that Todd's ideas were excellent. Todd then prepared and sent the final report for the systems analysis phase.

Before completing this part of the case, you should review the presentations section in the Systems Analyst's Toolkit.

This time, Mary Louise, the registrar, wanted a formal presentation. She requested that the college president and all the administrative vice presidents be invited to attend. The registrar wanted to be sure that she would have support for the new alumni system.

Unfortunately, Todd's car would not start the morning of the presentation. Therefore, he arrived 12 minutes late for the presentation, and was out of out of breath and disorganized. He immediately apologized and began to set out his notes. He then noticed that an easel was not in the room to hold his flip charts. Consequently, he moved a table closer to the front wall, placed the flip chart on the table, propped it against the wall, and began his presentation.

The flip chart was not very steady in that position, however, so Todd had to stand next to it to hold it. In order to flip to the next chart, Todd had to juggle the entire flip chart. He was so busy with the charts that he did not notice that people in the back of the room were straining to see the charts. The registrar finally interrupted to point out that not everyone was able to see the charts. Todd rushed out of the room to find an easel. When he finally returned with an easel, he found that several of the attendees had left. He did finish the presentation but with little of his original enthusiasm.

Assignments

1. List every mistake that Todd made.
2. For each mistake listed, describe what Todd should have done differently.
3. What might Mary Louise have done to help Todd?
4. What do you think Todd should do next to try to salvage the project?

HOOBER INDUSTRIES

M ichelle Quinn recently was hired as an information systems analyst at Hoober Industries. This new position was a promotion for her, because she had been a programmer at her previous job.

Michelle's first assignment at Hoober Industries was a preliminary investigation about improvements to an existing computer system. Michelle's boss was very pleased with her work and assigned her to work on the systems analysis phase.

During the preliminary investigation, Michelle had a brief interview with Raymond Morgan, who is the most knowledgeable person about existing system procedures at Hoober Industries. Now, she needed a more detailed interview with Raymond to learn about system operations. Michelle was nervous about her ability to remember the details, so she hid a small tape recorder in her purse and switched it on just before the interview. That night at home, Michelle replayed the tape many times, transcribing everything Raymond said. The next day at work she wrote up the interview documentation based on those transcribed interview notes, and then erased the tape.

Assignments

1. What do you think of Michelle's actions?
2. What would you have done in that situation?
3. What are the disadvantages to using a tape recorder to record the interview?
4. What else might Michelle have done to ensure that she understood and retained the information revealed during the interview?

Morgan could be suspicious.

CHAPTER 4

SDLC PHASES

Phase 1
Systems Planning

Phase 2
Systems Analysis

Phase 3
Systems Design

Phase 4
Systems Implementation

Phase 5
Systems Operation & Support

Analyzing Requirements

Analyzing requirements is the second of three chapters in the systems analysis phase.

OBJECTIVES

When you finish this chapter, you will be able to:

- Explain the structured analysis process and identify its elements
- Describe the symbols used in data flow diagrams and explain the rules for their use
- Explain the sequence of data flow diagrams, from general to specific, and what each data flow contains
- Explain how to level and balance a set of data flow diagrams
- Draw a complete set of data flow diagrams for an information system
- Describe how a data dictionary is used and what it contains
- Demonstrate the use of structured English, decision tables, and decision trees to develop information system process descriptions
- Explain the relationships among data flow diagrams, the data dictionary, and process descriptions

INTRODUCTION

The systems analysis phase has three stages. During the requirements determination stage described in Chapter 3, you used fact-finding techniques to gather and record data about the current system and user requirements. Now, in Chapter 4, you will learn about the second stage in systems analysis — analyzing requirements. When **analyzing requirements**, you use structured analysis tools to document the system requirements, analyze them, and develop a model of the system that you present to management. In the third stage, which is explained in Chapter 5, you will learn how to evaluate various development alternatives and prepare the system requirements proposal.

STRUCTURED ANALYSIS

Structured analysis examines a system in terms of its inputs, outputs, and processes and is the most common way to describe the requirements for a new system. Because it focuses on the flow of data as it is transformed into useful information, structured analysis is called a **process-centered** technique. Structured analysis uses three main tools: data flow diagrams, a data dictionary, and process descriptions. An analyst also can apply these structured methods using software packages called **computer-aided software engineering** (**CASE**) tools that provide automated support for many systems development tasks. You will learn how to use computer-aided software engineering tools in Chapter 5.

To learn more about
**Logical and
Physical Models,**
visit Systems
Analysis and
Design Chapter 4
More on the Web.

www.scsite.com/
sad3e/ch04/

The end product of structured analysis is a **logical model** that shows *what* the system must do, regardless of how it will be accomplished physically. Systems analysts sometimes refer to this model as a **business model**, because it must solve a business problem and meet the needs of managers and users. Later, in the systems design phase, the analyst builds a **physical model** that describes *how* the system will function, including hardware, software, data storage, and other operational details.

DATA FLOW DIAGRAMS

I n the Systems Analyst's Toolkit, you learn how to use visual aids during a presentation as shown in Figure 4-1. During the systems analysis phase, you will use a set of data diagrams as graphical aids that describe the system for management or other analysts.

A **data flow diagram** (**DFD**) shows how data moves through an information system. DFDs represent a logical model that shows *what* the system does, not *how* it does it. Data flow diagrams do not show program logic or processing steps. This distinction is important because focusing on implementation issues at this point would restrict your search for the most effective system design.

Figure 4-1   Systems analysts often use visual aids during presentations.

Data Flow Diagram Symbols

Data flow diagrams are drawn using four basic symbols that represent processes, data flows, data stores, and external entities. Several different versions of DFD symbols exist, but they all serve the same purpose. This text uses a popular version called the **Gane and Sarson** symbol set. Another popular symbol set is the **Yourdon** symbol set. Figure 4-2 shows examples of both versions. Symbols are referenced in the text using all capital letters for the symbol name.

APPLY
PAYMENT

PROCESS SYMBOL • A **process** receives input data and produces output that has a different content or form or both. For instance, the process for calculating pay uses two inputs (pay rate and hours worked) to produce one output (total pay). Processes can be very simple or quite complex. In a typical company, processes might include calculating sales trends, filing online insurance claims, ordering inventory from a supplier's system, or verifying e-mail addresses for Web customers.

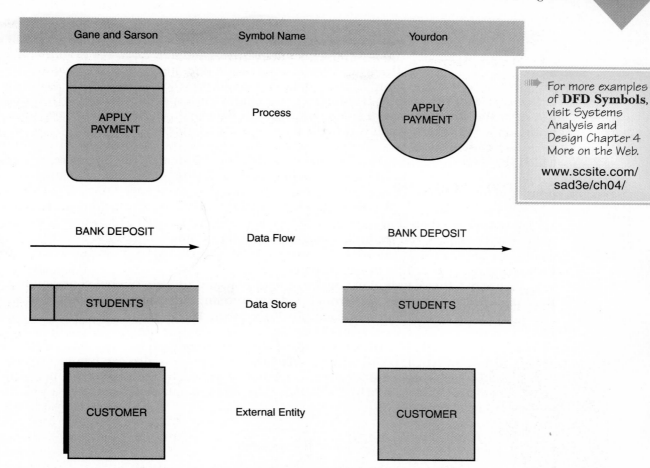

Figure 4-2 Data flow diagram symbols, symbol names, and examples for the Gane and Sarson and Yourdon symbol sets.

For more examples of **DFD Symbols**, visit Systems Analysis and Design Chapter 4 More on the Web.

www.scsite.com/ sad3e/ch04/

The Gane and Sarson symbol for a process is a rectangle with rounded corners; the name of the process appears inside the rectangle. The process name, which identifies the function it performs, consists of a verb, followed by a singular noun. If necessary, you can add an adjective to clarify the process name. Examples of process names are APPLY RENT PAYMENT, CALCULATE COMMISSION, ASSIGN FINAL GRADE, VERIFY ORDER, and FILL ORDER.

The details of a process are not shown in the data flow diagram; they are documented in a **process description**, which is discussed later in this chapter. For example, you might have a process symbol named DEPOSIT PAYMENT on your data flow diagram. Your DFD, however, would not show the actual data used, the detailed information output, or the specific steps performed in DEPOSIT PAYMENT. To understand these details, you would turn to the supporting process description called DEPOSIT PAYMENT.

In data flow diagrams, a process appears as a **black box**, where the inputs, outputs, and general function of the process are known, but the underlying details are not known. A black box approach shows an information system in a series of increasingly detailed pictures. By creating a separate description for every DFD process, you can explode each process and show the details without confusing the overall view of the system.

To learn more about **Black Box** approach, visit Systems Analysis and Design Chapter 4 More on the Web.

www.scsite.com/ sad3e/ch04/

BANK DEPOSIT

DATA FLOW SYMBOL • A **data flow** is a path for data to move from one part of the information system to another. A data flow in a DFD represents one or more pieces of data. For example, a data flow could represent a single data item, such as a student ID number, or a data flow could represent a *set* of data, such as a class roster with the student ID numbers and names for a specific class. The DFD does not show the structure and detailed contents of a data flow. These elements are defined in the data dictionary, which is described later in this chapter.

The symbol for a data flow is a line with an arrowhead that shows the direction in which the data flows. The data flow name, which should identify the data it represents, is placed above, below, or alongside the line. A data flow name consists of a singular noun and an adjective, if needed. Examples of data flow names are DEPOSIT, INVOICE PAYMENT, STUDENT GRADE, ORDER, and COMMISSION. Exceptions to the singular name rule are data flow names, such as GRADING PARAMETERS, where a singular name could mislead you to think a single parameter or single item of data exists. You would use the name CLASS DETAIL instead of CLASS DETAILS, however, because the former name could not be misrepresented.

Figure 4-3 shows typical examples of data flow and process symbol connections. Because a process changes data from one form into another, at least one data flow *must enter* and one data flow *must exit* each process symbol, as they do in the CREATE INVOICE process. A process symbol can have more than one outgoing data flow, as shown in the GRADE STUDENT WORK process, or more than one incoming data flow, as shown in the CALCULATE GROSS PAY process. A process also can connect to any other symbol, including another process symbol, as shown by the connection between VERIFY ORDER and ASSEMBLE ORDER. Therefore, a data flow *must* have a process symbol on at least one end.

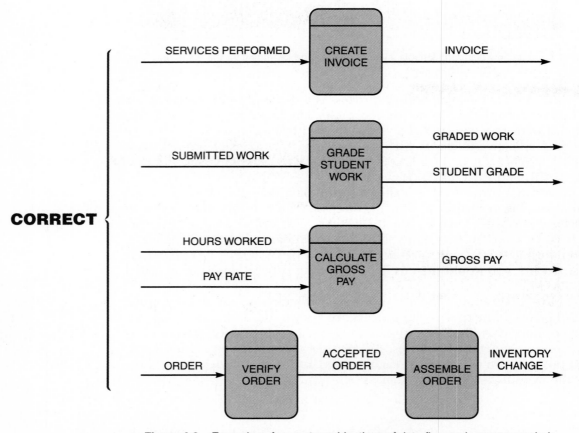

Figure 4-3   Examples of correct combinations of data flow and process symbols.

Figure 4-4 shows three data flow and process combinations that you must avoid. The APPLY INSURANCE PREMIUM process, for instance, has no input data flow. Because it has no input, this process is called a **spontaneous generation** process, or a **miracle**. The CALCULATE GROSS PAY is a **black hole** process, which is a process that has no output. A **gray hole** process is one that has at least one input and one output, but the input obviously is insufficient to generate the output shown. For example, a date of birth is not sufficient to output a final grade in the CALCULATE GRADE process.

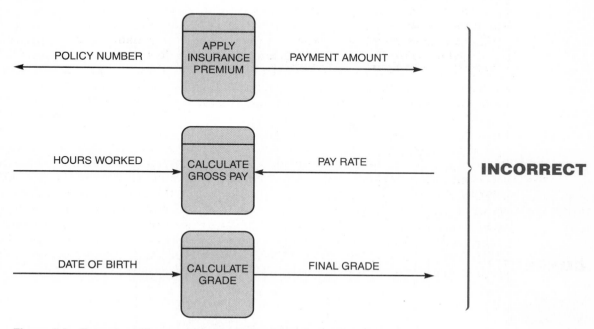

Figure 4-4 Examples of incorrect combinations of data flow and process symbols. APPLY INSURANCE PREMIUM has no inputs and is called a spontaneous generation process. CALCULATE GROSS PAY has no outputs and is called a black hole process. CALCULATE GRADE has an input that is obviously unable to support the output. This is called a gray hole.

Spontaneous generation, black holes, and gray holes are logically not possible in a DFD because a process must act on input data, shown by an incoming data flow, to produce output data represented by an outgoing data flow.

DATA STORE SYMBOL • A **data store**, or a **data repository**, is used in a data flow diagram to represent a situation when the system must retain data because one or more processes need to use the stored data at a later time. For instance, instructors need to store student scores on tests and assignments during the semester so they can assign final grades at the end of the term. In a payroll example, you would store employee salary and deduction data during the year so you can report total earnings and withholding at the end of the year. The detailed contents of a data store are not shown in the data flow diagram; the specific structure and data elements are defined in the data dictionary.

The specific storage location (such as disk, CD-ROM, or file folder) also is unimportant, because you are concerned with the logical requirements, and not the physical requirements, of the information system. The length of time that the data is stored also is unimportant — it can be seconds or years. What is important is that a process needs access to the data at some later time.

In a DFD, the Gane and Sarson symbol for a data store is a flat rectangle that is open on the right side and closed on the left side. The name of the data store is placed between the lines and identifies the data it contains. A data store name is a plural name consisting of a noun and adjectives, if needed. Examples of data store names are STUDENTS, ACCOUNTS RECEIVABLE, PRODUCTS, DAILY PAYMENTS, PURCHASE ORDERS, OUTSTANDING CHECKS, INSURANCE POLICIES, and EMPLOYEES. Exceptions to the plural name rule are collective nouns that represent multiple occurrences of objects. For example, GRADEBOOK represents a group of students and their scores.

A data store must be connected to a process with a data flow. Figure 4-5 illustrates typical examples of data stores. In each case, the data store has at least one incoming and one outgoing data flow and is connected to a process symbol with a data flow. Violations of the rule that a data store must have at least one incoming and one outgoing data flow are shown in Figure 4-6. In the first example, two data stores are connected incorrectly, and in the second and third examples, the data stores lack either an outgoing or incoming data flow.

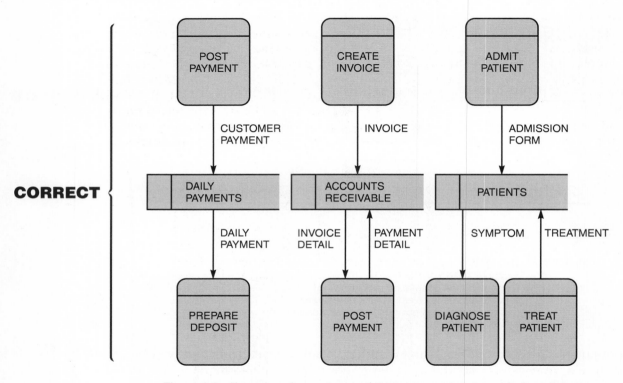

Figure 4-5   Examples of correct uses of data store symbols in a data flow diagram.

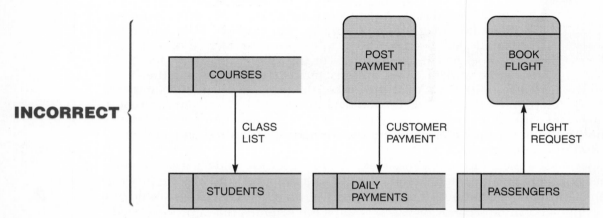

Figure 4-6   Examples of incorrect uses of data store symbols: two data stores cannot be connected by a data flow without an intervening process, and each data store should have an outgoing and incoming data flow.

EXTERNAL ENTITY SYMBOL • An **external entity** is a person, department, outside organization, or other information system that provides data to the system or receives output from the system. The Gane and Sarson symbol for an external entity is a square, which is usually shaded. The name of the external entity is placed inside the square.

For more information on **External Entities**, visit Systems Analysis and Design Chapter 4 More on the Web.

www.scsite.com/ sad3e/ch04/

External entities show the boundaries of the information system and how the information system interacts with the outside world. For example, a customer submitting an order is an external entity because the customer supplies data to the order system. Other examples of external entities include a patient who supplies medical data, a homeowner who receives a property tax bill, a warehouse that supplies a list of items in stock, and an accounts payable system that receives data from the company's purchasing system.

External entities also are called **terminators**, because they are data origins or final destinations. An external entity that supplies data to the system is called a **source**; an external entity that receives data from the system is called a **sink**. An external entity name is the singular form of a department, outside organization, other information system, or person. Examples of external entity names are CUSTOMER, STUDENT, EMPLOYEE, MEMBER, SALES REP, WAREHOUSE, ACCOUNTING, BANK, INTERNAL REVENUE SERVICE, PAYROLL SYSTEM, and GENERAL LEDGER SYSTEM. An external entity might be a source or a sink or both, as shown in Figure 4-7. An external entity must be connected to a process by a data flow. Figure 4-8 on the next page shows violations of this rule.

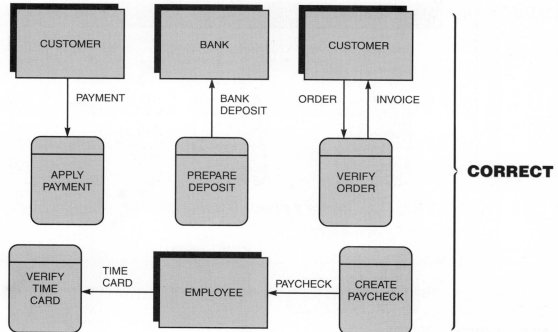

Figure 4-7   Examples of correct uses of external entities in a data flow diagram.

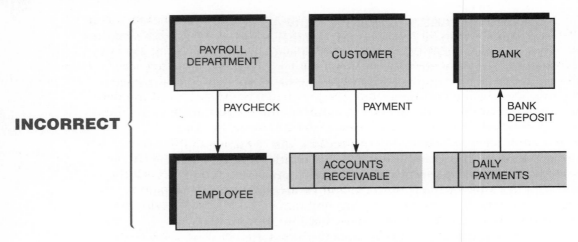

Figure 4-8 Examples of incorrect uses of external entity symbols. An external entity must be connected by a data flow to a process, and not directly to a data store or to another external entity.

With an understanding of the proper use of DFD symbols, you are ready to construct diagrams that use these symbols properly. A summary of the rules for using DFD symbols is shown in Figure 4-9.

DATA FLOW THAT CONNECTS	OK TO USE?	
	Yes	No
A process to another process	☑	☐
A process to an external entity	☑	☐
A process to a data store	☑	☐
An entity to another entity	☐	☑
An entity to a data store	☐	☑
A data store to another data store	☐	☑

Figure 4-9 Rules for connecting processes, data stores, and external entities in a DFD.

Context Diagrams

By using interviews, questionnaires, and other techniques to gather facts about the system, you learned how the various people, departments, data, and procedures fit together to support business operations. Now you are ready to create a graphical description of the information system based on your fact-finding results.

To learn how to construct data flow diagrams, you will use examples of three information systems. The simplest example is a grading system that instructors use to assign final grades based on the scores the students receive during the term. The second example is an order system that a company uses to enter orders and apply payments against a customer's balance. The most complex example is a manufacturing system that handles a company's production process.

The first step in constructing a set of data flow diagrams for an information system is to draw a DFD, called the context diagram. A **context diagram** is a data flow diagram that shows the boundaries or scope of the particular system. The context diagram is a top-level view of the information system. To draw a context diagram, you place *one* process symbol representing the entire information system in the center of the page. Then you draw all the external entities around the perimeter of the page and use data flows to connect the entities properly to the central process. You do not show any data stores in a context diagram because data stores are internal to the system.

How do you know what external entities and data flows to place in the context diagram? You can begin by reviewing the information system's requirements in detail to identify all external data sources and destinations. During this, be sure to record the name of all external entities, the name and content of the data flows, and the direction of the data flows. If you do this carefully, and you did a good job of fact-finding in the previous stage, you should have no difficulty drawing the context diagram.

Figure 4-10 shows the context diagram for the grading system. The GRADING SYSTEM process is at the center of the diagram. The three external entities of STUDENT RECORDS SYSTEM, STUDENT, and INSTRUCTOR are placed around this central process. Interaction among the central process and the external entities involves six different data flows. The STUDENT RECORDS SYSTEM external entity supplies data through the CLASS ROSTER data flow and receives data through the FINAL GRADE data flow. The STUDENT external entity supplies data through the SUBMITTED WORK data flow and receives data through the GRADED WORK data flow. Finally, the INSTRUCTOR external entity supplies data through the GRADING PARAMETERS data flow and receives data through the GRADE REPORT data flow.

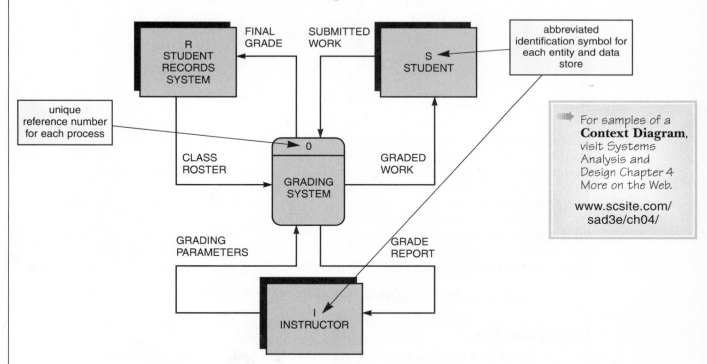

Figure 4-10   Context diagram DFD for the grading system.

The context diagram for an order system is shown in Figure 4-11 on the next page. Notice that the ORDER SYSTEM process is at the center of the diagram and five external entities surround the process. Three of the external entities, SALES REP, BANK, and ACCOUNTING, have single incoming data flows for COMMISSION, BANK DEPOSIT, and CASH RECEIPTS ENTRY, respectively. The WAREHOUSE external entity has one incoming data flow — PICKING LIST — that is a report that shows the items ordered and their quantity, location, and sequence to pick from the warehouse. The WAREHOUSE external entity has one outgoing data flow, COMPLETED ORDER. Finally, the CUSTOMER external entity has two outgoing data flows, ORDER and PAYMENT, and two incoming data flows, ORDER REJECT NOTICE and INVOICE.

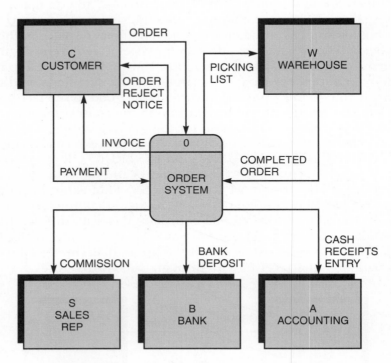

Figure 4-11 Context diagram DFD for the order system.

The context diagram for the order system appears to be more complex than the grading system because it has two more external entities and three more data flows. You cannot conclude that the order system is more complex, however, just by comparing the context diagrams. What makes one system more complex than another is that it has more components and more interaction among its processes, external entities, data stores, and data flows.

Figure 4-12 shows the context diagram for the manufacturing system. Because this information system supports the entire production of a company, you would expect the system to be very complex, and it is. If you analyze the context diagram, you can see that it has 13 external entities and 18 data flows.

To learn more about **DFD Rules**, visit Systems Analysis and Design Chapter 4 More on the Web.

www.scsite.com/ sad3e/ch04/

Conventions for Data Flow Diagrams

The data flow diagrams shown in Figures 4-10 (on the previous page) through 4-12 follow **conventions**, or rules, that you should use when constructing data flow diagrams. The six conventions include the following:

1. *Each context diagram must fit on one page.*

2. *The process name in the context diagram should be the name of the information system.* For example, the process names in Figures 4-10 through 4-12 are GRADING SYSTEM, ORDER SYSTEM, and MANUFACTURING SYSTEM. The system name is used as the process name because the context diagram shows the information system and its boundaries. For processes in lower-level DFDs, use a verb followed by a descriptive noun, such as UPDATE INVENTORY, CALCULATE OVERTIME, or PRODUCE REPORT.

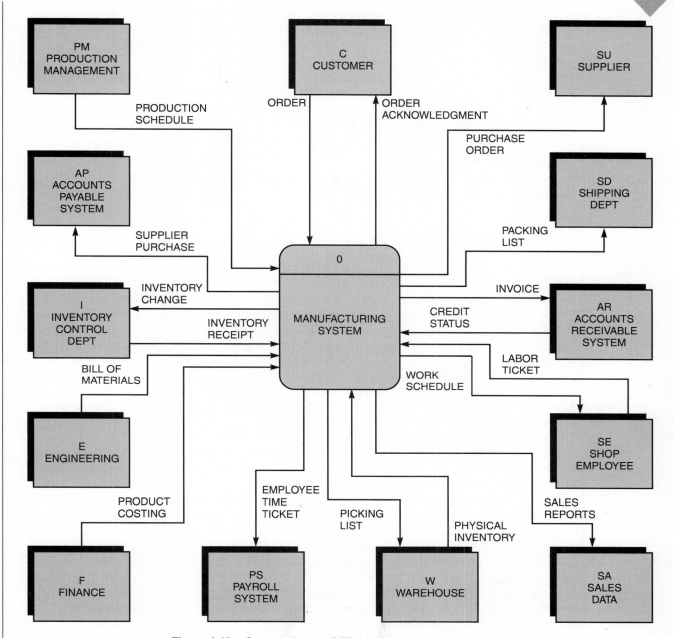

Figure 4-12   Context diagram DFD for the manufacturing system.

3. *Use unique names within each set of symbols.* For instance, the diagram in Figure 4-12 uses only one external entity named CUSTOMER and only one data flow named PURCHASE ORDER. Whenever you see the external entity CUSTOMER on one of the other manufacturing system's DFDs, you know that you are dealing with the same external entity. Whenever the PURCHASE ORDER data flow appears, you know that you are dealing with the same data flow. This naming convention also applies to data stores.

4. *Do not cross lines.* One way to achieve this goal is to restrict the number of symbols in any data flow diagram. On lower-level diagrams with multiple processes, you should not have more than nine process symbols. Including more than nine symbols usually is a signal that your diagram is too complex and that you should reconsider your analysis. Another way to avoid crossing lines is to duplicate an external entity or data

store. When duplicating a symbol on a diagram, make sure to document the duplication to avoid possible confusion. A special notation, such as an asterisk, next to the symbol name and inside of the duplicated symbols signifies that they are duplicated on the diagram.

5. *Use abbreviated identifications.* In the manufacturing system shown in Figure 4-12 on the previous page, for example, each external entity has a unique one- or two-character abbreviation that appears under the symbol. C represents CUSTOMER, AP represents the ACCOUNTS PAYABLE SYSTEM, and so forth. You can use the full name, but abbreviations usually are easier to remember. Similar to entities, each data store has an abbreviation inside the symbol along with the full data store name.

6. *Use a unique reference number for each process symbol.* You use the process number to point to the DFD that contains the next level of detail for that process. For example, on the highest-level DFD (the context diagram) always place a reference number of 0 (zero) inside the process symbol that represents the entire system. To find the detail for process 0, find the DFD identified as diagram 0.

Diagram 0

A context diagram provides the most general view of an information system because the entire information system is represented by a single process symbol. You can use additional data flow diagrams to show more details of the system. The first of these diagrams is called diagram 0. **Diagram 0** (the digit zero, and not the letter O) is a data flow diagram that zooms in on the context diagram to give a more detailed view. While the context diagram uses a single process symbol to represent the entire information system, diagram 0 goes a level deeper to show the major processes, data flows, and data stores within the system. Diagram 0 repeats the same external entities and data flows that appear in the context diagram.

When you expand the context diagram to look at the central process, you must retain all the other connections that flow into and out of that process. A generic example is shown in Figure 4-13. Notice that the inputs, outputs, data flows, and external entities are identical in both diagrams.

Returning to the grading system, a specific example is presented of the relationship between a context diagram and diagram 0, as shown in Figure 4-13. Notice that the three external entities (STUDENT RECORDS SYSTEM, STUDENT, and INSTRUCTOR) and the six data flows (FINAL GRADE, CLASS ROSTER, SUBMITTED WORK, GRADED WORK, GRADING PARAMETERS, and GRADE REPORT) appear in both diagrams. In addition, process 0 (GRADING SYSTEM) in the context diagram has been expanded in diagram 0 by showing greater detail. Specifically, four processes, one data store, and five new data flows have replaced this one process. The data store GRADEBOOK is abbreviated as D1.

Notice that each process in diagram 0 has a reference number: ESTABLISH GRADEBOOK is 1, ASSIGN FINAL GRADE is 2, GRADE STUDENT WORK is 3, and PRODUCE GRADE REPORT is 4. These reference numbers are important because they identify a series of data flow diagrams. If more detail is needed for ESTABLISH GRADEBOOK, for example, you would draw a diagram 1, because 1 is the reference number for this process.

The process reference numbers do not suggest that the processes are accomplished in a sequential order. Each process always is considered to be available and active and awaiting data to be processed. If a specific sequence in which the processes must be performed is required, you must document the sequence elsewhere, because data flow diagrams do not convey this information.

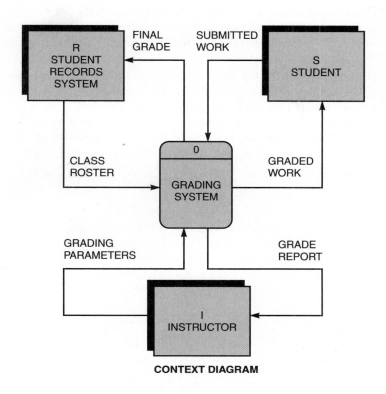

CONTEXT DIAGRAM

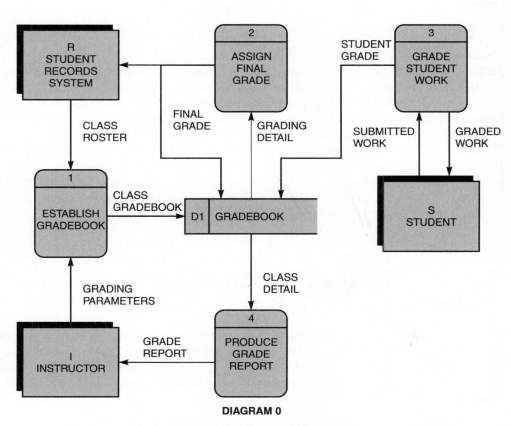

DIAGRAM 0

Figure 4-13   Context diagram and diagram 0 for the grading system.

The FINAL GRADE data flow output from the ASSIGN FINAL GRADE process is a diverging data flow that becomes an input to the STUDENT RECORDS SYSTEM external entity and to the GRADEBOOK data store. A **diverging data flow** is a data flow in which the same data travels to two or more different locations. In this situation, a diverging data flow is the best way to show this flow rather than showing two identical data flows, which could be misleading. Also, remember that if data flows both into and out of a symbol, you use separate data flows, and not one flow with two arrowheads. For example, in Figure 4-13 on the previous page the separate data flows (SUBMITTED WORK and GRADED WORK) go into and out of the GRADE STUDENT WORK process.

Because diagram 0 is a more detailed or expanded version of process 0 on the context diagram, diagram 0 is called an **exploded version of process 0**. Other names for exploded are **partitioned** and **decomposed**. Sometimes process 0 is said to be the **parent** of diagram 0, and diagram 0 is the **child** of process 0. Alternative names for diagram 0 are the **overview diagram** and the **level 0 diagram**.

The grading system is simple enough that you do not need any additional data flow diagrams to model the system. The details of the one data store and the ten data flows are placed in the data dictionary, and the details of the four processes are defined in process descriptions and also are placed in the data dictionary. Each of the four processes in Figure 4-13 is called a functional primitive. A **functional primitive** is a process that consists of a single function that is not exploded further. You outline the detailed specifications of a functional primitive in a process description in the data dictionary.

The order system's diagram 0 is shown in Figure 4-14. Process 0 on the order system's context diagram has been exploded to three processes (FILL ORDER, CREATE INVOICE, and APPLY PAYMENT), one data store (ACCOUNTS RECEIVABLE), two new data flows (INVOICE DETAIL and PAYMENT DETAIL), and one diverging data flow (INVOICE). In Figure 4-15, the mail-order firm, Land's End, uses a powerful, flexible order system to conduct business.

1. To ensure your understanding of what is being modeled in the data flow diagram shown in Figure 4-14, the following walkthrough will guide you. A CUSTOMER submits an ORDER. The FILL ORDER process acts on the order by either sending an ORDER REJECT NOTICE back to the customer or by sending a PICKING LIST to the WAREHOUSE. Notice that conditional or repetitive steps are not shown in data flow diagrams. Either a functional primitive for FILL ORDER or the process description for FILL ORDER clarifies any conditional or repetitive detail.

2. A COMPLETED ORDER from the WAREHOUSE is input to the CREATE INVOICE process, which outputs an INVOICE to both the CUSTOMER process and the ACCOUNTS RECEIVABLE data store.

3. A CUSTOMER makes a PAYMENT that is processed by APPLY PAYMENT. APPLY PAYMENT requires INVOICE DETAIL input from the ACCOUNTS RECEIVABLE data store along with the PAYMENT. APPLY PAYMENT also outputs PAYMENT DETAIL back to the ACCOUNTS RECEIVABLE data store and outputs COMMISSION to the SALES DEPT, BANK DEPOSIT to the BANK, and CASH RECEIPTS ENTRY to ACCOUNTING.

The walkthrough of diagram 0 illustrates the basic requirements of the order system. To learn more, you would examine the detailed description of each separate process. Notice that the CREATE INVOICE process is a functional primitive, but the other two processes shown in Figure 4-14 are not functional primitives because each has a more detailed data flow diagram.

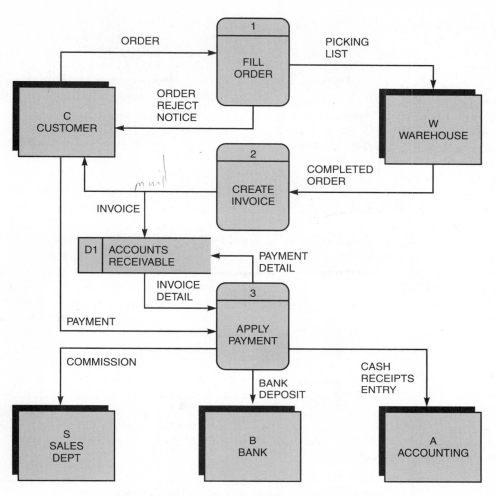

Figure 4-14   Diagram 0 DFD for the order system.

Figure 4-15   Companies such as Land's End depend on powerful order entry systems to handle thousands of daily orders and to maintain a high level of customer service and satisfaction.

Lower-Level Diagrams

When lower-level diagrams are needed to show detail, it is essential that they be leveled and balanced. **Leveling** is the process of drawing a series of increasingly detailed diagrams, until the desired degree of detail is reached. **Balancing** maintains consistency among the entire series of diagrams, including input and output data flows, data definition, and process descriptions.

A simple example of how a lower-level diagram is exploded from a parent diagram helps to explain leveling and balancing. Figure 4-16 shows PROCESS 1, which has two input flows and two output flows. The process itself is shown as a black box, with no details. In Figure 4-17, PROCESS 1 is exploded; it consists of three subprocesses and two internal data flows. Both Figures 4-16 and 4-17 were created with a CASE tool, which is described later in this chapter.

For more information on **Lower-Level Diagrams**, visit Systems Analysis and Design Chapter 4 More on the Web.

www.scsite.com/ sad3e/ch04/

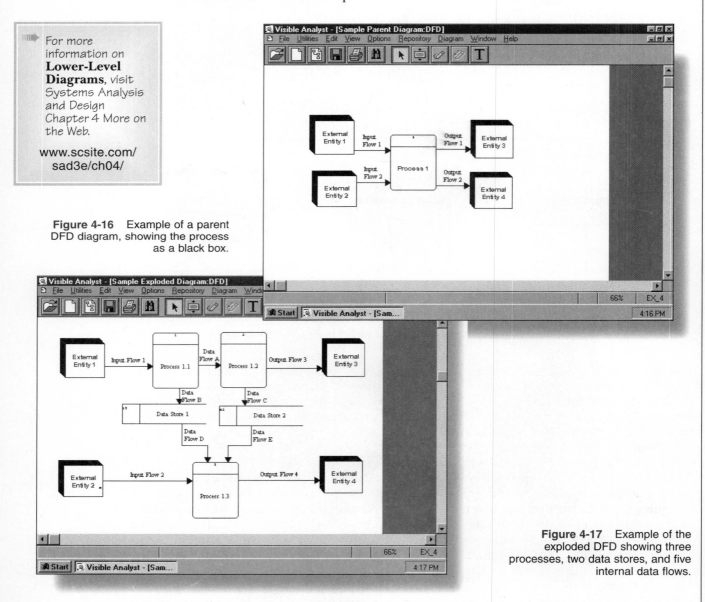

Figure 4-16 Example of a parent DFD diagram, showing the process as a black box.

Figure 4-17 Example of the exploded DFD showing three processes, two data stores, and five internal data flows.

The DFDs shown in Figures 4-16 and 4-17 are leveled and balanced. Each of the internal processes is numbered to show that it is a child of the parent process, and the four data flows into and out of PROCESS 1 are maintained.

Now consider another example. The exploded version of FILL ORDER from diagram 0 in Figure 4-14 on page 4.15 is shown in Figure 4-18. This new data flow diagram is called diagram 1 because it is the decomposition of the FILL ORDER process, which has a reference number of 1.

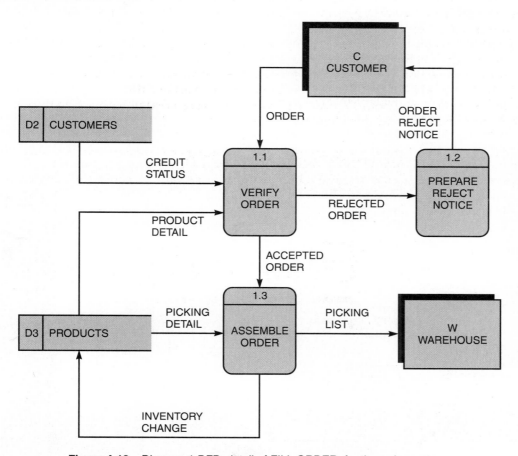

Figure 4-18 Diagram 1 DFD, detail of FILL ORDER, for the order system.

LEVELING • Leveling displays the information system as a single process, and then shows more detail until all processes are functional primitives. At this point, the set of DFDs is described as **leveled**. Leveling also is called **exploding**, **partitioning**, or **decomposing**. Because DFDs are created as a series of top-down pictures of an information system, each lower level provides additional details.

Figure 4-18 shows the exploded version of the FILL ORDER process. FILL ORDER consists of three detailed processes: VERIFY ORDER, PREPARE REJECT NOTICE, and ASSEMBLE ORDER. All processes on more detailed data flow diagrams are numbered using a decimal notation consisting of the parent's reference number, a decimal point, and a sequence number within the new diagram. The parent process of diagram 1 is process 1, so the processes in Figure 4-18 have reference numbers of 1.1, 1.2, and 1.3. If process 1.3, ASSEMBLE ORDER, is decomposed further, then it would appear in diagram 1.3 and the processes in diagram 1.3 would be numbered as 1.3.1, 1.3.2, 1.3.3, and so on. This numbering technique makes it easy to link all data flow diagrams in an orderly fashion.

Under the leveling concept, diagram 0 represents the highest-level view of an information system. Because the grading system is represented fully by a context diagram and a diagram 0, the grading system has just one DFD level. The order system needs two DFD levels. Both systems are relatively simple and need few DFD levels. Larger information systems, such as the manufacturing system, could require as many as six or more DFD levels.

Not all processes must be exploded to the same number of levels. The order system's diagram 0 shown in Figure 4-14 on page 4.15 has one functional primitive process, CREATE INVOICE, but the other two processes are exploded one additional level. Although it is not necessary to explode all processes down to exactly equivalent levels, uneven leveling often is a symptom of improper analysis. For example, if you develop a set of data flow diagrams that has one process that is exploded two levels and another process that is exploded six levels, then you should consider redrawing your DFD logical model of the information system. Making several sketches of a set of DFDs is a common occurrence; in fact, most systems analysts find that developing a set of DFDs requires trying various designs until you find the best overall approach.

Figure 4-19 is equivalent to Figure 4-18 on the previous page and is a common way of showing data flow diagrams below the context diagram level. The difference between these two diagrams is that the CUSTOMER and WAREHOUSE external entities have not been drawn in Figure 4-19. As a result, the data flows are missing a DFD symbol at one end. Many people draw DFDs this way because they feel that the missing symbols are not required, and removing them simplifies the diagram. Because the missing symbols appear on the parent, you can refer to that diagram if you need to know the source or destination of the data flows.

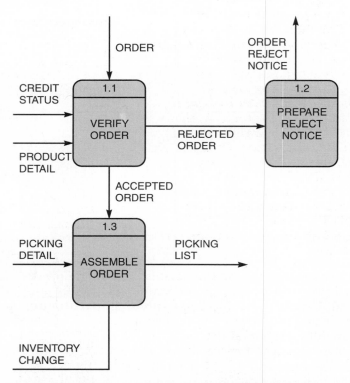

Figure 4-19   Diagram 1 DFD, detail of FILL ORDER, for the order system. In contrast to the DFD in Figure 4-18 on the prevous page, this diagram does not show the symbols that connect to data flows entering or leaving FILL ORDER on the context diagram.

On the other hand, many analysts prefer to show all the symbols. Either approach is acceptable, as long as you are consistent. You should follow whichever approach your instructor suggests or the method your company adopts as a standard.

When constructing DFDs, you might run into a special situation concerning data stores. Sometimes, a data store has output data flows only, which means that the information system accesses the data but does not change it in any way. In this case, the data store must be updated by some other system. For example, the CUSTOMERS data store shown in Figure 4-18 on page 4.17 provides credit status input to the order system, but is not maintained by that system.

BALANCING • Effective data flow diagrams must be accurate, clear, and consistent. One way to gain consistency is to define each functional primitive with a process description and see that each data store, data flow, external entity, and process is defined in the data dictionary. To achieve consistency, you also must balance your data flow diagrams properly.

In a **balanced data flow diagram**, the input and output data flows of the parent are preserved on the child DFD. Figure 4-19 shows a data flow diagram that is balanced because it has the same input and output flows as its parent process, FILL ORDER, as shown in Figure 4-14 on page 4.15. The ORDER data flow provides input to both FILL ORDER and diagram 1, and the PICKING LIST and ORDER REJECT NOTICE data flows serve as output from both FILL ORDER and diagram 1. Because the data flow diagrams do not show data dictionary entries, you would need to verify that all processes, data flows, and data stores are defined in the data dictionary to ensure that this data flow diagram is consistent.

DATA STORES • Figure 4-20 shows the order system's diagram 3, which is the detail of process 3, APPLY PAYMENT. The data store DAILY PAYMENTS appears on this diagram, but it did not appear on diagram 0 or on diagram 1. Why? When drawing data flow diagrams, you place a data store on the *highest-level* data flow diagram that has two or more processes using that data store. Neither diagram 0 nor diagram 1 requires the use of the DAILY PAYMENTS data store. Only when you reach diagram 3 do you have a need for DAILY PAYMENTS. The POST PAYMENT process in diagram 3 must store CUSTOMER PAYMENT data because both the DEPOSIT PAYMENT and PREPARE ACCOUNTING ENTRY processes require the use of this data at a later time.

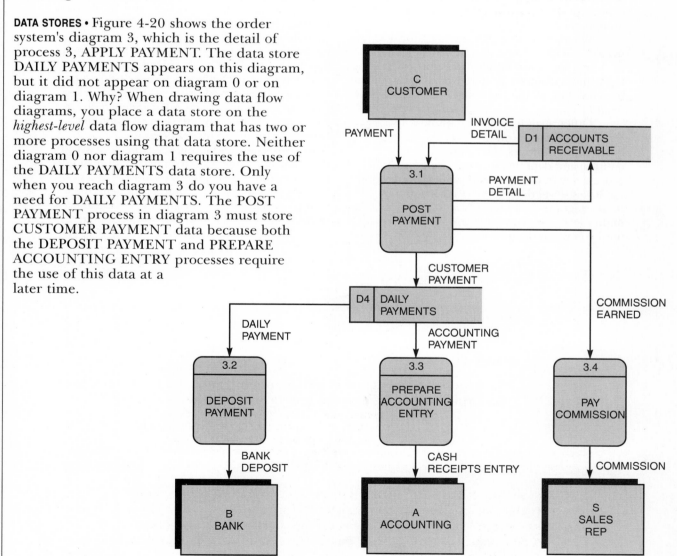

Figure 4-20   Diagram 3 DFD, detail of APPLY PAYMENT, for the order system.

How do you learn to develop a set of data flow diagrams for an information system? Start by practicing using the suggestions and guidelines discussed in this chapter. You must consider many tradeoffs as you develop the logical model of a system. Each system's requirements are unique, and experience will be your best teacher.

A set of data flow diagrams is a graphical, top-down model of an information system. To ensure that your model is accurate, you need to review the DFDs with users and obtain their approval. In doing this, you should start with the context diagram and work your way down to more detailed DFDs.

What about an overall strategy for developing a set of data flow diagrams? Most analysts work in a top-down fashion and start by creating the context diagram, followed by diagram 0, and then creating all the child diagrams for diagram 0, and so on.

Other analysts follow a bottom-up strategy. With a bottom-up strategy, you first identify all functional primitives, data stores, external entities, and data flows. Then, you group processes with other related symbols to develop the lowest-level diagrams. Next, you group these diagrams in a logical way to form the next higher level. You continue to work your way up until you reach diagram 0.

Now take a moment to review Figure 4-23 on page 4.22, which shows diagram 0 for the manufacturing system. In a large system like this, each process in diagram 0 actually represents an entire system. Using a diagram 0 is just one of dozens of acceptable ways you can partition a large system into its component systems. As you do so, remember that a diagram should have no more than nine process symbols. Figure 4-23 has only four process symbols, but you can imagine how complicated the figure would be with nine or more processes.

The manufacturing system is an example of a highly complex system with many processes, data stores, and data flows. As shown in Figure 4-21, any highly complex system requires many interactive processes and data sources to produce products efficiently. In such cases, you might use a combination of the top-down and the bottom-up strategies. You might begin with a bottom-up approach and then find problems and have to work your way back down before continuing back up again. Or, you could start at the top, working your way down and then back up repeatedly. In either case, you would find the diagramming process to be an iterative process.

If users and other analysts who review your data flow diagrams find them correct and simple to follow, you have chosen the proper strategy. Your particular strategy often will depend on your personal preferences and the circumstances of the information system you are modeling.

A KEY QUESTION

Take a look at the diagram 0 DFD shown in Figure 4-22. Based on the rules explained in this chapter, how many problems can you find?

Figure 4-21   Manufacturing systems require many interactive processes and data sources to produce the right product at the right time.

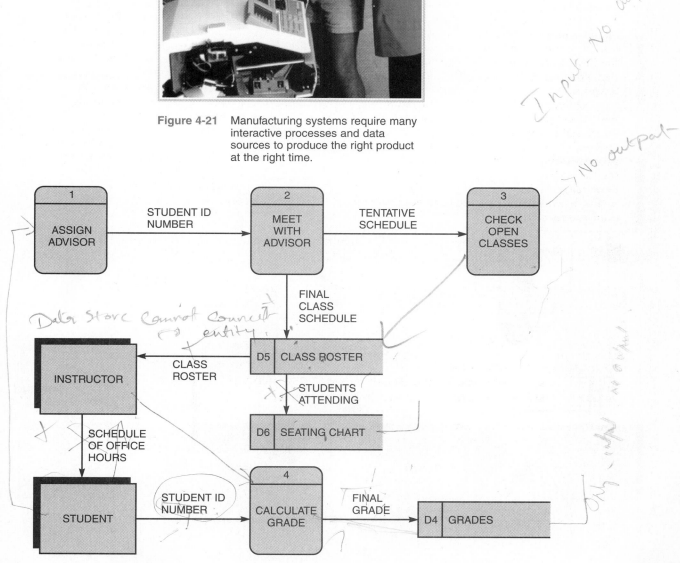

Figure 4-22   Based on the rules discussed in the text, what is wrong with this diagram 0 DFD?

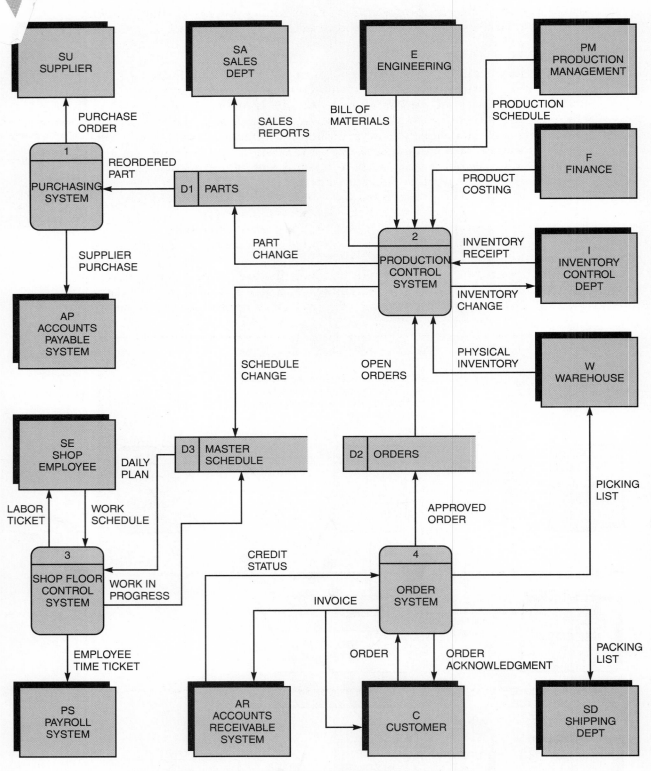

Figure 4-23 Diagram 0 for the manufacturing system.

DATA DICTIONARY

A set of data flow diagrams produces a logical model of the system, but all details within these DFDs must be documented carefully. The DFD details are stored and organized in the data dictionary, which is the second component of structured analysis.

A **data dictionary**, or **data repository**, is a central storehouse of information about the system's data. A data dictionary is used to collect, document, and organize specific facts about the system, including the contents of data flows, data stores, external entities, and processes. The data dictionary also defines and describes all data elements and meaningful combinations of data elements. A **data element**, or **data item** or **field**, is the smallest piece of data that has meaning within an information system. Examples of data elements are student grade, salary, Social Security number, account balance, and company name. Data elements are combined into **records** or **data structures**. A **record** is a meaningful combination of related data elements that is included in a data flow or retained in a data store. For example, an auto parts store inventory record might include part number, description, supplier code, minimum and maximum stock levels, cost, and list price.

Figure 4-24 shows a data dictionary and the items that are defined during structured analysis. Significant relationships exist among these items. Notice that the data stores and data flows are based on data structures that are composed of data elements.

> For an explanation of a **Data Dictionary**, visit Systems Analysis and Design Chapter 4 More on the Web.
>
> www.scsite.com/ sad3e/ch04/

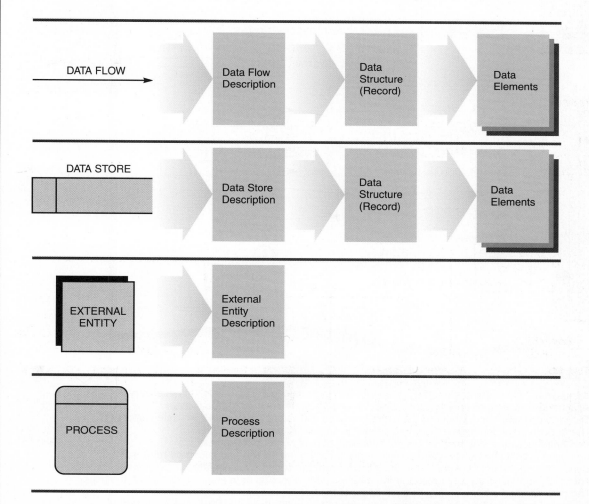

Figure 4-24 Contents of the data dictionary, including data flows, data stores, data structures and records, data elements, external entities, and processes.

Data flows are connected to data stores, external entities, and processes. Accurately documenting these relationships in a data dictionary is essential so the data dictionary is consistent with the DFDs.

Using CASE Tools to Document the System

Various software tools can help you create and maintain a data dictionary, and many of them are built into CASE products and database management systems. One example of a popular tool is a product from the Visible Systems Corporation, called the **Visible Analyst** (**VA**). Some of the DFDs and data dictionary entries that are shown in this chapter were created using this program. Although CASE tools from different software companies might use other terms or organize the documentation differently, the objective is the same: to provide clear, comprehensive information about the data and processes that make up the system.

Documenting the Data Elements

You must document every data element in the data dictionary. You can use a standard form to define a data element, such as SOCIAL SECURITY NUMBER, as shown in Figure 4-25, or you can use a CASE tool to record the same information.

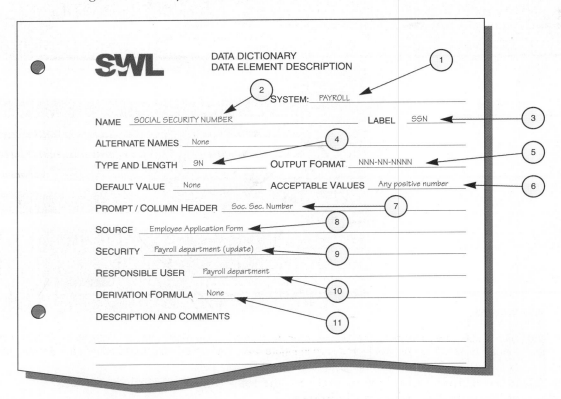

Figure 4-25   Data dictionary definition for a data element called SOCIAL SECURITY NUMBER.

1. Manual data dictionary entries often indicate which system is involved; this is not necessary in CASE data dictionaries because all information is stored in one file that is named for the system.
2. The data element has a standard name that provides consistency throughout the data dictionary.
3. The data element can have a label that usually is an abbreviation of the name.
4. This entry indicates that the data element consists of nine numeric characters.
5. An output format shows how the data will be displayed on the screen and in printed reports.
6. Depending on the data element, very strict limits might be placed on acceptable values, or none at all.
7. This entry is a standard way to refer to the data element in reports or interactive dialog with the user.
8. The data comes from the employee's job application.
9. This entry indicates that only the payroll department has authority to update or change this data.
10. Indicates the individual or department responsible for entering and changing data.
11. Indicates that this data does not need to be derived or calculated from other system data.

In Figure 4-26, two sample screens show how the SOCIAL SECURITY NUMBER data element might be recorded in the Visible Analyst data dictionary.

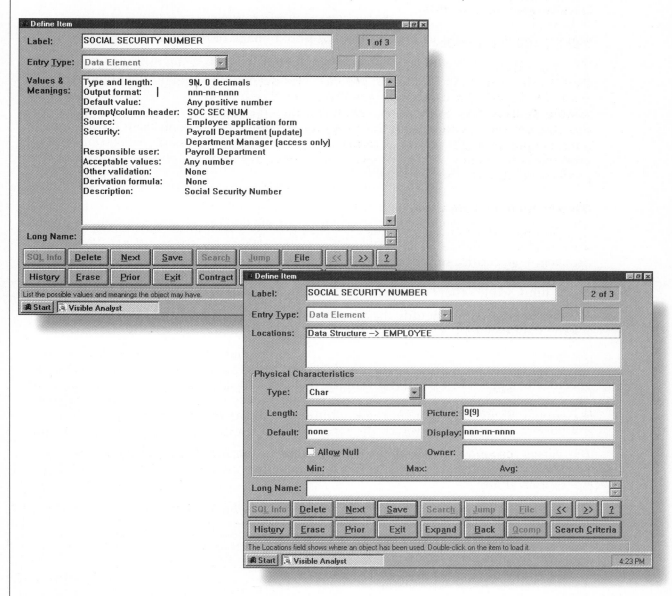

Figure 4-26   Two Visible Analyst screens that describe the data element named SOCIAL SECURITY NUMBER. Although the data display differs from the form shown in Figure 4-25, the same basic characteristics are documented.

Regardless of the terminology or method, the following characteristics usually are recorded and described in the data dictionary:

Data element name or label — The standard name for the data element; it should be meaningful to users.

Alternate name(s) — Any name(s) other than the standard data element name; these names are called **synonyms** or **aliases**. For example, if you have a data element named CURRENT BALANCE, various users might refer to this data element by alternate names such as OUTSTANDING BALANCE, CUSTOMER BALANCE, RECEIVABLE BALANCE, or AMOUNT OWED.

Type and length — **Type** refers to whether the data element contains numeric, alphabetic, or character values. **Length** is the maximum number of characters for an alphabetic or character data element or the maximum number of digits and number of decimal positions for a numeric data element. In addition to text and numeric data, sounds and images also can be stored in digital form. In some systems, these binary data objects are managed and processed just like traditional data elements. For example, an employee record might include a digitized photo image of the person.

Output format or edit mask — The arrangement of the data element when users see it printed on reports or displayed on the screen. For example, a telephone number might be stored as 9195559999, but its output format would be (919) 555-9999.

Default value — The value for the data element if a value otherwise is not entered for it. For example, all new customers might have a default value of $500 for the CREDIT LIMIT data element.

Prompt, column header, or field caption — The default display screen prompt or report column heading when the information system outputs the data element.

Source — The specification for the origination point for the data element's values. The source could be a specific form, a department or outside organization, another information system, or the result of a calculation.

Security — Identification for the individual or department that has access or update privileges for each data element. For example, only the credit manager might change a credit limit, while others could view the data in a read-only mode.

Responsible user(s) — Identify the user(s) responsible for entering and changing values for the data element.

Acceptable values and data validation — Specify the data element's **domain**, which is the set of values permitted for the data element; these values can be discrete and either specifically listed or referenced through a table of values, or the values can be continuous over a listed range of values. You also would specify if a value for the data element is optional. Some data elements have additional **validity rules**. For example, an employee's salary must be within the range defined for the employee's job classification.

Derivation formula — If the data element's value is the result of a calculation, then you show the formula for the data element, including significant digits and rounding operations, if any.

Description or comments — Part of the data element's documentation that allows you to provide additional definitions, descriptions, or notes.

 ## Documenting the Data Flows

In addition to documenting each data element, you must document every DFD data flow in the data dictionary. You can define the characteristics of each data flow using a standard form or with a software tool, as shown in Figure 4-27, that describes a data flow named COMMISSION. Although terms can vary, the typical characteristics of a data flow are:

Data flow name or label — The data flow name as it appears on the DFDs.

Alternate name(s) — Aliases for the DFD data flow name(s).

Abbreviation or ID — A code for the data flow name that provides a quick way of accessing a specific data flow in an automated data dictionary.

Description — Describes the data flow and its purpose.

Origin — The DFD beginning, or source, for the data flow; the origin can be a process, a data store, or an external entity.

Destination — The DFD ending point(s) for the data flow; the destination can be a process, a data store, or an external entity.

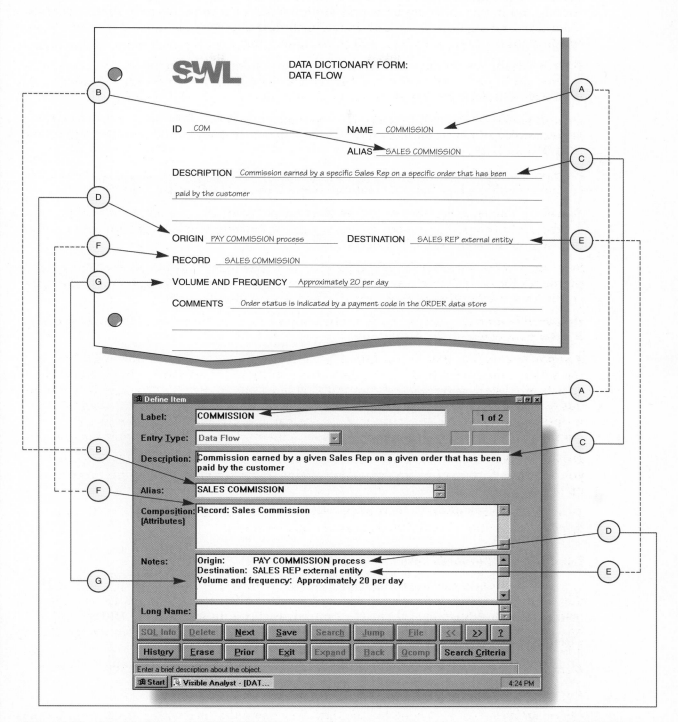

Figure 4-27   The data flow named COMMISSION is described in a sample data dictionary form and on a Visible Analyst screen. Notice that the letters indicate the same basic information.

Record — Each data flow represents a group of related data elements called a record. In most data dictionaries, records are defined separately from the data flows and data stores. Separating defining records is good documentation practice, so more than one data flow or data store can use the same record, if necessary.

Volume and frequency — Describes the expected number of occurrences for the data flow per unit of time.

Documenting the Data Stores

You must document every DFD data store in the data dictionary. You define the characteristics of each data store shown in Figure 4-28 that describes a data store named PRODUCTS. Typical characteristics of a data store are as follows:

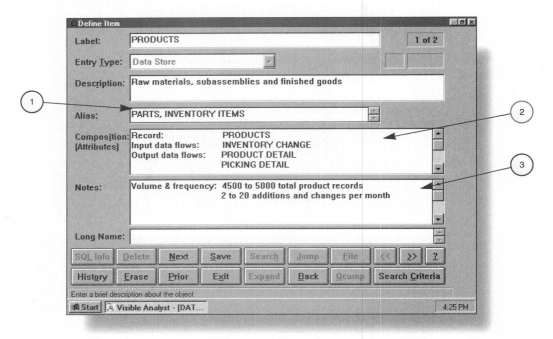

Figure 4-28   Visible Analyst screen that documents a data store named PRODUCTS.

1. This data store has two alternative names, or aliases.
2. For consistency, the data flow names are standardized throughout the data dictionary.
3. It is important to document these estimates, because they will affect design decisions in subsequent SDLC phases.

Data store name or label — The data store name as it appears on the DFDs.

Alternate name(s) — Aliases for the DFD data store name.

Abbreviation or ID — A code for the data store name that provides a quick way of accessing a specific data store in an automated data dictionary.

Description — Describes the data store and its purpose.

Input data flows — The standard DFD names for the data flows entering the data store.

Output data flows — The standard DFD names for the data flows leaving the data store.

Record — The record name in the data dictionary for the data store.

Volume and frequency — Describes the estimated number of records stored in the data store; specify any growth and change statistics for the data store.

Documenting the Processes

You must document every DFD process that is a functional primitive. You define a process as shown in Figure 4-29 that describes a process called VERIFY ORDER. Typical characteristics of a process are:

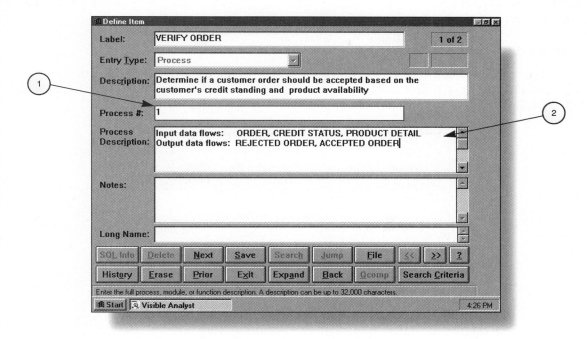

Figure 4-29 Visible Analyst screen that describes a process named VERIFY ORDER.

1. The process number identifies this process. Any subprocesses are numbered 1.1, 1.2, 1.3, and so on.
2. These data flows will be described specifically elsewhere in the data dictionary.

Process name or label — The process name as it appears on the DFDs.

Purpose or description — A brief statement of the process's general purpose; document the detailed steps that comprise the process in the process description.

Process number — A reference number that identifies the process and indicates relationships among various levels in the system.

Input data flows — The standard DFD names for the data flows entering the process.

Output data flows — The standard DFD names for the data flows leaving the process.

Process description — Document the detailed steps for the process; the detailed logic for the VERIFY ORDER process is not included in Figure 4-29, because process descriptions are described in the next section.

Documenting the External Entities

By documenting all external entities, the data dictionary can serve as a complete documentation package. You define each external entity shown in Figure 4-30 on the next page that describes an entity named WAREHOUSE (W). Typical characteristics of an external entity include the following.

External entity name — The external entity name as it appears on the DFDs.

Alternate name(s) — Any aliases for the external entity name.

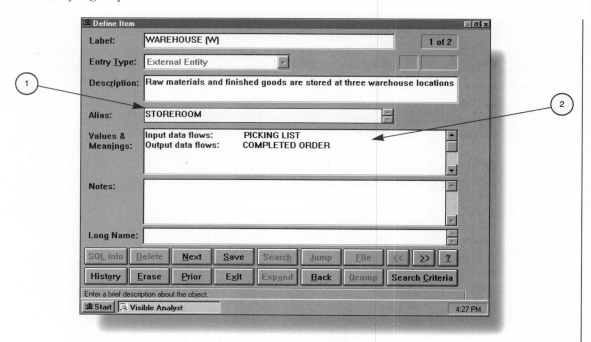

Figure 4-30 Visible Analyst screen that documents an external entity named WAREHOUSE.

1. The external entity also can have an alternative name, or alias, if properly documented.
2. For consistency, these data flow names are standardized throughout the data dictionary.

Description — Describe the external entity and its purpose.

Input data flows — The standard DFD names for the input data flows to the external entity.

Output data flows — The standard DFD names for the data flows leaving the external entity.

Documenting the Records

A **record** is a data structure that contains a set of related data elements that are stored and processed together. Data flows and data stores consist of records that you must document in the data dictionary. You define typical characteristics of each record, as shown in Figure 4-31.

Record name — The record name as it appears in the related data flow and data store entries in the data dictionary and include the following characteristics.

Alternate name(s) — Any aliases for the record name.

Definition or description — A brief definition for the record.

Record content or composition — A list of all the data elements included in the record. The data element names must match exactly with what you entered in the data dictionary. Identify any data element that will serve as a primary key. A **primary key** is a data element in a record that uniquely identifies that record. A primary key can consist of one data element or a combination of two or more data elements. The CREDIT STATUS record shown in Figure 4-31, for example, has a primary key of CUSTOMER NUMBER (PK is used to identify the primary key), which distinguishes one customer's record from all other customer records. In a video store, it might be necessary to use a primary key based on a combination of two fields, such as MOVIE NUMBER and COPY NUMBER, to identify each individual tape uniquely.

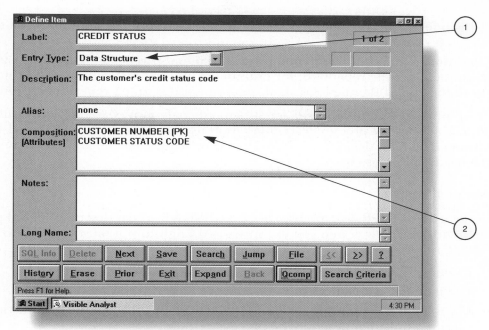

Figure 4-31   Visible Analyst screen that documents a record named CREDIT
STATUS.

1. The Visible Analyst tool defines a data structure as a group of related data
   elements that also can be referred to as a record.
2. The (PK) notation indicates that the CUSTOMER NUMBER is a primary key.

Data Dictionary Reports

The data dictionary serves as the central storehouse of documentation for an information system. In addition to describing each data element, data flow, data store, record, external entity, and process, the data dictionary documents the relationships among these components. You can obtain many valuable reports from a data dictionary, including these examples:

- An alphabetized list of all data elements by name
- A report by user departments of data elements that must be updated by each department
- A report of all data flows and data stores that use a particular data element
- Detailed reports showing all characteristics of data elements, records, data flows, processes, or any other selected item stored in the data dictionary

PROCESS DESCRIPTION TOOLS

Each data flow diagram functional primitive represents a specific procedure. You must document each functional primitive to have a complete logical model of the information system. In documenting the functional primitives, you must be accurate, complete, and concise. While you could use standard English narratives to document each functional primitive, a process description tends to be more precise and clear.

A **process description** documents the details of a functional primitive by using modular design. **Modular design** is based on combinations of three logical building blocks, or structures.

1. **Sequence** — the completion of one process step in sequential order, one after another.

For a review of
**Process
Description
Tools**, visit
Systems Analysis
and Design
Chapter 4 More on
the Web.

www.scsite.com/
sad3e/ch04/

2. **Selection** — the completion of one of two or more process steps based on the results of a test or condition.

3. **Iteration** — the completion of a process step that is repeated until the results of a condition end the repetition, for example, a process that continues to print checks until the end of the file is reached. Iteration also is called **repetition** or **looping**.

All process description tools for structured analysis are based on these three logical building blocks. The process description tools used most often are structured English, decision tables, and decision trees. You can use one or a combination of these tools for a given information system.

Structured English

Structured English is a subset of standard English that describes logical processes clearly and accurately. When you use structured English, you must conform to the following rules:

- Use only the three building blocks of sequence, selection, and iteration.
- Use indentation for readability.
- Use a limited vocabulary, including standard terms used in the data dictionary and specific words that describe the processing rules.

An example of structured English appears in Figure 4-32, which shows the VERIFY ORDER process that was illustrated earlier in Figure 4-29 on page 4.29. In Figure 4-32, structured English has been added to describe the processing logic.

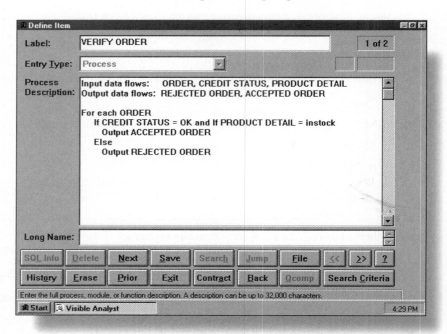

Figure 4-32   The VERIFY ORDER process description describes the logic rules and actions using structured English that users can understand easily.

Structured English might look familiar to you because it is similar to pseudocode, which is used in program design. The difference between structured English and pseudocode is that structured English is used to represent logical processes and must be understandable to users. Programmers who are concerned with coding, on the other hand, mainly use pseudocode.

Another example of structured English is shown is Figure 4-33. Notice that the capitalized words are all terms from the data dictionary to ensure consistency between process descriptions and the data dictionary. The other terms, such as *for*, *each*, *if*, and *output*, describe the processing logic. Following these structured English rules ensures that your process descriptions will be understandable to users who must confirm that the process is correct, as well as to other analysts and programmers who must design the information system from your descriptions.

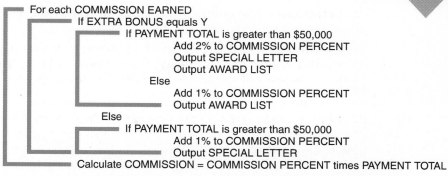

For each COMMISSION EARNED
  If EXTRA BONUS equals Y
    If PAYMENT TOTAL is greater than $50,000
      Add 2% to COMMISSION PERCENT
      Output SPECIAL LETTER
      Output AWARD LIST
    Else
      Add 1% to COMMISSION PERCENT
      Output AWARD LIST
  Else
    If PAYMENT TOTAL is greater than $50,000
      Add 1% to COMMISSION PERCENT
      Output SPECIAL LETTER
  Calculate COMMISSION = COMMISSION PERCENT times PAYMENT TOTAL

Figure 4-33 Sample structured English process description. Structured English is an organized way of describing what actions are taken on data. This structured English example describes a commission calculation policy.

Decision Tables

A **decision table** shows a logical structure, with all possible combinations of conditions and resulting actions. Analysts often use decision tables, in addition to structured English, to describe a logical process.

A simple example of a decision table is based on the VERIFY ORDER process shown in Figure 4-32. From the structured English description, we know that an accepted order requires that credit status is OK, and the product is in stock. Otherwise, the order is rejected. The decision table shown in Figure 4-34 shows all the possibilities. To create a decision table, follow the steps indicated in the figure.

For details on developing **Decision Tables**, visit Systems Analysis and Design Chapter 4 More on the Web.

www.scsite.com/ sad3e/ch04/

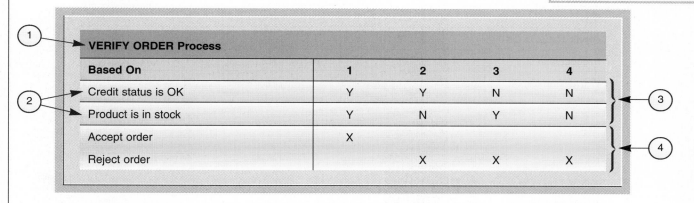

VERIFY ORDER Process

Based On	1	2	3	4
Credit status is OK	Y	Y	N	N
Product is in stock	Y	N	Y	N
Accept order	X			
Reject order		X	X	X

Figure 4-34 Example of a simple decision table showing the processing logic of the VERIFY ORDER process.
1. Place a heading at the top left that names the table.
2. Enter the conditions under the heading, with one condition per line, to represent the customer status and availability of products.
3. Enter all potential combinations of **Y/N** (for yes and no) for the conditions. Each column represents a numbered possibility called a **rule**.
4. Place an X in the action entries area for each rule to indicate whether to accept or reject the order.

Because each condition has two possible values, the number of rules doubles each time you add a condition. For example, one condition creates only two rules, two conditions create four rules, three conditions create eight rules, and so on. As you can see in Figure 4-34, four possible combinations exist, but only one rule — rule 1 — permits an accepted order output.

A more complex situation is presented in Figure 4-35 on the next page. In this example, the credit manager can waive the credit status requirement in certain situations. To be sure that all possibilities are covered, notice that the first condition provides an equal number of Ys and Ns, the second condition alternates Y and N pairs, and the third condition alternates single Ys and Ns.

The first table in Figure 4-35 shows eight rules. Because some rules are duplicates, however, the table can be simplified. To reduce the number of rules, you must look closely at each combination of conditions and actions. If you have rules with three conditions, only one or two of them may control the outcome, and the other conditions do not matter. You can indicate this with dashes (-) as shown in the second table in Figure 4-35. Then, you can combine and renumber the rules, as shown in the final table.

VERIFY ORDER Process with Credit Waiver (Initial version)

	1	2	3	4	5	6	7	8
Credit status is OK	Y	Y	Y	Y	N	N	N	N
Product is in stock	Y	Y	N	N	Y	Y	N	N
Waiver from credit manager	Y	N	Y	N	Y	N	Y	N
Accept order	X	X			X			
Reject order			X	X		X	X	X

VERIFY ORDER Process with Credit Waiver (With rules marked for combination)

	1	2	3	4	5	6	7	8
Credit status is OK	Y	Y	-	-	N	N	-	-
Product is in stock	Y	Y	N	N	Y	Y	N	N
Waiver from credit manager	-	-	-	-	Y	N	-	-
Accept order	X	X			X			
Reject order			X	X		X	X	X

(1) *(2)*

VERIFY ORDER Process with Credit Waiver (After rule combination and simplification)

	1 (Combines previous 1, 2)	2 (Previous 5)	3 (Previous 6)	4 (Combines previous 3, 4, 7, 8)
Credit status is OK	Y	N	N	-
Product is in stock	Y	Y	Y	N
Waiver from credit manager	-	Y	N	-
Accept order	X	X		
Reject order			X	X

Figure 4-35   A more complex example of a decision table for the VERIFY ORDER process showing the results of rule combination and simplification.

1. Because the product is not in stock, the other conditions do not matter.
2. Because the other conditions are met, the waiver does not matter.

In this example, rules 1 and 2 can be combined because credit status is OK and the waiver is not needed. Rules 3, 4, 7, and 8 also can be combined because the product is not in stock, and credit status does not matter. The result is that instead of eight possibilities, only four logical rules are created that control the VERIFY ORDER process.

In addition to multiple conditions, decision tables can have more than two possible outcomes. An example is presented in the PAY COMMISSION decision table shown in Figure 4-36. Here only two conditions exist: was an extra bonus given, and did the payment total exceed $50,000. Based on these two conditions, four possible actions can occur, as shown in the table.

PAY COMMISSION	1	2	3	4
EXTRA BONUS	Y	Y	N	N
PAYMENT TOTAL > $50,000	Y	N	Y	N
Add 2% to COMMISSION PERCENT	X			
Add 1% to COMMISSION PERCENT		X	X	
Output SPECIAL LETTER	X		X	
Output AWARD LIST	X	X		

Figure 4-36 Sample decision table based on the commission calculation policy described in structured English in Figure 4-32 on page 4.32. For example, if the payment total is more than $50,000 but no extra bonus is to be paid, the policy is to add 1% to the commission percent and to output a special letter to the sales representative.

Decision tables often are the best way to describe a complex set of conditions. Many analysts use decision tables because they are easy to construct and understand, and programmers find it easy to work from a decision table when developing code.

Decision Trees

A **decision tree** is a graphical representation of the conditions, actions, and rules found in a decision table. Decision trees show the logic structure in a horizontal form that resembles a tree with the roots at the left and the branches to the right. Decision trees are effective ways to present the system to management, as shown in Figure 4-37. You can consider a decision tree and a decision table to be equivalent, but in different forms — a graphic versus a table.

Figure 4-37 Analysts and managers use decision trees to show the outcomes of the process under consideration.

Figure 4-38 shows the same PAY COMMISSION conditions and actions shown in Figure 4-36 on the previous page. A decision tree is read from left to right, with the conditions along the various branches and the actions at the far right. Because this example has two conditions with four resulting sets of actions, the example has four terminating branches at the right side of the tree.

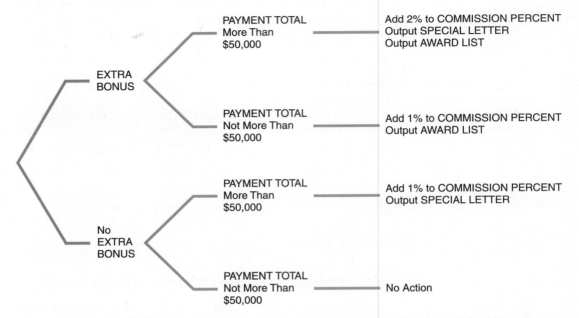

Figure 4-38   Sample decision tree process description. Similar to a decision table, a decision tree illustrates the action to be taken based on certain conditions, but presents it graphically. This decision tree is based on the commission calculation policy described in structured English in Figure 4-36 on the previous page. For example, if the payment total is more than $50,000 but no extra bonus is to be paid, the policy is to add 1% to the commission percent and to output a special letter to the sales representative.

A decision tree is easy to construct and understand. Whether to use a decision table or a decision tree often is a matter of personal preference. Many analysts, however, think a decision table is better for handling complex combinations of conditions. On the other hand, a decision tree is an effective way to describe a relatively simple process.

Logical vs. Physical Models

While structured analysis tools are used to develop a logical model for a new information system, these tools also can be used to develop physical models of an information system. A physical model shows how the system's requirements are implemented. During the systems design phase, you create a physical model of the new information system that follows from the logical model and involves operational tasks and techniques.

What is the relationship between logical and physical models? Think back to the begin-ning of the systems analysis phase when you were trying to understand the existing system. Rather than starting with a logical model, you first studied the physical operations of the existing system to understand how the current tasks were carried out. Many systems analysts create a physical model of the current system and then develop a logical model of the current system before tackling a logical model of the new system. By performing this extra step, they can understand the current system better.

If you follow this sequence when you develop an information system, you will develop a total of four models: a physical model of the current system, a logical model of the current system, a logical model of the new system, and a physical model of the new system. The major *benefit of the four-model approach* is that you will have a better grasp of the current system functions before making any modifications or improvements. This is important, because mistakes made early in systems development will affect later SDLC phases and can result in unhappy users and additional costs. Another *advantage* is that the requirements of a new information system often are quite similar to the current information system, especially where the proposal is based on new computer technology rather than a large number of new requirements. Adapting the current system logical model to the new system logical model in these cases is a straightforward process.

The major *disadvantage of the four-model approach* is the added time and cost needed to develop a logical and physical model of the current system. Most projects have very tight schedules that might not allow time to create the current system models. Additionally, users and managers want to see progress on the new system; spending too much time on the current system seems counterproductive. Finally, if you truly know the new system's requirements, then spending time documenting a system that is being replaced might not be necessary or wise.

A KEY QUESTION

In the SWL case study that follows, Rick Williams and Carla Moore are working on the logical model of SWL's payroll system, using DFDs, a data dictionary, and process descriptions. At some point while working on the logical model of the system, Rick considers some new enrollment forms that the human resources department might use to implement the Employee Savings and Investment Plan (ESIP). Was the subject of forms identified as a physical implementation issue? Is Rick going off on a tangent by considering *how* something will be done, instead of sticking to *what* will be done?

SOFTWEAR, LIMITED — ANALYZING REQUIREMENTS

Rick Williams, a systems analyst, and Carla Moore, a programmer/analyst, continued their work on the SWL payroll system project. After completing detailed interviews and other fact-finding activities, Rick and Carla now understand how the current system operates and the new requirements desired by users. They are ready to organize and document their findings by preparing a logical model of the payroll system.

Data Flow Diagrams

Rick and Carla reviewed the collected set of requirements and decided that the first step would be to prepare a context diagram. Rick was most familiar with the payroll system, so he prepared the diagram shown in Figure 4-39 on the next page. On a Friday afternoon, Rick walked Carla through the diagram and asked for her comments.

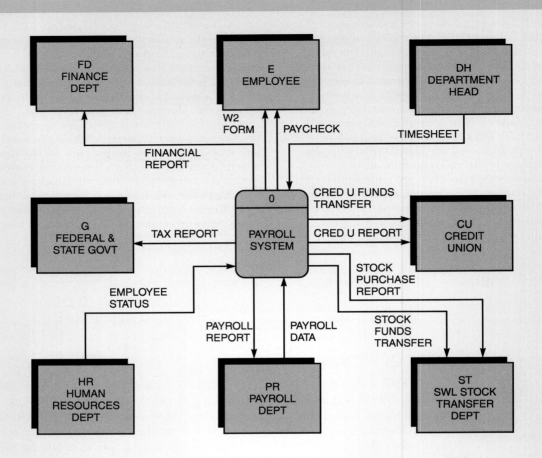

Figure 4-39 Initial version of context diagram for SoftWear, Limited's payroll system.

The diagram shows how the two analysts understood the system. They knew that an employee received a paycheck each week, based on a timesheet submitted by the department head, and that each employee receives a W-2 form at the end of the year. They knew that the human resources department prepares employee status changes, and the payroll department enters pay rate information. The diagram also noted the output of state and federal government reports and internal reports to SWL's finance and payroll departments. The credit union and the SWL stock transfer department reports and fund transfers also were included.

Carla, however, was not sure that they had covered everything. They both decided that it would be a good idea to review the system requirements over the weekend and discuss the diagram again on Monday.

The weekend review turned out to be a wise strategy. When she reviewed her interview documentation, Carla discovered that the payroll department enters the timesheet data received from department heads, as well as the pay rate information. So she removed the department head entity symbol and changed the existing input data flow from the payroll department, calling it PAY DETAIL.

After studying his notes, Rick also detected an error: the payroll system produces reports for the accounting department and this report is not shown on the diagram. They also realized that federal and state reporting requirements were different, so it would be more accurate to treat them as two separate entities. Rick revised the context diagram to reflect these changes, as shown in Figure 4-40.

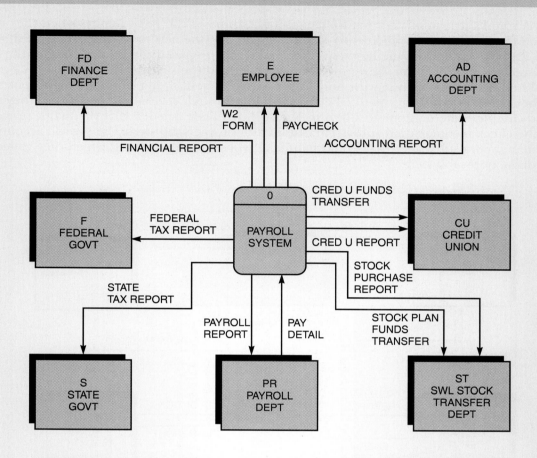

Figure 4-40 Second version of context diagram for SoftWear, Limited's payroll system.

Rick and Carla were comfortable with the context diagram and scheduled a meeting for the next day with Amy Calico, director of the payroll department, to discuss the diagram. In preparation for the meeting, they brainstormed their ideas about the payroll system's major processes, data stores, and data flows, and reviewed the system's requirements one more time.

The next day, Rick and Carla presented the context diagram with Amy, who had several suggestions. Amy noted that the human resources department generates employee status changes, including job title, pay rate, and exempt status. But the human resources group does not enter the data directly into the payroll system. Instead, all employee changes are sent to the payroll department for entry. Amy had several other comments:

- Periodic changes in state and federal government tax rates should be shown as inputs to the payroll system.

- All reports, except for a financial summary, should be distributed to the accounting department instead of to the finance department. Rick and Carla both recalled that Mr. Jeremy wanted this change.

- The bank returns cleared payroll checks to the payroll department once a month. Amy reminded the analysts that the payroll system handles the reconciliation of payroll checks.

- The human resources department would be setting up additional ESIP deduction choices for employees under a new 401(k) plan. Human resources also would receive ESIP reports from the payroll system.

Rick and Carla admitted that they had not considered the ESIP reports when they constructed the diagram. After discussing it, they agreed that the new functions should be shown in the diagram. Following the meeting, Rick and Carla prepared the final version of the payroll system context diagram shown in Figure 4-41 with all the suggested changes.

While their conversation with Amy Calico was still fresh in her mind, Carla proposed that they construct the diagram 0 DFD. After going through several draft versions, they were able to complete the diagram 0 shown in Figure 4-42. They decided that the major processes were the check reconciliation subsystem, the pay employee subsystem, the payroll accounting subsystem, and a subsystem that would handle all voluntary deductions, which they called the ESIP deduction subsystem.

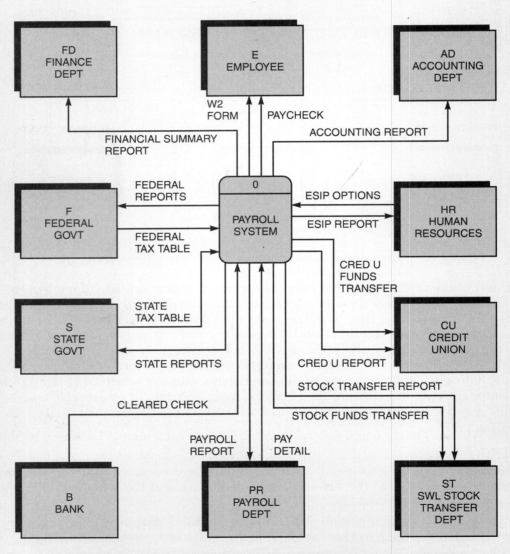

Figure 4-41   Final context diagram for SoftWear, Limited's payroll system.

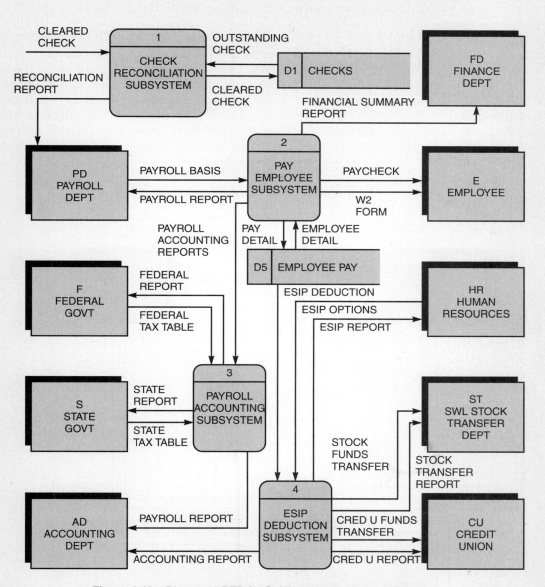

Figure 4-42   Diagram 0 DFD for SoftWear, Limited's payroll system.

Over the next few days, Rick concentrated on partitioning the pay employee subsystem and the ESIP subsystem, while Carla developed the lower-level diagrams for the other two subsystems.

At this point, Rick considered the problem of applying certain deductions on a monthly cycle, even though the deductions were made weekly. To provide flexibility, he decided to use two separate processes, as shown in Figure 4-43. When he finished, his diagram 4 DFD contained the two processes, EXTRACT DEDUCTION and APPLY DEDUCTION, as well as a local data store, UNAPPLIED DEDUCTIONS. Several local data flows also were included. The first process, EXTRACT DEDUCTION, would deduct the proper amount in each pay period. The deductions would be held in the temporary data store and then applied in the APPLY DEDUCTION process on a weekly or monthly basis, depending on the type of deduction. Rick decided that these processes were functional primitives and did not need to be partitioned further. This task completed the logical model of the new SWL payroll system.

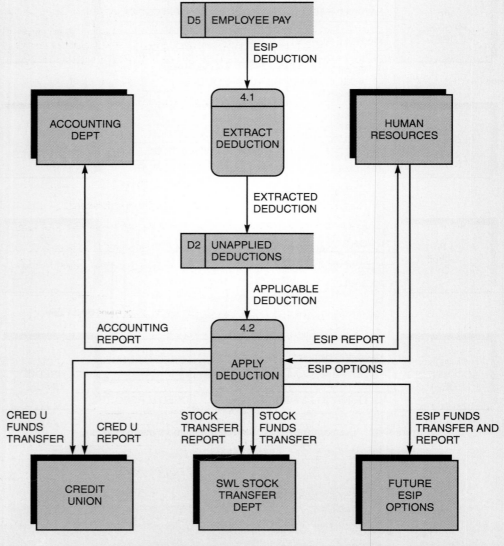

Figure 4-43   Diagram 4 DFD for SoftWear, Limited's payroll system shows the detail of the ESIP Subsystem.

Rick and Carla also considered the physical design of the ESIP deduction subsystem that would be completed later. They knew that it would be necessary to add some new forms and to redesign others. They saw that the human resources department would need a new form for enrollments or deduction changes for the credit union, SWL stock purchase plan, or any new ESIP choices that might be offered in the future. The payroll department then could use this form as its official notification. To provide for future expansion and add flexibility, the human resources department also would need a form to notify payroll of any new type of deduction, with a deduction code, the name of the deduction, and the payroll cycle involved. Rick anticipated that the new system would eliminate problems with improper deductions, while adding flexibility and reducing maintenance costs.

Data Dictionary and Process Descriptions

As they constructed the data flow diagrams for the payroll system, Rick and Carla also developed the data dictionary entries with supporting process descriptions.

Rick documented the ESIP deduction subsystem shown in Figure 4-44. Then, he defined the data flow called ESIP REPORT that originates in the APPLY DEDUCTION process and connects to the HUMAN RESOURCES entity, as shown in Figure 4-45 on the next page. He also documented the ESIP OPTIONS record shown in Figure 4-46 on the next page, which consists of eight data elements.

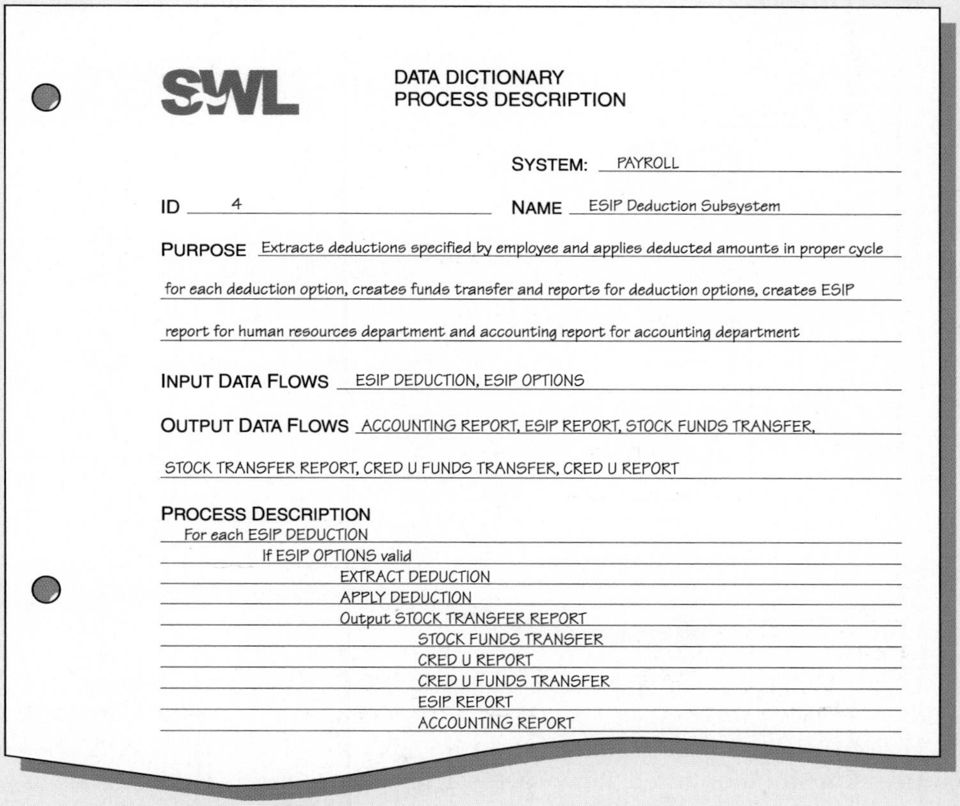

SWL   DATA DICTIONARY
PROCESS DESCRIPTION

SYSTEM: PAYROLL

ID ___4___   NAME ESIP Deduction Subsystem

PURPOSE Extracts deductions specified by employee and applies deducted amounts in proper cycle

for each deduction option, creates funds transfer and reports for deduction options, creates ESIP

report for human resources department and accounting report for accounting department

INPUT DATA FLOWS ESIP DEDUCTION, ESIP OPTIONS

OUTPUT DATA FLOWS ACCOUNTING REPORT, ESIP REPORT, STOCK FUNDS TRANSFER,

STOCK TRANSFER REPORT, CRED U FUNDS TRANSFER, CRED U REPORT

PROCESS DESCRIPTION
For each ESIP DEDUCTION
    If ESIP OPTIONS valid
        EXTRACT DEDUCTION
        APPLY DEDUCTION
        Output STOCK TRANSFER REPORT
            STOCK FUNDS TRANSFER
            CRED U REPORT
            CRED U FUNDS TRANSFER
            ESIP REPORT
            ACCOUNTING REPORT

Figure 4-44   Data dictionary definition for the ESIP Subsystem.

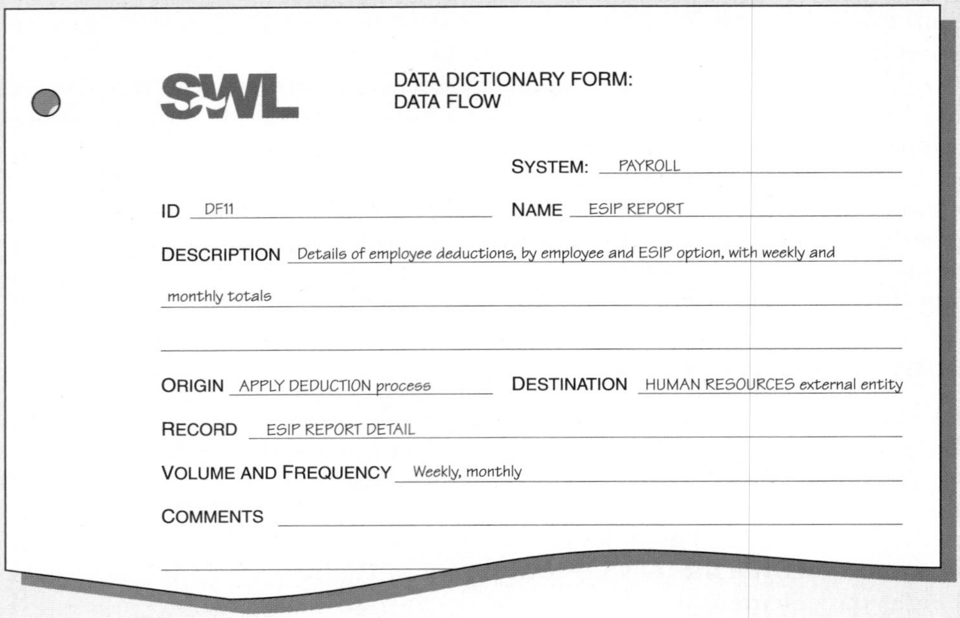

SWL   DATA DICTIONARY FORM:
DATA FLOW

SYSTEM: ___PAYROLL___

ID ___DF11___   NAME ___ESIP REPORT___

DESCRIPTION ___Details of employee deductions, by employee and ESIP option, with weekly and___

___monthly totals___

ORIGIN ___APPLY DEDUCTION process___   DESTINATION ___HUMAN RESOURCES external entity___

RECORD ___ESIP REPORT DETAIL___

VOLUME AND FREQUENCY ___Weekly, monthly___

COMMENTS _____

Figure 4-45   Data dictionary definition for the ESIP REPORT data flow.

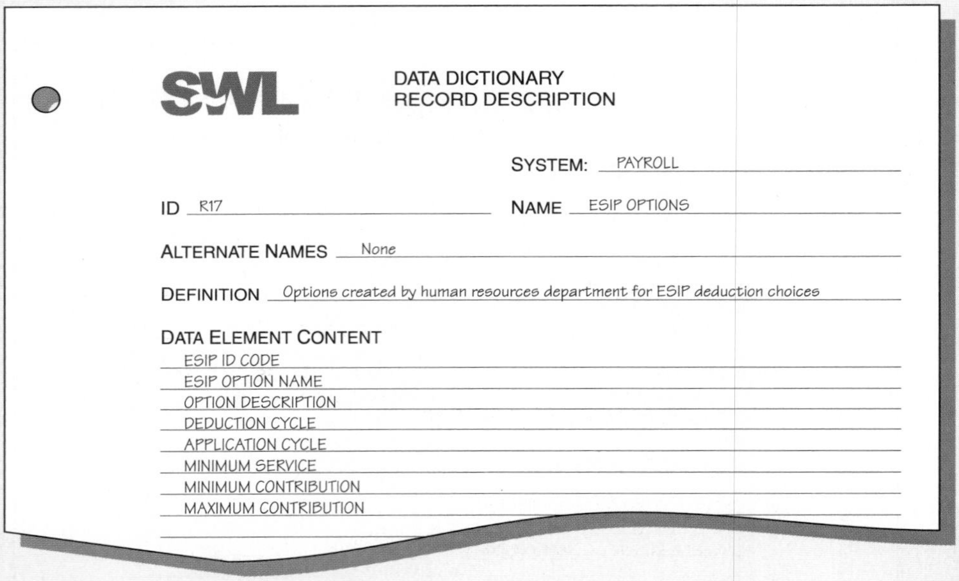

SWL   DATA DICTIONARY
RECORD DESCRIPTION

SYSTEM: ___PAYROLL___

ID ___R17___   NAME ___ESIP OPTIONS___

ALTERNATE NAMES ___None___

DEFINITION ___Options created by human resources department for ESIP deduction choices___

DATA ELEMENT CONTENT
___ESIP ID CODE___
___ESIP OPTION NAME___
___OPTION DESCRIPTION___
___DEDUCTION CYCLE___
___APPLICATION CYCLE___
___MINIMUM SERVICE___
___MINIMUM CONTRIBUTION___
___MAXIMUM CONTRIBUTION___

Figure 4-46   Data dictionary definition for the ESIP OPTIONS record.

Carla prepared the process description for EXTRACT DEDUCTION shown in Figure 4-47. Notice that she numbered this process 4.1, because it was exploded from process 4. The two analysts also completed the descriptions for the data element EXTRACTED DEDUCTION shown in Figure 4-48 and the ESIP ID CODE shown in Figure 4-49 on page 4.46. They spent the next two days documenting the rest of the data flows and external entities for the ESIP deduction subsystem, along with data elements and records.

SWL   DATA DICTIONARY
        PROCESS DESCRIPTION

SYSTEM: PAYROLL

ID 4.1   NAME EXTRACT DEDUCTION

PURPOSE During each payroll cycle, takes actual employee deductions for ESIP selections
and retains deducted amounts for further processing by the ESIP subsystem

INPUT DATA FLOWS ESIP DEDUCTION

OUTPUT DATA FLOWS EXTRACTED DEDUCTION

PROCESS DESCRIPTION
For each ESIP DEDUCTION
     EXTRACT DEDUCTION
     Output EXTRACTED DEDUCTION

Figure 4-47   Data dictionary definition for Process 4.1, EXTRACT DEDUCTION.

SWL   DATA DICTIONARY
        DATA ELEMENT DESCRIPTION

SYSTEM: PAYROLL

ID DE-18   NAME EXTRACTED DEDUCTION

ALTERNATE NAMES None

TYPE AND LENGTH 4N, 2 decimal   OUTPUT FORMAT Z9.99

DEFAULT VALUE None   ACCEPTABLE VALUES Any value

PROMPT / COLUMN HEADER EXTRACTED DEDUCTION

SOURCE Payroll department

SECURITY Payroll department (update)

RESPONSIBLE USER Payroll department

OTHER VALIDATION None

DERIVATION FORMULA None

DESCRIPTION AND COMMENTS

The EXTRACTED DEDUCTION is retained in UNAPPLIED DEDUCTIONS data store to be applied by
APPLY DEDUCTION process during application cycle

Figure 4-48   Data dictionary definition for the data element EXTRACTED DEDUCTION.

After completing the documentation of the ESIP deduction subsystem, Carla and Rick met with Amy to review the logical model for this subsystem. After a thorough discussion of all proposed changes and processing, Amy approved the model.

Rick and Carla continued their analysis and documentation of the payroll system over the next several days. As they completed a model of a portion of the information system, they would meet with the appropriate users at SWL to review the model, obtain user input, make necessary adjustments to the model, and obtain the users' approval. After Rick and Carla finished the complete payroll information system logical model, they turned their attention to completing the rest of the system requirements document.

YOUR TURN — Suppose that you are working with Rick and Carla when a new systems request comes in. SWL's vice president of marketing, Amy Neal, wants to change the catalog mailing program and provide a reward for customers who use the Internet.

Amy's plan specifies that customers will remain on SWL's mailing list if they either requested a catalog, ordered from SWL in the last two years, or signed the guest register on SWL's new Web site. To encourage Internet visitors, customers who register on the Web site also will receive a special discount certificate.

To document the requirements, Rick has asked you to design a decision table. Initially, it appears to have eight rules, but you notice that some of these rules are duplicates, or might not be realistic combinations.

1. Design the decision table with all possibilities.
2. Simplify the table by combining rules where appropriate.
3. Draw a decision tree that reflects Amy Neal's policy.
4. Create a set of structured English statements to show the policy.

ON THE NET

Rick asked you to do some research on companies that offer CASE products. He seems pleased with the memo you gave him. Now he wants you to determine whether these companies publish pricing information on their Web sites. He asked you for another brief memo with this information, and he also wants you to include URLs, telephone numbers, and e-mail addresses for his reference file. Use the Internet to contact these companies and find out whether they offer demonstration copies or student versions of their products.

SWL   DATA DICTIONARY
DATA ELEMENT DESCRIPTION

SYSTEM: _PAYROLL_

ID ___DE-039___   NAME ___ESIP ID CODE___

ALTERNATE NAMES ___None___

TYPE AND LENGTH ___A(3)___   OUTPUT FORMAT ___A(3)___

DEFAULT VALUE ___None___   ACCEPTABLE VALUES ___CRD, STK___

PROMPT / COLUMN HEADER ___ESIP CODE___

SOURCE ___Human resources department___

SECURITY ___Human resources department (update)___

RESPONSIBLE USER ___Human resources department___

OTHER VALIDATION ___None___

DERIVATION FORMULA ___None___

DESCRIPTION AND COMMENTS

___A three-character code identifies each ESIP deduction choice. The ESIP ID CODE must be unique.___

Figure 4-49   Data dictionary definition for the data element ESIP ID CODE.

CHAPTER SUMMARY

This chapter examines structured analysis, which is the most widely used requirements analysis methodology. You can use structured analysis to construct a logical model for a business information system of any size or level of complexity. Structured analysis has three main components: data flow diagrams, the data dictionary, and process descriptions.

Data flow diagrams graphically show the movement and transformation of data in the information system. Data flow diagrams use four symbols: the process symbol transforms data, the data flow symbol shows data movement, the data store symbol shows data at rest, and the external entity symbol represents someone or something connected to the information system. Various rules and techniques are used to name, number, arrange, and annotate the set of data flow diagrams to make them consistent and understandable.

Data flow diagrams are like a pyramid with the context diagram at the highest level. The context diagram represents the information system's scope and its external connections but not its internal workings. Diagram 0 displays the information system's major processes, data stores, and data flows and is the exploded version of the context diagram's process symbol, which represents the entire information system. Lower-level data flow diagrams show additional detail of the information system through the leveling technique of numbering and partitioning. Leveling continues until you reach the functional primitive processes, which are not decomposed further and are documented with process descriptions. All diagrams must be balanced to ensure their consistency and accuracy.

The data dictionary is the central documentation tool for structured analysis. All data elements, data flows, data stores, processes, external entities, and records are documented in the data dictionary. By consolidating documentation in one location, you can verify the information system's accuracy and consistency more easily and generate a variety of useful reports.

Each functional primitive process is documented using structured English, decision tables, and decision trees. Structured English uses a subset of standard English that defines each process with combinations of basic building blocks of sequence, selection, and iteration. You also can document the logic by using decision tables or decision trees.

Review Questions

1. What are the advantages of using structured analysis? Why is structured analysis most appropriate for use with business information systems?

2. Define data flow diagrams and name and draw the four symbols using the Gane and Sarson and the Yourdon styles.

3. Define process and draw both styles of symbols used for a process in a data flow diagram. Give four examples of typical process names.

4. Define data flow and draw both styles of symbols used for a data flow in a DFD. Give four examples of typical data flow names.

5. Define data store and draw both styles of symbols used for a data store in a DFD. Give four examples of typical data store names.

6. Define external entity and draw both styles of symbols used for an external entity in a DFD. Give four examples of typical external entity names.

7. What is a context diagram, and which symbol is *not* used in this diagram?

8. Explain how you would measure an information system's complexity.

9. What is the relationship between a context diagram and diagram 0?

10. What is meant by an exploded data flow diagram?

11. Where are the details of data flows, data stores, and processes documented?

12. Explain the data flow diagram leveling technique.

13. What is a balanced data flow diagram?

14. What do you document in a data dictionary when you use structured analysis?

15. Describe six characteristics you would define in a data dictionary for a data element.

16. List four characteristics you would define in a data dictionary for each of the following elements:
    a. data flow
    b. data store
    c. process
    d. external entity
    e. record

17. What is structured English?

18. What is the difference between a decision table and a decision tree, and when would you use each of these tools?

Discussion Questions

1. A balanced data flow diagram is defined as one that has the parent process's input and output data flows preserved on the child data flow diagram. In other words, balance is a downward attribute in that all data flows must be preserved as you level the data flow diagrams downward. What about the reverse? Must balance occur as you proceed upward in your leveling? Defend your position with examples and reasons.

2. None of the data flow diagrams in this chapter has two-headed data flows — that is, data flows with arrowheads on both ends. Is it appropriate to use two-headed data flows? If so, under what conditions and why? If not, give your reasons.

3. A systems analyst attended a weeklong workshop on structured analysis. When she returned to her job, she told her boss that structured analysis was not worth the time to learn and use on the job. Her view was that it was too academic and had too much new terminology to be useful in a practical setting. Do you agree or disagree? Defend your position.

4. Suppose a school has the following policy: to be eligible to take CIS 288, which is an advanced course, students must complete two prerequisites — CIS 110 and CIS 286. If a student completes one of these prerequisites and obtains the instructor's permission, however, he or she will be eligible to take CIS 288.

   a. Create a decision table to represent this policy.

   b. Draw a decision tree to represent this policy.

CASE STUDIES

NEW CENTURY HEALTH CLINIC — ANALYZING REQUIREMENTS

Y ou began the systems analysis phase at New Century Health Clinic by completing a series of interviews, reviewing existing reports, and observing office operations.

   As you learned, the doctors, nurses, and physical therapists provide services and perform various medical procedures. All procedures are coded according to the *Current Procedure Terminology (CPT)*, which is published by the American Medical Association (AMA). The procedure codes consist of five numeric digits and a two digit suffix, and are used for all billing and insurance claims.

   From your fact-finding, you determined that seven reports are required at the clinic. The first report is the daily appointment list for each provider. This list shows all scheduled appointment times, patient names, and services to be performed, including the procedure code and description. A second daily report is the call list that shows the patients who are to be reminded of their next day's appointments. The call list includes the patient name, telephone number, appointment time, and provider name. The third report is the weekly provider report that lists each of the providers and the weekly charges generated, plus a month-to-date (MTD) and a year-to-date (YTD) summary.

   The fourth report is the statement — a preprinted form that is produced monthly and mailed in a window envelope. Statement header information includes the statement date, household head name and address, the previous month's balance, the total household charges MTD, the total payments MTD, and the current balance. The bottom section of the statement lists all activity for the month in date order. For each service performed, a line shows the patient's name, the service date, the procedure code and description, and the charge. The statement also shows the date and amount of all payments and insurance claims. When an insurance payment is received, the source and amount are noted on the line. If the claim is denied, or only partially paid, a code is used to explain the reason. A running balance appears at the far right of each activity line.

   The associates also require two insurance reports: the weekly Insurance Company Report and the monthly Claim Status Summary. In addition to these six reports, the office staff would like to have mailing labels and computer-generated postcards for sending reminders to patients when it is time to schedule their next appointment. Reminders usually are mailed twice monthly. Now you are ready to organize the facts you gathered and prepare a system requirements document that represents a logical model of the proposed system. Your tools will include data flow diagrams, a data dictionary, and process descriptions.

Assignments

1. Prepare a context diagram for New Century's information system.

2. Prepare a diagram 0 DFD for New Century. Make sure to show subsystems for handling appointment processing, payment and insurance processing, report processing, and records maintenance.

3. Prepare lower-level data flow diagrams for the system.

4. Prepare a list of data stores and data flows needed for the system. Under each data store, list the data elements required.

5. Prepare a data dictionary entry and process description for one of the system's functional primitives.

RIDGEWAY COMPANY

Ridgeway Company, whose main business is the purchase and development of recreational land, has managed the Ridgeway Country Club successfully for the past three years. When Ridgeway originally acquired the club, it had twenty lighted tennis courts, an eighteen-hole golf course, a swimming pool, a pro shop selling tennis and golfing supplies and related items, and a clubhouse containing a restaurant, bar, and exercise room.

Over the past two years, Ridgeway Company expanded the facility by adding a second eighteen-hole golf course, a second swimming pool, and twenty more lighted tennis courts. Ridgeway Company has completed the construction of the first ten condominiums as part of a ten-year plan to build a total of sixty units on club property. Because the club overlooks Crystal Lake, Ridgeway recently changed the club's name to Lake View Country Club.

Membership at the facility is limited to 2,000 full members with unlimited privileges and 1,000 social members who are permitted to use only the clubhouse and swimming pools. A waiting list exists for both types of membership. A full member buys a share in the club. Each member pays monthly dues of $150 for a full member and $50 for a social member. A name and address file of all members is maintained on 3-by-5-inch index cards in the corporate accounting department.

Thomas McGee is the general manager and manages Lake View's operations. At his suggestion, Ridgeway management decided to develop a new membership billing system for Lake View. The requirements for the new system are as follows.

Two types of sales forms currently are used. Members and their guests use one sales form for recording tennis and golf lessons, purchases in the pro shop, and recording the rounds of golf played. This first sales form is a pressure-sensitive form that has two parts: the member is given the top copy, and the second copy is forwarded to the corporate accounting department. The second sales form is used for purchases made in the restaurant and bar. The bottom copy is given to the member, and the top copy is sent to Ridgeway's accounting department.

Members must sign both types of sales forms and place their member numbers on the form. The accounting department receives the sales slips and posts them to an account ledger for each member of the club. Posted on each account line is the date of the charge, a description of the charge including where the charge occurred, the amount of the charge, and the running balance.

The charges on the account ledger appear on a monthly statement sent to each member. The statement also includes the member's monthly dues. Each member is required to make a minimum amount of purchases each month of $100 for a full member and $35 for a social member. If a member's purchases for the month exceed the minimum, the member pays the amount of the purchases. Otherwise, the member pays the minimum amount. A member makes an average of 10 charges per month. Only the statement is mailed to the member. Corporate accounting retains copies of charge slips for one year in case a member questions a charge.

A monthly summary sales report is sent to Ridgeway's headquarters. This report shows total sales by club area (pro shop, restaurant, and tennis lessons) and an overall total. Thomas McGee receives three reports on a monthly basis:

- A daily sales report that shows total sales in the restaurant, the bar, and the pro shop by day, plus total sales by day. This report shows overall totals for the month for the three operations and a grand total.

- A monthly member sales report that lists all members alphabetically and their total purchases for the month.

- An exception report that lists alphabetically all members who made no purchases during the month.

Assignments

1. Prepare the context diagram for the billing system.
2. Prepare the diagram 0 data flow diagram for the billing system.
3. If any processes on diagram 0 need to be partitioned, prepare the second-level diagrams for these processes.
4. For each data store, list the data elements that would be found in that data store.

CHAPTER 5

SDLC PHASES

Phase 1
Systems Planning

Phase 2
Systems Analysis

Phase 3
Systems Design

Phase 4
Systems Implementation

Phase 5
Systems Operation/Support

Evaluating Alternatives and Strategies

Evaluating alternatives and strategies is the final step in the systems analysis phase of the systems development life cycle. Chapter 5 presents the systems analyst's review of software alternatives, consideration of various systems development approaches and techniques, preparation of the system requirements document, and planning of the transition to the next SDLC phase, systems design.

INTRODUCTION

The objectives of the systems analysis phase are to determine, analyze, organize, and document the requirements of a new information system. Chapters 3 and 4 covered the first two tasks — determining and analyzing the requirements. Chapter 5 covers the remaining tasks in the systems analysis phase, which include the evaluation of alternative solutions, the preparation of the system requirements document, and the presentation of the system requirements document to management. The chapter also describes several systems development tools, techniques, and strategies, including prototyping, computer-aided software engineering (CASE) tools, systems flowcharts, and state-transition diagrams.

The Systems Analyst's Toolkit has tools to help you evaluate the economic feasibility of various alternatives.

OBJECTIVES

When you finish this chapter, you will be able to:

- Evaluate various alternatives when planning systems development and acquisition
- Explain the advantages and disadvantages of in-house development versus purchasing a software package
- List the steps in purchasing and evaluating a software package
- Explain the differences between a request for proposal (RFP) and a request for quotation (RFQ)
- Describe the contents of the system requirements document and explain its purpose
- Explain the prototyping process and describe a typical situation where prototyping is used
- Describe computer-aided software engineering (CASE) tools and explain how they are used during the systems development life cycle
- Explain how systems flowcharts and state-transition diagrams are used

EVALUATING SOFTWARE ALTERNATIVES

Y ou learned that an information system requires hardware, software, people, procedures, and data to operate successfully. By this point in the systems analysis phase, you have analyzed the current system and developed a logical model of the proposed system. Your next task is to identify software that will support the requirements of the new system. Decisions about software are critical, because they affect every component in the system.

Companies can acquire software by developing an in-house system, buying a software package, or customizing a software package. The choice between developing software in-house and purchasing software often is called a **make or buy decision**. **In-house software** is developed by the company's own IS department. A **software package** is purchased or leased from another company. The package might be a standard version of a commercial program or it might be a customized package that was designed specifically for the purchaser. Companies that specialize in developing software for sale are called **software publishers**, or **software vendors**.

Software packages are available to handle almost every type of business activity. A software package that can be used by many different types of organizations is called a **horizontal application**. Accounting packages are good examples of horizontal applications because they can be utilized by most businesses.

In contrast, a software package developed to handle information requirements for a specific type of business is called a **vertical application**. Examples of organizations with special system requirements include colleges, banks, hospitals, insurance companies, construction companies, real estate firms, and airlines. For example, Hyatt Hotels, as shown in Figure 5-1, might use vertical application software for industry-specific systems and use horizontal application software for its basic business systems.

Of the software acquisition options available — developing in-house, buying a software package, or customizing a software package — each has advantages and disadvantages. These software acquisition options are described in detail in the next section.

To learn more about the **Make or Buy Decision**, visit Systems Analysis and Design Chapter 5 More on the Web.

www.scsite.com/ sad3e/ch05/

For an extensive list of **Vertical Applications**, visit Systems Analysis and Design Chapter 5 More on the Web.

www.scsite.com/ sad3e/ch05/

Developing Software In-House

Today, software packages are available to handle most horizontal and vertical needs. Why then would a company choose to develop its own software? As shown in Figure 5-2, reasons for choosing in-house development include unique business requirements, a need to avoid operational changes, the constraints of existing systems and technology, and a desire to develop internal resources and capabilities.

SATISFY UNIQUE REQUIREMENTS • Companies often decide to develop software in-house because no commercially available software

Figure 5-1   Organizations such as Hyatt Hotels require vertical applications to support the information management needs that are unique to the hotel industry.

Reasons for In-House Developed Software	Reasons for Purchasing a Software Package
Satisfy unique requirements	Lower costs
Minimize changes in business procedures and policies	Requires less time to implement
Meet constraints of existing systems	Proven reliability and performance benchmarks
Meet constraints of existing technology	Implemented by other companies
Develop internal resources and capabilities	Requires less technical development staff Future upgrades provided by the vendor

Figure 5-2 A number of factors must be considered before making the decision to develop a system in-house or purchase a commercial package.

package can meet their unique requirements. A college, for example, might need a course scheduling system based on curriculum requirements, student demand, classroom space, and available instructors. A package delivery company might need a system to identify the best combination of routes and loading patterns for the company's fleet of delivery trucks. If existing software packages cannot handle these requirements, then in-house developed software might be the only choice.

MINIMIZE CHANGES IN BUSINESS PROCEDURES AND POLICIES • A company also might choose to develop its own software if purchasing available packages would cause major changes to current operations, procedures, or data processing. While installing a new software package almost always requires some degree of change in how a company does business, if the installation of a package is too disruptive, then the organization might decide to develop its own software instead.

MEET CONSTRAINTS OF EXISTING SYSTEMS • Any new software that is installed must work with existing systems. For example, if a new budgeting system is needed to integrate an existing accounting system and update data stored in existing files, finding a software package that works correctly with the existing accounting system could be very difficult. An organization thus might choose to develop its own software.

MEET CONSTRAINTS OF EXISTING TECHNOLOGY • Another reason to develop software is that the new software must be compatible with existing hardware and operating environments. The major trend is toward **open architecture**, which is a nonproprietary design concept that allows many vendors to offer software and hardware that can run in the same operating environment. Each program, however, has its own specific requirements. For example, a program might require a 32-bit environment, a minimum of 32 megabytes of RAM, and 100 megabytes of disk storage.

Some companies have older microcomputer workstations that cannot handle graphics-intensive software or high-speed Internet access. In this situation, the firm either must upgrade the environment or develop in-house software that can operate within the constraints of the existing hardware. As a systems analyst, you addressed the issue of technical feasibility during the preliminary investigation. Now, in the systems analysis phase, you must reexamine the advantages and disadvantages of in-house software development to decide whether it is justifiable.

For an overview of **Open Architecture**, visit Systems Analysis and Design Chapter 5 More on the Web.

www.scsite.com/ sad3e/ch05/

DEVELOP INTERNAL RESOURCES AND CAPABILITIES • Many firms feel that in-house IS resources and capabilities provide a competitive advantage because they can respond quickly when business problems or opportunities arise. By designing a system in-house, companies can develop and train an IS staff that understands the organization's information support needs, which can be especially important when proprietary information is involved.

Buying a Software Package

During the systems analysis phase, you should investigate whether a commercially available software package could satisfy system requirements. Advantages of purchasing a software package over developing software in-house include lower costs, less time to implement, proven reliability and performance benchmarks, implementation by other companies, less need for technical development staff, and provision for future upgrades by the vendor.

LOWER COSTS • Because many companies use software packages, software vendors spread the development over many customers. Compared to software developed in-house, a software package almost always is less expensive.

REQUIRES LESS TIME TO IMPLEMENT • When you purchase a package, it already has been designed, programmed, tested, and documented. Therefore, the in-house time normally spent on these tasks is eliminated. Of course, you still must install the software and integrate it into your systems environment, which can require a significant amount of time.

PROVEN RELIABILITY AND PERFORMANCE BENCHMARKS • If companies have been using the package, critical errors already should have been detected and corrected by the vendor. If the product is popular, it probably has been rated and evaluated by independent sources, meaning that data on its performance is available from sources other than the vendor.

IMPLEMENTED BY OTHER COMPANIES • Using a commercial software package means you can contact users in other companies to get their impressions and input about the software package. You might be able to try the package or make a site visit to observe the system in operation before making a purchase decision.

REQUIRES LESS TECHNICAL DEVELOPMENT STAFF • Companies that use commercial software packages often are able to reduce the number of programmers and systems analysts on the IS staff. Using commercial software also means that the IS staff can concentrate on systems whose requirements cannot be satisfied by software packages.

FUTURE UPGRADES PROVIDED BY THE VENDOR • Software vendors regularly upgrade software packages by adding improvements and enhancements to create a new version or release. A new release of a software package, for example, might include drivers to support a new laser printer or a new type of data storage technology. In many cases, the vendor receives input and suggestions from current users when planning future upgrades.

If a company decides to install a new software release, the upgrade must be planned and coordinated carefully, just as with any other system change. Upgrades generally are less expensive than buying the entire package or acquiring new software, because vendors usually offer a lower price to current users. If you have modified the package, however, you must make similar modifications for any upgrades that you install later.

Customizing Software Packages

If you do not find a software package that satisfies your specific system requirements, you must decide whether to build your own software package or to acquire a software package that can be customized to meet your specifications. The three ways to customize a software package are as follows:

1. For some software packages, you might be able to purchase a basic package that can be customized to suit your needs. Many vendors offer basic packages that are available in a standard version, with add-on components that can be configured individually. A vendor offers this option when the standard application will not satisfy all customers. A human resources system is a typical example, because each company handles its employee compensation and benefits differently.

2. You might be able to negotiate directly with the software vendor to make enhancements to meet your systems needs by paying an extra fee for the changes. The vendor might agree to the modifications because it plans to include these enhancements in future versions of the standard package or because it feels that you are an important potential customer for other products.

3. Purchase the package and make your own modifications. This option might be attractive when the product comes close to satisfying your requirements and the vendor will not (or cannot) make the requested changes. A disadvantage of this approach is that systems analysts and programmers might be unfamiliar with the software and will need time to learn the package and make the modifications correctly.

Some advantages of purchasing a standard package are lost if the product needs to be customized. If the vendor does the customizing, the modified package will cost more, take longer to obtain, and might be less reliable. Although vendors regularly upgrade their standard software packages, they might not upgrade a customized version. When a new release of the package becomes available, the company might have to modify the new version.

Other Software Alternatives

Thus far, the three primary software alternatives have been discussed: developing in-house software, buying a software package, and customizing a software package. Other possibilities include outsourcing, end-user computing, and enterprise computing.

OUTSOURCING • **Outsourcing** is the use of outside companies to handle a portion of a company's workload on a temporary or long-term basis. In a manufacturing company, for example, outsourcing can be used to purchase parts that formerly were produced in-house. Outsourcing also is used in the IS area. Many firms have shifted IS work from employees to outside contractors as a way of controlling costs and dealing with rapid technological change. This trend can be especially important for a company whose volume fluctuates widely, such as a defense contractor. Outsourcing relieves the company of the responsibility of adding IS staff in busy times, only to lay off staff when the workload lessens.

> For additional information on **Outsourcing**, visit Systems Analysis and Design Chapter 5 More on the Web.
>
> www.scsite.com/ sad3e/ch05/

Companies often require additional programmers, systems analysts, and other technical personnel to handle peak workloads on a short-term basis. Rather than hire these people, companies can get assistance from a contract personnel firm. A **contract personnel firm** supplies technical help for specific periods of time at a set rate. A company also might turn to a contract personnel firm when it needs people with specialized skills or knowledge for a short-term project.

Outsourcing strategies can include everything from a temporary arrangement with a payroll service bureau to a long-term contract with a **systems management or facilities management** firm that provides IS support for an entire operation. A major disadvantage of outsourcing is that it raises concerns about job security. Talented people might seek positions where more commitment to in-house IS resources and development is offered.

Another type of outsourcing involves the joint development of a customized vertical application package where a company works together with an outside software vendor. Each party supplies specific expertise — the company knows the system requirements and the vendor knows how to build and market the system. The vendor develops the package to meet the specific requirements of a company and then sells it to other companies with similar systems needs in that vertical market. The original company recovers some of its investment by saving money on future maintenance, which the vendor performs, and possibly from royalties on package sales.

END-USER SYSTEMS • End-user systems have become a major factor in systems planning and development and should be considered when alternatives and strategies are being discussed. End-user systems are applications that can be operated and managed by end users on their own. For example, a firm's human resources department might acquire, learn, and use a commercial database package to manage a tuition reimbursement plan for employees. Without assistance from the IS department, the user shown in the example in Figure 5-3 can manage tasks independently so the IS department can focus on larger projects.

Figure 5-3   Employees who have end-user systems are able to manage their information needs better than when they must rely on the IS department for support.

Most IS departments have a backlog of development and maintenance work. Small systems for individuals or small groups often get a lower priority and are not developed unless users play an active role. At the same time, significant changes have taken place in the nature of application software. Application programs available today are more powerful, more flexible, and more user-friendly than ever. Companies such as Microsoft and Corel offer powerful **software suites** that include integrated applications that can exchange data. These programs include Help features to guide less experienced users who know what they need to do, but do not know how to make it happen.

As a result of end-user computing, many users can perform tasks that once required a programmer, and some users can even develop their own systems. End users typically utilize spreadsheets, database management programs, and other software packages to meet their information needs. Some programs have interactive Help features, called **wizards**, to assist the user in completing tasks. Figure 5-4 shows an example of a Microsoft Access wizard that identifies database design errors.

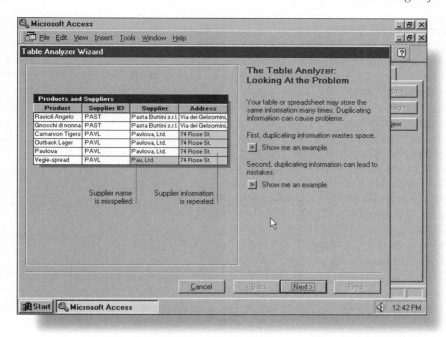

Figure 5-4 The Microsoft Table Analyzer Wizard points out errors in the end-user's database design. Notice that the user can request an example of the problem.

To make novice users more productive, the IS staff can create an opening screen, complete with menus, toolbar buttons, and user-defined options. With spreadsheet programs and predefined macros, users can import mainframe data and perform *what-if* analysis without assistance from the IS department.

In a system with end-user applications, you must include appropriate controls to ensure the security and accuracy of corporate data. Some files might be **read-only** so users can access, but not change, the data. Companies usually restrict end-user computing to PC-based systems within a user's department. In most large- and medium-sized companies, an **information center** (**IC**) within the IS department is responsible for supporting end-user computing. The IC staff can provide hotline assistance, training, and guidance to users who need software support.

Many companies empower lower-level employees by providing more access to data and more powerful data management tools. Empowerment also makes the IS department more productive because it can spend less time responding to the daily concerns of users and more time on high-impact systems development projects that support strategic business goals.

ENTERPRISE COMPUTING • As you learned during the discussion of strategic planning, many companies are designing systems solutions that involve the entire organization or enterprise. **Enterprise computing** is an overall information management strategy that supports group, departmental, and total company information needs. The key is the effective integration of information resources so users have controlled access to the mainframe data they need to support local systems. Centralized data remains secure and consistent but available to users who need it. Many enterprise-computing systems are based on a design concept called client/server architecture, which is explained in Chapter 9.

Selecting a Software Alternative

At this point in the SDLC, the company must decide whether to develop the software in-house, customize a software package, purchase a software package, or some combination of these solutions. The decision will affect the remaining SDLC phases and your involvement as a systems analyst. The decision to develop software in-house, for example, can require more participation from the systems analyst than choosing a commercial package. Figure 5-5 illustrates how systems analysts are involved in various software alternatives.

Management usually makes a determination after you present your written recommendations and deliver a formal presentation, which is described later in this chapter.

Degree of systems analyst involvement		
	HIGH	In-house developed software
		In-house customizations of a software package
		In-house software developed by contract personnel
		End-user computing
		Outsource a customized software package
		Software vendor customizes its software package
		Software vendor enhances its software package
	LOW	Software package used without modification

Figure 5-5 The system analyst's involvement depends on which alternative is selected.

If management decides to develop the system in-house, the systems design phase of the SDLC can begin. During the systems design, which is described in Chapters 6, 7, 8, and 9, you will develop the physical design for the system.

If management decides to buy a software package, you will perform a series of five steps: evaluate the information system requirements, identify potential software vendors, evaluate software package alternatives, make the purchase, and install the software package. These steps are described in detail in the next section.

If management decides to customize a software package, you will follow the same five steps described in buying a package, with one major difference. Because your system will require additional features or capabilities, you must design the specific changes, just as you would for an in-house developed project. Even though you are purchasing a package, you proceed to the systems design phase of the SDLC to design the modifications. Customizing a software package requires a combination of tasks, because you are purchasing *and* redesigning an essential part of the system.

STEPS IN EVALUATING AND PURCHASING SOFTWARE PACKAGES

he five steps in evaluating and purchasing a software package are described in this section.

Step 1: Evaluate the Information System Requirements

Based on your analysis of the system requirements, you must identify the system's key features, estimate volume and future growth, specify any hardware constraints, and prepare a request for proposal or quotation.

IDENTIFY THE KEY FEATURES OF THE SYSTEM • Evaluating system requirements first involves highlighting any critical features the system must have. For example, if a company operates nationwide, then its payroll system must be capable of deducting any applicable state income taxes. To be acceptable, a software package would have to include this essential feature.

ESTIMATE VOLUME AND FUTURE GROWTH • You need to know the current volume of transactions and processing and then forecast changes over a three- to five-year period. Figure 5-6 shows a one-year volume estimate for an order entry system, based on current procedures compared to the addition of a Web-based sales site. Volume figures are constraints for both the software package and the hardware platform. You must be sure that the package and the hardware can handle future transaction volumes and file storage requirements.

ONLINE ORDER ENTRY SYSTEM Estimated Activity During Next 12-Month Period			
	Current Level	**Future Growth Based on Existing Order Entry Procedures**	**Future Growth Assuming New Web Site Is Operational**
Customers	36,500	40,150	63,875
Daily Orders	1,435	1,579	2,511
Daily Order Lines	7,715	7,893	12,556
Sales Reps	29	32	25
Order Entry Support Staff	2	4	3
Products	600	650	900

Figure 5-6 A volume estimated for an order entry system showing current activity and future growth based on Web-based sales.

SPECIFY ANY HARDWARE CONSTRAINTS • As noted, the software must run properly on your current or proposed hardware platform. Whenever possible, you should make decisions about software first, because software is the main element in any system.

PREPARE A REQUEST FOR PROPOSAL OR QUOTATION • To obtain the information you need to make a decision, you should prepare a request for proposal (RFP) or a request for quotation (RFQ). These two documents are similar, but used in a different situations, based on whether or not you have selected a specific software product.

Typically, a **request for quotation** (**RFQ**) is used when you already know the specific product or package you want and you need to obtain price quotations or bids. RFQs can involve outright purchase or a variety of leasing options and can include maintenance or technical support terms.

A **request for proposal** (**RFP**), on the other hand, is a written list of specifications that is given to prospective vendors when you have *not* identified a specific product or package to use. Based on the RFP, vendors can decide if they have a product that will meet your needs and then respond with suggestions and alternatives. RFPs vary in size and complexity, just like the systems they describe. An RFP for a large system might have dozens of pages with unique requirements and features. You can use the RFP to designate some features as essential and others as desirable. The RFP, like the RFQ, will request specific pricing and payment terms. An example of a page from an RFP is shown in Figure 5-7 on the next page.

You can think of an RFQ as a shortened version of an RFP, because the RFQ refers to a specific product and does not contain a set of detailed specifications. With both methods, the objective is to obtain vendor replies that are *clear, comparable,* and *responsive* so you can make a well-informed selection decision.

Step 2: Identify Potential Software Vendors

The next step is to contact potential software vendors. If the software will be implemented on personal computers, a network, or as a widely used horizontal application, you might be able to purchase the package from a commercial software vendor. Preparing an RFP will help the vendor's sales representatives identify possible solutions.

SWL   **REQUEST FOR PROPOSAL**
ACCOUNTS PAYABLE

Features	Standard Feature	Comments
1. Interface to general ledger	✔	
2. Matching to receiving documents	✔	
3. Matching to purchase documents	✔	
4. Automatic check printing	✔	
5. Recurring payments		Planned For Next Release
6. Flexible payment selection	✔	
7. Checking statement reconciliation		Will Do On Custom Basis
8. Consolidated check preparation	✔	
9. Duplicate invoice check		No Plans For This Feature
10. Manual check processing	✔	

Reports

	Standard Feature	Comments
1. Vendor listing	✔	By Vendor Name
2. Invoice register	✔	
3. Check register	✔	
4. Cash requirements	✔	Weekly And Monthly
5. Detail aging	✔	30, 60, 90, 120 + Days
6. Form 1099 reports		Planned For Next Release
7. Account distribution	✔	
8. Bank statement reconciliation		Will Do On Custom Basis

Figure 5-7   In responding to a Request For Proposal (RFP), the vendor indicates whether or not key features are standard, with additional comments. Information on pricing and terms appear in another section of the RFP.

If software is needed for a minicomputer, mainframe computer, or as a vertical application, you might not be able to purchase it from a retail source. You can acquire this type of software, which can cost many thousands of dollars, in several different ways. First, you can contact the **computer manufacturer**, who may have a list of compatible software that has been certified to run on that particular platform.

Another way to find suppliers, especially for vertical applications, is to look in **industry trade journals**, which are publications written for specific types of businesses. Companies and individuals that develop industry-specific software often advertise in these magazines. For example, an auto parts store that wants an inventory control system might find several software packages advertised in automobile industry publications. You also will find many software firms that describe their products on Web sites. Some industry trade groups also maintain lists of companies that provide specific software solutions.

A third way to identify software suppliers is to work with a **systems consultant**. Using a consultant can be expensive, but can prevent mistakes that would be even more costly. Many consultants specialize in helping companies select software packages. A major advantage of using a consultant is that you can tap into broad experience that is difficult for any one company to acquire. Consultants can be located by contacting professional organizations in the industry, or by searching the Internet.

Step 3: Evaluate Software Package Alternatives

After identifying possible software packages, you must compare them and select the best one to fit system needs. First you should obtain information about the packages from as many sources as possible, including vendor presentations and literature, product documentation, trade publications, and companies that perform software testing and evaluation.

You also can contact existing users of the software package. For personal computer packages, ask your retail source for references, or call the software company directly. For minicomputer and mainframe software packages, software vendors will supply user references. **User references** are important because you need to know whether the software package has worked well for companies like yours. Vendors like to have satisfied clients on their reference lists, so do not be surprised if you receive mostly positive feedback.

If possible, ask users to try the software package. For horizontal applications or a small system, using a demonstration copy to enter a few sample transactions might be an acceptable test. For vertical applications or large systems, a team of IS

Figure 5-8   Many computer publications provide general information or specialized information, including reviews of individual software packages and benchmark tests. These reviews are important to the systems analyst because often they provide an unbiased opinion of the package's functions.

staff and users might need one or more days of testing. Testing can be done either at the vendor's location or your own, to ensure that the package meets business needs.

If you are concerned about the capability of the package to handle a certain transaction volume efficiently, a benchmark test can be performed. A **benchmark test** measures the time a package takes to process a certain number of transactions. For example, a benchmark might consist of measuring the time needed to post 1,000 sales transactions. If you are considering two or more packages, benchmark testing is a good way to measure relative performance.

For horizontal applications, computer magazines such as *InfoWorld*, *ComputerWorld*, *Datamation*, *Byte*, *PC Magazine*, and *PC World*, publish regular reviews of individual packages, including benchmark tests, and often have annual surveys covering various categories of software. Some of these publications are shown in Figure 5-8. You also can obtain information from independent firms that benchmark various software packages and sell comparative analyses of the results. These firms typically advertise in industry publications and on their own Web sites.

For more resources on **Benchmark Tests**, visit Systems Analysis and Design Chapter 5 More on the Web.

www.scsite.com/ sad3e/ch05/

ON THE NET

To find out about software packages and vendors, log onto the Internet and search using keywords that describe a specific package or application. You also can look for Web sites maintained by consultants, software publishers, and vendors.

The **Transaction Processing Performance Council** (**TPC**) is an example of a non-profit organization that publishes standards and reports for its members and the general public. Many of these reports can be viewed at the TPC Web site (Figure 5-9) or sent via mail. Companies such as **IDEAS International** develop competitive profiles and benchmark testing (Figure 5-10). The results are available to members, which include many large firms. **Usenet groups** are another source of information where you can exchange information and comments about various products of interest to analysts and programmers.

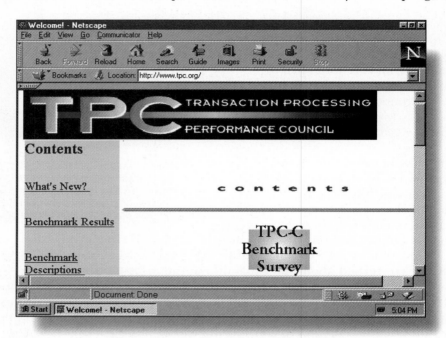

Figure 5-9   The Transaction Processing Performance Council (TPC) is a nonprofit group that publishes benchmark information.

Finally, you should match each package against the RFP features and rank the choices. If some features are more important than others, give them a higher weight. You can use a spreadsheet to perform the calculations and graph the results.

Step 4: Make the Purchase

When you purchase software, usually you do not own it — what you are buying is a **software license** that gives you the right to use the software under certain terms and conditions. For example, the license might allow you to use the software only on a single computer, a specified number of computers, a network, or an entire site, depending on the terms of the license.

Other license restrictions might prohibit you from making the software available to others or modifying the program. For personal computer users, software license terms and conditions usually cannot be modified. For minicomputer and mainframe users, terms of the license agreement can be negotiated and should be reviewed carefully by management and the legal department.

Although most software packages are purchased, some packages, especially mainframe systems software, such as database management systems, are leased for a fixed period of time with terms and payments described in a **lease agreement**.

You also can pay a monthly or annual fee for a maintenance agreement with the vendor. **Maintenance agreements** allow you to contact the vendor for assistance when you have system problems or questions. Many personal computer packages provide a

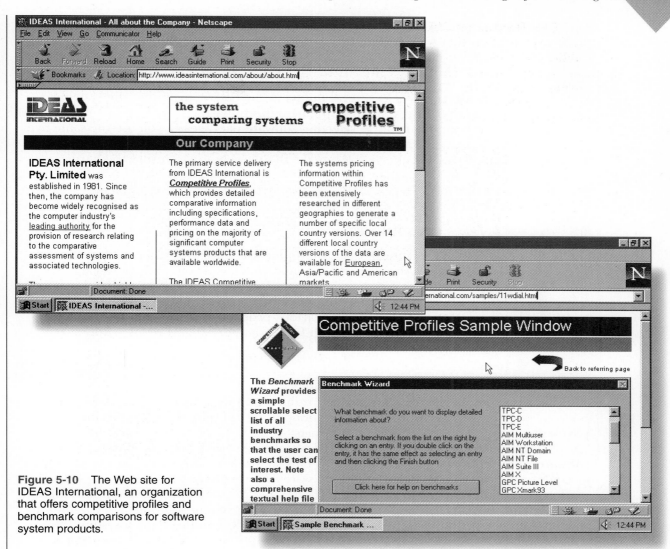

Figure 5-10 The Web site for IDEAS International, an organization that offers competitive profiles and benchmark comparisons for software system products.

mail-in registration card that entitles users to free technical support for a certain time period. Sometimes support is offered with a charge per occurrence, or per minute or hour of technical support time. Some software vendors also contact registered owners whenever a new release is available and usually offer the new release at a reduced price. For most minicomputer and mainframe packages, a maintenance agreement gives you the right to obtain new releases of the package at no charge or at a reduced rate.

Step 5: Install the Software Package

After purchasing the software package, the final step is installation. For small systems, installation might take one day or less. For large systems or network installations, the process can require more time and effort. Your installation strategy should be planned well in advance, especially if any disruption of normal business operations is expected. If the software package is customized, then the task will be more complex and difficult.

Before you can use the new software package, you must complete all implementation steps, including loading, configuring and testing the software, training users, and converting data files to the new system's format. Chapters 10 and 11 discuss implementation strategies and techniques in more detail.

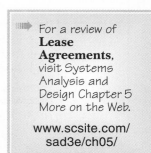

For a review of **Lease Agreements**, visit Systems Analysis and Design Chapter 5 More on the Web.

www.scsite.com/ sad3e/ch05/

HARDWARE ALTERNATIVES

The development of a new system can require decisions about hardware as well as software. As you have learned, these decisions require careful cost-benefit analysis and review of all the alternatives. As a systems analyst, you will consider **hardware alternatives** at several points in the SDLC, including the systems analysis, systems design, and systems implementation phases.

Selecting hardware is similar to selecting software packages — you use the same five-step approach. You must evaluate the system requirements, identify potential hardware vendors, evaluate hardware alternatives, make the purchase, and install the hardware.

ON THE NET

The Internet is a good place to search for information on hardware benchmarks and sources of comparative testing, just as you did when you selected software. Figure 5-11 shows a CPU comparison published by MDR Labs, an organization that conducts various product tests. Pricing for hardware also is available on the Web from commercial and retail vendors.

Because you often know the specific products and technical specifications required for your system, you can use a request for quotation (RFQ) to negotiate pricing and payment terms for specific hardware products.

Special situations might require that you select a combination of hardware and software from vendors as an integrated systems solution. In this case, you would prepare a request for proposal (RFP) for a turnkey system. A **turnkey system** is a complete information system that includes hardware, software, and documentation. System installation, training, and support also might be included. Turnkey system solutions are common in smaller companies that lack the technical staff to develop and support a system. The advantage of selecting a turnkey system is that a company can deal with a single vendor for the entire system. Many turnkey providers advertise in industry publications and maintain Web sites.

When purchasing hardware such as networks, computers, or printers, you might need to do site preparation. Depending on the size of the system, **site preparation** can include installing a new workstation, network cabling, raised floors, conditioned electrical lines, special fire extinguishing equipment, and **uninterruptible power supplies** (**UPSs**) that enable an orderly shutdown of the system in case of power outages.

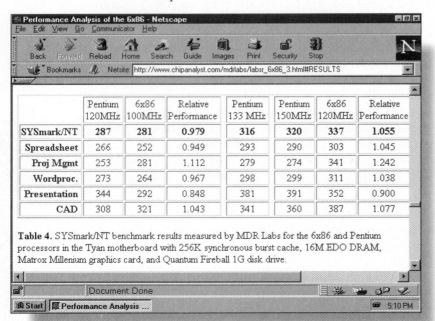

Table 4. SYSmark/NT benchmark results measured by MDR Labs for the 6x86 and Pentium processors in the Tyan motherboard with 256K synchronous burst cache, 16M EDO DRAM, Matrox Millenium graphics card, and Quantum Fireball 1G disk drive.

	Pentium 120MHz	6x86 100MHz	Relative Performance	Pentium 133 MHz	Pentium 150MHz	6x86 120MHz	Relative Performance
SYSmark/NT	287	281	0.979	316	320	337	1.055
Spreadsheet	266	252	0.949	293	290	303	1.045
Proj Mgmt	253	281	1.112	279	274	341	1.242
Wordproc.	273	264	0.967	298	299	311	1.038
Presentation	344	292	0.848	381	391	352	0.900
CAD	308	321	1.043	341	360	387	1.077

Figure 5-11 Internet site review of benchmark testing, published by MDR Labs.

Most companies use a combination of in-house developed software, software packages, outsourcing, and end-user systems. Even a single system might use a mix of software alternatives. For example, a company might purchase a standard software package to process its payroll, and then develop its own software to handle the interface between the payroll and in-house systems so users can access the information needed for departmental use.

The evaluation and selection of alternatives is not a simple process. Your objective is to obtain the best product at the best price, but actual cost and performance can be difficult to predict. With a large number of choices, how do you select the best alternative?

When selecting hardware, systems analysts often work as members of an evaluation and selection team. A **team approach** ensures that critical factors are not overlooked and that a sound choice is made. The evaluation and selection team also should include feedback from users, who should feel a sense of ownership in the new system and participate in the selection process.

The primary objective of the evaluation and selection team is to eliminate system alternatives that will not work, rank the system alternatives that will work, and then present the system alternatives to management for a final decision. Alternatives that are possible system solutions are called **viable alternatives**, which means they are workable or feasible. A viable alternative should include a specific recommendation with reasons. In some cases, more than one viable alternative exists and management must compare the relative strengths and weaknesses of several solutions. When evaluations are performed carefully and professionally, the team will provide management with the information needed to reach a sound decision.

A KEY QUESTION

Doug's Sporting Goods sells hunting and fishing supplies to customers nationwide. After 30 years of manual record keeping, the company finally is ready to introduce a computerized accounting system. Doug Sawyer, the company's founder and president, hired you to select an appropriate accounting system for the company and determine what hardware is required to run it.

Following a traditional SDLC approach, you completed the systems analysis phase and identified the requirements. You identified several software packages that could be customized easily to meet the company's needs. Doug wants you to develop the system yourself, however, because he does not want to depend on outside vendors and suppliers for technical support and upgrades. Doug wants to meet with you tomorrow to make a final decision. How will you prepare for the meeting? Should you try to influence him in a different direction? What is your strategy, and how will you present your alternatives to Doug during the meeting?

COMPLETION OF SYSTEMS ANALYSIS

 To complete the systems analysis phase, you must prepare the system requirements document and your presentation to management.

 The Systems Analyst's Toolkit includes a section with guidelines and suggestions for preparing the written report and the presentation to management.

System Requirements Document

The **system requirements document**, or **software requirements specification**, contains the requirements for the new system, describes the alternatives that were considered, and makes a specific recommendation to management. This important document is the starting point for measuring the performance, accuracy, and completeness of the finished system before entering the systems design phase. The system requirements document is like a contract that identifies what must be delivered by the system developers to users. The system requirements document, therefore, should be written in language that users can understand so they can offer input, suggest improvements, and approve the final version.

Because the system requirements document can be hundreds of pages in length, you should format and organize it so it is easy to read and use. The system requirements document should include a cover page and a detailed table of contents. You also can add an index and a glossary of terms to make the document easier to use. The content of the system requirements document will depend on the company and the complexity of the system. The Systems Analyst's Toolkit provides guidance and offers suggestions to help you create the system requirements document.

> To learn more about preparing a **System Requirements Document**, visit Systems Analysis and Design Chapter 5 More on the Web.
>
> www.scsite.com/ sad3e/ch05/

Presentation to Management

The presentation to management at the end of the systems analysis phase is one of the most critical milestones in the entire systems development life cycle. At this point, management makes key decisions that affect the future development of the system.

Prior to the management presentation, you might give two other presentations: one to the principal individuals in the IS department to keep them posted, and another presentation to users to answer their questions and seek their approval. The system requirements document is the basis for all three presentations and it should be distributed in advance of the presentations so the recipients can review it.

The object of the management presentation is to obtain approval for the development of the system and to gain management's full support, including the commitment of financial resources. Management will probably choose one of five alternatives: develop an in-house system, modify the current system, purchase or customize a software package, perform additional systems analysis work, or stop all further work. When these decisions are made, your next task as a systems analyst is as follows:

1. *Develop an in-house system*. Begin the systems design phase for the new system.
2. *Modify the current system*. Begin the systems design phase for the modified system.

3. *Purchase or customize a software package.* Negotiate the purchase terms with the software vendor for management approval. Then, if the package will be used without modification, you can begin planning the systems implementation phase. If you must make modifications to the package, your next step is to start the systems design phase. If the vendor will make the modifications, then your next step is to start planning the testing and documentation of the modifications as part of the systems implementation phase.

4. *Perform additional systems analysis work.* Management might want you to investigate certain alternatives further, explore alternatives that were not examined, reduce the project scope because of cost constraints, or expand the project scope based on new developments. If necessary, you will perform the additional work and schedule a follow-up presentation.

5. *Stop all further work.* This decision might be based on your recommendation, a shift in priorities or costs, or for other reasons.

When planning your presentation, you should review the guidelines and suggestions in the Systems Analyst's Toolkit, which will help you design and deliver a successful presentation. In addition to the techniques found in the Toolkit, also keep the following suggestions in mind:

- Begin your presentation with a brief overview of the purpose and primary objectives of the system project.
- Summarize the primary viable alternatives. For each alternative, describe the costs, advantages, and disadvantages.
- Explain why the evaluation and selection team chose the recommended alternative.
- Allow time for discussion and for questions and answers.
- Obtain a final decision from management or agree on a timetable for the next step in the process.

The project has progressed through the systems planning and systems analysis phases of the SDLC. After management makes a decision, you will begin a variety of tasks, depending on the strategy chosen. If you are developing an in-house system or modifying a package, you will build a model of the proposed system and start designing the system's outputs, inputs, files, and data structures. The following sections describe several tools and techniques that can assist you in this process. These include prototyping, CASE tools, and alternative graphical tools.

PROTOTYPING

The systems analyst must be sure that the system will satisfy user needs. To avoid problems, the analyst seeks input and feedback from users at every stage of the development process. Sometimes users have difficulty evaluating the system requirements document because it is only a *paper model* of the system. One of the more effective ways to help users understand it better is to design a system prototype. A **prototype** is an early, rapidly constructed working version of the proposed information system that is used to verify user requirements. The prototyping process often is used in the engineering field, where a less expensive working model is created to eliminate problems before the final version is produced.

For additional coverage of **Prototyping**, visit Systems Analysis and Design Chapter 5 More on the Web.

www.scsite.com/ sad3e/ch05/

Prototyping Software Tools

Prototyping is possible using modern nonprocedural software tools. When you use **nonprocedural** software tools, you specify the problem that the prototype must solve but not *how* to solve it. In contrast, when you use **procedural** software tools, you must specify the detailed steps, or procedures, to solve the specific problem. Examples of procedural tools are programming languages such as BASIC, Pascal, and COBOL.

Nonprocedural software tools used to create a prototype for a system include a CASE toolkit, report writer, query language, screen generator, program generator, and fourth-generation languages. In combination, these tools make up the fourth-generation environment. The **fourth-generation environment** also utilizes a relational database management system (DBMS) and a data dictionary to define all data used in the system, the data structure, and the relationships among the data elements. Figure 5-12 illustrates the fourth-generation environment and the software tools used in this environment. You will learn about databases and database management systems in Chapter 8.

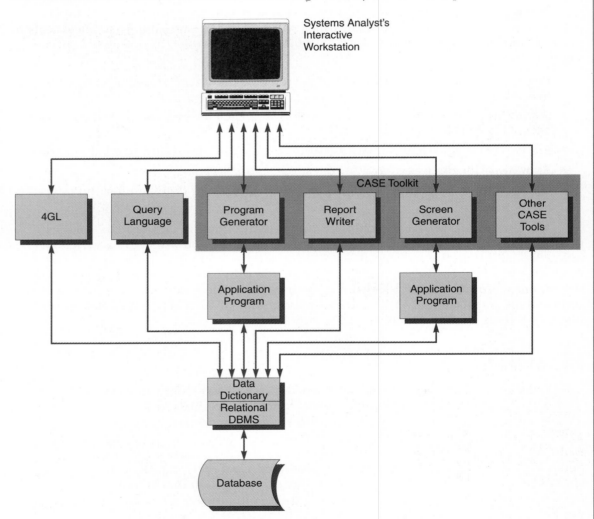

Figure 5-12   The fourth-generation (4GL) environment and its software components.

A **report writer**, or a **report generator**, is a tool for producing formatted reports using data from a database. In most cases, the report is printed on paper, but also can be displayed on a screen or saved to a file. The data is accessed by using a **query language**, which is a nonprocedural language for retrieving data from a database. The query language can display, sort, count, group, and total data in a specific manner so it can be printed, as shown in Figure 5-13, displayed on a screen, or saved to a file. Report writers include formatting capabilities for information that will be printed, while query languages are built for rapid response so users can retrieve data quickly and display it on their screens.

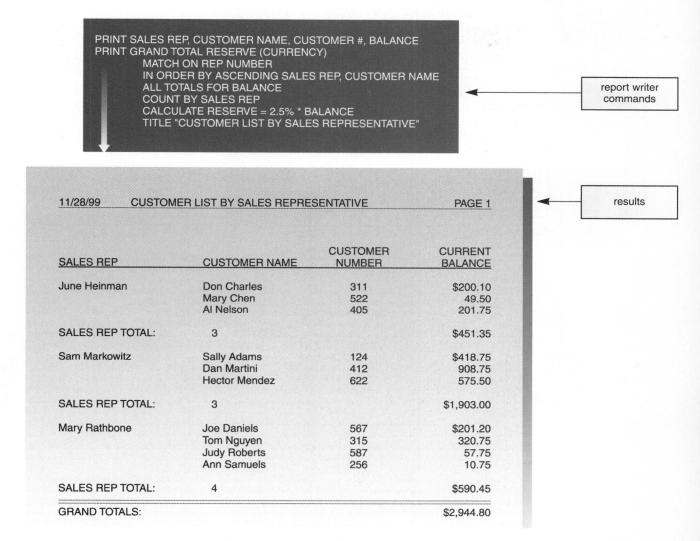

Figure 5-13 A sample of a report writer, shown above, and the output it produces. Notice that it includes subtotals, a grand total, and customer count for each sales rep. The output also could be the result of a query, as explained in the text.

A **screen generator**, or **screen painter**, **screen mapper**, or **form generator**, is an interactive software tool that helps you, as a systems analyst, to design a custom interface, create screen forms, and handle data entry format and procedures. The screen generator allows you to control how the screen will display captions, data fields, data, and other visual attributes. Also, by using a screen generator that interacts with the data dictionary, you can create screens to verify input data and perform calculations.

Some software packages have powerful screen generators that allow users to design their own data entry forms. For example, as shown in Figure 5-14 on the next page, Microsoft Access includes a Form Wizard tool that asks you a series of questions about the form you would like to create, and then creates the form for you. In this case, the form includes the same data elements as the report shown in Figure 5-13.

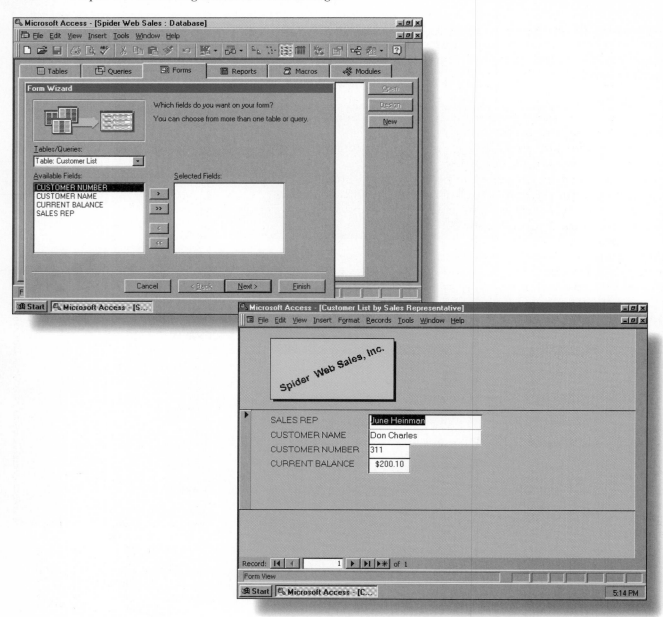

Figure 5-14   The top screen shows the Form Wizard in Microsoft Access, which can be used to design a custom data entry form. The bottom screen shows a data entry form for the CUSTOMER LIST shown in Figure 5-13 on the previous page.

A **program generator**, or **code generator**, is a software tool that generates program code to help a programmer or analyst develop and maintain programs. Instead of starting from scratch, the programmer uses the generated code as a template and then modifies it as required. This method can reduce the time and effort needed in program development significantly. CASE tools often include program generators, as you will learn in the next section.

A **fourth-generation language** (**4GL**) is a powerful, flexible programming language that has both procedural and nonprocedural features. A 4GL allows you to write computer programs faster and more accurately than in traditional languages, such as COBOL, because code can be developed directly from a logical model. Popular examples of 4GL languages include C++, Microsoft Visual J++, Java, and IBM's Cross System Product (CSP).

Prototyping During Systems Analysis

Prototyping can be used during the systems analysis phase while you are performing fact-finding. As you collect facts about the system, you can construct a prototype, as shown in Figure 5-15. Your goal is to develop a working model quickly that will satisfy user requirements. You can use program generators and other CASE tools to do this.

The initial prototype is given to users so they can provide feedback on how well it meets their needs. Users suggest changes or improvements to upgrade the prototype until they are satisfied. Encouraging users to participate actively in the systems analysis phase will increase costs, but this expense will be offset by lower costs during subsequent SDLC phases.

A prototype is a functioning system, but it is less efficient than a fully developed system. Because it is a model, rather than a completed system, the prototype will have slower processing speeds and response times. Your primary objective in prototyping is an early test of essential system features, so the prototype might lack security requirements, exception and error handling procedures, and other required functions. Despite these limitations, the prototype often can be upgraded to become the final information system. In this case, you would continue to improve and extend the prototype until it satisfies all user requirements. The object of prototyping is to reduce development time and cost by combining the systems design and systems implementation phases with the systems analysis phase.

The final system typically demands a higher-level performance than what can be obtained from the fourth-generation software tools used to create the prototype. If so, the prototype is abandoned and the remaining SDLC phases are completed. In this case, the prototype does not become the first version of the new system, but it ensures that the system will satisfy all requirements. Satisfying system requirements is the ultimate goal of systems development, and prototyping is an extremely valuable tool in this process.

COMPUTER-AIDED SOFTWARE ENGINEERING (CASE)

Y ou learned in Chapter 4 that computer-aided software engineering (CASE) tools enable systems analysts and programmers to be more productive, and you saw how CASE tools can handle certain tasks during the systems analysis phase. For example, individual CASE tools can create and integrate data flow diagrams, data dictionary entries, and process descriptions.

In addition to these specific tasks, a full set of CASE tools, called a **CASE toolkit**, can automate other systems development work, including logical and physical design and the generation of program code. The **Visible Analyst**, from the Visible Systems Corporation, is a CASE tool that integrates planning, analysis, design, code generation, and reverse engineering. Figure 5-16 on the next page shows the screen where you begin a project and select basic parameters, including the style of DFD symbols. Figure 5-17 on the next page shows a program generation feature, which was described earlier in this chapter. Visible Analyst offers either C or COBOL language options.

Figure 5-15 Steps followed by a systems analyst using a prototype during the systems analysis phase.

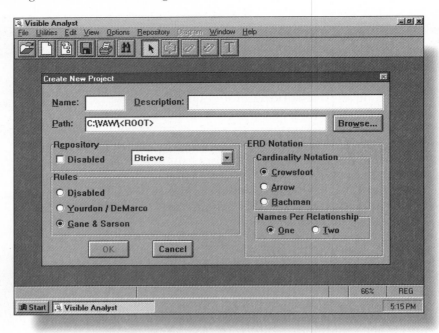

Figure 5-16 This is the initial screen you see when you create a new project using the Visible Analyst.

For a comprehensive resource on **CASE Tools,** visit Systems Analysis and Design Chapter 5 More on the Web.

www.scsite.com/ sad3e/ch05/

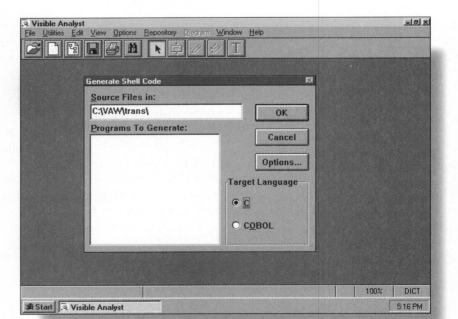

Figure 5-17 The Visible Analyst screen showing the program generator that can produce C or COBOL code.

Categories of CASE Tools

CASE tools can perform most of the tasks needed to develop and maintain a system, including diagramming tools, prototyping tools, a central repository, data design tools, programming tools, project management tools, and maintenance tools.

You can use a **diagramming tool** to draw, save, and modify a variety of diagrams, such as data flow diagrams that are leveled and balanced properly. Diagramming tools also can create other diagrams, including systems flowcharts and state-transition diagrams, which are described later in this chapter, and entity-relationship diagrams, which are explained in Chapter 8.

Figure 5-18 shows a DFD of a sample library system provided with the Visible Analyst. You can place, move, and connect the symbols, and you can save the DFDs in a project file. Other features let you link documentation to the data dictionary or explode a process to a lower-level DFD.

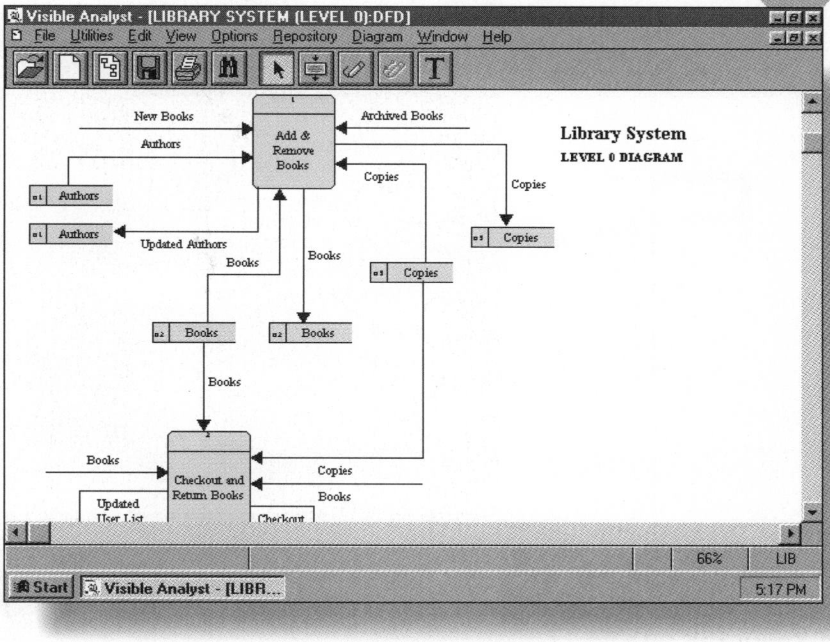

You also can use CASE tools to create a **central repository**,

Figure 5-18 Data flow diagram for a sample Library System provided with the Visible Analyst tool.

which is a data dictionary that tracks and manages your data. For example, if you are developing DFDs, then all information pertaining to your diagrams will be stored in the central repository. A CASE tool can analyze a set of DFDs for balance and ensure that all entities, data flows, data stores, and data elements have been entered properly in the central repository. For example, Figure 5-19 on the next page shows the central repository for an order processing system.

Another CASE toolkit is the **Hyper Analysis Toolkit** (**HAT**) shown in Figure 5-20 on the next page. This product allows the analyst to create a set of DFDs on the right side of the screen, with explanatory text including hypertext terms, on the left side of the screen. When you double-click a **hypertext** term, the program shows a detailed explanation for the term. You can navigate through a complex set of DFDs and the data repository with this feature, which is especially useful in a management presentation.

When selecting CASE tools, remember that the greater the number of tools integrated into the central repository, the greater the analysis and reporting capabilities.

Using CASE Tools

A **data design tool** assists you in the logical and physical modeling of files and databases. A **programming tool** assists you in the development of computer programs and includes testing tools, program debuggers, and code generators. A **program debugger** detects syntax errors and highlights them for the programmer. A **code generator** creates program code from program design specifications. A **project management tool** assists in the planning, tracking, controlling, and reporting of system projects. A **maintenance tool** analyzes, documents, or reengineers an existing computer program.

All of these CASE tools are examples of **forward engineering tools**, which support you as you work, phase by phase, through the systems development life cycle. A **reverse engineering tool** works in the other direction and converts program code into design specifications. A **reengineering** toolkit can use reverse and forward engineering to produce an improved version of the program. This powerful tool first converts the existing program to its design specifications. Then, the program analyzes the design specifications and permits you to make changes. When the specifications are acceptable, a code generator produces a new, improved version of a program.

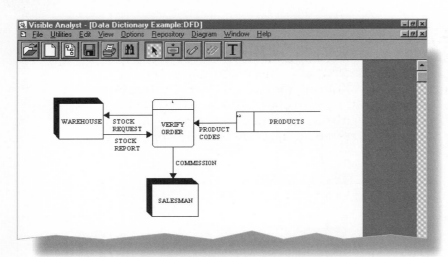

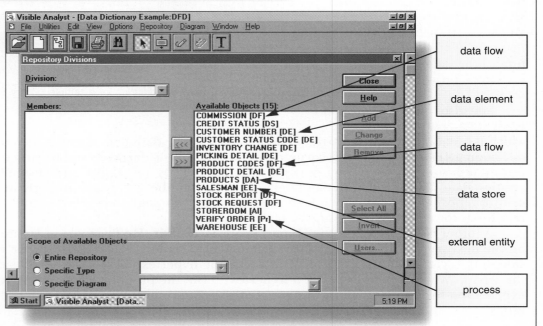

Figure 5-19 The data repository in the Visible Analyst allows the analyst to manage and organize objects, including data elements, data flows, data stores, external entities, and processes. Notice that objects in the data flow diagram shown in the top screen are documented in the repository shown in the bottom screen.

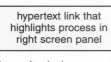

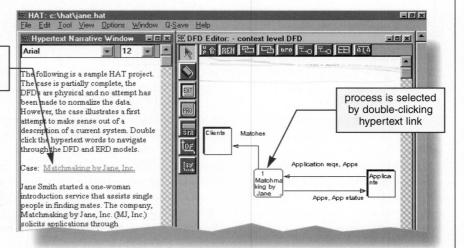

Figure 5-20 The Hyper Analysis Toolkit (HAT) offers hypertext descriptions that are linked to DFDs and the data repository. You can explore and navigate by double-clicking the hypertext terms. When you double-click a hypertext link, the program highlights the matching object in the DFD in the right screen panel. After you double-click a hypertext link, the text changes from green to red.

CASE tools also are classified as either front-end or back-end products, according to when they are used during the systems development life cycle. A **front-end tool**, or an **upper-CASE tool**, is used during the preliminary investigation, systems analysis, or systems design phases. A **back-end tool**, or a **lower-CASE tool**, is used during the systems development or systems implementation phases or during systems operation. Generally speaking, if your system runs on personal computers, then your CASE tools also will run on personal computers. If your system runs on minicomputers or mainframe computers, then the front-end tools usually will run on personal computers, and the back-end tools will run on minicomputers or mainframe computers.

ON THE NET

You can read a variety of reviews on CASE tools on the Internet to identify which ones will work best for your systems needs. Figure 5-21 shows a CASE tool index with hyperlinks to the vendors or manufacturers. You can explore several of these to learn the features of the products being offered.

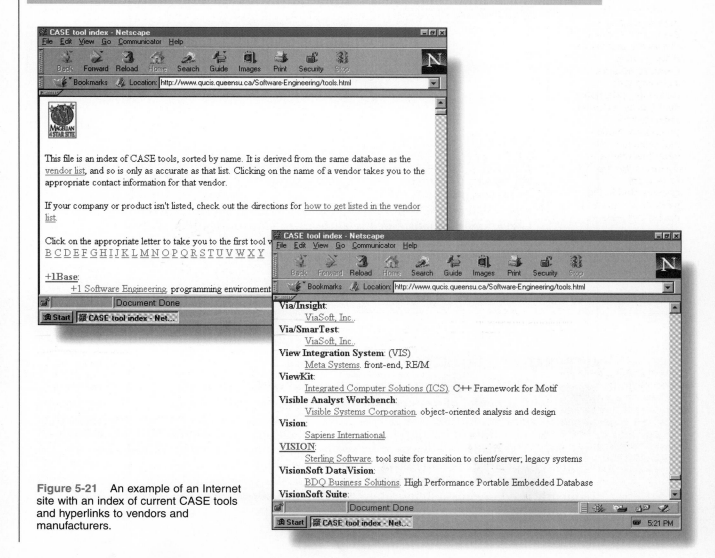

Figure 5-21 An example of an Internet site with an index of current CASE tools and hyperlinks to vendors and manufacturers.

CASE tools provide many advantages over manual development methods. CASE tools can automate manual tasks and encourage standard methods so systems analysts and programmers can follow each other's work easily. A final advantage is that CASE tools also can improve the accuracy and overall quality of the end product that is required at the end of each SDLC phase.

Although the pros of CASE far outweigh the cons, you also should keep in mind a few potential disadvantages, including the cost of the hardware and software needed to support a sophisticated CASE toolkit. The tradeoff is improved productivity, quality, and consistency, which will result in long-term cost savings.

Another possible disadvantage is a lack of CASE standards, which is not a problem if you use the same CASE tools consistently. If you use different CASE tools, you might have problems transferring your completed work between the CASE toolkits.

CASE products can affect the way you develop and maintain systems. Each product has a particular approach or methodology that you must follow. Although CASE technology replaces paper and pencil design work, it does not replace the planning and technical skills of a systems analyst. Even analysts and programmers who use CASE tools regularly must make careful, intelligent decisions. In addition, the solution must fit the size of the problem. A simple design might not require the creation of a full set of data flow diagrams and a data dictionary. To set up any CASE project, some amount of initial effort and preparation is required. Is it always worthwhile? The answer depends on the skills, experience, and preferences of the analysts and the IS management staff. Experience using CASE tools is now a requirement for many systems analysts positions, so you should study them carefully.

A KEY QUESTION

Sunnyside Beverages, a soft drink wholesaler, dispatches 30 retail delivery trucks daily. As a systems analyst, you have suggested that the company purchase the latest CASE tools to develop a new accounts receivable and billing system. Your supervisor has not worked in a CASE environment, but she authorized your purchase and then said, "Good, now we won't have to teach our new systems analysts how to create data flow diagrams. All they need to know is how to use the new CASE toolkit." Do you agree with her statement? How would you respond to her statement?

ALTERNATIVE GRAPHICAL TOOLS

Data flow diagrams are an integral part of structured analysis. DFDs show the logical model of a system and can be used for physical modeling during the systems design phase that follows. Data flow diagrams, however, are not the only graphical tools for developing systems. Other types of tools have existed for a long time, and many still are used by systems developers. Some graphical tools are designed to perform specific tasks during a particular phase of development, while other tools have a wider application. Of the alternative graphical tools, the two more frequently used during systems analysis are systems flowcharts and state-transition diagrams.

Systems Flowcharts

Systems developers have used systems flow-charts for many years. A **systems flowchart** displays the major processes, inputs, and outputs of a system. Systems flowcharts are used primarily for the physical modeling of a system where various symbols are used to represent data or files in different media such as disks, documents, and reports and to identify input and output operations. Many systems analysts still use systems flowcharts because they are easy to construct and understand, but data flow diagrams have become the most common way to represent logical and physical models.

A systems flow-chart for an order system is shown in Figure 5-22. The chart shows how a customer payment is posted and

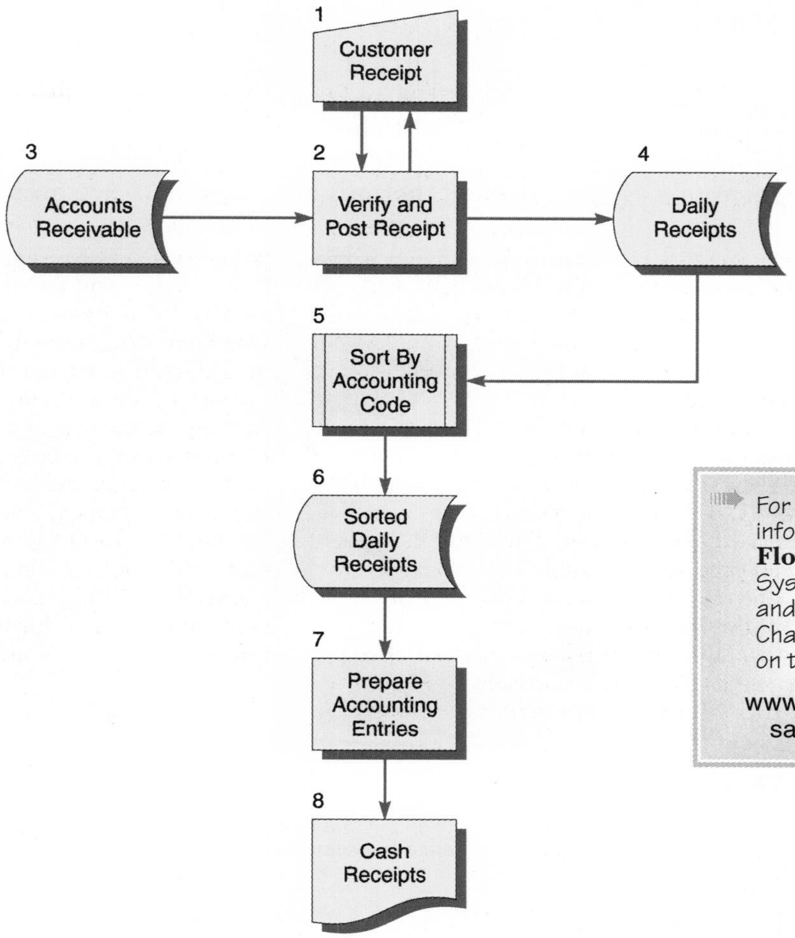

Figure 5-22 A systems flowchart for handling customer payments in an order system.

For more information on **Flowcharts**, visit Systems Analysis and Design Chapter 5 More on the Web.

www.scsite.com/ sad3e/ch05/

processed. Lines with arrowheads indicate the flow of data, just as they do in data flow diagrams. The flow of data and processing steps generally occurs from top to bottom and left to right.

Each symbol's *shape* indicates its purpose. The symbols are numbered for easier reference in this discussion. In Figure 5-22, symbols 1, 3, 4, 6, and 8 represent data or files stored in specific physical media. Symbol 1 is a workstation symbol. Symbols 3, 4, and 6 are disk symbols, and symbol 8 is a document or report symbol.

The other three symbols — 2, 5, and 7 — identify major processes that transform the data or files into another form. Symbols 2 and 7 are process symbols that represent programs, and symbol 5 is a predefined process symbol that represents a system utility program. Figure 5-22 shows three major processing steps that are completed in a sequence:

- The first step (symbol 2) verifies terminal-entered customer receipts (symbol 1) by reading from the accounts receivable file (symbol 3), reporting back to the workstation on the validity of the receipt, and then posting the valid receipts to the daily receipts file (symbol 4).

- The second step (symbol 5) sorts the daily receipts into accounting code sequence and then creates the sorted daily receipts file (symbol 6).

- The third step (symbol 7) reads the sorted daily receipts and then consolidates information to produce the cash receipts report (symbol 8).

State-Transition Diagrams

One drawback of data flow diagrams is that they do not show the time sequence that can be critical in real-time systems. A **real-time system** processes data and feeds it back to the operating environment. Examples of real-time systems include the monitoring system shown in Figure 5-23, automobile cruise control systems, microprocessor-controlled thermostats, and microwave oven control systems.

Figure 5-23   A hospital's intensive care unit monitoring system is an example of a real-time system that can be described using a state-transition diagram.

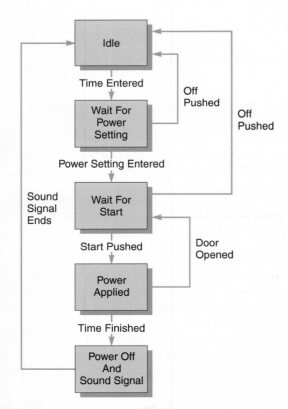

Figure 5-24   A state-transition diagram for a microwave oven.

Real-time systems change the state of the system when specific events occur. The events can be changes in environmental conditions or externally triggered signals. Examples of environmental conditions are changes in room temperature sensed by a thermostat and security devices that can detect motion. Examples of externally triggered signals are a person setting the cooking time on a microwave oven and a computer operator entering an operating system command to initiate a program.

A **state-transition diagram** (**STD**) is a graphic tool for showing the events, states, and time-dependent behavior of a real-time system. Figure 5-24 shows a state-transition diagram for a microwave oven. The lines with arrowheads show the events that occur and the boxes show the different states of the system. For example, the microwave oven sits idle until the *time entered* event occurs. The oven then waits for the *power setting entered* event, followed by a wait for the *start pushed* event. In any of these cases, the oven will return to its idle state if the *off pushed* event occurs. The *start pushed* event initiates the *power applied* state. If the *door opened* event occurs, the oven returns to its *wait for start* state. Otherwise, the oven continues applying power until the *time finished* event occurs. At this time, the power goes off, a sound is signaled, and then the oven returns to its *idle state*.

You can use a state-transition diagram as a lower-level DFD or to describe a process in a data flow diagram. By combining the tools, data flow diagrams and state-transition diagrams can help you describe a logical model for a real-time system.

TRANSITION TO SYSTEMS DESIGN

I f management decides to develop the system in-house, then the next phase of the SDLC — the systems design phase — can begin. In a smaller company, you might be assigned full responsibility for the project. In a large IS group, you might work as a member of a development team even though you had not participated in the earlier SDLC phases.

When systems design begins, it is essential to have an accurate and understandable system requirements document. Your document contains the design for the new system and is the starting point for the systems design phase. Errors, omissions, ambiguities, and other problems will affect the quality and completeness of the finished product. As you proceed to the next phase, you must be certain that you performed a thorough and accurate systems analysis and communicated the results in your system requirements document.

SOFTWEAR, LIMITED — EVALUATING ALTERNATIVES AND STRATEGIES

S ystems analyst Rick Williams and programmer/analyst Carla Moore continued to work on a logical model of the payroll system. Meanwhile, the information systems department recently purchased and installed Visible Analyst, a CASE toolkit that supports logical and physical modeling. Rick and Carla traveled to Massachusetts to attend a one-week workshop to learn how to use the package.

After returning from their trip, Rick and Carla decided to create the logical model for the payroll system with the Visible Analyst. They felt that the time spent now would pay off in later phases of the project. Rick and Carla used the manual DFDs they created in Chapter 4 to create computerized DFDs using the Visible Analyst. Now all related items for the new system are stored in the CASE tool.

Over the next month, Rick and Carla looked at various alternatives and spent their time evaluating the potential solutions. They determined that the best solution would be to purchase a payroll package, but the ESIP processing was so unique that none of the available software packages would handle SWL's specific requirements. They concluded that SWL should purchase a payroll package and develop the ESIP system in-house. Jane Rossman and Ann Hon agreed with their recommendation.

The systems analysts completed work on the logical model, alternative evaluations, and cost and time estimates and then prepared the system requirements document for the payroll system. The document was printed and distributed and a management presentation was scheduled at the end of the following week.

At this point, the IS team members were confident that they had done a good job. They had worked closely with SWL users throughout the development process and received user approval on important portions of the document as it was being prepared. They developed visual aids, rehearsed the presentation, and then tried to anticipate questions that might be asked.

Carla gave the management presentation. She recommended that SWL purchase a payroll package sold by Pacific Software Solutions and that ESIP processing be developed in-house to interface with the payroll package.

During the presentation, Carla and Rick answered questions on several points, including the economic analysis they had done. Michael Jeremy, vice president of finance, was especially interested in the method they used to calculate payback analysis, return on investment, and net present value for the new system.

SWL's president, Robert Lansing, arrived for the last part of the presentation. When the presentation ended, he asked the top managers how they felt about the project, and they indicated support for the proposal made by the IS department. The next step would be to negotiate a contract with Pacific Software Solutions and for Rick and Carla to begin systems design for the ESIP processing component.

YOUR TURN

Although the presentation was successful, Rick and Carla both feel that the IS department should have a checklist that could serve as a suggested model to help IS staff people who must prepare management presentations. They asked you to suggest a list of *"Do's and Don'ts"* for presentations. They also want you to review the DFDs that they prepared using the Visible Analyst to see if you have any suggestions for improvement. If you have access to a copier, make a copy of the DFDs shown in Chapter 4, and then write your notes directly on the diagrams. Otherwise, you can present a brief memo listing your comments.

CHAPTER SUMMARY

In this chapter, you studied the evaluation of alternatives and strategies, the preparation of the system requirements document, and the management presentation of the systems analysis phase.

The most important software alternatives are developing an in-house system, buying a software package, and buying a customized software package. Compared to developing an in-house system, an existing commercial software package is an attractive alternative, because a package generally costs less, takes less time to implement, has fewer errors, has a proven track record, requires fewer systems developers, and is upgraded frequently. In-house development might be the best choice when a software package cannot meet system requirements or constraints. A customized software package also might be an appropriate alternative in these situations.

The process of acquiring software and hardware is similar: evaluate the needs, identify all possible solutions, evaluate the feasible solutions, make the purchase, and install the product. In addition to the three main alternatives, you also can consider outsourcing, end-user computing, and enterprise computing as possible solutions.

The system requirements document is the end product of the systems analysis phase. This document details all systems requirements and constraints, recommends the best solution, and provides cost and time estimates for future development work. The system requirements document is the basis for the management presentation. Based on the analyst's findings and recommendations, management decides on the next step in system development.

You also learned about various tools and techniques that can assist you in systems development, including prototyping, the use of 4GL tools, CASE tools, and alternative graphic tools such as systems flowcharts and state-transition diagrams.

Prototyping is an effective way to verify the system requirements with users. You can use 4GL tools, which are nonprocedural languages, to construct a limited, working version of the proposed system, called a prototype. A nonprocedural language speeds up the development process by allowing you to specify what you want the program to do, without having to spell out the detailed code. The resulting prototype either is abandoned or used as the basis for the new system. The fourth-generation environment software tools used in prototyping are a data dictionary, relational database management system, report writer, query language, screen generator, program generator, and a fourth-generation language.

Computer-aided software engineering (CASE) describes a set of tools for developing and maintaining systems. Specific tasks in the systems development life cycle can be automated using specific CASE tools, such as a diagram generator or a full set of CASE tools called a CASE toolkit. Because they often replace manual tasks, CASE products are important in making systems development more efficient and faster.

Systems flowcharts are used to show the physical model of an information system graphically. State-transition diagrams are used to show the events, states, and time-dependent behavior of real-time systems graphically.

Review Questions

1. Explain the difference between horizontal application software and vertical application software.
2. What is the most common reason for a company to choose to develop its own information system? Give two other reasons why a company might choose the in-house approach.
3. Discuss four advantages of buying a software package.
4. Describe two ways that a software vendor can customize its package.
5. What problems can a company encounter when it uses a customized software package?
6. What is an RFP and how does it differ from an RFQ?
7. What is one resource for identifying potential software vendors?
8. What is the purpose of a benchmark test?
9. Explain the difference between a software license and a maintenance agreement.
10. Is the use of outsourcing increasing or declining? Why?
11. Define a turnkey system.
12. To what different groups of people do you give presentations at the end of the systems analysis phase?
13. What are the different decisions management could reach at the end of the systems analysis phase? What is the next step in each of these cases?
14. Give three reasons why change to the requirements of an information system is inevitable.
15. What is a prototype?
16. What are the prototyping software tools?
17. What is a 4GL?
18. What is CASE?
19. List and describe five different categories of CASE tools.
20. Define reengineering and describe its steps.
21. Give three advantages of using a CASE tool.
22. What is the purpose of a systems flowchart? Is its use increasing or declining and why?
23. What is a real-time system? Give two examples of real-time systems.
24. Give a definition for a state-transition diagram.

Discussion Questions

1. When discussing computer-aided software engineering (CASE) in this chapter, it was indicated that the solution must fit the size of the problem. A simple design might not require the creation of a full set of data flow diagrams and a data dictionary. To set up any CASE project, some amount of initial effort and preparation is required. Is it always worthwhile? As a systems analyst, how would you answer this question? Be prepared to state specific reasons for your position.
2. For many years, IS professionals have said that COBOL is outdated and that modern, third- and fourth-generation languages would soon replace it. Due to the enormous investment in existing

COBOL programs, however, COBOL still is used for business information systems. What are your views about the future of COBOL as a primary business information system language?

3. Visit the data center at your school or at a local company and investigate the use of CASE tools. Present to your class what tools are being used. How satisfied are the systems developers and management with the results of their use of CASE tools?

4. Select a specific type of horizontal application software to investigate. Visit local libraries and computer stores and use the Internet to determine what software packages are available. Describe the common features of these packages and the features that distinguish one product from another.

CASE STUDIES

NEW CENTURY HEALTH CLINIC — EVALUATING ALTERNATIVES AND STRATEGIES

ased on your earlier recommendations, New Century decided to continue the systems development process for a new information system that would improve operations, decrease costs, and provide better service to patients.

Facts

Now, at the end of the systems analysis phase, you are ready to prepare a system requirements document and give a presentation to the New Century associates. Many of the proposed system's advantages were described during the fact-finding process. These include smoother operation, better efficiency, and more user-friendly procedures for patients and New Century staff.

You also must examine tangible costs and benefits to determine the economic feasibility of several alternatives. If New Century decides to go ahead with the development process, the main options are to develop the system in-house or purchase a vertical package and configure it to meet New Century's needs. You have studied these choices and put together some preliminary figures.

You know that New Century's current workload requires 3 hours of office staff overtime per week at a base rate of $8.50 per hour. Also, based on current projections, it will be necessary to add another full-time clerical position in about six months. Neither the overtime nor the additional job will be needed if the new system is implemented, however. The current manual system also causes an average of three errors per day, and each error takes about 20 minutes to correct. The new system should eliminate these errors.

Based on your research, you estimate that you could complete the project in about 12 weeks, working full-time. Your consulting rate, which New Century agreed to, is $30 per hour. If you design the new system as a database application, you can expect to spend about $2,500 for a networked commercial DBMS package. After the system is operational and the staff is trained, you hope that New Century will be able to handle routine maintenance tasks without your assistance.

As an alternative to in-house development, a vertical software package is available for about $9,000. The vendor offers terms of $3,000 down, followed by two annual installments of $3,000 each. If New Century buys this package, it would take you about four weeks to install, configure, and test it, working full-time. The vendor provides free support during the first year of operation, but then New Century must sign a technical support agreement at an annual cost of $500. Although the package contains many of the features that New Century wants, most of the reports are pre-designed and it would be difficult to modify the layouts.

No matter which approach is selected, New Century probably will need you to provide about 10 hours of initial training and support each week for the first three months of operation. After the new system is operational, it will need routine maintenance, file backups, and updating. These tasks will require about four hours per week, and can be performed by a clinic staff member. Also, in both cases, the necessary hardware and network installation will cost about $5,000. In your view, the useful life of the system will be about five years, including the year in which the system becomes operational.

Assignments

You are scheduled to make a presentation to New Century in one week, and you will be expected to submit a system requirements document during the presentation. To give a successful presentation, you will need to learn the skills described in the Systems Analyst's Toolkit. Your oral and written presentation must include the following:

- An overview of proposed system, including the costs and benefits, with an explanation of the various cost and benefit types and categories
- An economic feasibility analysis, using payback analysis, ROI, and present value (assume a discount rate of 10 percent)
- A context diagram and diagram 0 for the proposed system
- A brief explanation of the various alternatives that should be investigated if development continues, including in-house development and any other possible strategies

In addition, you may wish to include other material that will help your audience understand the new system and make a decision on the next step.

Presentation Rules

The following presentation rules should be considered.

- Use suitable visual aids
- Use presentation software, if you wish
- Distribute handouts before, during, or after the presentation
- Follow the guidelines in the Systems Analyst's Toolkit
- Keep your presentation length to 30 minutes, including five minutes for questions

Rules for the System Requirements Document

The following rules should be considered in preparation of the system requirements document.

- Follow the guidelines in the Systems Analyst's Toolkit
- Pay special attention to the Reports section and the description of the various sections of the systems analysis report
- Include any charts, graphs, or other visual information in the document that would be helpful
- Spell check and carefully proofread everything you submit

RIDGEWAY COMPANY

 he Ridgeway Company requirements were described in Chapter 4. The following assignments are based on those same requirements.

Assignments

1. If you have access to a CASE tool for preparing data flow diagrams, use the tool to create the entire set of data flow diagrams for the Ridgeway Company's billing system.
2. If you have access to prototyping software tools, prototype the monthly statement and the daily sales report.
3. Thomas McGee has asked you to give a presentation about the new membership billing system to Ridgeway's management team. Prepare a short overview of the proposed system, including the costs and benefits, with discussion of the suggested software alternative (make or buy).

The Systems Analyst's Toolkit discusses software change control, which is the process of managing and controlling changes after presenting the system requirements document to management. You should review the material about this topic now, before completing the Cutting Edge Incorporated case.

CUTTING EDGE INCORPORATED

Cutting Edge Incorporated is a company engaged in the development of CASE packages. Product manager Michele Kellogg is the main user for a new software package being developed for sale to the furniture industry. Santiago Benitez is the lead systems analyst for this effort, which now is one month into the systems design phase that began on October 6. The completion and first installation of the package is scheduled for August 1 of the following year.

On November 6, Michele received a request from the vice president of development for a new functional capability that needs to be added to the package. She asked Santiago to analyze this change and determine its impact to the project.

Michele and Santiago reviewed the results of the analysis at a meeting on November 15. Adding the new requirements to the package at this time would increase the developmental costs by $28,000 and would add one month to the schedule. Santiago evaluated a second alternative, which is to continue to develop the package without the requested changes and to incorporate the changes into the package as part of a follow-up release. This second alternative would take three months time and $66,000 to accomplish.

Assignments

1. Because the project is in the systems design phase and no programming has been started, why would incorporating the requested change add one month and $28,000 to the project?
2. Why would it take two extra months and $38,000 more if the changes were performed after package development has been completed?
3. What are the advantages and disadvantages of each alternative?
4. Suppose you are Michele and you must recommend action on the change request. What factors would you consider, and what would you recommend?

Phase 3
Systems Design

386 —

8

7

Phase 1
Systems Planning

Phase 2
Systems Analysis

Phase 3
Systems Design

Phase 4
Systems Implementation

Phase 5
Systems Operation & Support

Output Design
Input Design
File and Database Design
System Architecture

SDLC PHASES

Systems design is the third phase in the systems development life cycle. In the previous phase — systems analysis — you developed a logical model of the system that would satisfy user needs and meet business requirements. Based on this logical model, you then considered various development alternatives and strategies, prepared the system requirements document, and presented it to management. Now you are ready to begin the physical design of the system and focus on designing an information system that satisfies the criteria specified in the system requirements document. In the next phase — systems design — you will review general design requirements and then work on four tasks: output design, input design, file and database design, and system architecture.

CHAPTER 6

SDLC PHASES

Phase 1
Systems Planning

Phase 2
Systems Analysis

Phase 3
Systems Design

Phase 4
Systems Implementation

Phase 5
Systems Operation Support

Output Design

Output design is the first of four chapters in the systems design phase. During output design, you create a physical design of the information system based on the logical model you developed in the systems analysis phase. In this chapter, you will focus on various forms of system output that support business objectives and satisfy user requirements.

OBJECTIVES

When you finish this chapter, you will be able to:

- Explain the differences between logical and physical design
- Discuss the objectives of systems design and provide guidelines for good design
- List and describe the major activities of the systems design phase
- Design and use appropriate codes in systems design and development
- Provide examples of types of output, including new technology-based methods of information delivery
- Describe the classifications of output reports and explain the differences among them
- Design effective printed reports that will meet user requirements
- Design screen reports that are easy to understand and use
- Explain output control concepts and methods

INTRODUCTION

Output design is the first of four chapters covering the systems design phase of the systems development life cycle. This chapter begins with an overview of systems design, including basic concepts, design tasks, the use of codes, and general guidelines for designing information systems. The chapter then covers specific tasks in output design, including designing printed reports, screen output, and other system outputs. Finally, the chapter concludes with a discussion of the importance of output control and a description of automated output design tools.

SYSTEMS DESIGN OVERVIEW

The **logical design** of an information system defines the logical functions and features of the system and the relationships among its components. The logical design includes the output that must be produced by the system, all the input needed by the system, and the processes that must be performed by the system *without regard to how tasks will be accomplished physically*. Because the logical design defines the necessary, or *essential*, requirements of a system, it also is known as the **essential model.**

As previously discussed, a logical design defines *what* must take place, not *how* it is to be accomplished. Logical designs, thus, do not address the actual methods of implementation. The logical design for a customer system, for example, describes the data that must be entered, specifies that records must be displayed in customer number order, and explains what information to produce for a customer status report. Specifications for the actual input, or entry, of data, the sort method, the physical process of creating the report, and the exact format of the report are *not* part of the logical design.

In contrast, the **physical design** of an information system is a plan for the actual implementation of the system. The physical design is built on the system's logical design and describes the implementation of a specific set of system components. In the customer system, for example, the physical design describes actual processes of entering, verifying, and storing data; the physical layout of data files; the sorting procedures; the exact format of reports; and so on. Whereas logical design is concerned with *what* the system must accomplish, physical design is concerned with *how* the system will meet these requirements.

The logical design is completed during the systems analysis phase of the SDLC. To create the logical design, you investigated, analyzed, and documented the input, processing, and output requirements and constraints. Now, in the systems design phase, you are ready to complete the physical design of the system.

The Relationship between Analysis and Design

Because logical and physical designs are related so closely, good systems design is impossible without careful, accurate systems analysis. In fact, the design phase typically cannot begin until the analysis work is complete. Although some overlap is possible, it is much better to finish the analysis phase before moving on to systems design.

During systems design, you should return to the analysis phase only in very limited situations. You might need to return to fact-finding, for example, if you discover that you overlooked an important fact, if users have significant new needs, or if legal or governmental requirements change. Or, you might have to return to requirements analysis if you encounter unforeseen design issues or problems. Such cases are the exception to the rule, however. If an analyst develops a pattern of returning to prior phases, it might indicate that the earlier work was inaccurate or incomplete.

Systems Design Activities

As defined in Chapter 1, an information system has five basic components: data files, people, procedures, hardware, and software (Figure 6-1). These components are interdependent, and the interaction among them has an enormous impact on the design process. The analyst must understand the entire logical design of the system before beginning the physical design of any one component.

The first step is to review the system requirements document that was prepared at the end of the systems analysis phase. Reviewing this document is especially important if you did not work on the previous phase or if a substantial amount of time has passed since the analysis phase was completed.

After you review the system requirements, you are ready to start the actual design process. What should you do first, and why?

The best place to begin is with the system output. Of all the system specifications, the output requirements best define the system. The **output requirements** drive the design process because they describe what the system must produce to meet business needs.

To learn more about the **Relationship between Analysis and Design**, visit Systems Analysis and Design Chapter 6 More on the Web.

www.scsite.com/ sad3e/ch06/

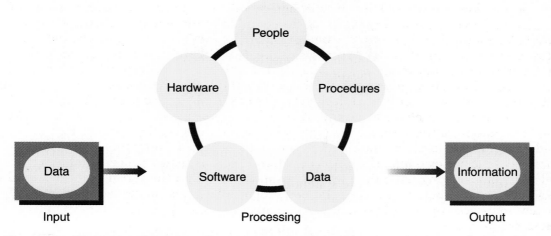

Figure 6-1   All elements of an information system must work together to turn data into useful information.

After completing output design, you will work on input, data files and databases, systems processing, and architecture for the system. Because the components of a system are interdependent, however, the design phase is not a series of clearly defined steps. Although you might start with one component, it is not unusual to work on several components at the same time. For example, making a decision to change a report might require other changes in file design or input screens.

The final step in systems design is to prepare a system design specification report and present your results to management. These tasks and other systems design activities are listed and described in Figure 6-2.

STEP	ACTIVITY	DESCRIPTION
1	**Review the system requirements**	Become thoroughly familiar with the complete logical design.
2	**Design the system**	
	• Design the output	Design the physical layout for each systems output and define the physical disposition and handling of the output.
	• Design the input	Determine how the data will be input to the system, design source documents for capturing the data, design the input data records, audit trails, and system security measures.
	• Design the files and databases	Design the systems data stores by considering organization, access, storage, and usage requirements.
	• Design the system architecture	Design the processing methods, including batch, online, centralized, distributed, and client/server processing together with necessary network configurations.
3	**Present the systems design**	Create the system design specification document, in which you detail the complete proposed systems design, the anticipated benefits of the system, and the estimated development and implementation costs of the design.

Figure 6-2   The systems design phase consists of three main steps. The process depends on five key design activities.

GENERAL GUIDELINES FOR SYSTEMS DESIGN

The goal of **systems design** is to build a system that is effective, reliable, and maintainable. To be **effective**, the system must satisfy the defined requirements and constraints. The system also must be accepted by users who use it to support the organization's business objectives.

A system is **reliable** if it adequately handles errors, such as input errors, processing errors, hardware failures, or human mistakes. Ideally, *all* errors can be prevented. Unfortunately, no system is completely foolproof, whether it is a payroll system, a telephone switching system, an Internet access system, or a space shuttle navigation system. A more realistic approach to building a reliable system is to plan for errors, detect them as early as possible, allow for their correction, and prevent them from damaging the system itself.

A system is **maintainable** if it is well designed, flexible, and developed with future modifications in mind. No matter how well a system is designed and implemented, at some point, it will need to be modified. Modifications will be necessary to correct problems, to adapt to changing user requirements, to enhance the system, or to take advantage of changing technology. Your systems design must be capable of handling future modifications or the system soon will be outdated and fail to meet requirements.

For a review of
Systems Design Guidelines, visit
Systems Analysis
and Design
Chapter 6 More on
the Web.

www.scsite.com/
sad3e/ch06/

Design Suggestions

The following suggestions will help you design effective, reliable, and maintainable systems. Figure 6-3 shows three categories of considerations, according to whether they affect users, data, or processing.

Systems Design Considerations
User Considerations
• Consider points where users interact with the system
• Anticipate future user, system, and organizational needs
Data Considerations
• Enter data where and when it occurs
• Verify data where it is input
• Use automated data-entry methods whenever possible
• Control access for data entry
• Report every instance of entry and change to data
• Enter data only once
Processing Considerations
• Use a modular design
• Design independent modules that perform a single function

Figure 6-3   Design considerations can be grouped into three main categories.

USER CONSIDERATIONS • Of the many issues you must consider during systems design, your most important goal is to make the system acceptable to users, or **user-friendly**. Throughout the design process, the essential factor to consider is how decisions will affect users. Always remember that you are designing the system for the user, and keep these basic points in mind:

Carefully consider any point where users receive output from or provide input into the system. Output should be attractive and easy to understand, with an appropriate level of detail. Input processes should be well documented, easy to follow, intuitive, and forgiving of errors. Screens or other mechanisms known as **user interfaces** enable users to enter input, issue commands, request specific actions, and receive responses. User interfaces must be clear and well documented.

Anticipate future needs of the users, the system, and the organization. Suppose that an employee master file contains a one-character field to indicate each employee's category. The field currently has two valid values: *F* indicates a full-time employee, and *P* indicates a part-time employee. Depending on the field value, either FULL-TIME or PART-TIME will print as the value on various reports. While these two text values could be programmed, or **hardcoded**, into the report programs, designing a separate table with category codes and captions is a better choice. The hardcoded solution is straightforward, but if the organization adds another value, such as *S* for job-sharing, a programmer would have to change all the report programs. If a separate table for codes and captions is used, however, it can be changed easily without requiring modifications to the reports.

Suppose that a user wants a screen display of all customer balances that exceed $5,000 in an accounts receivable system. How should you design this feature? The program could be hardcoded to check customer balances against a fixed value of 5,000. This approach is a simple solution for the programmer and the user because extra keystrokes or commands are not entered to produce the display. This approach, however, is inflexible. For instance, if a user later needs a list of customers whose balances exceed $7,500 rather than $5,000, the existing system cannot provide the information. To accommodate the request, the program would have to be changed and retested and new documentation would have to be written.

On the other hand, the program could be designed to produce a report of all customers whose balance exceeds a specific amount entered by the user. For example, if a user wants to display customers with balances over $7,500, he or she can enter the number 7,500 in a parameter query. A **parameter** is a value that the user enters whenever the query is run. This solution provides flexibility, enables users to access information without assistance from the IS staff, and is less expensive to maintain.

A good system design might combine both approaches. In this example, you could design the program to accept a variable amount entered by the user, but start with a default value of 5,000. Then users can press the Enter key to accept the default value, or enter another value. Often, the best design strategy is to come up with several alternatives, so users can decide what will work best for them. Again, remember that you should design the system with the user in mind.

A KEY QUESTION

Experienced analysts sometimes complain that users request many reports, but use only a small portion of the data. In many offices you see in-boxes filled with reports and stacks of reports sitting on desks. Why? Suppose you are interviewing users about what reports they want or need. What questions would you ask? What if users could design most of their own reports without assistance from the IS staff, by using a powerful, user-friendly report generator program? Do you think they would request as many reports or the same types of reports? What are the pros and cons of giving end users total control over output?

DATA CONSIDERATIONS • Data entry and storage considerations are important parts of the system design. Some guidelines to follow include:

Data should be entered into the system where and when it occurs because delays cause data errors. For example, employees in the receiving department should enter data about incoming shipments when the shipments arrive, and sales clerks should enter data about new orders when they take the orders.

Data should be verified when it is entered, so errors are caught immediately. The input design should specify a data type, such as numeric, alphabetic, or character, and a range of acceptable values for each data entry item. If an incorrect data value is entered, the system should recognize and flag it immediately. The system also should allow corrections at any time. Some errors, for example, are corrected most easily right at entry while the original source documents are at hand or the customer is on the telephone. Other errors may need further investigation, so users must be able to make corrections at a later time, as well.

Automated methods of data entry should be used whenever possible. Receiving department employees in many companies, for example, use hand-held scanners to capture data about merchandise received. Automated data entry methods, such as the bar code scanner shown in Figure 6-4, reduce input errors and improve employee productivity.

Access for data entry should be controlled and all entries or changes to critical data values should be reported. Dollar fields and many volume fields are considered critical data fields. Examples of critical volumes might include the number of checks processed, the number of medical prescriptions dispensed, or the

Figure 6-4   Using a scanner to track products reduces input errors and increases employee productivity.

number of insurance premium payments received. Reports that trace the entry of and changes to critical data values are called **audit trails** and are essential in every system.

Every instance of entry and change to data should be reported. Without this step, documentation becomes incomplete and inaccurate.

Data should be entered into a system only once. If input data for a payroll system also is needed for a human resources system, you should design a program interface between the systems so data can be transferred automatically.

Data duplication should be avoided. In an inventory file, for example, the suppliers' addresses should not be stored with every part record. Otherwise, the address of a vendor who supplies 100 different parts would be repeated 100 times in the data file. Additionally, if the vendor's address changes, all 100 part records must be updated. Data duplication also can produce inconsistencies. If those 100 stored addresses for the vendor are not identical, how would a user know which version is correct?

PROCESSING CONSIDERATIONS • In addition to the issues affecting users and data, you should consider the following guidelines in your processing design.

Use a modular design. In a **modular design**, or **structured design**, you create individual processing components, called **modules** that connect to a higher-level program or process. Each module represents a specific process or subprocess shown on a DFD and documented in a process description.

Design modules that perform a single function. Modules that perform a single function are easier to understand, implement, and maintain. Independent modules also provide greater flexibility because they can be developed and tested individually, and then combined at a later point in the development process. Modular design is especially helpful when developing large-scale systems because separate teams of analysts and programmers can work on different areas of the project, and then integrate the modules to create a finished system.

> For an overview on **Modular Design**, visit Systems Analysis and Design Chapter 6 More on the Web.
>
> www.scsite.com/ sad3e/ch06/

Design Tradeoffs

You will find that design goals often conflict with each other. In the systems design phase, you must analyze alternatives and weigh tradeoffs constantly. To make a system easier to use, for example, programming requirements might be more complex. Making a system more flexible might increase maintenance requirements. Meeting one user's requirements could make it harder to satisfy another user's needs.

Most design tradeoff decisions that you will face can be reduced to the basic conflict of *quality versus cost*. Although every project has budget and financial constraints, you should avoid decisions that will achieve short-term savings but might mean higher costs later. For example, steps you take to reduce implementation costs might create higher operational costs. If necessary, you should document and explain these situations carefully to management, and discuss the possible risks if the design is compromised. Each tradeoff must be considered individually, and the final result must be acceptable to users, the systems staff, and company management.

DESIGNING AND USING CODES

A **code** is a set of letters or numbers that represents an item of data. Codes are used in output from or input into the system. You probably noticed some codes during the systems analysis phase. Now, in systems design, you will work with existing codes and develop any new ones that are required.

Because codes often are used to represent data you encounter them constantly in your everyday life. Student numbers, for example, are unique codes used in a college registration system to identify students. Three students with the name John Turner might be enrolled at your school, but only one of them has student number 268960.

Your ZIP code is another type of code that contains multiple pieces of information compressed into nine digits. The first digit identifies one of ten geographical areas of the United States. The combination of the first three digits identifies a major city or major distribution point. The first five digits identify an individual post office, an area within a city, or a specific delivery unit. The last four digits identify a post office box or a specific street address.

For example, consider the ZIP code 27906-2624 shown in Figure 6-5. The first digit, 2, indicates a broad geographical area in the eastern United States. The digits, 790, indicate Elizabeth City, North Carolina. The fifth digit, 6, identifies the post office that services the College of the Albemarle. The last four digits, 2624, identify the post office box for the college.

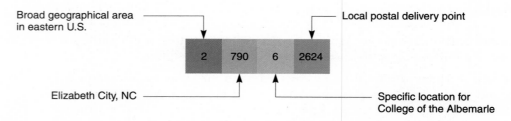

Figure 6-5   A ZIP code is an example of a significant digit code that uses a series of subgroups to provide information.

As you can imagine, codes serve many useful purposes. Because codes often are shorter than the data they represent, they save storage space and costs, reduce data transmission time, and decrease data entry time. For example, ZIP codes are used to classify and sort mail efficiently. Codes also can be used to reveal or conceal information. The last two digits of a seven-digit part number, for example, might represent the supplier number. By contrast, the coded wholesale price on a retail price tag is read easily by salespeople but not by customers. Finally, codes can reduce data input errors in situations when the coded data is easier to remember and enter than the original source data, when only certain valid codes are allowed, and when something within the code itself can provide immediate verification that the entry is correct.

Because users must deal with coded data, the coding methods must be acceptable to them. If you plan to use new codes or change existing ones, you first should obtain comments and feedback from users.

Types of Coding

The ten common coding schemes are described in this section.

1. **Sequence codes** are numbers or letters assigned in a specific order. Sequence codes contain no additional information other than an indication of order of entry into the system. For example, consecutive employee numbers might be issued to identify employees. Because the codes are assigned in the order in which employees are hired, you can use the code to see that employee number 584 was hired after employee number 433. The code, however, does not indicate the starting date of either person's employment.

2. **Block sequence codes** use blocks of numbers for different classifications. College course numbers usually are assigned using a block sequence code. 100-level courses, such as Chemistry 110 and Mathematics 125, are freshman-level courses, whereas course numbers in the 200s indicate sophomore-level courses. Within a particular block, the sequence of numbers might have some additional meaning, such as when English 151 is the prerequisite for English 152.

3. **Classification codes** distinguish one group of items from another. For example, a local department store might use a two-character code to identify the department in which a product is sold: GN for gardening supplies, HW for hardware, and EL for electronics.

4. **Alphabetic codes** are abbreviations. For example, standard codes include NY for New York, ME for Maine, and MN for Minnesota.

5. **Mnemonic codes** use a combination of letters and symbols that are easy to remember. The three-character airport codes shown in Figure 6-6 that you see on luggage tags are mnemonic codes: LAX represents Los Angeles International Airport, DFW is Dallas/Ft. Worth Airport, and ORD is Chicago O'Hare International Airport. Obviously, some codes, such as DFW, are easier to recognize than others, such as ORD.

Figure 6-6   Codes are used to identify baggage in the airline industry. Codes are machine-readable using the bar code that is printed when the baggage is checked. Airline employees recognize the unique three-character code that identifies the destination. A bar code reader scans a code that also represents the employee number who checked in the baggage, the passenger's name, and other pertinent information.

6. **Significant digit codes** distinguish items by using a series of subgroups of digits. ZIP codes, for example, are significant digit codes. Other such codes might include inventory location codes that consist of a two-digit warehouse code, followed by a one-digit floor number code, a two-digit section code, a one-digit aisle number, and a two-digit bin number code. Figure 6-7 illustrates the inventory location code 11205327. What appears to be a large eight-digit number is actually five separate numbers, each of which has significance.

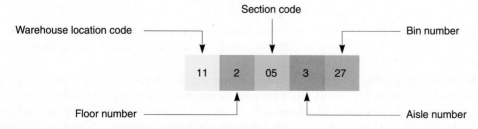

Figure 6-7   Sample of a code that uses significant digits to pinpoint the location of an inventory item.

7. **Derivation codes** combine data from different item attributes, or characteristics, to build the code. Most magazine subscription codes are derivation codes. One popular magazine's subscriber code consists of the subscriber's five-digit ZIP code, followed by the first, third, and fourth letters of the subscriber's last name, the last two digits of the subscriber's house number, and the first, third, and fourth letters of the subscriber's street name. The magazine's subscriber code for one particular subscriber is shown in Figure 6-8.

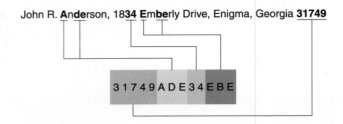

Figure 6-8   A magazine subscriber code is derived from various parts of the name and address.

8. **Cipher codes** use a keyword to encode a number. A retail store might use a ten-letter word, such as CAMPGROUND, to code wholesale prices, where the letter C represents 1, A represents 2, and so on. Thus, the code, GRAND, indicates that the store paid $562.90 for the item.

9. **Action codes** indicate what action is to be taken with an associated item. For example, a computerized query/update program might require you to enter a student number and an action code to act on the record in a certain manner. The code *D* indicates that you want to display the student's record, the code *A* indicates that you want to add a record for the student number, and the code *X* indicates that you want to exit the program.

10. **Self-checking codes** use a check digit to verify the validity of a numeric code. One method of using a four-digit self-checking code is to calculate a check digit by multiplying the first digit by 1, the second digit by 2, and so on. Then, those products are summed. If the sum contains more than one digit, the digits in the sum are added until they produce a one-digit answer. That final answer is the check digit that is appended to the numeric code. The code 1302-6 is valid because the result of the calculation is 6, which matches the given check digit, as shown in Figure 6-9. Figure 6-9 also shows the erroneous code 7198-3. At least one of the five digits in this code is wrong because the calculation result is 5, which does not match the given check digit 3.

You could build a useful code by using a combination of two or more of these coding schemes, but simpler coding schemes usually work better.

Developing a Code

Devising a code with too many features makes it difficult to remember, decipher, and verify. Keep the following suggestions in mind when developing a code.

1. **Keep codes concise.** Do not create codes that are longer than necessary. For example, if you need a code to identify each of 250 customers, you will not need a six-digit code.

2. **Allow for expansion.** A coding scheme must allow for reasonable growth in the number of assigned codes. If the company currently has eight warehouses, you should not use a one-digit code for the warehouse number. If three more warehouses are added, the code must be increased to two digits or changed to a character code in order to identify each location. This rule also applies to using a single letter as a character code; you might need more than 26 codes in the future.

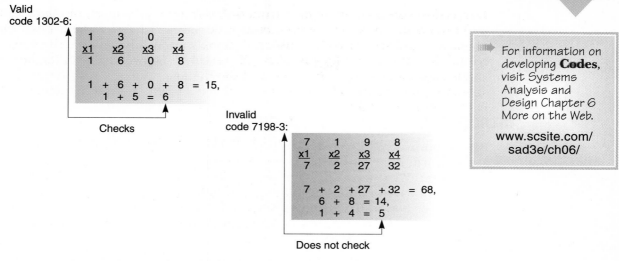

Figure 6-9   The first code is valid and it checks, but in the second code the check digit is invalid.

For information on developing **Codes**, visit Systems Analysis and Design Chapter 6 More on the Web.

www.scsite.com/ sad3e/ch06/

3. **Keep codes stable.** Codes that have to be changed cause major problems when they are implemented and replace the old codes. During the changeover period, you will have to change all the stored occurrences of a particular code and all documents containing the old code, as users switch to the new code. Usually, both the old and new codes are used for an interim period, and special procedures might be required to handle the two codes. For example, when area codes change, you can use either area code for a certain time period.

4. **Make codes unique.** Codes used for identification purposes must be unique to have meaning. If the code HW can indicate Hardware or Housewares, the code has no utility.

5. **Use sortable codes.** If products with three-digit codes in the 100s or the 300s are of one type, while products with codes in the 200s are a different type, a simple sort will not group all the products of one type together. Also be careful that single-digit character codes will sort properly with double-digit codes — you can add a leading zero (01, 02, 03, and so on) to make sure that codes sort correctly.

6. **Avoid confusing codes.** Do not code some part numbers with two letters, a hyphen, and one digit, and others with one letter, a hyphen, and two digits. Avoid allowing both letters and numbers to occupy the same positions within a code because it is easy to confuse the number zero (0) and the uppercase letter O, or the number one (1) and the lowercase letter L (l) or uppercase letter I. For example, the five-character code 5Z081 easily can be misread as 5ZO8I, or 52081, or even totally incorrectly as S20BI.

7. **Make codes meaningful.** Codes must be easy to remember, useful for users, convenient to use, and easy to encode and interpret. Using SW as a code for the southwest sales region, for example, has far more meaning than the code 14. Also, using ENG as the code for the English department is easier to interpret and remember than either XQA or 132.

8. **Use a code for a single purpose.** Do not use a single code to classify two or more unrelated attributes. For example, if you use a single code to identify the combination of an employee's department *and* the employee's insurance plan type, it will be difficult to identify all the subscribers of a particular plan, or all the workers in a particular department, or both. A separate code for each separate characteristic makes much more sense.

9. **Keep codes consistent.** If the payroll system already is using two-digit codes for departments, do not create a new, different coding scheme to be used in the personnel system. If these two systems already are using two different coding schemes, you should try to convince the users of the two systems to adopt just a single and consistent department coding scheme.

INTRODUCTION TO OUTPUT DESIGN

The purpose of a system is to provide users with the information they need to perform their jobs. Most users will not care about the technical details of system design. What they will see is the finished product, and they will judge the entire system based on how well the output helps them carry out their job responsibilities. No matter how well a system is designed, the *critical* test of its success is whether it meets the users' and the organization's business needs. For the system to be successful, the output must be useful, accurate, understandable, and timely.

Checklist for Output Design

Before considering the output details of a report or screen form, ask yourself several questions:

- What is the purpose of the output?
- Who or what wants this information, why it is it needed, and how will it be used?
- What specific information will be included?
- What format should be used?
- When will the information be provided, and how often must it be updated?
- Will simultaneous user access be required for screen forms?
- Are security or confidentiality issues involved that need to be considered?

The design process should not begin until you have answered these questions. Some of this information probably was gathered during the systems analysis phase. To complete your understanding, you should meet with users to find out exactly what kind of output is needed. You can use prototypes and mock-ups to obtain feedback and suggestions throughout the design process. Your answers will affect your output design strategies, as you will see next.

TYPES OF OUTPUT AND INFORMATION DELIVERY

Although most system output is printed in reports or displayed on screens, new technology has had an enormous impact on how people communicate and obtain information. This change especially is true in business information systems that require significant interaction by users.

As shown in Figure 6-10, in addition to traditional forms of output, information is delivered to users in the form of audio output, automated facsimile systems, e-mail, and links to Web pages, among others. The type of output and the technology needed usually is decided during the systems analysis phase, based on user requirements. Now, in the systems design phase, you must design the actual reports, screen forms, and other output delivery methods.

Information Delivery Method	Description
Printer	Produces text and graphics on various types of paper
Screen	Displays text and graphics on a monitor
Plotter	Produces graphic output on special paper or charts
Audio output	Transforms digital information into speech that can be understood by the user
E-mail	Electronic messaging systems that use local or wide area networks, including the Internet
Links to Web pages	Provides access to information linked to a Web site; can include hypertext and file transfer protocols
Automated facsimile system	User-controlled system for requesting and receiving specific information by facsimile
Computer output microfilm (COM)	Records information as images on microfiche sheets or microfilm rolls
Other specialized devices	Output for specialized applications, including ATMs, point-of-sale terminals, and other industry-specific uses

Figure 6-10 Common output devices and methods.

Printed Output

Technological advances have resulted in printers that are faster, better, and less expensive than their predecessors. **Impact printers** are used for multiple form output. If speed is critical and draft quality is acceptable, high-speed printers are available. **Laser printers** now are standard in most businesses because they offer speed, excellent quality, and graphical output at an affordable price.

Despite these advances in printing technology, however, many companies are trying to reduce the amount of paper they use and create a *paperless office*. Most businesses have been unable to achieve this goal and still rely on printed output in their daily operations. Why is this so? Part of the answer lies in the unique advantages of working with a piece of paper. Many people prefer to work with paper for tasks such as proofreading, rather than reading the document on the screen. Paper also has the added advantage of being highly portable. Printed output, for example, is necessary for **turnaround documents,** which are output documents from a system that are later entered back into the same or another information system. Your telephone or electric bill, for example, is a turnaround document that is printed by the company's billing system, and then when you return the bill with your payment, the bill is scanned into the company's accounts receivable system to record your payment accurately.

Printed output, however, does have certain disadvantages. For instance, paper is expensive to purchase, print, store, and dispose of. Printed information has a short shelf life, and might be outdated quickly. An inventory status report, for example, is correct only until a single item is added to or removed from inventory. Adding to this concern is that often a delay is experienced between the request for and delivery of printed information.

For a guide to selecting a **Printer**, visit Systems Analysis and Design Chapter 6 More on the Web.

www.scsite.com/ sad3e/ch06/

Screen Output

The **screen**, or **monitor, CRT** (cathode ray tube), **LCD** (liquid crystal display), or **VDT** (video display terminal), is the most familiar computer output device. Early computer monitors could display only monochrome text in a format 80 characters wide and 24 lines high. Today, monitors can display high-resolution color graphics in millions of colors. Software publishers and programmers take advantage of this capability by designing output that is attractive, easy to read, and colorful. By combining a variety of graphics, special effects, and features, program designers strive to create programs that are attractive for users.

Screen output is the most popular output medium because users constantly work with monitors at their computers, whether they are multiuser terminals or personal computers. An important advantage of screen output is timeliness because the display can reflect the status of information on a real-time basis. For example, consider an online database that is updated every time an item is added to or removed from inventory. The screen display reflects this change immediately and a sales representative can tell a customer whether an item is in stock at that time. This type of information is essential in the highly competitive, customer-oriented marketplace of today.

Other Types of Information Delivery

Within the two major categories of output — printed and screen — many specialized types of output exist. Some of the newer types of output include audio output, automated facsimile systems, e-mail, links to Web pages, and other specialized forms of output discussed next.

AUDIO OUTPUT • Many firms use automated telephone systems to handle voice transactions and provide information to customers. For example, using a Touch-Tone™ telephone, you can confirm an airline seat assignment, check your credit card balance, or find out the current price of a mutual fund. In addition, audio output consisting of words and other sounds can be designed into a program or inserted into a document. For example, Figure 6-11 shows how a user can add a voice annotation to a Microsoft Word 97 document.

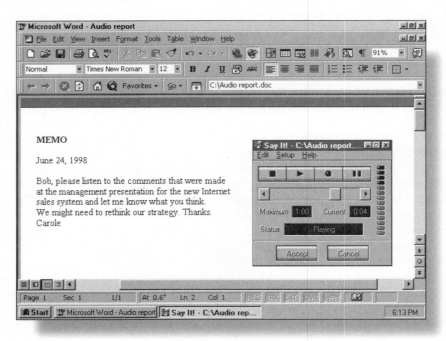

Figure 6-11 By inserting an audio annotation, you can integrate audio output into a Microsoft Office 97 document.

AUTOMATED FACSIMILE AND FAXBACK SYSTEMS • Some firms use automated facsimile and faxback systems, whereby a customer can use a Touch-Tone™ telephone to request printed output in the form of a fax. The fax is transmitted in a matter of seconds to the user's fax machine. A computer firm, for example, might allow users to request product data, information on new device drivers, or technical assistance via fax. This type of automated output is inexpensive, available 24 hours a day, and provides immediate response to customers.

E-MAIL • As companies develop more powerful Internet capabilities, e-mail has become an important means of transmitting information, both for internal and external communications. A sales organization, for example, could send new product announcements or periodic updates to customers via e-mail, and a financial services company can send e-mail messages to confirm the purchase or sale of securities. Experts forecast enormous growth in e-mail as a form of screen output.

LINKS TO WEB PAGES • Many firms use the Internet and the World Wide Web to reach new customers and markets around the world. For example, a business can link its inventory system to its Web site so the output from the inventory system is input directly into an online Web-based catalog. Then, customers visiting the Web site can use the catalog to obtain current price quotes and check product availability. Other forms of screen output used on the Internet might include customized responses to technical support questions that are generated when a user enters a set of specific symptoms or problems.

SPECIALIZED FORMS OF OUTPUT • Today's retail point-of-sale terminals actually are computer terminals that handle credit card transactions, print detailed register receipts, and update inventory records. Automatic teller machines (ATMs) process bank transactions and print deposit slips and cash withdrawal receipts. Computer terminals record and print lottery tickets. Driver's licenses are printed on special-purpose printers, and digitized photos can be printed on employee identification cards. Programmable devices such as television sets, VCRs, and microwave ovens produce visual output displays.

As noted in the previous examples, output from one system often becomes input into another system, either inside or outside the organization. Within a company, payment data from the accounts receivable system becomes input to the general ledger system. These same companies might send tax statement records to the IRS on magnetic media or transmit them electronically. As shown in Figure 6-12, many individual taxpayers submit their returns electronically to receive faster refunds that can be deposited directly into their bank accounts. Local and wide area networks are the most common transmission methods, but magnetic media such as disks and tapes also are used to transfer data between systems.

Next, you will learn about the specific considerations and steps in the design of outputs from a system. First you will examine the design of printed reports, then screen output, and finally other system outputs.

For more detail about **Faxback Systems**, visit Systems Analysis and Design Chapter 6 More on the Web.

www.scsite.com/ sad3e/ch06/

To view an example of **Web Page Output**, visit Systems Analysis and Design Chapter 6 More on the Web.

www.scsite.com/ sad3e/ch06/

Figure 6-12   Data can be input using a one system (a PC) and sent over a network to become input into another system (the IRS system). When a taxpayer files electronically, data is input into the receiving system without the need for input operations by IRS employees. Electronic input saves time and money while ensuring data accuracy.

DESIGNING PRINTED REPORTS

Reports are classified in two ways: by content and by distribution. Classification by content includes detail, exception, and summary reports. Classification by report distribution includes internal or external reports.

Reports Classified by Content

To be useful, a report must include the information that the recipient needs. From a user's point of view, a report with too little information is of no value. Too much information, however, can make a report confusing and difficult to understand. In designing reports, the essential objective is to match the report to the user's specific information needs. Depending on their job functions, users might need one or more of the reports described below.

DETAIL REPORTS • In a **detail report**, one or more lines of output is produced for each record processed. Each line of output that is printed is called a **detail line**. Figure 6-13 shows a simple detail report of employee hours for a chain of retail shops. Notice that one detail line prints for each employee. All the fields in the record do not have to be printed, nor do the fields have to be printed in the sequence in which they appear in the record. An employee paycheck that has multiple output lines for a single record is another example of a detail report.

03/15/99		EMPLOYEE HOURS WEEK ENDING DATE: 03/12/99				PAGE 1
SHOP NUMBER	EMPLOYEE NAME	POSITION	REGULAR HOURS	OVERTIME HOURS	TOTAL HOURS	
8	Andres, Marguerite	Clerk	20.0	0.0	20.0	
8	Bogema, Michelle	Clerk	12.5	0.0	12.5	
8	Davenport, Kim	Asst Mgr	40.0	5.0	45.0	
8	Lemka, Susan	Clerk	32.7	0.0	32.7	
8	Linquist, Linda	Clerk	16.0	0.0	16.0	
8	Ramirez, Rudy	Manager	40.0	8.5	48.5	
8	Ullery, Ruth	Clerk	20.0	0.0	20.0	
11	Byrum, Cheri	Clerk	15.0	0.0	15.0	
11	Byrum, Mary	Clerk	15.0	0.0	15.0	
11	Deal, JoAnn	Clerk	4.8	0.0	4.8	
11	Gadzinski, Barbara	Manager	40.0	10.0	50.0	detail lines
11	Huyhn, Loc	Clerk	20.0	0.0	20.0	
11	Schuller, Monica	Clerk	10.0	0.0	10.0	
11	Stites, Carol	Clerk	40.0	12.0	52.0	
11	Thompson, Mary Kay	Asst Mgr	40.0	1.5	41.5	
17	De Martini, Jennifer	Clerk	40.0	8.4	48.4	
17	Haff, Lisa	Manager	40.0	0.0	40.0	
17	Rittenbery, Sandra	Clerk	40.0	11.0	51.0	
17	Wyer, Elizabeth	Clerk	20.0	0.0	20.0	
17	Zeigler, Cecille	Clerk	32.0	0.0	32.0	

Figure 6-13   A detail report, with one detail line per employee.

A well-designed detail report should include totals for numeric fields for control and accounting purposes. The report shown in Figure 6-13, for example, lacks grand totals of regular hours, overtime hours, total hours, and subtotals by shop.

Figure 6-14 shows the same report with subtotals and grand totals added. In this example, the shop number field is called a **control field**, because it controls the output. When the value of a control field changes, a **control break** occurs. A control break usually causes specific actions, such as printing subtotals. This type of report is called a **control break report**. To produce a control break report, the records *must* be sorted, or arranged, in proper order based on the control field. This ordering can be done by the report program or in a previous sort procedure.

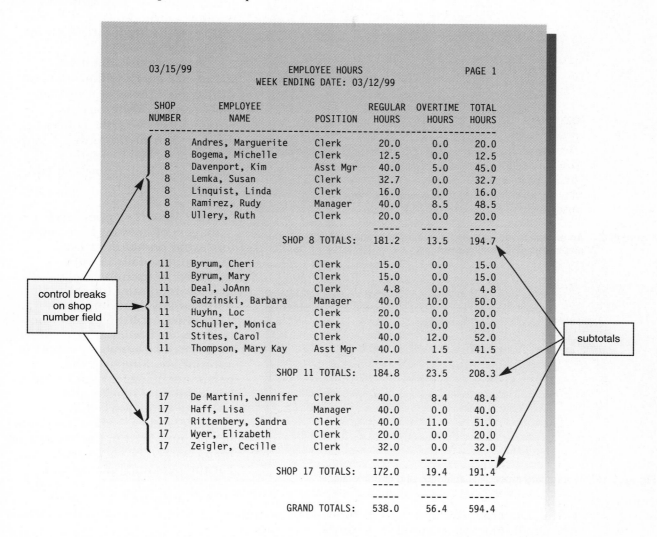

```
03/15/99                    EMPLOYEE HOURS                    PAGE 1
                       WEEK ENDING DATE: 03/12/99

     SHOP       EMPLOYEE                    REGULAR   OVERTIME   TOTAL
    NUMBER        NAME          POSITION     HOURS     HOURS     HOURS
    ----------------------------------------------------------------
      8      Andres, Marguerite   Clerk       20.0      0.0      20.0
      8      Bogema, Michelle     Clerk       12.5      0.0      12.5
      8      Davenport, Kim       Asst Mgr    40.0      5.0      45.0
      8      Lemka, Susan         Clerk       32.7      0.0      32.7
      8      Linquist, Linda      Clerk       16.0      0.0      16.0
      8      Ramirez, Rudy        Manager     40.0      8.5      48.5
      8      Ullery, Ruth         Clerk       20.0      0.0      20.0
                                             -----     -----    -----
                        SHOP 8 TOTALS:       181.2     13.5     194.7

     11      Byrum, Cheri         Clerk       15.0      0.0      15.0
     11      Byrum, Mary          Clerk       15.0      0.0      15.0
     11      Deal, JoAnn          Clerk        4.8      0.0       4.8
     11      Gadzinski, Barbara   Manager     40.0     10.0      50.0
     11      Huyhn, Loc           Clerk       20.0      0.0      20.0
     11      Schuller, Monica     Clerk       10.0      0.0      10.0
     11      Stites, Carol        Clerk       40.0     12.0      52.0
     11      Thompson, Mary Kay   Asst Mgr    40.0      1.5      41.5
                                             -----     -----    -----
                       SHOP 11 TOTALS:       184.8     23.5     208.3

     17      De Martini, Jennifer Clerk       40.0      8.4      48.4
     17      Haff, Lisa           Manager     40.0      0.0      40.0
     17      Rittenbery, Sandra   Clerk       40.0     11.0      51.0
     17      Wyer, Elizabeth      Clerk       20.0      0.0      20.0
     17      Zeigler, Cecille     Clerk       32.0      0.0      32.0
                                             -----     -----    -----
                       SHOP 17 TOTALS:       172.0     19.4     191.4
                                             -----     -----    -----
                                             -----     -----    -----
                        GRAND TOTALS:        538.0     56.4     594.4
```

control breaks on shop number field

subtotals

Figure 6-14   This detail report contains the same data as Figure 6-13, but provides more information. Control breaks are used to separate the data for each shop, with subtotals and grand totals for numeric fields.

Because it contains one or more lines for each record, a detail report can be quite lengthy. Consider, for example, a large auto parts business. If the firm stocks 3,000 parts, then the detail report would include 3,000 detail lines on approximately 50 printed pages. A user who wants to locate any part in short supply has to examine 3,000 detail lines to find the critical items. A much better alternative is to produce an exception report.

EXCEPTION REPORTS • An **exception report** shows only those records that meet a specific condition or conditions. Exception reports are useful when the user wants information only on records that might require action, but does not need to know the details. For example, a credit manager would use an exception report to identify only those

```
03/15/99              OVERTIME REPORT                PAGE 1
                 WEEK ENDING DATE:  03/12/99

  SHOP                          EMPLOYEE         OVERTIME
 NUMBER      POSITION             NAME             HOURS
-----------------------------------------------------------
   8        Asst Mgr        Davenport, Kim          5.0
            Manager         Ramirez, Rudy           8.5
                                                   -----

                              SHOP 8 TOTAL:        13.5

  11        Manager         Gadzinski, Barbara     10.0
            Clerk           Stites, Carol          12.0
            Asst Mgr        Thompson, Mary Kay      1.5
                                                   -----

                             SHOP 11 TOTAL:        23.5

  17        Clerk           De Martini, Jennifer    8.4
            Clerk           Rittenbery, Sandra     11.0
                                                   -----

                             SHOP 17 TOTAL:        19.4
                                                   -----
                                                   -----

                               GRAND TOTAL:        56.4
```

Figure 6-15   An exception report that shows information for *only* the employees who worked overtime.

```
03/15/99         EMPLOYEE HOURS SUMMARY       PAGE 1
             WEEK ENDING DATE:  03/12/99

    SHOP        REGULAR      OVERTIME      TOTAL
   NUMBER        HOURS         HOURS       HOURS
---------------------------------------------------
     8           181.2         13.5        194.7

     11          184.8         23.5        208.3

     17          172.0         19.4        191.4
        ------------------------------------------
 TOTALS:         538.0         56.4        594.4
```

Figure 6-16   A summary report lists subtotals and grand totals.

customers with past due accounts, or a customer service manager might want a report on all packages that were not delivered within a specified time period. Figure 6-15 shows an exception report that includes information for only those employees who worked overtime, instead of listing information for all employees.

As previously discussed, parameter queries allow users to display only those records that meet certain conditions or parameters. The same concept applies to printed reports. A parameter query can be used to determine which records should appear in a report.

SUMMARY REPORTS • Upper-level managers often want to see only totals and do not need the supporting details. A sales manager, for example, might want to know total sales for each sales representative, but might not want a detail report listing every sale made by each sales representative. In this case, a **summary report** is appropriate. Similarly, the personnel manager might need to know the total regular and overtime hours worked by employees in each shop but might not be interested in the number of hours worked by each employee. For the personnel manager, a summary report such as the one shown in Figure 6-16 is most useful. Generally, reports used by individuals at higher levels in the organization include less detail than reports used by lower-level employees.

Reports Classified by Distribution

In addition to classifying reports by the level of detail shown, a report can be classified by where it is distributed — either inside or outside of the organization.

INTERNAL REPORTS • **Internal reports** are distributed within the organization and rarely are sent outside the organization or seen by individuals who are not employees of the organization. The examples shown in Figures 6-13 through 6-16 on pages 6.18 through 6.20 are internal reports.

To avoid unnecessary expense, internal reports usually are printed on **stock paper**, which is blank, single-ply, standard-sized, continuous-form paper. Not only is stock paper less expensive than other types of paper, it can be used for a wide variety of reports to avoid the expense of changing paper each time a new report is run.

EXTERNAL REPORTS • External reports are distributed outside the organization. Statements, invoices, tax reports, paychecks, and mailing labels are examples of external reports.

External reports usually are printed on special forms instead of on stock paper. **Special forms** can include paper that is standard size and single-ply or paper that is preprinted with some type of information. Special forms typically are more expensive than stock paper, and the time needed to load and unload special forms from a printer creates an additional cost. Every time special forms are used for printing, a computer operator must stop the printer, remove the stock paper, insert and align the new forms, and restart the printer. When the printing is completed, the entire process is reversed. Multi-part forms also require an extra step, called **decollating**, to separate the copies after printing.

Because external reports are used outside the organization, they should be well-organized, useful, and professional in appearance. Invoices produced on special forms preprinted with the company's logo look much better than reports printed on plain paper. Most companies believe that the benefits of using preprinted forms far outweigh their higher costs. Figure 6-17 shows an example of a preprinted invoice form.

> For examples of different **Types of Reports**, visit Systems Analysis and Design Chapter 6 More on the Web.
>
> www.scsite.com/ sad3e/ch06/

HILL MACHINE WORKS, INC.
1033 BALDWIN STREET
TOLEDO, OH 42511

ORDER #:

ORDER DATE:

HILL

SOLD TO:

SHIP TO:

QUANTITY	PART #	PART DESCRIPTION	# SHIPPED	UNIT PRICE	AMOUNT
				SUBTOTAL	
				SALES TAX	
				TOTAL	

Figure 6-17   A sample of a preprinted invoice. The report program prints data in the correct location on the form.

For large applications such as catalog mailings, many companies use mailing labels printed on continuous sheets with one to four columns of gummed mailing labels. Some firms use special labels preprinted with the company logo and other information, as shown in Figure 6-18 on the next page. Many companies now use production laser printers that print customer mailing information directly on the brochure, catalog, or mailing envelope to avoid having to affix labels.

External requirements sometimes influence the format and paper used for external reports. Bank checks, such as the one shown in Figure 6-19 on the next page, must

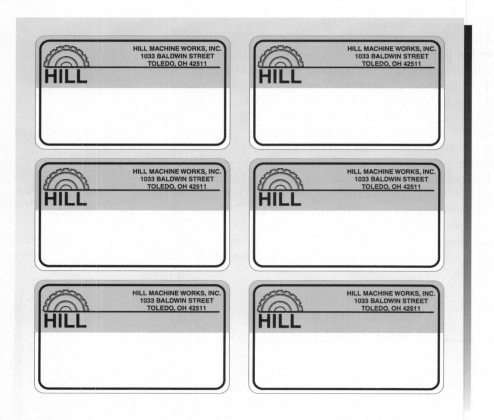

Figure 6-18 A sample preprinted mailing label. This form is called a two-up form because the form consists of two columns of labels.

PERIOD ENDING	# HRS	EARNINGS			DEDUCTIONS					NET AMOUNT	EMP #
		regular	overtime	total	fed. with.	F.I.C.A.	st. with.	cr. union	union dues		
YEAR TO DATE		EARNINGS			DEDUCTIONS					NET AMOUNT	
		regular	overtime	total	fed. with.	F.I.C.A.	st. with.	cr. union	union dues		

HILL MACHINE WORKS, INC.
1033 BALDWIN STREET
TOLEDO, OH 42511

7841

20-311
4256

HILL

Date: _____

Pay to the Order of _____ $ _____

_____ Dollars

1st Fidelity Bank   185 MAIN STREET
TOLEDO, OHIO 42510   (Not Negotiable)
■❙ 8903 >> 1552-4456 ◆ 7841❙

Figure 6-19 A sample preprinted paycheck.

conform to industry standards, and many government reports must be printed on special forms.

Designing the Report

Today, most reports are designed in a graphical environment with a choice of typefaces and scalable fonts, which gives the designer more freedom than a character-based environment. Many information systems, however, still use character-based reports that are produced on high-speed impact printers. These printers have fixed size fonts and lack the output flexibility of laser printers. For this reason, printer spacing charts still are used to design new reports and modify existing ones, although they are much less important as design tools. A **printer spacing chart**, as shown in Figure 6-20, is a grid of rows and columns that represents the lines and positions on a page of printer paper. Most high-speed impact printers provide up to 132 characters per line, so printer spacing charts must include at least that many positions.

Printer spacing charts provide a standard method for visually documenting a report so programmers can use them when writing the report program. To design a report, you decide where a specific field will be printed and

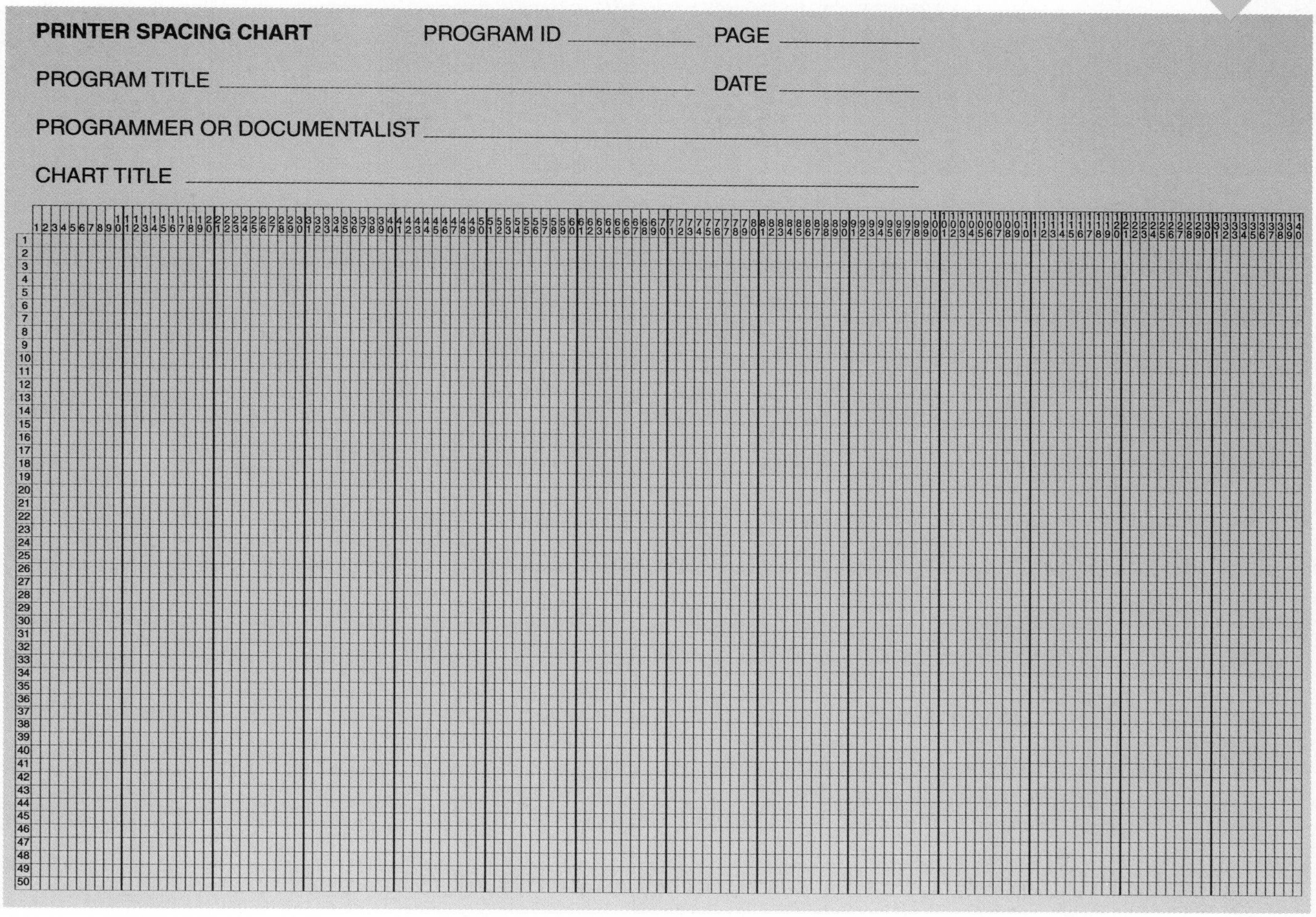

Figure 6-20   A printer spacing chart.

then mark the boxes on the chart. You can specify constant information, such as titles and headings, by entering it on the chart exactly as it will appear on the printed page. In Figure 6-21 on the next page, the column headings LAST NAME, FIRST NAME, AGE, and BIRTH DATE appear on the first print line.

You indicate print positions for variable information by entering a standard format code to show the output requirements and field sizes. In Figure 6-21, the third and fifth lines on the printer spacing chart show variable output specifications for the detail lines on the report. The first output field on line 3 is a 15-character field named LAST NAME. The format specification for that field is written as XXXXXXXXXXXXXXX. The second output field, FIRST NAME, has 10 characters, so the format specification is written as XXXXXXXXXX. You also can write long, alphanumeric formats by marking the first and last positions with an X and connecting the Xs with a line. For example, you can indicate the FIRST NAME field as X————————X.

The third field on the detail line is a two-digit field named AGE. In Figure 6-21, the format is written as Z9; the Z indicates that any leading zero in the age is to be suppressed. The fourth field is a six-digit field named BIRTH DATE; its format is Z9/99/99.

Notice that the specification for the fifth line is identical to that of the third line. The information was repeated to indicate the line spacing desired. The fourth line was left blank to tell the programmer that the detail lines should be double-spaced. The detail line specifications appear on consecutive lines to indicate single-spacing.

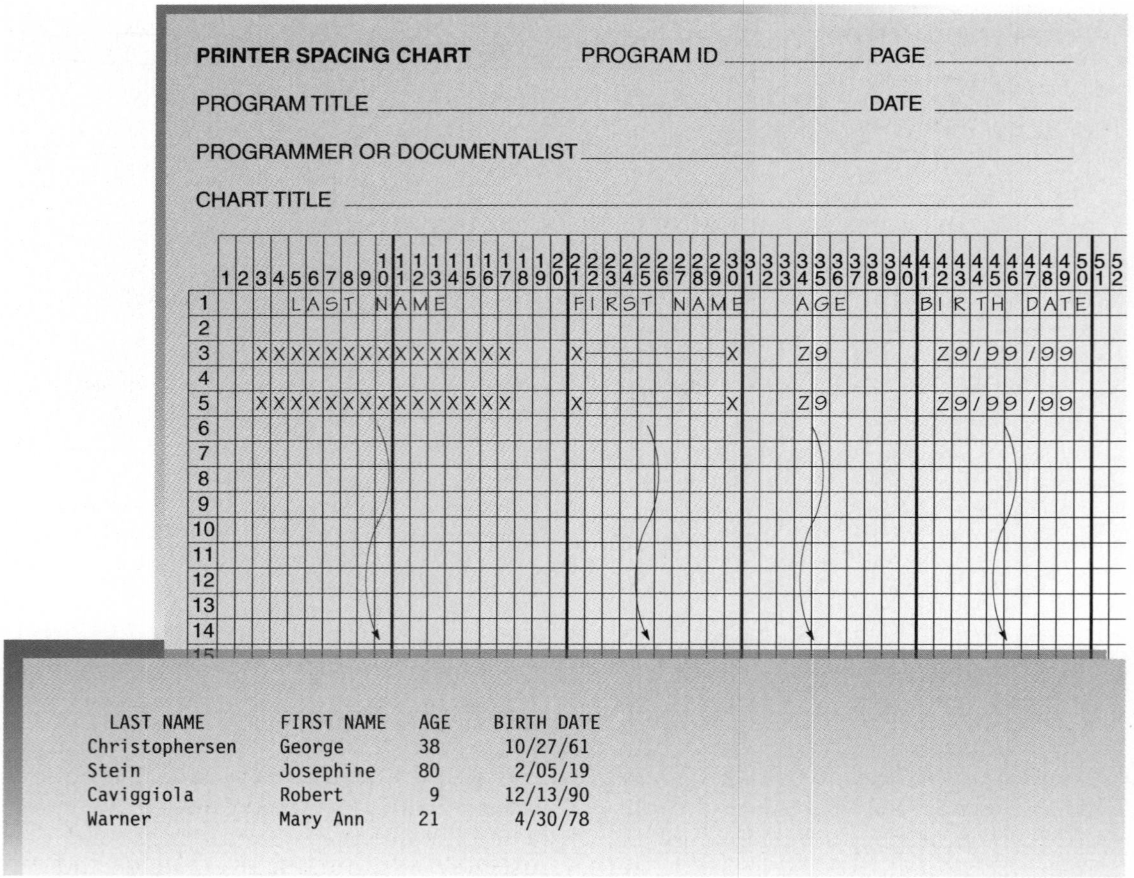

Figure 6-21 A printer spacing chart and report sample, with both constant and variable information.

The wavy vertical lines drawn under each output field on the fifth line indicate that detail line output continues using the same format. Thus, a third detail line with the same format specifications would be printed on line 7 of the report, a fourth on line 9, and so on.

In addition to showing line spacing, you must show detail line information when other output, such as totals, will follow that line. If reports span multiple pages, you should prepare charts for the following pages if they differ from the first report page.

STOCK PAPER REPORTS • Several principles apply when designing a stock paper report so it will be attractive and easy to understand and use.

Page heading lines. Because stock paper is blank, the report program must generate the title and heading lines. Every page should include the report title and identification code, the page number, the printing date, and the time if the report is produced more than once a day. The information that uniquely identifies a report is called a **page header**.

Column heading lines. Column headings identify the data below each column name and should be short and descriptive. You should avoid abbreviations unless they are understood easily by users.

Column heading alignment. Figure 6-22 shows several column heading alignment options. In Example 1, the left-justified column headings do not work well with numeric fields because the amount 1.25 would print past the right edge of the AMOUNT heading. In Example 2, the right-justified headings cause a problem with alphanumeric fields, because none of the characters in a short name would print under any part of the

Example 1: Column headings are left-justified over maximum field widths.	NAME XXXXXXXXXXXXXXXXXXXXXXXX	NUMBER ZZZ9	AMOUNT ZZZ,ZZ9.99
Example 2: Column headings are right-justified over maximum field widths.	NAME XXXXXXXXXXXXXXXXXXXXXXXX	NUMBER ZZZ9	AMOUNT ZZZ,ZZ9.99
Example 3: Column headings are centered over maximum field widths.	NAME XXXXXXXXXXXXXXXXXXXXXXXX	NUMBER ZZZ9	AMOUNT ZZZ,ZZ9.99
Example 4: Column headings are centered over average field widths.	NAME XXXXXXXXXXXXXXXXXXXXXXXX	NUMBER ZZZ9	AMOUNT ZZZ,ZZ9.99
Example 5: Column headings are left-justified over alphanumeric fields and right-justified over numeric fields.	NAME XXXXXXXXXXXXXXXXXXXXXXXX	NUMBER ZZZ9	AMOUNT ZZZ,ZZ9.99

Figure 6-22   Five different column heading alignment options.

NAME heading. Centering headings over *maximum* field widths, as shown in Example 3, is not ideal when many of the actual values are shorter than the maximum width. Most experienced designers prefer Example 4, which centers headings over *average* field widths or Example 5, where headings are left-justified over alphanumeric fields and right-justified over numeric fields.

Some designers use a combination of these techniques by centering headings for alphanumeric fields over average field widths, right-justifying headings over shorter numeric fields, and centering headings over average widths for larger numeric fields.

Spacing between columns. Columns of information should be spaced carefully. A crowded report is hard to read, and large gaps between columns make it difficult for the eye to follow a line. Placing two or three positions between columns and headings usually works well to correct this problem.

Sometimes enough print positions are not available on the page. What are your options?

When space permits printing all detail values, but there is not enough room for full column headings, you can print a legend at the bottom of each page that explains the headings. This solution usually requires that you reserve two or three lines of every page for the legend.

When there is enough width for the detail values, but not enough room for subtotal or grand total lines, you can print the subtotals and totals on the following lines. For example, consider a report with sales figures for each of 12 months on every detail line. A detail line contains just enough room to fit the three-digit monthly sales detail values. How should you print the monthly subtotals and grand totals? You could use the entire page width and as many lines as you need to present the subtotals or totals, captioning each one individually, such as JAN TOTAL: ZZ,ZZ9, FEB TOTAL: ZZ,ZZ9, and so on, as shown in Figure 6-23. Or, as shown in Figure 6-24, you could use two lines for the subtotals and totals and then print the values for the odd-numbered months on one line and the values for the even-numbered months on a second line.

What should you do when there are not enough positions on one line to print the detail values? One possible solution is to split the report into two or more versions, as shown in Figure 6-25. Each report version would include only as many detail values that fit on a single line. The output will be attractive and readable, but readers will need to refer to several versions.

Figure 6-26 on page 6.28 shows a second potential solution, which is to print all the information in a single report using two or more single-spaced print lines for each detail. This solution requires that you stack column headings for all the detail lines at the top of each page, with a blank line between each detail set. The advantage is that a single report contains all the information needed by any user. Reading a multiline report is difficult. You can reduce confusion and improve readability by stacking alphanumeric fields over numeric fields and vice versa.

Figure 6-27 on page 6.28 shows a third solution that uses a single set of column headings for the identifying fields, followed by a set of single-spaced print lines for each detail. On the first line, the identifying fields are printed with left captions, such as ITEM#: XXXXX ITEM DESCRIPTION: XXXXXXXXXXXXXXXXXXXXX. The rest of the detail values are printed on the second line and aligned under their column headings. This solution has the advantage of producing a single report with all the information and is less confusing.

Each of these three approaches has advantages and disadvantages. You should try each solution to see which one will be the most readable by users.

A KEY QUESTION

Lynn Jennings is the IS manager at Lazy Eddie, a chain that specializes in beanbag chairs and recliners. She asked Jan Lauten, a senior systems analyst, to review the large number of printed reports that are distributed to Lazy Eddie's 35 store managers. "Jan, I just can't believe that our people really read all of these reports," Lynn said. "We constantly add new reports, and we never seem to eliminate the old ones. Sometimes I think all we're doing is keeping the paper companies in business!"

Jan replied, "I agree, but what can we do? The managers say they want the reports, but I always see them stacked on top of file cabinets. I've never seen anyone read a report."

"I have an idea," Lynn said. "I want you to come up with a procedure that requires users to review and justify their information needs to see if they really use the reports we send them. You could design a form that asks whether the information still is required, and why. Try to get users to decide whether a report is worth the cost of producing it. Do you think you can do it?"

"Sure I can," Jan replied. When Jan returned to her office, she wondered where to begin. What advice would you give to Jan?

```
01/15/99                          ITEM SALES ANALYSIS                                    PAGE 1

                 UNIT  SELLING --------------------MONTHLY SALES--------------------------YEARLY
ITEM# ITEM DESCRIPTION     COST  PRICE   JAN  FEB  MAR  APR  MAY  JUN  JUL  AUG  SEP  OCT  NOV  DEC   TOTAL
----------------------------------------------------------------------------------------------------

218CW CHROME WIDGET              1.23   8.95  241  134  198  180  187  294  295  159  268  352  378  400   3,086
227DS DOUBLE-TWISTED ANGLE STOPPER 11.20 34.80  0   80  270  512  717  732  882  890  735  913  901  879   7,511
                .                  .              .              .              .
                .                  .              .              .              .
                .                  .              .              .              .
297PB PLASTIC BASE                .87   5.98  812  801  813  860  501  981  992  879  899  888  940  979  10,345

        ITEM CLASS SUBTOTALS:  JAN TOTAL:  21,916   APR TOTAL:  24,003   JUL TOTAL:  25,027   OCT TOTAL:  25,897
                               FEB TOTAL:  22,113   MAY TOTAL:  20,880   AUG TOTAL:  23,632   NOV TOTAL:  25,371
                               MAR TOTAL:  24,291   JUN TOTAL:  24,765   SEP TOTAL:  24,111   DEC TOTAL:  24,669

                                                                            YEARLY TOTAL:  286,675
```

Figure 6-23 A report designed with subtotals and captions printed on multiple lines.

```
01/15/99                          ITEM SALES ANALYSIS                                    PAGE 1

                 UNIT  SELLING --------------------MONTHLY SALES--------------------------YEARLY
ITEM# ITEM DESCRIPTION     COST  PRICE   JAN  FEB  MAR  APR  MAY  JUN  JUL  AUG  SEP  OCT  NOV  DEC   TOTAL
----------------------------------------------------------------------------------------------------

218CW CHROME WIDGET              1.23   8.95  241  134  198  180  187  294  295  159  268  352  378  400   3,086
227DS DOUBLE-TWISTED ANGLE STOPPER 11.20 34.80  0   80  270  512  717  732  882  890  735  913  901  879   7,511
297PB PLASTIC BASE                .87   5.98  812  801  813  860  501  981  992  879  899  888  940  979  10,345

        ITEM CLASS SUBTOTALS:         21,916    24,291    20,880    25,027    24,111    25,371    286,675
                                          22,113    24,003    24,765    23,632    25,897    24,669
```

Figure 6-24 A report designed with subtotals printed on alternating lines to reduce the print width.

subtotals on alternating lines

```
01/15/99                          ITEM SALES ANALYSIS                                    PAGE 1

                 UNIT  SELLING --------------------MONTHLY SALES--------------------------YEARLY
ITEM# ITEM DESCRIPTION     COST  PRICE   JAN  FEB  MAR  APR  MAY  JUN  JUL  AUG  SEP  OCT  NOV  DEC   TOTAL
----------------------------------------------------------------------------------------------------

218CW CHROME WIDGET              1.23   8.95  241  134  198  180  187  294  295  159  268  352  378  400   3,086
227DS DOUBLE-TWISTED ANGLE STOPPER 11.20 34.80  0   80  270  512  717  732  882  890  735  913  901  879   7,511
```

```
01/15/99                          ITEM SALES ANALYSIS               PAGE 1

               QTY ON     QTY      QTY     QTY ON  UNIT   SELLING
ITEM# ITEM DESCRIPTION    HAND  ALLOCATED  AVAILABLE  ORDER  COST    PRICE
------------------------------------------------------------------------

218CW CHROME WIDGET               183      4        179       300   1.23    8.95
227DS DOUBLE-TWISTED ANGLE STOPPER 322    121       201       500  11.20   34.80
```

the two sections must be joined to create a complete report

Figure 6-25 A report that is split into two sections because the detail values cannot fit on one print line.

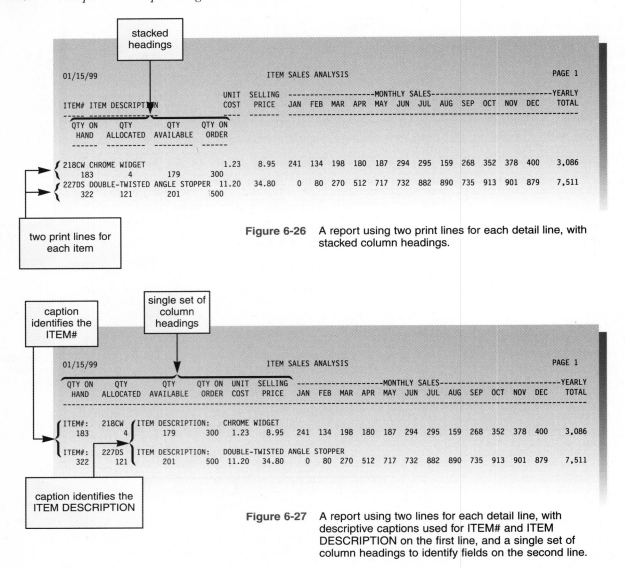

Figure 6-26 A report using two print lines for each detail line, with stacked column headings.

Figure 6-27 A report using two lines for each detail line, with descriptive captions used for ITEM# and ITEM DESCRIPTION on the first line, and a single set of column headings to identify fields on the second line.

Order of data items on detail lines. Reports generally are read from left to right, so the order of items on the detail line should be presented in the same order. If one or more fields identify the detail line, they should appear first. Logically related items should be grouped. The report shown in Figure 6-28, for example, shows detail lines printed in alphabetical order within shop number, so the shop number is in the left column, followed by the employee name. The employee position relates to the name, so the items are printed together. The hours information also is grouped.

Grouping detail lines. If detail groups are meaningful, they should be highlighted in some way. You can print a special heading above the first detail line and a footer after the last detail line in a group. In some report programs, these headings are called **group headers** and **group footers**.

The report shown in Figure 6-28 consists of three footing lines for each shop. In the first footing line, hyphens serve as a visual clue to the totals printed below them. In the second footing line, the group totals for these fields are printed. To identify the line as a group total line, the words, SHOP *nn* TOTALS: also are printed. The third group footing line is just a blank line that serves to separate a group from the one that follows.

Report footing. Every stock paper report that includes more than one printed page should have a report footing to identify the end of the report. A **report footing**, together with consecutive page numbers on every page, ensures that report users have a complete copy of the report. A report footing might include field totals, as shown in Figure 6-28, or the footing can be as simple as a line that indicates, END OF REPORT.

Improving a report design. The Employee Hours report shown in Figure 6-28 has met each of the design considerations discussed, but it still could be improved. Too much detail is contained on the page, forcing readers to search for the information they need. Can you see any material that could be eliminated?

If most employees do not work overtime, then overtime hours should stand out. You can do this by *not* printing 0.0 when overtime hours are zero. Repeating the same shop number for all employees of each shop also is unnecessary. Finally, most of the employees in a shop are clerks. The managers and assistant manager titles would stand out better if the word, Clerk, is not printed for all clerical employees. These changes have been made in Figure 6-29. The name and position columns also were exchanged to avoid a large gap between clerk names and clerk hours.

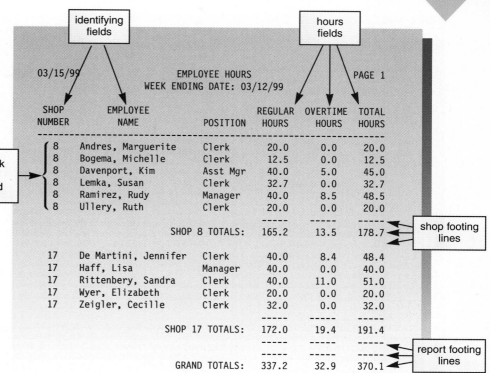

Figure 6-28   The Employee Hours report is a detail report with control breaks. Subtotals and totals are included for appropriate numeric fields.

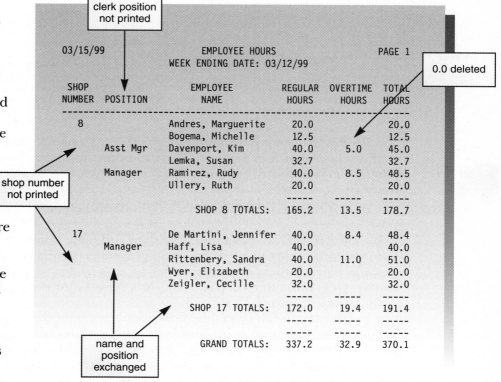

Figure 6-29   An improved version of the Employee Hours report shown in Figure 6-28.

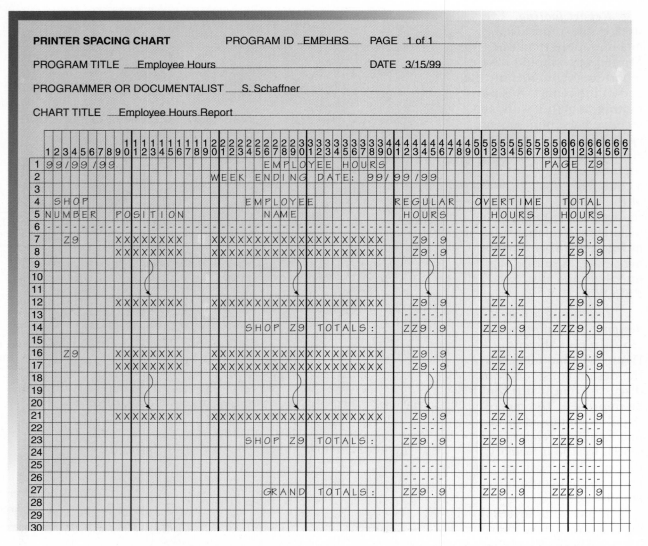

Figure 6-30 The printer spacing chart for the Employee Hours report shown in Figure 6-29 on the previous page.

Documenting a report design. Figure 6-30 shows the final printer spacing chart for the report shown in Figure 6-29 on the previous page. After a report design is finished and approved, you must document the design in a **report analysis form**, as shown in Figure 6-31.

Design consistency. Good design standards produce reports that are uniform and consistent. When several reports are produced by a single system, each report should have a similar style. For example, the date and page numbers should print in the same place on each report page. Abbreviations used in reports should be consistent. For example, when indicating a number value, it is confusing for one report to use #, another NO, and a third NUM. Items in a report also should be consistent. If one report prints inventory location fields as floor number followed by bin number, then printing bin number followed by floor number on another report creates confusion.

Most of the design principles for stock paper reports also apply to reports on preprinted or special forms, with a few exceptions. For example, heading information usually is preprinted for reports such as bank checks, invoices, and customized mailing labels, or it is not necessary for some reports, such as blank mailing labels.

SYSTEM DOCUMENTATION

NAME OF SYSTEM	DATE	PAGE 1 OF 1
payroll	April 5, 1999	

ANALYST	PURPOSE OF DOCUMENTATION
S. Schaffner	Report Analysis-Employee Hours Report

FIELD	FIELD TYPE	FIELD LENGTH
Shop Number	Numeric	2
Employee Position	Alphanumeric	8
Employee Name	Alphanumeric	20
Regular Hours	Numeric	3 (1 decimal position)
Overtime Hours	Numeric	3 (1 decimal position)
Total Hours	Numeric	3 (1 decimal position)

COMMENTS

Week ending date is printed at the top of the report.
Detail lines are in order by employee name within shop number.
Shop totals for regular, overtime, and total hours are printed, identified by Shop Number.
Grand totals for regular, overtime, and total hours are printed.

Shop Number is printed only for the first employee detail line for a shop and for the first employee detail line on a page.

Employee Position is printed only for nonclerks. If Employee Position is equal to "Clerk", eight blank characters are printed.

Only nonzero Overtime Hours are printed. If Overtime Hours is equal to 0.0, four blank characters are printed.

The report is printed on single-ply, standard white stock paper.

FREQUENCY

The report is printed weekly on the first working day of the week or before 10:00 a.m. on the second working day of the week.

DISTRIBUTION

The report is to be delivered to the director of personnel no later than 11:00 a.m. of the second working day of each week.

ATTACHMENTS

Printer spacing chart and mock-up report are attached.

Figure 6-31   The report analysis form for the Employee Hours report shown in Figure 6-29 on page 6.29.

SPECIAL FORM REPORTS • Special form output, such as blank paper reports, consists of detail lines, subtotals, and totals. You can use a printer spacing chart to indicate the format and position of output fields, just as you would for stock paper reports. First, you would draw the outline of the form with any preprinted information in its proper position. Then, you indicate where the variable information will be printed, just as you do for stock paper reports. For example, Figure 6-32 shows a printer spacing chart for the preprinted invoice shown in Figure 6-17 on page 6.21. A systems analyst drew the form outline and then identified the placement of the logo, title, and heading to match how these items appear on the form. Then output fields and format specifications were placed on the chart in the proper positions.

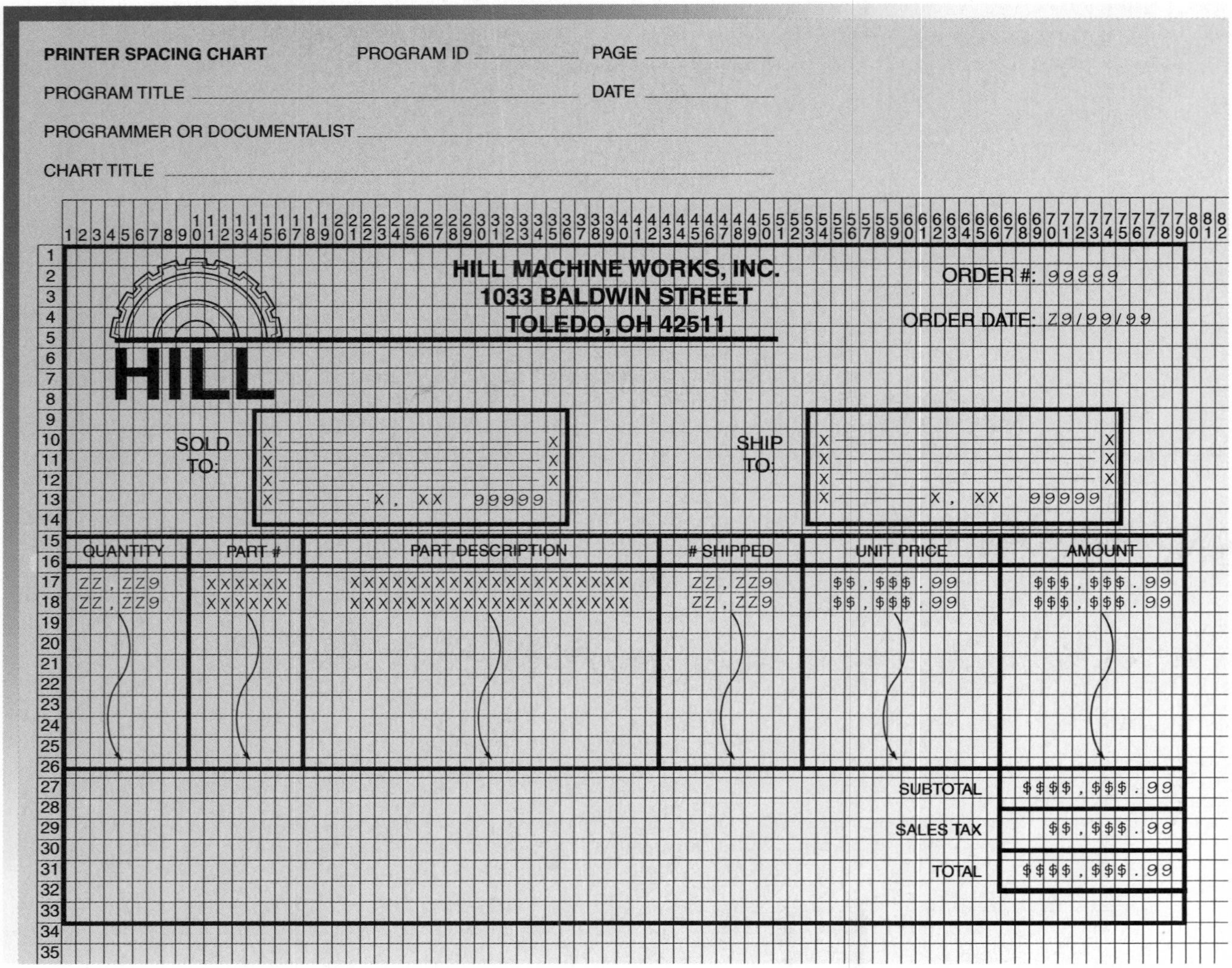

Figure 6-32   The printer spacing chart for the preprinted invoices shown in Figure 6-17 on page 6.21.

The functional and aesthetic design principles for stock paper reports also apply to preprinted forms. Your field labels should be short but descriptive and avoid nonstandard abbreviations. Use reasonable spacing between columns for better readability. The order and placement of printed fields should be logical, and totals should be identified clearly.

When designing a preprinted form, you should contact the forms vendor or printer for advice on paper sizes, type styles and sizes, paper and ink colors, field placement, and other important form details. Your goal is to design a form that is attractive, readable, and useful, at the lowest possible cost. To reduce expense, you might be able to use a standard invoice form on which your company logo can be printed instead of designing a new form.

Report Volume and Time Calculations

As a systems analyst, you must determine whether printing capacity is adequate for reports generated by the system. Efficient printing operations, timely delivery of finished reports, and accurate forecasts of paper and storage needs all depend on accurate estimates of print volumes and times. You also will need to consider the specifications of the printer being used, the length of the report, and the type of output that is required.

TYPES OF PRINTERS • Although the majority of companies use laser printers for business reports and documents, many organizations still use high-speed impact printers for certain types of reports, invoices, checks, labels, and other high-volume requirements, especially if multiple copies are needed. Companies that produce large mailing lists use production laser printers to print information directly on the mailing piece. You must consider the volume, printing time, and overall costs when selecting the best printer. To compare alternatives, you should calculate a cost per copy that takes into account the cost of paper, supplies (such as toner), and other expenses.

ON THE NET

You can obtain information about high-speed printers by searching the Web. You can start with a general search for printer information and then narrow your search by adding more specific terms. Make a list of at least three companies, their URLs, and examples of products they offer.

PRINT VOLUME CALCULATIONS • After completing the report design, it is important to estimate the length of the report. For example, consider the Employee Hours report shown in Figure 6-29 on page 6.29. Assume that this company has a total of 380 employees in six shops. The stock paper will have 66 lines per page. Six lines are reserved for the top and bottom margins, leaving 60 printed lines per page. In this report, every page begins with six lines of heading information. This leaves 54 lines per page for printing employee detail lines, shop footing lines, and grand total footing lines.

Because there are 380 employees, 380 detail lines will print. Each of the six shops has three footing lines, for a total of 18 shop footing lines. Finally, the grand total requires three additional lines. The complete report will include 401 detail and total lines. At 54 lines per page, the report will require 7.4 pages. Therefore, the final estimate for the paper requirements for this weekly report is eight printed pages per week. Figure 6-33 on the next page shows these volume calculations.

CALCULATING THE LENGTH OF THE REPORT

	66	total lines available per page of stock paper
-	6	lines reserved for top and bottom margins
-	6	lines per page for 2 title lines, 1 blank line, 2 column heading lines, and 1 hyphen line
	54	available detail lines per page
	3	lines per shop for 1 line with hyphens, 1 line of shop totals, and 1 blank line
X	6	shops
	18	shop footing lines
+	3	lines per report for 2 lines with hyphens and 1 line of grand totals
	21	footing lines
+	380	detail lines
	401	report lines
÷	54	lines per page
	7.4	**printed pages**

Figure 6-33   Report volume calculations for the Employee Hours report shown in Figure 6-29 on page 6.29.

Figure 6-34   Printer manufacturers provide a pages-per-minute (ppm) rating that you can use to estimate printing time.

PRINT-TIME CALCULATIONS • You also can estimate the time required to print the report. If the high-speed laser printer shown in Figure 6-34 is used to print a report, you can estimate the time by using the printer's **ppm rating**, which represents the number of pages printed per minute. For example, at 12 ppm, a laser printer would print the eight-page Employee Hours report in about 40 seconds. If the report is printed on a line printer with a speed of 2,000 lines per minute, you would divide 401 lines by 2,000 lines per minute, for a total time of .20 minutes, or 12 seconds of printing time.

The paper requirements and printer time calculations for a much larger report are shown in Figure 6-35. This example dramatically shows the value of volume and time estimates. Imagine the problems that might occur when the report is printed for the first time if no one estimated that it would take nearly 19 hours to print 38,889 pages.

Both of the time calculation examples are for reports printed on stock paper. If special forms are used, the calculation process is similar, but you must add a time factor for loading and unloading the forms. Also, if you use multiple-part forms, you must estimate the time needed to separate the pages.

Report Approvals

Printed reports are an important way of delivering information to users, so recipients should approve all report designs in advance. To avoid major problems, you should submit each design for approval as you complete it, rather than waiting until you finish all report designs.

When designing a report, you should prepare a mock-up, or prototype, for users to review. The **mock-up** should include sample field values with enough records to show all the design features. Depending on the type of printed output, you can use a word processor, a report generator, or a printer spacing chart to create mock-up reports. You might have to submit several designs to satisfy user requirements, but it is better to make changes in the design process now, rather than later, when the system is operational.

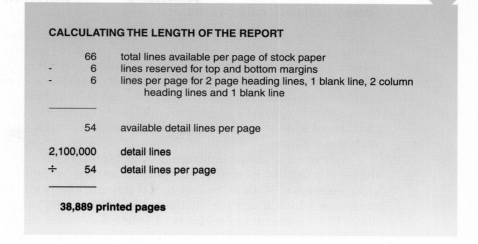

CALCULATING THE LENGTH OF THE REPORT

66	total lines available per page of stock paper	
- 6	lines reserved for top and bottom margins	
- 6	lines per page for 2 page heading lines, 1 blank line, 2 column heading lines and 1 blank line	
54	available detail lines per page	
2,100,000	detail lines	
÷ 54	detail lines per page	
38,889 printed pages		

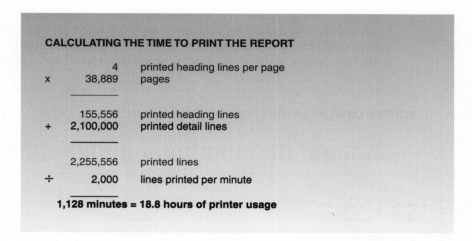

CALCULATING THE TIME TO PRINT THE REPORT

4	printed heading lines per page	
x 38,889	pages	
155,556	printed heading lines	
+ 2,100,000	printed detail lines	
2,255,556	printed lines	
÷ 2,000	lines printed per minute	
1,128 minutes = 18.8 hours of printer usage		

Figure 6-35   Report volume calculations for a monthly report of 2,100,000 customer accounts.

DESIGNING SCREEN OUTPUT

I n today's dynamic business world, decisions are made quickly. In most organizations, people have access to personal computers or terminals that provide up-to-date information to support company operations and objectives.

Screen output offers several major advantages over printed output, the most important of which is timeliness. A user can view a report within seconds, instead of hours or days, and the output can reflect current information. Because it is available instantly, screen output can be produced when and where it is needed.

Screen Design Considerations

Many of the design principles for printed output also apply to screen design. For example, screens should be visually attractive and easy to read. You should present information logically and consistently, and clearly identify all output items.

Screen output has one requirement that is not needed for printed reports — you must provide onscreen instructions for users about how to use the display. In many cases, several actions will be available, and the choices must be easy to understand. On character-based screens, the top or the bottom screen display line usually is reserved for such instructions.

You need to communicate messages to users on a screen display. If a user presses the wrong key, for example, you might want the system to display an error message and offer assistance. With character-based screens, the bottom line typically is reserved for messages, which limits the available screen space to an area of about 80 columns by 22 lines. Error messages also can be displayed in boxes on the screen.

For character-based screen design, systems analysts use a special screen display layout form, such as the one shown in Figure 6-36. The form consists of 80 columns and 24 lines, matching the 80 x 24 line limits of most standard character-based screens. If you are designing output for a screen with more columns or lines, or if screen design layout forms are not available, you can mark the necessary screen limits on a printer spacing chart. When designing graphical screens, analysts usually plot screen locations by using inches, metric values, or special measurement units instead of columns and lines.

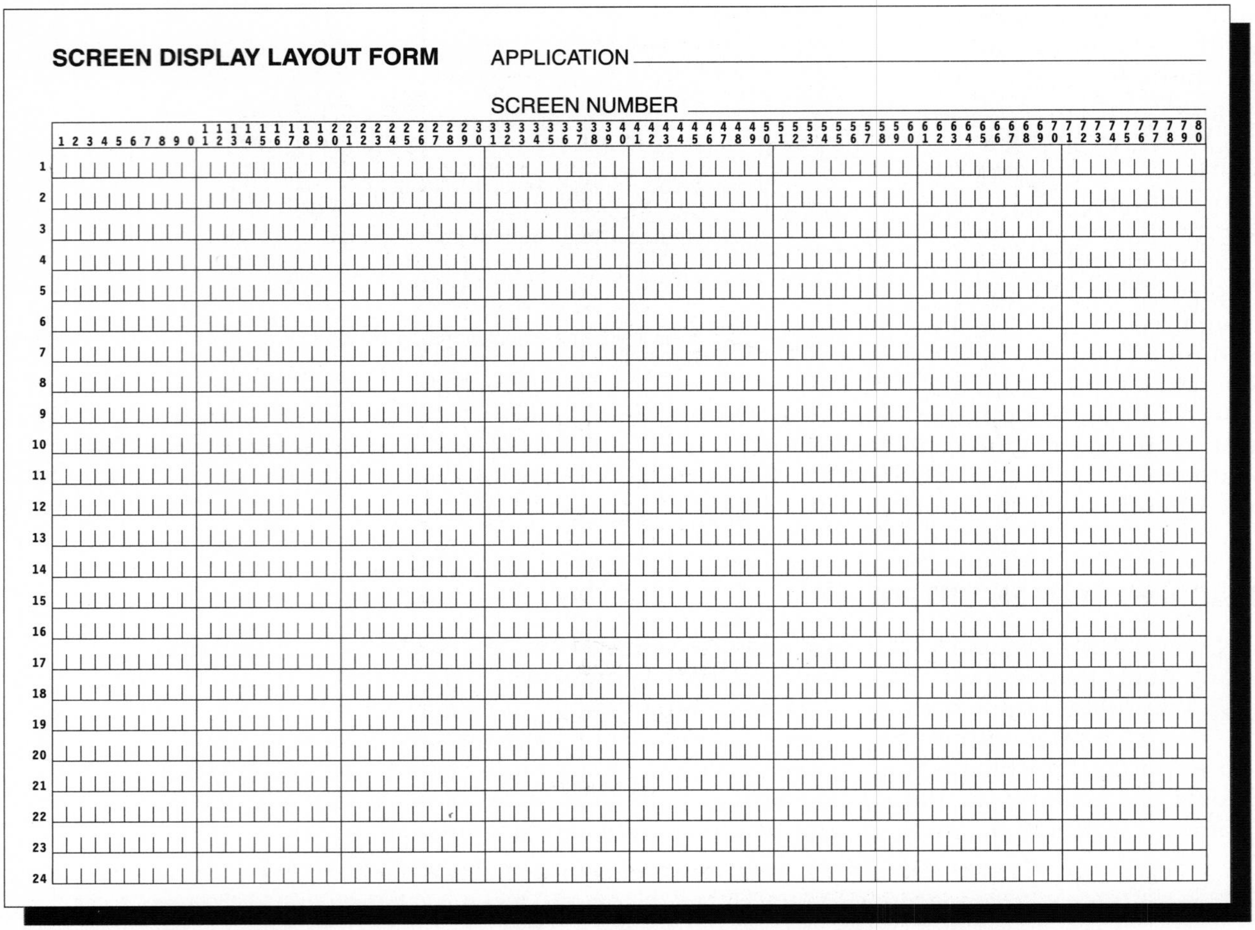

Figure 6-36 A sample screen display layout form.

Character Output

When designing traditional character-based screens, the systems analyst was limited to an 80-column format. Now, with scalable fonts and graphical displays, these constraints no longer apply, but some important limitations still exist. Because users will get information from the screen, the display must be clear and easy to read. Even when users have high-resolution monitors, the analyst still must choose fonts and typefaces carefully. Some screen design guidelines are discussed later in this chapter and also in Chapter 7.

A complete screen report is shown in Figure 6-37. The screen display is similar to the printed version of the report, except the column headings on the screen display on a single line.

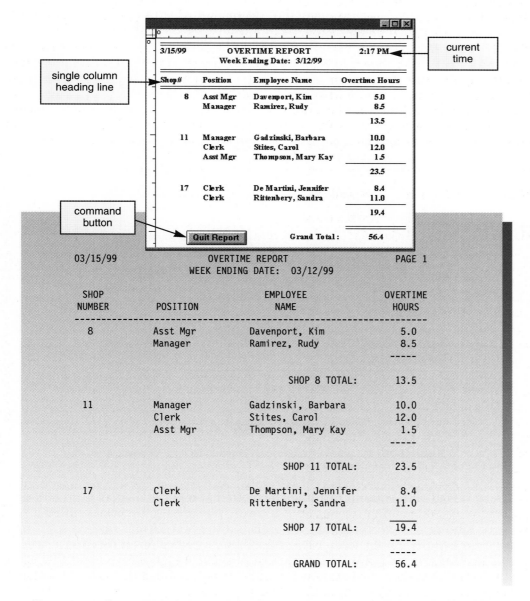

Figure 6-37   A screen version and a printed report version of an exception report that lists employees who worked overtime.

Because a screen is smaller than a printed page, you might have to rearrange the information. The report shown in Figure 6-37 on the previous page was small enough to fit on a single screen, with some minor charges in the column headings. In other cases, you might have to create several screens to display the information from a single printed page. Another difference is the command button at the bottom of the screen. In this case, only one action is available — when the user is finished with the report, clicking the Quit Report button clears the screen and displays another menu.

Single-screen reports, such as the one shown in Figure 6-37, are not typical. The printed report shown in Figure 6-37, for example, would fit across a screen but is too long to fit on a single screen. A solution might be to show information for only one shop per screen. The full report would use as many screens as there are shops, and you would provide options to allow users to move from one shop display to another.

Sometimes an entire screen is needed to display information for a single record. Figure 6-38 shows a screen display for a single inventory item. Notice that this screen layout is different from those used in printed reports. The field captions display to the left of the fields instead of in column headings, and the fields are presented vertically instead of horizontally.

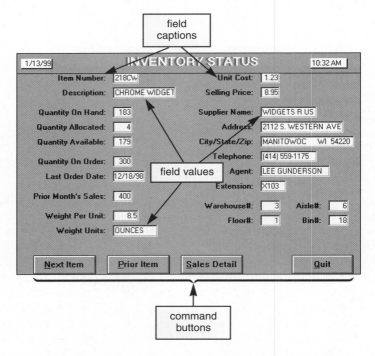

Figure 6-38   A sample screen report showing all data for a single inventory item.

A screen layout with column headings formatted across the display is an efficient way of presenting information for multiple records. This design format is called a **columnar** or **tabular** design. A tabular design is not the best format when displaying information for a single entity, such as an individual customer or an inventory item.

Figure 6-39 shows several different ways to present the information. Option 1 uses column headings, and the other options use left captions. Notice that all five options require five screen lines to display the information, but Option 1 requires more columns. Because screen space is limited, a presentation that requires less space generally is better. When you want to display only one field value for each caption, left captions are the best choice.

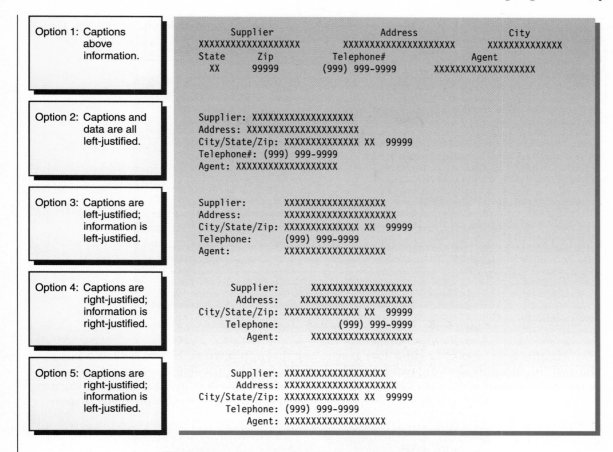

Figure 6-39   Five examples of screen presentation options.

Options 2 through 5, shown in Figure 6-40 on the next page, show various ways of aligning left captions and field values. Most users feel that Option 5 is the easiest to read, because it uses right-justified captions and left-justified field values. This method is shown in Figure 6-40.

Notice the command buttons at the bottom of the screen shown in Figure 6-40. The user has four options: display the values for the previous or the following inventory item, display a graph of the prior year's sales detail for the current item, or terminate the program. If the screen for the prior year is selected, a command button is needed to return the user to the original screen. Two display screens are needed because the information for an item does not fit on a single screen. When multiple screens are required for a single item, you must provide a way for the user to move from one screen to another.

Graphical Output

So far you have seen character information displayed on a screen, but many workstations also can display information graphically. For example, look at the screen shown in Figure 6-40. The top of the screen includes character information from Figure 6-39. The bottom of the screen includes a table that shows units sold by each store for each month. The table displays the data clearly, but assume that users also would like to see the data represented in a graph. If the user clicks the Graph button, a chart of the data displays.

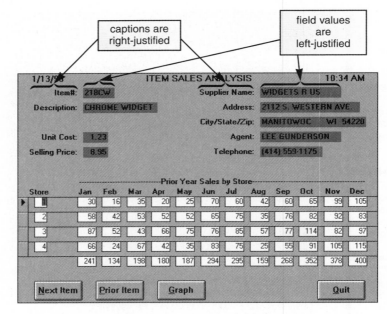

Figure 6-40 A tabular presentation of sales information on a screen.

Figures 6-41 and 6-42 show two graphs for this application. Figure 6-41 is a bar chart of the monthly sales figures for each store. Notice that the legend identifies which pattern represents each store. Figure 6-42 shows a line graph of total sales for all stores for each month. Both screens have a Table button that returns to the previous display.

For information on designing **Graphical Output**, visit Systems Analysis and Design Chapter 6 More on the Web.

www.scsite.com/ sad3e/ch06/

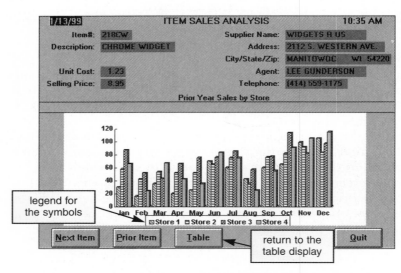

Figure 6-41 A bar chart presentation of the sales information in Figure 6-40.

Many graphic formats are possible, including pie charts, maps, bar charts, area charts, and scatter diagrams. Regardless of the style you choose, remember to give the chart a descriptive title, label each axis, and include a legend to explain any symbols or shapes.

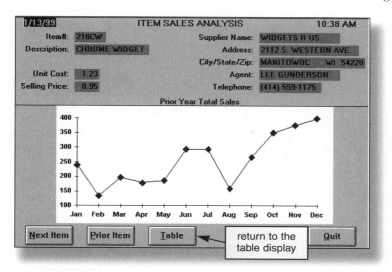

Figure 6-42   A line graph of the sales information in Figure 6-40.

Special Effects

You can add special video or audio effects to screen displays. On older character-based systems, selected areas of the screen could be highlighted by using high brightness, blinking, reverse video (swapping the text and background colors), and displaying different colors for emphasis. A modern graphical environment provides many more possibilities, including command buttons, boxes and borders, unlimited use of color, and other special features, such as custom menus, icons, and multiple windows. Several of these effects are shown in Figure 6-43.

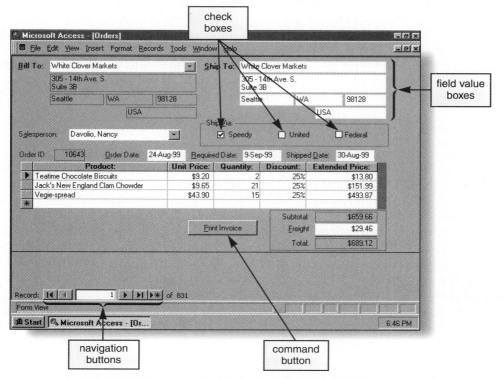

Figure 6-43   Sample screen that displays information about current orders. The screen includes a command button, check boxes, and navigation buttons that help the user move around the screen.

In addition to video effects, you can use sound to attract the user's attention or to provide information. In the most common use of audio effects, the system alerts a user with a beep or other sound. Many commercial packages allow the user to select different sounds to represent specific situations. A system also might play a digital sound file when the user wants to access stored audio information, as shown in Figure 6-11 on page 6.16.

When special effects are used appropriately and correctly, they can enhance a screen display, but they are not a replacement for good design. First, you must develop a basic design that is logical and user-friendly. Only then should you add special effects.

DESIGNING OTHER OUTPUTS

Sometimes output from one system is used as input to another system. Using a printed report from the first system as input to the second system is expensive and prone to error. In an integrated business environment, data transfer typically is handled by a communications network that connects users and allows interaction between systems. If network data transfer is not possible in some situations, however, you could use tapes or disks as a method of transferring information from the first system to the second system.

Output to Tapes and Disks

In the systems analysis phase, you identify various data elements, and how they form data structures, or records, that allow data to flow between system processes, data stores, and entities. During systems design, you can create an output **file format**, which is a data structure that can be understood by another program or system. An output file designed to be used by another program or system also is called an **export file**.

If you are developing a new accounts receivable system, for example, an output file becomes input into the general ledger system. An output or export file also might be used as input by a spreadsheet or a presentation graphics package. In these examples, the format for the output file is driven by the input format requirements of the other system or program.

In addition to describing the file format, your design must calculate the output file volume. The volume calculations for tape and disk output files are the same as for system data stores and are discussed in Chapter 8.

Other Output Media

For output exported to other devices, the format and contents depend on the output device and its requirements. Output directed to a plotter, for example, consists of a series of commands that are formatted for the particular plotter being used. As with tape and disk output formats, your design objective is to provide output information in the specific format required.

Computer output microfilm (COM) consists of computer output that is recorded as images on roll or sheet film. For example, an insurance company might scan policies into a computer system as input, store them in digital form for a period of time, and then use COM as a permanent storage medium. To design for COM output, you must design, size, and document the output as you would any printed report.

OUTPUT CONTROL

T he objective of output control is to ensure that information is correct, complete, and secure. Effective output control is essential to every organization — its importance cannot be overemphasized.

Output Integrity

Output must be both correct and complete. If data integrity is lost during processing or output, the problem must be recognized and corrected. You should take several steps to ensure that output is correct and complete.

Every report should have an appropriate title and include the date the report was prepared and the dates for the covered time period. Report pages should be numbered consecutively. The end of the report should be identified. Control totals and record counts should be printed and reconciled against input totals and counts. Reports should be selected at random for a thorough check of correctness and completeness. All processing errors or interruptions must be logged so they can be analyzed and corrected.

Some special measures apply to output errors. You should review error reports periodically to investigate possible causes. To maintain system integrity, you should print error control totals and record counts, and reconcile them with the totals produced after the errors have been corrected and reentered. You also should create an independent error file to flag records that were not corrected and reentered.

Output Security

Output security protects the privacy rights of individuals and organizations and protects the organization's proprietary data from theft or unauthorized access. To assure output security, you must perform several important tasks. First, ensure that only the required number of report copies are produced. Reports should be distributed to authorized personnel only. All sensitive reports should be stored in secure areas. All pages of confidential reports should be labeled appropriately. Burn or shred sensitive reports, out-of-date reports, and output from aborted runs. Ensure that blank check forms receive special security treatment and are stored in a secure location. Blank checks should be inventoried regularly to check for missing forms. Finally, store signature stamps in a secure location away from the forms storage location.

In most organizations, the information systems department is responsible for nearly all of the previously identified security control measures. Systems analysts must be concerned with security issues in all phases of their work.

AUTOMATED DESIGN TOOLS

M any database management packages, fourth-generation languages (4GLs), and CASE products include powerful online report and screen generators that can help you design reports and screen displays.

Report Generators

Most CASE tools and database management packages include a report generator. A **report generator** allows you to enter constant information such as report titles and page and column headings and specify a print position for each item. If you are using a CASE tool, you select fields to be printed from the data dictionary and specify each field's location. The report generator can use the field sizes, edit masks, and captions from the data dictionary to lay out the detail lines and column headings for the report. Using a report generator, you can modify the report design easily at any time in the design process.

To learn more about the **Report Generators**, visit Systems Analysis and Design Chapter 6 More on the Web.

www.scsite.com/ sad3e/ch06/

When you are satisfied with the report layout, the report generator produces a report definition that is similar to a printer spacing chart. You also can input sample field values to create a *mock-up report* that users can review before final report design decisions are made.

Many database management systems include powerful report generators that allow you to select a variety of fonts, type styles, and graphics to include in the report. You also can control the placement of all objects in the report. Based on your design, the report generator creates program code that actually produces the report. You even can use a report generator to produce an initial design and make the necessary modifications to customize the report for your needs.

Screen Generators

A **screen generator** is similar to a report generator because you can create displays using onscreen layout tools. You also can produce screen mock-ups for users to review and approve. In addition to output design, screen generators also are important tools that you can use to design input screen forms for data entry. Input design is discussed in Chapter 7.

Completing the Report and Screen Designs

Report and screen generators ensure consistency with the data dictionary. These generators automate routine design tasks such as counting field lengths, centering information, and positioning form boxes. Although it produces rapid results, a screen generator does not guarantee good design. You still must know and apply all the principles of effective design to produce reports and screens that satisfy user requirements.

Designing effective output is the first step in systems design. Now you can continue your work by designing the inputs to the system as discussed in Chapter 7, the system files and databases as discussed in Chapter 8, and the system architecture as discussed in Chapter 9. An effective combination of these designs is necessary for a successful and high-quality system.

SOFTWEAR, LIMITED — OUTPUT DESIGN

After completing the systems analysis phase, systems analyst Rick Williams and programmer/analyst Carla Moore began working on the design for the payroll system. SoftWear, Limited's management decided to negotiate with Pacific Software Solutions to purchase an appropriate payroll package. Meanwhile, Rick and Carla began to design the Employee Savings and Investment Plan (ESIP) system. Because most of the payroll requirements would be handled by the Pacific payroll package, they decided that Carla would work on the new ESIP modules and Rick would concentrate on the rest of the payroll system.

Fortunately, the negotiations with Pacific Software Solutions were completed successfully, and a new systems analyst, Becky Evans, was assigned to help Rick develop the payroll package.

Carla spent her time on the design of the ESIP system and its interaction with the payroll package. Her first step was to design the outputs. She had to design several reports: the ESIP Deduction Register, the ESIP Payment Summary, and the checks that SWL sends to the credit union and the Stock Purchase Plan. Carla also needed to develop an ESIP accounting summary as a file that will be loaded into the accounting system.

Carla learned that standard SWL company checks were used to make the payments to the credit union and stock purchase department. Also, the output entry to the accounting system had been specified by the accounting department in a standard format for all entries into that system.

To prepare the new ESIP Deduction Register, Carla reviewed the documentation from the systems analysis phase to be sure that she understood the logical design and the available data fields.

Carla decided to use a monthly format because some deductions would be applied on a monthly cycle. She started her design with a standard SWL report heading. Then she added a control heading and footing for each employee's Social Security number. The total of employee deductions would be compared with the transferred ESIP funds to be sure they matched. After preparing a rough layout, she used a report generator shown in Figure 6-44 to prepare the mock-up report shown in Figure 6-45 on the next page. She used both actual and test data to produce the mock-up report so it would be realistic when she presented it to users for their approval.

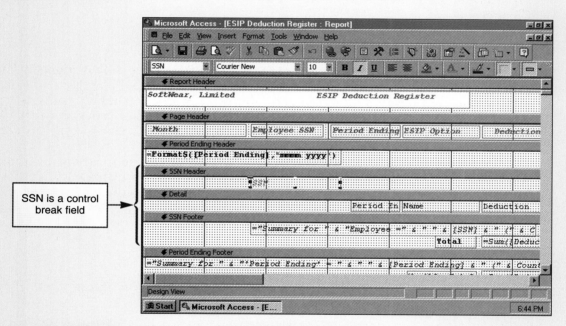

Figure 6-44   The layout for the ESIP Deduction Register that Carla created using a report generator. Notice that SSN is a control break field, and an SSN Header and SSN Footer are included, where subtotals will display.

When she showed the mock-up report to Mike Feiner, director of human resources, he said that he wanted to see the data grouped by the type of ESIP deduction with the appropriate subtotals. Carla was able to use a different sort option to satisfy his request. Then she sent the revised mock-up report shown in Figure 6-46 on page 6.47 to Mike, which he later approved. Carla also sent the mock-up report to Amy Calico, director of payroll. Several days later, she received an e-mail message from Amy that approved both versions without any changes.

During the systems analysis phase, Carla learned that the accounting department required a control report to show the ESIP deduction amounts that were not yet applied. This control report is used to verify the amount of the checks or fund transfers SWL makes to the Credit Union and Stock Purchase Plan. The accounting department needs this control report to verify the accounting system outputs and balance the ESIP deduction totals against the payroll system's Payroll Register report.

```
SoftWear, Limited          ESIP Deduction Register

Month              Employee SSN     Period Ending ESIP Option        Deduction
March 1999
                   000-00-0000
                                    3/05/99  Stock Purchase           $15.00
                                    3/05/99  Credit Union             $20.00
                                    3/12/99  Credit Union             $20.00
                                    3/12/99  Stock Purchase           $15.00
                                    3/19/99  Stock Purchase           $15.00
                                    3/19/99  Credit Union             $25.00
                                    3/26/99  Stock Purchase           $15.00
                                    3/26/99  Credit Union             $20.00

          Summary for Employee = 000000000 (8 detail records)
                                             Total                   $145.00

                   123-45-6789
                                    3/05/99  Stock Purchase           $10.00
                                    3/05/99  Credit Union             $30.00
                                    3/12/99  Stock Purchase           $10.00
                                    3/12/99  Credit Union             $30.00
                                    3/19/99  Stock Purchase           $10.00
                                    3/19/99  Credit Union             $30.00
                                    3/26/99  Credit Union             $30.00
                                    3/26/99  Stock Purchase           $10.00

          Summary for Employee = 123456789 (8 detail records)
                                             Total                   $160.00

                   999-99-9999
                                    3/05/99  ESIP: Option 1            $9.99
                                    3/12/99  ESIP: Option 1            $9.99
                                    3/19/99  ESIP: Option 1            $9.99
                                    3/26/99  ESIP: Option 1            $9.99

          Summary for Employee = 999999999 (4 detail records)
                                             Total                    $39.96

      Summary for 'Period Ending' = 3/26/99 (20 detail records)
                                        Monthly Total                $344.96
                                        Grand Total                  $344.96
```

Figure 6-45   Mock-up report for the ESIP Deduction Register.

Figure 6-47 on page 6.48 shows a mock-up of the ESIP Payment Summary Report. Carla met with Buddy Goodson, director of accounting, to review the design. Buddy was pleased with the report and felt it would be acceptable to the company's outside auditors. Buddy met with the auditing firm later that week and secured the team's approval.

Carla is finished with the output design for the ESIP system. She is ready to design the other system components.

SoftWear, Limited	ESIP Deduction Register by ESIP Option		
Name	**SSN**	**Period Ending**	**Deduction**
Credit Union	000-00-0000	3/05/99	$20.00
	000-00-0000	3/12/99	$20.00
	000-00-0000	3/19/99	$25.00
	000-00-0000	3/26/99	$20.00
	123-45-6789	3/05/99	$30.00
	123-45-6789	3/12/99	$30.00
	123-45-6789	3/19/99	$30.00
	123-45-6789	3/26/99	$30.00
		ESIP Option Total	$205.00
ESIP: Option 1	999-99-9999	3/05/99	$9.99
	999-99-9999	3/12/99	$9.99
	999-99-9999	3/19/99	$9.99
	999-99-9999	3/26/99	$9.99
		ESIP Option Total	$39.96
Stock Purchase Plan	000-00-0000	3/05/99	$15.00
	000-00-0000	3/12/99	$15.00
	000-00-0000	3/19/99	$15.00
	000-00-0000	3/26/99	$15.00
	123-45-6789	3/05/99	$10.00
	123-45-6789	3/12/99	$10.00
	123-45-6789	3/19/99	$10.00
	123-45-6789	3/26/99	$10.00
		ESIP Option Total	$100.00
		Grand Total:	$344.96

Figure 6-46   Version 2 of the ESIP Deduction Register, as requested by Mike Feiner. Note that detail lines now are grouped by ESIP option.

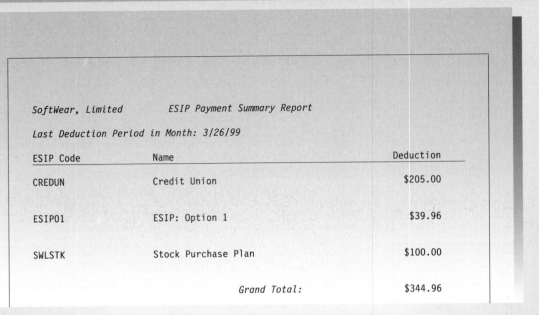

Figure 6-47   Mock-up of the ESIP Payment Summary Report.

 YOUR TURN — Suppose Carla asked you to design the ESIP Deduction Register. She wants you to prepare an initial layout on a printer spacing chart. If you do not have access to a pre-printed chart, use graph paper. Follow the guidelines in this chapter, and use your own ideas, too. Submit your design to Carla with a brief cover memo telling her what you did, and why.

CHAPTER SUMMARY

I n this chapter, you began your study of the systems design phase. The purpose of the systems design phase is to create a physical design of the system that satisfies the logical design requirements that were defined during the systems analysis phase.

The three major activities in systems design are reviewing the system requirements document, designing the system components, and presenting the completed design. During the design process, you follow guidelines that help you achieve a system design that is efficient, reliable, and maintainable. Your design should consider user needs, data entry and storage methods, and use a modular, structured processing design. Because the information produced by the system must satisfy user requirements, the design process usually begins with the output.

You learned that a code is a set of letters or numbers that is used to represent data in a system. By using codes, you can speed up data entry, reduce data storage space, and reduce transmission time. Codes also can be used to reveal or to conceal information. The main types of codes are sequence codes, block sequence codes, classification codes, alphabetic codes, mnemonic codes, significant digit codes, derivation codes, cipher codes, action codes, and self-checking codes.

A system can produce various types of output. In addition to printed output and screen output, which are the most common form, other examples include audio output, automated facsimile and faxback, e-mail, and links to Web pages. Other specialized forms of output are produced by retail point-of-sale terminals and ATMs, for example.

Several types of reports were illustrated. Output reports are classified as detail, exception, or summary reports, and as internal or external reports. You learned about printed report designs for both stock paper and specialty forms and saw how to perform report volume calculations. Screen output design was described for both character and graphical output.

Next, you learned about output control and the various measures you can take to achieve adequate output control to ensure that information is correct, complete, and secure. Finally, you saw how report and screen generators are automated tools that are useful to the output design process.

Review Questions

1. What is a physical information system design? What is a logical information system design? During which systems development life cycle phases are they created?

2. After you begin working on the systems design phase, what situations might cause you to return to the systems analysis phase? Is this a common occurrence?

3. What is the first activity of the systems design phase? Why?

4. What does it mean to say that an information system is effective, reliable, and maintainable?

5. What is a code? For what purposes are codes used?

6. What are the more commonly used coding schemes? Describe each type of scheme.

7. Discuss the advantages and disadvantages of printed output.

8. List and describe various types of output, including the technology-based forms of information delivery.

9. What is a detail report?

10. What is a control-break report? Define the terms control field and control break.

11. What is an exception report? When is it appropriate to use an exception report?

12. What is a summary report? When is it appropriate to use a summary report?

13. What is an internal report? An external report? In what ways do their design considerations differ?

14. Define the terms specialty form and preprinted form. Are they synonymous? Why or why not?

15. When using a printer spacing chart or screen display layout form, how do you indicate the following objects: constant fields, variable fields, and line spacing?

16. What is a mock-up report? When is it used, and why?

17. What additional information must be provided on a screen display that does not need to be present on a printed report for the same data?

18. List three or more special video effects and describe how they might be used to improve the user interface.

Discussion Questions

1. Some systems analysts argue, "You must give users what they ask for. If they want long reports with reams of data, then that is what you give them. Otherwise, users will be unhappy and feel that you are trying to tell them how to do their jobs." Others say, "The systems analyst should dictate to users what information can be obtained from the system. If you listen to users, you'll never get anywhere, because they don't really know what they want and don't understand information systems." What do you think of these arguments? Why?

2. Obtain copies of one or more computer output documents, such as computer-printed invoices, form letters, or student grade reports. Analyze the design and appearance of each document, and try to identify at least one possible improvement for each.

3. Suppose your organization employs dozens of technical support representatives who travel constantly and work at customer sites. Your task is to design an information system that provides technical data and information to this field team. What types of output and information delivery would you suggest for this system and why?

4. A systems analyst designed the report layout shown in Figure 6-48 on the next page. He asks you to review it, identify any flaws in the report design, and suggest specific improvements.

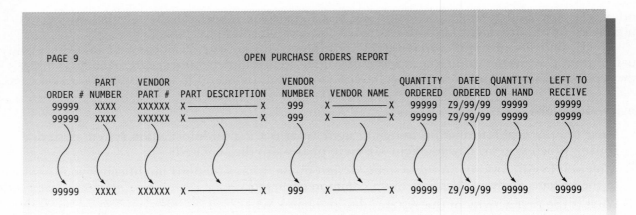

Figure 6-48   Sample report layout.

CASE STUDIES

NEW CENTURY HEALTH CLINIC — OUTPUT DESIGN

T he associates at New Century Health Clinic approved your recommendations for a new computer system. Your next step was to develop a design for the new system, starting with the system's outputs. After reviewing the earlier documentation and talking to the New Century staff, you decide to design the following outputs, with the information as shown.

Report Title	Report Contents
Daily appointment list for each provider	Provider name, patient name, patient telephone numbers, appointment time, procedure name
Weekly provider report	Provider number, provider name, patient number, date procedure performed, procedure code, fee (with subtotals by provider and grand total)
Monthly preprinted statement patients	Patient number, patient name, address, date procedure performed, provider name, procedure code, procedure name, fee (with total)
Mailing labels for twice a month mailing	Patient name, address

Assignments

1. Design the daily appointment list (using a printer spacing chart or graph paper), a mock-up report, and a report analysis form.

2. Design the weekly provider report (using a printer spacing chart or graph paper), a mock-up report, and a report analysis form.

3. The monthly statement will be a new preprinted form that you must design using a printer spacing chart or graph paper. Also prepare a report analysis form for your design.

4. Design the daily appointment list as a screen output instead of a printed report. Explain the advantages and disadvantages of this approach.

5. What output controls are needed for the New Century information system?

6. Dr. Jones has asked you to create a monthly Claim Status Summary report. He wants you to include the insurance company number, the patient number and name, the procedure date, the procedure code and description, the fee, the date the claim was filed, the amount of the claim, the amount of reimbursement, and the amount remaining unpaid. He wants you to group the data by insurance company number, with subtotals by company and grand totals, for each numeric field. When you design the report, be sure to include printer spacing charts, a mock-up report, and a report analysis form.

CARL'S CORVETTES

Carl Dekker owns a sales and service shop for Corvettes. Last year, Carl purchased a computer system to manage data for customers, sales, and service appointments. In addition to the main computer in his own office, which he shares with his assistant Linda, Carl also installed a workstation at the service desk. Throughout the year, Carl and Linda entered service data for every job that was performed. Appointment records contain the appointment number, date, customer name, and automobile registration number. Every appointment has one or more task records. Each task record contains the following information:

Appointment number	5 numeric digits
Mechanic	15 alphanumeric digits
Task code	4 numeric digits
Task description	20 alphanumeric digits
Standard task time	3 numeric digits
Actual task time	3 numeric digits

Carl would like to have a report of each of his mechanics' service logs for the past three months. The report should list all the tasks performed by each mechanic, listed in order by date. For each task, Carl wants to see the code, description, date, standard time, actual time, and the percent by which the actual task time was over (or under) the standard task time. He wants a total line for each mechanic, giving the total number of tasks and the percent that the total of the mechanic's actual task times is over (or under) the total of the standard task times. He also wants a grand total line, giving similar totals for the entire service operation. In an average month, the four mechanics at Carl's Corvettes work on a total of 120 appointments, and each appointment averages 2.35 tasks.

Assignments

1. Design the report on a printer spacing chart or on graph paper.

2. Perform volume and time calculations for the report you designed. Carl recently bought a new laser printer with an 8 ppm rating, but Linda also uses the original printer that came with the system, which is a dot matrix printer that can handle about 150 lines per minute. Assume that the report will be printed on stock paper, and develop a volume and time estimate for both printers.

3. Consider the report Carl has requested. Classify the report by content (detail, exception summary), and distribution (internal, external) and explain the reasons for your choices. Would you suggest any changes or improvements to the report Carl has requested? If so, what?

4. Carl also would like a screen display for the appointment scheduler's use. For any specified task, he wants to see the task code, description, standard task time, the 10 most recent (or all, if fewer than 10) actual times achieved for that task along with the assigned mechanic, and the average actual time of the displayed tasks. Design a screen display for the appointment scheduler.

G. H. AMES & COMPANY

The marketing department at G. H. Ames & Company has requested a new report for the sales analysis system. Users want a biweekly report that shows the following information for the most recent two-week period for each of the company's 62 sales representatives: sales representative name (20 characters), number of sales calls, number of orders taken, total of the order amounts, and total miles driven. For each sales call, they would like to see the name (25 characters) and city (15 characters) of the customer visited, the date of the visit, the date of the previous visit (if any) to that same customer, and the amount of the order (if any) resulting from that visit. Each sales representative visits 38 customers in an average two-week period; a visit produces an order about 60 percent of the time. The average order total is $1,200; $9999.99 is a reasonable maximum single order value. The information for each sales representative should start on a new page.

Assignments

1. Design the requested report on a printer spacing chart or graph paper. Prepare a mock-up for one page of your designed report.
2. Perform volume and time calculations for the report you designed. Assume the report will be printed on stock paper either on a line printer that effectively prints 300 lines per minute, or on a laser printer rated at 12 ppm.
3. Prepare a report analysis form for your report.
4. Use a printer spacing chart or graph paper to design a biweekly exception report that shows only those sales representatives who have an order-per-visit ratio of less than 60%.

RIDGEWAY COMPANY

 homas McGee, vice president of operations for the Ridgeway Company, has the responsibility of running the Blue Waters Country Club. He recently requested three new reports to be produced by the club's billing system.

1. A report listing sales for the month at the pro shop, restaurant, and bar, to be printed in order by date within facility.
2. A report listing the monthly sales total for each member with purchases, printed in order by member number.
3. A report listing each member who made no purchases during the month, printed in order by member number.

The following information is available on a billing record.

Field	Description
Charge date	8 numeric digits, YYYYMMDD form
Charge amount	6 numeric digits, including 2 decimal positions
Charge location code	1 numeric digit: 1 = restaurant, 2 = bar, 3 = pro shop
Charge description	25 characters
Member number	4 numeric digits
Member last name	18 characters
Member first name	15 characters

Assignments

1. Design each of the three management reports using printer spacing charts or graph paper. Include any control totals you feel are appropriate.
2. Explain how the control totals included in your report designs should be calculated, and how McGee should use them.
3. Classify each report by content (detail, exception summary) and explain the reasons for your choices.
4. Thomas decides that he wants the second report (monthly sales total by member) printed in order of highest to lowest sales. What modifications need to be made to the report?

CHAPTER 7

Input Design

Input design is the second of four chapters in the systems design phase. During input design, you will focus on designing a user-friendly interface and processes that ensure the quality, accuracy, and timeliness of system input.

OBJECTIVES

When you finish this chapter, you will be able to:

- Discuss the objectives of systems input design
- Explain the differences among data capture, data entry, and data input
- Explain the differences between batch and online input
- List and describe the different types of data validation checks
- Discuss effective source document design
- Design input records
- Discuss guidelines for effective screen design
- Describe and design data entry screens, process control screens, graphical user interfaces, and Help screens
- Explain input control techniques

INTRODUCTION

Over the past three decades, input technology has changed enormously. Today, many input techniques and devices are available, as shown in Figure 7-1 on the next page. One basic rule, however, remains true: the quality of the output from an information system is only as good as the quality of the input. This concept, sometimes known as **garbage in, garbage out** (**GIGO**), is familiar to IS professionals, who recognize that inaccurate input leads to inaccurate output. The main objective of input design is to develop a user-friendly interface and input processes that ensure the quality, accuracy, and timeliness of input.

During input design, a systems analyst selects the best strategy for getting data into the information system in a timely and accurate fashion. Chapter 7 focuses on input design objectives and the key tasks that must be performed. You will learn about batch and online input methods and validation techniques. The chapter also offers suggestions for designing effective source documents, input records, and various types of screens, including graphical user interface (GUI) design. The chapter concludes with a discussion of input control techniques and automated input design tools.

Input Device	Description
Keyboard	Most common input device.
Mouse	Pointing device that allows the user to move the insertion point to a specific location on the screen and select options.
Internet workstation	Enables the user to provide input to Web-based intranet or Internet recipients; can be integrated with information system output or personal computer applications.
Terminal	Device that might be dumb (screen and keyboard only) or intelligent (screen, keyboard, independent processing).
Touch screen	Sensors that allow users to interface with the computer and select options by touching specific locations on the screen.
Telephone	Technology that allows users to press telephone buttons or speak selected words to choose options in a system, such as electronic funds transfer, shop-at-home purchases, or registration for college courses.
Graphic input device	Includes light pens, digitizers, and graphics tablets that allow drawings to be translated into digital form that can be processed by a computer.
Voice input device	Device that allows users to enter data and issue commands using spoken words; also can be used in connection with telephone input, so a user can *press,* or *say,* a number to select a processing option.
MICR (magnetic ink character recognition)	Technology used primarily in the banking industry to read magnetic ink characters printed on checks.
Scanner/optical recognition	Various devices that read printed bar codes, characters, or images.
Data collection device	Fixed or portable devices that can read data on-site; fixed devices include ATMs and warehouse inventory control points; portable devices include terminals used by package delivery drivers, some of which can capture and store a signature digitally.
Electronic whiteboard	Electronic version of standard whiteboard that uses scanners to record and store text or graphics that are written or drawn on the board.
Video input	Video camera input, in digital form, that can be stored and replayed later.
Biological feedback device	Device that creates a digital image of biological data such as fingerprints or retina patterns.
Digital camera	Device that records photographs in digital form rather than using traditional film; the resulting data file can be stored, displayed, or manipulated by the computer.

Figure 7-1 Examples of common types of input devices.

INPUT DESIGN OBJECTIVES

I **nput design** involves defining the methods used for data capture, data entry, and data input. **Data capture** is the identification and recording of source data. **Data entry** is the process of converting source data into a computer-readable form. **Data input** is the process by which the computer-readable source data actually enters the information system. During input design, the systems analyst has four main objectives:

1. To select the most suitable input media and methods
2. To develop efficient input procedures
3. To reduce input volume
4. To reduce input errors

Most input problems occur when data is captured and entered. Designing easy-to-use entry documents, capturing data at its source, reducing input volume, and streamlining data entry procedures are steps that can ensure data quality and reduce data entry bottlenecks.

➡ For examples of devices used for **Source Data Automation**, visit Systems Analysis and Design Chapter 7 More on the Web.

www.scsite.com/ sad3e/ch07/

Input Media and Data Entry Methods

One of the analyst's first decisions is whether to use batch or online input. Using **batch input** methods, data entry is performed over a period of time, which might be hours, days, weeks, or longer. A common example of the batch input method occurs when a data entry clerk enters data from source documents during a work shift. At the end of the day, the resulting collection, or **batch**, of source data is input into the system, all at one time.

In today's dynamic business environment, **online data entry**, such as the portable device shown in Figure 7-2, is a necessity. The online method — or **direct data entry** — offers several major advantages, including the immediate validation and availability of data. Another input method is **source data automation,** which combines online data entry with **online data capture**, using direct input devices such as **magnetic data strips**, or **swipe scanners**. Some common examples of source data automation are:

- Businesses use point-of-sale (POS) terminals with keyboards or keypads, wands or holographic bar code scanners, or magnetic swipe scanners to input credit card numbers.

- Automatic teller machines (ATMs) read data strips on bankcards.

- Factory employees use magnetic ID cards to clock on and off specific jobs, so the company can track production costs accurately.

- Hospitals imprint bar codes on patient identification bracelets and use portable scanners when gathering data on patient treatment and medication.

- Retail stores use portable bar code scanners to log new shipments and and take inventory.

- Libraries use handheld scanners to read optical strips on books.

Figure 7-2   When a customer's signature is stored in digital form, it becomes input into the information system.

Direct data entry has been a major trend in recent years because it reduces the need for human interaction. Online data capture is faster, more accurate, and involves less human involvement than batch input. The combination of source data automation and modern day communication, such as the Internet enables businesses to manage operational data almost instantly on a global basis.

Although online input often is more desirable than batch input, it does have some disadvantages. For instance, manual online data entry can be slower and more expensive than batch input because it is performed as the transaction occurs and often must be completed when computer demand is at its highest. In addition, some business processes, such as weekly payroll, do not require a sophisticated, costly online system.

The decision to use batch or online input should depend on the type of system and the requirements of the business. Airline reservations must be entered and processed immediately, for example, but monthly invoices can be entered and processed later, in a batch. In fact, some input occurs naturally in batches. A typical catalog sales firm, for example, receives mail orders and payments in batches when the mail arrives.

The choice of batch versus online data entry also can be affected by hardware factors. For example, when personal computers are used as data entry terminals, input data often is uploaded to a central computer in files or batches.

To learn more on various **Data Input and Entry Methods**, visit Systems Analysis and Design Chapter 7 More on the Web.

www.scsite.com/ sad3e/ch07/

Develop Efficient Input Procedures

Input procedures should be efficient, timely, and logical. Suppose, for example, that each time an order arrives, one person receives and dates the incoming order and a second person checks the individual items and approves the order. The time spent transferring documents from one person to another might amount to only a few seconds per transaction, but thousands of orders must be processed, and the total time could be significant. In addition, if only one person can approve orders, delays might occur if that person is unavailable or busy with other responsibilities.

As noted in the previous example, you must watch out for potential *bottlenecks* in your input design, such as having only one person designated to review input documents. Good input design also requires realistic estimates of order volumes. If input delays are common, then your data capture procedures must be changed. Perhaps a second person could share approval responsibility, or approvals could be required only for orders over a certain amount. Another solution is to reduce input volume.

For guidelines on developing **Input Procedures**, visit Systems Analysis and Design Chapter 7 More on the Web.

www.scsite.com/ sad3e/ch07/

Reduce Input Volume

To reduce input volume, you must reduce the number and size of input data items for each transaction. Data capture and data entry require time and effort, so when you reduce data volume, you reduce labor costs. You also get the data into the system more quickly so it can be processed and used as soon as possible.

The number of errors in a given set of data is related directly to data volume. As volume increases, the number of errors also increases. By reducing data volume, you reduce the number of errors that must be located and corrected. The following guidelines will help reduce input volume.

1. **Input necessary data only**. Do not input a data item unless it is needed by the system. A completed order form, for example, might contain the name of the clerk who took the order. If that data is not needed by the system, it should not be entered.

2. **Do not input data that can be retrieved from system files or calculated from other data**. In the order system example shown in Figure 7-3, the customer number, item numbers, and quantities must be entered for all orders, but all other information can be retrieved or calculated. The input of the customer number causes the system to retrieve the customer's name and address from the customer master file. When an item number is entered, the description and current price can be retrieved from the item master file. The extended price is calculated by multiplying the input quantity times the item price, and the sum of the extended prices produces a total. Finally, a stored sales tax rate is applied to produce a grand total.

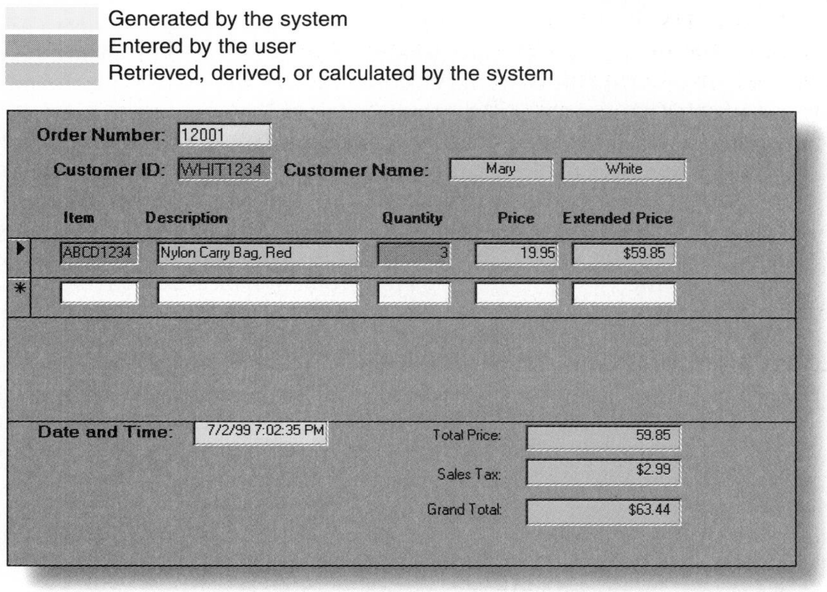

           Generated by the system
           Entered by the user
           Retrieved, derived, or calculated by the system

Order Number: 12001

Customer ID: WHIT1234   **Customer Name:**   Mary   White

Item	Description	Quantity	Price	Extended Price
ABCD1234	Nylon Carry Bag, Red	3	19.95	$59.85

Date and Time: 7/2/99 7:02:35 PM

Total Price: 59.85

Sales Tax: $2.99

Grand Total: $63.44

Figure 7-3   In this data entry screen for customer orders, the system generates an order number and the date and time. The user enters a customer ID. If the entry is valid, the system displays the customer name so the user can verify it. The user enters the item and quantity. Note that the description, price, extended price, total price, sales tax, and grand total are retrieved automatically or calculated by the system.

3. **Do not input constant data**. If orders are in batches with the same date, then the order date should be entered only once for the first order in the batch. If orders are entered online, then the order date is retrieved automatically using the current system date.

4. **Use codes**. You learned in Chapter 6 that codes usually are shorter than the data they represent, so one advantage of using codes is reduced data entry time. In the order example in Figure 7-3, the customer ID and item numbers are codes.

     Discussing data volume at this point is important because all the data items were specified during the systems analysis phase. Now, during systems design, you must determine *when* and *how* these data items will be input. For example, if the system requirements document specifies that an item description must be printed when an invoice is printed, your goal during the systems design phase is to decide whether users will input the item description or the system will retrieve it from a file.

In the section on input volume, you learned that you should input only necessary data. The example used an order form that contained space for a customer name and a customer number. The customer name does *not* have to be entered because it is retrieved from a customer master file when the customer number is entered. Does that mean that users should not enter retrievable data? If the customer name is entered, is this a good way to verify the customer number?

Online data entry allows the operator to see a customer's name immediately after entering the customer's number. Then the operator can verify the name that is retrieved by the system against the source document. If the customer name does not match the customer number, then something obviously is wrong. The operator immediately can reject the source document and set it aside for further investigation. An online data entry program always should allow the operator to avoid entering incorrect data.

What if you use batch input methods? With batch input, data must be verified when it is input to the system, rather than when the user physically enters the source data. What if the customer number on the source document is wrong, but it matches another customer's number? If the customer name has not been entered, how would the system detect the error? Unfortunately, this mistake might not show up until the wrong customer receives the shipment, or an invoice. To avoid such situations, you should have a way to check the validity of a batch-input customer number.

A possible solution to this problem is to enter the customer name *and* the customer number, which, unfortunately, can create a different type of problem. Each time you add characters to a data item, you increase data entry time, storage requirements, and costs. You also introduce the possibility of rejecting correct records in addition to those records that contain problems, because the customer number is correct but the name does not match exactly. For example, if the input customer name is Tamisha Ward and the stored customer name is Tamisha J. Ward, then a correct record will be rejected. Similarly, a record that you enter for Dynamic Systems, Inc. will not match a stored record for Dynamic Systems, Incorporated.

This problem typically is handled in one of two ways. First, batch source documents can be checked carefully before data entry. For example, several employees could be assigned to verify customer numbers and correct any errors found on the source documents. The same staff also would be responsible for correcting any customer name variations.

Second, to help avoid false rejections, only a portion of the customer name could be entered. For example, if the data entry person inputs only the first three characters of a customer name, then the previously described correct records would not be rejected.

By using both input methods, you can avoid most problems or at least detect and correct them during input.

A KEY QUESTION

Prowler Products is a leading manufacturer of scale model airplanes, with more than 50,000 mail-order customers worldwide. Recently, the sales department has been receiving complaints of incorrect bills and shipping mistakes because of customer number errors. Prowler uses a batch input system for mail and telephone orders. Data entry people enter the orders into a batch input file as they are received during the day, and then the batch input file is entered into the system each evening. Systems analyst Kerry Whidbey has suggested that Prowler change to an online data entry system. While it will be more expensive, Kerry believes that it will improve data accuracy, increase Prowler's customer satisfaction levels, and help promote the firm's image as a customer-oriented company. Are these valid reasons to change to a more expensive system? What cost-benefit issues, if any, should you analyze? What factors would affect your recommendation?

Reduce Input Errors

Reducing the number of input errors increases data quality. As previously mentioned, one effective way to reduce input errors is to reduce input data volume. A customer name cannot be misspelled if it is not entered. Similarly, an outdated item price cannot be used by mistake if the item price is retrieved from a master file instead of being input by the operator.

Good input design also reduces errors. For example, a document's layout, captions, and instructions can be designed to make the data capture and data entry processes easier and more error-free. Well-designed screen layouts also help reduce errors.

Even with the best input design and procedures, some data errors still will occur. The final defense to prevent incorrect data is by identifying and correcting errors before inputting data into the system. Data should be validated as soon as possible, so errors can be detected and corrected quickly.

At least eight types of data validation checks can be applied to data.

> To learn ways to reduce **Input Errors,** visit Systems Analysis and Design Chapter 7 More on the Web.
>
> **www.scsite.com/ sad3e/ch07/**

1. **Sequence checks** are used when the data must be in some predetermined sequence. If orders must be input in order-number sequence, for example, then an out-of-sequence order number indicates an error. If transactions must be input in date order, then a transaction with an out-of-sequence date indicates an error.

2. **Existence checks** are used for data items that must be input, such as a required field. If a record is entered with a blank value for a required field, the existence check would report the error.

3. **Data type checks** test to ensure that a data item fits the required data type or class. For example, a numeric field must have only numbers or numeric symbols, and an alphabetic field can contain only the characters *A* through *Z* or *a* through *z*.

4. **Range checks** test data items to verify that they fall between a minimum and a maximum value. The weekly hours worked by an employee, for example, must fall within the range of 0 to 168 hours, because there are only 168 hours in a week. When the validation check involves a minimum or a maximum value, but not both, it is called a **limit check.** Checking that a payment amount is greater than zero, but not specifying a maximum value, is an example of a limit check.

5. **Reasonableness checks** identify values that are questionable, but not necessarily wrong. For example, input payment values of $.05 and $5,000,000.00 both pass a simple limit check for a payment value greater than zero, and yet both values might be errors. Similarly, an hours worked value of 160 passes a 0 to 168 range check, but the value seems unlikely and should be verified by a reasonableness check.

6. **Validity checks** are used for data items that must have certain values. For example, if an inventory system has 20 valid item classes, then any input item that does not match one of those 20 item classes will fail the validity check. Verifying that a customer number on an order matches a customer number in the customer master file is another type of validity check. Because the value entered must refer to another value, this type of check also is called **referential integrity.** (Referential integrity will be discussed in more detail in Chapter 8.) Another validity check might verify that a new customer number does *not* match a number already stored in the customer master file.

7. **Combination checks** are performed on two or more fields to ensure that they are consistent or reasonable when considered together. Even though all the fields involved in a combination check might pass their individual validation checks, the combination of the field values might be inconsistent or unreasonable. For example, if an order input for 30 units of a particular item has an input discount rate applicable only for purchases of 100 or more units, then the combination is invalid; either the input order quantity or the input discount rate is incorrect.

8. **Batch controls** are totals used to verify batch input. Batch controls might check data items such as record counts and numeric field totals. For example, before entering a batch of order forms, a data entry person might calculate the total number of orders and the sum of all the order quantities. When the batch of orders is input into the ordering system, the system also calculates the same two totals. Then the system's totals can be compared against the control totals. If the totals do not match, then a data entry error has occurred. Unlike the other validation checks, batch controls do not identify specific errors. For example, if the sum of all the order quantities does not match the batch control total, you know only that one or more orders in that batch was entered incorrectly or not input. The control totals often are called **hash totals,** because they are not meaningful numbers themselves, but are useful for comparison purposes.

KEY TASKS IN INPUT DESIGN

To meet the previously described input design objectives, you must select suitable input media and methods, develop efficient input procedures, and reduce input volume and errors. The input design process includes these six tasks.

1. Design data entry and input procedures.
2. Design source documents for data capture, or devise other data capture methods.
3. Design input data records.
4. Design data entry screens.
5. Design user interface screens.
6. Design audit trails and system security measures.

For additional guidelines on **Input Design**, visit Systems Analysis and Design Chapter 7 More on the Web.

www.scsite.com/ sad3e/ch07/

In addition to automated methods, a variety of media — print, screen, and other types — can be used to collect input data. During input design, you must determine whether users will input information directly into the system using data entry screens, or whether input data will be collected on paper forms and automated data capture, before it enters the system. While many businesses are moving toward online input, some firms still use source documents to collect input data.

SOURCE DOCUMENT DESIGN

A source document is a form used to request and collect input data, to trigger or authorize an input action, and to provide a record of the original transaction. During the input design stage, you develop source documents that are easy to complete and inexpensive.

Consider a time when you struggled to complete a poorly designed form. You might have encountered insufficient space, confusing instructions, or poor organization. All of these are symptoms of incorrect **form layout**.

A good form layout, by contrast, makes the form easy to complete. You must provide enough space, both vertically and horizontally, for users to enter the data. If the form will be completed using a computer printer or a typewriter, the lines should be spaced in multiples of one-sixth of an inch, because six lines per inch is a common printing standard. If the form will be completed by hand, the lines should be spaced at least one-quarter of an inch apart. Lines that are spaced one-third of an inch apart work well for both machine-printed and handwritten entry.

Entry lines on the form should be long enough to contain the requested data. A general guideline is that you should provide one inch of space for every five or six characters of handwritten data, or one inch of space for every ten characters for data that will be printed using a computer printer or typewriter.

Data entry positions should be indicated clearly by blank lines or boxes and descriptive captions. Figure 7-4 shows several techniques for line and box captions.

For forms that are completed with a typewriter, avoid placing captions below the entry spaces, because they will not be visible when the typewriter is positioned on the entry line. Figure 7-4 also shows two presentation methods for check boxes that are effective when a user must select choices from a list.

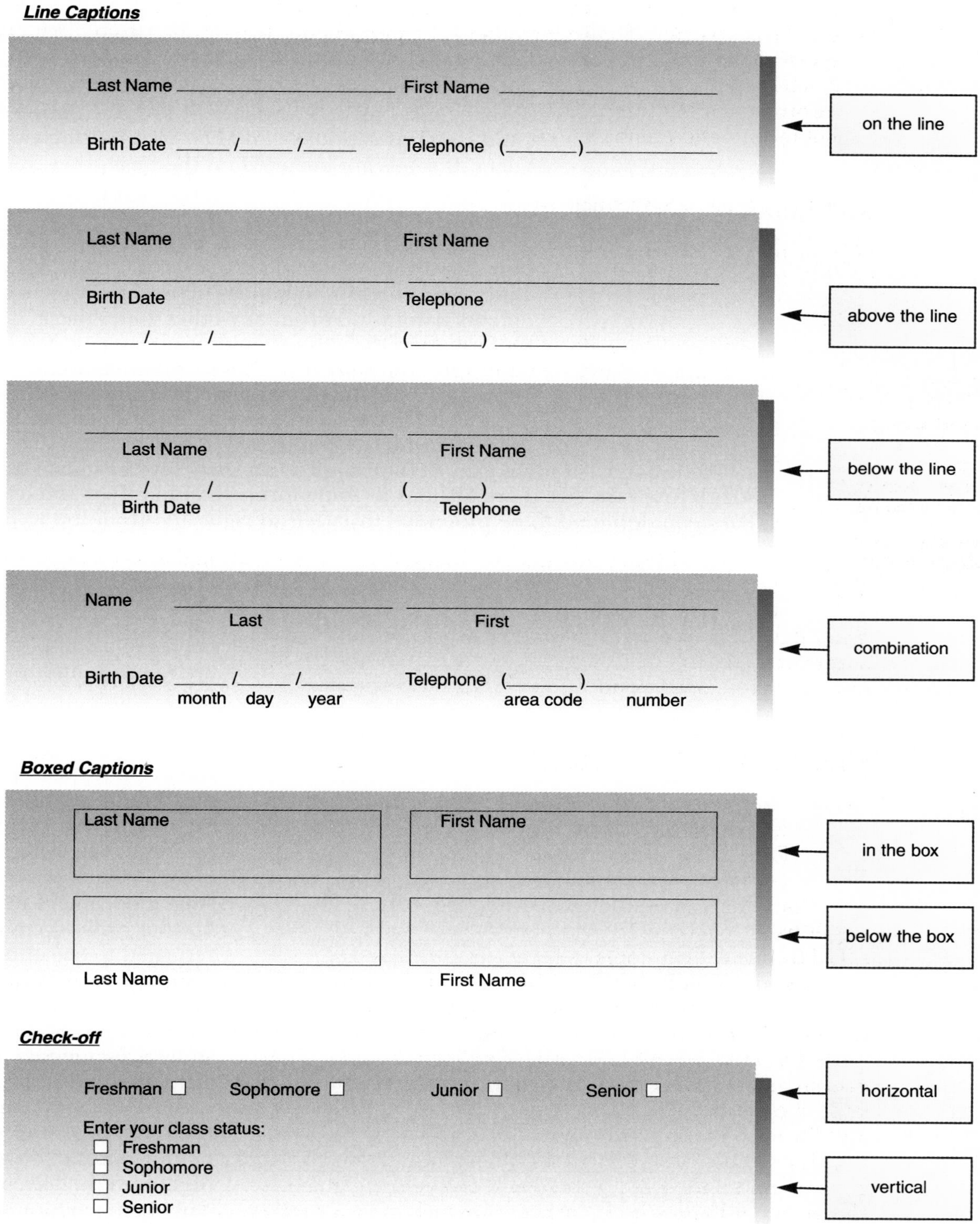

Line Captions

Last Name _____ First Name _____

Birth Date _____ / _____ / _____ Telephone (_____)_____   ⟵ on the line

Last Name

First Name
_____

Birth Date

Telephone
_____ / _____ / _____

(_____) _____   ⟵ above the line

_____
    Last Name

_____
    First Name

_____ / _____ / _____
    Birth Date

(_____) _____
    Telephone   ⟵ below the line

Name _____ _____
             Last   First

Birth Date _____ / _____ / _____ Telephone (_____)_____   ⟵ combination
          month   day   year   area code   number

Boxed Captions

Last Name First Name   ⟵ in the box

    ⟵ below the box

Last Name First Name

Check-off

Freshman ☐   Sophomore ☐   Junior ☐   Senior ☐   ⟵ horizontal

Enter your class status:
- ☐ Freshman
- ☐ Sophomore
- ☐ Junior
- ☐ Senior   ⟵ vertical

Figure 7-4   Common source document caption techniques.

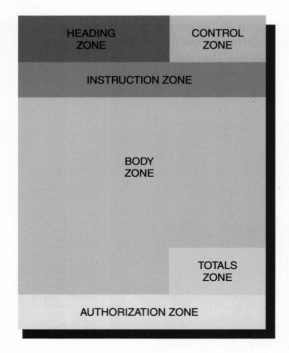

Figure 7-5 Source document zones.

The sequence of information on a form also is important. Source documents typically include most of the zones shown in Figure 7-5. The **heading zone** usually contains the company name or logo and the title and number of the form. The **control zone** contains codes, identification information, numbers, and dates that are used for storing completed forms. The **instruction zone** contains instructions for completing the form. The main part of the form, called the **body zone**, usually takes up at least half of the space on the form and contains captions and areas for entering variable data. If totals are included on the form, they appear in the **totals zone**. Finally, the **authorization zone** contains any required signatures.

Figure 7-5 uses a typical form layout. Notice how the flow of information on the form is from left to right and top to bottom to match the way users read documents naturally. Within any other zone, the information flow also should progress from left to right and from top to bottom. This layout makes the form easy to use for the individual who completes the form and also for the operators who input data into the system using the completed forms.

Figures 7-6 through 7-9 (on pages 7.10 through 7.12) show several source documents. Although the zones are more obvious in some forms than in others, notice that each form has been designed to be processed from left to right and from top to bottom.

To reduce form printing and storage costs, source documents usually are designed in standard sizes, such as 3" x 5", 5" x 7", 8" x 10", or 8 1/2" x 11". The appropriate paper type depends on how the form will be used. Forms that will be routed to many people or used in harsh environments should be printed on heavier paper. When several copies of a completed form are needed, multipart forms can be used with different paper colors for each copy. For example, the two-part dog license application shown in Figure 7-6 also serves as a receipt; the top (white) copy is retained as the source document and the bottom (yellow) copy is returned to the applicant.

Source documents can be external or internal, just like reports. **External source documents** must be attractive and professional because they represent the company's image to people outside the organization. The video club membership application shown in Figure 7-7 is an example of an external document. Form

DOG LICENSE 1999 — PARKER COUNTY STATE OF MICHIGAN — LICENSE NUMBER: 00001

THIS LICENSE EXPIRES: DECEMBER 31, 1999 — City / Twnshp

Received of _____ (Name of Dog Owner) — Telephone _____

_____ (Complete Mailing Address of Dog Owner)

the sum of $_____, amount due for DOG LICENSE for one dog, hereinafter described, which, upon compliance with the Dog Law of 1979 and all Amendments thereto, you are authorized to keep without further payment, until this license expires. State law requires all dogs 6 months and older to have a current license.

Beagle [ ] Doberman [ ] Poodle [ ] — Dog's Name _____
Boxer [ ] Hound [ ] Samoyed [ ] — Color _____
Bull [ ] Labrador [ ] Setter [ ]
Chihuahua [ ] Pekinese [ ] Shepherd [ ] — Age _____ Today's Date _____
Cockerpoo [ ] Pointer [ ] Spaniel [ ]
Collie [ ] Police [ ] Terrier [ ] — Rabies Vac. No. _____ Expires _____
Dachshund [ ] Pomeranian [ ] Weimaraner [ ]
Other [ ] — Veterinarian _____

[ ] MALE, $7.50   [ ] FEMALE, $15.00   [ ] ALTERED, $5.00

Figure 7-6 Sample source document for a dog license application and receipt.

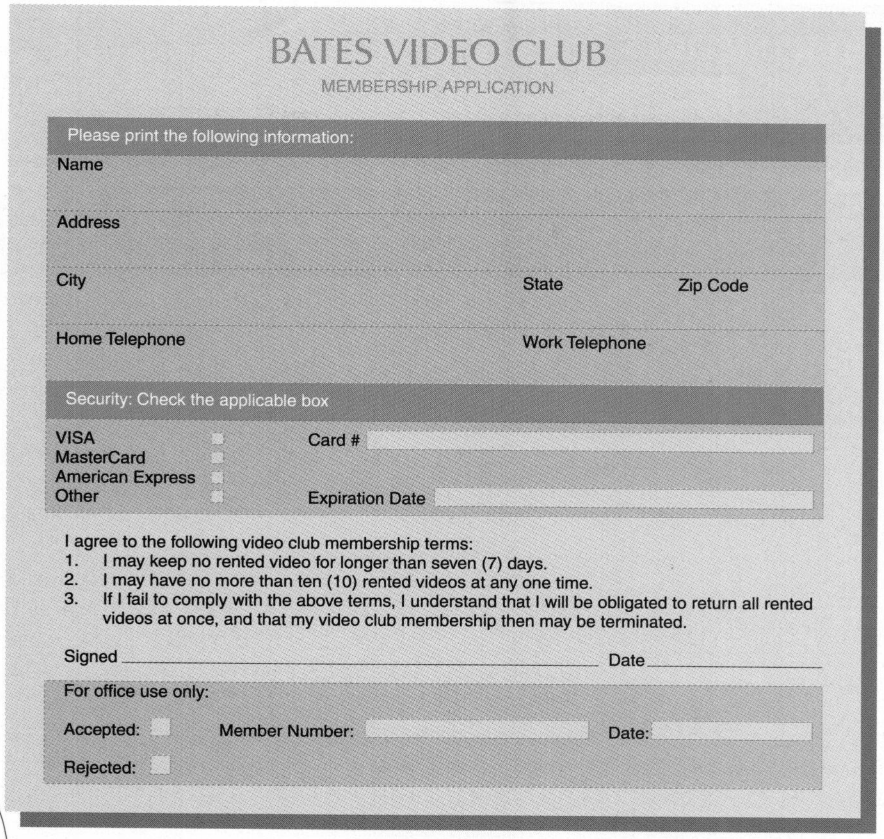
BATES VIDEO CLUB

MEMBERSHIP APPLICATION

Please print the following information:

Name

Address

City | State | Zip Code

Home Telephone | Work Telephone

Security: Check the applicable box

VISA
MasterCard
American Express
Other

Card #

Expiration Date

I agree to the following video club membership terms:

1. I may keep no rented video for longer than seven (7) days.
2. I may have no more than ten (10) rented videos at any one time.
3. If I fail to comply with the above terms, I understand that I will be obligated to return all rented videos at once, and that my video club membership then may be terminated.

Signed ______________________ Date ________

For office use only:

Accepted: Member Number: Date:

Rejected:

Figure 7-7 Sample source document for a video club membership application.

appearance usually is less critical for **internal source documents**, such as the student registration form shown in Figure 7-8, or the employee expense report shown in Figure 7-9 on the next page.

Although you should try to design source documents at a reasonable cost, the price of a form is *not* the most important design consideration. The cost of using a poorly designed document is much greater than any expense saved on the form itself. The typical form has many users, including the person who completes it, the person who checks it, the person who approves it, and the person who uses it for data entry. A poorly designed form often can result in higher labor costs and data errors. The best form is the one that does the best job of collecting data.

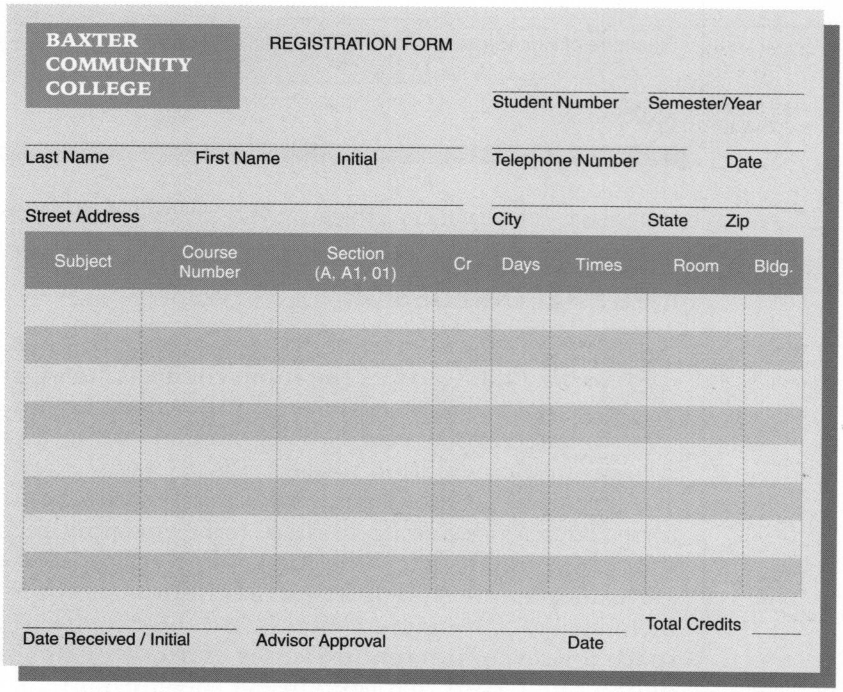
BAXTER COMMUNITY COLLEGE

REGISTRATION FORM

Student Number | Semester/Year

Last Name | First Name | Initial | Telephone Number | Date

Street Address | City | State | Zip

Subject	Course Number	Section (A, A1, 01)	Cr	Days	Times	Room	Bldg.

Date Received / Initial | Advisor Approval | Date | Total Credits

Figure 7-8 Sample source document for student registration form.

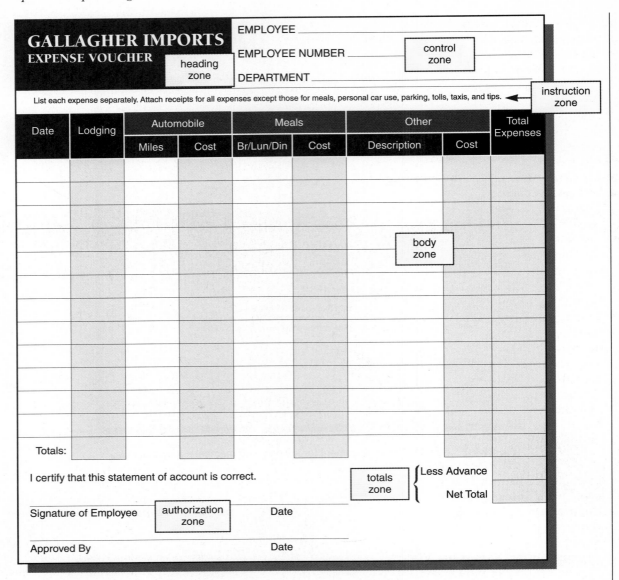

Figure 7-9 Sample source document for an employee expense report.

INPUT RECORD DESIGN

hen data is entered into a system in batches, data is placed in a temporary file that becomes the input file for data entry. You can use a word processor, a data dictionary, or an **input record layout chart** to design and document batch input records. Programmers will use your record layouts during the systems implementation phase.

Figure 7-10 shows a typical input record layout chart of a student registration form. You can define up to three different input records on one chart page. Many source documents allow the input of several related data items, called **repeating fields**. For example, the student registration form shown in Figure 7-8 on the previous page includes space for eight courses, and the expense report shown in Figure 7-9 includes space for seven different expenses entries. For this type of source document, you can design one record that contains all the **constant**, or **non-repeating,** data such as name and identification number and a second record that will repeat as necessary to contain the recurring data.

Consider again the student registration form shown in Figure 7-8 on page 7.11. This form has three parts: one copy becomes the source document for data entry, the advisor receives the second copy, and the student keeps the third copy. A student record and a course record are needed to capture the data from this form. Figure 7-10 contains the record layouts and Figure 7-11 is a system documentation form that describes the record designs. In both records, the first field is a one-character code that indicates the record type, which is the first data item the operator must input.

The student record includes the data from the top of the source document. Only the first four characters of the name are input. The telephone number, date, and address fields will not be entered, because they can be retrieved from other files on the system. By storing the data in only one place, you avoid data duplication, which was one of the guidelines discussed earlier in Chapter 6.

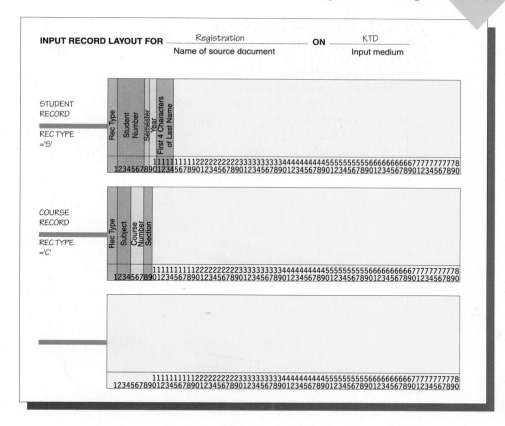

Figure 7-10   Input record layouts for the student registration form.

SYSTEM DOCUMENTATION

NAME OF SYSTEM REGISTRATION	DATE 2/17/99	PAGE 1 OF 1
ANALYST M. Friedman	PURPOSE OF DOCUMENTATION Registration Input Record Layouts	

STUDENT RECORD — One record is created for each registration form

FIELD	TYPE	POSITION	COMMENTS
REC TYPE	A	1	="S" for a student record
STUDENT NUMBER	N	2-7	
SEMESTER	A	8	="F" for Fall, "W" for Winter, "S" for Summer
YEAR	N	9-10	Last two digits of the year
NAME	X	11-14	Only the first four characters of the last name are entered

COURSE RECORDS — One record is created for each course on the form

FIELD	TYPE	POSITION	COMMENTS
REC TYPE	A	1	="C" for a course record
SUBJ	A	2-4	Standard department abreviation
COURSE NUMBER	N	5-7	
SECTION	X	8-9	Left-justified

Figure 7-11   Input record documentation for the student registration form.

The course record contains data from the table on the form. Only the first three fields of the table are included in the course record. The fourth field — number of credits — can be retrieved from the system. The last four fields, which specify course meeting times and locations, appear on the form only for the convenience of the student and are not entered into the system.

Figure 7-12 shows a completed registration form. A data entry operator will use this form to create six records: one student record and five course records. Notice that the records and fields are entered in the order in which they appear across and down the form to make data entry easier.

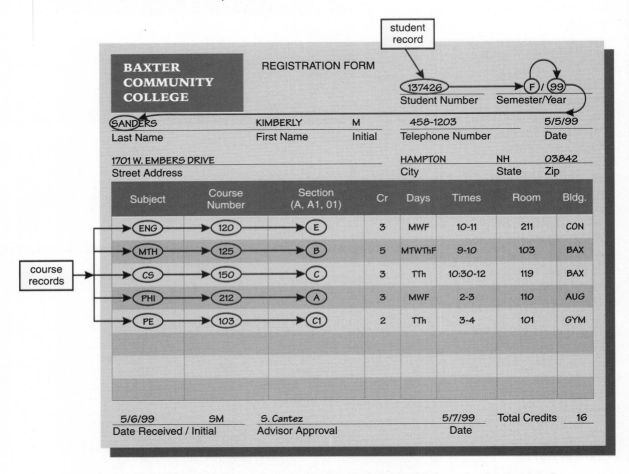

Figure 7-12   Example of a completed student registration form showing the data flow.

For suggestions on **Form Layout and Design**, visit Systems Analysis and Design Chapter 7 More on the Web.

www.scsite.com/ sad3e/ch07/

Figure 7-13 shows two different data flows for a hypothetical form layout. Notice that the job will be more difficult, time-consuming, and prone to error if data entry clerks must follow the first example rather than the second because they would have to move around the form to locate the input data.

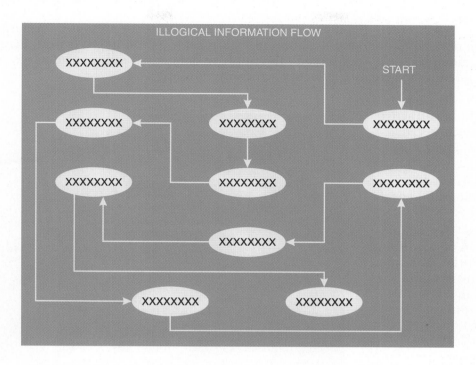

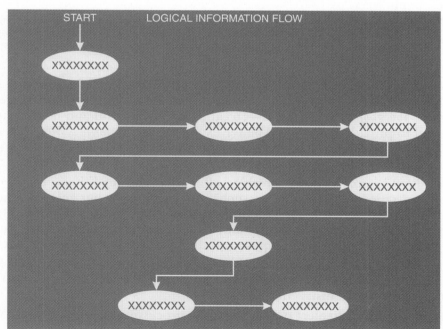

Figure 7-13   Compare the two information flows. The top diagram might be confusing to a user, while the bottom one is logical and easy to follow.

SCREEN DESIGN

Y ou first considered screen design in Chapter 6, when you learned about output screen displays. Next you will learn about design principles for data entry screens and other types of user interface screens.

All **screen displays** serve the same purpose — to present information and assist the data entry operator, as shown in Figure 7-14. As you might expect, many design guidelines for output screens also apply to data entry and user interface screens. Some guidelines for creating effective screen designs are:

1. Screen displays should be attractive and uncluttered.

2. Information on a single screen should be displayed in a meaningful, logical order.

3. Screen presentations should be consistent, with titles, messages, and instructions in the same general locations on all screen displays. Use consistent terminology — for example, do not use the terms *delete*, *cancel*, and *erase* to indicate the same action.

Figure 7-14 Effective screen designs are important. A good screen design ensures that data is collected accurately and efficiently and makes the order entry process easier for operators.

4. Messages should be specific, understandable, and professional. You should avoid using messages that are cute, cryptic, or insulting. Do not use error messages such as *WRONG! You goofed!* or *Error DE4-163* that are not helpful and might antagonize users or fail to provide help. Some better examples are: *Enter a number between 1 and 5*; *Customer number must be numeric - please re-enter*; and *Call the Accounting Department, Ext. 239 for assistance.*

5. Messages should remain on the screen so all readers can read them. Display messages for a specific length of time — such as 10 seconds — but keep in mind that if the operator is distracted, he or she might not see the messages. On the other hand, if the operator is familiar with the system, 10 seconds might be too long. One solution might be to display messages until the operator takes some further action.

6. Special effects such as color, blinking, high brightness, reverse video, and sound should be used sparingly. You should make the form interesting and easy to use, but too many effects will be distracting to users.

7. Feedback is important to alert users to lengthy processing times or delays. Messages can be used to indicate the anticipated delays and the time remaining for completing tasks.

8. Input screen designs should be documented on a **screen display layout** form for later use by programmers. Screen designs should be approved as soon as they are developed — do not wait until you finish all the screens before presenting them to users. Make sure that all of your designs are consistent, so if a user does not like one screen, you can make similar modifications to other screens.

Screen display layout forms should not be shown to end users. Instead, prepare screen mock-ups to simulate the forms that users will see. An ideal screen mock-up is a prototype that users actually can test and evaluate.

Data Entry Screen Design

Users work constantly with screen displays when they interact with the information system. Screen designs should be clear, easy to use, and support the way users prefer to work with data. Good user-friendly screen design can boost productivity and affect user attitudes toward the information system. For example, well-designed screens help the workers shown in Figure 7-15 to accomplish their goals.

Figure 7-15   Well-designed, user-friendly screens allow these customer service agents to be more productive.

The traditional method of online data entry is **form filling**, in which the form is completed on the screen. The user enters the data and then moves to the next field. Figure 7-16 shows a data entry screen form in which the user already has entered the first field value and is entering the value for the second field, as indicated by the position of the insertion point. Refer to Figure 7-16 as you review the following guidelines for effective data entry screen design.

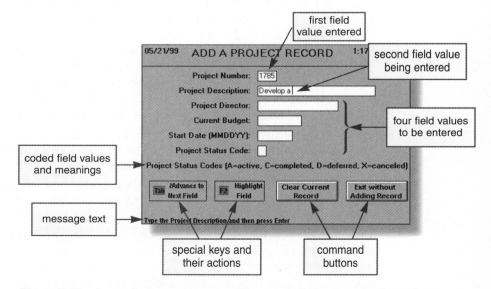

1. Restrict user access to screen locations where data is entered. When the screen in Figure 7-16 displays, the insertion point should be positioned in the first entry location. After the operator enters a project number, the insertion

Figure 7-16   A sample data entry screen. The user is in the process of entering a project description.

point should move automatically to the entry location for the next field. A user should be able to position the insertion point only in places where data is entered on the form.

2. Provide a descriptive caption for every field, and show the user where to enter the data, including the required or maximum field size. In Figure 7-16 on the previous page, the white boxes — called **field text boxes** — indicate the location and maximum length of each field. Other methods to indicate field locations are to use video highlighting, underscores, special symbols, or a combination of these features.

3. Show a sample format if values in a field must be entered in a specific format. For example, in Figure 7-16, the Start Date field caption indicates that the date format is MMDDYY. For example, November 30, 1999 is entered as 113099.

4. Require an ending keystroke for every field. Pressing the ENTER key or the TAB key normally signifies the end of a field entry. Unfortunately, some data entry programs require the user to type an ending keystroke *only* when the data entered is less than the maximum field length. Full-length entries automatically move the insertion point to the next field. This difference can be confusing to users, because they will have to decide whether they should press a key to move to the next field.

5. Do not require users to enter special characters, such as slashes in date fields. To enter a project start date of November 30, 1999, for example, the operator should enter 113099 and then the system redisplays the input in a standardized format, such as 11/30/99. The input format can be changed by using an **input mask** that contains slashes, hyphens, or other characters that serve as **separators**. For example, the input mask for a Social Security number is 999-99-9999.

6. Do not require users to type leading zeroes for numeric fields or trailing spaces for alphanumeric fields. For example, if the project number is 45, the operator should type 45 instead of 0045 before pressing the ENTER key. Similarly, entering a date as 11799 should be allowed; the entry should be interpreted and redisplayed by the system as 01/17/99. Be careful about omitting characters, however. Entering a date as 10599 indicates January 5, 1999, and not October 5, 1999. The omission of the leading zero for the date (05) indicates a completely different date to the system.

7. Do not require users to type trailing zeroes for numbers that include decimals. For example, when a user types a value of 98, the system should interpret the value as 98.00 if the field has been formatted to include numbers with two decimal places. The decimal point is needed *only* to indicate nonzero decimal places, such as 98.76.

8. Display default values so operators can press the ENTER key to accept the suggested value. If the default value is not appropriate, the operator can change it.

9. Use a default value when a field value will be constant for successive records or throughout the data entry session. For example, if records are input in order by date, the date used in the first transaction should be used as the default date until a new date is entered, at which time the new date becomes the default value.

10. Display a list of acceptable values for fields with a limited number of valid values. In Figure 7-16, all values and meanings for the Project Status Code field are displayed on the data entry screen. In some graphical data entry programs, described later in the chapter, the user can click a value in a list of valid values to enter it automatically on the form.

11. Provide a way to leave the data entry screen at any time without inputting the current record. In Figure 7-16, clicking the Exit without Adding Record button cancels the current record. Clicking the Clear Current Record button moves the insertion point back to the beginning of the form.

12. Provide operators with an opportunity to confirm the accuracy of input data before entering it by displaying a message such as, Add this record? (Y/N). A positive response (Y) adds the record, clears the entry fields, and positions the insertion point in the first field so another record can be input. If the response is negative (N), the current record is not added and the operator must be allowed to correct the errors.

13. Provide a means for operators to move among fields on the form in a standard order or in any order they choose. For example, the TAB key is used to move the insertion point to the next field, as shown in Figure 7-16 on page 7.17; you also can indicate that pressing the SHIFT+TAB keys together moves the insertion point to the previous field.

14. Design the screen form layout to match the layout of the source document. If student registration data is entered online, the data entry screen might look like the one shown in Figure 7-17, which is similar to the registration form itself.

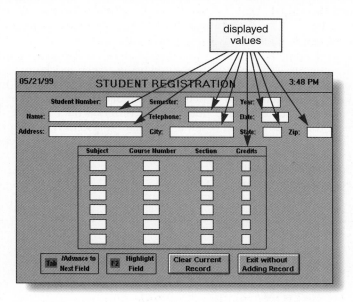

Figure 7-17   A data entry screen for the student registration form.

15. Allow the operator to add, change, delete, and view records. Screens similar to the one shown in Figure 7-16 can be used for changing, deleting, and viewing project records. In all three cases, after the operator enters a project number, the appropriate record displays with the current values for all the fields. Then the operator can change field values. Messages such as, Apply these changes? (Y/N) or Delete this record? (Y/N), should display after the operator changes or deletes a record to confirm these actions. Highlighting the letter N as the default response in these situations is wise in case the operator presses the ENTER key by mistake. When viewing a data record, the field values are displayed until the user types a special key, positively answers a prompt, or clicks a command button. One screen can be used to let users choose to add, change, delete, or view records. Then, you can provide special keys or command buttons to start the add process, to confirm a deletion, and so on.

16. Design a method to allow operators to search for a specific record. As described later in the chapter, multipurpose screens with menus and prompts can provide a powerful, flexible way to search on specific fields.

At what point during online data entry should data fields be validated? Should all appropriate field checks be applied as soon as a field is entered, or should you wait until all fields are input before validating any one of them?

Sometimes, the system environment is an important factor in selecting the validation method. In some environments, the data entry process operates much faster if fields are entered and transmitted first and then validated later. In other situations, the time difference might not be significant.

When the operating environment allows a choice, which practice is better? Some fields always should be validated upon entry, especially if the field values provide unique identification values or control the retrieval of other fields. For example, when the student number is entered on the student registration screen, the system should verify immediately that the student number is valid.

Some fields, however, cannot be verified immediately. A field involved in a combination check, for example, cannot be validated completely until all fields for that check have been entered. When your design uses immediate validation, users can correct a keystroke error immediately. If the data on the source document is obviously incorrect or missing, the user can set the source document aside and move on to the next one, to avoid entering other data for a source document that will be rejected later anyway.

On the other hand, validating data after all fields have been entered avoids the problems associated with immediate validation, but new problems can occur. If the validation occurs after the last field on the form is entered, no way exists to validate data that is entered out of sequence on the form.

The issue of validation timing should be presented using screen mock-ups so users can choose the best validation method for their needs. Remember that using different validation methods for different data entry screens in the same information system is not a good practice, however. Inconsistent screens will cause operator confusion and errors.

A KEY QUESTION

When should a design issue be decided by a systems analyst, and when should end users be allowed to select what works best? The field of **ergonomics** is concerned with improving the work environment and studying how users interact with their environment. Does this field also include input screens?

Suppose you are a systems analyst working on the input design for a new order entry system at Boolean Toys, the fastest-growing computer software developer for children in the United States. You designed and presented mock-ups of input screen designs to the data entry operators and explained their validation procedures. Some operators prefer to validate each field as data is entered and others want validation to occur after all fields have been entered. Should you include an on-screen option for users to choose their preferred method? What are the pros and cons of allowing different validation methods in the same information system?

Process Control Screen Design

In many online information systems, users can enter commands or requests using interactive input screens called **process control screens**, or **dialog screens**. Process control screens enable the user to initiate or control system actions. Two common types of process control screen designs are menu screens and prompted screens. Next, you will learn how to create effective screen designs and see how these methods can be used together.

MENU SCREENS • A **menu screen** displays a list of processing options and allows a user to choose an option. An **option** might be selected by entering an option number, pressing a function key, or by using an input device such as a keyboard, mouse, or a touch screen. This screen design is a **menu-driven system** because it uses one or more menus for process control.

Figure 7-18 shows a menu for an online project tracking system. Selecting option 1 leads the user to the data entry screen shown in Figure 7-16 on page 7.17. Selecting option 2, 3, or 4 will display the change, delete, and view screens, respectively. Selecting option 5 or 6 will print the report or display the report on the screen. Finally, selecting option 7 exits the system.

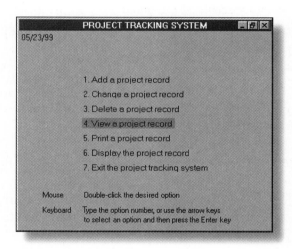

Figure 7-18   A menu for the project tracking system.

Most online information systems are more complex than the example shown in Figure 7-18. Too many options on a single screen can complicate the display. A better approach is to use a series of menus and arrange them in a logical way. The **main menu**, or top-level menu, displays several groups of options. Selecting one of these options leads to other menus, called **submenus**, with specific processing choices. In more complex systems, submenus might lead to other submenus. Eventually, every menu path leads to a specific action.

Figure 7-19 on the next page shows the menu design for an online student grading system. The main menu options are shown at the left. Each main menu option leads to a submenu shown at the right. Each submenu option leads to a specific system process. Notice that each submenu includes an option to return to the main menu. A function key or other control key also can be specified for this purpose.

Screen displays in a menu-driven system have numbers based on their level, just like data flow diagrams. The main menu is screen 0. Screens for the submenus are numbered 1.1, 1.2, and so on. For example, in Figure 7-19 the Student Score Processing menu is screen 1.0, the Class List Processing menu is screen 2.0, and so on. The data entry screen for adding a set of scores is screen 1.1, which indicates that a user must choose option 1 on the main menu, followed by option 1 on the 1.0 screen. Similarly,

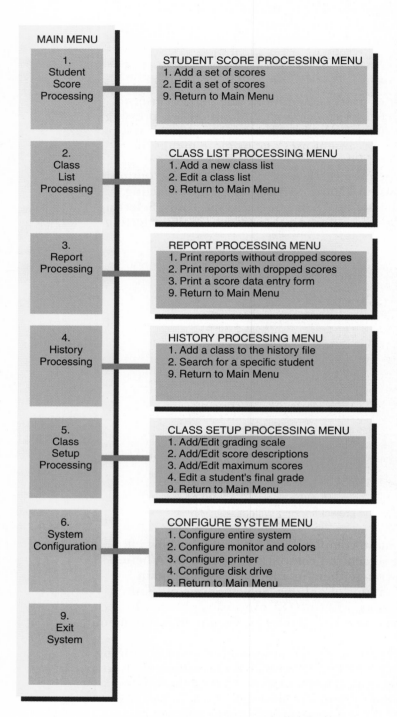

Figure 7-19   Menu hierarchy for a student grading system.

screen 1.2 is used to edit a set of scores. Screen 5.4 edits a student's final grade. This method of screen numbering is very useful for documentation purposes.

The menu method has several advantages. First, menus are easy to understand. With menus, users do not need to know all available options because they can select the option they need from a short list. Menus also make it easier to select choices — the user typically presses a single key, or clicks a menu choice, command button, or icon. Menus also can provide a logical succession of choices. For example, when a user selects the **F**ile menu, the system responds by displaying a series of options that relate to files.

Multiple-level menus can be confusing unless they are structured in a way that makes sense to users. Your menu design must reflect groupings that are logical from a user's perspective, even if the menu hierarchy does not match the system's internal processing logic.

For experienced users, multiple-level menus can be burdensome. For example, screen number 1.3.4 might be used often, but the user must go through three other menu screens to reach that screen. You can solve this problem by providing a shortcut to the screen that allows the operator to enter an option of 1.3.4 at the main menu to skip all the intermediate menu screens. A shortcut often is based on a combination of keys, such as CTRL+A to add a record. You always should provide menu navigation shortcuts for multiple-level menu systems to give operators the choice of using the menus or the shortcuts.

PROMPT SCREENS • With prompted input process control methods, the user types a response to a prompt that displays on the screen. For many years, the most familiar prompt was the DOS system prompt (**C:\>**). To respond to a computer system's prompt, the operator typed an operating system command, such as the **DIR** command to display a list of files.

Command language processors also are used for process control. **Structured Query Language (SQL)** is a popular command language. Typing an INSERT command at the SQL prompt creates a new data record. SQL queries can be saved and executed on personal computers that are networked to the company's mainframe.

Unlike a menu screen, which displays a list of options, a prompt screen might display as a blank screen with a single prompt. After the user responds to the first prompt, another prompt might appear. The screen display scrolls down and data is displayed as more commands are entered.

One type of prompted input is the **question/answer screen**, in which the system asks specific questions and provides instructions for the user. Figure 7-20 shows a question/answer screen as it might display after several questions have been asked by the system and answered by the user. Default values often are used to make it easier for the user to respond. For example, when the user is asked about another report, the default answer is N. To accept the default value, the operator presses the ENTER key. To replace the default value, the operator types another value.

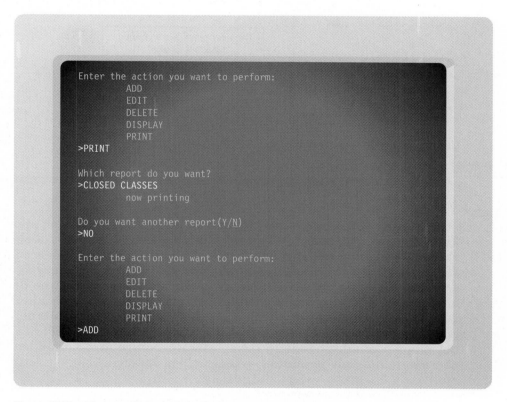

```
Enter the action you want to perform:
        ADD
        EDIT
        DELETE
        DISPLAY
        PRINT
>PRINT

Which report do you want?
>CLOSED CLASSES
        now printing

Do you want another report(Y/N)
>NO

Enter the action you want to perform:
        ADD
        EDIT
        DELETE
        DISPLAY
        PRINT
>ADD
```

Figure 7-20   The user has typed several responses to reply to screen prompts and questions. After typing ADD and pressing the ENTER key, the screen in Figure 7-21 on the next page displays.

In Figure 7-20, the user typed **PRINT** as a response to the first question, and **CLOSED CLASSES** as a response to the follow-up question. When the user types **ADD** and presses the ENTER key, the data entry screen shown in Figure 7-21 on the next page displays. Although they are not as user-friendly as menu screens, question/answer screens can be effective alternatives to menus for process control if operators know the available options and can provide the necessary responses.

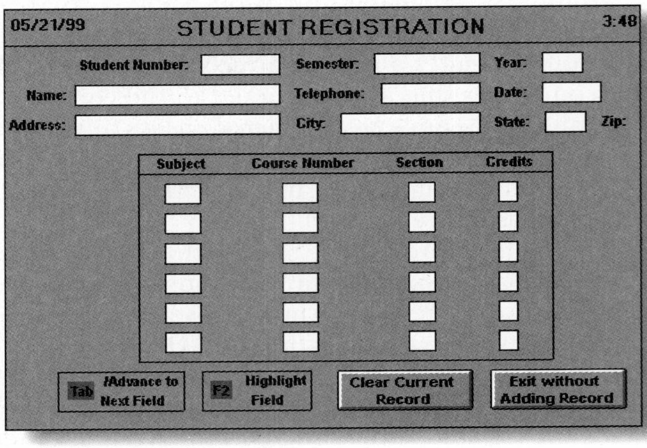

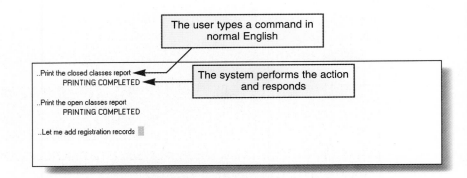

Figure 7-21 The data entry screen displays when the user enters the ADD command.

Figure 7-22 A natural language prompt screen.

For a comprehensive resource on **Natural Languages**, visit Systems Analysis and Design Chapter 7 More on the Web.

www.scsite.com/ sad3e/ch07/

Another type of prompted input uses **natural language** that allows users to type commands or requests in normal English phrases, as shown in Figure 7-22. A natural language that you might be familiar with is an online Help system that lets you ask a question and receive a response from the system. This feature makes data input easier for the operator, who does not have to memorize a series of complex commands and syntax. Natural language technology still is evolving and is being used in many Internet browsers and search engines. Figure 7-23 shows a Web site for PLS, a leading supplier of information retrieval software. Notice that natural language queries are not only permitted — they are encouraged.

ON THE NET

Natural language techniques help users find relevant information in large amounts of data by employing intelligent and intuitive search technologies. Many firms maintain Web sites that describe their natural language products and many articles have been written on the subject. Search the Internet using the phrase "natural language" and see if you can locate sites that offer more information on this topic.

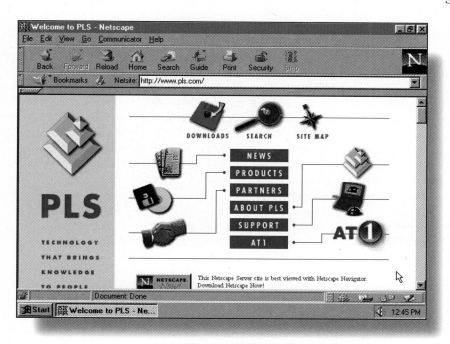

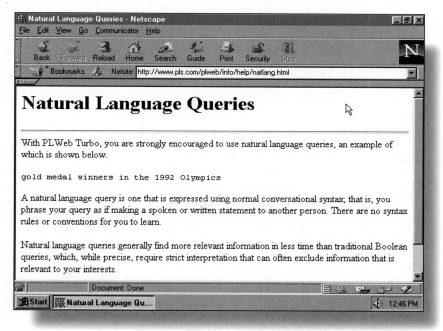

Figure 7-23   PLS offers information retrieval software that allows natural language queries.

Compared to menus, command language prompts can provide users with more control of system processes. Users need to be familiar with the commands, however, and might need training to use the command language effectively.

COMBINATION SCREENS • Menu and prompt screens often can be combined to guide a user through the selection process. For example, consider the menu system for the student grading system shown in Figure 7-19 on page 7.22. When the user selects a menu processing option under the main menu option 1, such as adding or editing a set of scores, the system responds with a prompt that asks for the name of the specific class.

To learn more about designing **User Interfaces**, visit Systems Analysis and Design Chapter 7 More on the Web.

www.scsite.com/ sad3e/ch07/

Graphical User Interfaces

Most screen designs today use a graphical user interface. A **graphical user interface (GUI)** uses graphics, such as windows, menus, and boxes, to allow users to communicate with the system. Microsoft Windows and the Apple Macintosh operating system are examples of GUIs. In Microsoft Windows, for example, a user double-clicks an icon that represents a command to start the program. A major advantage of using GUI programs is that the menus are similar in several application programs. Most software programs use a graphical interface, and many companies use GUIs for their internal systems. The most significant advantage of a GUI is the ease of learning the system, but this advantage is lost if users must work with inconsistent GUIs. Therefore, all application systems within a particular company should have a similar look and feel.

In a GUI environment, no clear distinction exists between process control screens and data entry screens. Instead, windows within a single screen are displayed, changed, or erased as required by the user. These windows can contain processing options, or data entry options, or both. To make the interface even more powerful, several programs can be open at once, and data can be transferred between programs. Because GUIs are used for data entry as well as for process control, they must follow the guidelines for good data entry screen design that you learned earlier in this chapter.

Figure 7-24 shows a GUI version of the main menu for the student grading system. The main menu options display at the top of the screen in a **menu bar**. Some software packages provide a menu builder feature that allows you to create customized menu bars and toolbars. A **toolbar** contains icons or buttons that represent shortcuts for executing common commands. These commands might be navigation shortcuts or can trigger other actions, as shown in Figure 7-24. For example, users can press the E-mail button to retrieve and read their e-mail. When they exit the e-mail program, the system will return to the desktop. A user can select a menu command either by clicking the desired choice or by pressing the ALT key and the underlined letter.

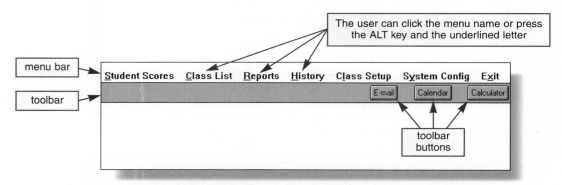

Figure 7-24   A GUI interface with a menu bar and toolbar for the student grading system.

In Figure 7-25, the user has selected the History menu name and additional commands are displayed in a **drop-down menu**. After the user decides to search for a specific student, Figure 7-26 shows a dialog box that prompts the user to enter a student name. A **dialog box** allows users to enter information about a task to be performed. Figure 7-27 shows eight methods for communicating with GUI programs. A **text box** is used for entering alphanumeric data such as an employee name. A **toggle button** is used to represent a function's status as either on or off; clicking the toggle button switches to the other status. A **list box** displays a list of choices. If the list of available choices does not fit in the box, a scroll bar like the one shown in Figure 7-27 allows the user to move quickly through the available choices. A **drop-down list box** displays the current selection; when the user clicks the arrow, a list of the available choices displays. **Option buttons** (or

radio buttons) represent groups of options. Only one option can be selected at a time; selected options contain a black dot. A **check box** is used to select one or more options from a group. Selected options are represented by a check mark. **Command buttons** initiate an immediate action such as canceling an action or saving a file. A command button name followed by an ellipsis (...) opens a dialog box that is used to gather more information about the request. Finally, a **spin bar** includes an up and a down arrow that allows the user to increase or decrease the value in the spin box.

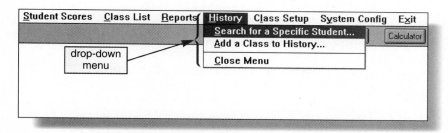

Figure 7-25   A drop-down menu for the student grading system.

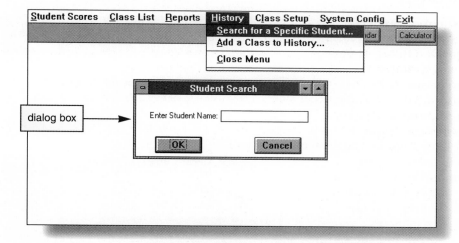

Figure 7-26   A dialog box.

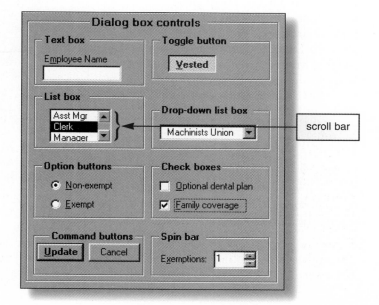

Figure 7-27   Common controls for dialog boxes.

Figure 7-28 shows a switchboard that is an alternative to process control menus. A **switchboard** contains command buttons or menus to select system options; a switchboard is like a graphical version of a main menu. The command buttons might have text labels, such as those shown in Figure 7-28 or they can be icons that represent various tasks. Some systems use a mix of menus, toolbars, and switchboards to accommodate users who prefer one method to another.

Help Screen Design

Even the most experienced users will sometimes need assistance. Online Help screens are used to display information about menu choices, procedures, function keys, concepts, and formats. Typically, users can request help by clicking a command button, toolbar button, or menu command or pressing a special key. Many information systems use several of these methods.

Help information can be provided in two ways: context-sensitive or user-selected. **Context-sensitive Help** provides instant assistance for the task in progress. Figure 7-29 shows a Help screen that displays if an end user requests help while entering data into the SEMESTER field. Notice that the Help screen describes the field and lists all valid field values and their descriptions. Clicking the Close button returns the user to the task. Context-sensitive Help is a quick way to learn more about the current task.

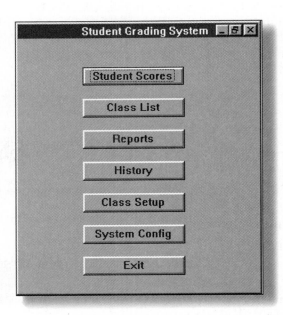

Figure 7-28 A switchboard for the student grading system.

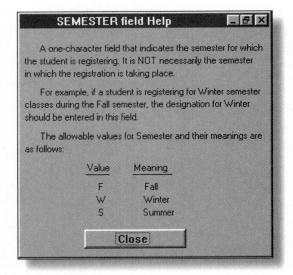

Figure 7-29 A context-sensitive Help screen for a data entry field in the student registration system.

User-selected Help displays a Help switchboard or menu when the user requests help. By making appropriate choices through the menus and submenus, the user eventually reaches a screen with the desired information. Figure 7-30 shows the main Help switchboard for the grading system.

Many information systems provide both context-sensitive and user-selected Help. Numerous commercial packages also include a hypertext feature that can be used in internal software development. **Hypertext** allows a user to click a selected term in the Help text, called a **link**, and then the system displays additional information about that term. Hypertext is a series of links that permit users to navigate various Help topics. Hypertext is a powerful, user-friendly feature that will enhance any Help system.

The guidelines for designing menu, prompt, and switchboard screens also apply to Help menu screens. In addition, keep the following suggestions in mind when designing text Help screens.

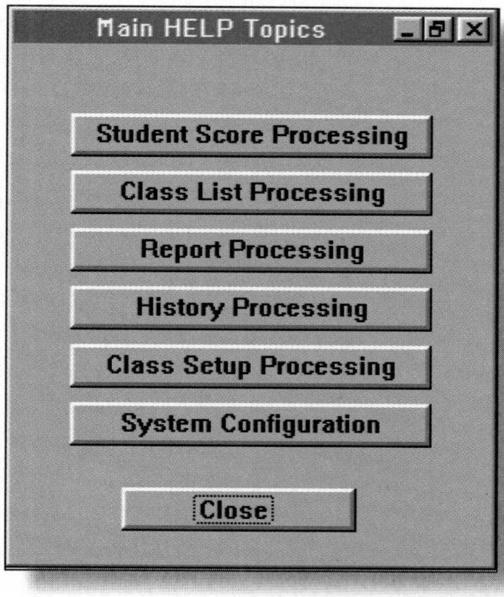

- Provide a direct route for the user to return to the point from where help was requested.
- Title every Help screen to identify the Help text that follows.
- Keep the Help text simple, concise, and easy to understand.
- Present attractive screens — Help screens should not be cluttered or confusing. Inserting blank lines between paragraphs makes text easier to read.
- Provide examples when appropriate.
- Use hyperlinks to provide links to related Help topics, both within and outside of the system.
- If a person or department in the organization is responsible for providing help to users, include a reference to the location, telephone number, or e-mail address of the Help support group.

Figure 7-30   A main Help switchboard for the grading system.

INPUT CONTROL

Input control includes the necessary measures to ensure that input data is correct, complete, and secure. Input control must be stressed during every phase of input design. Many input control measures already have been discussed. Effective source document design promotes the accuracy and quality of data. When using a batch input method, critical source document fields can be checked and validated during data capture. When input takes place, batch control totals can be used. The batch input program should write all rejected records to a log file that then must be checked periodically to ensure that all rejected records are corrected and reentered later. When using online data entry, the program can validate all data fields, and refuse to accept any incorrect values.

Every piece of information in the system should be traceable back to the input data that produced it. This means that you must provide an **audit trail** that records the source of all data and the date it was input. In addition to recording the original source, an audit trail must show how and when data is accessed or changed, and by whom. All these actions must be logged in an audit trail file and monitored carefully.

A company must have procedures for handling source documents to ensure that data is not lost before it enters the system, and these rules must be followed throughout the organization. All source documents that originate from outside the organization should be logged when they are received. Whenever source documents pass between

For additional information on **Audit Trails**, visit Systems Analysis and Design Chapter 7 More on the Web.

www.scsite.com/ sad3e/ch07/

departments, the transfer should be recorded. To prevent duplicate data from entering the system, a source document should be stamped or otherwise marked as it goes through a data entry process.

Data security protects data from loss or damage and recovers data when it is lost or damaged. Once data is transferred to another source, such as the microfilm shown in Figure 7-31, source documents should be stored in a safe location for some specified length of time. The company should have a **records retention policy** that meets all legal requirements and business needs.

Audit trail files and reports should be stored and saved. Then, if a data file is damaged, you can reconstruct the lost data. Data security also involves protecting data from unauthorized access. System sign-on procedures should prevent unauthorized individuals from entering the system. Data files should be given passwords that are changed regularly. Having several levels of access also is advisable. For example, a data entry person might be allowed to *view* a credit limit, but not allowed to *change* it. Sensitive data can be **encrypted**, or coded, in a process called **encryption**, so only users with decoding software can read it.

For an overview of **Encryption**, visit Systems Analysis and Design Chapter 7 More on the Web.

www.scsite.com/ sad3e/ch07/

Figure 7-31 Organizations can use microfilm copies of source documents for security purposes and to provide an audit trail. The U.S. Government, for example, stores census data forms on microfilm for later reference.

ON THE NET

Data encryption technology is changing rapidly. To be up to date, you should search for the latest information on this subject. Data encryption involves several major issues: individual privacy, government concerns about security, and the technology itself. Some Web search engines such as Yahoo! have a dedicated category for Internet security and encryption. Choose one of these key issues and use the Yahoo! search engine to learn about the latest developments.

The information systems department usually is responsible for the output and input control measures covered in Chapters 6 and 7. As a systems analyst, you must develop controls that ensure the quality and accuracy of data, which in turn will affect the quality of the information produced for the business needs of the organization.

AUTOMATED DESIGN TOOLS

In Chapter 6, you learned about screen and form generator software provided with many DBMS, 4GL, and CASE products. A screen or form generator can be useful during input design as well. When you design a screen using one of these tools, the program produces specifications that can serve as documentation so screen layout forms are not needed. Screen mock-ups can be used to show users what the final design will look like during the design stage. Because they interact with the data dictionary, screen or form generators can ensure consistency and help you develop better designs.

Many screen or form generators create programs with field validation checks. When a mock-up is developed, users or operators can use the generated program to simulate a realistic data entry session, or a combination of menu screens and switchboards can be used to simulate a user interface. Feedback and comments from users and IS staff members will be extremely valuable in the actual implementation of the information system.

SOFTWEAR, LIMITED — INPUT DESIGN

The management at SoftWear, Limited decided to use the payroll package developed by Pacific Software Solutions and customize it by adding its own ESIP system to handle all the features of the Employee Savings and Investment Plan.

Pacific Software Solutions offers free training for new customers of its payroll package, so systems analysts Rick Williams and Becky Evans attended a three day *train-the-trainer* workshop at the company's site in Los Angeles. When they returned, they began developing a one-day training session for SWL users, including people from the accounting, payroll, and human resources departments. The initial training would include the features and processing functions of the new payroll package that was scheduled to arrive the following week.

Meanwhile, programmer/analyst Tom Adams began to design the inputs for the ESIP system. Tom needed to develop four inputs. Two of these inputs were new forms that also would serve as source documents: an ESIP Option Form and an ESIP Deduction Authorization Form. The other two inputs would be data entry screens based on the new forms.

Tom started by designing the ESIP Option Form. He included an ESIP ID code, an option name, and other information. For each field, he established a range of acceptable values. Tom intended that the new form shown in Figure 7-32 could be used for adding new ESIP

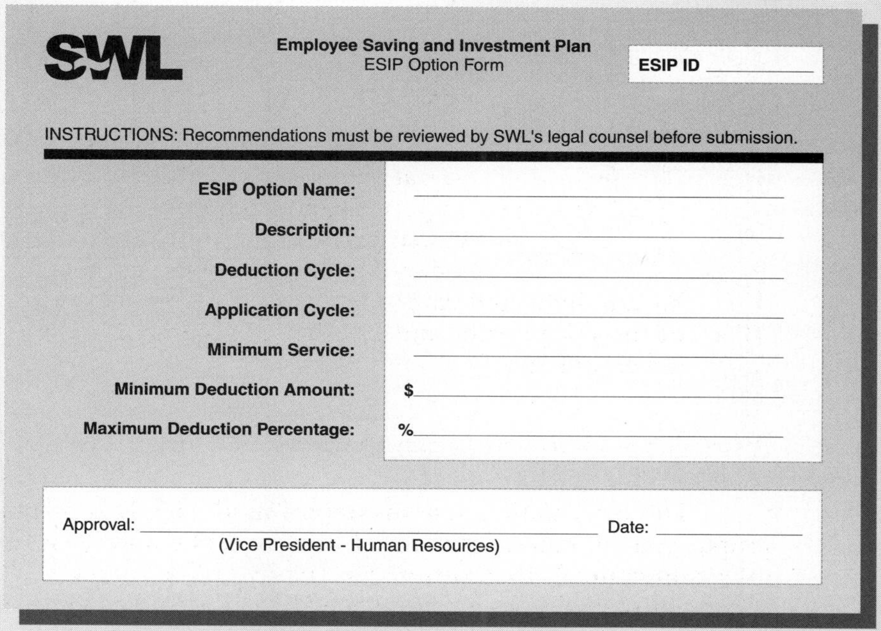

SWL
Employee Saving and Investment Plan
ESIP Option Form
ESIP ID ________

INSTRUCTIONS: Recommendations must be reviewed by SWL's legal counsel before submission.

ESIP Option Name: ________
Description: ________
Deduction Cycle: ________
Application Cycle: ________
Minimum Service: ________
Minimum Deduction Amount: $________
Maximum Deduction Percentage: %________

Approval: ________ Date: ________
(Vice President - Human Resources)

Figure 7-32 The design for a form to add or change ESIP system options.

options and modifying existing ones when authorized by the vice president of human resources.

Next, Tom worked on a data entry screen based on the ESIP Option Form. Using SWL's existing screen design standards, he quickly developed the screen shown in Figure 7-33. Tom decided that the screen would be more useful if data on existing options could be viewed. By entering the appropriate action codes to add, delete, or find a record, the user could perform these actions.

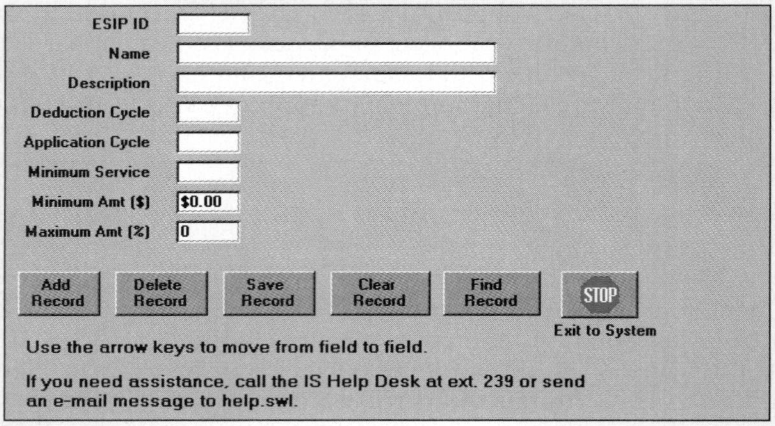

Figure 7-33   Data entry screen for adding and changing ESIP options.

Instead of waiting until all input design was finished, Tom decided to create mock-ups to show Tina Pham, vice president of human resources and Mike Feiner, director of human resources. The two mock-ups are shown in Figure 7-34. Tom reasoned that if any comments or suggestions were offered, they also would apply to other input screens.

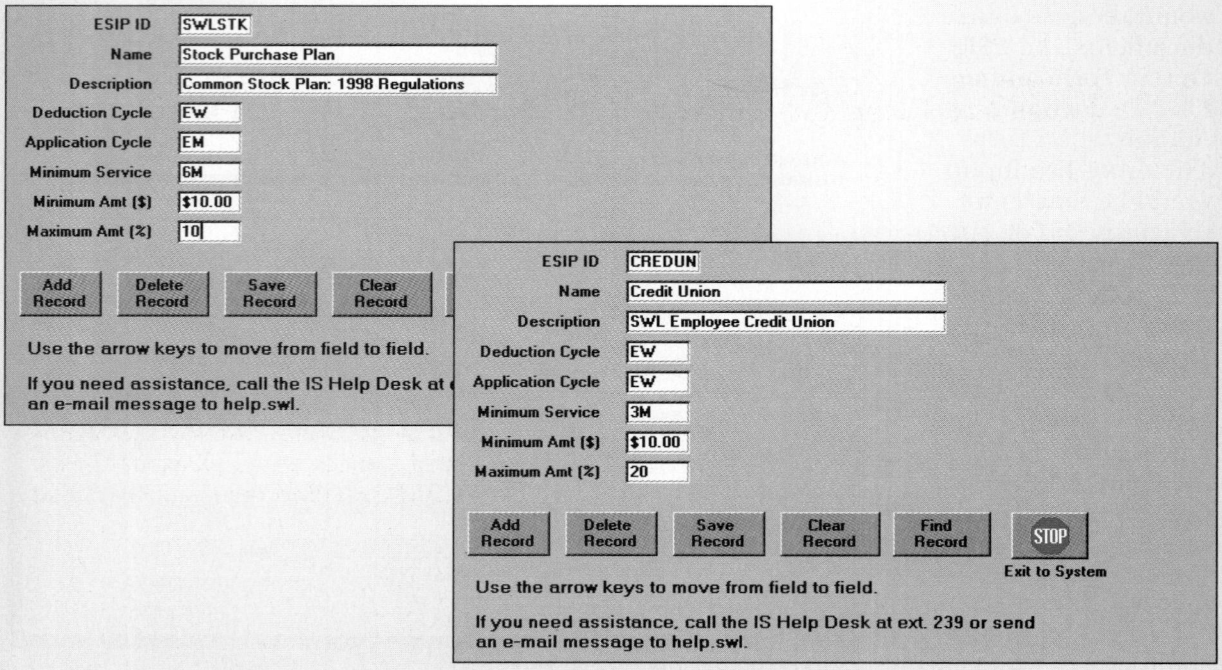

Figure 7-34   Tom's mock-up screens with actual data to obtain user approval.

The ESIP Deduction Authorization Form was a more complicated form than the ESIP Option Form, because it required more data and signatures. It took several hours for Tom to design the form shown in Figure 7-35. He divided the form into three sections: the employee completes the information in the top section; human resources completes the middle section; and payroll representatives completes the bottom section.

SWL

Employee Saving and Investment Plan
ESIP Deduction Authorization Form

Name

Social Security Number

☐☐☐-☐☐-☐☐☐☐

Option (Check One):

SWL Credit Union ☐
Employee Stock Purchase ☐
Other ________ ☐

Deduction Amount:

$________

I want to select the ESIP option and deduction amount specified above, and I authorize the company to make this deduction from my regular earnings. I have read the plan description and I understand that SWL's ESIP plan is subject to company policies and various federal and state regulations that might change in the future.

Signed ________ Date ________

Human Resources Department Approval:

By ________ Date ________

Payroll Department Verification:

By ________ Date ________

Effective Date ________

Figure 7-35 The design for the ESIP Deduction Authorization Form.

Tom next designed a data entry screen based on this form. He made the screen consistent with the other ESIP screen designs. Now a user could add, delete, save, clear, or find a record by clicking the appropriate command buttons. Tom also provided instructions to the operator for exiting from the system.

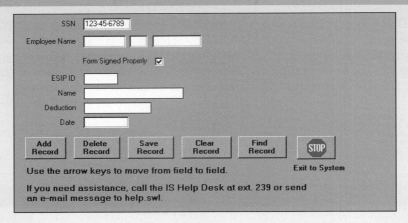

Figure 7-36 Data entry screen for ESIP deductions. Here, the user has just entered an employee's Social Security number, and is about to press the ENTER key. Notice that the form features various command buttons, including a STOP button that exits the program.

Tom decided to create a series of mock-ups to show users how the new ESIP deduction screen would work. Figure 7-36 shows the screen after the user has entered an employee's Social Security number. In Figure 7-37, the system has retrieved the employee's name, Sean Fitzpatrick, so the user can verify it against the source document. Figure 7-38 shows that the user has entered the stock purchase plan code, SWLSTK, and the system has supplied the name. Finally, the user enters the $10.00 deduction and the current date.

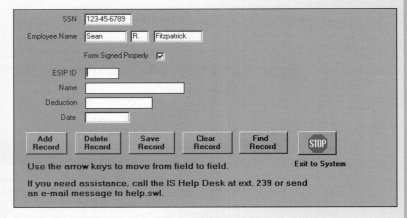

Figure 7-37 After the user presses the ENTER key, the system retrieves the employee's name from the master file and displays it so the user can validate it. Note that the user must check a box to verify that the form has been signed properly.

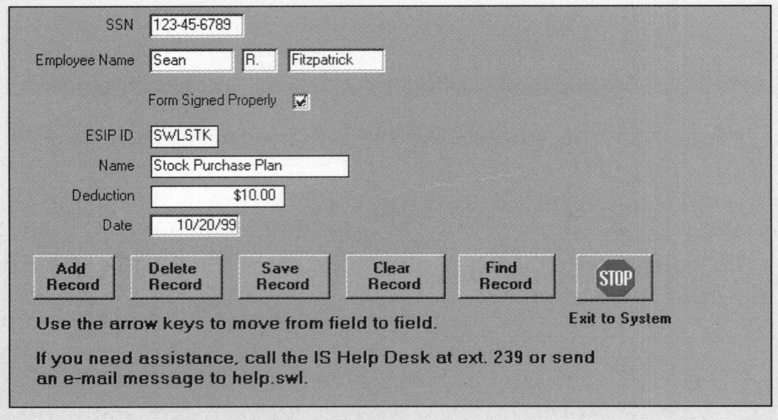

Figure 7-38 In this step, the user enters a stock purchase deduction of $10.00 for the employee and is ready to save the record.

The users approved the new design, with one suggestion — the system date should be added automatically as the entry date. Tom proceeded to make this change.

As part of the final design, Tom realized that he needed a menu screen to link the two data entry screens, so he designed the switchboard screen shown in Figure 7-39. The switchboard allows the user to perform various other tasks based on comments that users made during the design process. Now that he had a working model of the input system, Tom went back to the users again to show them the complete package.

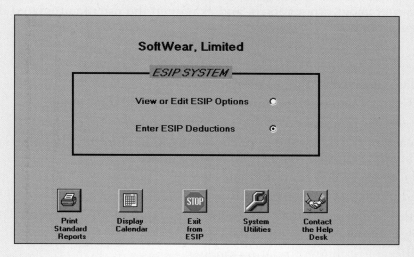

Figure 7-39 The new ESIP switchboard design features command buttons for various user options.

 YOUR TURN — Tom Adams has a potential problem that he wants you to help him solve. Tom planned to have the new ESIP Deduction Authorization Form handle all current and future deductions, including the employee stock purchase plan. SWL's legal counsel, however, says that in her opinion, the Employee Stock Purchase Plan might require a separate enrollment and change form, because of certain governmental regulations. While she is studying that possibility, Tom wants you to design a separate input source document for the stock purchase plan and a data entry screen so the designs will be ready, if needed, and the overall project will not be delayed. You will need to start by reviewing the existing stock purchase form that is shown in Chapter 3 in Figure 3-19 on page 3.28.

CHAPTER SUMMARY

In this chapter, you studied the input design stage of the systems design phase. Input quality and accuracy are essential for every successful information system. With today's technology, a wide variety of input media is available, including optical, voice, and magnetic recognition devices; special-purpose terminals; and graphical input devices.

Input design includes selecting appropriate input media and methods, developing efficient input procedures, reducing input volume, and avoiding input errors. In carrying out these tasks, the systems analyst must consider three key procedures: data capture, data entry, and data input. Data capture involves identifying and recording source data. Data entry involves converting source data into a computer-readable form. Data input involves the actual introduction of data into the information system.

To help reduce input errors, data is validated by one or more checks of sequence, existence, range and limit, reasonableness, validity, combination, and batch control.

You learned about source document design features, followed by input record design for batch input data and various types of input screen design. Form-filling screens are the most common method of online data entry. Both menu-driven and prompted-input screens enable end users to access data and request system actions. Graphical user interfaces (GUIs) are the most popular approach to screen design. A GUI combines the functions of data entry and process control by using powerful graphical and windowing capabilities. Online Help screens provide context-sensitive or user-selected assistance to system users.

Finally, you learned about input control and examined the use of automated design tools in the systems input design process.

Review Questions

1. What are the main objectives of input design?
2. Explain the differences among data capture, data entry, and data input.
3. List and briefly discuss four ways of reducing input volume.
4. Briefly discuss each of the data validation checks mentioned in this chapter. Is data validation performed during data capture, data entry, or data input?
5. What is a control total? What is a hash total?
6. What is included in each of the typical source document zones?
7. Briefly discuss the design guidelines applicable to all types of input screens.
8. Discuss the design guidelines for online data entry.
9. Describe two different prompted input techniques.
10. What does it mean when an information system is said to be menu-driven?
11. What is a GUI? How does a GUI differ from character-based screen design? Consider data entry screens and process control screens in your answer.
12. Briefly describe the different types of screens and screen controls that can be used in a GUI for inputting information.
13. What does context-sensitive Help mean?
14. What is meant by input data security? List and briefly discuss several different input data security measures.

Discussion Questions

1. Some systems analysts maintain that when converting from a manual system, the new computerized system should use the existing source documents. If new source documents are designed, data entry operators must be retrained and the probability of errors is much higher. On the other hand, if the system is designed around current source documents, then less chance exists for error in the capture and input of data. Costs also will be lower because new forms will not have to be designed or printed, and training will not be necessary. Others argue that the analyst should determine whether more effective source documents are needed. In this case, savings resulting from increased efficiency will offset any of the costs associated with new source documents. Which position do you support? Why?

2. At Baxter Community College, whenever a faculty member contacts the Records Office for a student's address or telephone number, a clerk accesses the online student information system to retrieve the data stored for that student. Faculty members complain that the addresses and telephone numbers they are given often are outdated.

   When a student enrolls at Baxter, his or her current address and telephone number are entered into the student information system. If the student moves, he or she must obtain, complete, and return a change-of-address form to the Records Office. In practice, it has been determined that few students submit these forms. Therefore, much of the student information system data is out of date.

The registration form (see Figure 7-8 on page 7.11) includes spaces for the student's current address and telephone number. These fields are ignored during the data entry of the registration forms, which is accomplished using the screen shown in Figure 7-17 on page 7.19. After all the registration forms have been entered, they are filed and stored. When time permits, a Records Office clerk examines each registration form and enters corrected addresses and telephone numbers when appropriate, so that final grade reports sent at the end of the semester are addressed correctly. This lengthy process is necessary because change-of-address forms rarely are submitted.

Faculty members have requested that address and telephone corrections be entered as the registration forms are entered, so the student information system always contains current data. Records Office personnel argue that they already are swamped with work during registration, and the current practice is the best they can do. Do you have any suggestions for resolving this problem?

3. Obtain copies of one or more actual source documents used to capture data, such as credit card charge slips, application forms, tax forms, and so on. Comment on each form's design and consider its layout, spacing, zoning, and appearance. Discuss how well the document would serve as the basis of an online data entry form.

CASE STUDIES

NEW CENTURY HEALTH CLINIC — INPUT DESIGN

 fter completing the output design for the system at New Century Health Clinic, you are ready to turn your attention to input design. Based on what you have learned in this chapter, complete the following assignments.

Assignments

1. Determine the data required for a new patient. Design an input source document that will be used to capture this data.

2. Design a data entry screen to handle the entry of data for a new patient.

3. Besides the data entry screens required for a new patient, what other data entry screens are required? Design data entry screens for each.

4. What input controls are needed for the system? Write a report to the associates of New Century Health Clinic to describe your recommended input controls.

BATES VIDEO CLUB

 he Bates Video Club has hired you to design two online data entry screens. Based on what you have learned in this chapter, complete the following assignments.

Assignments

1. Design a data entry screen for entering new members, using the source document shown in Figure 7-7 on page 7.11. Assume that name and address are both 30-character fields, city is a 25-character field, credit card numbers can contain up to 16 digits, and member number is a 5-digit number.

2. You were not consulted when the membership application form shown in Figure 7-7 on page 7.11 was designed originally. Do you have any criticisms about its design? What improvements can you suggest? Justify your suggestions.

3. The owner of Bates Video Club also would like you to design a video rental form (the input source document). Use your word processor or graph paper to design the form. In addition to the video information, the video rental form must include the following fields from the membership application form: Name, Address, City, State, Zip Code, Home Telephone, Work Telephone, and Member Number. Assume that a member can rent only five videos at one time.

4. Design a data entry screen for the video rental form you designed. Note that the Name, Address, City, State, Zip Code, Home Telephone, Work Telephone, and Member Number fields will be retrieved from the Member file on the system.

CARL'S CORVETTES

 arl Dekker, owner of Carl's Corvettes, recently started computerizing his customer, sales, and service record keeping. In the Chapter 6 case study, the contents of appointment and task records were listed and the Mechanic's Service Record report and the appointment scheduler's Task History display were described.

Assignments

1. Design a data entry screen for creating new customer records. The customer file records designed by Carl include the following fields:

Customer Name	40 characters
Street Address	30 characters
City	15 characters
State	2 characters
ZIP code	5 numeric digits
Home Telephone Number	7 numeric digits
Work Telephone Number	7 numeric digits

   and, for each Corvette owned by the customer:

Vehicle Identification No.	17 characters
Year	4 characters
Color	10 characters

2. Design a data entry screen for adding a new task code record that contains a task code, task description, and a standard time for each task.

3. Design one data entry screen for adding a new appointment record and its associated task records. Assume a maximum of 10 tasks per appointment.

4. Outline a menu system for controlling the processing for Carl's Corvettes. Provide options for adding, changing, deleting, or viewing either customer records, task code records, or appointment records; printing lists of all current customers and tasks; displaying task histories; and printing the Mechanic's Service Record report. Design all necessary prompt screens.

CHAPTER 8

SDLC PHASES

Phase 1
Systems Planning

Phase 2
Systems Analysis

Phase 3
Systems Design

Phase 4
Systems
Implementation

Phase 5

Operations Support

OBJECTIVES

When you finish this chapter, you will be able to:

- Define the terms entity, file, record, and attribute and discuss the various types of keys
- Draw an entity-relationship diagram, and explain the types of entity relationships
- Define cardinality, cardinality notation, and crow's foot notation
- Explain normalization, including examples of first, second, and third normal form
- Compare and contrast database management and file processing environments
- Explain various types of database organization, including hierarchical, network, and relational design
- Describe various types of files, including master, transaction, table, work, history, and security
- Evaluate methods of file organization, including sequential, direct, and indexed
- Calculate file sizes and storage requirements
- Discuss file and database control measures

File and Database Design

File and database design is the third of four chapters in the systems design phase. During file and database design, you will study data management issues and data structures that are necessary to support the information system objectives.

INTRODUCTION

I n the systems analysis phase, you created data flow diagrams and identified data elements, data flows, and data stores to build a logical design for the information system. Now, in the systems design phase, you will develop a physical plan for data organization, storage, and retrieval.

This chapter begins with a review of data terminology and concepts. Then you will study the relationships among various data objects and learn how to draw entity-relationship diagrams that describe these associations. You also will learn how to use normalization concepts to build an effective database design. The chapter explains file organization and access methods, including various file types and concludes with a discussion of physical design issues, such as file media, sizing, and controls.

DATA TERMINOLOGY AND CONCEPTS

T he systems analyst must understand the basic elements of **data design** — entities, fields, records, files, and keys — and how to build these elements into a data management system. Figure 8-1 on the next page shows an entity named CUSTOMER, and a data file that consists of fields, records, and various keys.

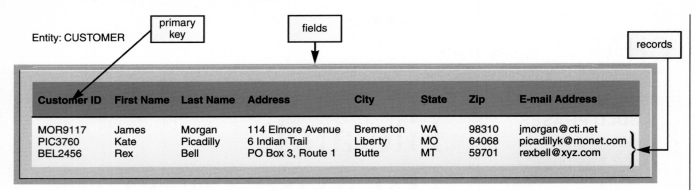

Figure 8-1   A file for an entity named CUSTOMER includes records, fields, and a primary key.

Definitions

An **entity** is a person, place, thing, or event for which data is collected and maintained. For example, an online sales system would include entities named CUSTOMER, ORDER, PRODUCT, and SUPPLIER. When you prepared DFDs during the systems analysis phase, you identified various entities and data stores. Now you must analyze their relationships as part of a database.

A **field**, or an **attribute**, is a single characteristic or fact about an entity. In the example shown in Figure 8-1, the entity named CUSTOMER has fields to store data about each customer, such as the First Name, Last Name, and Address.

A **record** is a collection of fields that describes one instance of an entity, such as one customer, one order, or one product. A record might have one or dozens of fields, depending on what information is needed for business purposes. If the online sales system offers 1,500 items, the product file has 1,500 records — one record for each product.

A **file** is a set of records that contains data about a specific entity. For example, files might consist of data for all customers, products, orders, or suppliers.

A **key field** is a field that is used to locate, retrieve, or identify a specific record. A key that *uniquely* identifies each record in an entity is called a **primary key**, which can be composed of one or more fields. Other types of keys are explained in the next section.

Key Fields

Key fields are identified during the systems analysis phase. During the systems design phase, you use keys to organize, access, and maintain data structures. The four types of keys are primary keys, candidate keys, foreign keys, and secondary keys.

PRIMARY KEYS • A **primary key** is the field or combination of fields that *uniquely* and *minimally* identifies a particular member of an entity. In a customer file, for example, the customer number is a **unique** primary key because no two customers can have the same customer number. This key also is **minimal** because it contains no information beyond what is needed to identify the customer. In Figure 8-1, Customer ID is an example of a primary key based on a single field.

A primary key also can be composed of two or more fields. For example, if a student registers for three courses, his or her student number will appear in three records in the registration system. If one of those courses has 20 students, 20 separate records will exist for that course number — one record for each student who registered.

In the registration file, neither the student number nor the course number is unique, so neither field can be a primary key. To identify a specific student in a specific course, the primary key must be a *combination* of student number and course number. In this case, the primary key is a combination key, or a **multivalued key**.

Figure 8-2 shows four different record designs. The first three designs have single-field primary keys. In the fourth record, however, the primary key is a combination key of the STUDENT-NUMBER and COURSE-ID fields.

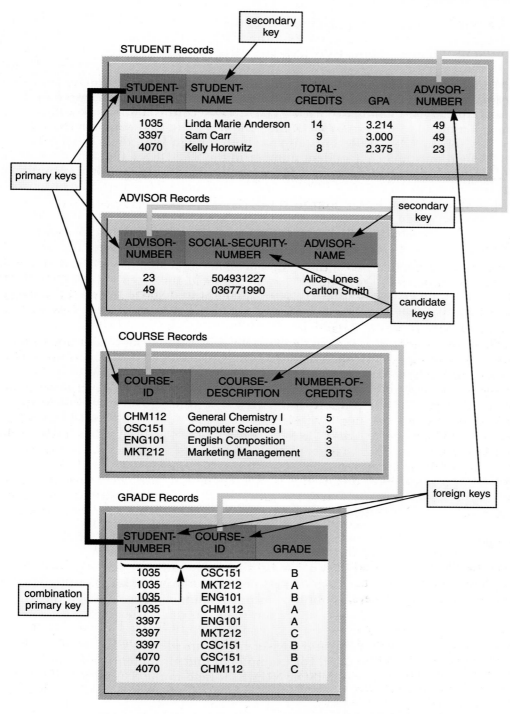

Figure 8-2 Examples of primary keys, candidate keys, foreign keys, and secondary keys.

CANDIDATE KEYS • Sometimes you have a choice of fields or field combinations to use as the primary key. Any field that *could* serve as a primary key is called a **candidate key**. For example, if every employee has a unique employee number, then either the employee number or the Social Security number could be used as a primary key. Because you can designate only one field as a primary key, you should select the field that contains the least amount of data and is the easiest to use. Any field that is not a primary key or a candidate key is called a **nonkey field**.

The primary keys shown in Figure 8-2 on the previous page also are candidate keys. Two other candidate keys are pointed out: the SOCIAL-SECURITY-NUMBER field in the ADVISOR Records and the COURSE-DESCRIPTION field in the COURSE Records.

FOREIGN KEYS • A **foreign key** is a field in one file that must match a primary key value in another file in order to establish a relationship, or a link, between the two files. In Figure 8-2, the advisor number in each STUDENT Record is a foreign key because it must match a number in the ADVISOR file. The two fields that combine to form the primary key for the GRADE Records also are both foreign keys: the STUDENT-NUMBER field must match a student number in the STUDENT file, and the COURSE-ID field must match one of the course IDs in the COURSE file. Another example of a foreign key occurs in an ORDER file where the customer ID for a specific order must match a customer ID in the CUSTOMER file.

In Chapter 7, you learned that validity checks can help avoid data input errors. One type of validity check, called **referential integrity**, ensures that a foreign key value cannot be entered unless it matches an existing primary key in another file. In the example shown in Figure 8-2, referential integrity will not allow a user to enter an advisor number in the STUDENT file unless a valid advisor number exists in the ADVISOR file. Referential integrity also can deny a user request to delete a record if the record has a primary key that matches foreign keys in other files. For example, you cannot delete an advisor number from the ADVISOR file while records in the STUDENT file still refer to that advisor number. In this case, students must be reassigned to other advisors, and *then* the advisor record could be deleted.

As shown in Figure 8-2, foreign keys do not need to be unique. A particular advisor number can appear several times in the STUDENT file — once for each student assigned to that advisor. In the GRADE file, the foreign keys based on student numbers and course IDs can appear any number of times. Because the two foreign keys form a unique primary key, however, only *one* combination of a specific student and a specific course can exist.

SECONDARY KEYS • A **secondary key** is a field or combination of fields that can be used to access or retrieve records. Secondary key values do not need to be unique. For example, if you need to access records for only those customers in a specific ZIP code, then the ZIP code field is used as a secondary key. Secondary keys also can be used to sort or display records in a certain order. For example, you could use the GPA field in a STUDENT file to display records for all students in grade point order.

The need for a secondary key arises because a file can have only one primary key. In a CUSTOMER file, the customer number is the primary key. You might know a customer's name, however, but not the customer's number. If you assign the CUSTOMER-NAME field as a secondary key, then you can retrieve records by using the CUSTOMER-NAME field.

In Figure 8-2, student name and advisor names are identified as secondary keys, but other fields also could be used. For example, to find all students who have a particular advisor, you could use the ADVISOR-NUMBER field in the STUDENT file as a secondary key.

DATA RELATIONSHIPS AND ENTITY-RELATIONSHIP DIAGRAMS

ecall that an entity is a person, place, thing, or event for which data is collected. A **relationship** is a logical link between entities based on how they interact. For example, a relationship exists between the entities PRODUCT and WAREHOUSE because products are stored in warehouses.

Entity-Relationship Diagrams

An **entity-relationship diagram (ERD)** is a graphical model of the information system that shows the relationships among system entities. Figure 8-3 shows the basic format of an ERD. Each entity is represented as a rectangle and a diamond represents the **relation**, or relationship, that connects the entities. The entity rectangles are labeled with singular nouns, and the relationship diamonds are labeled with active verbs. For example, in Figure 8-4, a doctor *treats* a patient. You also might say that a patient is *treated by* a doctor, but it is better to use the active voice. Some CASE tools permit two references — one in each direction.

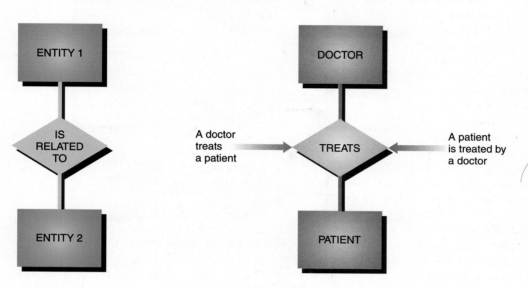

Figure 8-3 An entity-relationship diagram (ERD).

Figure 8-4 In an entity-relationship diagram, entities are labeled with singular nouns and relationships are labeled with verbs. The ERD is interpreted as a simple English sentence.

Unlike data flow diagrams and systems flowcharts, entity-relationship diagrams do not depict data or information flows. An ERD has no arrowheads. One of the entities must be positioned above or to the left of the other entity, but this positioning does not imply a superior/inferior relationship between the entities or a flow from the first entity to the second entity.

Three main types of relationships can exist between entities. A **one-to-one relationship**, abbreviated **1:1**, exists when exactly one of the second entity occurs for each instance of the first entity. ERDs for several possible 1:1 entity relationships are shown in Figure 8-5 on the next page. A number 1 is placed alongside each of the two lines connecting a rectangle to the diamond to indicate the 1:1 relationship.

A **one-to-many relationship**, abbreviated **1:M**, exists when one occurrence of the first entity can be related to many occurrences of the second entity, but each occurrence of the second entity can be associated with only one occurrence of the first entity. For example, the relationship between DEPARTMENT and EMPLOYEE is one-to-many: one department can have many employees, but each employee works in only one department. Several possible 1:M entity-relationship diagrams are shown in Figure 8-6 on the next page. The line connecting the *many* entity to the relationship is labeled with an M, whereas a *1* labels the other connecting line.

How many is *many*? The first 1:M relationship shown in Figure 8-6 shows the entities INDIVIDUAL and AUTOMOBILE. One automobile is owned by one individual, but one person might own twenty automobiles, or one, or even none. Thus, *many* can mean any number, including zero.

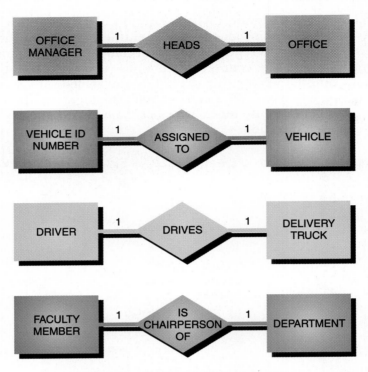

Figure 8-5   One-to-one (1:1) relationships.

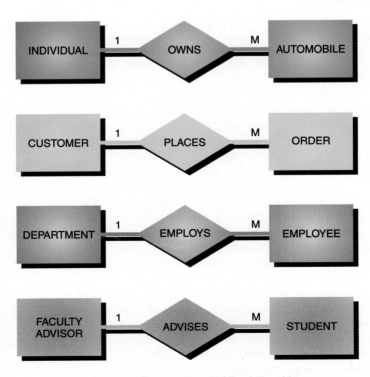

Figure 8-6   One-to-many (1:M) relationships.

A **many-to-many relationship**, abbreviated **M:N**, exists when one instance of the first entity can be related to many instances of the second entity, and one instance of the second entity can be related to many instances of the first entity. The relationship between STUDENT and CLASS, for example, is many-to-many — one student can take many classes, and one class can have many students enrolled in it. Figure 8-7 shows several M:N entity-relationships. One of the lines connecting an entity to a relation is labeled with an *M*; an *N* labels the connection between the other entity and the relation.

A complete ERD shows all system entities and relationships. Figure 8-8 has five entities: SALES REP, CUSTOMER, ORDER, WAREHOUSE, and PRODUCT. In this example, the relationship between SALES REP and CUSTOMER is one-to-many. In some organizations, however, a customer might be served by more than one sales rep, in which case this relationship changes to a many-to-many relationship. The relationship between WAREHOUSE and PRODUCT is many-to-many, but the relationship would be one-to-many if the company has only one warehouse in which to store all products.

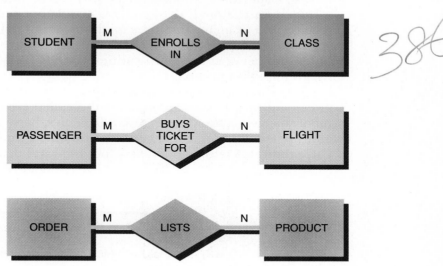

Figure 8-7 Many-to-many (M:N) relationships.

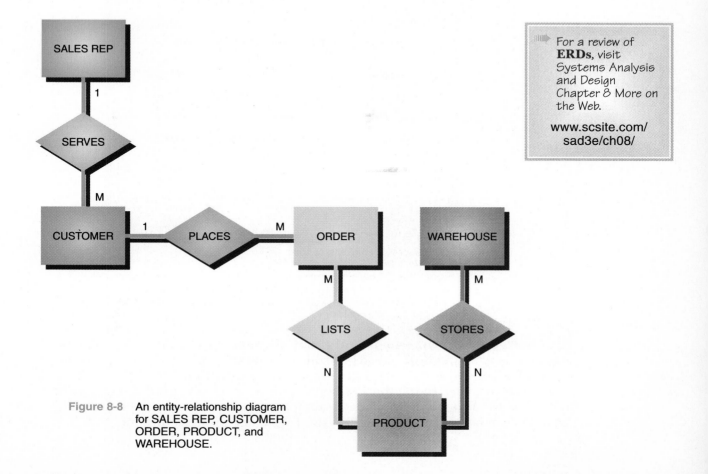

For a review of **ERDs**, visit Systems Analysis and Design Chapter 8 More on the Web.

www.scsite.com/ sad3e/ch08/

Figure 8-8 An entity-relationship diagram for SALES REP, CUSTOMER, ORDER, PRODUCT, and WAREHOUSE.

Cardinality

Figures 8-5, 8-6, and 8-7 on pages 8.6 and 8.7 describe various relationships among entities: one-to-one, one-to-many, and many-to-many. The nature of these links also is called cardinality. As an analyst, you must understand cardinality in order to design files and databases that reflect accurately all relationships among entities.

Cardinality describes how instances of one entity relate to instances of another entity. In a specific relationship, an entity can be **mandatory**, which means that it always is required, or **optional**. If an entity is mandatory, only one instance might be allowed in a relationship, or many instances might be permitted. For example, one customer can have many orders, or none, but each order *must* have one and only one customer. In the relationship between these two entities, the CUSTOMER entity is mandatory and the ORDER entity is optional.

Several different types of **cardinality notation** can be used to show relationships between entities. One common method is called **crow's foot notation** because of the symbol shapes. As shown in Figure 8-9, circles, bars, and symbols are used to indicate various possibilities. A single bar indicates one, a double bar indicates one and only one, a circle indicates zero, and a crow's foot indicates many.

One and only one CUSTOMER can have anywhere from zero to many of the ORDER entity.

One and only one CLIENT can have one ADDRESS or many.

One and only one EMPLOYEE can have one SPOUSE or none.

One EMPLOYEE, or many employees, or none, can be assigned to one PROJECT, or many projects, or none.

Figure 8-9 Crow's foot notation is a common method of indicating cardinality. The four examples show how you can use various symbols to describe the relationship between two entities.

In Figure 8-9, four examples of cardinality notation are shown. In the first example, one and only one CUSTOMER can have anywhere from zero to many of the ORDER entity. In the second example, one and only one CLIENT can have one ADDRESS or many. In the third example, one and only one EMPLOYEE can have one SPOUSE or none. In the fourth example, one EMPLOYEE, or many employees, or none, can be assigned to one PROJECT, or many projects, or none.

Most CASE products support the drawing of ERDs from entities in the data repository. Figure 8-10 shows part of a library system ERD drawn using the Visible Analyst CASE tool. Notice that crow's foot notation cardinality has been used to show the nature of the relationships, which are described in both directions.

Creating an ERD

Entity-relationship diagrams are easy to construct if you follow these steps:

1. *Identify the entities.* Review your DFDs and list the people, places, things, or events for which data is collected. Be sure to identify all data stores. For example, consider the rental car company shown in Figure 8-11. People might include customers and employees; places might include rental locations and return points; things would include vehicles, rental contracts, and customer reservations; events would include making a reservation, executing a rental contract, and returning a car. Information about customer preferences and past rental history might be maintained in a data store.

2. *Determine all significant events or activities for two or more entities.* This task requires you to analyze the business operations and identify the entities and the nature of the relationship between them. For example, a CUSTOMER makes a RESERVATION and a LOCATION has various VEHICLES available for rental.

3. *Analyze the nature of the interaction.* Does the interaction involve one instance of the entity or many? Is the pattern always the same or does it depend on some factor? For example, consider the relationship between CUSTOMER and RESERVATION. One and only one customer can have one, many, or no reservations, but each reservation must have one and only one customer. Also, a LOCATION can have one VEHICLE, or many, or none — but each vehicle must have one and only one assigned location.

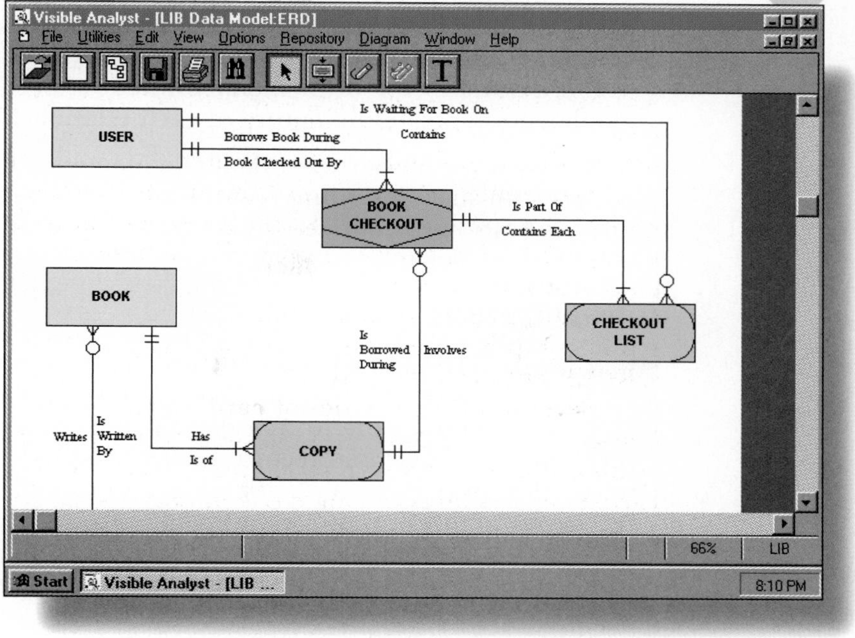

Figure 8-10   An ERD for a library system drawn with Visible Analyst. Notice that crow's foot notation has been used and relationships are described in both directions.

Figure 8-11   When a customer rents or returns a car, several entities are involved, including the customer, the reservation, the vehicle, and the location.

4. *Draw the ERD.* You can draw the ERD manually or by using a CASE tool. Study the diagram carefully to ensure that all entities and relationships are shown accurately. If you are using a type of cardinality notation, be sure that you have used the correct symbols to indicate the nature of each relationship.

Now that you understand database elements, including entities and their relationships, you can start designing records and constructing database files. The first step is the normalization of your record designs, as you will see next.

NORMALIZATION

Normalization is a process by which you identify and correct inherent problems and complexities in your record designs. A **record design** specifies the fields and identifies the primary key, if any, for all records in a particular file. Working with a set of initial record designs, you use normalization to develop an overall database design that is simple, flexible, and free of data redundancy.

The normalization process typically involves three stages: first normal form, second normal form, and third normal form. These three normal forms constitute a progression in which a record in first normal form is better than one that is unnormalized; a record in second normal form is better yet; and a record in third normal form represents the best design.

First Normal Form

A record is in **first normal form (1NF)** if it does not contain a repeating group. A **repeating group** is a set of data items that can occur any number of times in a single record. As an example, consider the order record shown in Figure 8-12. In addition to the order number and date, the record contains repetitions of the product number, description, and number ordered. An **unnormalized** record is one that contains a repeating group, which means that a single record has multiple values in a particular field. A format for an unnormalized record layout is:

ORDER (<u>ORDER-NUM</u>, ORDER-DATE, (PRODUCT-NUM, PRODUCT-DESC, NUM-ORDERED))

RECORD#	<u>ORDER- NUM</u>	ORDER- DATE	PRODUCT- NUM	PRODUCT- DESC	NUM- ORDERED
1	40311	03111999	304	All-purpose gadget	7
			633	Trangam	1
			684	Super gismo	4
2	40312	03111999	128	Steel widget	12
			304	All-purpose gadget	3
3	40313	03121999	304	All-purpose gadget	144

repeating groups

Figure 8-12   Three unnormalized ORDER records. Records 1 and 2 have repeating groups because they contain several products.

This notation indicates that the ORDER record design contains five fields, which are listed within the outer parentheses. The ORDER-NUM field is underlined to indicate that it is the primary key. The PRODUCT-NUM, PRODUCT-DESC, and NUM-ORDERED fields are enclosed within an inner set of parentheses to indicate that they are fields within a repeating group. If a customer orders three different products in one order, then the set PRODUCT-NUM, PRODUCT-DESC, and NUM-ORDERED will repeat three times, as shown in record 1 in Figure 8-12. Notice that the second record also has a repeating group. In a 1NF record, each field has only *one* value.

Eliminating one or more repeating groups greatly simplifies the record design. To convert an unnormalized record to 1NF, you expand the primary key to include the key of the repeating group. Therefore, the 1NF form of the ORDER record is:

ORDER (<u>ORDER-NUM</u>, ORDER-DATE, <u>PRODUCT-NUM</u>, PRODUCT-DESC, NUM-ORDERED)

RECORD#	ORDER- <u>NUM</u>	ORDER- DATE	PRODUCT- <u>NUM</u>	PRODUCT- DESC	NUM- ORDERED	
1	40311	03111999	304	All-purpose gadget	7	
2	40311	03111999	633	Trangam	1	
3	40311	03111999	684	Super gismo	4	repeating groups have been eliminated
4	40312	03111999	128	Steel widget	12	
5	40312	03111999	304	All-purpose gadget	3	
6	40313	03121999	304	All-purpose gadget	144	

Figure 8-13   The ORDER records as they appear in 1NF. Repeating groups have been eliminated. Now one record exists for each instance.

Figure 8-13 shows the 1NF form for the ORDER records. The primary key of the 1NF records cannot be the ORDER-NUM field alone, because multiple records can have the same order number value when many items are ordered at the same time. Similarly, PRODUCT-NUM cannot be the primary key. Because each record reflects a specific item in a specific order, you need a *combination* of ORDER-NUM and PRODUCT-NUM to identify a single record uniquely. Therefore, the combination of ORDER-NUM and PRODUCT-NUM is the primary key.

Second Normal Form

To understand second normal form (2NF), you first must understand the concept of functional dependence. The field X is **functionally dependent** on the field Y if a value for Y determines a single value for X. For example, an order date is dependent on an order number; for a particular order number, there is only one value for the order date. In contrast, the product description is not dependent on the order number. For a particular order number, there might be several product descriptions — one for each item ordered.

A record design is in **second normal form (2NF)** if it is in 1NF and if all fields that are not part of the primary key are dependent on the *entire* primary key. If any field in a 1NF record depends on only one of the fields in a combination primary key, then the record is not in 2NF. A 1NF record with a primary key that is a single field is automatically in 2NF.

Now reexamine the 1NF design for the ORDER record:

ORDER (<u>ORDER-NUM</u>, ORDER-DATE, <u>PRODUCT-NUM</u>, PRODUCT-DESC, NUM-ORDERED)

The primary key is the combination of the order number and the product number. The NUM-ORDERED field depends on the *entire* primary key. For the number ordered to be meaningful, you need to know the product number *and* a specific order number. The ORDER-DATE field, however, depends only on the order number, which is a part of the primary key, and the PRODUCT-DESC field depends only on the product number, which is another part of the primary key. Because all fields are not entirely dependent on the primary key, this record design is *not* in 2NF.

Why is it important to move from 1NF to 2NF? Four kinds of problems are found with records in 1NF that do not exist in 2NF. First, consider the work that is necessary to change a particular product's description. Suppose 1,000 current orders exist for product number 304. Changing the product description involves modifying 1,000 records for product number 304. Thus, updating all 1,000 records would be cumbersome and expensive.

Second, 1NF records can contain inconsistent data. Nothing prevents product number 304 from having two or more different product descriptions in two or more different records. In fact, if product number 304 appeared in 30 order records, 30 different product descriptions could exist for the same product number.

The third problem arises when you want to add a new product for your customers to order. Because the primary key must include an order number *and* a product number, you need values for *both* fields to add a record. What value do you use for the order number when you want to add a new product that has not been ordered by any customer? You could use a dummy order number, and then replace it with a real order number when the product is ordered to solve this problem, but this solution also is problematic.

The fourth problem concerns deletions. If all the related records are deleted once an order is filled and paid for, what happens if you delete the only record that contains product number 633? The information about that product number and its description is lost.

A standard process exists for converting a record design from 1NF to 2NF. First, create a new record design for each field in the primary key. Then, create new record designs for all combinations of primary key fields taken two at a time, three at a time, and so on, until you have a record with the *entire* original primary key. For each new record, designate a field (or a combination of fields) as a primary key. In our sample 1NF record, you begin by creating these three partial records:

(ORDER-NUM,
(PRODUCT-NUM,
(ORDER-NUM, PRODUCT-NUM,

Finally, place each of the remaining fields with its appropriate primary key, which is the *minimal* key upon which it depends. When you have finished placing all the fields, remove any record that has had no additional field placed into it. The *remaining* records are the 2NF version of your original record design. For the example record, this process yields:

ORDER (ORDER-NUM, ORDER-DATE)
PRODUCT (PRODUCT-NUM, PRODUCT-DESC)
ORDER-LINE (ORDER-NUM, PRODUCT-NUM, NUM-ORDERED)

For an additional example of **Normalization**, visit Systems Analysis and Design Chapter 8 More on the Web.

www.scsite.com/ sad3e/ch08/

Instead of one 1NF record design, you now have three records that are in 2NF. These records then are assigned new, descriptive names: ORDER, PRODUCT, and ORDER-LINE, respectively. The 2NF versions are shown in Figure 8-14.

Has the 2NF design eliminated all potential problems? To change a product description, now you change just one PRODUCT record. Multiple, inconsistent values for the product description are impossible because the description appears in only one location. To add a new product, you simply create a new PRODUCT record, instead of creating a dummy order record. When you remove the last ORDER-LINE record for a particular product number, you do not lose that product number and its description because the PRODUCT record still exists. The four potential problems have been eliminated, and the three 2NF record designs are superior to both the original unnormalized record and the 1NF record design.

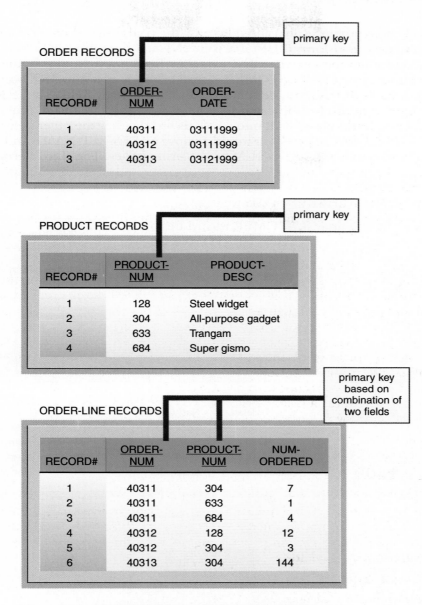

Figure 8-14   ORDER RECORDS, PRODUCT RECORDS, and
ORDER-LINE RECORDS in 2NF. All fields are
functionally dependent on the primary key.

Third Normal Form

Now consider the following CUSTOMER record design:

CUSTOMER (<u>CUSTOMER-NUM</u>, CUSTOMER-NAME, ADDRESS, SALES-REP-NUM, SALES-REP-NAME)

This record is in 1NF because it has no repeating groups. The record is also in 2NF because the primary key is a single field. But this design still has four potential problems similar to the four 2NF problems described earlier. Changing the name of a sales rep still requires changing every record in which that sales rep name appears. Nothing about the design prohibits a particular sales rep from having different names in different records. In addition, because the sales rep name is part of the CUSTOMER record, you must create a dummy CUSTOMER record to add a new sales rep who has not yet been assigned any customers. Finally, if you delete all the records for customers of sales rep number 22, you will lose that sales rep's number and name.

These potential problems are caused because the record design is not in 3NF. A record design is in **third normal form** (**3NF**) if it is in 2NF *and* if no nonkey field is dependent on another nonkey field. Remember that a **nonkey field** is a field that is not a candidate key for the primary key. The CUSTOMER record example is not in 3NF because one nonkey field, SALES-REP-NAME, depends on another nonkey field, SALES-REP-NUM.

To convert this record to 3NF, remove all fields from the 2NF record that depend on another nonkey field and place them into a new record that has the other field as a primary key. For our CUSTOMER record, you would remove SALES-REP-NAME and place it into a new record with SALES-REP-NUM as the primary key. The third normal form is:

CUSTOMER (<u>CUSTOMER-NUM</u>, CUSTOMER-NAME, ADDRESS, SALES-REP-NUM)

SALES-REP (<u>SALES-REP-NUM</u>, SALES-REP-NAME)

By converting the one CUSTOMER record design to 3NF, you created two record designs: CUSTOMER and SALES-REP. Sample records for the 2NF design and the 3NF version of the same data are shown in Figure 8-15. Only the key identifies 3NF records.

> in 2NF, the nonkey field SALES-REP-NAME is functionally dependent on another nonkey field SALES-REP-NUM

CUSTOMER IN 2NF

RECORD#	CUSTOMER-NUM	CUSTOMER-NAME	ADDRESS	SALES-REP-NUM	SALES-REP-NAME
1	108	Benedict, Louise	San Diego, CA	41	Kaplan, James
2	233	Corelli, Helen	Nashua, NH	22	McBride, Jon
3	254	Gomez, J.P.	Butte, MT	38	Stein, Ellen
4	431	Lee, M.	Snow Camp, NC	74	Roman, Harold
5	779	Paulski, Diane	Lead, SD	38	Stein, Ellen
6	800	Zuider, Z.	Greer, SC	74	Roman, Harold

Figure 8-15a 2NF record design for the CUSTOMER data.

CUSTOMER IN 3NF

RECORD#	CUSTOMER-NUM	CUSTOMER-NAME	ADDRESS	SALES-REP-NUM
1	108	Benedict, Louise	San Diego, CA	41
2	233	Corelli, Helen	Nashua, NH	22
3	254	Gomez, J.P.	Butte, MT	38
4	431	Lee, M.	Snow Camp, NC	74
5	779	Paulski, Diane	Lead, SD	38
6	800	Zuider, Z.	Greer, SC	74

SALES-REP IN 3NF

> in 3NF, no nonkey field is dependent on another nonkey field

RECORD#	SALES-REP-NUM	SALES-REP-NAME
1	22	McBride, Jon
2	38	Stein, Ellen
3	41	Kaplan, James
4	74	Roman, Harold

Figure 8-15b When CUSTOMER data is transformed from 2NF to 3NF, the result is two records: CUSTOMER and SALES-REP.

A Normalization Example

To show the normalization process, consider the familiar situation shown in Figure 8-16, which is a system with three entities: ADVISOR, STUDENT, and COURSE, as shown in the ERD in Figure 8-17.

Figure 8-16   A faculty advisor, who represents an entity, can advise many students, each of whom can register for one or many courses.

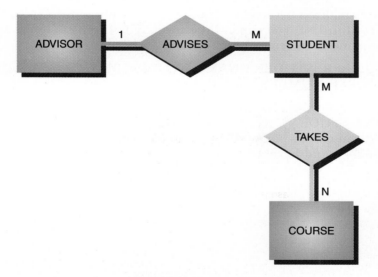

Figure 8-17   An initial entity-relationship diagram for ADVISOR, STUDENT, and COURSE.

The initial design of the record for the STUDENT entity includes the student number, student name, total credits taken, grade point average (GPA), advisor number, advisor name, and, for every course the student has taken, the course number, course description, and grade received.

Figure 8-18 on the next page shows three unnormalized STUDENT record designs. The STUDENT record design can be written as:

STUDENT (<u>STUDENT-NUMBER</u>, STUDENT-NAME, TOTAL-CREDITS, GPA, ADVISOR-NUMBER, ADVISOR-NAME, (COURSE-NUMBER, COURSE-DESC, GRADE))

STUDENT

STUDENT-NUMBER	STUDENT-NAME	TOTAL-CREDITS	GPA	ADVISOR-NUMBER	ADVISOR-NAME	COURSE-NUMBER	COURSE-DESC	GRADE
1035	Linda	17	3.647	49	Smith	CSC151	Computer Science I	B
						MKT212	Marketing Management	A
						ENG101	English Composition	B
						CHM112	General Chemistry I	A
						BUS105	Introduction to Business	A
3397	Sam	9	3.000	49	Smith	ENG101	English Composition	A
						MKT212	Marketing Management	C
						CSC151	Computer Science I	B
4070	Kelly	14	2.214	23	Jones	CSC151	Computer Science I	B
						CHM112	General Chemistry I	C
						ENG101	English Composition	C
						BUS105	Introduction to Business	C

repeating groups

Figure 8-18   Three unnormalized STUDENT records with repeating groups because each student has several classes.

The record designs for the ADVISOR and COURSE entities are:

ADVISOR (<u>ADVISOR-NUMBER</u>, ADVISOR-NAME)

COURSE (<u>COURSE-NUMBER</u>, COURSE-DESC, NUM-CREDITS)

The ADVISOR and COURSE records already are in 3NF. The STUDENT record, however, is unnormalized because it contains a repeating group. To convert the STUDENT record to 1NF, you expand the primary key to include the key of the repeating group and then remove the repeating group, producing:

STUDENT (<u>STUDENT-NUMBER</u>, STUDENT-NAME, TOTAL-CREDITS, GPA, ADVISOR-NUMBER, ADVISOR-NAME, <u>COURSE-NUMBER</u>, COURSE-DESC, GRADE)

Figure 8-19 shows the 1NF version of the sample STUDENT data. Do any of the fields in the 1NF STUDENT record depend on only a portion of the primary key? The student name, total credits, GPA, advisor number, and advisor name all relate only to the student number, and have no relationship to the course number. The course description depends on the course number, but not on the student number. Only the GRADE field depends on the *entire* primary key.

STUDENT

STUDENT-NUMBER	STUDENT-NAME	TOTAL-CREDITS	GPA	ADVISOR-NUMBER	ADVISOR-NAME	COURSE-NUMBER	COURSE-DESC	GRADE
1035	Linda	17	3.647	49	Smith	CSC151	Computer Science I	B
1035	Linda	17	3.647	49	Smith	MKT212	Marketing Management	A
1035	Linda	17	3.647	49	Smith	ENG101	English Composition	B
1035	Linda	17	3.647	49	Smith	CHM112	General Chemistry I	A
1035	Linda	17	3.647	49	Smith	BUS105	Introduction to Business	A
3397	Sam	9	3.000	49	Smith	ENG101	English Composition	A
3397	Sam	9	3.000	49	Smith	MKT212	Marketing Management	C
3397	Sam	9	3.000	49	Smith	CSC151	Computer Science I	B
4070	Kelly	14	2.214	23	Jones	CSC151	Computer Science I	B
4070	Kelly	14	2.214	23	Jones	CHM112	General Chemistry I	C
4070	Kelly	14	2.214	23	Jones	ENG101	English Composition	C
4070	Kelly	14	2.214	23	Jones	BUS105	Introduction to Business	C

Figure 8-19   1NF STUDENT records. The repeating groups have been eliminated.

Creating records for each field and combination of fields in the primary key, and then placing the other fields with their appropriate key produces the following record designs:

STUDENT (<u>STUDENT-NUMBER</u>, STUDENT-NAME, TOTAL-CREDITS, GPA, ADVISOR-NUMBER, ADVISOR-NAME)

COURSE-X (<u>COURSE-NUMBER</u>, COURSE-DESC)

GRADE (<u>STUDENT-NUMBER</u>, <u>COURSE-NUMBER</u>, GRADE)

The original STUDENT record now has been expanded to three records, all in 2NF. One of these records, COURSE-X, has the same primary key as the original COURSE record. At any time during normalization, if you have two records with identical primary keys, you should merge them into a single record that includes all fields from both records. In this case, the new COURSE-X record has no field that was not already in the original COURSE record design, so you can keep the original COURSE record and discard the COURSE-X record.

Figure 8-20 shows the 2NF STUDENT, COURSE, and GRADE records for the sample data. Are all three records in 3NF? COURSE and GRADE are in 3NF. STUDENT is not in 3NF, however, because the ADVISOR-NAME field depends on the advisor number, which is not part of the STUDENT primary key. To convert STUDENT to 3NF, you remove the ADVISOR-NAME field from the STUDENT record and place it into a new record with ADVISOR-NUMBER as the primary key. The new record duplicates your original ADVISOR record, however, so a new record is not needed.

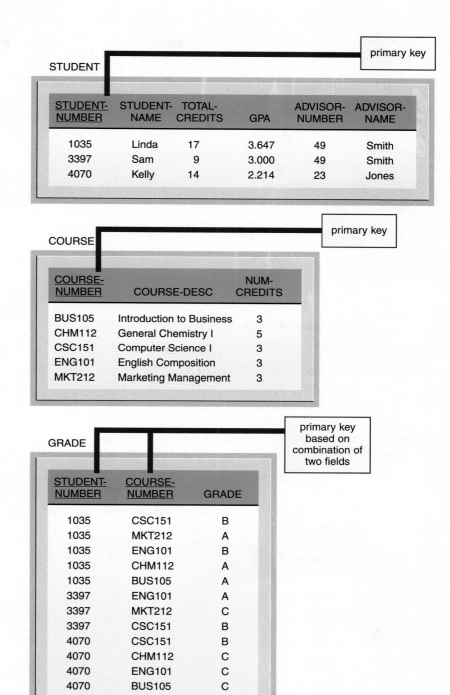

Figure 8-20   STUDENT, COURSE, and GRADE records in 2NF. All fields are functionally dependent on the primary key.

STUDENT

STUDENT-NUMBER	STUDENT-NAME	TOTAL-CREDITS	GPA	ADVISOR-NUMBER
1035	Linda	17	3.647	49
3397	Sam	9	3.000	49
4070	Kelly	14	2.214	23

in 3NF, no nonkey field is dependent on another nonkey field

Professor

ADVISOR

ADVISOR-NUMBER	ADVISOR-NAME
23	Jones
49	Smith

COURSE

COURSE-NUMBER	COURSE-DESC	NUM-CREDITS
BUS105	Introduction to Business	3
CHM112	General Chemistry I	5
CSC151	Computer Science I	3
ENG101	English Composition	3
MKT212	Marketing Management	3

GRADE

STUDENT-NUMBER	COURSE-NUMBER	GRADE
1035	CSC151	B
1035	MKT212	A
1035	ENG101	B
1035	CHM112	A
1035	BUS105	A
3397	ENG101	A
3397	MKT212	C
3397	CSC151	B
4070	CSC151	B
4070	CHM112	C
4070	ENG101	C
4070	BUS105	C

Figure 8-21 STUDENT, ADVISOR, COURSE, and GRADE records in 3NF. When STUDENT records are transformed from 2NF to 3NF, the result is two records: STUDENT and ADVISOR.

Figure 8-21 shows the 3NF versions of the sample data for STUDENT, ADVISOR, COURSE, and GRADE. The final 3NF design for all the entity records is:

STUDENT (STUDENT-NUMBER, STUDENT NAME, TOTAL-CREDITS, GPA, ADVISOR-NUMBER)

ADVISOR (ADVISOR-NUMBER, ADVISOR-NAME)

COURSE (COURSE-NUMBER, COURSE-DESC, NUM-CREDITS)

GRADE (STUDENT-NUMBER, COURSE-NUMBER, GRADE)

Now there are four entities: STUDENT, ADVISOR, COURSE, and GRADE. Figure 8-22 shows the complete ERD after normalization. If you go back to Figure 8-17 on page 8.15, which was drawn before you identified GRADE as an entity, you can see that the M:N relationship between STUDENT and COURSE has been converted into two 1:M relationships: one relationship between STUDENT and GRADE and the other relationship between COURSE and GRADE.

To create 3NF designs, you must understand the nature of first, second, and third normal forms. In your work as a systems analyst, you will encounter designs that are much more complex than the examples in this chapter. You also should know that normal forms beyond 3NF exist, but they rarely are used in most business-oriented systems.

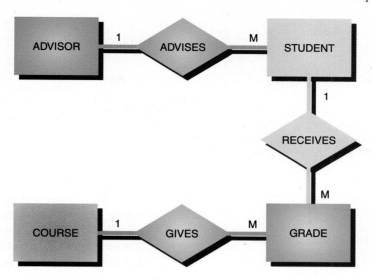

Figure 8-22   The entity-relationship diagram for STUDENT, ADVISOR, and COURSE after normalization. the entity GRADE was identified during the normalization process.

STEPS IN DATABASE DESIGN

After normalizing your record designs, you are ready to create the database. The following four analysis and design steps can be used to create database and file designs. To highlight the steps, consider another familiar situation shown in Figure 8-23, which is an information system for a video rental store.

1. *Create the initial ERD.* Review your data flow diagrams to identify all entities and data stores. Typically, each data store will be represented as an ERD entity. Next, create a rough draft of the ERD. Carefully analyze each relationship to determine if it is 1:1, 1:M, or M:N. Figure 8-24 shows the initial ERD for the entities MEMBER and VIDEO in the video rental system.

2. *Assign all data elements to entities.* Verify that every data element in the data dictionary is associated logically with an entity. For the video rental system, the initial record designs with all data elements are listed under the ERD in Figure 8-24.

Figure 8-23   A video rental involves several entities, including a member, a video, and a rental agreement. In the video store's information system, each entity is represented by a data record that contains various fields.

```
MEMBER (MEMBER-NUMBER, NAME, ADDRESS, CITY, STATE, ZIP, HOME-PHONE,
  WORK-PHONE, CREDIT-CARD-CODE, CREDIT-CARD-NUMBER, (VIDEO-ID, TITLE,
  DATE-RENTED, DATE-RETURNED))
VIDEO (VIDEO-ID, TITLE)
```

Figure 8-24   The initial entity-relationship diagram and unnormalized record designs for the video rental system.

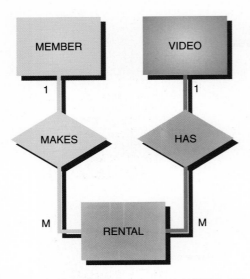

MEMBER (<u>MEMBER-NUMBER</u>, NAME, ADDRESS, CITY, STATE, ZIP, HOME-PHONE,
  WORK-PHONE, CREDIT-CARD-CODE, CREDIT-CARD-NUMBER)
VIDEO (<u>VIDEO-ID</u>, TITLE)
RENTAL (<u>MEMBER-NUMBER</u>, <u>VIDEO-ID</u>, DATE-RENTED, DATE-RETURNED)

Figure 8-25 The final entity-relationship diagram and normalized record designs for the video rental system.

3. *Create 3NF designs for all records, taking care to identify all primary, secondary, and foreign keys.* Generate the final ERD that will include new entities identified during normalization. Figure 8-25 shows the final ERD and the normalized records. Notice that a new entity, RENTAL, was identified during normalization and the M:N relationship is simplified into two 1:M relationships.

4. *Verify all data dictionary entries.* Make sure that the data dictionary entries for all data stores, records, and data elements are documented completely and correctly.

After creating your final ERD and normalized record designs, you can transform them into a database. First, you simply consider the design, elements, and characteristics of database management systems.

DATABASE MANAGEMENT

In a **file processing** environment, each user department has its own information system and each system has its own collection of files. Three potential problems exist in a file processing environment. The first problem is **data redundancy**, which means that data common to two or more information systems is stored in multiple files. Data redundancy requires more storage space, and maintaining and updating data in several locations is expensive.

Secondly, potential for **inconsistent data** exists if updates are not applied in every system. For example, a company with independent payroll and personnel systems is shown in Figure 8-26. The payroll and personnel files have many data items in common, including employee name and number, department number, and position. When an employee is transferred to a new department, that change affects data in both systems. Changing the data in only one of the systems will cause a loss of data integrity and result in incorrect information in the second system.

The third problem with the typical file processing environment concerns the need for information for management decisions that span the entire business enterprise. A top-level manager might need to relate information from several departments or make comparisons among business divisions that are continents apart. In a file processing environment, this task would mean retrieving information from several independent systems, which is slow and inefficient.

Database Management Design

Database technology offers a solution to the problems of file processing. A **database** is a structure that can store data about many entities and the relationships among them. A database is a complete and logically integrated framework that avoids data redundancy and also provides a shared environment that allows many users to access information at the same time.

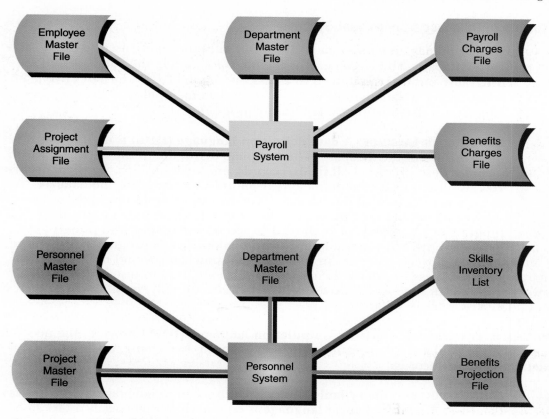

Figure 8-26   A typical file processing environment. Each information system maintains a separate set of files.

In a file processing environment, data files are designed to fit individual applications. In contrast, in a database environment, the application systems are built around the database. Figure 8-27 shows a database environment with a single database serving five separate information systems.

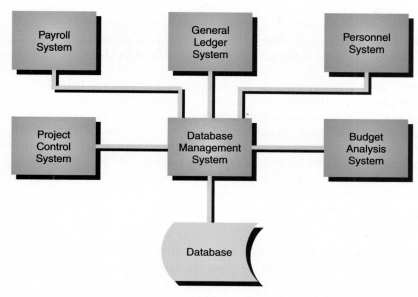

Figure 8-27   In a database environment, several systems can access a central data resource, which is important in a design that encompasses the entire company or enterprise.

Elements of Database Management Systems

A **database management system** (**DBMS**) is a software system used to create, access, and control a database. The DBMS acts as the interface among the database and the programs and users that need to access the data. A DBMS includes five main components: a data definition language, a data manipulation language, a query language, a data dictionary, and utility programs.

For additional information on **DBMSs**, visit Systems Analysis and Design Chapter 8 More on the Web.

www.scsite.com/ sad3e/ch08/

DATA DEFINITION LANGUAGE • A **data definition language** (**DDL**) is used to describe the structure of the database. The complete definition of the database, which includes descriptions of all fields, records, and relationships, is called a **schema**. You also use the DDL to define one or more subschemas for the database. A **subschema** is a view of the database used by one or more programs or users. A subschema defines only those portions of the database that a particular program or user needs or is allowed to access. For example, to protect individual privacy, you would not want to allow certain programs or employees to retrieve an employee's pay rate. In this case, the subschema would not include the pay rate field so access is restricted. Subschemas also are used to restrict the kind of access permitted. In some cases, access is for data retrieval only; in other cases, the user can update and retrieve data.

DATA MANIPULATION LANGUAGE • A **data manipulation language** (**DML)** provides the necessary commands for all database operations, including storing, retrieving, updating, and deleting database records.

For more detail on performing **Queries**, visit Systems Analysis and Design Chapter 8 More on the Web.

www.scsite.com/ sad3e/ch08/

QUERY LANGUAGE • A **query language** is a nonprocedural language used to access a database. A **nonprocedural language** is one in which you specify a task to be done without specifying *how* the task will be accomplished. With some query languages, the user enters complete commands; many of these query languages use **natural languages** that accept commands that resemble ordinary English sentences. Using a **query-by-example (QBE) language**, the user describes the desired database access by specifying an example. The most popular query language is **SQL (Structured Query Language**), which is available on most platforms and has powerful capabilities. All types of query languages are designed to be simple to learn and use, so users can access the database themselves.

DATA DICTIONARY • A **data dictionary** serves as a central repository for information about the database. The schema and all subschemas are stored in the data dictionary.

UTILITY PROGRAMS • Most DBMSs include the necessary support for interactive processing, database security, backup and recovery, audit trails, data integrity, and shared update. To say that a DBMS supports **shared update** means that two or more users can access and update the database simultaneously.

Most DBMSs also provide several utility programs to assist in the general maintenance of the database. These programs typically include utilities for creating a database, changing the structure of the database, gathering and reporting patterns of database usage, and detecting and reporting database structure irregularities.

Characteristics of Database Management

A **database management approach** offers many advantages, and some disadvantages, compared to traditional file processing designs. Some database strengths include the following:

1. *Scalability.* **Scalability** means that a system can be expanded, modified, or downsized easily to meet the rapidly changing needs of a business enterprise.

2. *Better support for client/server systems.* In **client/server design**, processing control can be distributed to users, called **clients**, throughout the organization. Client/server systems require the power and flexibility of a database design. You will learn more about client/server systems in Chapter 9.

3. *Economy of scale.* Database design can allow better utilization of hardware capability, which results in **economy of scale**. In many systems where a corporate-wide database is maintained, it is less expensive to use larger, more powerful hardware for transaction processing rather than using several smaller computers.

4. *Sharing of data.* Data can be **shared** across the enterprise, allowing more users to access more data. Because the database is flexible, users can view the same information in different ways. Users are empowered because they have access to the information they need to do their jobs.

5. *Balancing conflicting requirements.* To function effectively, a database must be managed by a **database administrator (DBA)**. This person or group assesses the overall needs of the organization and manages the database for the benefit of the entire organization and not just for the needs of a single department or user.

6. *Enforcement of standards.* Effective database administration ensures that **standards** for data names, formats, and documentation are followed uniformly throughout the organization.

7. *Controlled redundancy.* Because the data is stored in a single database, data items do not need to be duplicated in separate files for various systems. Even where some duplication might be allowed for performance reasons, the database approach allows control of the redundancy. **Data consistency** depends on avoiding unnecessary redundancy.

8. *Security.* The DBA can define **authorization procedures** to ensure that only legitimate users can access the database and can allow different users to have different levels of access. Most DBMSs provide sophisticated security support.

9. *Increased programmer productivity.* Programmers do not have to create the underlying file structure for a database. Because they can concentrate on logical design, a new database application can be developed more quickly than a file-oriented system.

10. *Data independence.* Programs that interact with a DBMS are relatively **independent** of how the physical data is maintained. This design provides the DBA flexibility to improve data structures without modifying application programs that use the data.

Although the database approach has many advantages, some concerns are common. Because DBMSs are so powerful, hardware that is more expensive is required, including more memory, more disk space, faster access and retrieval devices, and multitasking processors.

A DBMS is a complex product; systems analysts must understand the features of a package fully to use it effectively. This knowledge can require more training and increase overall development costs. As with any project, an analyst must make design choices carefully because a weak design can lead to a failed project. DBMS software also can be expensive — a mainframe DBMS package can cost thousands of dollars. Even DBMSs for personal computers cost more than other applications and can require additional hardware to run properly.

Finally, procedures for security, backup, and recovery are more complicated and critical in a database environment. When a company maintains its vital information resources in a database, a DBMS failure will seriously disrupt business operations.

Although the major trend is toward large-scale database design, the typical corporation still has a combination of independent databases and file-based systems. Why is this so? It exists, on the one hand, because of pressure to manage data as a company-wide resource. There also is considerable interest in a new approach, called **data mining**, which enables users to extract information from a variety

To learn more about **Data Mining**, visit Systems Analysis and Design Chapter 8 More on the Web.

www.scsite.com/ sad3e/ch08/

of business units and operations throughout the corporation without having to know where the data is or what form it is in. At the same time, other factors have influenced information systems planners, including hardware expenses, a reluctance to move away from established information systems, and a realization that large-scale databases can be highly complex and expensive to maintain. As with many design decisions, the best solution depends on the individual circumstances.

DATABASE MODELS

The four basic models of database organization are hierarchical, network, relational, and object-oriented. Hierarchical and network databases generally are used on mainframes. Relational databases can run on many platforms, including personal computers. Relational databases are well-suited to client/server computing because they are so powerful and flexible. The object-oriented model is modular and cost-effective and is used in many new DBMS systems.

Hierarchical Databases

In a **hierarchical database**, data is organized like a family tree or organization chart, with branches of parent records and child records. A parent record can have multiple child records, but each child record can have only one physical parent. The parent record at the top of the hierarchy is called the **root record**. Figure 8-28 shows a hierarchical database for departments, faculty, students, and majors. DEPARTMENT is the parent of two types of records: FACULTY and MAJOR. FACULTY is the parent of STUDENT. Notice that a dotted line — instead of a solid line — connects MAJOR and STUDENT. MAJOR cannot be a parent to a STUDENT record, because STUDENT already has FACULTY as a physical parent. To establish an effective relationship between students and their majors, MAJOR can be defined as a logical parent, rather than a physical parent.

Relationships in a hierarchical database are defined by parent/child associations. To access records, the DBMS follows pointers from the root down, up, and along the branches in a process called **navigation**. For example, to find the name of a particular student's faculty advisor, you execute a command to find that STUDENT record. The DBMS retrieves records starting from the root until it finds the desired STUDENT record. At that point, the most recently read FACULTY record becomes the parent record. To determine all the students that a particular faculty member advises, you execute a command to find a specific FACULTY record, and then execute commands to find the STUDENT records associated with that record.

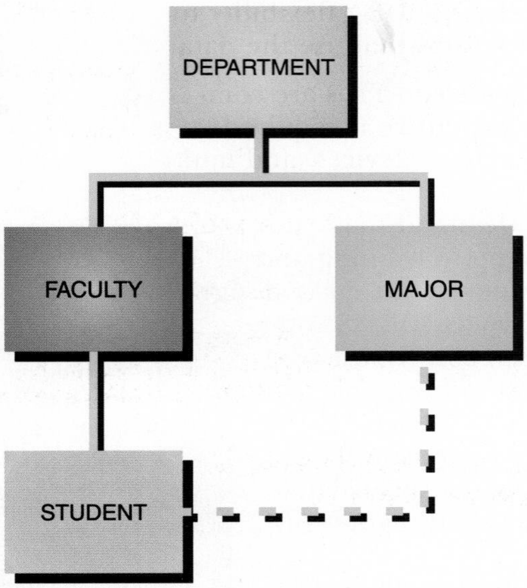

The hierarchical model has several disadvantages. First, each child record must have one, and only one parent. For example, in the model shown in Figure 8-28, a student without an assigned faculty advisor cannot be stored unless a dummy advisor record is created. Second, changes to the structure of a record require reorganizing the database and modifying the application programs. Finally, the hierarchical data model is complex, and application programs that interact with a hierarchical DBMS usually are complicated and difficult to maintain.

Figure 8-28 A hierarchical database for DEPARTMENT, FACULTY, STUDENT, and MAJOR records.

Network Databases

The **network database model** is shown as a set of records arranged in one-to-many relationships. Most network DBMSs conform to standards established by the **CODASYL** (Conference on Data Systems Languages) organization as shown in Figure 8-29.

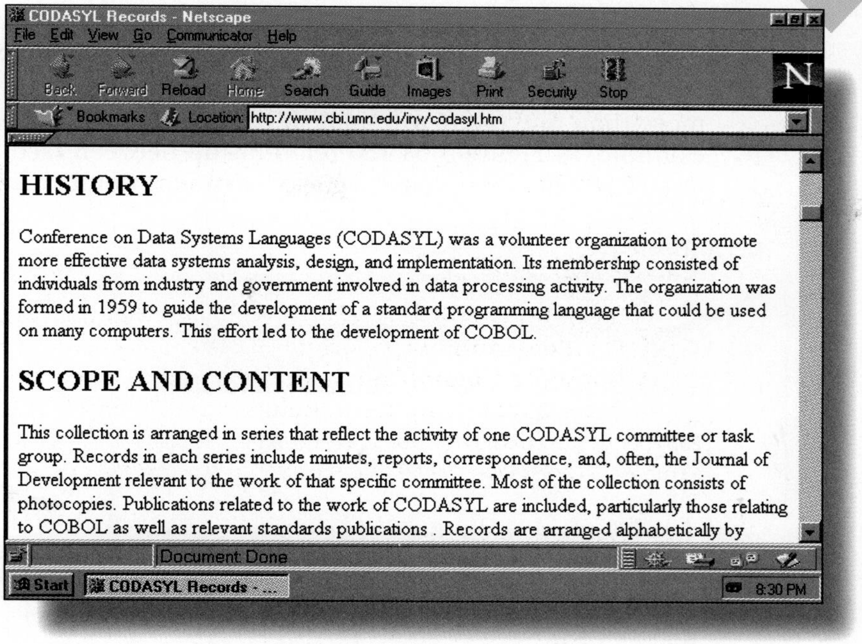

The terms *record* and *field* are used in the network model exactly as they are used in a file processing environment. A relationship between two records is defined as a **set**. For example, if a faculty member advises a number of students, the one-to-many relationship between FACULTY and STUDENT is represented by a set called ADVISES. One occurrence of the ADVISES set includes one faculty member and every student advised by that faculty member. In this example, the FACULTY record is called the **owner** record, and the STUDENT records are called **member** records.

In the network model, a record can be a member of multiple sets, without a restriction similar to the hierarchical model's limitation of one physical parent per child. Figure 8-30 illustrates a network database design for DEPARTMENT, FACULTY, STUDENT, and MAJOR records.

A particular member record can exist without an owner record in a network database. A student who has no assigned advisor, for example, still can be stored in the database, but the record is not represented in the ADVISES set.

Many successful systems use the network database model. The performance of well-designed network DBMSs is better than that of many relational and object-oriented models. The network design, however, has some of the same disadvantages as the hierarchical model. Any changes made to the data structure require rebuilding the database and recompiling the affected programs. In addition, as with the hierarchical database, programs that interact with a network DBMS usually are complex.

Figure 8-29   CODASYL (Conference on Data Systems Languages) developed various standards for data systems used by industry and government.

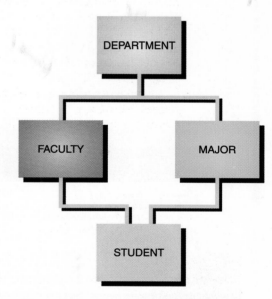

Figure 8-30   A network database for DEPARTMENT, FACULTY, STUDENT, and MAJOR records.

Relational Databases

In a **relational database**, data is organized in two-dimensional tables, or **relations**. Each row in a table is called a **tuple** and each column is called an **attribute**. You can think of a relation as a file, tuples or rows as records, and attributes or columns as fields.

Figure 8-31 shows four tables from a relational database — one for each of the four relations of DEPARTMENT, FACULTY, MAJOR, and STUDENT.

A relational database uses a **common field**, which is an attribute that appears in more than one table, to establish relationships between tables in the database. For example, in Figure 8-31 the relationship between faculty members and their departments is created by matching a department number in the FACULTY table to a department number in the DEPARTMENT table. Notice that DEPARTMENT NUMBER is the primary key of the DEPARTMENT table and a foreign key in the FACULTY table.

Similarly, matching a FACULTY NUMBER, which is a foreign key in the STUDENT table, to a primary key FACULTY NUMBER in the FACULTY table, creates the relationship between students and their advisors. To find the name of the advisor for a particular student, the DBMS locates that student in the STUDENT table and uses the faculty number to locate the appropriate row in the FACULTY table. To find all students for a particular advisor, the DBMS finds all rows in the STUDENT table with that advisor's number.

An important advantage of a relational database is simplicity. You can add a new entity, attribute, or table at any time without restructuring the entire database. Because it so powerful and flexible, the relational database model is the predominant design approach today.

Object-Oriented Databases

The **object-oriented approach** to systems development is a design strategy that focuses on data rather than processes by using an object library to reduce development and maintenance costs. Many DBMSs add object-oriented features to a relational structure.

DEPARTMENT

DEPARTMENT-NUMBER	DEPARTMENT-NAME	CHAIRPERSON-NUMBER
103	Business	35
285	Chemistry	93
297	Computer Science	06
414	Mathematics	49

FACULTY

FACULTY-NUMBER	FACULTY-NAME	DEPARTMENT-NUMBER
06	Kolhapur	297
18	Jones	103
23	Smith	297
35	Martino	103
49	Paulson	414
87	O'Leary	103
93	Hoffman	285

MAJOR

MAJOR	MAJOR DESCRIPTION	DEPARTMENT-NUMBER
ACC	Accounting	103
FIN	Finance	103
IS	Information Systems	297
MGT	Management	103
MKT	Marketing	103
SE	Software Engineering	297

STUDENT

STUDENT-NUMBER	STUDENT-NAME	TOTAL-CREDITS	GPA	MAJOR	FACULTY-NUMBER
1035	Linda	17	3.647	MKT	18
3397	Sam	46	2.400	ACC	87
4070	Juan	35	3.000	IS	23
5166	Catherine	117	2.877	FIN	87
8892	Kelly	93	2.214	ACC	35

Figure 8-31   A relational database with DEPARTMENT, FACULTY, MAJOR, and STUDENT tables.

To learn more about **Object-Oriented Databases**, visit Systems Analysis and Design Chapter 8 More on the Web.

www.scsite.com/ sad3e/ch08/

An **object-oriented definition** includes objects, methods, messages, and inheritance. An **object** is a unit of data, along with the actions that can affect that data. A CUSTOMER object, for example, consists of the data relevant to customers (number, name, address, credit limit, and so on) along with the actions that can be performed on customer data (add a customer, change a credit limit, and so on). An **object library** is a collection of objects that can be accessed by various programs and information systems.

The actions defined for an object are called methods. **Methods** are identified when data is defined. In contrast to the traditional approach, actions are created as part of data processing rather than data definition.

A **message** is a request to execute a method. As part of sending a message, you must send the required data. For example, to add a customer, you send a message that includes all data items for the new customer.

To illustrate the concept of **inheritance**, analyze the database shown in Figure 8-32. You begin by defining an object named PERSON that consists of relevant data, such as an identifying number, name, and so on. Then you define all appropriate actions for the PERSON object, such as adding or deleting a person from the database. This object definition is stored in the DBMS object library, which contains reusable objects and code.

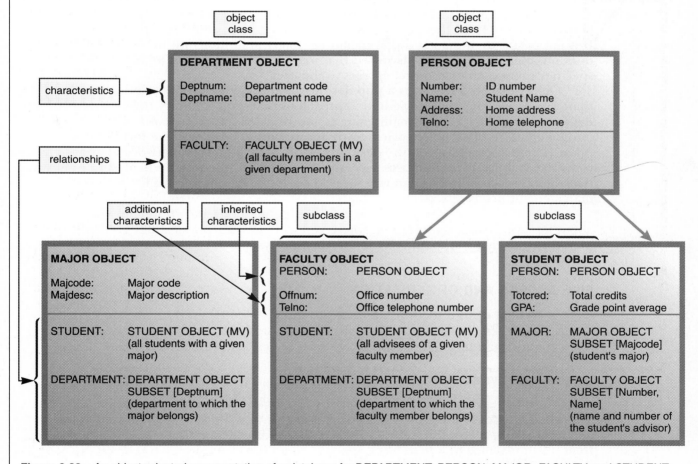

Figure 8-32 An object-oriented representation of a database for DEPARTMENT, PERSON, MAJOR, FACULTY, and STUDENT.

Now, you can use the library definition to define FACULTY as a subclass of the PERSON object. Because of inheritance, a subclass takes on all characteristics of the object on which it is based. In addition, you can define additional properties for a subclass. For the FACULTY object, for example, you can add data items such as title, department number, office number, and office telephone number. Similarly, you can add actions specific to a faculty member, such as changing his or her position as a result of a promotion.

The advantage of the reusability of objects becomes clear when you add students to your database definition. A student also is a person, so you now define STUDENT as another subclass of PERSON. Again, all data and actions for PERSON automatically become characteristics of STUDENT. You only need to add the data items and actions that apply specifically to a student, such as total credits, GPA, and the action of calculating a GPA.

Figure 8-32 on the previous page shows an object-oriented definition of the database. The first specification line for the FACULTY and STUDENT objects indicates that both of these objects are based on the PERSON object. The second and third lines in the STUDENT object define two additional data items that are relevant to students: total credits and GPA.

Relationships are accomplished by including related objects within each other's object definitions. For example, the DEPARTMENT definition includes the FACULTY object with the letters MV, indicating that the relationship is multivalued. Therefore, a single occurrence of a DEPARTMENT object can contain multiple occurrences of the FACULTY object — one for each faculty member assigned to that department. Conversely, the FACULTY definition includes the DEPARTMENT object. This definition does not include the notation MV because a particular faculty member is assigned to only one department, and the relationship is not multivalued in this direction.

Other examples include relationships between departments and their majors, between students and their faculty advisors, and between students and their majors. It is important to understand that including object definitions within other definitions does not mean that the data is stored that way physically. Instead, an object definition specifies the way that an object *appears* to the user.

Object-oriented design is a popular design strategy that focuses on data rather than processes. The object-oriented approach uses an object library that provides a high degree of flexibility, ease of maintenance, and reduced operating costs. The initial implementation of an object-oriented design requires considerable effort because it places so much emphasis on the design process. Also, because object-oriented design views data totally apart from the processes that affect it, the systems analyst must ensure that the object-oriented design will support business operations and information management needs effectively.

Now that you have reviewed database design methods and strategies, you will learn about file access and organization, where you will consider physical design issues and plan the underlying structure of the information system.

FILE ACCESS AND ORGANIZATION

 Physical design requires an understanding of file types, data storage formats, file access methods, and how files can be organized. The process begins with understanding the difference between logical and physical records.

Logical and Physical Records

The smallest amount of data is one binary digit, called a **bit**. A group of eight bits is a called a **byte,** or a **character**. A set of bytes forms a **field**, which is an individual fact about a person, place, thing, or event. A field also is called a **data element** or a **data item**. Each instance of a field has a specific value. For example, CUSTOMER NUMBER is a field. One customer number might have the value 123, and another customer number might have the value 647.

A **logical record** contains field values that describe a single person, place, thing, or event. Application programs see a logical record as a set of fields, regardless of how or where the data is stored physically. For example, a logical customer record contains specific values for customer number, customer name, credit limit, and so on — values that relate to a single customer. Most often, the term *record* indicates a logical record.

Whenever an application executes a read or write command, the operating system supplies one logical record to the program or accepts one logical record from the program.

A **physical record**, or a **block**, is the smallest unit of data that is accessed by the operating system. The operating system reads or writes one physical record at a time. When the operating system reads a physical record, it transfers the record from the file to a **buffer**, which is a block-sized segment of computer memory. Similarly, when the system writes a physical record, all data in the buffer is written to the file.

A physical record consists of one or more logical records. The **blocking factor** is the number of logical records in one physical record. If the blocking factor is more than one, the execution of a read or write command does not always result in the physical action of reading or writing. Sometimes, the read or write command requires only a transfer of data from one memory location to another.

Types of Files

A **file** is a set of logical records that contains data about an entity. For example, an inventory system has an entity called PRODUCT. The product file contains logical records and each record stores data about one instance of the PRODUCT entity. Figure 8-33 shows a file with fields, logical records, and physical records, or blocks.

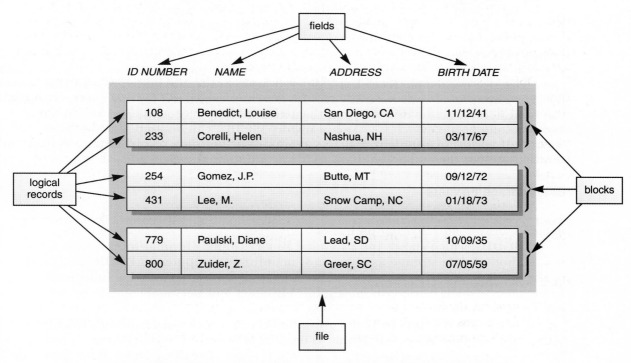

Figure 8-33 A file stores information about an entity. The file consists of physical blocks that contain logical records. Each logical record is a set of related field values.

An information system uses one or more of each of the following types of files: master files, table files, transaction files, work files, security files, and history files.

MASTER FILES • A **master file** stores relatively permanent data about an entity in the information system. For example, a product master file contains one logical record for each product the company sells. The quantity-on-hand field in each record might change daily, but the number of product master file records does not change unless the company offers a new product or discontinues an old product. Master files might include data for customers, sales representatives, students, employees, or patients.

TABLE FILES • A **table file** contains reference data used by the information system. As with master files, table files usually are permanent. Table files, however, are not updated by the system. Instead, special table update programs change the values in a table file. Examples of table files include tax tables, postage rate tables, and department code tables.

TRANSACTION FILES • A **transaction file** stores records that contain day-to-day business and operational data. A transaction file is an input file that updates a master file; after this update is completed, the transaction file has served its purpose. Unless it is saved for security or backup reasons, transaction files usually are temporary files. Examples of transaction files include orders, new employees, patient releases, cash receipts, commissions, and customer payments.

WORK FILES • A **work file** is a temporary file created by an information system for a single task. Most often a work file is created by one process in the information system and used by another process within the same system. Work files also are called **scratch files** or **temporary files**. Work files can contain copies of master file records or various other records that are needed temporarily. Example of work files include **sorted files** and **report files** that hold output reports until they are printed.

SECURITY FILES • A **security file** is created and saved for backup and recovery purposes. Examples of security files include audit trail files and backups of master, table, and transaction files. New security files must be created regularly to replace outdated files.

HISTORY FILES • A **history file** is a file copy created and saved for historical or archiving reasons. New history files, unlike new security files, do not replace the old files. In some cases, inactive master file records are deleted periodically and added to a special history file. For example, records for students who have not registered for any course in the last two semesters might be deleted from the active student master file and added to an inactive student file, which is a type of history file that can be used for queries or reports. If an inactive student registers again, his or her data record is deleted from the inactive student file and added back to the active student master file.

Data Storage Formats

Data can be stored in five basic data storage formats: EBCDIC, ASCII, packed decimal, binary, and floating point.

EBCDIC, which stands for Extended Binary Coded Decimal Interchange Code, is a method of data storage used on most mainframe computers. EBCDIC can handle character data. **ASCII** is an acronym for American Standard Code for Information Interchange, which is used on most minicomputers and personal computers. ASCII also can handle character data.

The **packed decimal** format stores numbers in a compact form, with each digit occupying one half-byte. This format is used in most business information systems because it saves storage space and makes the process of reading and writing data faster than using ASCII or EBCDIC. Because packed decimal data is ready for computation, the operating system does not need to convert a packed decimal number to another form for arithmetic operations and then convert it back again for storage.

A **binary format** can be used to store numeric integers. On most computers, you can specify binary field storage lengths of two bytes (a halfword), four bytes (a fullword), or even eight bytes (a doubleword). A **halfword** can store integer values between -32768 and +32767, and integer values as large as four billion can be stored in a binary **fullword**. For all but the smallest integers, a binary format requires less storage space than a packed decimal format. Most computer systems, however, must convert binary fields to packed decimal form for computation.

Floating point format is used primarily in scientific applications, and is not typically found in business information systems.

What is the best way to store date fields? Most users in the United States enter dates in the format MM/DD/YY and want output in the same form. Is this method the best way to store dates?

For many years, systems were designed with only two digits for the year because data storage was expensive. As IS professionals in business and government plan for the year 2000, enormous concern exists that many systems will not handle dates after 1999 properly. In some cases, expensive modifications will be needed to accommodate the change in century. To avoid future problems and achieve consistency, the **International Organization of Standardization** (**IOS**) has proposed a format of four digits for the year, two for the month, and two for the day (YYYYMMDD).

What is the best way to store dates? Storing a year as four digits might make sense, because years can be displayed as needed with either two or four digits. If users prefer to input only two-digit years, programs can supply the century digits. Rules would have to be established on a field-by-field basis, however. Birth dates, for example, would be treated differently from sales forecast dates.

If a date never needs to be sorted, compared to another date, or used in a calculation, it could be stored in a MMDDYYYY form. Dates in this form can be sorted and compared, but only if you separate the year from the month and day and then treat them as separate fields.

Alternatively, a date stored as YYYYMMDD can be sorted easily and used in comparisons. If a date in this form is larger than another date in the same form, then the first date is later. For example, 19990815 is later than 19990131, just as August 15, 1999 is later than January 31, 1999.

What if dates must be used in calculations? For example, if a manufacturing order placed on June 23 takes three weeks to complete, when will the order be ready? If a payment due on August 13 is not paid until April 27 of the following year, exactly how late is the payment and how much interest is owed? Julian dates and absolute dates are easier to use in such calculations.

A standard **Julian date** is a five-digit number in which the first two digits represent the year and the last three digits represent the day of the year. Thus, the Julian date form of January 1, 1999 is 99001, while June 23 of that same year is 99174. An **extended Julian date** is a seven-digit number in which the first four digits represent the year. Thus, the extended Julian date for June 23, 1999 is 1999174, and three weeks later is 1999195 (1999174 + 21). Julian dates work well for calculations with dates that fall in the *same* year, but extra steps are needed to add five weeks to December 3 or to calculate the number of days between August 13 and April 27.

An **absolute date** is the total number of days from some specific base date. To calculate the number of days between two absolute dates, you subtract one date from the other. For example, if you use a base date of January 1, 1900, then August 13, 1999 has an absolute date value of 36385. April 27, 2000 has an absolute date of 36643. If you subtract the earlier date value from the later one, the result is 258 days. You can use a simple calculation or a spreadsheet function to determine absolute dates easily.

Which is the best method? The answer depends on how the specific date will be printed, displayed, or used in a calculation. You must consider how the date will be used most often — in calculations or in a display — to determine the right format to use.

For more information on **IOS**, visit Systems Analysis and Design Chapter 8 More on the Web.

www.scsite.com/ sad3e/ch08/

A KEY QUESTION

SoccerMom Company sells a patented seat that spectators can take to youth soccer games. The seat folds so it is small enough to fit in the glove box of most vehicles. The company operates a factory in Kansas and also contracts its manufacturing projects to small firms in Canada and Mexico.

An unusual problem has occurred for this small multinational company: people are getting confused about dates in internal memos, purchase orders, and e-mail. Towson Hopkins handles all IS functions for SoccerMom. When he designed the company's database, he was not aware that the format for dates in Canada and Mexico was different from the format used in the United States. For example, in Canada and Mexico, the notation 2/1/99 indicates January 2, 1999, whereas in the United States the same notation indicates February 1, 1999. Although it seems like small point, this confusion has resulted in several order cancellations.

Towson has asked for your advice. You could suggest writing a simple program to convert the dates automatically or designing a keyboard macro that would allow users to select a date format as data is entered. You realize, however, that SoccerMom might want to do business in other countries in the future. What would be the best course of action? Should SoccerMom adapt to the standard of each country, or should it maintain a single international format? What are the arguments both ways?

ON THE NET

Before responding to Towson, you decide to search the Internet to see if you can find information about the problem of inconsistent date formats and determine whether international standards are available. Research the topic of international date standards and respond to Towson in a memo. You can begin by using a Web search engine such as Yahoo! to search for the phrase, "date format". You also can look for information about the International Organization of Standardization (IOS).

FILE ACCESS

In any data management system, you must determine the data structure, logical record design, and relationships between entities. In addition, in a file processing system, you must make decisions about file access and organization. **File access methods** concern how programs read and write records. The file access method usually is determined by the characteristics of the file management system and whether a specific relationship exists between access methods and file organization. The two basic access methods are sequential access and random access.

A program using the **sequential access method** starts by reading or writing a record, which usually is the first record in the file, and proceeds to read or write all the records in sequence until the end of the file is reached.

With the **random access method**, a program can read any logical record without having to access all preceding records. Random access often is called **direct access** because a program accesses any desired record directly. Random access is comparable to locating a song instantly on a music CD, while sequential access is similar to using the fast forward button to find the same song on a cassette tape.

If you need to find a large number of records in a file, sequential access is faster than random access. For instance, you normally would process a transaction file sequentially because all records will be read. To decide how to process the master file, for example, you estimate file activity. If a large percentage of the records need to be accessed, you would process the master file sequentially. In that case, the transaction file must be sorted so the records are in master file order. Typically, sequential access is used for batch processing, while random access is used for online processing.

FILE ORGANIZATION

F **ile organization** is the way that logical records are stored in a file. The three alternatives are sequential organization, direct organization, and indexed organization. The decision to use a method usually depends on a number of factors, including access and retrieval speed, efficient use of storage, ease of expansion, and how much routine maintenance or file reorganization is needed.

Sequential Organization

When a program creates a file using **sequential organization**, records are stored in physical sequence as they occur during processing. Two different types of sequential organization are possible. In the first example, shown in Figure 8-34, the records are stored in no special sequence except the chronological order in which they were entered. Using the second type of sequential organization, records are created and physically stored in primary key order, much like a telephone directory. Figure 8-35 shows a customer file with this type of organization.

Sequential organization allows very fast access, but if you need to retrieve a specific record, you must retrieve all records physically ahead of that record, because random access cannot be used in this type of file. Clearly, sequential organization is

Figure 8-34 Sequential organization with records stored in no specific order as the data was entered. Using a blocking factor or three, one physical record has three logical records.

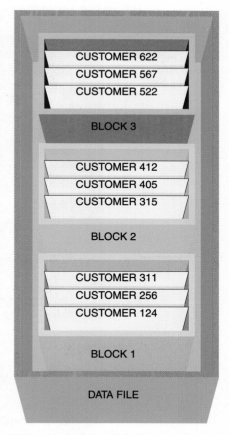

Figure 8-35 Sequential organization by primary key of customer number. Again, using a blocking factor of three, one physical record has three logical records.

not suited for an online environment. Also, whenever records are added, deleted, or modified in a sequential file, the file must be recopied to maintain the correct position for all records.

Direct Organization

With **direct organization**, a record is stored at an address based on a formula that uses the record's primary key, which must be numeric. Two types of direct organization are used: key-addressing and hashing.

KEY-ADDRESSING TECHNIQUES • With **key-addressing techniques**, the formula is based on the primary key and results in a unique record number. Figure 8-36 shows an example of this technique. The nine records have a key value of the actual customer numbers 1 through 9. Each record is stored at the relative record number that corresponds to its key.

To retrieve the record for customer number 8, a program reads the record with the relative record number 8. This example uses the primary key value without any change. Although direct addressing permits fast access, a major problem is that mapping the primary key to a relative record number can create large gaps that waste storage space because space is reserved for records that might not exist.

HASHING TECHNIQUES • **Hashing techniques** are similar to key-addressing in that the primary key of a record is part of a formula that determines the address for storing and retrieving the record.

Hashing techniques sometimes are called **randomizing techniques**. The formula used to transform the primary key into a record address also is known as a **hashing algorithm**, a **hashing routine**, a **randomizing routine**, or simply a **hash function**. The objective of hashing is to spread the records as evenly as possible throughout the file, in no particular sequence. Hashing uses storage efficiently, which allows rapid random access. The hashing formula, however, does *not* guarantee a unique storage address and might designate the same address for two or more records. No matter how well you choose your hashing algorithm, you will have some collisions. A variety of methods, called **collision management techniques**, are used to minimize the number of collisions and minimize the effects when they do occur.

Indexed Organization

In every type of file organization, logical records are stored in a data file. With **indexed organization**, you also have a separate index file that contains the key value and data file location for each logical record. Several types of indexed organization exist.

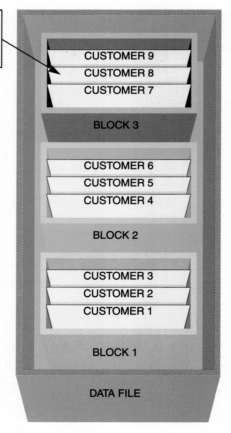

the primary key value is the relative record number in the file

CUSTOMER 9
CUSTOMER 8
CUSTOMER 7

BLOCK 3

CUSTOMER 6
CUSTOMER 5
CUSTOMER 4

BLOCK 2

CUSTOMER 3
CUSTOMER 2
CUSTOMER 1

BLOCK 1

DATA FILE

Figure 8-36   Direct organization where the customer number serves as the relative record number.

INDEXED RANDOM ORGANIZATION • When the data records of an indexed file are not stored in any significant sequence, the organization is called **indexed random organization**, or **indexed nonsequential organization**. An example of indexed random organization is shown in Figure 8-37. The nine records of the customer file are stored in random order in the data file. The index also has nine records — one for each data file record. Each index record contains a customer number, which is the primary key, and the data file block number that specifies where the record is stored.

An index file requires additional storage space but its use has several advantages. For instance, the index allows sequential retrieval of randomly stored data records. Although the logical records in the data file in Figure 8-37 are not stored in any meaningful order, the *index* records are stored in primary key order. When you use the index, you will access the data records in customer number sequence, just as if they had been stored that way.

The DBMS reads index records more quickly than it reads data records because index records are much smaller. Data records can be hundreds or thousands of bytes long, but each index record needs only a few bytes to store the primary key and the data record address. As the number of data records increases, the number of index records increases at the same rate. Index search time will increase, but this method still is much faster than searching the entire data file, especially if the entire index can be loaded into main memory.

An additional advantage of indexed random organization is that a program does not need to access the data file if you need to know only whether a specific record exists. You can determine this from the index itself. If the primary key value is found in the index, you know the record exists; if the record does not exist in the index, then it does not exist in the database. A final advantage of indexed random organization is that data file records do not need to be in sequence. When records are added, they are stored at the end of the file.

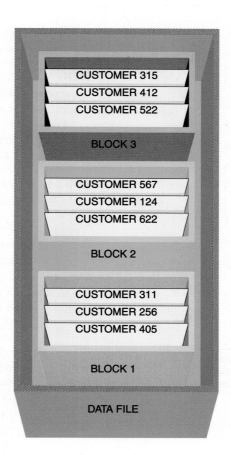

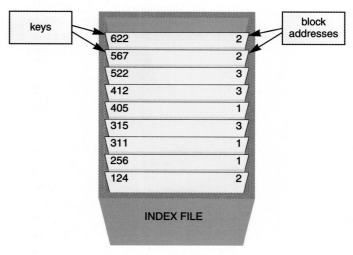

Figure 8-37 Indexed random organization. Each record in the index file contains the primary key and the corresponding block where the record is located in the data file.

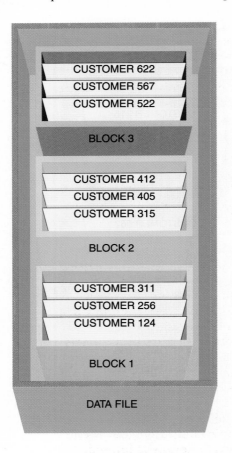

Figure 8-38 Indexed sequential organization with a sparse index.

For more information on **ISAM**, visit Systems Analysis and Design Chapter 8 More on the Web.

www.scsite.com/ sad3e/ch08/

INDEXED SEQUENTIAL ORGANIZATION • Indexed sequential organization means that the file is indexed with data records in primary key sequence. In Figure 8-38, the customer records are in sequence by the primary key of customer number. The index looks much like the one for the indexed random organization shown in Figure 8-37 on the previous page. Because the data file records are in sequence, however, you need only one index record for each data file block, rather than one for each individual record. This method means faster access and retrieval and a smaller index file, called a **sparse index**.

Because indexed sequential organization is faster and takes less space, why would you ever want to use indexed random organization? The reason is that you might need another way to access a data file. In addition to the primary index, you can create secondary indexes on other fields. For example, the primary key for products is the product number, but you might want to retrieve records based on description, price, or vendor fields. If they are organized sequentially, the data records will be in primary key order based on product number. Therefore, all secondary indexes must use indexed random organization to relate secondary key values to records containing those values.

When indexed sequential organization is used, where does the system insert a record when the block is full, and what happens to the index? The answer depends on the specific file organization system. For example, the **indexed sequential access method (ISAM)** uses a mapping technique to store records in available locations on the disk. Other methods for managing record insertions use a splitting technique that divides a physical record between blocks. IBM's **virtual storage access method (VSAM)** uses mapping and block splitting to allocate storage space dynamically.

File Organization Advantages and Disadvantages

Files with sequential organization require the least space because no index files are stored. Sequentially organized files, however, cannot be accessed randomly.

Direct file organization provides fast random access but has several drawbacks. Key-addressing is the most efficient way to determine record locations because a separate index is not required. Key-addressing techniques, however, sometimes are impractical because space is wasted and more storage is needed. Hashing techniques provide a tradeoff between the fastest access and the most efficient use of storage space, but because of collisions, the performance of hashed direct files can be affected.

Indexed organization provides an efficient means of both sequentially and randomly accessing records. Random access with indexed files, however, is slower and extra file storage space is required to store the index. Indexed sequential organization usually is preferable to indexed random organization, but this method is based only on the primary key. If other fields are needed to select records for retrieval, random access must be used. Also, to be efficient, indexed sequential files must be reorganized periodically.

If all the programs in the information system need to access a file sequentially, then the file should use *sequential organization*. If all the programs need to access the file randomly, then *direct organization* would be appropriate. If programs use various access methods, then *indexed organization* is the most flexible alternative.

FILE MEDIA TYPES

 ith technology advances, data storage costs have decreased sharply and data storage capacities have increased. Storage media include magnetic tape, floppy disks, optical discs, and mass storage devices. Each alternative has advantages and disadvantages.

Magnetic tape was once the primary method for storing large amounts of data. That is no longer true, but tape still is a reliable, inexpensive, and transportable storage medium. Tape storage, however, has a significant disadvantage. All the other file media allow for either random or sequential access, but tape files can be accessed *only* sequentially. For that reason, magnetic tape can be used for transaction and work files, but it rarely is used for master files or table files. Tape often is used for backup, security and history files, and for transferring data from one system to another. Originally, tape was only available in reel-to-reel form, but today various types of cartridge tapes have replaced reel-to-reel devices on many mainframes and minicomputers. Magnetic tape still is less expensive, byte for byte, than other devices, but its characteristics make it unsuitable for many applications.

Floppy disks are relatively inexpensive, portable, mailable, and easy to store. Floppy disks can be used on personal computers and mainframe computers, but their transferability between systems with different operating systems generally is limited. Also, disk storage space is limited, and the disks can be damaged by magnetism, temperature extremes, and contaminants such as dust and smoke.

Hard disks, or **fixed disks** or **direct access storage devices** (**DASDs**), provide larger and faster storage capabilities than floppy disks. Hard disks commonly are used in all types of computers. The storage capacities, access and transfer speeds, and other physical characteristics of hard disks vary greatly, depending on the manufacturer and type of disk. One type of hard disk storage is an integrated group of small disks called a **RAID**, which stands for Redundant Array of Inexpensive Disks. RAIDs can be used in various ways to speed up data access and reduce the risk of data loss.

Another device that is being used increasingly is the **removable disk cartridge** that combines the storage capacity of a hard disk and the portability of a disk. Where data security is critical, the cartridge can be removed and safely stored. One type of disk cartridge is the **Bernoulli disk cartridge**, which uses an air cushion to keep the read and write heads from touching the flexible disk surface where the data is stored.

Optical technology also is an important means of data storage. **Optical discs** are better known as **CD-ROMs,** which stands for compact disc read-only memory. Large quantities of information are stored on an optical disc by burning microscopic holes on its surface with a laser. Although advances in drive technology have increased the reading process, CD-ROMs still are slower than hard drives, especially those that use the **small computer system interface** (**SCSI**). As optical disc technology advances, storage capacities also will increase.

In general, data stored on a standard optical disc cannot be modified. Optical discs often are called **WORM** devices, for write once, read many. Standard optical discs are practical, therefore, only for files that are not updated. Rewritable optical discs now are available that allow users to update data, just as on a hard disk. As prices decrease, these devices are expected to be in wide use.

To learn more about **RAID**, visit Systems Analysis and Design Chapter 8 More on the Web.

www.scsite.com/ sad3e/ch08/

As their name suggests, mass storage devices offer enormous storage capacity. A **mass storage system** consists of a library of storage media and an automated device for access and retrieval. Most mass storage systems use a library of tapes or data cartridges. When access to a particular file is requested, the device selects the appropriate cartridge from the library and transfers the file to magnetic disk. When the program is finished, the file is copied onto the tape cartridge and returned to the library by the system. Mass storage offers the random access capability of disks, but uses less expensive tape media for storage. Mass storage devices usually are expensive and the access is too slow for most online applications.

CALCULATING FILE SIZES AND VOLUMES

ne of the final steps in physical design is estimating file sizes. You need to verify that data storage capacity is available for current and future needs. You must plan for reasonable growth when sizing a file. For example, if your company's customer base is expected to increase by 15 percent annually, then in five years you will need to store twice as many customer records. Also, business organizations require more data and hence more data storage for decision-making, marketing, and operational needs. Systems analysts must consider growth when planning data storage and access requirements.

Sizing Tape Files

Traditional reels of magnetic tape are available in lengths of 300 to 3,600 feet, with typical recording densities of 800, 1,600, 3,200, or 6,250 **bits per inch** (**bpi**). Newer cartridge tapes have even higher densities and can store much more data; it is not uncommon for data cartridges to hold one gigabyte or more.

To allow space for stopping and starting the tape between blocks, an unused area called an **interblock gap** exists between each block. Typical interblock gaps are from 0.3 to 0.6 inch in length. You must know the recording density and the size of the interblock gap to estimate the size of a tape file. Figure 8-39 shows the calculation for a tape file of 20,000 records, each with 275 bytes of data. For calculation A, the records are unblocked. A blocking factor of 20 was used in calculation B, and a blocking factor of 40 was used for calculation C. Notice the dramatic difference between the unblocked file and the file with a blocking factor of 20: the unblocked file needs nearly eight times as much tape.

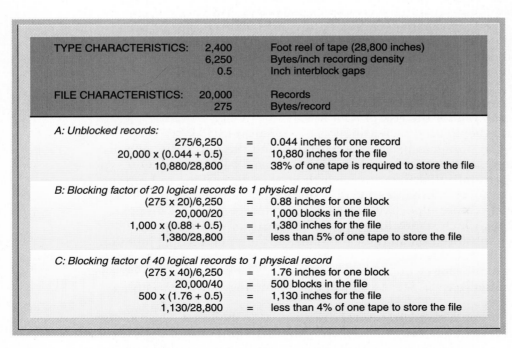

TYPE CHARACTERISTICS:	2,400	Foot reel of tape (28,800 inches)
	6,250	Bytes/inch recording density
	0.5	Inch interblock gaps
FILE CHARACTERISTICS:	20,000	Records
	275	Bytes/record

A: Unblocked records:

275/6,250	=	0.044 inches for one record
20,000 x (0.044 + 0.5)	=	10,880 inches for the file
10,880/28,800	=	38% of one tape is required to store the file

B: Blocking factor of 20 logical records to 1 physical record

(275 x 20)/6,250	=	0.88 inches for one block
20,000/20	=	1,000 blocks in the file
1,000 x (0.88 + 0.5)	=	1,380 inches for the file
1,380/28,800	=	less than 5% of one tape to store the file

C: Blocking factor of 40 logical records to 1 physical record

(275 x 40)/6,250	=	1.76 inches for one block
20,000/40	=	500 blocks in the file
500 x (1.76 + 0.5)	=	1,130 inches for the file
1,130/28,800	=	less than 4% of one tape to store the file

Figure 8-39   Calculation for tape storage requirements using unblocked records and blocking factors of 20 and 40 records.

Sizing Disk Files

Volume calculations for disk files are more complex because the storage capacities and characteristics of disks vary greatly. On hard disks, data is organized physically into either sectors or cylinders. Depending on the specific method used, data storage always results in some amount of unused space. Many disk manufacturers supply charts or programs for determining optimum file blocking factors, based on the record length and the presence or lack of record keys. **Keyed files**, which include both direct files and indexed files, require several additional bytes for each record for direct addressing. Figure 8-40 shows an example of a calculation for a typical disk. Notice that the result depends on the type of file and whether it is indexed.

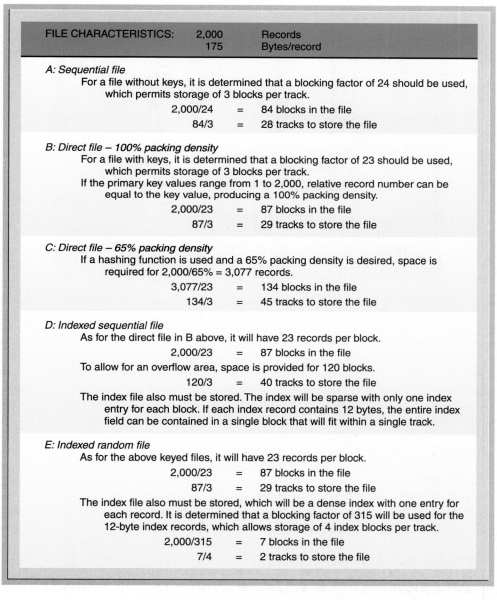

Figure 8-40   Calculations for disk file storage requirements.

Data Compression

Data compression reduces storage needed by using codes to represent repeating data patterns so more data can be stored on hard disks or tapes. Many vendors offer data compression utilities for disk and tape storage.

FILE AND DATABASE CONTROL

Just as it is important to secure the physical part of the system, as shown in Figure 8-41, file and database control must include all measures necessary to ensure that data storage is correct, complete, and secure. File and database control also is related to input and output techniques discussed earlier.

Figure 8-41 System security involves the physical controls shown here and a range of software controls including access codes, data encryption, passwords, and audit trails.

For an overview of **Database Security**, visit Systems Analysis and Design Chapter 8 More on the Web.

www.scsite.com/ sad3e/ch08/

Most database management systems provide built-in control and security features, including passwords, encryption, audit trail files, and backup and recovery procedures to maintain data. Your main responsibility is to ensure that the DBMS features are used properly. With traditional file processing systems, however, you also must design the needed security measures.

Limiting access to files and databases is the most common way of protecting stored data. Only those users who furnish an appropriate code, or **password**, are allowed to access a file or database. Different privileges can be associated with different codes, so some users can be limited to read-only access, while other users might be allowed to update or delete data. For highly sensitive data, additional access codes can be established at the record or field level. Stored data also can be **encrypted** to prevent unauthorized access; special decoding software that is available only to authorized users is used to interpret encrypted data.

All system files and databases must be backed up regularly, and a series of **backup** copies must be retained for a specified period of time. In the event of a file catastrophe, **recovery procedures** can be used to restore the file or database to its current state at the time of the last backup. **Audit trail files**, which record details of all accesses and changes to the file or database, then are used to recover changes made since the last backup.

You also can include **audit fields**, which are special fields within data records to provide additional control or security information. Typical audit fields include the date the record was created or modified, the name of the user who performed the action, and the number of times the record has been accessed.

SOFTWEAR, LIMITED — FILE AND DATABASE DESIGN

At his next meeting with Tom Adams and Becky Evans, Rick Williams shared a message that he received from Ann Hon, director of information systems. Attached to Ann's note was the memo shown in Figure 8-42 from Michael Jeremy.

SWL   **MEMORANDUM**

Date: January 7, 1999
To: Ann Hon, Director of Information Systems
From: Michael Jeremy, Vice President, Finance
Subject: Strategic Planning for Information Systems

As you know, SWL conducts an annual review of the company's strategic plan. Next month, the board of directors will meet with all SWL department heads to discuss our plans and how they fit together.

SWL's president, Robert Lansing, has asked me to submit a specific plan for the information systems department. He feels strongly that SWL's future success will depend on information management and technology.

Please draft a proposal based on the following assumptions:

- SWL must provide its employees with technology, training, and information access to empower them and boost their productivity.

- Information management must be distributed throughout the company, while maintaining necessary security, controls, and quality. This will require the study of networking and client/server architecture.

- SWL's organization will change frequently in response to business needs and competitive pressures.

- SWL must focus on building alliances with customers and suppliers that include IS integration.

- Information technology must be flexible, affordable, and readily available to meet the information needs of users.

- We must identify specific critical success factors to measure our progress and make changes when necessary.

I realize this is a major assignment, but it is vital to SWL's future success. Please plan to meet with me in three weeks to discuss your proposal. Thank you.

Figure 8-42   Michael Jeremy's memo requesting an information systems plan for SWL.

After reading the memo, Tom and Becky were excited because they would be working on an overall strategy for information management at SWL. Rick said they would need to study various approaches that could support SWL's current and future business requirements. He said they would examine several alternatives, including a client/server design. Tom and Becky both had heard of client/server design, but neither person had worked on such a system.

Rick also said that he discussed the memo with Ann Hon, and she wanted to use the ESIP system as a prototype for developing other SWL systems in the future. Ann said that the new design would have to be powerful, flexible, and scalable. With this in mind, the team decided that a database management strategy would be the best solution for SWL's future information systems requirements.

Meanwhile, work continued on the ESIP system. Rick asked Tom and Becky to draw an entity-relationship diagram with normalized record designs. Tom and Becky used the Visible Analyst, a CASE tool, to produce the diagram shown in Figure 8-43. Rick noticed that only two entities were shown: EMPLOYEE and DEDUCTION. Rick suggested that the ESIP-OPTION and the HUMAN RESOURCES entities should be added. Tom and Becky agreed. The second version of their ERD is shown in Figure 8-44. With the ERD completed, Tom turned to the design of the EMPLOYEE record. He suggested the following design:

EMPLOYEE (<u>SSN</u>, EMPLOYEE-NAME, HIRE-DATE)

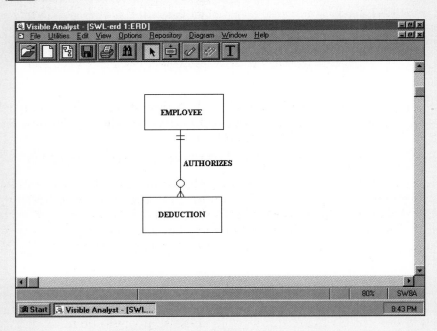

Figure 8-43 Initial ERD showing two entities: EMPLOYEE and DEDUCTION. Notice that crow's foot notation shows that one and only one employee can authorize anywhere from zero to many deductions.

"The record obviously is in 1NF, because it has no repeating groups," Tom said. "It's also in 2NF, because it has a single field as the primary key. And I'm sure it's in 3NF, because the employee name and the hire date both depend on the Social Security number." Everyone agreed that this was the correct design. Tom and Becky turned their attention to designing the ESIP-OPTION record, and later suggested the following design:

ESIP-OPTION (<u>OPTION-CODE</u>, OPTION-NAME, DESCRIPTION, DEDUCTION-CYCLE, APPLICATION-CYCLE, MIN-SERVICE, MIN-DEDUCTION, MAX-DEDUCTION)

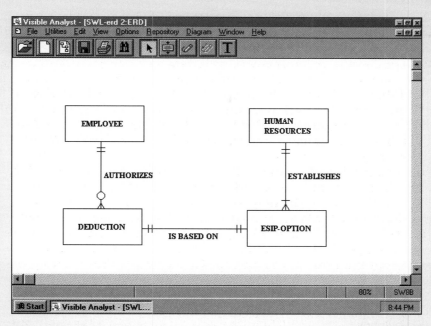

Figure 8-44   Second version of the ERD. Now, DEDUCTION has relationships to two other entities: EMPLOYEE and ESIP-OPTION. Notice that one and only one deduction can apply to one and only one ESIP option.

The design appeared to meet the test for 3NF. Although seven fields existed in addition to the primary key, each field appeared to depend entirely on the key. Finally, Becky proposed the following design for the DEDUCTION record:

DEDUCTION (<u>SSN</u>, <u>ESIP-OPTION</u>, <u>DATE</u>, EMPLOYEE-NAME, AMOUNT)

This time, Rick felt that the record was in 1NF, but not in 2NF because the employee name field only depends on a part of the key rather than the entire key. Becky agreed with him and suggested that the EMPLOYEE-NAME field could be removed and accessed using the EMPLOYEE table. The (SSN) field could be used as a foreign key to match values in the EMPLOYEE table's primary key. To put the record in 2NF, she rewrote the DEDUCTION record design as follows:

DEDUCTION (<u>SSN</u>, <u>ESIP-OPTION</u>, <u>DATE</u>, AMOUNT)

With this change, everyone agreed that the record was also in 3NF because the AMOUNT field depended on the entire key. The next step would be to work on a system design to interface with the payroll system and provide support for SWL's long-term information technology goals.

While Rick, Tom, and Becky were working on ERDs and record normalization, Pacific Software delivered the payroll package that SWL ordered. Tom was assigned to work on installing and configuring the package and training users on the new payroll system.

Meanwhile, Rick felt that SWL should get more information about client/server design. With Ann Hon's approval, he contacted several IS consulting firms that advertised their client/server design expertise on the Internet. Rick and Becky met with three firms and recommended that SWL work with True Blue Systems, a consulting group with a local office in Raleigh, not far from SWL's headquarters. In addition to the design for the ESIP system, Rick suggested that the agenda should include a general discussion about a future SWL intranet, with support for Web standards and the possibility that employees could access their ESIP accounts from home via the Internet.

Assignments

Rick has asked you to help him put together a brief progress update for Michael Jeremy and several other top managers. Specifically, Rick wants you to explain the concept of normalization without using a lot of technical jargon with which managers might be unfamiliar. He says that some managers do not understand why it takes so much time to develop the final design for the system. Rick is confident that you will be able to summarize the concept of normalization in a paragraph or two, using plain English and simple examples. You do not have to describe all the details — just the basic idea of normalization and why it is so important.

CHAPTER SUMMARY

A logical record is composed of fields. The primary key of a file is the field or field combination that uniquely and minimally identifies a particular logical record, and a candidate key is any field that could serve as a primary key. A foreign key is a field or field combination that must match the primary key of another file. A secondary key is a field or field combination that is used as the basis for sorting or retrieving file records.

An entity-relationship diagram (ERD) is a graphic representation of all system entities and the relationships among them. The ERD is based on entities and data stores in DFDs prepared during the systems analysis phase. The three basic relationships represented in an ERD are one-to-one (1:1), one-to-many (1:M), and many-to-many (M:N).

The relationship between two entities also is referred to as cardinality. A common form of cardinality notation is called crow's foot notation, which uses various symbols to describe the characteristics of the relationship.

Normalization is a process for avoiding problems in record design. A first normal form (1NF) record has no repeating groups. A record is in second normal form (2NF) if it is in 1NF and all non-key fields depend on the entire primary key. A record is in third normal form (3NF) if it is in 2NF and if no field depends on a nonkey field.

File and database design tasks include creating an initial ERD, assigning data elements to an entity, normalizing all record designs, and completing the data dictionary entries for files, records, and data elements. Files should be sized to estimate the amount of storage space they will require.

Compared to traditional file processing designs, the database approach offers scalability, support for organization-wide access, economy of scale, data sharing among end-user groups, balancing of conflicting user requirements, enforcement of standards, controlled redundancy, effective security, flexibility, better programmer productivity, and data independence. Databases often are complex and require extensive security and backup/recovery features.

The four basic database models are hierarchical, network, relational and object-oriented. The hierarchical model uses a hierarchy, or family tree. A parent record type can have many children, but a child record type can have only one physical parent. In the network database model, entities are stored in a network of owner and member record types. Each owner-member relationship is defined as a set. The relational model is powerful, flexible, and provides the best support for client/server architecture. Object-oriented databases define data objects, together with the actions (called methods) that can affect the data objects. Through inheritance, a new object obtains all the characteristics of the object upon which it is based.

Common file media types include magnetic tape, floppy disks, hard disks, CD-ROMs, and mass storage systems. As part of the physical design, you must estimate file sizes and plan for future growth. Tape capacities depend on recording density, in bits per inch, and the blocking factor. Disk capacities vary widely, according to the characteristics of the particular disk, the type of file, and how it is indexed.

File access either can be sequential or random. Sequential access requires the storage and retrieval of records in a specific order, while random access permits the records accessed directly, regardless of the order in which records are stored.

The three major file organizations are sequential, direct, and indexed. Sequential organization permits sequential access only. Records within a data file with sequential organization can be unordered or in sequence by primary key value.

Direct organization uses a formula to determine a location for the storage and later retrieval of records. Key-addressing techniques produce a unique physical storage location but can leave storage gaps that waste disk storage. Hashing techniques use an algorithm that does not guarantee a unique disk storage location, and various methods of collision management are necessary.

Indexed organization provides an efficient way of sequentially and randomly accessing records. The logical records are stored in a data file, and a separate index is used to locate records in the data file. Indexed organization either can be random or sequential.

File and database control measures include limiting access to the data, data encryption, back-up/recovery procedures, audit-trail files, and internal audit fields. A file consists of physical records, or blocks, that contain one or more logical records. Typical information system file types include master files, table files, work files, transaction files, history files, and security files.

Review Questions

1. Define the terms primary key, candidate key, secondary key, and foreign key. Which of these, if any, is a nonkey field?

2. What are entity-relationship diagrams? How are they used?

3. What symbol is used for an entity in an entity-relationship diagram? What symbol is used for a relationship?

4. What is cardinality, and what symbols do you use in the crow's foot notation method?

5. What are the three basic types of relationships among entities? What is the abbreviation for each of these basic relationship types?

6. In a one-to-many relationship, for one occurrence of the *one* entity, what is the minimum number of occurrences of the *many* entity?

7. What is the criterion for a record design to be in first normal form? How do you convert an unnormalized record design to 1NF?

8. What are the criteria for a record design to be in second normal form? How do you convert a non-2NF record design to 2NF?

9. What are the criteria for a record design to be in third normal form? How do you convert a non-3NF record design to 3NF?

10. What is a DBMS? Briefly describe the five components of a DBMS.

11. What is a DBMS schema? What is a subschema?

12. List and briefly discuss the advantages and disadvantages of the database approach.

13. How are relationships defined or created in the hierarchical database model, the network model, the relational model, and in the object-oriented model?

14. What are the specific disadvantages associated with the hierarchical database model? Which of these disadvantages are shared by the network database model?

15. What are the specific advantages and disadvantages of the network database model?

16. Explain the difference between a logical record and a physical record.

17. List and briefly describe the six types of information system files. Indicate which types are relatively permanent files and which types usually are temporary files.

18. What is a Julian date? What is an absolute date? How would a specific date, such as March 1, 1999, be represented in each form?

19. What are the two types of file access, and what are the main advantages and disadvantages of each?

20. What are the three general classifications of file organization?

21. How does the size calculation for an indexed file differ from that for a sequential file?

22. What is an audit field? List three typical audit fields.

Discussion Questions

1. In the discussion of third normal form as shown in Figures 8-15a and 8-15b on page 8.14, one 2NF customer record design was converted to two 3NF records. Verify that the four potential problems identified for non-3NF records have been eliminated in the 3NF design.

2. Figure 8-31 on page 8.26 showed sample data for a system with four entities: DEPARTMENT, FACULTY, MAJOR, and STUDENT. Assume that this system will be implemented as a nondatabase, standard file-based system. Are the entities DEPARTMENT and MAJOR potential candidates for combining into a single data file? What would the one record for the combined file look like? Is that record in 1NF, 2NF, or in 3NF? What is gained by combining the entities? What is lost by combining the entities? Would you recommend combining those two entities? Why?

3. In the section on access methods, the following statement appears: *If you need to find a large number of records in a file, sequential access is faster than random access.* Explain why this statement is true.

4. A mail-order company recently expanded its toll-free telephone sales system to include 24-hour customer sales and product support. At the same time, the order and customer master files were reorganized as direct files for rapid online access by the customer representatives. The system performed well during the first several weeks of operation. But recently, accessing a specific order in the order master file has been taking longer. What could be the cause of the access delays?

5. Consider an automobile dealership that maintains an inventory system of cars and trucks in stock at its three locations. Record fields exist for stock number, vehicle identification number, make, model, year, color, and invoice cost. Identify the possible candidate keys, the likely primary key, a probable foreign key, and potential secondary keys. Justify your choices.

CASE STUDIES

NEW CENTURY HEALTH CLINIC — FILE AND DATABASE DESIGN

After completing the output and input designs for the new information system at New Century, you turned your attention to file and database design to consider whether to use a database approach or a file processing system. Begin by studying the data flow diagrams you prepared previously and the rest of the documentation from the systems analysis phase. Perform the following tasks.

Assignments

1. Create an initial entity-relationship diagram for the New Century Health Clinic system.

2. Normalize your record designs.

3. If you identified any new entities during normalization, create a final entity-relationship diagram for the system.

4. Write a memo for your documentation file that contains the following items:

- Your recommendation as to whether to use a file processing or a database environment
- The estimated size of the patient, insurance company, and provider files, based on your record designs and information that you learned previously about New Century's operations
- Copies of your ERD(s) and normalized designs

CUTTING EDGE INCORPORATED

utting Edge Incorporated is a company engaged in the development of computer-aided design (CAD) software packages. The management of Cutting Edge wants to develop a project tracking system to accumulate and report data on current projects, employees, and departments. Systems analyst Penny Binns developed the following initial record design:

(<u>PROJECT-NUMBER</u>, PROJECT-NAME, START-DATE, PROJECT-STATUS, (EMPLOYEE-NUMBER, EMPLOYEE-NAME, DEPARTMENT-NUMBER, DEPARTMENT-NAME, JOB-TITLE, PROJECT-HOURS))

Penny believes the only system entities are PROJECT, DEPARTMENT, and EMPLOYEE; but because she is assigned to two other projects, she has not had time to consider the relationships among those system entities or to normalize the record design.

Assignments

1. For each of the three entities, design files and identify the possible candidate keys, the likely primary key, a probable foreign key, and potential secondary keys. Use sample data to populate the fields for three records.
2. Draw an initial entity-relationship diagram for the system, using the entities Penny identified. State any assumptions you must make about the Cutting Edge organization to determine the types of the relationships. (*Hint*: Penny's situation provides a clue for one of the assumptions you must make.)
3. Convert the record design to third normal form.
4. Draw a final entity-relationship diagram for the system.

FASTFLIGHT AIRLINES

astFlight Airlines is a small air carrier operating in three northeastern states. FastFlight is in the process of computerizing its passenger reservation system. The following data items have been identified: reservation code, flight number, flight date, origin, destination, departure time, arrival time, passenger name, seat number, reservation agent number, and reservation agent name. For example, flight number 303, which is scheduled every Tuesday and Thursday, leaves Augusta, Maine, at 9:23 A.M. and arrives in Nashua, New Hampshire, at 10:17 A.M. You can assume that the FastFlight reservations system will detect automatically whether empty seats are available.

Assignments

1. Draw the entity-relationship diagram for the system.
2. Create third normal form records for the system.
3. If you identified any new entities during normalization, create a final entity-relationship diagram for the system.
4. For each of the entities identified, design files and identify the possible candidate keys, the likely primary key, a probable foreign key, and potential secondary keys. Use sample data to populate the fields for three records.

RIDGEWAY COMPANY

 he Ridgeway Company requirements were discussed in a Chapter 4 case study. The following assignments are based on the work you did for that case study.

Assignments

1. Create an initial entity-relationship diagram for the Ridgeway Company billing system.
2. Normalize your record designs.
3. For each file, determine the file type (master file, transaction file, and so on), and then identify all key fields.
4. For each file, determine the appropriate file organization, and then specify the access method for every process using the file.

CHAPTER 9

SDLC PHASES

Phase 1
Systems Planning

Phase 2
Systems Analysis

Phase 3
Systems Design

Phase 4
Systems
Implementation

Phase 5
Operation & Support

System Architecture

OBJECTIVES

When you finish this chapter, you will be able to:

- Define the term system architecture and describe how it relates to the organization and functions of a business system

- Discuss major processing methods, including batch, online, centralized, and distributed processing

- Describe local and wide area networks, and explain various network configurations, including hierarchical, bus, star, and ring

- Explain the characteristics of distributed systems and client/server architecture

- Discuss the major processing functions of data input, validating, updating, sorting, and reporting

- Describe standard backup and recovery methods for batch and online processing systems

- Discuss the differences between traditional systems development and object-oriented development

- Define the contents of the system design specification document

System architecture is the last of four chapters in the systems design phase. In Chapter 9, you will learn about processing methods, functions, and support. You also will examine network design, client/server systems, and software design. At this point in the SDLC, your objective is to determine an overall architecture that will support the information management requirements of the business effectively.

INTRODUCTION

An information system requires hardware, software, data, procedures, and people to accomplish an organized set of functions. An effective system combines these elements into a design that meets the information management needs of the organization. You have learned about systems design strategies for data, information, and data stores in other chapters and about integrated systems design considerations for people, procedures, and hardware throughout the systems design chapters.

In Chapter 9, you will learn about information system architecture and software design, including major processing functions. **System architecture** refers to the logical design and physical structure of the system, including hardware, software, design, and processing methods. The end product of the systems design phase is the preparation of the system design specification document and its delivery to management and IS department staff.

PROCESSING METHODS

Each information system operates in an environment that includes one or more specific platforms. Both terms, **environment** and **platform**, refer to a particular combination of hardware and systems software. The environment influences system architecture and processing design, including various combinations of online and batch processing methods.

For many years, organizations had two primary environments. Terminals were connected to mainframes to provide **multiuser access** or individual users operated PCs as **stand-alone** workstations. Stand-alone systems typically ran under the control of operating systems such as DOS that allowed a user to run one program at a time. Today, most personal computers use powerful multitasking operating environments, and stand-alone PCs are increasingly rare in the interconnected business world.

Tremendous technological advances in hardware, software, and networking have created entirely new ways of communicating information. At the same time, business is more dynamic than ever due to competitive pressure, corporate restructuring, mergers, and downsizing. Employees at all levels of the organization now are expected to take responsibility for their own information needs, so companies must provide users with the necessary technology and resources. In this environment, systems must be cost-effective, flexible, and user-friendly. In addition, systems must be scalable, so they can support a constantly changing environment.

Most importantly, the operational requirements of the business will determine the best processing strategy. As a systems analyst, your job is to examine various processing methods to select the most effective solution.

Online Processing

Early computer systems relied mostly on batch processing, but the vast majority of systems today use online processing. An **online processing** system handles transactions when and where they occur and provides output directly to users. Because it is interactive, online processing avoids delays and allows a dialog between the user and the system that increases productivity.

An airline reservations system is a familiar example of an online system. When the travel agent shown in Figure 9-1 wants to check on flights for a customer, she enters the origin, destination, and travel dates. The travel agent uses *what-if* analysis to locate the least expensive fare based on the departure dates or length of stay. The system searches a database and responds by displaying possible flights, times, prices, and seat availability. If the customer makes a reservation, the agent enters the customer's name, address, and other required data, and the system assigns a specific seat and updates the flight database immediately.

Figure 9-1 A customer can contact a travel agent who uses an online processing system to retrieve up-to-date flight schedules and other airline information. If the customer books the flight, the system is updated immediately.

Online processing also can be used with file-oriented systems. Figure 9-2 shows what happens when a customer uses an ATM to inquire about an account balance. After the ATM verifies the customer's card and password, the customer enters the request (Step 1). Then, the system accesses the account master file using the account number as the primary key, and retrieves the customer's record (Step 2). The system verifies the account number and displays the balance (Step 3). Data is retrieved and the system transmits the current balance to the ATM, which prints it for the customer. Online processing systems have four typical characteristics: transactions are processed completely when and where they occur, users interact directly with the information system programs, random access is used to access a database or files that have direct or indexed organization, and the information system must be available continuously whenever users require processing of transactions or requests for information.

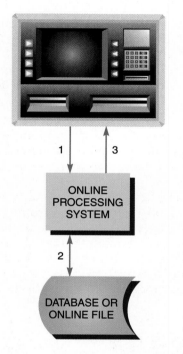

ATM QUERY PROCESS

Step 1: Customer enters his or her account number and requests an account balance

ONLINE SYSTEM

Step 2: Retrieves current account balance

Step 3: Verifies bank account number and displays balance on ATM screen

ACCOUNT MASTER FILE

> To learn more about various **Processing Methods**, visit Systems Analysis and Design Chapter 9 More on the Web.
>
> www.scsite.com/ sad3e/ch09/

Figure 9-2   When a customer requests a balance using an ATM, the system submits the query, retrieves the current balance, verifies the account number, and displays the balance on the ATM screen.

Batch Processing

In a **batch processing** system, data is collected and processed in groups, or *batches*. Although online processing is used for interactive business systems that require immediate data input and output, batch processing can handle other situations more efficiently. For example, batch processing typically is used for large amounts of data that must be processed on a routine schedule, such as paychecks or credit card transactions.

In batch processing, input transactions are grouped into a single file and processed together. For example, when a firm produces customer statements at the end of the month, a batch application might process many thousands of records in one run of the program. A batch processing system has several main characteristics: transactions are collected, grouped, and processed periodically; computer operators can run batch programs on a predetermined schedule, without user involvement, during regular business hours, at night, or on weekends; and batch programs can access files and databases either sequentially or randomly.

Combined Online and Batch Processing

Many online systems also use batch processing to perform certain routine tasks. Figure 9-3 shows how a retail chain might use both online and batch methods. This system uses an online system to handle data entry and inventory updates, while reports and accounting entries are performed in a batch.

This application illustrates both online processing and batch processing of data. During business hours, the salesperson enters a sale on a **point-of-sale** (**POS**) terminal, such as the one shown in Figure 9-4, which is part of an information system that handles daily sales transactions and maintains the online inventory file. When the salesperson enters the transaction, online processing occurs. The system performs calculations, updates the inventory file, and produces output on the point-of-sale terminal in the form of a screen display and a printed receipt. At the same time, each sales transaction creates input data for day-end batch processing.

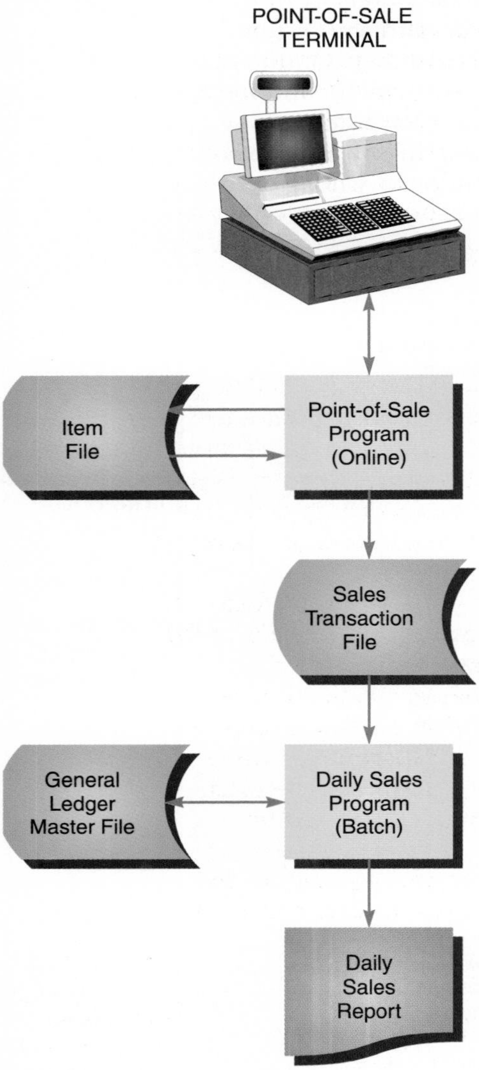

POINT-OF-SALE
TERMINAL

Item File

Point-of-Sale Program (Online)

Sales Transaction File

General Ledger Master File

Daily Sales Program (Batch)

Daily Sales Report

Figure 9-3 Many retail stores use both online and batch processing. When the sales clerk enters the sale on the point-of-sale terminal, the online system retrieves data from the item file, updates the quantity in stock, and produces a sales transaction record. At the end of the day, a batch processing program produces the daily sales report and updates the general ledger master file.

Figure 9-4 Customer transactions are handled online so the retailer's inventory can be updated immediately. At the end of the day, a batch of input data is transmitted to a central computer, which triggers restocking actions and tracks the movement of fast-selling items.

When the store closes, the sales transactions are used to produce the daily sales report and related accounting entries, using batch processing. Performing this processing online before all sales transactions are completed would not make sense. In this situation, a batch method is better for routine transaction processing, while an online approach is needed for point-of-sale processing, which must be done as it occurs.

In the retail store example, both online and batch processing are integral parts of the information system. Online processing has an inherent advantage because data is entered and validated as it occurs, so the stored data is available sooner and is always up to date. Online processing is more expensive, however, and the effects of computer system downtime are far more disruptive. Also, backup and recovery for online processing is more difficult. In many situations, batch processing is cost-effective, less vulnerable to system disruption, and less intrusive to normal operations. Most information systems will continue to use a combination of online and batch processing for some time to come.

Centralized and Distributed Processing

Centralized processing typically involves a mainframe and terminals located at one central location to provide information for an entire organization. In the past, centralized processing was the only alternative because communications networks were not available to transmit input and output data from remote locations. As network technology advanced and became affordable, however, processing methods changed so that data could be entered and accessed anywhere in the organization, regardless of where the processing computer was located.

A **distributed system** consists of data resources that are accessible at many locations. Distributed systems provide instant access to data, regardless of the location of the user or the data. Data can be stored at one or more locations that are connected by a data communication network. A **data communication network** is a collection of terminals, computers, and other equipment that uses communication channels such as telephone lines or the Internet to share data. The network is transparent to online users because users see the data as if it is stored on their own workstations. Networks also permit **distributed processing**, which allows certain tasks to be performed by decentralized computers instead of by a central computer.

The capabilities of a distributed system depend on the power and capacity of the underlying data communication network. Distributed systems, however, raise concerns about data security and system reliability because operations are performed at many locations. As a systems analyst, your objective is to design a system that is secure and dependable as well as flexible and powerful.

Distributed system design involves two separate issues: where to perform system processing and where to store data. Traditionally, data was stored on central computers to control data security and integrity better. Just as processing can be done at various places, however, data can be stored in more than one location using a **distributed database management system** (**DDBMS**).

Using a DDBMS offers several advantages. Data is stored closer to users to reduce network traffic. Also, a DDBMS system is easily scalable and new data sites can be created without affecting network operation. With data stored in various locations, the system is less likely to experience a catastrophic failure. One major disadvantage of a DDBMS is data security. When data is stored in various locations, the system lacks a central set of controls and standards. In addition, the architecture of a DDBMS is more complex and difficult to manage.

Many IS professionals feel that DDBMS is an emerging technology with enormous potential, and many software vendors, including Oracle, Sybase, and IBM, offer products that support distributed data management systems.

To learn more about **Distributed Database Management Systems,** visit Systems Analysis and Design Chapter 9 More on the Web.

www.scsite.com/ sad3e/ch09/

Figure 9-5 shows various stages in the development and evolution of distributed systems. When centralized mainframe computers were used to store systems and data, many companies performed data processing at a central location called a **data processing center**. Source documents were sent there for data entry, and then printed reports were distributed throughout the company.

1. Central mainframe at a data processing center handles all data entry, processing, and reports.

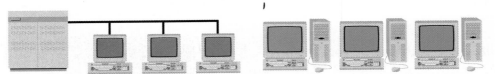

2. Central mainframe with remote terminals attached for data entry and stand-alone PCs.

3. Mainframe file server with networked PCs running local applications.

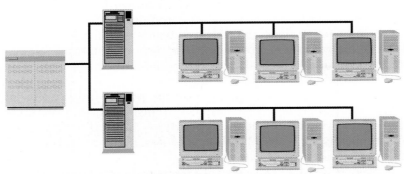

4. Client/server architecture combines shared data and processing on wide and local area networks based on minicomputer servers and PCs.

Figure 9-5   The evolution from a central mainframe to client/server information systems.

With the introduction of data transmission networks, users were able to enter and access data remotely. For example, using terminals connected to a central computer, sales clerks entered orders from many locations. Then, as networks become more powerful, a main computer often functioned as a file server, allowing users to download stored data and run system software locally at their workstations. Using this approach, known as a **file server design**, data can be shared across various local and wide area networks. Finally, with **client/server architecture**, data and processing can be shared throughout the organization.

LOCAL AREA NETWORKS AND WIDE AREA NETWORKS

Networks usually are described as either local area networks (LANs) or wide area networks (WANs). A **local area network** (**LAN**) connects a group of personal computers in a limited area such as an office or a department to a server that is a powerful personal computer or a minicomputer. A **wide area network** (**WAN**) uses a combination of telephone lines, fiber-optic cables, microwave transmission, and satellites to connect personal computers and LANs into a network that can span the globe.

A **network** allows hardware, software, and data resources to be shared to reduce expenses and provide more capability to users. Figure 9-6 shows a LAN that includes a file server, several clients, a laser printer, and a tape backup unit that can be accessed by any personal computer connected to the network.

For a comprehensive resource on **LANs**, visit Systems Analysis and Design Chapter 9 More on the Web.

www.scsite.com/ sad3e/ch09/

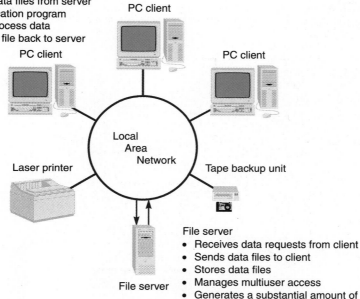

PC client
- Handles user interface
- Sends data request to server
- Receives data files from server
- Runs application program locally to process data
- Sends data file back to server

PC client

PC client

PC client

Local Area Network

Laser printer

Tape backup unit

File server
- Receives data requests from client
- Sends data files to client
- Stores data files
- Manages multiuser access
- Generates a substantial amount of LAN traffic

File server

Figure 9-6   Example of a LAN file server design. The server stores and manages the data, while the client PCs run the application program and perform all the processing.

As shown in Figure 9-6, a data file on the LAN file server is sent to a personal computer that runs its own copy of the program and processes the data locally. After processing, the data file is sent back to the server where it is stored and backed up. A file server design requires a powerful data communications network because the entire data file is transmitted to a client. In contrast, in client/server systems that are discussed later in this chapter, the server transmits only the results of the data request and not the entire file.

When considering any network design, it is important to investigate software licensing restrictions. Various types of individual and site licenses are available from software vendors. Some vendors limit the number of users or the number of computers that can access the program simultaneously. You also must investigate the capabilities of network software carefully to ensure that it can handle the anticipated system traffic.

The way a network is configured is called the network **topology**. LAN and WAN networks typically are arranged in four patterns: hierarchical, bus, star, and ring. The concepts are the same regardless of the size of the network, but the implementation is different in a large-scale WAN that spans an entire business enterprise versus a small LAN in a single department. In all cases, the network must use a **protocol**, which is a set of standards that govern data transmission on the network. A popular network protocol is **TCP/IP**, which was developed originally by the U.S. Department of Defense to permit interconnection of military computers.

Individual locations on the network usually are referred to as **nodes**. Individual networks can be integrated into larger networks, which is how the Internet is organized. The four topologies are shown in Figures 9-7 through 9-10 on pages 9.8 through 9.10.

For more detail about **TCP/IP**, visit Systems Analysis and Design Chapter 9 More on the Web.

www.scsite.com/ sad3e/ch09/

Hierarchical Network

In a **hierarchical network**, as shown in Figure 9-7, one computer that typically is a mainframe controls the entire network. Individual satellite processors control lower levels of processors and devices.

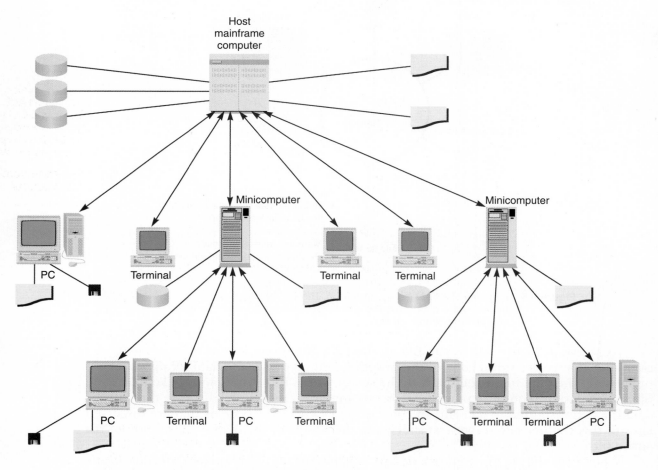

Figure 9-7   A hierarchical network with a single computer that controls the network.

Bus Network

In a **bus network**, as shown in Figure 9-8, a single communication path connects the mainframe computer, minicomputer, workstations, and peripheral devices.

Information is transmitted in either direction from any workstation to another workstation, and any message is directed to a specific device. An advantage of the bus network is that devices can be attached or detached from the network at any point without disturbing the rest of the network. In addition, a failure in one workstation on the network does not necessarily affect other workstations on the network.

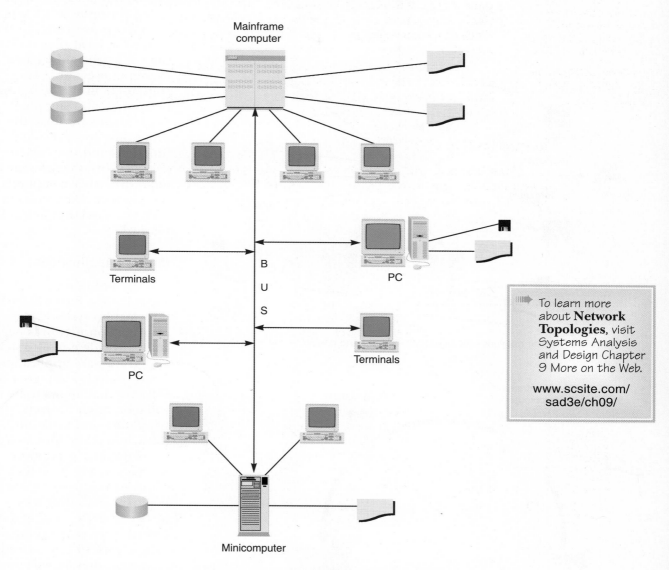

To learn more about **Network Topologies**, visit *Systems Analysis and Design* Chapter 9 More on the Web.

www.scsite.com/
sad3e/ch09/

Figure 9-8   A bus network with all devices connected to a single communication path.

Star Network

A **star network** has a central computer with one or more workstations connected to it that form a star. A star configuration, as shown in Figure 9-9 on the next page, often is used when the central computer contains all data required to process the input from the workstations. The central computer in a star network does not have to be the primary data storage point, however, it also can serve as a network coordinator that enables the other devices to transmit and receive data from each other.

A star network provides efficiency and close control over the data processed on the network. A major disadvantage is that the entire network depends on the central computer. In most large star networks, backup systems are available in case of a failure in the central computer.

Ring Network

A **ring network**, as shown in Figure 9-10, resembles a circle of computers that communicate with each other. A ring network often is used when processing is performed at local sites rather than at a central location. For example, users accessing computers in the accounting, personnel, and shipping departments perform the processing for individual functions and then use the ring network to exchange data with other computers on the network. Data flows in only one direction in a ring network.

Network Applications

In addition to supporting a firm's business information systems, data transmission networks enable companywide e-mail systems and groupware applications. **Groupware** is a category of software that allows users to collaborate on projects, share schedules, and work effectively as a team. One of the more popular groupware products is Lotus Notes, which can be used by small departmental groups or across an entire multinational company. As more companies assign work to groups and teams, groupware will continue to grow in importance.

Advances in network technology enable companies to create information management strategies that span an entire company. With powerful network resources, companies have found new ways of integrating data, people, and operations. One major design strategy involves client/server systems, which you will learn about in the next section.

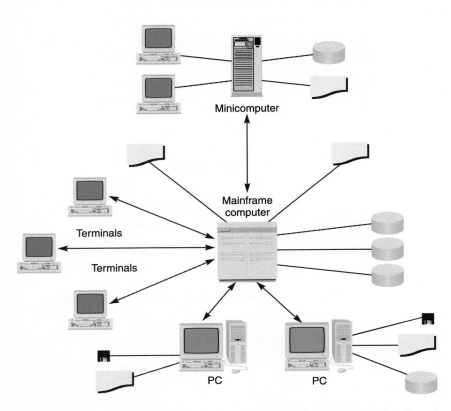

Figure 9-9   A star network with a central computer and connected workstations.

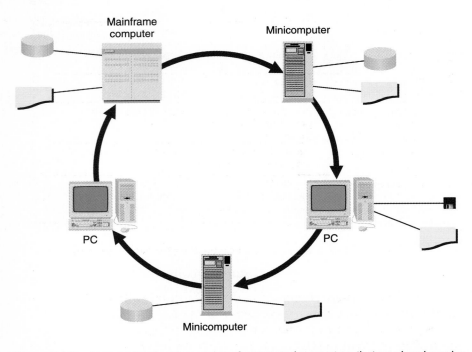

Figure 9-10   A ring network with a series of connected computers that send and receive data that flows in one direction.

CLIENT/SERVER SYSTEMS

A **client/server system** divides processing between one or more clients and a central server. A client handles the entire user interface, including data entry, editing, and data query, and the server provides data access, processing, and database management functions. In a typical interaction, the client submits a request for information from the server, which carries out the operation and responds to the client. As shown in Figure 9-11, the data file is not transferred from the server to the client — only the request and the result are transmitted across the network. To fulfill a request from a client, the server might contact other servers for data or processing support, but this process is transparent to the client. The analogy can be made to a restaurant where the customer gives an order to a server, who relays the request to a cook who actually prepares the meal.

Figure 9-12 lists some major differences between client/server and traditional mainframe systems. Many early client/server systems did not produce expected savings because few clear standards existed, and development costs often were higher than anticipated. Implementation was expensive because clients need powerful hardware and software to handle shared processing tasks. In addition, in many cases, the installed base of mainframe data, called **legacy data**, was difficult to access and transport to a client/server environment.

As large-scale networks grew more powerful and IS professionals gained design experience, client/server systems became more cost-effective. Many companies invested in client/server systems to achieve a unique combination of computing power, flexibility, and support for changing business operations.

File server system

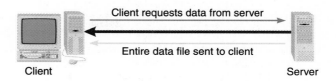

Client/server system

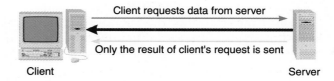

Figure 9-11   A file server system compared to a client/server system.

CHARACTERISTICS OF CLIENT/SERVER VERSUS MAINFRAME SYSTEMS		
Characteristic	**Client/Server**	**Mainframe**
Basic architecture	Very flexible	Very rigid
Application development	Flexible Fast Object-oriented	Highly structured Slow Traditional
User environment	PC-based GUI Empowers the user Improves productivity	Uses terminals Text interface Constrains the user Limited options
Security and control features	Decentralized Difficult to control	Centralized Easier to control
Processing options	Can be shared and configured in any form desired	Cannot be modified
Data storage options	Can be distributed to place data closer to users	All data is stored centrally
Hardware/software integration	Very flexible Multivendor model	Very rigid Single proprietary vendor

Figure 9-12   Characteristics of mainframe and client/server systems.

Today, enormous interest exists in client/server systems by users, IS staff, and managers. In a merger of two technologies, companies are studying ways to base client/server designs on Internet protocols, as well as on traditional network models. As businesses formed new alliances with customers and suppliers, the client/server concept expanded to include clients and servers outside the organization. By using **electronic data interchange** (**EDI**) to support these links, many companies have changed the way they interact with customers and suppliers.

IBM's Web site recently reported two examples of successful client/server systems. In the first case, Boston Market, a nationwide food chain shown in Figure 9-13, was experiencing rapid growth, adding more than 300 stores per year. The company decided to create a central support center where servers use a data communication network to poll all Boston Market locations for daily sales, marketing, and productivity data. This storehouse of data is accessed by 25 client area offices that manage information to make rapid decisions about inventory, product promotions, and pricing. Boston Market reported that the client/server design resulted in new ways of capturing, sharing, and managing information and contributed significantly to the company's success.

For an overview of **Client/Server Systems**, visit Systems Analysis and Design Chapter 9 More on the Web.

www.scsite.com/ sad3e/ch09/

Figure 9-13 Because of its rapid growth and expansion, Boston Market, a nationwide restaurant chain, created a central support center where servers use a data communications network to poll all Boston Market locations for daily sales, marketing, and productivity data. Twenty-five client offices access this data to manage information to make rapid decisions about inventory, product promotions, and pricing.

The second IBM example involved Maytag Corporation's Customer Service Division, as shown in Figure 9-14. Maytag used rapid application development (RAD) to design a client/server solution with two AS/400 R servers and more than 100 personal computer clients. The goal was to set up a world-class customer service telephone center.

Previously, with a volume of more than one million calls per year, service representatives manually entered parts requests, customer comments, and complaint resolutions. The new system uses a sophisticated touch-tone menu to give telephone customers quick access to a customer consultant at a client workstation that is connected to a server. The consultant can access an enormous amount of information, including a database of answers to questions, repair histories, and personalized customer data. Each call is logged to add more data to the troubleshooting database.

To support business requirements, future information systems need to be scalable, powerful, and flexible. Client/server systems have many characteristics that meet these needs. First, whether a business is expanding or downsizing, client/server systems enable

Figure 9-14   Maytag Corporation used rapid application development (RAD) to design a client/server solution with two AS/400 R servers and more than 100 personal computer clients. The goal was to set up a world-class customer service telephone center. The system uses touch-tone menus to give telephone customers access to a consultant at a client workstation that is connected to a server.

the firm to scale the system to a rapidly changing environment. As the size of the business changes, it is easier to adjust the number of clients and the processing functions they perform than it is to alter the capability of a large-scale central server.

Client/server computing also allows companies to transfer applications from expensive mainframes to less expensive client platforms. Also, using common languages such as SQL, clients and servers can communicate across multiple platforms. This difference is important because many businesses have substantial investments in a variety of hardware and software environments.

Finally, client/server systems reduce network load and improve response times so users have faster access to data. For example, consider a user at a company headquarters who wants information about total sales figures. In a file server design, the system might need to transmit three separate sales transaction files from three regional offices in order to provide sales data that the client would process — but in a client/server system, the server locates the data, performs the necessary processing, and responds immediately to the client's request. The data retrieval and processing functions are transparent to the client because they are done on the server, and not by the client.

ON THE NET

Many firms offer software and consulting services to assist companies in the planning, design, and implementation of client/server systems. You can search the Internet to locate some of these firms and make a list of products and services that are available. For example, using a Web search engine, search for the term "client/server." If necessary, you can add other terms to narrow the scope of the search.

The major difference between file server designs and client/server systems is that file servers enable the sharing of data, while client/server systems support the sharing of data *and* processing. Thus, two systems might have the same physical devices — a server, a network, and several workstations — but have entirely different designs. Why would a company choose one approach or the other?

One of the main questions is whether the system requires a large number of users to access the same data at the same time. If so, a client/server design has a major advantage because the server, rather than the clients, manages all concurrent data access. If a system does not require heavy multiuser access, however, then a file server design might be a simpler, less expensive alternative. For example, a file server design would support a company e-mail system that allows each user to access his or her personal mailbox, but does not require multiuser sharing of data.

The size and characteristics of the data files also are important factors. For example, if users need information from a large relational database, a file server must transfer the entire database to the client, while a client/server system can respond with only the results of the client's query. On the other hand, if the system uses separate files rather than a database design, a file server design can be efficient and cost-effective.

Finally, the analyst must consider the processing requirements and physical characteristics of the system. A client/server system allows shared processing, which provides operational flexibility in a multi-platform environment. For example, some client workstations might handle certain processing tasks, while others with different capabilities can be assigned other functions. In contrast, a file server design requires all client workstations to handle similar processing tasks.

The issue of file server versus client/server design, like many others, requires the systems analyst to balance various factors, including power, flexibility, and cost. The main objective is to select a design that will support current and future business operations effectively.

A KEY QUESTION

You are the new IS manager at R/Way, a small but rapidly growing trucking company headquartered in Cleveland, Ohio. The company slogan is "Ship It R/Way — The State of the Art in Trucking and Customer Service."

R/Way's information system currently consists of a file server and three workstations where freight clerks enter data, track shipments, and prepare freight bills. To perform their work, the clerks obtain data from the server and use database and spreadsheet programs stored on their local PCs to process the data.

Unfortunately, your predecessor did not design a relational database. Instead, data is stored in several files, including one for shippers, one for customers, and one for shipments. The system has worked well in the past, but you are concerned about the future. The company president is supportive of making changes, but he is reluctant to spend money on major IS improvements unless you can convince him that they are necessary.

You realize that a relational database is essential, and you suspect that a client/server system is appropriate for the future. The data file sizes are relatively small, however, and a file server design probably could handle current R/Way operations for the next year or two.

Should you present a recommendation for a new client/server system at this point, or would it be better to design a relational database and see how it runs on the file server platform before changing the underlying design? What would you recommend and why?

Client/server systems represent a major trend in systems development. Many IS professions, however, see the transition from centralized processing to client/server systems as a journey, not to be achieved all in one step. Future growth of client/server systems will be driven by business needs, the way that users interact with information systems and advances in technology. Successful client/server projects will need clear objectives, total support from management, adequate resources, and reasonable time frames. The best client/server systems will be those that are customer-centered, championed by strong managers, and reflect the way the company actually does business.

PROCESSING FUNCTIONS

hen designing a system, you must document all processing functions in the system requirements document. All information systems have four basic processing functions: data input and validating, updating, sorting, and reporting.

Data Input and Validating

For online processing, the same program handles data entry, data input, and validation as a transaction is entered. For example, in an online banking system, one program might handle entry, input, and validation for deposits, while another program handles the same functions for withdrawals. Other systems might have one large program that handles data entry, data input, and validation functions for both types of transactions.

Batch systems also can have one or more programs for each type of transaction. Data entry and validation in batch processing, however, differs from online systems in two ways. First, data entry and data validation are two separate functions in a batch processing system. Second, the batch processing system needs a specific way to handle transaction errors.

In some systems, valid transactions are processed immediately, while incorrect transactions are listed in an error report that data entry clerks use to correct and reprocess the transactions. In some systems, however, *all* transactions must be correct before *any* additional processing can occur. A payroll system, for instance, typically requires that all errors be corrected before processing the payroll run.

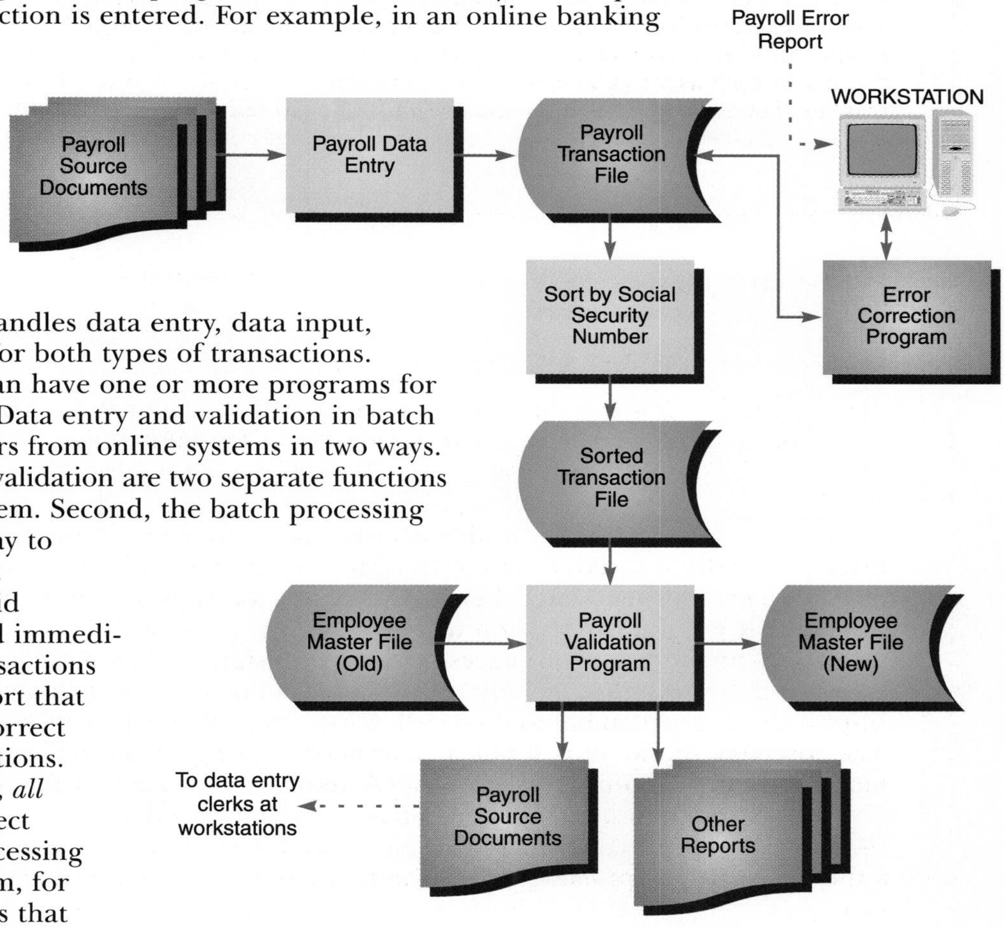

Figure 9-15   An error correction program can be used to correct a payroll transaction file. Then, the corrected transaction file is sorted again and input to the payroll validation program, along with the current employee master file.

Another method for handling errors is a program that allows corrections to the transaction file. Figure 9-15 shows a program that allows data entry clerks to use the payroll error report to enter corrections. The corrected transaction file is sorted and run through the payroll validation program again. Although this method is an easy way to make corrections, sorting, reading, and validating the entire transaction file a second time is a major disadvantage. With small transaction files, the additional processing might not be a problem, but a large transaction file might require excessive processing time.

Another common method for handling corrections is to have the payroll validation program create an error transaction file, called a **suspense file**, as shown in Figure 9-16. The error correction program allows corrections to the suspense file, which is sorted and processed through the validation program.

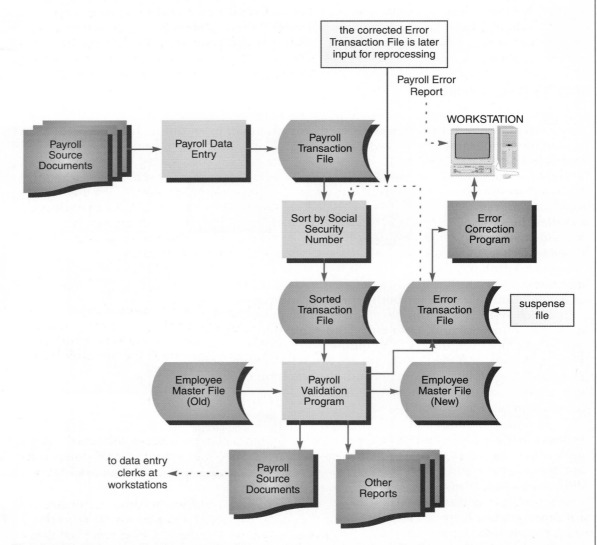

Figure 9-16 An error correction program allows corrections to a suspense file that contains error transactions. The corrected transactions are sorted and reprocessed, and the previous employee master file is the new input to the payroll validation program.

Online and batch validation programs often need to access other master files to verify that an input value matches a valid primary key. For example, the payroll validation program shown in Figure 9-16 might need to access a department master file to verify that the department number is correct.

Updating

Updating, or **file maintenance**, is the process of adding, changing, and deleting records in a master or table file. An **online update program** randomly updates a master file and handles all data entry, data input, validation, and update functions. Because it is critical to record the modifications that occur to master files, an online update program creates an audit file that identifies master file changes and produces an audit transaction report. The batch system is similar, but when a batch transaction file is used to update a master file, both files must be in the primary-key sequence of the master file.

Some update programs logically delete records from master files instead of physically deleting them. **Logical deletion** uses a special field, or **flag**, to indicate whether the record has been deleted. Logical deletions are used when the file organization does not permit physical deletions or when records cannot be deleted immediately. Payroll systems, for instance, need to retain employee records for year-end processing to produce W-2 reports for former employees who worked during the year. Logical deletion also permits restoration of deleted records. Records that were logically deleted are physically deleted at a specified time. For example, employee payroll records that were logically deleted during the year are physically deleted after year-end processing is completed.

Sorting

In file-based systems, sorting records is a major task that requires a substantial amount of computer processing time. Transaction files must be sorted before running a batch update program, and sorting also is done to put master files and other files in the sequence needed for various reports. For example, in a file-based system, suppose you want to produce a payroll report by employee name within department. The employee master file might be in Social Security number order, so it must be sorted first by department and then by name. In a database environment, sorting is not necessary because the DBMS uses indexes when processing and displaying records.

Reporting

Producing reports is a major function of both batch and online processing systems. In file processing systems, whether batch or online, a systems analyst can design reports by using a report generator program or a 4GL language. If the system uses a commercial database program, the analyst also can use report creation tools that are built into the package.

PROCESSING SUPPORT

No matter how well it is designed, every system will experience some problems, such as hardware failures, systems software errors, user mistakes, and power outages. As part of the systems design, you must anticipate these future problems and plan for ways to recover from them.

You already are familiar with data validation, audit trail files, security measures, and other control features to help ensure that data is entered and processed correctly. You must provide additional means, however, to deal with situations where files or databases are damaged or when processing is interrupted before completion.

When system problems occur, safeguards must be in place to prevent permanent damage to or loss of vital data, and processing must restart properly. Four support functions can handle these concerns: backup and recovery, file retention, restart, and start-up processing.

Online Backup

Step 1: Make a nightly backup of the online master file.

Step 2: Create the log file during online processing.

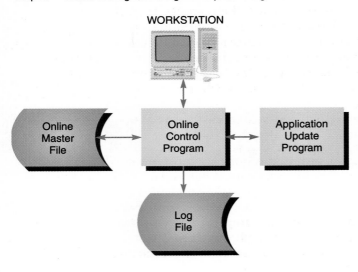

Online Recovery

Step 1: Use the most recent nightly backup file to restore the online master file.

Step 2: Reprocess the day's transactions from the current log file.

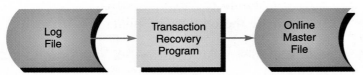

Figure 9-17 Backup and recovery steps in an online processing environment. The backup process involves making a backup copy of the master file and creating a log file during online processing. Recovery consists of restoring the online master file from the backup copy and processing the day's transactions from the log file.

Backup and Recovery

Backup refers to making copies of data files so if data is lost, a timely **recovery** can be made and processing can continue. Batch processing presents few backup and recovery problems. The transaction file and the previous version of the master file are saved as backup files in case the new master file is damaged or the update program execution is interrupted. Any problems are corrected by executing the update program again with the transaction file and the previous master file as inputs. A backup should be made immediately each time the master file is updated. The most common backup medium is magnetic tape in various forms.

Online processing presents greater backup and recovery problems than batch processing. With online systems, as shown in Figure 9-17, you must perform backups when the system is inactive — usually at nights or on weekends. In addition, transactions processed since the time of the last backup must be captured. Most online systems can recreate transactions using copies of modified master file records that are stored in special files called log files, or journal files. A **log file**, or **journal file**, contains a copy of each record as it appears before and after modification. If a master file is damaged, the current backup is used to recover, or restore, the master file. Then, a special transaction recovery program processes the log file to bring the master file forward to its state at the time the damage occurred. The total recovery time can take many hours for master files with large numbers of records and transactions.

Rather than using a log file, some companies use other methods to record online transactions. A common technique is to use multiple high-capacity disks that mirror the data file while processing continues. Another variation is to use a streaming tape device that constantly records all data file activity as it occurs. If processing is interrupted, data is recovered by restoring the file from the backup media.

File Retention

File retention refers to the length of time a file needs to be stored. Online master and table files are permanent files, so they are retained for the life of the information system. File retention for transaction files, backup files, and master files is determined by a combination of processing and legal requirements. Processing requirements dictate that files be retained long enough to permit the recovery of all master file data. Many companies retain sequentially organized master files that are updated during batch processing for three updating cycles, or **generations**. This concept is called the **grandparent, parent, and child strategy**. The **grandparent file** represents the oldest master file retained, the **parent file** represents the second oldest file, and the **child file** represents the current master file. Retaining these three files and the transactions that were used to update the files usually is adequate backup retention.

Legal requirements also affect file retention policies. If a government rule specifies that a record of all payments to the company must be kept for three years, then your design must retain the records for that period. Designing a payment history file or retaining monthly backup copies of the payment file for three years are common strategies.

One other issue concerns lost reports. If the report is recreated easily, you can run the report program again to produce another copy. Another solution is to output the report initially to a disk or tape file from which the report can be printed. When the retention period is over, the file is deleted.

Restart

When an error occurs while a program is running, the first step is to correct the problem. If a disk master file is damaged, you must recover the file from the latest backup and restart the program. Your design must include specific steps for restarting programs depending on where the error occurred.

Restarting online processing systems is relatively simple. For single-user systems, the user reenters the transactions processed since the last backup. For multiuser systems, the log file is processed to the point of interruption.

If you need to restart a relatively short batch processing program, you can rerun the program from the beginning. If the program runs for a longer period, you should consider the use of **checkpoints**. At a processing checkpoint, **program status indicators** are saved on disk. These indicators include the records being processed, the contents of main memory, and other information necessary to restart the program from that point. Checkpoints occur periodically while the program executes. If the program needs to be restarted, the program does not need to rerun completely; it can be restarted at the last checkpoint before the error occurred.

Because the printing of special outputs, such as paychecks or invoices, might be interrupted due to a power failure or a printer problem, you should design restart procedures for these jobs. One method is for the print program to request the computer operator to enter check numbers for the last check printed correctly. Then, the program bypasses all employees whose paychecks were printed correctly and resumes printing the next check.

Start-Up Processing

Another design task involves start-up processing. **Start-up processing** is needed when making the transition from the current system to a new system. The main objective is to create new master files from existing data, which may require special data conversion programs. Start-up processing and conversion programs are discussed during the systems implementation phase in Chapter 11.

For additional guidelines on **System Backup**, visit Systems Analysis and Design Chapter 9 More on the Web.

www.scsite.com/ sad3e/ch09/

For more information on **File Retention** policies, visit Systems Analysis and Design Chapter 9 More on the Web.

www.scsite.com/ sad3e/ch09/

SOFTWARE DESIGN

Software design involves two distinct levels. This chapter continues the first design level, which began during the systems analysis phase when all functions were identified and documented with process descriptions. Now, during the design phase, the systems analyst determines which programs are needed to perform these functions and what each program will do. In a traditional file-oriented system, the analyst must describe each program in detail and its relationship to other system programs. Similarly, if a DBMS is used, the systems analyst identifies all procedures, modules, and macros, and decides whether the code will be written by programmers or generated by the program.

The second level of software design is performed during the systems implementation phase when a programmer determines exactly *how* each program will accomplish its objectives. This process is discussed in Chapter 10, which describes programming, testing, and documentation.

> To learn more about **Software Design**, visit Systems Analysis and Design Chapter 9 More on the Web.
>
> www.scsite.com/ sad3e/ch09/

Programs Required

During systems design, you must identify the specific functions that will be performed in each program in a process called **partitioning**. You start by reviewing the process descriptions developed during the systems analysis phase and listing the processes that must be handled by software programs.

When developing a database using a DBMS, you will not need to create special programs to update files or validate transactions because these functions are handled by the DBMS. You might design modules, however, to perform certain types of processing that can be done more efficiently with program code.

In a file-based system, you will need to partition the system software functions into programs. During this process, keep the following guidelines in mind.

Use a separate update program to maintain each master file. In general, every master file needs its own update program to maintain that file. Consider a batch program that uses a transaction file to write to a customer master file and a customer invoice file. As shown in Figure 9-18, you also would need a program to update the customer master file and another program to update the customer invoice file.

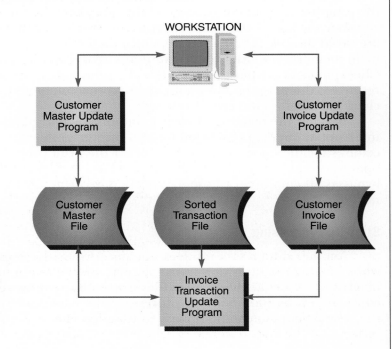

Figure 9-18 The customer master file and the customer invoice file both have update programs that handle additions, changes, and deletions of records. In this example, a third update program receives input from a transaction file and updates both master files.

Provide a validation program for each update program that does not perform its own validation. All transactions must be validated, and you must be sure that all update programs are supplied with valid transactions. This rule usually applies only to batch updates because online update programs generally handle their own validation.

Reduce the number of report programs if possible. You can reduce the number of programs if several reports are based on the same file or files. Suppose an invoice system has two reports — one report printed in invoice number sequence and another report printed in customer name order. If the reports are based on the same customer invoice file, you should consider designing one program to produce both reports, which would save time and be more cost-effective.

Identify any programs required to perform special processing. As you identify update, validation, report, and menu procedures, you should match the process descriptions with specific programs. In some cases, you might need to design additional programs to handle special processing situations. For example, many master files have accumulation fields, such as month or year-to-date fields. An employee master file has monthly, quarterly, and yearly accumulations for taxes, earnings, and deductions; one or more programs will be needed to initialize these fields at the beginning of each month, quarter, and year.

Program Documentation

In a file-based system, after deciding which programs are required, you must assemble the necessary documentation. Figure 9-19 on the next page shows a sample documentation form for an Employee Hours Report in a payroll system. As the form illustrates, you must provide the following specific information:

Program identification. Each program has two means of identification: an English version program name and a computer program name. The computer program name is the system name of the program and usually is determined by IS department standards. The computer program name for an inventory update program, for example, might be INVUPD or IN205.

Purpose of the program. Provide a brief description of the program's purpose.

Files. Each file that is input, output, printed, and updated by the program must be identified by name. You should use the data dictionary name for the file, and refer to printer spacing charts, screen layouts, and source documents used by the program for other file names.

Processing requirements. The process descriptions were developed during systems analysis and describe the program's processing tasks. If any requirements were added during the systems design phase, they must be documented in the data dictionary.

OBJECT-ORIENTED DESIGN

A significant difference exists between traditional methods of systems analysis and an object-oriented approach, as you learned in Chapter 8. In conventional systems analysis, an analyst focuses on data flows and procedures, using CASE tools or other graphical techniques to assist in top-down modeling. In contrast, the object-oriented analysis phase uses a bottom-up approach that emphasizes data rather than data flows. Traditional tools such as DFDs and ERDs are used in object-oriented design, but in different ways. The line separating systems analysis, design, and implementation is not as clear as in the traditional SDLC because more overlap exists among the phases, especially when prototyping is used.

An object-oriented approach to systems analysis is especially useful if the analyst knows that the system will be developed in an object-oriented programming environment.

For more information on **Object-Oriented Design**, visit Systems Analysis and Design Chapter 9 More on the Web.

www.scsite.com/sad3e/ch09/

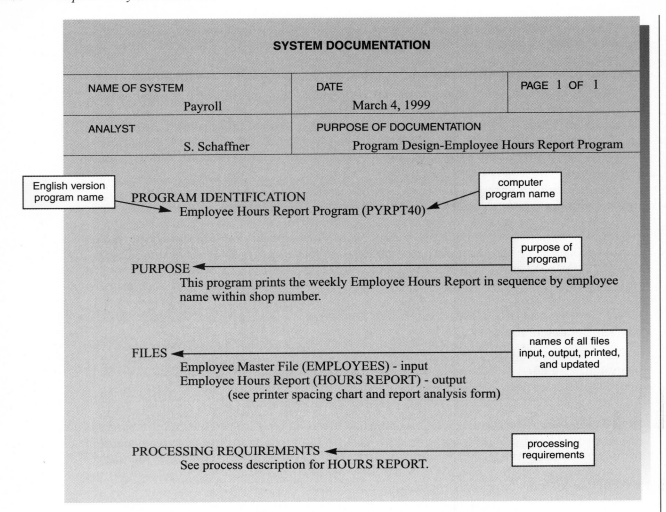

Figure 9-19   An example of program documentation for the Employee Hours Report.

SYSTEMS DESIGN COMPLETION

T
he preparation of the system design specification and its presentation to management and other IS people are the final activities in the systems design phase. Before the presentation, you need to obtain the support and approvals from IS department management and technical staff and from users on all design issues that affect them.

System Design Specification

The **system design specification**, also called the **technical design specification** or the **detailed design specification**, is a document that presents the complete design for the new information system along with detailed costs, staffing, and scheduling for completing the next SDLC phase — systems implementation.

The system design specification is the baseline against which the operational system will be measured. Unlike the system requirements document, which is written to be read and understood by users, the system design specification is oriented toward the programmers who will use it to create the necessary programs. Some sections of the system requirements document are repeated in the system design specification, such as process descriptions, data dictionary entries, and data flow diagrams.

The system design specification varies in length, so you must organize it carefully. and number all pages in sequence. You should include a cover page, a detailed table of contents, and an index.

The contents of the system design specification will depend on company standards and the complexity of the system. Most system design specifications have a structure similar to that shown in Figure 9-20, which is described next.

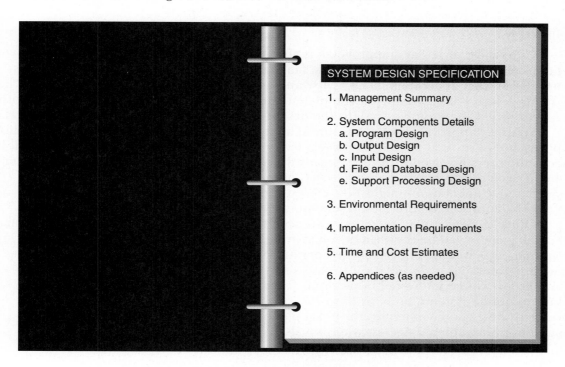

Figure 9-20   The organization of a system design specification.

1. **Management Summary.** The management summary provides an overview of the project. It outlines the development efforts to date, provides a current status report, summarizes current project costs and costs for the remaining phases, reviews the overall benefits of the new system, presents the systems development phase schedule, and highlights any issues that need to be addressed by management.

2. **System Components Details.** This section contains the complete design for the new system, including all programs, outputs, inputs, files, and databases. You should include source documents, printer spacing charts, screen layouts, DFDs, and all other relevant documentation. You also should include the requirements for all support processing, such as backup and recovery, file retention, and restart processing. If the purchase of a software package is part of the strategy, you must include any interface information required between the package and the system you are developing. If you use a CASE design tool, you can print design diagrams and most other documentation directly from the tool.

3. **Environmental Requirements.** This section describes the constraints affecting the system, including any requirements that involve operations, hardware, systems software, or security. Operational constraints include volumes, sizes, frequencies, and timing such as reporting deadlines, online response times, and processing schedules.

4. **Implementation Requirements**. You specify start-up processing requirements, user training plans, and software test plans in this section.

5. **Time and Cost Estimates.** This section provides detailed schedules, estimates, and staffing requirements for the systems development phase and revised projections for

the remainder of the SDLC. You also present total costs to date for the project and compare these costs with your prior estimates.

6. **Appendices.** Supplemental material can be included in appendices at the end of the system design specification as needed. Copies of important documents from the first three phases, a copy of the change request procedure, and copies of government regulations are examples of the information you might want to include.

Approvals

Users must review and approve all report and output screen designs, menu and data entry screen designs, source documents, manual processing, and other parts of the systems design that affect them. The review and approval process continues throughout the systems design phase. When you complete the design for a report, you should meet with users to review the prototype, adjust the design if necessary, and obtain written approval.

Securing approvals from users throughout the design phase is very important. This approach ensures that you do not have a major task of collecting approvals at the end, it keeps the users involved with the system's development, and it gives you feedback about whether you are on target. Some portions of the system design specification, such as program documentation, might not interest users, but anything that does affect them should be approved before the presentation you will conduct at the end of the phase.

Other IS department members also need to review the system design specification. IS management will be concerned with staffing, costs, hardware and systems software requirements, and the effects on the operating environment of adding the new system. The programming team will want to assess all the programming tasks, and the operations group will be interested in program scheduling, report distribution, additional loads to online systems, and any hardware or software issues they need to prepare for. You must be a good communicator to keep people up to date, obtain their input and suggestions, and obtain necessary approvals.

When the system design specification is complete, you distribute the document to a target group of users, IS department personnel, and company management. You should distribute the document at least one week before your presentation to allow the recipients enough time to review the material.

Technical and Management Presentations

Usually, you will give several presentations at the end of the systems design phase. These presentations will give you an opportunity to explain the system, answer, consider any comments, and secure approval. The first presentation is to the systems analysts, programmers, computer operators, and technical support staff who will be involved in future project phases or operational support for the system. Because of the audience, this presentation is technically oriented.

You give the next presentation to top IS department management and major users from all departments affected by the system. As in the first presentation, your primary objective is to obtain support and approval for the systems design. This is not a technical presentation; it is aimed at user interaction with the system and management's interest in budgets, schedules, staffing, and impact on the production environment.

The final presentation is given to company management. By the time you give this presentation, you should have obtained all prior approvals from previous presentations, and you should have the support of users and the IS department. Just like the management presentation at the end of the systems analysis phase, this presentation has a key objective: to get management's approval and support for the next development step — systems implementation — including a solid commitment for financial and other resources needed.

Based on the presentation and the data you submitted, management might reach one of three decisions: proceed with systems development, perform additional work on the systems design phase, or terminate the project. The next chapter discusses systems implementation, which is the fourth SDLC phase.

SOFTWEAR, LIMITED — SYSTEM ARCHITECTURE

Jane Rossman, manager of applications, and Rick Williams, systems analyst, had several meetings with True Blue Systems, the consulting firm that was hired to assist SWL in implementing the new ESIP system. As requested by Michael Jeremy, SWL's finance vice president, True Blue also was asked to make recommendations about a possible SWL intranet that would link all SWL locations and support client/server architecture.

The initial report from True Blue indicated that the new ESIP system should be designed as a DBMS so it could interface with the new mainframe payroll package. True Blue suggested that the ESIP system be implemented on a server in the payroll department and developed as a Microsoft Access application. They felt this approach would provide a relational database environment, client/server capability, and SQL command output to communicate with the mainframe. Figure 9-21 shows the proposed design of the system.

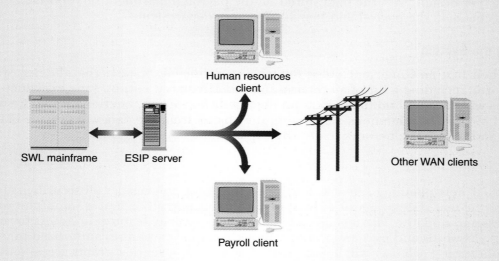

Figure 9-21　The proposed ESIP system.

Jane Rossman met with Ann Hon to review True Blue's report and get her approval for training for IS staff members. Jane had some prior experience in Access application development, but Rick had none, so Jane suggested that he and Becky Evans attend a one-week workshop. Ann agreed.

Ann, Jane, and Rick met with Michael Jeremy to get his approval before proceeding further. He asked them to develop a specific budget and timetable including all necessary hardware, software, and training costs. They had most of the information, but they needed some help from True Blue to estimate the cost of network implementation, installation, and physical cabling.

The first phase of the project would use a local area network to link the various headquarter departments to the mainframe. A second phase, proposed by True Blue, would connect all SWL locations to a wide area network, with the possibility that employees could access their individual ESIP accounts over the internal network or from outside the company using the Internet.

A week later, Ann received a memo from Mr. Jeremy that said the project had been approved and she should start work immediately.

System Architecture

The ESIP development team included Jane, Rick, and Becky. The group discovered that developing a Microsoft Access application is different from using a traditional programming language. Instead of developing a main program and subprograms to manage the data, they would create a series of interactive objects, including tables, queries, forms, reports, macros, and code modules.

They would begin by reviewing the entity-relationship diagrams they prepared previously to determine the overall structure of the DBMS design. Then they would identify the tables, review the relationship among them, and analyze the record designs they had developed. They also would review output requirements, input screen designs, processing considerations, backup and recovery procedures, and controls that must be built into the new system.

As recommended by True Blue Systems, the new ESIP system would be implemented as a client/server design, with the data stored on the payroll department server, which would be linked to clients in the payroll and human resources department.

Planning the System

In their first meeting, Jane asked the team to define all the tasks that the new system will perform, including a list of all reports and other required output. Jane explained that ESIP data will be stored on the server, but objects such as forms, queries and reports would be stored on client workstations. Separating the objects from the data will provide better security, and reduce the network loads, she explained.

Security

In their next planning session, Jane asked the group to consider all security issues to build into the new system. Because the system contains payroll data, it is important to control user access and updates. The team decided to use the security features in Access for control, including passwords and user and workgroup accounts for employees authorized to use the ESIP application. Each user will be assigned a permission level that grants access only to certain objects.

Rick suggested that they should design the basic security features before proceeding further, but Jane disagreed. "We'll create the security features later, when we create the database. Meanwhile, let's go back to the department heads, Michael Jeremy and Tina Pham, to get their input on security levels," Jane said. "Users will be allowed to create and modify certain forms and reports, but most other actions will be permitted only by authorized IS department members," she added.

Creating the Objects

Before creating the objects, the team reviewed the ERDs and normalized record designs to ensure their design accuracy. Also, they verified that the new payroll system permitted cross-platform access because the ESIP system would use data from the payroll master file. They discovered that the payroll package used a standard data format called **open database connectivity** (**ODBC**) that would support links to the Access database. After planning the system, they will start creating the objects.

Planning the User Interface

From earlier interviews, the IS team knew that users in the payroll and human resources departments wanted an interface that would be simple and easy to operate. Jane asked Becky to start designing a main form, or switchboard, that would display automatically when the

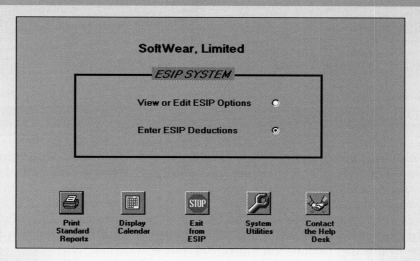

Figure 9-22　Sample of a main switchboard that displays when the ESIP system starts.

ESIP application started. All ESIP screen forms would use buttons, menus, and icons as shown in Figure 9-22.

Becky created a prototype of the input screens to show to users. After securing user approval, the screen designs were added to the system specification document for the ESIP system.

Using Access Basic for Procedures and Macros

Because she was a programmer before her promotion to systems analyst, Becky wanted to know whether they would be using Access Basic as a program development language. Jane told her that they would write many of the procedures in the Access Basic language because it allows more powerful data manipulation than macros and makes it easier to customize error messages. Jane explained that they still would use macros to speed up development time — and that certain actions can be done *only* with macros. Becky was looking forward to learning Access Basic because it is related closely to Visual Basic, which is used as a macro language in other Microsoft products.

Completing the Systems Design Phase

The IS team completed the systems design phase by writing the documentation and designing backup and recovery, file retention, restart procedures, and start-up procedures. The final step was to develop a system design specification for the ESIP system, and then to complete output, input, file, and program designs.

Rick and Becky showed a draft of the system design specification to Jane and Ann Hon. After incorporating their changes, they printed the final document, sent it to the review committee, and scheduled a presentation for the following week. The presentation went well, and management approved the design phase of the ESIP system.

 YOUR TURN — Rick Williams documented the backup and recovery and file retention procedures for the ESIP system, but these procedures were not described in the SoftWear, Limited case study.

1. What should be the backup and recovery procedures?
2. Suggest a file retention policy for SWL.

3. Who is ultimately responsible for security — users, management, or the IS department? Write a brief memo to Jane explaining your views.

CHAPTER SUMMARY

A successful information system combines hardware, software, data, procedures, and people. The hardware and software environment, or platform, and the methods of processing determine the system's design.

The primary processing methods are online, batch, centralized, distributed, single-user, and multiuser. Users interact directly with online systems that continuously process their transactions when and where they occur and randomly update files and databases. In contrast, batch systems process transactions in groups, execute on a predetermined schedule, and either randomly or sequentially access files and databases. Most information systems use online processing to handle normal business transactions and queries. Batch processing is used to generate regularly scheduled reports. Centralized processing takes place at one location, whereas distributed processing locates computer resources at multiple sites connected by data communication networks. Single-user systems are used by one person at a time on a single computer, whereas multiuser systems have two or more people using the same computer.

Data communication networks either can be LANs (local area networks) or WANs (wide area networks). Networks permit workstations to share hardware devices such as printers and backup systems as well as data. Networks are categorized by their configuration, or topology. A single mainframe computer usually controls a hierarchical network, a bus network connects workstations in a single-line communication path, a star network connects workstations to a central computer, and a ring network connects workstations in a circular communication path.

In file server systems, a server transmits the stored data files or database to a client workstation that performs the processing and transmits the data files or database back to the server. Client/server systems differ from file servers because they support the sharing of processing, as well as data, between the server and client workstations. In a client/server system, the client handles the user interface and submits a data query to the server. The server responds with the results of the query, and not the entire data file. Compared to file server designs, client/server systems are more scalable and flexible. They can reduce costs and network traffic, and they can connect with customer and supplier systems using electronic data interchange.

All information systems have the four basic processing functions of data input and validating, updating, sorting, and reporting. Each of these functions is handled differently based on the processing methods used. Each information system also must include support functions that can handle backup and recovery, file retention, restart, and start-up processing.

Although each information system has unique requirements, a system must have programs to update files and databases, validate input data, produce reports, control online interaction, and handle special processing situations. Program documentation is an extension of other systems analysis and design documentation and specifies the program's identification, purpose, files, and processing requirements.

In a file-based system, the analyst identifies the programs that will carry out the processing functions and the specific work that each program must perform, while a DBMS environment typically handles these tasks.

Software design depends on the overall systems analysis approach. In traditional structured analysis, the focus is on data flows and procedures, while object-oriented analysis emphasizes data characteristics and relationships.

The system design specification presents the complete systems design for an information system and is the basis for the presentations that complete the systems design phase. Following the presentations, the project either proceeds on to the systems development phase, requires additional systems design work, or is terminated.

Review Questions

1. What is an environment, or platform?
2. What is an online processing system? Describe four characteristics of an online processing system.
3. What is a batch processing system? Give three characteristics of a batch processing system.
4. Are most information systems online, batch, or combined online and batch processing systems? Why?
5. What is centralized processing?
6. What is distributed processing?
7. What is a data communication network?
8. What is the difference between a LAN and a WAN?
9. What is a distributed database management system?
10. Name and describe the various network topologies.
11. What are client/server systems? How do they differ from file server designs?
12. What is electronic data interchange?
13. Name the four major processing functions.
14. What is a logical deletion? Give two reasons for using logical deletions.
15. Describe how the process of backup and recovery differs between batch and online processing systems.
16. What is a log file?
17. What two types of requirements do you use to determine a file's retention period?
18. What is a checkpoint?
19. What is start-up processing?
20. What information is placed in the system components details section of the system design specification?

Discussion Questions

1. Some authorities feel that programming, documentation, and design standards must be imposed on the information systems profession. These authorities argue, "Millions of dollars and thousands of hours of time are wasted in retraining whenever individuals change jobs because every installation is different. Standards would eliminate this problem." Other authorities argue, "Standards stifle creativity. We will never progress as a profession if all people in information systems are required to follow prescribed standards. Standards imply a best way — we haven't found the best way yet in information systems. Information systems is much too young as a profession to begin to impose standards." What is your opinion?

2. An executive from one of the country's leading accounting firms recently remarked, "It is virtually impossible for accountants in our firm to properly audit any large-scale computerized financial or inventory system. For one thing, most systems are not designed for any type of efficient auditing and, even if they are, the multitude of data that can be processed on a large computer would take hundreds of work-years to audit the system." What do you think of this opinion?

3. After spending 11 months as the systems analyst in charge of a major IS project, you are scheduled to give the final management presentation for the systems design phase. Two days before the presentation, you learn of a major new hardware announcement. After investigating, you realize that this new product could reduce the cost and increase the effectiveness of the system.

The new product, however, will require a substantial redesign of the system and at least three months of additional effort. What would you do, and why?

4. One senior executive states, "When a new system is proposed, all I want is a written report, not an oral presentation. I want to see the facts about costs, the time to implement, and the resulting benefits. On that basis, I'll make my decision as to whether the system should be implemented. Systems analysts don't get paid to make management-level decisions, and that's exactly what they try to do when they try to sell a system in an oral presentation. I've seen too many systems implemented because smooth-talking analysts convinced management that a system is an absolute necessity when the facts just don't justify it." Do you agree with this point of view? Justify your position.

CASE STUDIES

NEW CENTURY HEALTH CLINIC — SYSTEM ARCHITECTURE

The New Century clinic associates accepted your output, input, and file designs and your recommendation to install a server and four personal computers as clients on a local area network. The server will include a tape backup unit and a modem to exchange data with insurance companies. A high-speed laser printer and an impact printer for multipart forms will be accessible by any of the four PCs. Now you will determine the processing strategy and system architecture.

When you created ERDs and record designs for the New Century system earlier in the systems design phase, you also considered whether to use a file-processing or database approach. As you know, each strategy has advantages and disadvantages, depending on the specific hardware and software environment and business requirements. Dr. Jones does not have a background in systems design, and he is willing to accept your recommendation (with your instructor's approval).

If you use a file-based approach, you will review the process descriptions that you created during the systems analysis phase, describe the programs needed, and create a systems flowchart to provide a clear picture of the system.

If you have experience with relational database design and use that approach, you will identify the system functions and determine how they will be performed in a database environment.

After you select an alternative (with your instructor's approval) you will review the DFDs and other documentation you prepared in the systems analysis phase (Chapter 4) and the entity-relationship diagrams and record designs you created earlier in the systems design phase (Chapter 8). Then you will perform the following assignments.

Assignments

If you use a file-based approach, perform the following tasks:

1. Based on the procedures you have identified, determine the programs required for the system. Prepare documentation for each program including the program's name, purpose, and files used.

2. Prepare a diagram of the system using either a systems flowchart or another diagramming method recommended by your instructor.

If you use a database design approach, perform the following tasks:

1. Based on the entity-relationship diagrams and record descriptions you created earlier in the systems design process, identify all entities, design the database tables required, and indicate the common fields that will link the tables.

2. Identify all system functions and determine how these functions will be handled by the database management system. You should include the following functions in your list: data input and validating, updating, sorting, and reporting. Depending on the software environment, you might be able to use features built into the software package for some of these functions. In other cases, it will be necessary to create queries, forms, reports, macros or modules with coded procedures and routines.

Regardless of which design approach you select, also perform the following tasks:

1. Document the backup and recovery procedures for system data and files.
2. Document the file retention periods for system data and files.
3. Prepare the system design specification. The document should include:
   a. A management summary
   b. Documentation for output, input, files, programs, and support processing
   c. Environmental requirements
   d. Implementation requirements
   e. Time and cost estimates

NAUGATUCK INDUSTRIAL SUPPLY COMPANY

Naugatuck Industrial Supply Company (NISC) distributes maintenance tools and supplies, cleaning materials, and general-purpose equipment to companies in the Naugatuck River Valley region. NISC has had a minicomputer for the past six years that runs systems using batch and online processing in a multiuser environment. NISC also has seven personal computers that run single-user programs and are connected to the minicomputer in a star configuration. When interacting with the minicomputer, the personal computers download and upload data and act as terminals to the users for online processing against the central files and programs stored on the minicomputer.

The IS department is concerned about the difficulties of backup and recovery on the minicomputer because recovery of the online system takes at least two hours, during which time the users cannot access the system. The first hour is spent restoring the master files from backup files, and the rest of the time is spent reprocessing transactions from the log file. The systems analysts are studying various alternatives to reduce the recovery time.

NISC is developing a new online purchase order system on the minicomputer. The purchase order system will have two master files: a purchase order master and a vendor master. The systems analyst for this project has proposed a new method for updating these two master files. Transactions will be entered and validated online, as is the case with all current online systems. Rather than updating the master files directly at this point, the online program will store the valid transactions in a file on disk. Then, during nightly batch processing, the transactions will be processed to update the master files.

Assignments

1. What are the advantages of this deferred method of updating?
2. What additional processing must the online validation program perform?
3. What are the potential problems with this approach?
4. Draw a diagram illustrating the backup and recovery processing that would be used for this system.

RIDGEWAY COMPANY

he Ridgeway Company requirements were described in a Chapter 4 case study. The following assignments are based on the work you did for that case study.

Assignments

1. Determine the programs required for the billing system. Prepare program documentation for each program by specifying the program's name, purpose, files used, and processing requirements.
2. Document the backup and recovery requirements for all files in the system.
3. Document the file retention period for all the files in the system.
4. Document the restart procedures that will be used in the system.

Phase 4
Systems Implementation

Phase 1
Systems Planning

Phase 2
Systems Analysis

Phase 3
Systems Design

Phase 4
Systems Implementation

Phase 5
Operation & Support

Systems Implementation

Application Development

Installation and Evaluation

SDLC PHASES

Systems implementation is the fourth phase in the systems development life cycle. In the previous phase, you completed the design of the system. Now, in systems implementation, you will perform a series of application development tasks, followed by the system installation and evaluation. During application development, all necessary system programs and code modules are designed, written, tested, and documented. The system installation and evaluation stage includes user training, file conversion, the actual changeover to the new system, and an evaluation of the results. You will learn about application development in Chapter 10 and about installation and evaluation in Chapter 11.

CHAPTER 10

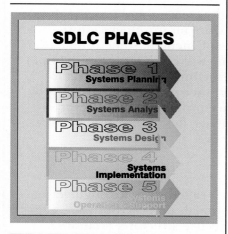

SDLC PHASES

Phase 1
Systems Planning

Phase 2
Systems Analysis

Phase 3
Systems Design

Phase 4
Systems
Implementation

Phase 5
Systems
Operational Support

OBJECTIVES

When you finish this chapter, you will be able to:

- Describe the major tasks and activities that are completed during the systems implementation phase
- Discuss the role of the systems analyst during application development
- Explain the importance of quality assurance and the role of software engineering in software development
- Describe the different types of documentation the systems analyst must prepare
- Explain the different phases of testing including unit testing, link testing, and system testing
- Describe top-down design and modular design and the advantages of these approaches

Application Development

Application development is the first of two chapters in the systems implementation phase. Chapter 10 emphasizes the process of constructing the necessary programs and code modules for the system.

INTRODUCTION

At the conclusion of the previous SDLC phase (systems design), you prepared a system design specification that contains the complete design for the new information system. Now, in the systems implementation phase, the systems design specification serves as a blueprint for constructing the new system. During this phase, the IS department plans, develops, documents, integrates, and tests all new programs and code modules. If the design is based on a commercial software package, IS staff members can add custom features by using the application's built-in development tools or by creating additional programs and modules.

At this point in systems development, programmers and systems analysts assume different responsibilities. An analyst must deliver a clear, accurate set of specifications to a programmer. Depending on the organization, these specifications might be highly detailed or generalized. A programmer codes, tests, and documents the individual program modules, while the systems analyst plans the integration of the programs and assures that they work together to meet business requirements. Programmers and analysts often work as a team to test and document the entire system. Chapter 10 stresses the analyst's role during application development and does not cover programming skills, techniques, or activities, which are a separate area of study.

QUALITY ASSURANCE

I n today's competitive business environment, businesses are intensely concerned with the quality of their products and services. To be successful, an organization constantly must improve quality in every area, including its business information systems. Top management must support the quality concept and provide the leadership, encouragement, and resources needed for quality improvement efforts.

No matter how carefully a system is designed and implemented, some problems will occur, especially in a complex system. Rigorous testing will catch errors in the final stages, but it is much better and far less expensive to correct mistakes earlier in the development process. The main objective of **quality assurance** is to avoid problems or to detect problems as early as possible. A quality assurance program must address several types of problems, including inaccurate requirements, design or coding errors, faulty documentation, and ineffective testing.

For an overview of the **Software Engineering** process, visit Systems Analysis and Design Chapter 10 More on the Web.

www.scsite.com/ sad3e/ch10/

Software Engineering

Because quality is so important, an approach called software engineering has emerged to manage and improve the development process. **Software engineering** stresses quality through solid design, effective structure, accurate documentation, and careful testing (Figure 10-1). In addition to these basic concepts, advanced methods of software development are available. For example, the **Software Engineering Institute** (**SEI**) at Carnegie Mellon University was established with the goal of finding better, faster, and less expensive methods of software engineering and providing leadership to software developers and systems analysts. SEI designed a technique called the **Capability Maturity Model** (**CMM**^{SM}) to improve quality, reduce development time, and cut costs. Figure 10-2 shows the SEI home page and mission statement.

For additional detail on **Capability Maturity Model**^{SM}, visit Systems Analysis and Design Chapter 10 More on the Web.

www.scsite.com/ sad3e/ch10/

Figure 10-1 Thorough testing is a critical part of software engineering. Software engineers will put a system or program such as the battle simulation software shown here — through a series of tests before releasing it for use.

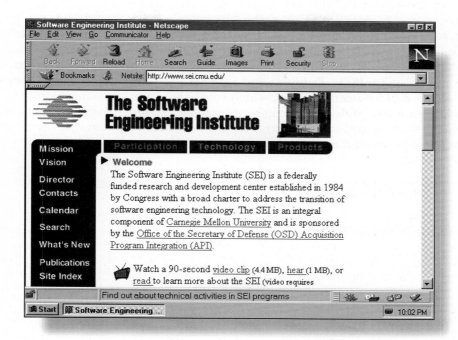

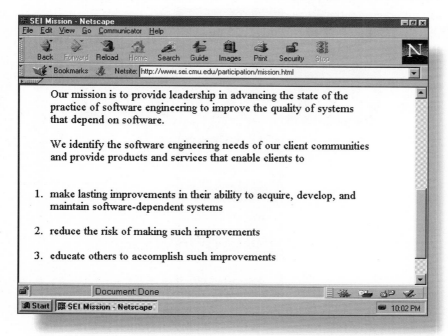

➤ For information on ensuring **Quality**, visit Systems Analysis and Design Chapter 10 More on the Web.

www.scsite.com/ sad3e/ch10/

Figure 10-2   The Software Engineering Institute's (SEI) Web page describes the organization and explains that the purpose of software engineering is to improve the quality of software-based systems.

ON THE NET

More than ever, the success of a business depends on the quality of its products and services. In the global market-place, specific quality standards exist that are promulgated by the **International Organization for Standardization** (**ISO**). Products and services that meet these requirements are entitled to ISO certification, which can be an important marketing advantage. Use a Web search engine to search for information on ISO standards, including any standards that apply specifically to computer software. Summarize your findings in a brief memo.

APPLICATION DEVELOPMENT

A new system requires planning, construction, and testing. After an overall strategy is established, programs, and modules must be designed, coded, tested, and documented, as shown in Figure 10-3. After developing the programs and code modules, systems analysts and programmers perform link testing of modules, system testing, and complete all documentation.

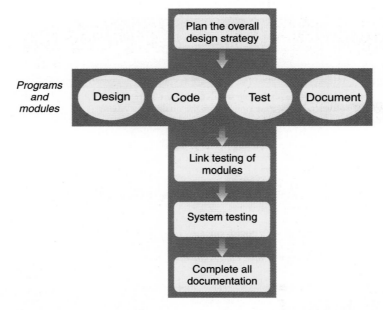

To learn more about the **Top-Down Approach**, visit Systems Analysis and Design Chapter 10 More on the Web.

www.scsite.com/ sad3e/ch10/

Figure 10-3 The main steps in application development.

When planning the system, most analysts use a top-down approach, which proceeds from a general design to a detailed structure in a series of logical steps. In a **top-down approach**, the systems analyst defines the overall objectives of the system, and then breaks them down into subsystems and modules in a process called **partitioning**. This approach also is called **modular design** and is similar to constructing a leveled set of DFDs that show individual elements in a complete, working structure.

A **module** is a set of program instructions that can be executed as a group. By assigning modules to different programmers, several areas of development can proceed at the same time. Using project management software, each module can be plotted on a Gantt chart, based on estimated development times and available IS resources, and the critical path can be calculated for the project. The Systems Analyst's Toolkit shows how to use these techniques.

Although the top-down approach has many advantages, the analyst must proceed carefully, with constant input from programmers and IS management to achieve a sound, modular structure. All modules must function properly as an overall information system, so the analyst must ensure that integration capability is built into each design and thoroughly tested during the development process.

> To learn more about programming **Modules**, visit Systems Analysis and Design Chapter 10 More on the Web.
>
> www.scsite.com/ sad3e/ch10/

Documentation Review and Application Design

With an overall strategy in place, the next step is to review documentation from prior SDLC phases and create a set of **program designs**. In addition to the system design specification, the systems analyst can refer to DFDs, process descriptions, screen layouts, report layouts, source documents, data dictionary entries, and anything else that will help a programmer understand what functions the program or module must perform and its relationship to other programs and modules. Based on these requirements, the main responsibility for actually coding and constructing the program or module belongs to the programmer.

After reviewing the design, a programmer develops a step-by-step logical solution by using **structure charts** or **hierarchy charts**, **program flowcharts**, and **pseudocode**. For example, to develop a program for sales commission processing, a programmer could use the structure chart shown in Figure 10-4, the program flowchart shown in Figure 10-5 on the next page, and the pseudocode shown in Figure 10-6 on page 10.9. Traditionally this work is handled by programmers, but some companies assign a team of analysts and programmers to work together on application development.

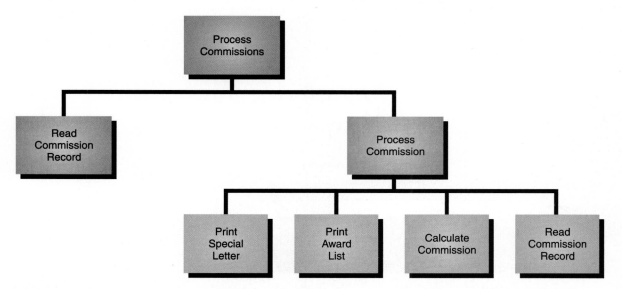

Figure 10-4   Example of a structure chart for sales commission processing shows the program modules and the functions they perform.

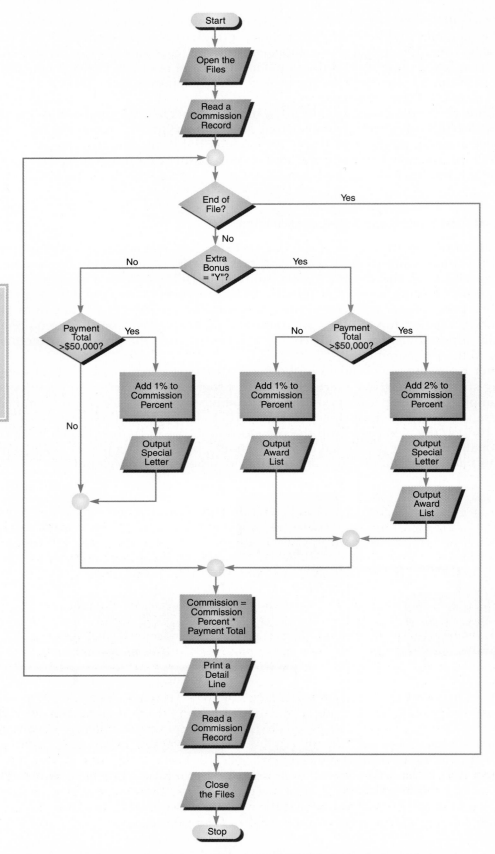

For an example of using **Flowcharts**, visit Systems Analysis and Design Chapter 10 More on the Web.

www.scsite.com/ sad3e/ch10/

Figure 10-5   An example of a program design flowchart shows the logic needed to calculate commissions and perform related tasks.

```
Open the files
Read a COMMISSION record
Do until end of file
        If EXTRA BONUS equals Y
                If PAYMENT TOTAL is greater than $50,000
                        Add 2% to COMMISSION PERCENT
                        Output SPECIAL LETTER
                        Output AWARD LIST
                Else
                        Add 1% to COMMISSION PERCENT
                        Output AWARD LIST
            ENDIF
          Else
            If PAYMENT TOTAL is greater than $50,000
                    Add 1% to COMMISSION PERCENT
                    Output SPECIAL LETTER
            ENDIF
        ENDIF
        Calculate COMMISSION = COMMISSION PERCENT times PAYMENT TOTAL
        Print a detail line
        Read a COMMISSION record
ENDDO
Close the files
End the program
```

Figure 10-6 An example of pseudocode that documents the logical steps in sales commission processing.

If a programmer believes that the design needs changes, he or she must contact the systems analyst to review the suggested revisions. For example, the programmer might notice that certain information is duplicated in a report design. If the analyst determines that users might be affected by the changes, they must be informed in advance. All modifications must be documented in the system design specification.

Coding

Coding is the process of turning program logic into specific instructions that can be executed by the computer system. If a programmer has prepared a careful design, the coding process is a simple translation of logical functions into program code. Small programs usually are coded by a single programmer, whereas larger programs are divided into modules that can be assigned to different individuals or groups.

Each IS department has its own standards for programming languages and coding. Visual C++, Access Basic, Visual Basic, and SQL are examples of commonly used programming languages, and many commercial packages use a proprietary set of commands. As more companies use Internet protocols for company intranets, HTML, Java, and other development tools will be used extensively.

For helpful **Coding** tips, visit Systems Analysis and Design Chapter 10 More on the Web.

www.scsite.com/ sad3e/ch10/

A strong trend exists toward using report writers, screen generators, program generators, fourth-generation languages, and other CASE tools that produce code directly from program design specifications. Some commercial applications can generate editable program code directly from macros, keystrokes, or mouse actions. Figure 10-7 on the next page shows an example of a Visual Basic code module in Microsoft Access that opens a customer order form and produces a beep sound. The code was generated automatically by a macro, which itself was created by a series of keystrokes and mouse actions. Notice that the module shown in Figure 10-7 includes program commands, comments, and error-handling procedures.

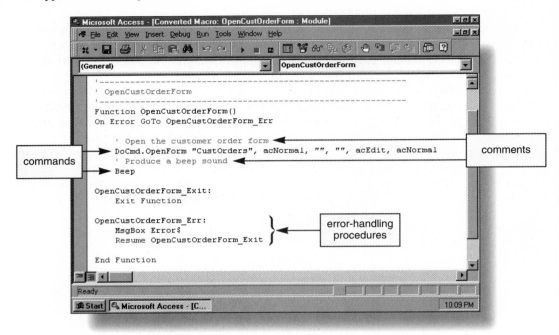

Figure 10-7 A Visual Basic code module that opens a customer order form and produces a beep sound. First, the programmer creates a Microsoft Access macro by using keystrokes and mouse actions, and then Access converts the macro to editable code — complete with commands, comments, and error-handling procedures.

Testing the Application

After coding, a programmer must test the program to be sure that it functions correctly. Later, programs are tested in groups, and finally the entire system must be tested, as shown in Figure 10-8.

For an overview of **Software Testing**, visit Systems Analysis and Design Chapter 10 More on the Web.

www.scsite.com/ sad3e/ch10/

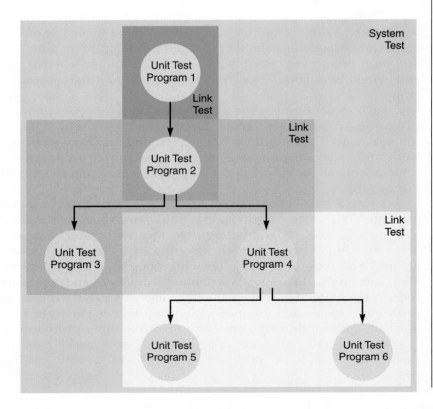

Figure 10-8 The first step in testing is unit testing, followed by link testing, and then system testing.

The programmer's first step is to compile the program using a CASE tool or a language compiler. This process detects **syntax errors**, which are language grammar errors. The programmer corrects the errors until he or she obtains a **clean compilation**, which indicates that the program code can be executed properly.

Next, the programmer desk checks the program. **Desk checking** is the process of reviewing the program code to spot **logic errors**, which produce incorrect results. This process can be performed by the person who wrote the program or by other programmers. Many organizations require a more formal type of desk checking called a **structured walkthrough**, or **code review**, as shown in Figure 10-9. Other programmers on the team and the systems analyst who designed the program usually participate in the code review. The objective is to identify errors, maintain IS standards, and verify that the program meets all requirements as set forth in the system design specification.

Figure 10-9   Teamwork is important in all phases of the SDLC, including program development. Both programmers and systems analysts, for example, participate in the process of code review.

UNIT TESTING • Finally, a programmer tests the program. The testing of an individual program or module is called **unit testing**. The objective is to identify and eliminate execution errors that cause the program to terminate abnormally and logic errors that might have been missed during desk checking.

Test data should contain both correct data *and* erroneous data and should test all possible situations that the program must handle. For example, for a field that allows a range of values, the test data should contain minimum values, maximum values, and values outside the acceptable range. During testing, programmers can use CASE tools, such as **online debuggers** to determine the location and potential causes of program errors and **code analyzers** to assess the logical flow.

Programs that interact with other programs and files must be tested individually before they are integrated into the system, using a process called stub testing. In **stub testing**, the programmer simulates each program outcome or result and displays a message to indicate whether the program executed successfully. Each stub represents an entry or exit point that will be linked later to another program or data file.

To obtain an independent analysis, someone other than the programmer who wrote the program usually creates the test data and reviews the results. Systems analysts frequently create test data during the systems design phase as part of an overall **test**

> For more information on **Debugging**, visit Systems Analysis and Design Chapter 10 More on the Web.
>
> www.scsite.com/ sad3e/ch10/

plan that prepares the test sequences that occur during systems implementation. Regardless of who creates the test data, the project manager or a designated analyst also reviews the final test results. Some organizations also require users to approve final unit test results.

LINK TESTING • Testing two or more programs that depend on each other is called **link testing**, **string testing**, **series testing**, or **integration testing**. For example, consider an information system with a transaction validation program and a separate master file update program. The output from the validation program must be formatted properly and becomes input to the update program. Testing the programs independently does not guarantee that the file passed between them is correct. Only by performing a link test for this pair of programs can you be sure that the programs work together properly. Figure 10-8 on page 10.10 shows link testing for several groups of programs. Notice that a program can be a member of two or more groups.

Another reason for link testing in a minicomputer or mainframe environment is to ensure that the job streams are correct. A **job stream** is a series of statements that control programs, files, and devices that must work together properly. Testing these commands is just as important as testing the actual programs.

Systems analysts usually develop the data they use in link testing. As is the case with all forms of testing, link test data must consider both normal and unusual situations. For example, link testing might include passing a file with a dozen records between two programs, followed by a file with zero records to simulate an unusual event. You should use test data that simulates actual conditions because you really are testing the interface and not the actual programs. Even so, you should verify that programmers check the individual programs thoroughly and that a project manager or a systems analyst approves the unit test results. A program should not move to the link test stage unless it has performed properly in all unit tests.

SYSTEM TESTING • After completing link testing, you must run a series of system tests that involve the entire information system, as shown in Figure 10-8. A **system test** includes all typical processing situations. During a system test, users enter data, including samples of actual, or **live** data, perform queries, and print reports to simulate actual operating conditions. All processing options and outputs are verified by users and the IS project development team to ensure that the system functions correctly. Commercial software packages must undergo system testing similar to that of in-house developed systems, although unit and link testing usually are not performed. Regardless of how the system was developed, the major objectives of system testing are:

- Perform a final test of all programs
- Ensure that the IS staff has the documentation and instructions needed to operate the system properly and that backup and restart capabilities of the system are adequate
- Demonstrate that users can interact with the system successfully
- Verify that all system components are integrated properly and that actual processing situations will be handled correctly
- Confirm that the information system can handle predicted volumes of data in a timely and efficient manner

Successful completion of system testing is the key to user and management approval — this is why system tests sometimes are called **acceptance tests**. Final acceptance tests, however, are performed during systems installation, which is described in Chapter 11.

How far should you go with system testing? In many cases, demands from users who anxiously are waiting for the new system and pressure from management to reduce development costs and gain the benefits of the new system as soon as possible have a bearing on the length and type of system testing that takes place. The IS development team might be eager to begin a new project. At the same time, you should not conclude system testing prematurely and run the risk that a major error will not be discovered until the system is operational. You must use good judgment and obtain input from other analysts, programmers, and IS management before finishing the system testing. If a project manager has been designated, he or she probably will make the final decision.

Very few systems are totally error-free, and each system test might reveal some new problems, even if they are relatively minor. Some users want the system to be a completely finished product, while others realize that minor changes can be treated as maintenance items after the system is operational. Clearly, any errors that affect the integrity or accuracy of data must be corrected immediately. Minor errors, such as typographical errors in screen titles, can be corrected later. In the final analysis, you must decide whether to postpone system installation if major problems are discovered. If conflicting views exist, the decision to install the system will be determined by management after a full discussion of the options.

A KEY QUESTION

You are a lead systems analyst shown in Figure 10-10 and your team is almost finished testing an important new system. During two weeks of system testing, team members discovered and corrected a number of minor problems. Users are calling daily to see when the new system will be operational. One manager wants system testing to continue until all problems — major and minor — are resolved. She says that she does not want to take risks with her department's operational data, and she wants you to guarantee that she will not encounter any major problems in the future. How should you respond to her concerns?

Figure 10-10   Systems analysts must use good judgment and get input from other analysts, programmers, and IS management before deciding to end system testing.

DOCUMENTATION

D ocumentation is essential for successful system operation and maintenance. Accurate documentation helps a programmer who needs to carry out a future program change and makes maintenance easier, faster, and less expensive. **Documentation** explains the system, helps people interact with it, and includes program documentation, system documentation, operations documentation, and user documentation.

Program Documentation

Program documentation starts in the systems analysis phase and continues during systems implementation. Systems analysts prepare overall documentation, such as process descriptions and report layouts, early in the SDLC. Programmers provide documentation by constructing modules that are well-supported by internal and external comments and descriptions that can be understood and maintained easily. A systems analyst usually verifies that program documentation is complete and accurate.

System Documentation

System documentation describes the system's functions and how they are implemented. The analyst prepares most system documentation during the systems analysis and systems design phases. System documentation includes data dictionary entries, data flow diagrams, screen layouts, source documents, and the systems request that initiated the project.

During systems implementation, an analyst must review system documentation to verify that it is complete, accurate, and up to date, including any changes made during systems implementation. For example, if a screen or report is modified, the analyst must update the system documentation. Updates to the system documentation should be made in a timely manner to prevent oversights.

Operations Documentation

If the information system environment involves a minicomputer or mainframe, the analyst must prepare documentation for the IS group that supports centralized operations. A mainframe installation might require the scheduling of batch jobs and the distribution of printed reports. In this type of environment, the IS operations staff serves as the first point of contact when users experience problems with the system.

Operations documentation tells the operations group how and when to run the programs in the information system. For example, a **program run sheet** contains all the information needed for processing and distributing output. A typical program run sheet includes the following information:

- Program, job, systems analyst, programmer, and system identification
- Scheduling information, such as run frequency and deadlines
- Input files and where they originate and output files and destinations
- Report distributions
- Special forms required
- Error and informational messages to operators and restart procedures
- Special instructions, such as security requirements

Operations documentation should be clear, concise, and available online whenever possible. If the IS department has an operations group, you should review the documentation with them as early as possible to locate any problems. If you keep the operations group informed during early phases of the SDLC, it will be easier to develop the documentation they need.

User Documentation

Analysts are responsible for preparing documentation to help users learn and operate the system (Figure 10-11). **User documentation** includes the following items:

- System overview that clearly describes all major system features, capabilities, and limitations
- Source document content, preparation, processing, and samples
- Menu and data entry screen options, contents, and processing instructions
- Reports that are produced regularly or available at the user's request with samples
- Security and audit trail information
- Responsibility for specific input, output, or processing requirements
- Procedures for requesting changes and reporting problems
- Examples of exceptions and error situations
- Frequently asked questions (FAQs)
- Explanations of how to get Help and procedures for updating the manual

For guidelines on developing **User Documentation**, visit Systems Analysis and Design Chapter 10 More on the Web.

www.scsite.com/ sad3e/ch10/

Figure 10-11   Whether written or online, clear user documentation is needed to help users learn and operate the system. Systems analysts are responsible for preparing the documentation, but often ask users to participate in developing the material.

The written documentation material often is called a **user manual**. A sample user manual page is shown in Figure 10-12. Systems analysts usually prepare the manual but many companies ask users to review the material and participate in developing the manual.

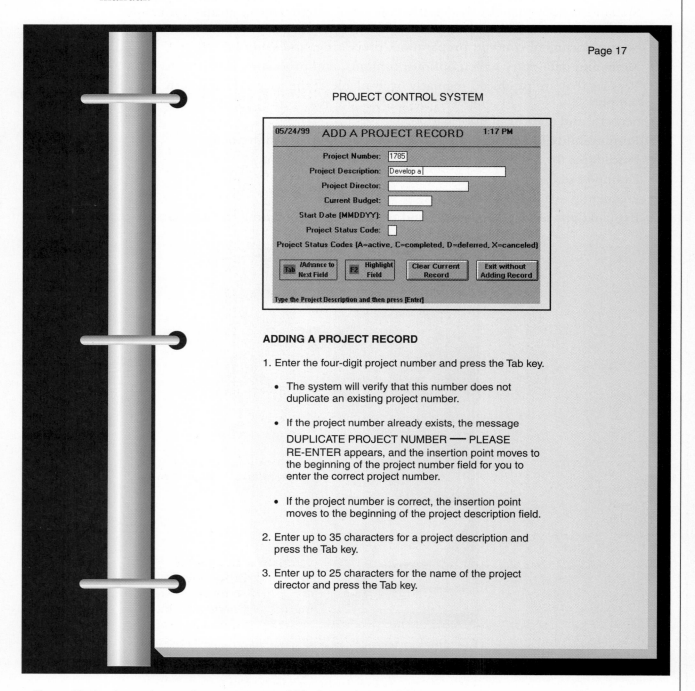

Figure 10-12   A sample page from a user manual. The instructions explain how to add a new project record to the system.

For a user, one of the more valuable sources of information is **online documentation**, which is available readily to users, as shown in Figure 10-13. Many users are accustomed to context-sensitive Help screens, interactive tutorials, hints and tips, hypertext, onscreen demos, and other user-friendly features in popular software packages, and they expect the same kind of support for in-house developed software. Powerful online documentation actually is a productivity tool because it helps users take full advantage of the program and reduces the time that IS staff members must spend in providing telephone, e-mail, or face-to-face assistance.

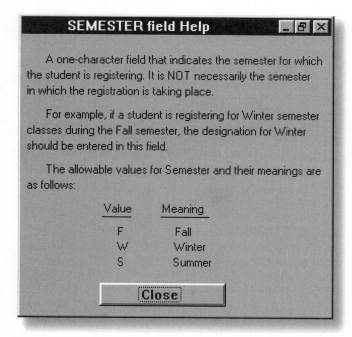

Figure 10-13   A context-sensitive Help screen for data entry
into the student registration system.

User training typically is scheduled when the system is installed; these training sessions offer an ideal opportunity to distribute the user manual and explain how it will be updated in the future.

MANAGEMENT APPROVAL

A fter system testing is complete, you present the results to management. You should highlight the test results, the status of all required documentation, and input from users who participated in system testing. You also must provide detailed time schedules, cost estimates, and staffing requirements for making the system fully operational. If system testing produced no technical, economical, or operational problems, then management will determine a schedule for system installation and evaluation, which is discussed in Chapter 11.

SOFT WEAR, LIMITED — APPLICATION DEVELOPMENT

T he ESIP development team of Jane Rossman, Tom Adams, and Becky Evans started work on the ESIP system, which would be a Microsoft Access application in a client/server environment. Jane and Tom scheduled additional meetings with the consulting firm, True Blue Systems, while Becky started designing the main switchboard and the data input screens.

The ESIP system design included a server to interact with various SWL clients and an interface with the new payroll package from Pacific Software. By now, the payroll package was implemented successfully on SWL's mainframe, and several payroll cycles were completed without any processing problems.

When the ESIP development team met on Monday morning, the members studied the overview that True Blue submitted (Figure 10-14). Jane said they would use a top-down design approach. Their first step was to partition the system and break it down into a set of modules on a structure chart. Each module would represent a program or function to be performed by one or more macros or Visual Basic procedures.

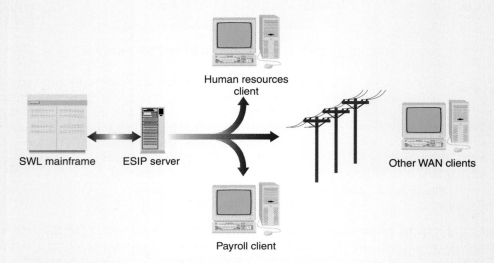

Figure 10-14 The ESIP system plan as submitted by True Blue Systems.

The team reviewed its documentation carefully, using the DFDs they prepared during the systems analysis phase. The team determined that the ESIP system needed to perform five main tasks: extract the ESIP deductions during payroll processing, apply the extracted deductions to specific ESIP options, update employee deduction selections, update ESIP option choices, and handle fund transfers to internal and external ESIP entities. To accomplish these tasks, the system would need a variety of reports, controls, query and display capabilities, input screens, security provisions, and other features.

Of the five main ESIP processes, only the extracting of payroll deductions would be done on SWL's mainframe. Jane said they would need to develop an interface program to control the extraction processing, but all the other functions would run on the ESIP server and clients. By afternoon, they had produced the draft structure chart shown in Figure 10-15.

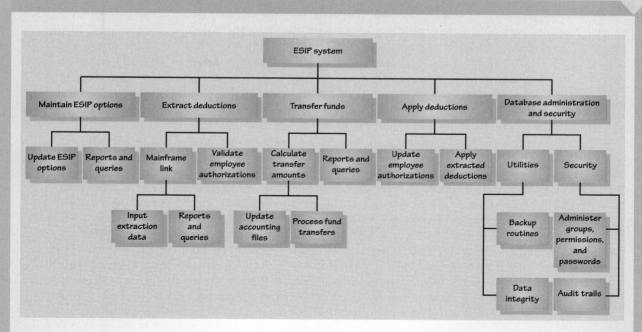

Figure 10-15   Draft of a structure chart for the ESIP system.

After studying the tasks and requirements, Jane estimated the time needed to design, code, unit test, and document each module. Further, she estimated additional time for link and system testing, completing the ESIP system documentation, and receiving management approval. Jane used Microsoft Project to organize the information into a Gantt chart to manage and track the project and show the individual assignments. The chart indicated that many tasks could be done concurrently and displayed the critical path. The development team agreed that they would meet daily to review their progress and discuss any problems.

Mainframe Interface

Jane's next step was to meet with Rick Williams, who was familiar with the new payroll package, to discuss the ESIP deduction extract program that executes when the mainframe runs the weekly payroll. Jane learned that the new payroll package was developed as a database application and she could write the extract module in Visual Basic.

Working together, Jane and Becky prepared a design, wrote the commands, and unit tested the ESIP program modules with test files they created. They used stubs to indicate inputs and outputs to files with which the extract program would interact. After verifying the results, Jane created a procedure for downloading the deduction file from the mainframe to the ESIP server in the payroll department. She tested the download procedure and updated the documentation.

ESIP Server

The team started developing the Access database application that would handle the other ESIP functions. The plan was that Becky would finish the basic switchboard and screen designs, then add features that users had requested, including custom menus and icons for frequently used functions. Becky also would design all the reports documented in the data dictionary.

Meanwhile, Jane and Tom worked on the other modules. Their first task was to examine the ERDs developed in the systems design phase to ensure that the entities and normalized record designs still were valid. Then they would start creating individual objects, including tables, queries, macros, and code modules, using the application design tools in Access.

Jane and Tom defined the data tables, identified primary keys, and linked the tables into a relational structure. They used online Access Help to make sure they were using the correct field types, sizes, and names, and that the tables would work properly with the input screens created by Becky. Jane and Tom used an agreed-upon naming convention for all objects to ensure consistency among the systems.

After the tables were designed and loaded with test data, Jane and Tom developed queries that would allow users to retrieve, display, update, and delete records. Some queries affected only individual records, such as ESIP options, while other queries were designed to update a specific batch of records, such as all deductions made during a certain period.

Jane and Tom also developed macros that performed specific actions when certain events occurred. They tested each macro by stepping through it to make sure the commands executed properly. The macros later would be linked to various buttons and menus that Becky was designing into her switchboard and input screens. To save coding time, Tom converted several macros to Visual Basic in order to work on additional features and capabilities.

Jane and Tom also completed work on various security features, including password protection and several levels of permission required to view, modify, or delete specific objects. Later, when the system became operational, management would authorize specific permission levels, and Jane would designate a system administrator to maintain security and system policies.

Completing Application Development

In three weeks, the ESIP development team finished design and unit testing. Becky tested the switchboard, macros, queries, screen forms, menus, submenus, and code modules to ensure that they functioned correctly. Now, it was time to join all the system objects and perform link testing. Because the design was modular and used a consistent naming convention, the testing process ran smoothly and they encountered no significant problems.

After the link testing, the analysts asked several principal users to participate in system testing. During this process, some minor screen changes were suggested and implemented after checking with users who would be affected. Also, it turned out that one of the reports did not include a federally required Employer Identification Number (EIN). Because the reports had been designed with the Access report generator, this change was corrected easily.

The team members prepared user documentation as they completed each task. To produce a clear, understandable user manual, they decided to ask Amy Calico, SWL's payroll director, to review their notes and help them write a draft for current and future users. They wanted to explain the system in nontechnical terms, with adequate illustrations, screen shots, and a set of frequently asked questions. Jane said that the entire manual could be put online after SWL's intranet was developed.

 YOUR TURN — Although the systems testing at SWL resulted in no major problems, Rick asked you to help him develop a recommendation for future testing of this type. One of his concerns is that in systems testing, it is virtually impossible to simulate every system transaction and function. Specifically, Rick wants you to suggest some guidelines that will produce the most reliable test results.

He suggested that you should consider *who* should be involved in the testing, *what* types of transactions should be tested, and *when* the testing should be done. Based on what you already have learned about the ESIP system in prior chapters, what would you recommend? Write a brief memo to Rick with your suggestions.

CHAPTER SUMMARY

T he systems implementation phase consists of application development and installation and evaluation of the new system. During application development, analysts determine the overall design strategy and work with programmers to complete the design, coding, testing, and documentation of all programs, modules, and macros.

In addition to system documentation, analysts also prepare operations and user documentation. Operations documentation provides instructions and information, such as a program run sheet, to the IS operations group. User documentation consists of instructions and information to users who will interact with the system and includes user manuals, Help screens, and tutorials.

Programmers perform desk checking, code review, and unit testing tasks during application development. Link testing is necessary for programs that depend on each other, and the final step is overall system testing, which usually includes users. The application development stage ends with a presentation to management. If management approves the results, the development team can begin work on system installation, which concludes the systems implementation phase of the SDLC.

Review Questions

1. What five steps does a programmer complete during application development?
2. Give three examples of program design tools.
3. What types of tests might a programmer conduct in the testing of an individual program?
4. What is a program run sheet, and what information does the program run sheet supply to the operations group?
5. What types of information do you need to provide in the user documentation?
6. What is link testing? What are other names commonly used for link testing?
7. Who participates in system testing?
8. What are the major objectives of system testing?

Discussion Questions

1. A systems analyst recently asserted, "Link testing is a waste of time. If each program is tested adequately and if program specifications are prepared properly, link testing is not needed. Only system testing is required to check out the system procedures." Do you agree or disagree with this comment? Justify your position.
2. Analysts often use live data during system testing. Are there circumstances where simulated data is preferable to live data? What are these circumstances?

CASE STUDIES

NEW CENTURY HEALTH CLINIC — APPLICATION DEVELOPMENT

Y ou completed the systems design for the insurance system at New Century Health Clinic. The associates at the clinic have approved your design specification, and you have hired two programmers, Bill Miller and Celia Goldring, to assist you with the programming and testing of the insurance system.

Assignments

1. Design the testing that will be required for the system. You should consider unit, link, and system testing in your test plan and determine who should participate in the testing.

2. Design the test data that you will use. You should include data for all tests that will be performed on the system in all phases of testing.

3. Prepare a structure chart that shows the main program functions for the New Century system.

4. You have asked Anita Davenport, New Century's office manager, to contribute to the user manual for the insurance system. She suggested you include a section of frequently asked questions (FAQs), which you also could include in the online documentation. Prepare ten FAQs and answers for use in the printed user manual and context-sensitive Help screens.

GREEN PASTURES LIMITED

T he management at Green Pastures has decided to replace Kirby Ellington, who had developed the company's new billing information system. Kirby had used the C programming language to develop the programs for the system. He did not prepare the operations or user documentation for the system. Green Pastures discovered that the billing statements created by Kirby's system contained errors and had to be revised.

Green Pastures has hired you to correct the billing system problems. Kirby's last day at Green Pastures coincides with your first day on the job; you will meet with Kirby for two hours in the morning and one hour in the afternoon before he leaves.

Assignments

1. What specific information would you ask Kirby during your meetings with him?

2. In addition to an interview with Kirby, what other fact-finding techniques would you use to learn more about the billing system? Why?

3. What are your options for completing the billing system, and what are the most important factors you should consider in recommending the appropriate course of action?

4. Green Pastures management has asked for you to briefly present the results of your interview with Kirby and your recommended course of action. Prepare a brief outline of your presentation, highlighting your planned activities in the next month.

RIDGEWAY COMPANY

T he Ridgeway Company requirements were described in a Chapter 4 case study. The following assignments are based on the work you did for that case study.

Assignments

1. Design the testing that will be required for the billing system. You should consider program, link, and system testing in your test plan.

2. Design the test data that will be used for the testing of the billing system. You should include data for all tests that will be performed on the system in all phases of testing.

3. During systems testing, team members found several errors in the billing system report, including one subtotal field that calculates incorrectly. Thomas McGee would like to go ahead and install the system and correct this error later. As lead analyst on the project, what would be your recommended course of action? Why?

4. Design three sample context-sensitive online Help screens to help a user add a new customer to the billing system.

CHAPTER 11

SDLC PHASES

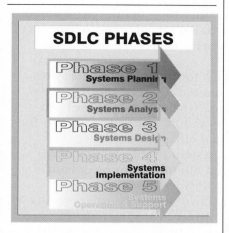

Phase 1
Systems Planning

Phase 2
Systems Analysis

Phase 3
Systems Design

Phase 4
Systems Implementation

Phase 5
Systems Operation & Support

OBJECTIVES

When you finish this chapter, you will be able to:

- Discuss the main tasks in the installation and evaluation process

- Explain why it is important to maintain separate operational and test environments

- Develop an overall training plan with specific objectives for each group of participants

- Explain three typical ways to provide training, including vendors, outside resources, and in-house staff

- Describe online tutorials and other user training techniques

- Create an outline for a training manual and describe the contents of each section

- Describe the file conversion process

- Identify four system changeover methods and discuss the advantages and disadvantages of each

- Explain the purpose of a post-implementation evaluation and list the specific topics covered during the evaluation

- Specify the contents of the final report to management

Installation and Evaluation

Installation and evaluation is the second of two chapters in the systems implementation phase. Chapter 11 describes the actual installation of the information system and its initial evaluation by users.

INTRODUCTION

Chapter 11 describes the actual installation of the new system and the evaluation that follows. These tasks complete the implementation phase of the SDLC and are performed for every information systems project, whether you develop the application in-house or purchase it as a commercial package.

The new system now is ready to go to work. Your earlier design activities produced the overall architecture and processing strategy, and you have consulted users at every stage of development. Programs were developed and tested individually, in groups, and as a complete system. You prepared the necessary documentation and checked it for accuracy, including support material for IS staff and users. Now, you will carry out the remaining steps in systems implementation.

- Prepare an operational environment and install the new system
- Provide training for users, IS staff, and managers
- Perform file conversion and system changeover
- Carry out a post-implementation evaluation of the system
- Present a final report to management

OPERATIONAL AND TEST ENVIRONMENTS

T he hardware and software environment for the actual system operation is called the **operational environment** or **production environment**. The environment that analysts and programmers use to develop and maintain programs is called the **test environment**. A separate test area is necessary to maintain system security and integrity and protect the operational environment. An effective testing process is essential, whether you are examining an information system or a batch of computer chips, as shown in Figure 11-1.

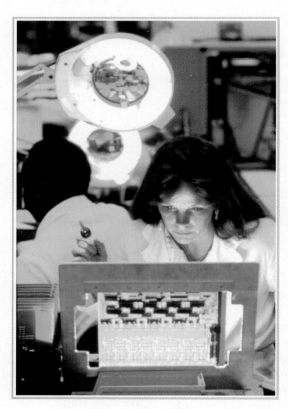

Figure 11-1 The basic concepts of testing are the same regardless of whether hardware or information systems are being evaluated. The objective is to verify that the product meets all specifications.

Access to the operational environment is limited to users and is strictly controlled. Systems analysts and programmers should not have access to the operational environment except to correct a system problem or to make authorized modifications or enhancements. Otherwise, IS department members have no reason to access the day-to-day operational system.

The test environment for an information system contains copies of all programs, procedures, and test data files. Before making any changes to an operational system, you must verify them in the test environment and obtain user approval. Figure 11-2 shows the differences between the test and operational environments.

Every experienced systems analyst can tell you a story about an apparently innocent program change that was introduced without being tested properly. After any modification, you should repeat the same acceptance tests you ran when the system was developed. By restricting access to the operational area and performing all tests in a separate environment, you can protect the system and avoid problems that could damage data or interrupt operations.

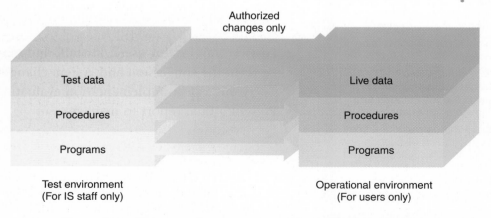

Figure 11-2   The test environment versus the operational environment.

To prepare the operational environment, you must examine carefully all hardware and software configurations, operating system programs and utilities, network resources, and any other components that affect system performance. Data communications is an essential element of the operational platform, and you must verify network capabilities before installing any applications. You should check all communications features in the test environment carefully, and then check them again after loading the programs into the operational environment. Your documentation should identify all network specifications clearly, including technical and operational requirements for communications hardware and software. If you have to build or upgrade network resources to support the new system, you must test the platform rigorously before system installation begins.

TRAINING

N o system can be successful without proper **training** whether it involves software, hardware, or manufacturing, as shown in Figure 11-3. A successful information system requires training for users, managers, and IS staff members. The entire systems development effort can depend on whether people understand the system and know how to use it effectively.

Figure 11-3   In any situation, training must fit the needs of users and help them carry out their job functions.

You should start to consider a training plan early in the systems development process. As you create documentation, you should think about how to use the material in future training sessions. Now, when you implement the system, it is essential to provide the right training to the right people at the right time. The first step is to identify who should receive training and what training is needed. You must look carefully at the organization, how the system will support business operations, and who will be involved or affected. Figure 11-4 on the next page is an example of specific training topics for users, managers, and IS staff. Notice that each group needs a mix of general background and detailed information to understand and use the system.

As shown in Figure 11-4, the three main groups are users, managers, and IS staff. A manager does not need to understand every submenu or feature, but he or she does need to know that users are trained properly. Similarly, users need to know how to perform their day-to-day job functions, but do not need to know how system operational charges are allocated among user departments. IS staff people probably need the most information. To support the new system, they must have a clear understanding of how the system functions, how it supports business requirements, and the skills that users need to operate the system and perform their tasks.

USERS

System overview
Key terms
Start-up and shut down
Main menu and submenus
Icons and shortcut keys
Major system functions
Online and external Help
Frequently asked questions
Troubleshooting guide
Handling emergencies

MANAGERS

Project origin
Cost-benefit analysis
Support for business goals
Key IS contact people
Handling system charges
Major reports and displays
Requesting enhancements
User training

TRAINING

Project history and justification
System architecture
System documentation
Typical user questions
Vendor support
Logging and resolving problems
Technical training for IS staff
User and management training

IS STAFF

For an example of **Vendor Training** courses, visit Systems Analysis and Design Chapter 11 More on the Web.

www.scsite.com/ sad3e/ch11/

Figure 11-4 Examples of training topics for three separate groups. Users, managers, and IS staff have different training needs.

Figure 11-5 Users must be trained on the new system. Training sessions might be one-on-one or group situations such as the one shown here. Many vendors provide product training as part of an overall service to customers.

After you identify the objectives, you must determine how the training will be provided. The main choices are to obtain training from vendors, outside training firms, or use IS staff and in-house resources.

Vendor Training

If the system includes the purchase of software or hardware, then vendor-supplied training is one of the features you should investigate or request in the RFPs (requests for proposal) or RFQs (requests for quotation).

Many hardware and software vendors offer training programs free or at a nominal cost for the equipment and systems they sell. In other cases, the price might be negotiable, depending on the relationship with the vendor and the prospect of future purchases. These courses usually are conducted at the vendor's site by experienced trainers who provide valuable hands-on experience. If a large number of people must be trained, you might be able to arrange classes at your location.

Vendor training, as shown in Figure 11-5, often gives the best return on your training dollars because it is focused on products that the vendor developed. The scope of vendor training, however, usually is limited to a standard version of the vendor's software or hardware. You might have to supplement the training in-house, especially if your IS staff customized the package.

Outside Training Resources

You also can look into an independent training firm to provide in-house hardware or software training. If vendor training is not practical and your organization does not have the internal resources to perform the training, outside training consultants can be a desirable alternative. Professional outside trainers, however, usually are not practical for an information system that you developed in-house.

The rapid expansion of corporate information systems and PCs has produced tremendous growth in the field of computer training. Many training consultants, institutes, and firms are available that provide either standardized or customized training packages. If you decide to investigate this alternative, you can contact several firms and obtain references for their consulting and training work. You also can seek assistance from nonprofit sources with an interest in training, including universities, industry associations, and information management organizations. For example, Figure 11-6 shows the Web site for the **Center for the Application of Information Technology** (**CAIT**) that describes a variety of information technology (IT) education and training.

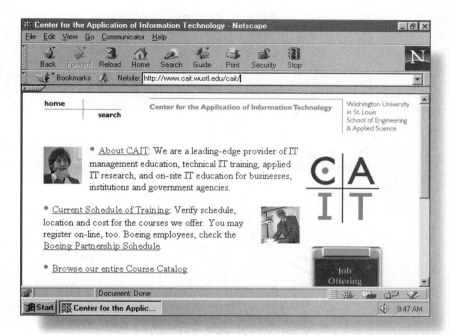

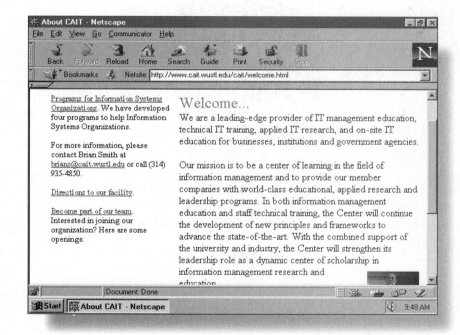

Figure 11-6   The Center for the Application of Information Technology (CAIT) uses its Web site to present information technology (IT) education and training and describes the organization's mission.

ON THE NET

Suppose you have no experience with large-scale training programs and you need some help to develop user training for a major new information system at your company. You can use a Web search engine to locate firms that offer consulting assistance of this type. Try to find a Web site that describes the specific services that are available using key terms such as, training, and, information systems. Write a brief memo that describes the results of your search.

In-House Training

The IS staff and user departments often share responsibility for developing and conducting training programs for internally developed software. If the organization has an information center, that group might be able to handle user training.

Multimedia can be an effective method for user training. With presentation software such as Microsoft PowerPoint you can design training sessions that combine slides, animation, and sound. You also can use programs that capture actual keystrokes and mouse actions, and then replay the screens as a demonstration for users. If your firm has a media or graphic arts group, they can help you prepare training aids, such as videotapes, charts, and other instructional materials. When developing a training program, you should keep the following guidelines in mind.

Train people in groups, with separate training programs for distinct groups. Group training makes the most efficient use of time and training facilities. In addition, if the group is small, trainees can learn from the questions and problems of others. A training program must address the job interests and skills of a wide range of participants. For example, IS staff personnel and users require very different information. Problems often arise when some participants have technical backgrounds and others do not. A single program will not meet everyone's needs.

Select the most effective place to do the training. Training employees at your own location offers several advantages. Employees incur no travel expense, they can respond to local emergencies that require immediate attention, and training can take place in the actual environment where the system will operate. You are likely to encounter some disadvantages, however. Employees who are distracted by telephone calls and other duties will not get the full benefit of the training. Also, using the organization's computer facilities for training can disrupt normal operations and limit the amount of actual hands-on training.

Provide for learning by hearing, seeing, and doing. Some people learn best from lectures, discussions, and question-and-answer sessions. Others learn best from viewing demonstrations or from reading documentation and other material. Most people learn best from hands-on experience. You should provide training that supports each type of learning.

Prepare a training manual. A typical training manual outline is shown in Figure 11-7. The Introduction chapter includes a section titled, Who Should Read This Manual, that describes the information system and its features. The Information System chapter consists of the Getting Started section, which contains basic introductory information such as how to start the system and the Lessons section, which includes step-by-step instructions for using all the features of the information system. Figure 11-8 on page

For more information on **Outside Training Resources**, visit Systems Analysis and Design Chapter 11 More on the Web.

www.scsite.com/ sad3e/ch11/

To learn more about **Multimedia Training Materials**, visit Systems Analysis and Design Chapter 11 More on the Web.

www.scsite.com/ sad3e/ch11/

11.8 shows a sample first lesson for a PC-based sales prospect management system. In Lesson One, the user learns how to enter and exit the system. In Lesson Two, as shown in Figure 11-9 on page 11.9, the user learns how to add a sales prospect and return to the main menu.

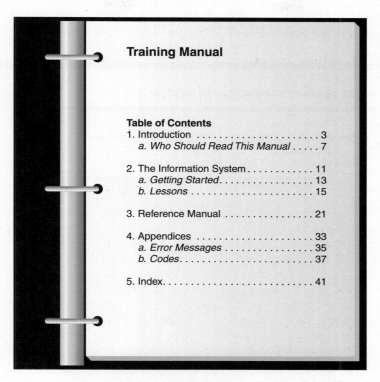

Training Manual

Table of Contents

Figure 11-7   Typical organization for a training manual.

The Reference Manual chapter summarizes all options and commands. After becoming familiar with the system, a user can use the Reference Manual to find an answer to a question. In the Appendices, the Error Messages section explains what happens when system errors occur and what action the user should take. Finally, all codes used by the system are listed and explained in the Codes section. As with any instructional materials, the manual concludes with the Index.

Develop interactive tutorials and training tools. Studies show that people learn best when they participate actively in the training process. A **tutorial** is a series of online lessons that present material and provide a dialog with users. Simple tutorials resemble the training manual pages shown in Figure 11-8 on the next page and Figure 11-9 on page 11.9. More sophisticated tutorials might offer interactive sessions where users can practice various tasks and get feedback on their progress. Even if you lack the resources to develop interactive tutorials, you might design a series of dialog boxes that respond with Help information and suggestions when users select various menu topics.

Rely on previous trainees. After one group of users has been trained, they can assist others. Users often learn more quickly from coworkers who share common interests. Using a **train-the-trainer** strategy, you can select knowledgeable users who then conduct sessions for others.

To view an **Interactive Tutorial**, visit Systems Analysis and Design Chapter 11 More on the Web.

www.scsite.com/ sad3e/ch11/

To learn more about **Train-the-Trainer Strategies**, visit Systems Analysis and Design Chapter 11 More on the Web.

www.scsite.com/ sad3e/ch11/

When training is complete, many organizations conduct a full-scale test as a dress rehearsal for users and IS support staff. The system development team might observe the process but does not participate. All procedures, including those that are executed only at the end of a month, quarter, or year, are included in this **simulation**. As questions or problems arise, the participants consult the documentation or each other to determine appropriate answers or actions. This system test provides valuable experience and can build confidence for everyone involved with the new system.

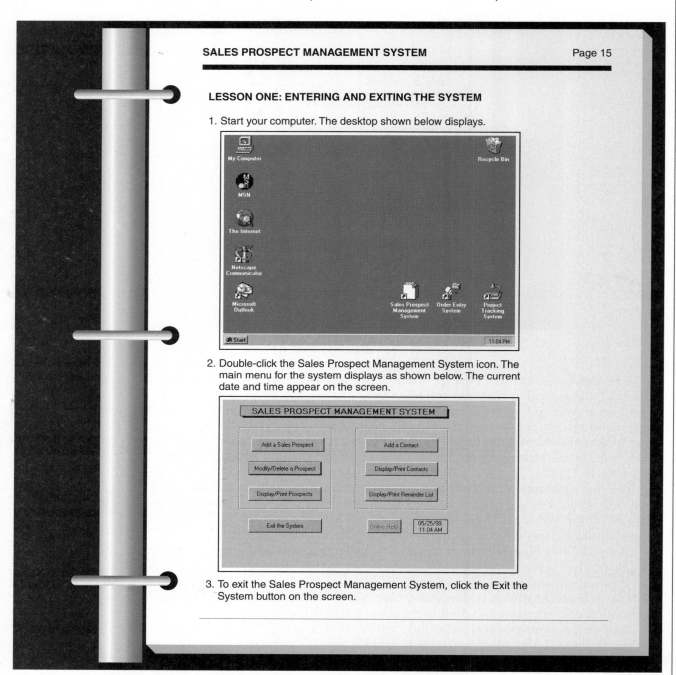

Figure 11-8 A sample lesson in a user training manual for a sales prospect management system. In the first lesson, the user learns how to enter and exit the system.

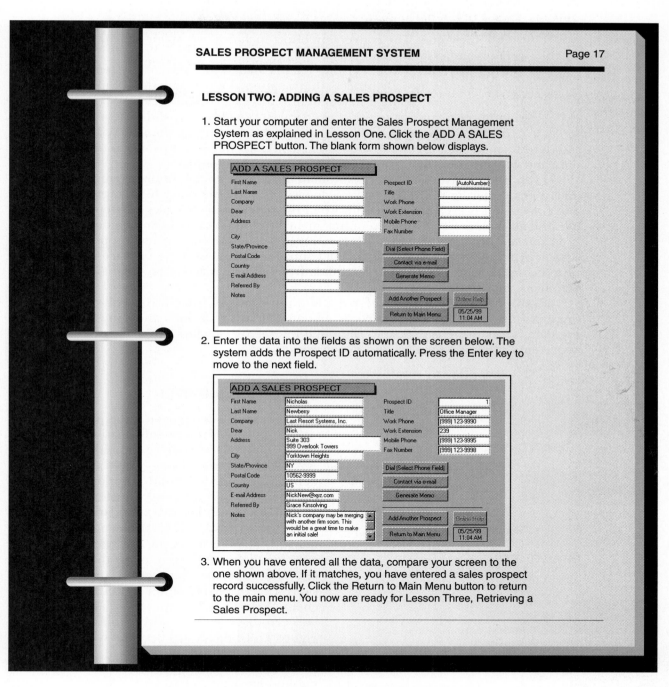

Figure 11-9   A second sample lesson in a user training manual.

FILE CONVERSION

For more information on **File Conversion Software**, visit Systems Analysis and Design Chapter 11 More on the Web.

www.scsite.com/ sad3e/ch11/

A fter establishing the new system's operational environment and performing the necessary training, you can begin the conversion process. During **conversion**, you transfer operations from the old system to the new one. The conversion effort includes two major activities: file conversion and system changeover.

During **file conversion**, existing data is loaded into the new system. This conversion can be a costly process that requires the participation of users and the IS project team. When a new system replaces a computerized system, you should try to automate file conversion, if possible. The old system might be capable of **exporting** data in an acceptable format for the new system or in a standard format, such as ASCII. Otherwise, you must develop a program to extract the data and convert it to the format required by the new system.

Even if file conversion can be automated, the new system often requires additional data items. Entering this data can be a major task and temporary help might be required. File conversion is even more difficult when the new system replaces a manual system because all data must be entered online or by batch data entry of source documents.

You should maintain strict input controls during the file conversion process, when data is extremely vulnerable. All system control measures must be in place and in operation during file conversion to protect data from unauthorized access and to help prevent erroneous input.

Even with careful file conversion and input controls, some errors will occur. Most organizations require that users verify all data, correct all errors, and supply every missing data item during conversion. Although interactive displays can make the task easier, conversion often is a lengthy and expensive process.

SYSTEM CHANGEOVER

S ystem changeover is the process of putting the new information system online and retiring the old system. Changeover can be rapid or slow, depending on the method. The four changeover approaches are direct cutover, parallel operation, pilot operation, and phased.

Direct cutover is like throwing a switch that instantly changes from the old system to the new. Parallel operation requires that both systems run for a specified period, resulting in the slowest method. The other options, phased changeover and pilot operation, are somewhere between direct cutover and parallel operation. Figure 11-10 illustrates the four system changeover methods.

Figure 11-11 shows that each changeover method has its own cost and risk factors. As a systems analyst, you must weigh the advantages and disadvantages of each method and recommend the best choice in a given situation. The final changeover decision will be based on input from the IS staff, users, and management.

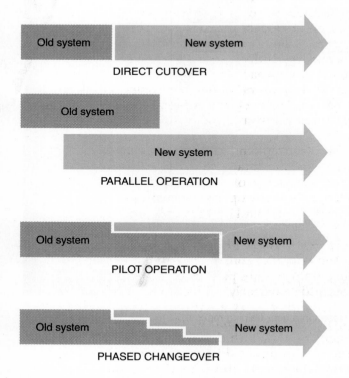

Figure 11-10   The four system changeover methods.

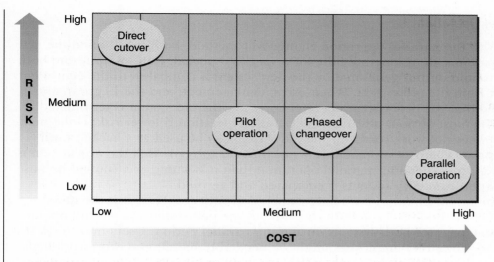

Figure 11-11   Relative risk and cost characteristics of the four changeover methods.

For an overview of **System Changeover Methods,** visit Systems Analysis and Design Chapter 11 More on the Web.

www.scsite.com/ sad3e/ch11/

Direct Cutover

With the **direct cutover** approach, the changeover from the old system to the new system occurs immediately when the new system becomes operational. Direct cutover usually is the least expensive changeover method because the IS group has to operate and maintain only one system at a time.

Direct cutover, however, involves more risk than other changeover methods. Regardless of how thoroughly and carefully you conduct testing and training, some difficulties might arise when the system goes into operation. Problems can result from data situations that were not tested or anticipated or from errors caused by users or operators. A system also can encounter difficulties because live data typically occurs in much larger volumes than test data.

Although initial implementation problems are a concern with all four changeover methods, they are most significant when the direct cutover approach is used. Detecting minor errors also is more difficult with direct cutover because users cannot verify current output by comparing it to output from the old system. Major errors can cause a system process to terminate abnormally, and with the direct cutover method, you cannot revert to the old system as a backup option.

Companies often choose the direct cutover method for implementing commercial software packages because these applications involve less risk of total system failure. For systems developed in-house, most organizations use direct cutover only for noncritical situations. Direct cutover might be the only choice, however, if the operating environment cannot support both the old and new systems or if the old and new systems are incompatible.

Timing is very important when using a direct cutover strategy. Most systems operate on weekly, monthly, quarterly, and yearly cycles. For example, consider a payroll system that produces output on a weekly basis. Some employees are paid twice a month, however, so the system also operates semimonthly. Monthly, quarterly, and annual reports also require the system to produce output at the end of every month, quarter, and year. When a cyclical information system is implemented in the middle of any cycle, complete processing for the full cycle requires information from both the old and the new systems. To minimize the need to require information from two different systems, cyclical information systems usually are converted using the direct cutover method at the beginning of a quarter, calendar year, or fiscal year.

To read about a successful changeover using **Parallel Operation**, visit Systems Analysis and Design Chapter 11 More on the Web.

www.scsite.com/

Parallel Operation

With the **parallel operation** changeover method, both the old and the new information systems operate fully for a specified period. Data is input into both systems, and output generated by the new system is compared to the equivalent output from the old system. When users, management, and the IS group are satisfied that the new system operates correctly, the old system is terminated.

The most obvious advantage of parallel operation is lower risk. If the new system does not work correctly, the old system can be used as a backup until appropriate changes are made. It is much easier to verify that the new system is working properly under parallel operation than it is with direct cutover because the output from both systems is compared and verified.

Parallel operation, however, does have some disadvantages. First, it is the most costly changeover method. Because both the old and the new systems are in full operation, the company pays for both systems during the parallel period. Users must work in both systems and temporary employees might be needed to handle the extra workload. In addition, running both systems might place a burden on the operating environment and cause processing delays.

Parallel operation is not practical if the old and new systems are incompatible technically, or if the operating environment cannot support both systems. Parallel operation also is inappropriate when the two systems perform different functions or if the new system involves a new method of business operations. For example, until a company installs new data scanners in a factory, it would be impractical to launch a new production tracking system that requires this technology.

Pilot Operation

With the **pilot operation** changeover method, you implement the complete new system at a selected location of the company. A new sales reporting system, for instance, might be implemented in just one branch office, or a new payroll system might be installed in only one department. In these examples, the group that uses the new system first is called the **pilot site**. During pilot operation, the old system continues to operate for the entire organization, including the pilot site. After the system proves successful at the pilot site, it is implemented in the rest of the organization, usually using the direct cutover method. Therefore, pilot operation is a kind of semiparallel operation that combines the parallel operation and direct cutover methods.

Restricting the implementation to a pilot site reduces the risk of system failure, compared to a direct cutover method. Operating both systems for only the pilot site is less expensive than a parallel operation for the entire company. Also, if you later use a parallel approach to complete the implementation, the changeover period can be much shorter if the system proves successful at the pilot site.

For more information on a **Phased Changeover Approach**, visit Systems Analysis and Design Chapter 11 More on the Web.

www.scsite.com/
sad3e/ch11/

Phased Changeover

With a **phased changeover** method, you implement the new system in stages, or modules. Instead of implementing a new manufacturing system all at once, for example, you might first install the materials management subsystem, then the production control subsystem, then the job cost subsystem, and so on. You can implement each subsystem by using any of the other three changeover methods.

Analysts sometimes confuse the phased changeover and pilot operation methods. Both methods combine direct cutover and parallel operation to reduce risk and costs. With phased changeover, however, you give a part of the system to all users, while pilot operation provides the entire system, but only to some users.

One advantage of phased changeover is that the risk of errors or failures is limited to only the implemented module. For instance, if a new production control subsystem fails to operate properly, that failure might not impact the new purchasing subsystem or the existing shop floor control subsystem.

Phase 4

Post-Implementation Evaluation   **11.13**

Phased changeover is less expensive than full parallel operation because you have to deal with only one part of the system at a time. Phased changeover is not possible, however, if the system cannot be separated easily into logical modules, or phases. On the other hand, if a large number of phases are to take place, this method might be more costly than a pilot approach.

POST-IMPLEMENTATION EVALUATION

nce the new system is operational, you must perform two additional tasks: prepare a post-implementation evaluation and deliver a final report to management.

A **post-implementation evaluation**, as shown in Figure 11-12, assesses the overall quality of the information system. The evaluation verifies that the new system meets specified requirements, complies with user objectives, and achieves the anticipated benefits. In addition, by providing feedback to the development team, the evaluation also helps improve IS development practices for future projects.

Figure 11-12   An important function of the post-implementation phase is an evaluation. This task requires one-to-one communication with users so the IS staff can learn as much as possible about the strengths and possible weaknesses of the new system.

A post-implementation evaluation should examine all aspects of the development effort and the end product — the developed information system. A typical evaluation includes feedback for the following areas:

- Accuracy, completeness, and timeliness of information of system output
- User satisfaction
- System reliability and maintainability
- Adequacy of system controls and security measures
- Hardware efficiency and platform performance
- Effectiveness of database implementation
- Performance of the IS team
- Completeness and quality of documentation
- Quality and effectiveness of training
- Accuracy of cost-benefit estimates and development schedules

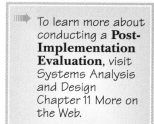

To learn more about conducting a **Post-Implementation Evaluation**, visit Systems Analysis and Design Chapter 11 More on the Web.

www.scsite.com/ sad3e/ch11/

You can apply the same fact-finding techniques in a post-implementation evaluation that you used to determine the system requirements during the systems analysis phase. When evaluating a system, you should:

- Interview members of management and key users
- Observe users and computer operations personnel actually working with the new information system
- Read all documentation and training materials
- Examine all source documents, output reports, and screen displays
- Use questionnaires to gather information and opinions from a large number of users
- Analyze maintenance and help desk logs

Figure 11-13 shows the first page of a sample user evaluation form for the new information system. In the form, users evaluate 18 separate elements on a numerical scale, so the results can be tabulated easily.

1 of 3

USER EVALUATION FORM

System:	Evaluator:	Date:

Please evaluate the information system project by circling the one number for each factor that best represents your assessment.

	Unsatisfactory		Acceptable			Excellent
SYSTEM OUTPUT						
1. Accuracy of information	1	2	3	4	5	6
2. Completeness of information	1	2	3	4	5	6
3. Ease of use	1	2	3	4	5	6
4. Timeliness of information	1	2	3	4	5	6
USER INTERFACE						
5. Clarity of instructions	1	2	3	4	5	6
6. Quality of Help messages	1	2	3	4	5	6
7. Ease of use	1	2	3	4	5	6
8. Appropriateness of options	1	2	3	4	5	6
9. Clarity of error messages	1	2	3	4	5	6
10. Prevention of input errors	1	2	3	4	5	6
INFORMATION SYSTEMS STAFF						
11. Cooperation	1	2	3	4	5	6
12. Availability	1	2	3	4	5	6
13. Knowledge	1	2	3	4	5	6
14. Reporting of progress	1	2	3	4	5	6
15. Communication skills	1	2	3	4	5	6
TRAINING						
16. Completeness	1	2	3	4	5	6
17. Appropriateness	1	2	3	4	5	6
18. Schedule	1	2	3	4	5	6

Figure 11-13 Sample user evaluation form.

Whenever possible, the post-implementation evaluation should be conducted by people who were not directly involved in developing the system. The evaluation usually is done by IS staff and users, although some firms use an internal audit group or independent auditors to ensure the accuracy and completeness of the evaluation.

When should post-implementation evaluation occur? Is it better to wait until the new system has been in operation for one month, six months, one year, or longer? Details of the developmental effort can be forgotten if too much time elapses before the evaluation. After several months or a year, for instance, users might not be able to remember whether they learned a procedure through training, from user documentation, or by experimenting with the system themselves.

Users also might forget their impressions of IS team members over time. An important purpose of the post-implementation evaluation is to improve the quality of IS department functions, including interaction with users, training, and documentation. Consequently, the evaluation team should perform the assessment while users are able to recall specific incidents, successes, and problems so they can offer suggestions for improvement.

In contrast, post-implementation evaluation primarily is concerned with assessing the quality of the new system. If the team performs the evaluation too soon after implementation, users will not have enough time to learn the new system and appreciate its strengths and weaknesses. Although many IS professionals recommend conducting the evaluation after at least six months of system operation, pressure to finish the project sooner usually results, so the IS department can move on to other tasks.

A KEY QUESTION

Cindy Winslow likes her new job as lead systems analyst at Yorktown Industries. She is pleased that her development team completed the new human resources system ahead of schedule and under budget. Cindy looked forward to receiving the post-implementation evaluation because she was confident that both the system and the development team would receive high marks from users and managers.

After the system operated for one month, Cindy received a call from her supervisor, Ted Haines. Ted told her that she would have to handle the evaluation, even though she headed the development effort. Cindy told Ted that she didn't feel comfortable evaluating her own team's work. She explained that someone who wasn't involved in its development should do an independent evaluation.

Ted responded that he had full confidence in Cindy's ability to be objective and explained that no one else is available and he needs the evaluation quickly so he can move forward with the next stage in the corporate development plan.

Cindy was troubled about the situation, and she called you, a professional acquaintance, for your advice. What would you tell her, and why?

Ideally, conducting a post-implementation evaluation should be standard practice for all information systems projects. Sometimes, however, evaluations are skipped for various reasons — users are eager to use the new system to complete their work, IS personnel are assigned to other projects, or qualified people are not available to perform the evaluation. In some organizations, management might not recognize the importance and benefits of a post-implementation evaluation.

FINAL REPORT TO MANAGEMENT

A t the end of each SDLC phase, you produce a report to management, and the systems implementation phase is no exception. Your report should include the following items:

1. Final versions of all system documentation
2. Planned modifications and enhancements to the system that have been identified
3. A recap of all systems development costs and schedules
4. A comparison of actual costs and schedules to the original estimates
5. The post-implementation evaluation, if it has been performed

The final report to management marks the end of systems development work. In the next chapter, you will study the role of a systems analyst during systems operation and support, which is the final phase of the SDLC.

SOFTWEAR, LIMITED — INSTALLATION AND EVALUATION

A fter a successful period of parallel processing, the payroll package purchased by SWL from Pacific Software was implemented fully. Now, the installation of the ESIP system was ready to begin.

In preparation, the IS development team of Jane Rossman, Tom Adams, and Becky Evans confirmed that SWL's existing network could handle the additional traffic generated by the new system. True Blue Systems, the outside consulting firm, noted in its report that the network might need to be upgraded in the future, especially if SWL expanded the number of networked applications and users.

Tom's first task was to install the ESIP application on the server in the payroll department, and to verify that the system could communicate properly with SWL's mainframe. Then he installed and tested a new high-speed tape cartridge backup system for the ESIP system.

Next, Tom loaded the ESIP application on a client PC in the human resources department. He checked all hardware and system software settings and used several test files to be sure that the client communicated with the ESIP server in the payroll department.

Meanwhile, Becky Evans and Rick Williams worked together on the interface between the ESIP system and the mainframe. They previously created a module called an extract program that directed the mainframe payroll system to capture the ESIP payroll deductions, store them in a file, and transmit the file back to the ESIP system. They already tested the interface using stubs to represent actual input and output files. Now, they would use a test data file with examples of every possible combination of permissible deductions, and several deductions that would not be allowed.

As soon as Rick confirmed that the payroll package was ready for the interface test, Tom set up the ESIP server and sent the test file to the mainframe. Then he ran the module that sent processing commands to the payroll system. Everyone was pleased to see that the mainframe handled the test data properly and generated an extracted deduction file, which it downloaded to the ESIP server.

Becky and Rick now were ready to conduct hands-on training with the payroll group, so they arranged an early morning session with Amy Calico, Nelson White, Britton Ellis, and Debra Williams. Becky walked them through the steps, which were described clearly in the user manual, and then answered several questions. The payroll employees seemed pleased with the explanation and commented on how much easier the new system would be.

Next, Becky went to see Mike Feiner, director of human resources. Mike would be the only person allowed to add, change, or delete any of the ESIP options. Based on written authorization from Tina Pham, vice president of human resources, Mike would have a special password and permission level to allow him to perform these actions. Becky described to Mike how the system worked and then showed him how to enter, modify, and delete a test option she prepared. For security reasons, the special documentation for these functions will not be printed in the user manual itself; it will be retained in the IS department files.

Becky and Tom met again with the payroll group to show users how to enter the deduction authorizations for individual employees. Although the new payroll system was operational, ESIP deductions still were being handled manually. Using the ESIP server and another networked payroll PC, the payroll clerks were able to enter actual payroll data during a three-day test period. The built-in edit and validation features detected the errors that the team purposely inserted as test data and even identified several invalid authorizations that were not noticed previously. Printed reports were produced and verified by other payroll department members.

Jane Rossman had a last minute idea: perhaps it would be wise to send a notice to all SWL employees describing the new ESIP system. The flyer also could remind employees how to select options and invite their questions or comments. Michael Jeremy, vice president of finance, thought that Jane's idea was excellent.

Up to this point, no final decision was made about the changeover method for the new system. Because the ESIP system replaced a series of manual processing steps, the main question was whether to run the manual system in parallel operation for a specified period. Managers in the payroll, human resources, and accounting departments wanted the new system operational as soon as possible and everyone agreed that a direct cutover would take place on May 7, 1999, when the weekly payroll was processed.

Starting on Monday, May 3, the IS team met again with each of the users and reviewed a final checklist. No problems appeared and the system now was ready to interface with the mainframe and handle live data in an operational environment. On Friday morning, May 7, the payroll department ran the ESIP module that sent the processing commands to the payroll system. Later that morning, during the weekly processing cycle, the payroll package created a file with the extracted deductions and passed it back to the ESIP server.

With the ESIP system using real input data, IS department members visited each of the recently trained users to be sure they were experiencing no difficulties. They received good reports — users in the payroll and human resources departments seemed pleased with the new system. They were able to access the ESIP data, enter new deductions, and had no problems with screen output or printed reports.

The direct cutover to the ESIP system occurred without major problems. By the end of June 1999, the system completed eight, weekly payroll cycles, produced all required reports and outputs, and properly handled the monthly transfer of funds to the credit union and the SWL stock purchase plan.

During the first part of July, the IS department conducted a post-implementation evaluation with a team that consisted of two people: Katie Barnes, a systems analyst who had not been involved in the ESIP system development, and Ben Mancuso, a member of the finance department who was designated by Michael Jeremy. The evaluation team reviewed system operations, conducted interviews, and asked users to complete a brief questionnaire. The results were favorable, and it appeared that users were very satisfied with the new ESIP system. When the evaluation was completed in mid-July, Ann Hon sent the cover memo shown in Figure 11-14 on the next page to Michael Jeremy with a copy of the final report. The systems development effort for the ESIP system was completed successfully.

MEMORANDUM

Date: July 15, 1999
To: Michael Jeremy, Vice President, Finance
From: Ann Hon, Director of Information Systems
Subject: Report on the ESIP System

The payroll system and the ESIP project were developed as a result of your systems request dated September 15, 1998.

As you know, the payroll system from Pacific Software was implemented in January 1999 and has operated without any major problems. The new system has resulted in accurate, faster processing and has eliminated overtime by payroll employees.

The ESIP system became operational on May 7, 1999 and has handled all employee payroll deductions and ESIP processing successfully. The system was installed in a direct cutover from the prior manual system and can be extended to all SWL locations as a client/server application in the future.

Both systems have received very favorable post-implementation reviews from users and managers, as shown in the attached report and some enhancements already have been suggested. The report also includes a recap of all estimated and actual costs and an estimate of operation and maintenance support costs.

Mike Feiner, director of human resources, asked me whether we could design a way for employees to access their ESIP account data from SWL offices or from home using the Internet. I recommended that the SWL computer resources committee discuss this item at our next meeting. This could tie into our recent discussions about an SWL intranet based on Web standards.

If you have any questions about the report, please let me know.

Attachment: Final Report

Figure 11-14 Cover memo for Ann Hon's report to management.

YOUR TURN — During the systems analysis phase, you learned how to use fact-gathering techniques to determine system requirements. Before completing this assignment, you should review the material on interviews and questionnaires.

Suppose you are selected as a member of the post-implementation evaluation team at SWL. You are given two specific assignments: you must prepare a list of interview questions for users and design a brief questionnaire that measures the effectiveness of the new system. Develop the interview questions and questionnaire by following the guidelines suggested in the chapter and in the Systems Analyst's Toolkit.

In the Systems Analyst's Toolkit, you learned how to use project management techniques, including PERT charts, to plan a project and make sure it stays on schedule. Before completing this assignment, you should review the project management section of the Toolkit.

Although the installation and evaluation tasks are complete, Rick wants to give you a training exercise. Suppose you are just starting this phase and you want to use a PERT chart to help manage the work. You need to make a list of the specific tasks, a list of who will be assigned to these tasks, and an estimate of the duration of the project. Later, you will determine a specific sequence for the tasks and whether certain tasks are dependent on others being completed first.

To practice your skills, Rick wants you to prepare a list of the tasks that are involved in this phase of the project. He understands that you do not have enough information to make an accurate estimate of the task durations — but he wants you to use your best judgment based on what you know about the ESIP system and the capabilities of the IS team. He gave you the form shown in Figure 11-15 and he included the first four tasks as examples to get you started. You should examine the SWL case carefully and complete the list for Rick.

ESIP System: Systems Installation and Evaluation Tasks

Task	Description	IS people assigned	Duration in hours
1	Install the ESIP application on the server	Tom	3
2	Verify that the ESIP server can communicate properly with the mainframe	Tom	1
3	Install and test tape backup system	Tom	4
4	Load the ESIP application on the client PCs in the payroll and human resources departments	Tom	4
5	...	...	...

Figure 11-15   Systems installation and evaluation tasks for the ESIP system.

CHAPTER SUMMARY

D uring installation and evaluation, you establish an operational, or production, environment for the new information system that is completely separate from the test environment. The operational environment contains all the programs, procedures, and live data files and is accessible only by authorized users. Once the operational environment is established, members of the IS department can access that environment only to apply authorized corrections, modifications, and enhancements. The test environment, which the project team created to develop and test the new system, continues to exist even after the operational environment is established. All future changes to the system must be verified using the test environment before the changes are applied to the operational environment.

Everyone who interacts with the new information system must receive training that is appropriate to his or her role and skills. Sometimes, much of the training is provided by software or hardware vendors or by professional training organizations. The responsibility for training, however, often falls on the members of the information systems department. When you develop a training program, remember the following guidelines: train people in groups; utilize people already trained to help train others; develop separate programs for distinct employee groups; and provide for learning by using discussions, demonstrations, documentation, training manuals, and interactive tutorials.

File conversion often is a lengthy, complicated process. During file conversion, all data for the new system is loaded into files or a database and is verified by users. If the new system is replacing a computerized system, special programs that translate the data into a form the new system can use often can perform the conversion effort.

System changeover is the process of putting the new information system into operation and retiring the old system. Four changeover methods exist. With direct cutover, the old system stops and the new system starts simultaneously; direct cutover is the least expensive and most risky changeover method. With parallel operation, users operate both the old and new information systems for some period of time; parallel operation is the most expensive and least risky of the changeover methods. Pilot operation and phased changeover represent compromises between direct cutover and parallel operation; both methods are less risky than direct cutover and less costly than parallel operation. With pilot operation, a limited part of the organization uses the new system for a period of time, while the old system continues to operate for the entire organization. After the system proves successful at the pilot site, it is implemented throughout the organization. With phased changeover, you implement the system in the entire organization, but only one module at a time, until the entire system is operational.

A post-implementation evaluation assesses and reports on the quality of the new system and the work done by the project team. Although it is best if people who were not involved in the systems development effort perform the evaluation, this is not always possible. The evaluation should be conducted early so users have a fresh recollection of the development effort, but not before users have experience using the new system.

The final report to management includes the final system documentation, describes any future system enhancements that already have been identified, and details the project costs. The report represents the end of the development effort and the beginning of the new system's operational life.

Review Questions

1 What is the purpose of an operational environment?

2. By what other name is an operational environment known?

3. Who must receive training before a new information system is implemented?

4. What is included in a typical training manual? How is a tutorial different from a training manual?

5. Is file security more or less important during file conversion than during subsequent system operation?

6. List and describe the four system changeover methods.

7. Which of the system changeover methods generally is the most expensive? Why?

8. Which of the system changeover methods generally is the most risky? Why?

9. How does phased changeover differ from pilot operation?

10. Who should perform a post-implementation evaluation? Who usually performs the evaluation?

11. List four investigative techniques that can be used when performing a post-implementation evaluation.

12. What information usually is included in the final report to management?

Discussion Questions

1. Obtain and evaluate an online tutorial or reference manual lesson for some software product. Are the instructions and lesson steps clear? Are the illustrations appropriate and helpful? What level of computer sophistication does the lesson assume from the user? If the lesson requires some prior computer knowledge, are novice users told where to find supplementary information? What specific suggestions do you have for improving the lesson?

2. Prepare a tutorial to train someone in the use of specific software or hardware, such as a Web browser or an ATM machine.

3. Prepare a one-page questionnaire to distribute to users in a post-implementation evaluation of a recent information system project. Include at least 12 questions that cover the important information you want to obtain.

CASE STUDIES

NEW CENTURY HEALTH CLINIC — INSTALLATION AND EVALUATION

 ll the programs and procedures for the new computerized office information system for New Century Health Clinic have been prepared, tested, and approved. A powerful personal computer server and six client PCs have been purchased, installed, and networked in the clinic offices. You now are ready to begin installation and evaluation of the system.

Assignments

1. Identify the specific people who will require training on the new system. Describe the type and level of training you recommend for each person or group.

2. Recommend a changeover method for New Century's system and justify your recommendation. If you suggest phased changeover or pilot operation, specify the order in which you would implement the modules or how you would select a pilot workstation or location.

3. Develop a file conversion plan that identifies what data must be entered during the conversion process, and the order in which data should be entered.

4. Should the associates perform a post-implementation evaluation? If an assessment is done, who should perform it? What options are available and which would you recommend?

 You can use the project management techniques described in the Systems Analyst's Toolkit to help you with the assignment in the following case study.

HOOBER INDUSTRIES

 ou are the project manager for the development of a new mainframe information system at Hoober Industries that will operate on a weekly cycle. The new system will be implemented with a direct cutover and should start operation on a Monday, which marks the beginning of a new pay period. Before the system changeover takes place, two activities must be completed: training and file conversion.

You must train 22 users, four IS operations staff people, and three managers. In addition, users must complete the file conversion process, which can begin as soon as you train at least one IS operations person and one user.

You estimate that each training session will take two complete work days and that no more than eight people can be involved in any one session. You developed three different types of training sessions: one for users, one for managers, and one for the IS staff. Assume that all IS people attend the same training session and that the session occurs during regular business hours on two consecutive weekdays. Each user can spend up to 20 hours of a 40-hour week in training or file conversion; the remaining 20 hours are required for other job duties.

You decide to use person-weeks to help you plan the schedule. One person-week means one person is occupied for a one-week period. You estimate that file conversion will require 21 person-weeks: 19 person-weeks to enter and verify existing data, and two person-weeks to enter and verify current data, which can be accomplished only on the weekend prior to the cutover. Hoober's computer center will be fully operational throughout the weekend. A maximum of 100 overtime hours has been approved for the file conversion effort.

Assignments

1. Prepare a training and file conversion plan that will result in the earliest possible implementation and minimize the need for overtime.

2. For each of the three groups that need training on the system, describe the type of training you would recommend and the topics you would cover.

3. One of Hoober's top managers is nervous about using the direct cutover method; he has asked you to clarify why you chose this approach. Draft a memo outlining the reasons for using a direct cutover approach. (In addition to the information outlined here, use your imagination to add detail on the type of system best suited to direct cutover).

4. Six months after the system changeover, the system is operating largely error-free. To assess the system's overall quality, you decide to perform a post-implementation evaluation. Prepare two evaluation forms for the new information system, one for users and managers, and one for the IS operations staff.

RIDGEWAY COMPANY

 he Ridgeway Company requirements for the new billing system for the Lake View Country Club were described in case studies in Chapters 4, 8, 9, and 10. The following assignments are based on the work you already have done in those chapters.

Assignments

1. Identify the specific groups of people who need training on the new system. For each group, describe the type of training you would recommend and list the topics you would cover.

2. Suggest a changeover method for the new billing system and provide specific reasons to support your choice. If you recommend phased changeover, specify the order in which you would implement the modules. If your recommendation is for pilot operation, specify the department or area you would select as the pilot site, and justify your choice.

3. Develop a file conversion plan that specifies which data items in which files must be entered, the order in which the data should be entered, and which data items are the most time-critical.

4. You decide to perform a post-implementation evaluation to assess the quality of the system. Who would you involve in the process? What investigative techniques would you use and why?

Phase 5
Systems Operation and Support

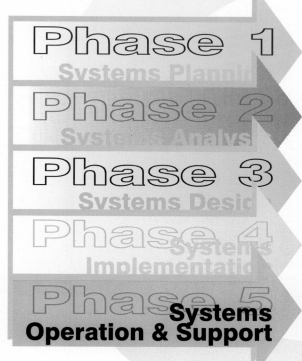

Phase 1
Systems Planning

Phase 2
Systems Analysis

Phase 3
Systems Design

Phase 4
Systems Implementation

Phase 5
Systems Operation & Support

Systems Operation and Support

SDLC PHASES

Systems operation and support is the last phase in the systems development life cycle. The systems operation and support phase includes maintenance and improvements to the system after it becomes operational, and provides ongoing support for users to help them solve problems and obtain the most value from the system.

CHAPTER 12

SDLC PHASES

Phase 1
Systems Planning

Phase 2
Systems Analysis

Phase 3
Systems Design

Phase 4
Systems
Implementation

Phase 5
Systems
Operation & Support

Systems Operation and Support

OBJECTIVES

When you finish this chapter, you will be able to:

- Explain how the systems operation and support phase relates to the rest of the SDLC
- Describe the information center concept and how it supports user needs
- Discuss the three main categories of systems maintenance
- Describe standard maintenance procedures
- Discuss the role of configuration management in systems operation
- Describe the process of capacity planning, including workload and performance measurements
- Recognize the signs of system obsolescence

INTRODUCTION

Now that the system is operational, the real test begins. The key question is whether the system meets user expectations and provides support for business objectives. Systems must be maintained and improved to meet changing business demands, and users constantly require assistance. Chapter 12 describes how companies meet these needs.

In addition to performing maintenance, a systems analyst is like an internal consultant who provides guidance, support, and training. Successful, robust systems often need the most support because users want to learn the features, try all the capabilities, and discover how the system can help them perform their business functions. Higher levels of system activity cause users to want more features, more enhancements, more maintenance, and more support. In most organizations, more than half of all IS department effort goes into supporting existing systems and making them more valuable to users.

This chapter begins with a discussion of systems support, including the information center concept. You will study the three main types of maintenance: corrective, adaptive, and perfective. You also will learn how the IS group delivers operational support, including maintenance teams, configuration management, and maintenance releases. Finally, you will examine system performance issues, CASE maintenance tools, and how to recognize system obsolescence.

OVERVIEW OF SYSTEMS SUPPORT AND MAINTENANCE ACTIVITIES

T he systems operation and support phase begins when a system becomes operational and ends when it is replaced. The systems analyst's most important goal is a system that meets business needs and is efficient, easy to use, and affordable.

After delivering the system, the analyst has two other important tasks. The first objective is to provide guidance and user training, which can include formal training sessions, technical support, and the creation of a centralized information center. The second responsibility is to perform necessary maintenance to keep the system operating properly and increase its value to users.

SUPPORT ACTIVITIES

User Training and Assistance

Y ou already are familiar with initial user training that is performed when a new system is introduced. For example, an airline provides training for mechanics when new aircraft are purchased, as shown in Figure 12-1. In addition, new employees must learn how to use the company's information systems. In most firms, newly hired employees are trained by user departments, rather than IS staff members.

To read more on the importance of **User Training**, visit Systems Analysis and Design Chapter 12 More on the Web.

www.scsite.com/ sad3e/ch12/

Figure 12-1   The training process for any type of organization, whether the users are data entry staff, customer service reps, airline mechanics, or NASA technicians, is essentially the same. The main objective is to give users the best possible support so they can use the system efficiently to perform their job functions.

If significant changes take place in the existing system or if a new version is released, the IS department might develop a **user training package**. Depending on the nature of the changes, this package could include special online Help via e-mail or the company's intranet, a revision to the user guide, a training manual supplement, or formal training sessions. Training users about system changes is similar to initial training. The main objective is to show users how the system can help them perform their jobs.

Information Centers

As systems and data structures become more complex, users need constant support and guidance. To make data more accessible and to empower users, many IS departments create information centers. An **information center** (**IC**), as shown in Figure 12-2, has three main objectives: to help people use system resources more effectively, to provide answers to technical or operational questions, and to make users more productive by teaching them how to meet their own information needs. In some organizations, an information center is called a **help desk**, which is the first place users contact when they need assistance.

Figure 12-2 An information center (IC) or help desk performs many important functions, including assisting users to identify and correct system problems. Users should be able to contact the IC or help desk easily to get support.

For a complete reference on **Help Desk** resources, visit Systems Analysis and Design Chapter 12 More on the Web.

www.scsite.com/ sad3e/ch12/

An information center does not replace traditional IS maintenance and support activities. Instead, ICs enhance productivity and improve utilization of a company's information resources.

To work in an information center, you need strong interpersonal and technical skills plus a solid understanding of the business, because you will interact with users in many departments. During a typical day, the information center staff shown in Figure 12-2 might be required to carry out the following tasks:

- Show a user how to create a data query or report with specific business information
- Demonstrate an advanced feature of a system or a commercial package
- Help a user recover damaged data
- Offer tips for better operation
- Explain an undocumented software feature
- Show a user how to write a macro
- Explain how to access the company's intranet or the Internet

- Assist a user in developing a simple database to track time spent on various projects
- Answer questions about software licensing and upgrades
- Provide information about system specifications and the cost of new hardware or software
- Recommend a system solution that integrates data from different locations to solve a business problem

In addition to functioning as a valuable link between IS staff and users, the information center is a contact point for all IS maintenance activities. The information center is where users report system problems, ask for maintenance, or submit new systems requests. An information center can utilize many types of automated support, just as outside vendors do, including e-mail responses, on-demand fax capability, an accessible knowledge base, publication of frequently asked questions (FAQs), electronic bulletin boards, and a voice mail system for user questions.

Whether the system involves computer applications or building high-performance automobile engines, it is essential to monitor performance and provide support, as shown in Figure 12-3.

Figure 12-3 Performance for any system must be recorded carefully, measured, and analyzed, regardless of the type of information system.

MAINTENANCE ACTIVITIES

The overall cost of an information system includes the systems operation and support phase. Figure 12-4 shows a typical pattern of operational costs and maintenance expenses during the useful life of a system. **Operational costs** include items such as supplies, equipment rental, and software leases. Notice that the lower area shown in Figure 12-4 represents fixed operational costs.

Maintenance expenses vary significantly during the system's operational life and include spending to support maintenance activities. **Maintenance activities** include changing programs, procedures, or documentation to ensure correct system performance, adapting the system to changing requirements, or making the system operate more efficiently. These needs are met by corrective, adaptive, and perfective maintenance. Corrective maintenance is done to fix errors, adaptive maintenance adds new capability and enhancements, and perfective maintenance improves efficiency. Although some analysts use the term *maintenance* to describe only corrective maintenance, the definition

For an overview of **Maintenance Activities**, visit Systems Analysis and Design Chapter 12 More on the Web.

www.scsite.com/ sad3e/ch12/

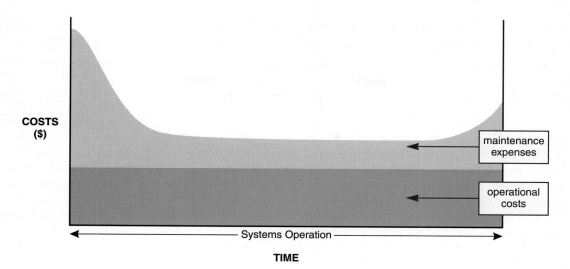

COSTS ($)

maintenance expenses

operational costs

Systems Operation

TIME

Figure 12-4   The total cost of an information system during the systems operation and support phase includes operational and maintenance costs. Operational costs are relatively constant, while maintenance expenses vary over time.

of maintenance also can include adaptive or perfective maintenance. The main idea is to understand that different types of support activities and goals exist.

Maintenance expenses usually are high when a system is implemented because problems must be detected, investigated, and corrected. Afterward, costs usually remain low and involve minor adaptive maintenance. Eventually, both adaptive and perfective maintenance activities increase in a dynamic business environment.

Near the end of a system's useful life, maintenance expenses increase rapidly due to adaptive maintenance and a higher level of perfective maintenance. Figure 12-5 shows the typical patterns for each of the three classifications of maintenance activities over a system's life span.

	Immediately After Implementation	Early Operational Life	Middle Operational Life	Later Operational Life
Corrective Maintenance	High	Low	Low	High
Adaptive Maintenance (Minor Enhancements)	None	Medium	Medium	Medium
Adaptive Maintenance (Major Enhancements)	None	None	Medium to High	Medium to High
Perfective Maintenance	Low	Low to Medium	Medium	Low

Figure 12-5   Information systems maintenance depends on two major factors: the type of maintenance and the age of the system.

Corrective Maintenance

Corrective maintenance diagnoses and corrects errors in an operational system. In addition to errors in the original version of the system, corrective maintenance often is needed to resolve issues created by previous maintenance changes. To avoid introducing new problems, all maintenance work requires careful analysis before making changes. The best maintenance approach is a scaled-down version of the SDLC itself, where investigation, analysis, design, and testing are performed before implementing any solution.

You can respond to errors in various ways, depending on the nature and severity of the problem. Most organizations have standard procedures for minor errors, such as an incorrect report title or an improper format for a data element. In a typical procedure, a user submits a systems request that is evaluated, prioritized, and scheduled by the systems review committee. If the request is approved, a maintenance team designs, tests, documents, and implements a solution. Figure 12-6 shows a systems request to correct a relatively minor error in a monthly sales report.

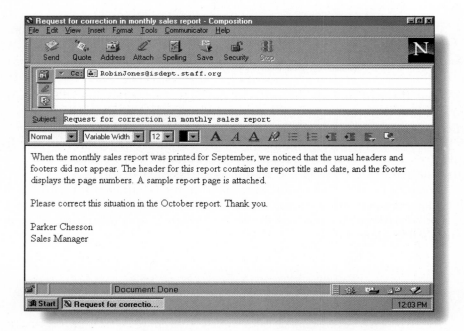

Figure 12-6   An e-mail request for the correction of a formatting error in a report.

For more serious situations, such as incorrect output totals or missing customer records, a user submits a systems request with supporting evidence. These situations get a high priority and a maintenance team begins work on the problem immediately. Severe errors sometimes occur because the system developers did not test for certain data combinations or processing situations.

The worst case is a total system failure, which is an emergency situation. When this occurs, the maintenance team bypasses the initial steps and tries to correct the failure immediately. Meanwhile, a written systems request is prepared by a user or a member of the IS department and added to the maintenance log. When the system is operational again, the maintenance team determines the cause, analyzes the problem, and designs a permanent solution. The IS response team updates the test data files, thoroughly tests the system, and prepares full documentation.

Adaptive Maintenance

Adaptive maintenance adds enhancements to an operational system. An **enhancement** is a new feature or capability or a change that improves efficiency or maintainability. The need for adaptive maintenance usually arises from business environment changes such as new products or services, new manufacturing technology, or support for a new Web site.

The procedure for adaptive maintenance is similar to minor corrective maintenance. A user submits a systems request that is evaluated and prioritized by the systems review committee. A maintenance team then analyzes, designs, and implements the enhancement. Although the procedures for the two types of maintenance are alike, adaptive maintenance requires more IS department resources than minor corrective maintenance.

An adaptive maintenance project is like a small-scale SDLC project, because the development procedure is similar. Adaptive maintenance can be more difficult than new systems development because the enhancements must work within the constraints of an existing system.

> For more information on **Adaptive Maintenance** processes, visit Systems Analysis and Design Chapter 12 More on the Web.
>
> www.scsite.com/ sad3e/ch12/

Perfective Maintenance

Perfective maintenance involves changing an operational system to make it more efficient, reliable, or maintainable. Figure 12-7 shows several examples of perfective maintenance. Requests for corrective and adaptive maintenance normally come from users, while perfective maintenance usually is initiated by the IS department.

Examples of Perfective Maintenance Projects

- Install additional high-speed memory
- Write a macro to handle repetitive tasks
- Upgrade modems to the latest models
- Replace network cabling with fiber optics
- Create a code module that compresses all data files before network transmission
- Rewrite a program in a new, nonprocedural language
- Redesign a graphical interface to provide greater flexibility
- Reorganize program modules to interact more efficiently
- Develop a library of reusable code modules
- Create multiple desktop settings so several users can share the same workstation
- Replace older storage devices with high-speed disk cartridge tape units
- Use object-oriented language for application development
- Convert slower batch processing tasks to online procedures
- Replace older CD-ROM drives with the latest models

Figure 12-7   Typical examples of perfective maintenance projects that improve a system's efficiency, reliability, or maintainability.

During system operation, changes in user activity or data patterns can cause a decline in efficiency, and perfective maintenance might be needed to restore performance. When users are concerned about performance, you should determine whether a perfective maintenance project might improve response time and system efficiency.

Perfective maintenance also can improve system reliability. For example, input problems might cause a program to terminate abnormally. By modifying the data entry process, you can highlight errors and notify the user that proper data must be entered. When a system is easier to maintain, support is less costly and less risky. In many cases, you can simplify a complex program to improve maintainability.

Two important techniques that can be used in perfective maintenance and other stages of the SDLC are reverse engineering and reengineering. A **reverse engineering tool** is a CASE tool that translates program source code into a series of logic diagrams, structure charts, and text descriptions that allow the analyst to study the program from a design viewpoint rather than from a coding level.

Some reverse engineering tools also suggest coding modifications to improve a program's quality or performance. These tools are called **reengineering tools** and an analyst uses them interactively to correct program errors or change the program design. Programs that need a large number of maintenance changes usually are good candidates for reengineering or restructuring. The more a program changes, the more likely it is to become inefficient and difficult to maintain. Detailed records of all maintenance work help identify systems with a history of frequent corrective, adaptive, or perfective maintenance.

In many organizations, perfective maintenance is not performed frequently enough. Companies with limited resources often consider new systems development, adaptive maintenance, and corrective maintenance more important than perfective maintenance. Managers and users constantly request new projects so few resources are available for perfective maintenance work. As a practical matter, perfective maintenance can be performed as part of another project. For example, if a new function must be added to a program, you can include perfective maintenance in the adaptive maintenance project.

Perfective maintenance usually is cost-effective during the middle of the system's operational life. Early in systems operation, perfective maintenance usually is not needed. Later, perfective maintenance might be necessary, but high in cost. Most benefits of perfective maintenance are less valuable if the company already plans to discontinue the system.

For additional information on **Reverse Engineering**, visit Systems Analysis and Design Chapter 12 More on the Web.

www.scsite.com/ sad3e/ch12/

For an overview of **Reengineering**, visit Systems Analysis and Design Chapter 12 More on the Web.

www.scsite.com/ sad3e/ch12/

MANAGING SYSTEMS OPERATION AND SUPPORT

ystems operation, like all other phases in the SDLC, requires effective management. During the operational phase, many companies use a maintenance team, a configuration management process, and a maintenance release procedure.

Maintenance Team

A **maintenance team** consists of one or more systems analysts and programmers. The analysts must have a solid background in information technology, strong analytical abilities, and a solid understanding of business operations and management functions. Analysts also need effective interpersonal and communications skills and they must be creative, energetic, and eager for new knowledge.

Maintenance systems analysts are like skilled detectives who investigate and rapidly locate the source of a problem by using analysis and synthesis skills. **Analysis** means examining the whole in order to learn about the individual elements, while **synthesis** involves studying the parts to understand the overall system. A systems analyst must understand the system elements and how to maintain them without affecting the overall system.

IS managers often divide systems analysts and programmers into two groups: one group performs new system development and the other group handles all maintenance. One advantage of this approach is the maintenance group develops strong support skills.

Some organizations, however, use a more flexible approach and assign IS staff members to various projects as they occur. By integrating development and support work, the people developing the system also assume responsibility for maintaining it. Because the team is familiar with the project, additional training or expense is unnecessary, and members are likely to have a sense of ownership from the onset.

Unfortunately, many analysts feel that maintenance work is less attractive than developing new systems, which they see as more interesting and creative. Also, it can be more challenging to deal with someone else's work that might be poorly documented and organized.

Some organizations with separate maintenance and new systems groups rotate people from one area to the other. When analysts learn different skills, the organization is more versatile and people can shift to meet changing business needs. For instance, systems analysts working on maintenance projects learn why it is important to design easily maintainable systems. Similarly, analysts working on new systems get a better appreciation of the development process and the design compromises necessary to meet business objectives. This knowledge can help them become better maintenance systems analysts.

One disadvantage of rotation is it increases overhead costs because time is lost when people move from one job to another. When systems analysts constantly shift between maintenance and new development, they have less opportunity to become highly skilled at any one job. Another disadvantage is that with the rotation method, some analysts must spend a substantial amount of time in a job that is less desirable to them personally.

Newly hired and recently promoted IS staff members sometimes are assigned to maintenance projects because most IS managers believe that maintenance work offers the best learning experience. Studying existing systems and documentation is an excellent way to learn program and documentation standards. In addition, the mini-SDLC used in many adaptive maintenance projects is good training for the full-scale systems development life cycle. Some disadvantages exist, however. For a new systems analyst, maintenance work often is more difficult than new systems development, and it might make more sense to assign a new person to a development team where more experienced analysts are available to provide training and guidance.

In most organizations, the training value of maintenance work outweighs the other factors, and IS managers usually assign new employees to maintenance activities.

Configuration Management

Configuration management is a process for controlling changes in system requirements during the development phases of the SDLC. Configuration management also helps a company manage support resources and costs after the system becomes operational. Usually three steps are performed when handling maintenance requests: the request is submitted, a manager makes an initial decision, and the systems review committee renders a final determination.

1. The **maintenance request.** Users submit most requests for corrective and adaptive maintenance when the system is not performing properly or if they want new features. IS staff members usually initiate requests for perfective maintenance. To keep a complete maintenance log, all work must be covered by a specific request that users submit in writing or by e-mail.

2. **Initial action on the request.** Most organizations designate a systems operation manager with responsibility for configuration management on specific systems. When a user submits a maintenance request, the manager makes an initial decision. If the request involves a severe problem, a team is assigned immediately to perform corrective maintenance. In noncritical situations, the manager either accepts or rejects the request or postpones action pending fur-

For more information on **Configuration Management**, visit *Systems Analysis and Design* Chapter 12 More on the Web.

www.scsite.com/ sad3e/ch12/

ther study. The manager notifies the requester and the systems review committee of the decision and the reasons for the determination.

3. **Final disposition of the request.** The systems review committee evaluates the request and either rejects it or assigns it a priority and schedules the maintenance work. To reduce paperwork and unnecessary effort, the committee often delegates final authority to the systems operation manager for requests that fall within a certain cost range.

To learn more on improving **Maintenance** processes, visit Systems Analysis and Design Chapter 12 More on the Web.

www.scsite.com/ sad3e/ch12/

Configuration management is an effective tool for managing different versions of a system. A system implemented in multiple environments often has different versions for each platform and thus requires different maintenance updates. The IS department must keep track of all system versions, to ensure that all maintenance updates are applied correctly, and to see that all versions of the system work correctly.

Configuration management also helps to organize and handle documentation. An operational system has extensive documentation that covers development, modification, and maintenance for all versions of the installed system. Most documentation material, including the initial systems request, project management data, end-of-phase reports, the data dictionary, and the IS operations and user manuals, is stored in the IS department.

Most maintenance projects require documentation changes. You must be especially careful to issue updates whenever you make adaptive changes or perform major corrective maintenance. It is important to avoid surprises for users and IS staff members. Keeping track of all documentation and ensuring that updates are distributed properly is an important part of configuration management.

TRADE OFF

In many companies, the systems review committee separates maintenance requests from new systems development requests when evaluating requests and setting priorities. In other organizations, all requests for systems services are put into one group and considered together. The most important project is given top priority, whether it is maintenance or new development.

Many IS managers believe that evaluating all projects together leads to the best possible decisions because maintenance and new development require similar IS department resources. In IS departments where systems analysts and programmers are organized into separate maintenance and new development groups, however, it might make sense to evaluate requests separately. Another advantage of a separate approach is that maintenance is more likely to receive a proportional share of IS department resources.

Neither approach guarantees an ideal allocation between maintenance and new systems development. The most important objective is to have a procedure that balances new development and necessary maintenance work to provide the best support for business requirements and priorities.

A KEY QUESTION

As IS manager at Brightside Insurance Company, you organized your IS staff into two separate groups — one team for maintenance projects and the other team for new systems work. This arrangement worked well in your last position at another company. At Brightside, however, systems assignments previously were made with no particular pattern.

At first, the systems analysts in your group did not comment about the team approach. Now, one of your best analysts might quit if he is assigned to work on the maintenance team because he is not interested in this type of work. You decide that if you match the right analyst with the right assignment, there would be no problems. What could you do? Should assignments be voluntary? Why or why not? If you have to make assignments, what criteria should you use?

Maintenance Releases

Coordinating maintenance changes and updates can be difficult, especially for a complex system with several versions. Many organizations, and especially software vendors, use numbered releases to designate different versions. When a **maintenance release methodology** is used, all noncritical changes are held until they can be implemented at the same time. Each change is documented and installed as a new version of the system that is called a **release**.

For an in-house developed system, the time between releases usually depends on the level of maintenance activity. A new release to correct a critical error, however, might be implemented immediately or saved for the next scheduled release. The decision depends on the nature of the error and the possible impact.

When a release method is used, a numbering pattern distinguishes the different releases. In a typical system, the initial version of the system is 1.0, and the release that includes the first set of maintenance changes is version 1.1. A change from version 1.4 to 1.5 indicates relatively minor changes, while whole number changes, such as from version 1.0 to 2.0 or from version 3.4 to 4.0, indicate a significant upgrade.

The release methodology offers several advantages, especially if two teams perform maintenance work on the same system. When a release methodology is used, all changes are tested together before a new system version is released. The release method also reduces costs because only one set of system tests is needed for all maintenance changes. This approach results in fewer versions, and means less expense and interruption for users.

Using a release methodology also reduces the documentation burden. Every time a new version of a system is implemented, all documentation must be updated, and some users feel that they spend too much time filing documentation changes. Even worse, some users let the upgrades pile up and eventually ignore them. With a release methodology, all documentation changes are coordinated and become effective simultaneously. Users and IS staff members integrate a package of updates into their documentation for each release.

The release methodology also has some potential disadvantages. Users expect a rapid response to their problems and requests, but with a release methodology, new features or upgrades are available less often. Even when changes would improve system efficiency or user productivity, the potential savings must wait until the next release date, which might increase operational costs.

MANAGING SYSTEM PERFORMANCE

A system's **performance** directly affects users who rely on it to perform their job functions. To ensure satisfactory support for business operations, the IS department monitors current system performance and anticipates future needs.

When most firms used a central computer for all data processing, it was relatively simple to measure the efficiency of the system. Today, companies use complex networks and client/server systems to support business information needs. A user at a client workstation often interacts with an information system that depends on other clients, servers, networks, and data located throughout the company. Rather than a single computer, it is the integration of all these system components that determines the system's capability and performance.

Various statistics are available to assess system performance, including capacity planning, which is a process that uses operational data to forecast system capabilities and future needs.

Performance and Workload Measurement

You already are familiar with several **workload measurements**, including the number of lines printed, the number of records accessed, and the number of transactions processed in a given time period. An analyst working on any system needs to analyze performance by measuring response time, turnaround time, and throughput time.

Response time is the overall time between a request for system activity and the delivery of the response. In the typical online environment, response time is measured from the instant the user presses the Enter key or clicks a mouse button until the requested screen display appears or printed output is ready.

Response time is affected by the system design, capabilities, and processing methods. If a user requests a batch processed report, for example, the batch processing schedule will determine the response time. Response time includes three elements: the time necessary to transmit or deliver the request to the system, the time that the system needs to process the request, and the time it takes to transmit or deliver the result back to the user. If the request involves network or Internet access, response time is affected by data communication factors.

Online users expect an immediate response and they are frustrated by any apparent lag or delay. Of all performance measurements, response time is the one that users notice and complain about most.

Turnaround time measures the efficiency of central computer operations. Turnaround time is the amount of time between the arrival of a request at a computer center and the availability of the output for delivery or transmission. Although turnaround time usually is associated with traditional data processing at central locations, some companies still use central batch methods for certain tasks, such as customer billing or credit card transaction processing.

Throughput measures the efficiency of the computer itself, which usually is a mainframe, minicomputer, or powerful PC server. Throughput is the time from the input of a request to the central processor until the output is delivered to the system. Throughput also can refer to the efficiency of a data communication network.

The IS department often measures average response time, turnaround time, or throughput for a particular system to evaluate performance before and after changes in the system or business information requirements have occurred. Performance data also is used for cost-benefit analysis of proposed maintenance and to evaluate systems that are nearing the end of their economically useful lives. Finally, management uses current performance and workload data as input to the capacity planning process.

Capacity Planning

Capacity planning is a process that monitors current activity and performance levels, anticipates future activity, and forecasts the resources needed to provide desired levels of service.

As a first step in capacity planning, you develop a current model based on the system's present workload and performance specifications. Then you project demand and user requirements over a one- to three-year time period and analyze the model to see what is needed to maintain satisfactory performance and meet requirements. To assist you in this process, you can use a technique called *what-if* analysis.

Using ***what-if*** analysis, you can vary one or more of the elements in a model to measure the effects on other elements. For example, you might use *what-if* analysis to answer questions such as, How will response time be affected if we add more PC workstations to the network? Will our client/server system be able to handle the growth in sales from the new Web site? What will be the effect on server throughput if we add more memory?

Powerful spreadsheet tools also can assist you in performing *what-if* analysis. For example, Microsoft Excel contains a feature called Goal Seek that determines what changes are necessary in one value to produce a specific result for another value. In the example shown in Figure 12-8, a capacity planning worksheet indicates that the system can handle 34,560 transactions per day, at 2.50 seconds each. The user wants to know the effect on processing time if the number of transactions increases to 50,000. The second figure shows the Goal Seek solution.

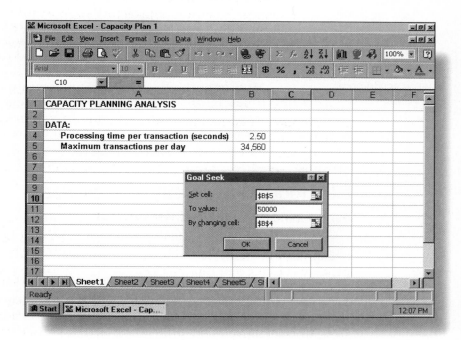

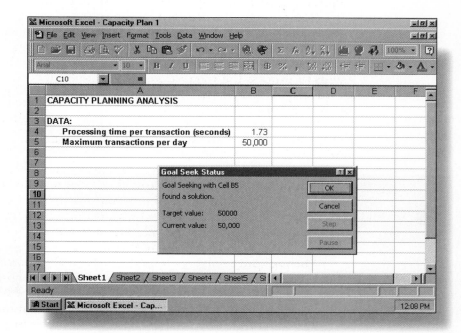

Figure 12-8   Microsoft Excel provide a Goal Seek feature that permits *what-if* analysis. In the first example, an analyst has asked the program to calculate how much faster the processing must be to handle 50,000 transactions per day than 34,560. The second figure shows the new processing time.

To learn more about ***What-if*** **Analysis**, visit Systems Analysis and Design Chapter 12 More on the Web.

www.scsite.com/ sad3e/ch12/

For more detail on **Capacity Planning**, visit Systems Analysis and Design Chapter 12 More on the Web.

www.scsite.com/ sad3e/ch12/

When you plan capacity, you need detailed information about the number of transactions; the daily, weekly, or monthly transaction patterns; the number of queries; and the number, type, and size of all generated reports. If the system involves a LAN, you need to estimate network traffic levels to determine whether or not the existing hardware and software can handle the load. If the system uses a client/server design, you need to examine performance and connectivity specifications for each platform.

Most importantly, you need an accurate forecast of future business activities. If new business functions or requirements are possible, you should develop contingency plans based on input from users and management. The main objective is to ensure that the system meets all future demands and provides effective support for business operations.

CASE TOOLS FOR SYSTEMS MAINTENANCE

You can use automated tools that provide valuable assistance during the operation and support phase. A typical CASE maintenance toolkit provides various tools for systems evaluation and maintenance, including the following:

- A performance monitor that provides data on program execution times
- A program analyzer that scans source code, provides data element cross-reference information, and helps evaluate the impact of a program change
- An interactive debugging analyzer that locates the source of a programming error
- A restructuring tool or a reengineering tool
- Automated documentation tools
- Network activity monitors
- Workload forecasting software

In addition to CASE tools, you also can use spreadsheet and presentation software to calculate trends, perform *what-if* analyses, and create attractive charts and graphs to display the results. Information technology planning is an essential part of the business planning process, and you probably will deliver presentations to management. You can use the Systems Analyst's Toolkit for more information on using spreadsheet and presentation software to help you communicate effectively.

SYSTEM OBSOLESCENCE

Even with the best support, at some point every system becomes obsolete. For example, you might not remember the punch cards shown in Figure 12-9, which were essential in the 1960s. System obsolescence can be anticipated in several ways and should never come as a complete surprise.

A system becomes **obsolete** when its functions are no longer required by users or when the platform becomes outmoded. The most common reason for discontinuing a

Figure 12-9   At one time, punch cards represented state-of-the-art processing. As technology changed, punch cards became obsolete. To be competitive, companies must use the newest information systems technology and invest in the future.

system is that it has reached the end of its economically useful life, as indicated by the following signs.

1. The system's maintenance history indicates that adaptive and corrective maintenance is increasing steadily.
2. Operational costs or execution times are increasing rapidly, and routine perfective maintenance does not reverse or slow the trend.
3. A software package is available that provides the same or additional services faster, better, and less expensively than the current system.
4. New technology offers a way to perform the same or additional functions more efficiently.
5. Maintenance changes or additions are difficult and expensive to perform.
6. Users request significant new features to support business requirements.

Systems operation and support continues until a replacement system is installed. Toward the end of a system's operational life, users are unlikely to submit new requests for adaptive maintenance because they are looking forward to the new release. Similarly, the IS staff usually does not perform much perfective maintenance because the system will not be around long enough to justify the cost. A system in its final stages only requires corrective maintenance to keep the system operational. Figure 12-10 shows typical levels of maintenance for a system at this point in the SDLC.

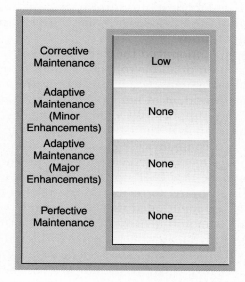

Figure 12-10 All maintenance activities decrease significantly during the final phase of operations as a replacement system is being developed.

In the end, user satisfaction determines the life span of a system. A system will be unable to continue unless users believe that it helps them reach their operational and business goals. If users have problems, the IS staff will be notified. Negative feedback is very important, however, and should be documented because it can be the first signal of system obsolescence.

At some point in a system's operational life, maintenance costs start to increase, users begin to ask for more features and capability, new systems requests are submitted, and the SDLC begins again.

SOFTWEAR, LIMITED   SYSTEMS OPERATION AND SUPPORT

I n mid-December 1999, five months after the final report to management, the payroll package and the ESIP system were operating successfully and users seemed satisfied with both systems.

During this time, users requested minor changes in reports and screen displays, which were handled easily by the IS staff. Jane Rossman, manager of applications, continued to assign a mixture of new systems and maintenance tasks to the IS team, and the members indicated that they enjoyed the variety and challenge of both types of work.

The only operational problem was reported by Debra Williams, the payroll clerk who prints the ESIP checks. She could not load and align the special check stock in the printer correctly. Becky Evans visited Debra to study the situation, and then wrote a specific procedure to solve the problem.

No overtime has been paid in the payroll department since the new system was implemented and errors in payroll deductions have stopped. Michael Jeremy, SWL's vice president of finance, who initiated the payroll and ESIP projects, is very pleased with the system's operation and output. He recently visited an IS department staff meeting to congratulate the entire group personally.

Some requests for enhancements also occurred. Mike Feiner recently submitted a systems request for the ESIP system to produce an annual employee benefits statement with the current value of all savings plan deductions, plus information on insurance coverage and other benefits data. Mike also indicated that several new ESIP choices would be offered during 2000, including various mutual funds.

On December 15, Pacific Software announced the latest release of its payroll package. The new version supports full integration of all payroll and human resources functions and data. Ann Hon, director of information systems, was interested in this announcement because she knew that Tina Pham, SWL's vice president of human resources, wanted a human resources information system (HRIS) to support SWL's long-term needs. At Ann's request, Jane Rossman assigned Becky Evans to analyze the new payroll package to determine if SWL could implement the latest version as a companywide client/server application.

Becky began the preliminary investigation by reviewing the current system and meeting with Mike Feiner to learn more about the new ESIP options. Next, she met with Marty Hoctor, a representative from Pacific Software, to review the features of the new release. After describing the new software, Marty mentioned that the package recently was implemented at a large Midwestern retail chain and invited Becky to contact Fred Brown, director of IS at that company, to discuss the new release. Becky spoke with Fred and he agreed to e-mail her a summary of comments that users had made about the new software.

Becky completed her preliminary investigation, including a cost-benefit analysis, and worked with Jane Rossman and Ann Hon to prepare a report and presentation to SWL's newly formed systems review committee, which had been created at Ann's suggestion. In their presentation, the IS team recommended that SWL upgrade to the new release of the payroll package and build a client/server application for all of SWL's payroll and personnel functions, including the ESIP system. They also suggested that a team of IS and human resources people get together to study preliminary economic, technical, and operational factors involved in a human resources information system, and report back to the systems review committee. They pointed out that if this project is approved, the same team could handle the systems development using JAD or RAD techniques. After the presentation, the committee approved the request and Ann called an IS department staff meeting for the next morning to start planning the systems analysis phase.

During the meeting, Ann and Jane thanked the entire department for its efforts on the payroll and ESIP projects. Ann pointed out that although the payroll package and the ESIP system support SWL's current needs, the business environment changes rapidly and a successful, growing company must investigate new information management technology constantly. At this point, the systems development life cycle for SWL begins again.

YOUR TURN — Now that the new ESIP system is operational, Jane Rossman wants you to track system performance by using various measurements. At a minimum, she expects you to monitor operational costs, maintenance frequency, technical issues, and user satisfaction. You can add other items if you choose.

Write a proposal for Jane that lists each factor you will measure. Be sure to explain why the item is important and how you plan to obtain the information.

ON THE NET

A human resources information system (HRIS) helps a company manage information about its people. Many firms have replaced older personnel record-keeping systems with powerful, state-of-the-art HRIS products. Suppose you are assigned to the SWL team that will study the feasibility of a human resources information system. Your job is to identify several commercial packages and the names of firms or consultants who specialize in HRIS implementation. You can start by using a Web search engine to search for the phrase, human resources information system. Write a brief memo with your findings.

CHAPTER SUMMARY

Systems operation and support covers the entire period from the implementation of an information system until the system is no longer used. A systems analyst's primary involvement with an operational system is to manage and solve user support requests.

Corrective maintenance includes changes to correct errors. Adaptive maintenance satisfies new systems requirements, and perfective maintenance makes the system more efficient. Adaptive and perfective maintenance changes often are called enhancements.

The typical maintenance process resembles a miniature version of the systems development life cycle. A systems request for maintenance work is submitted and evaluated. If it is accepted, the request is prioritized and scheduled for the IS group. The maintenance team then follows a logical progression of investigation, analysis, design, development, testing, and implementation.

Corrective maintenance projects occur when a user or an IS staff member reports a problem. Standard maintenance procedures usually are followed for relatively minor errors, but work often begins immediately when users report significant errors.

In contrast to corrective maintenance, adaptive and perfective maintenance projects always follow the organization's standard maintenance procedures. Adaptive maintenance projects occur in response to user requests for improvements to meet changes in the business or operating environments. Perfective maintenance projects usually are initiated by the IS staff to improve performance or maintainability. Automated program restructuring and reengineering are forms of perfective maintenance.

A maintenance team consists of one or more systems analysts and programmers. Systems analysts need the same talents and abilities for maintenance work as they use when developing a new system. Many IS departments are organized into separate new development and maintenance groups where staff members are rotated from one group to the other.

Configuration management is necessary to handle maintenance requests, to manage different versions of the information system, and to distribute documentation changes. Maintenance changes can be implemented as they are completed or a release methodology can be used in which all non-critical maintenance changes are collected and implemented simultaneously. A release methodology usually is cost-effective and advantageous for users because they do not have to work with a constantly changing system.

System performance measurements include response time, turnaround time, and throughput time. Capacity management uses these measurements to forecast what is needed to provide necessary future levels of service and support.

CASE tools are available to assist you in many aspects of systems operation and support. Maintenance toolkits provide a wide selection of system evaluation and maintenance support tools.

All information systems eventually become obsolete. The end of a system's economic life usually is signaled by rapidly increasing maintenance or operating costs, the availability of new software or hardware, or new requirements that cannot be achieved easily by the existing system. When a certain point is reached, an information system must be replaced, and the entire systems development life cycle begins again.

Review Questions

1. What percentage of an information systems department staff's time typically is spent on maintenance activities?
2. What are the three standard classifications of maintenance?
3. How is enhancement different from maintenance?
4. During which stages of systems operation is corrective maintenance most common?
5. How does adaptive maintenance differ from perfective maintenance?
6. List six typical perfective maintenance projects.
7. Why is perfective maintenance rarely undertaken late in the life of an information system?
8. Which of the three kinds of maintenance is most likely to generate changes to user documentation? Which type is least likely to generate changes?
9. Why are newly hired and recently promoted systems analysts and programmers sometimes assigned to maintenance projects?
10. What is a release methodology? What are the advantages and disadvantages of using a release methodology?
11. Define the following terms: response time, turnaround time, throughput time, and throughput. How are these terms related?
12. What is the purpose of capacity planning?
13. What is a *what-if* analysis? How is *what-if* analysis used in capacity planning?
14. What kinds of tools are found in a CASE maintenance toolkit?
15. List six indications that an information system is nearing the end of its economically useful life.

Discussion Questions

1. Updates to a particular operational inventory control system are controlled with a release methodology. The current version of the system is version 2.3. For each of the maintenance changes listed below, decide whether the release including only that change should be numbered as version 2.4 or version 3.0.

   a. Added optional report
   b. Added graphical screen display
   c. Added input validation check

d. Added interface to the budget control system
e. Additional valid product classification code
f. Additional level in the inventory classification scheme
g. Added capability for producing graphical output on a laser printer
h. Changed order of the printed fields in an existing report
i. More efficient sort procedure
j. Increased limit on the number of different warehouses
k. Renaming a data element
l. Rewriting a program to streamline its execution

2. A manager of new development in the information systems department said, "Maintenance systems analysts and programmers don't need any of the new software tools because they are just patching programs." What arguments would you use to try to change that manager's mind?

3. An IS manager assigns programmers and systems analysts to maintenance projects if they have less than two years of experience or if they received an average or below average rating in their most recent performance evaluation. What misconceptions do you suspect that manager holds?

4. Visit the information systems department at your college or at a local company and investigate which performance and workload measurements are used in its production environment. Present to your class a report of the measurements used and the department's assessment of its effectiveness. If the department does not use any performance or workload measurements, explain its reasons for not doing so.

CASE STUDIES

NEW CENTURY HEALTH CLINIC — SYSTEMS OPERATIONS AND SUPPORT

You implemented the new system at New Century Health Clinic successfully, and the staff has used the system for nearly four months. New Century is pleased with the improvements in efficiency, office productivity, and patient satisfaction.

Some problems have surfaced, however. The office staff members call you almost daily to request assistance and changes in the way certain reports and forms are organized. You try to be helpful, but now you are busy with a major project for a local distributor of exercise equipment. Actually, your contract only required you to provide support during the first three months of operation. Anita Davenport, New Century's office manager, reported that the system seems to slow down at certain times during the day, making it difficult for the staff to keep up with its workload.

Assignments

1. You are willing to provide ongoing support with a lower rate for your services because you designed the system. You want New Century to use a specific procedure for requesting assistance and changes, however. Prepare a complete, written procedure for New Century Health Clinic maintenance change requests. Include appropriate forms with your procedure.

2. What could be causing the periodic slowdowns at New Century? If a problem does exist, which performance and workload measures would you monitor to pinpoint the problem?

3. At the end of the systems analysis phase you studied the economic feasibility of the system and estimated the future costs and benefits. Now that the system is operational, should these costs and benefits be monitored? Why or why not?

4. To your surprise, you receive a call from a large IS consulting firm that wants to interview you for a systems analyst position. The position would involve handling projects for several major corporations, and you are quite excited about the opportunity.

You know that the firm will ask you about your experiences on the New Century project. To prepare for the meeting, write a memo that describes the highlights of your work at New Century. You should list any significant experiences, including the following:

- What was the most difficult part of the project, and why?
- What was the easiest part of the project, and why?
- If you had the project to do again, what would you do differently?
- List the most important skills you gained during the project.
- Will this project help you in your future IS career? How?
- Suppose that three years from now you are working as a manager outside of the IS department. Will your experiences on the New Century project be of value to you? Why or why not?

HOOBER INDUSTRIES

The production support system is a complex online information system that runs 24 hours a day in all production shop areas at Hoober Industries. The current production support system was developed in-house and implemented less than two months ago. Last Monday morning, the system developed a problem. When a screen display of certain part master file records was requested, the displayed values were garbled.

When she was alerted to the situation, Marsha Stryker, manager of applications maintenance in the information systems department at Hoober Industries, immediately assigned Eric Wu, a maintenance systems analyst, to the problem. Marsha instructed Eric to fix the system and resume operations as soon as possible. Eric previously worked on two small maintenance projects for the production control system so he was somewhat familiar with the application.

Eric worked the rest of the day on the problem and by 6:30 in the evening, he developed and implemented a fix. After verifying that the production support system again was capable of producing correct part master file record displays, Eric went home. Early the following morning, Eric and two other members of the applications maintenance group were called to a meeting in Marsha's office, where she briefed them on a new adaptive maintenance project for another high-priority system. She asked them to begin work on the new project immediately.

Several nights later, the production control system crashed shortly after midnight. Every time the system was reactivated by a computer operations operator, it crashed again. Finally, around 2:30 A.M., all production lines were shut down and all third-shift production workers were sent home. The production support system finally was corrected and full production was restored at noon, but by that time, Hoober Industries had incurred thousands of dollars in lost production costs. The cause of the production support system crash was identified as a side effect of the fix that Eric made to the system.

Assignments

1. Is the second production support system failure entirely unexpected?
2. Who is most to blame for the second system failure?
3. What might Marsha have done differently to avoid this situation? What might Eric have done differently?
4. Outline a new set of maintenance procedures that will help Hoober Industries avoid such problems in the future.

GALLAGHER IMPORTS

An online sales information system recently was developed and implemented at Gallagher Imports. Using a client/server design, the PCs in each of Gallagher's 12 retail stores were networked with a minicomputer located in the sales support center at the main office. Salespeople in the retail stores use the customer sales information system to record sales transactions; to open, close, or query customer accounts; and to print sales receipts, daily sales reports by salesperson, and daily sales reports by merchandise code. The sales support staff uses the system to query customer accounts and print various daily, weekly, and monthly reports.

When the customer sales system was implemented, the IS department conducted extensive training for the salespeople and the sales support center staff. One member of the systems development team also prepared a user manual, but users are familiar with the system so the manual rarely is used.

Two weeks ago, Gallagher Imports opened two additional stores and hired six new sales representatives. The new sales representatives were given the user manual and asked to read it and experiment with the system.

Now, the salespeople in both new stores are having major problems using the sales system. When a representative from the main office visited the stores to investigate the problem, she discovered that the new people could not understand the user manual. When she asked for examples of confusing instructions, several salespeople pointed to the following samples:

1. Obtaining the authorization of the store manager on Form RBK-23 is required before the system can activate a customer charge account.

2. Care should be exercised to ensure that the Backspace key is not pressed when the key on the numeric keypad with a left-facing arrow is the appropriate choice to accomplish nondestructive backspacing.

3. To prevent report generation interruption, the existence of sufficient paper stock should be verified before any option that requires printing is selected. If not, the option must be reselected.

4. The F2 key should be pressed in the event that a display of valid merchandise codes is required. That same key terminates the display.

Assignments

1. What policies or procedures could have been established to avoid this situation?

2. Should the sales support staff ask the IS department to rewrite the user manual as a maintenance project, or should they request a training session for the new salespeople? Can you offer any other suggestions?

3. Rewrite the user manual instructions so they are clear and understandable for new users. What steps might you take to ensure the accuracy of the new user manual instructions?

4. In the process of rewriting the user manual instructions, you discover that some of the instructions were not changed to reflect system maintenance and upgrade activities. Form RBK-23, for example, has been replaced by a request form on the firm's intranet. Gallagher also has phased out printed reports in favor of online reports, which users can view by entering a user name and password. Rewrite the user manual instructions to reflect these changes.

The Systems Analyst's Toolkit

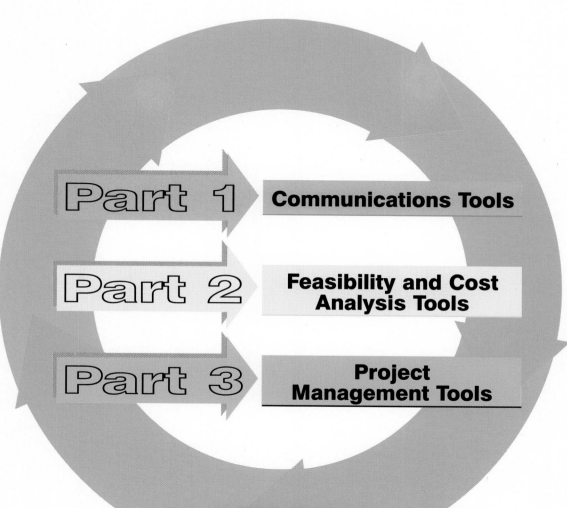

Part 1 — Communications Tools

Part 2 — Feasibility and Cost Analysis Tools

Part 3 — Project Management Tools

TOOLKIT

The Systems Analyst's Toolkit presents a valuable set of cross-phase skills and techniques that you can use throughout the systems development life cycle. The Toolkit includes three important keys to success as a systems analyst. Part 1 describes communications tools that can help you write clearly, speak effectively, and deliver powerful presentations. Part 2 demonstrates economic analysis tools you can use to measure project feasibility, develop accurate cost-benefit estimates, and make sound decisions. Part 3 explains project management tools that can help you organize, plan, and manage IS projects to a successful conclusion.

PART 1

The Systems Analyst's Toolkit

Communications Tools

 *In Part One, you will learn about communications skills that are important to the systems analyst.*

OBJECTIVES

When you finish this section, you will be able to:

- List the guidelines for successful communications
- Explain the importance of effective letters, memos, and e-mail communication
- Describe the organization of written reports that are required during the SDLC and explain each report section
- List the guidelines for effective oral communication
- Organize and plan an oral presentation
- Review important speaking techniques

INTRODUCTION

A successful systems analyst must have good written and oral communications skills to perform his or her job effectively. Never underestimate the importance of effective communications whether you are using a memo, e-mail, or an oral presentation to convey your ideas. The following guidelines will help you prepare and deliver effective presentations. Remember, however, that nothing increases your ability to communicate better than practicing these skills.

GUIDELINES FOR SUCCESSFUL COMMUNICATIONS

When you are planning your communications, concentrate on making sure that your communication answers the questions of *why, who, what, when,* and *how.*

1. **Know *why* you are communicating, and *what* you want to accomplish.** Ask yourself the question, Is this communication necessary, and what specific results am I seeking? Your entire communication strategy depends on the results that you need.

2. **Know *who* your targets are.** Chapter 1 describes how the information needs of managers depend on their organizational and knowledge levels. When communicating with management, sometimes a fine line exists between saying enough and saying too much. Each situation is different, so you must use good judgment. You should plan a communication strategy and be alert for feedback from your audience.

3. **Know *what* is expected of you, and *when* to go into detail.** This is directly related to knowing who your targets are and the organizational and knowledge levels of your audience. For example, a vice president might expect less detail and more focus on how a project supports the company's strategic business goals. You must design your communications just as carefully as your systems project. For example, will the recipients expect you to address a specific issue or topic? Will they expect cost estimates or charts? Design your communications based on the answers to these questions.

4. **Know *how* to communicate effectively.** Use the Toolkit and your own experiences and observations of successful and unsuccessful techniques used by others to become a better communicator.

Most importantly, know your subject. Before any presentation, consider what others expect you to know and what questions they will ask. No matter how well you prepare, you will not have an answer for every question. Remember that it is better to say, "I don't know, but I'll find out" rather than to guess.

WRITTEN COMMUNICATIONS

Good writing is important because others often judge you by your writing. If you make a mistake while speaking, your audience probably will forget it. Your written errors, however, might be around for a long time. Grammatical, typographical, and spelling errors distract readers from your message.

If you have not taken a writing course, you should consider doing so. If you have a choice of courses, select one that focuses on business writing. *Any* writing class, however, is worth the effort. Bookstores and libraries have many excellent books on communicating effectively. As you prepare written documents, keep in mind the following suggestions.

For guidelines on enhancing **Written Communication** skills, visit Systems Analysis and Design Toolkit More on the Web.

www.scsite.com/ sad3e/chTK/

1. *Know your audience.* If you are writing for nontechnical readers, use terms that readers will understand.

2. *Use active voice whenever possible.* For example, Tom designed the system, is better than, The system was designed by Tom.

3. *Keep your writing concise.*

4. *Use one paragraph to convey a single idea.*

5. *Use the right style.* Use a conversational tone in informal documents and a business tone in formal documents.

6. *Use lists.* When you must enumerate a number of subtopics related to the same topic, lists are an organized way to present them.

7. *Use short, easy-to-understand words.* Your objective is not to impress your audience with the size of your vocabulary.

8. *Check your work.* Look for grammatical and typographical mistakes and correct them.

9. *Avoid repeating the same word too often.* Use a **thesaurus** to locate synonyms for frequently repeated words. Many word processing programs include a thesaurus and other tools to help you write better.

10. *Check your spelling*. You can use the **spell checker** in your word processing program to check your spelling, but remember that a spell checker identifies only those words that do not appear in the program's dictionary. You should proofread your documents. The spell checker will not identify instances when you use the word, their, instead of the word, there.

Memos, Letters, and E-mail

Most companies have a standard format for internal letters and memos. When you are preparing documents, you can use a word processor to create templates with specific layouts, fonts, and margin settings. **Templates** will give your work a consistent look and make your job easier. Some word processing programs even provide a feature that allows you to fill in the blanks as you work.

Many companies now use e-mail as a standard form of written correspondence. **E-mail** usually is less formal than other written communication, but you still must follow the rules of good grammar, spelling, and clear writing. Although many authors use a more conversational style for e-mail, you should remember that e-mail messages often are forwarded to other recipients or groups, and so they are as important as any other form of written communication. If you regularly exchange messages with a specific group of users, most e-mail programs allow you to create a distribution list that includes the members and their e-mail addresses. For example, Figure 1 shows how to use Microsoft Outlook to send a memo to a four-person systems development team.

> For more information on using **E-mail** effectively, visit Systems Analysis and Design Toolkit More on the Web.
>
> **www.scsite.com/ sad3e/chTK/**

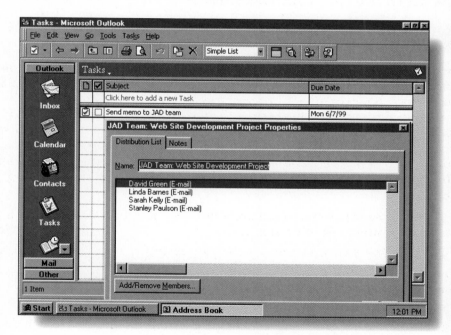

Figure 1   Microsoft Outlook is a desktop information management program that allows users to create distribution lists for sending e-mail messages.

Reports

You must prepare many reports during the SDLC, including the preliminary investigation report, the system requirements document at the end of the systems analysis phase, the system design specification at the end of the system design phase, and the final report to management when the system goes into operation. You also might submit other reports such as status reports, activity reports, proposals, and departmental business plans.

You can use a basic format for all your reports and make modifications as needed. Depending on the type of report and the subject matter, the written document can include the following elements: cover letter, title page, table of contents, summary, findings and conclusions, alternatives, recommendations, and an appendix. Figure 2 shows a typical binder for a system requirements document that includes all these sections. The elements of this report are described next.

A **cover letter** usually is addressed to the systems review committee or to management. Use the cover letter to identify the attached report and set a date, time, and place

Figure 2   Typical binder for a system requirements document.

for the oral presentation. You also can request that the recipients read the report in advance of the presentation.

The **introduction** usually includes a title page, table of contents, and brief description of the proposal. The **title page** should be clean and neat and contain the name of the proposal, the subject, the date, and the names of the development team members. If the project already has a recognized name or acronym, use it. Include a **table of contents** when the report is long or includes many exhibits. Many word processing programs include a tool that can generate a table of contents automatically.

The **summary** is used to summarize the entire project, including your recommendations, in several paragraphs. Generally, the summary should not exceed 200 words or one page.

Use the **findings** section to describe the major conclusions that you or the team reached during the systems analysis phase. The findings section can be detailed or summarized, depending on the project. You must explain the logical design of the new system in a way that nontechnical managers can understand clearly. With a management audience, the most important task is to explain how the proposed system supports the company's business needs.

The **recommendations** section presents the best system alternative, with a brief explanation that does not disparage anyone who favors a different alternative. The essential factors of economic, technical, and operation feasibility should be mentioned in your recommendation.

The **alternatives** section can be a separate section, or part of the recommendations section. The alternatives section identifies various strategies and alternatives, as discussed in Chapter 5. In the alternatives section, you should list the advantages and disadvantages of each major system alternative. In this section, you should include the cost-benefit results, with a clear description of the economic analysis techniques that were used. You can use tables or graphs to support and clarify your alternatives when necessary.

When you have a large number of supporting documents such as questionnaires or sampling results, you should put these items in an **appendix**. Make sure you include only relevant information, and provide references for interested readers.

ORAL COMMUNICATION

An **oral presentation** is required at the end of the preliminary investigation and again at the conclusion of the systems analysis phase. You might need to give more than one presentation in some situations to present technical material to members of the IS department or to present an overview for top managers. When preparing an oral presentation, keep in mind the following suggestions: define the audience, define the objectives for your presentation, organize the presentation, define any technical terms you will use, prepare your presentation aids, and practice your material.

Define the Audience

Before you develop a detailed plan for a management presentation, you must define the audience. For vice presidents and senior managers, you should provide less detail and a strategic overview.

Define the Objectives

When you communicate, you should focus on your objectives. In the management presentation for the systems analysis phase, your goals are to:

- Inform management of the status of the current system
- Describe your findings concerning the current system problems
- Explain the alternative solutions that you developed
- Provide detailed cost and time estimates for the alternative solutions
- Recommend the best alternative and explain the reasons for your selection

Organize the Presentation

Plan your presentation in three stages: the introduction, the information, and the summation. First, you should introduce yourself and describe your objectives. During the presentation, make sure that you discuss topics in a logical order. Be as specific as possible when presenting facts — your listeners want to hear your views about what is wrong, how it can be fixed, and how much it will cost. In your conclusion, briefly summarize the main points, and then ask for questions.

Define Any Technical Terms

You should avoid specialized or technical terminology whenever possible. If your audience might be unfamiliar with a term that you plan to use, either define the term or find another way to say it so your material will be understood.

Prepare Presentation Aids

For additional suggestions on giving **Presentations**, visit Systems Analysis and Design Toolkit More on the Web.

www.scsite.com/ sad3e/chTK/

Studies show that 75 percent of everything learned is acquired visually, so you should use helpful, appropriate visual aids to help the audience follow the logic of your presentation and hold their attention. Visual aids also can direct audience attention *away* from you, which is helpful if you are nervous when you give the presentation. You can use a visual aid with an outline of topics that will help you stay on track.

Visual aids can help you display a graphical summary of performance trends, a series of cost-benefit examples, or a bulleted list of important points. You can use whiteboards, flip charts, overhead transparencies, slides, films, and videotapes to enhance your presentation. When preparing your visual aids, make sure that the content is clear, readable, and easy to understand. Verify ahead of time that the visual material can be seen from anywhere in the room. Remember that equipment can fail unexpectedly, so be prepared with an alternate plan.

With a computer and a projection system, you can use presentation graphics software, such as Microsoft PowerPoint, to create slides with sounds, animation, and graphics. A sample PowerPoint slide is shown in Figure 3, along with an example of the Presentation Conference Wizard, which allows you to deliver a presentation over a company network or the Internet.

When you create a slide show, you should concentrate on preparing the content of your presentation first, and then focus on visual aids. You should select special effects carefully — too many graphics, colors, or audio and special effects will distract the audience.

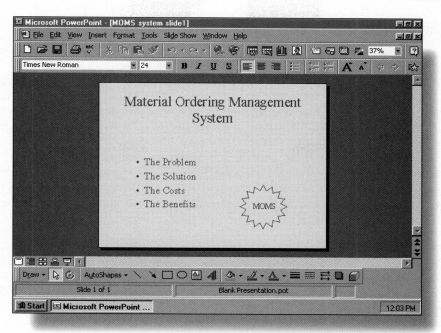

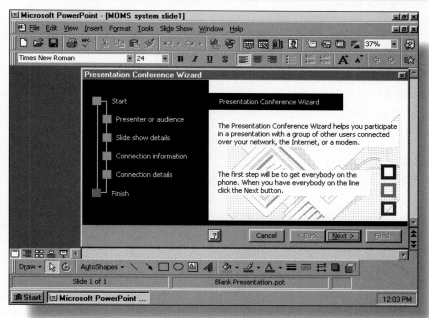

Figure 3   A sample slide created in Microsoft PowerPoint is shown on the top screen. The first Presentation Conference Wizard dialog box displays on the bottom screen.

Practice

The most important part of your preparation is practice. You should rehearse several times to be sure that the presentation flows smoothly and the timing is correct. **Practicing** will make you more comfortable and build your confidence.

Do not be tempted to write a script. If you read your presentation, you will be unable to interact with your audience and adjust your content based on their reactions. Instead, prepare an outline of your presentation and practice from the outline. Then, when you deliver the actual presentation, you will not have to struggle to remember the exact words you planned to say, and you will be able to establish a good rapport with your audience.

The Presentation

When you give the presentation, the following points will help you succeed.

SELL YOURSELF AND YOUR CREDIBILITY • To be successful in a presentation, you must sell yourself and your credibility. A brilliant presentation will not convince top managers that the system should be approved if they are not sold on the person who gave the presentation. On the other hand, many systems projects are approved because the systems analyst did an excellent sales job.

Your presentation must show confidence about the subject and your recommendations. You should avoid any conflicts with the people attending the presentation. If anyone directs critical remarks to you, address the criticisms honestly and directly. You will have a successful presentation only if you know the material thoroughly, prepare properly, and sell yourself and your credibility effectively.

CONTROL THE PRESENTATION • During the presentation, you must control the discussion, maintain the pace of the presentation, and stay focused on the agenda — especially when answering questions. Although you might be more familiar with the subject material, you must not appear to be taking a superior attitude toward your listeners. Maintain eye contact with the audience and use some humor, but do not insert irrelevant jokes or make a joke at someone else's expense.

ANSWER QUESTIONS APPROPRIATELY • Let your audience know whether you would prefer to take questions as you go along or have a question and answer session at the end. Sometimes the questions can be quite difficult. You must listen carefully and respond with a straightforward answer. Try to anticipate the questions your audience will ask so you can prepare your responses ahead of time.

When answering a difficult or confusing question, repeat the question in your own words to make sure that you understand it. For example, you can say, "If I understand your question, you are asking whether …". This will help avoid confusion and give you a moment to think on your feet. To make sure that you gave a clear answer, you can say, "Have I answered your question?" Allow follow-up questions when necessary.

USE GOOD SPEAKING TECHNIQUES • The delivery of your presentation is just as important as its content. You can strengthen your delivery by speaking clearly and confidently and projecting a relaxed approach. You also must control the pace of your delivery. If you speak too fast, you will lose the audience and if the pace is too slow, people lose their concentration and the presentation will not be effective.

Many speakers are nervous when facing an audience. If this is a problem for you, keep the following suggestions in mind.

1. *Control your environment.* If you are most nervous when the audience is looking at you, use visual aids to direct their attention away from you. If your hands are shaking, do not hold your notes. If you are delivering a computer slide show, use the keyboard to advance to the next slide instead of using the mouse. Concentrate on using a strong, clear voice. If your nervousness distracts you, take a deep breath and remind yourself that you really do know your subject.

2. *Turn your nervousness to your advantage.* Many people do their best work when they are under a little stress. Think of your nervousness as normal pressure.

3. *Avoid meaningless filler words and phrases.* Using words and phrases such as okay, all right, you know, like, um, and ah are distracting and serve no purpose.

4. *Practice! Practice! Practice!* Some people are naturally gifted speakers, but most people need lots of practice. You must work hard at practicing your presentation and building your confidence. Many schools offer a speech or public speaking course that is an excellent way of practicing your skills.

SUMMARY

our success as a systems analyst depends on your ability to communicate effectively. You must know why you are communicating, what you want to accomplish, who your targets are, what is expected of you — and when to go into detail. You must know your subject and how to use good written and oral communications techniques.

You will be judged by your written work, so it must be free of grammatical, spelling, and punctuation errors. Your letters and memos should be written clearly and the writing style should match the situation. Many companies have standard formats for letters and memos, and you can use word processing templates to achieve consistency.

You will prepare various reports during the SDLC and the format will vary depending on the nature of the report. Your reports should have a cover memo and might include a title page, table of contents, summary or abstract, description of alternatives, your recommendations, and an appendix.

In addition to written communications, you must communicate effectively in person. You might be required to deliver several presentations to different audiences at different times during the SDLC. Presentations are an important form of oral communication and you should follow specific guidelines in preparing your presentation. You prepare by defining your audience, identifying your objectives, and organizing the presentation itself. You also need to define technical terms and prepare visual aids to help your audience understand the material. Most importantly, you must practice your delivery to gain confidence and strengthen your presentation skills.

When you give the presentation, you are selling your ideas and your credibility. You must control the discussion, build a good rapport with the audience, answer all questions clearly and directly, and try to use good speaking techniques. Again, the best way to become a better speaker is to practice.

Review Questions

1. Describe the *who, what, when, where,* and *why* of communications. Explain each term and give an example.

2. Mention five specific techniques you can use to improve your written documents.

3. What is the role of e-mail communication? What techniques can you use to become an effective e-mail communicator?

4. What are the main sections of a written report to management, and what is the purpose of each section?

5. What are five things you can do to prepare an effective oral presentation?

6. When you organize your presentation, what three main stages do you plan?

7. Why are visual aids important? Give at least three examples of different types of visual aids, with a specific example of how you would use each type in an actual presentation. You can use the SWL case or make up your own scenario.

8. What should you do during the delivery of your presentation to improve the success of the presentation?

9. Name three specific activities you can do if you get nervous during a presentation.

10. Why is practice so important when preparing a presentation?

PART 2

The Systems Analyst's Toolkit

Feasibility and Cost Analysis Tools

In Part Two, you will learn about the feasibility and cost analysis tools that are used in the preliminary investigation and during the systems analysis phase.

OBJECTIVES

When you finish this section, you will be able to:

- Define economic feasibility
- Identify the cost considerations that analysts consider throughout the SDLC
- Understand chargeback methods and how they are used
- Use cost-benefit analysis, payback analysis, return on investment analysis, and present value analysis

INTRODUCTION

Chapter 2 contains a brief overview of economic feasibility. A project is **economically feasible** if the future benefits outweigh the estimated costs of developing or acquiring the new system. In this section of the Systems Analyst's Toolkit, you will learn how to calculate a project's costs and benefits. As a systems analyst, you need to know how to calculate a project's costs and benefits when conducting a preliminary investigation, evaluating projects, and making recommendations to management.

DESCRIBING COSTS AND BENEFITS

As a systems analyst, you must analyze a project's costs and benefits at the end of each SDLC phase so management can decide whether or not to continue the development effort. Before you can use the economic analysis tools described in this section of the Toolkit, you must learn how to identify and classify all costs and benefits.

Cost Classifications

Costs can be classified as tangible or intangible, direct or indirect, fixed or variable, and developmental or operational. **Tangible costs** are costs for which you can assign a specific dollar value. Examples of tangible costs include employee salaries, hardware and software purchases, and office supplies. In contrast, **intangible costs** are costs whose dollar value cannot be calculated easily. The cost of customer dissatisfaction, lowered employee morale, and reduced information availability are examples of intangible costs. If the analyst examines an intangible item carefully, however, it sometimes is possible to estimate a dollar value. For example, users might dislike a system because it is difficult to learn. Their dissatisfaction is an intangible cost, but if it translates into an increase in errors that must be corrected, you probably could assign a tangible dollar cost. You should try to work with tangible costs whenever possible.

Direct costs are costs that can be associated with the development of a specific system. Examples of direct costs include the salaries of project team members and the purchase of hardware that is used only for the new system. In contrast, **indirect costs**, or **overhead expenses**, cannot be attributed to the development of a particular information system. The salaries of network administrators, copy machine rentals, and insurance expenses are examples of indirect costs.

Fixed costs are costs that are relatively constant and do not depend on a level of activity or effort. Many fixed costs recur regularly, such as salaries and hardware rental charges. **Variable costs** are costs that vary depending on the level of activity. The costs of printer paper, supplies, and telephone line charges are examples of variable costs.

Developmental costs are incurred only once at the time the system is developed or acquired. These costs might include salaries of people involved in system development, software purchases, initial user training, and the purchase of necessary hardware or furniture. **Operational costs** are incurred after the system is implemented and continue while the system is in use. Examples might include system maintenance, ongoing training, annual software license fees, and communications expense.

Some costs apply to more than one category of expenses. For example, overtime pay for clerical help during the systems analysis phase might be developmental, variable, and direct; or a monthly fee for maintaining the company's Web site might be operational, fixed, and indirect.

Managing Information Systems Costs and Charges

Management wants to know how much an information system costs, so it is important for the systems analyst to understand direct costs, indirect costs, and methods of allocating IS charges within the company.

Direct costs usually are easier to identify and predict than indirect costs. For example, the salaries of project team members and the purchase of hardware, software, and supplies for the new system are direct costs. After a new information system goes into operation, other direct costs might include the lease of system-specific hardware or software.

Many IS department costs cannot be attributed directly to a specific information system or user group. These indirect costs can include general hardware and software acquisition expenses, facility maintenance, air conditioning, security, rent, insurance, general supplies, and the salaries of operations, technical support, and information center personnel.

A **chargeback method** is a technique that uses accounting entries to allocate the indirect costs of running the IS department. Most organizations adopt one of four chargeback methods: no charge, a fixed charge, a variable charge based on resource usage, or a variable charge based on volumes.

To view an example of a **Chargeback Policy,** visit Systems Analysis and Design Toolkit More on the Web.

www.scsite.com/ sad3e/chTK/

1. **No charge.** Some organizations treat information systems department indirect expenses as a necessary cost of doing business, and IS services are seen as benefiting the entire company. Thus, indirect IS department costs are treated as general organizational costs and are not charged to other departments. In this case, the information systems department is called a **cost center** because it generates accounting charges with no offsetting credits for IS services.

2. **Fixed charge.** With this method, the indirect IS costs are divided among all the other departments in the form of a fixed monthly charge. The monthly charge might be the same for all departments or based on a relatively constant factor such as department size or number of workstations. By using a fixed charge approach, all indirect costs are charged to other departments and the IS group is regarded as a profit center. A **profit center** is a department that is expected to break even or show a profit. Under the profit center concept, company departments purchase services from the IS department and receive accounting charges that represent the cost of providing the services.

3. **Variable charge based on resource usage. Resource allocation** is the charging of indirect costs based on the resources used by an information system. The allocation might be based on connect time, CPU time, data communication lines required, printer use, or a combination of similar factors. **Connect time** is the total time that a user is connected actively to a remote computer — many Internet service providers use this as a basis for charges. In a mainframe-based system, **CPU time** is the time that an information system actually executes and uses the central processing unit. The amount a particular department is charged will vary from month to month, depending not only on that department's resource usage, but also on the total resource usage. The information systems department is considered a profit center when an organization uses the resource allocation method.

4. **Variable charge based on volume.** The indirect information systems department costs are allocated to other departments based on user-oriented activity, such as the number of transactions or printing volume. As with the resource allocation method, a department's share of the costs varies from month to month, depending on the level of activity. In this case, the information systems department is considered a profit center.

Benefit Classifications

In addition to classifying costs, you must classify the benefits that a project is expected to provide. Like costs, benefits can be classified as tangible or intangible, fixed or variable, and direct or indirect. Another useful benefit classification relates to the nature of the benefit: positive benefits versus cost-avoidance benefits. **Positive benefits** increase revenues, improve services, or otherwise contribute to the organization as a direct result of the new information system. Examples of positive benefits include improved information availability, greater flexibility, faster service to customers, higher employee morale, and better inventory management.

In contrast, **cost-avoidance benefits** refer to expenses that would be necessary if the new system is *not* installed. Examples of cost-avoidance benefits include handling the work with current staff instead of hiring additional people, not having to replace existing hardware or software, and avoiding problems that would otherwise be faced with the current system. Cost-avoidance benefits are just as important as positive benefits, and you must consider both types when performing cost-benefit analysis.

COST-BENEFIT ANALYSIS

Cost-benefit analysis is the process of comparing the anticipated costs of an information system to the anticipated benefits. Cost-benefit analysis is performed throughout the SDLC to determine the economic feasibility of an information system project and to compare alternative solutions. Many cost-benefit analysis techniques exist. This section covers discussion of only the three most common methods: payback analysis, return on investment analysis, and present value analysis. Each of these approaches analyzes cost-benefit figures differently, but the objective is the same: to provide reliable information for making decisions.

For more information on **Cost-Benefit Analysis**, visit Systems Analysis and Design Toolkit More on the Web.

www.scsite.com/ sad3e/chTK/

Payback Analysis

Payback analysis is the process of determining how long it takes an information system to pay for itself. The time it takes to recover the system's cost is called the **payback period**. To do a payback analysis, you perform the following steps:

1. Determine the initial development cost of the system.
2. Estimate annual benefits.
3. Determine annual operating costs.
4. Find the payback period by comparing total development and operating costs to the accumulated value of the benefits produced by the system.

When you plot the system costs over the potential life of the system, you typically see a curve like the one shown in Figure 4. After the system is operational, costs decrease rapidly and remain relatively low for some period. Eventually, as the system requires more maintenance, costs begin to increase. The period between the beginning of systems operation and a point when operational costs are rapidly increasing is called the **economically useful life** of the system. When you plot the benefits provided by an information system against time, the resulting curve usually resembles the one shown in Figure 5 on the next page. Benefits start to appear when the system becomes operational, might increase for a time, and then level off or begin to decline.

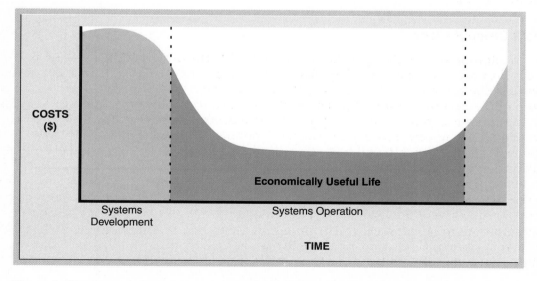

Figure 4   The costs of a typical system vary over time. At the beginning, system costs are high due to initial development expense. Costs then drop during systems operation. Maintenance costs begin to increase until the system reaches the end of its economically useful life. The area between the two dashed lines shows the economically useful life of this system.

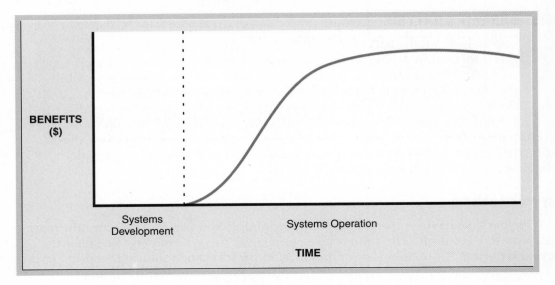

Figure 5   The benefits of an information system change over time. Benefits are not realized until the system becomes operational. Then, benefits usually increase rapidly at first before leveling off.

When conducting a payback analysis, you calculate the time it takes for the accumulated benefits of an information system to equal the accumulated costs of developing and operating the system. In Figure 6, the cost and benefit curves are plotted on the same graph. The dashed line indicates the payback period. Notice that the payback period is *not* the point when current benefits equal current costs, where the two lines cross. Instead, the payback period compares *accumulated* costs and benefits. If you graph current costs and benefits, the payback period corresponds to the time at which the *areas* under the two curves are equal.

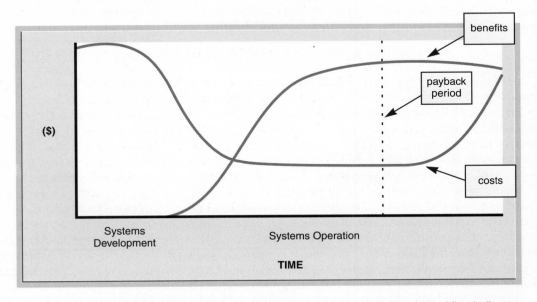

Figure 6   A system's costs and benefits are plotted on the same graph. The dashed line indicates the payback period, when accumulated benefits equal accumulated costs.

Figure 7 contains two cost-benefit tables. The tables show the anticipated annual costs, cumulative costs, annual benefits, and cumulative benefits for two information systems projects. Year 0 (zero) corresponds to the year in which systems development begins. The development of Project A takes less than one year, so some benefits are realized in Year 0. Systems development for Project B requires more than one year, so the benefits do not begin until some time in Year 1.

PROJECT A:

YEAR	COSTS	CUMULATIVE COSTS	BENEFITS	CUMULATIVE BENEFITS
0	60,000	60,000	3,000	3,000
1	17,000	77,000	28,000	31,000
2	18,500	95,500	31,000	62,000
3	19,200	114,700	34,000	96,000
4	21,000	135,700	36,000	132,000
5	22,000	157,700	39,000	171,000
6	23,300	181,000	42,000	213,000

Payback period is approximately 4.2 years

PROJECT B:

YEAR	COSTS	CUMULATIVE COSTS	BENEFITS	CUMULATIVE BENEFITS
0	80,000	80,000	——	——
1	40,000	120,000	6,000	6,000
2	25,000	145,000	26,000	32,000
3	22,000	167,000	54,000	86,000
4	24,000	191,000	70,000	156,000
5	26,500	217,500	82,000	238,000
6	30,000	247,500	92,000	330,000

Payback period is approximately 4.7 years

Figure 7   Payback analysis data for two information systems proposals: Project A and Project B.

In Project A, by the end of Year 4, the cumulative costs are $135,700, which slightly exceeds the $132,000 cumulative benefits through that year. By the end of Year 5, however, the $171,000 cumulative benefits far exceed the cumulative costs, which are $157,700. At some point in time, between the end of Year 4 and the end of Year 5, closer to the beginning of Year 5, the accumulated costs and benefits are equal. The payback period for Project A is, therefore, approximately 4.2 years. By a similar process, the payback period for Project B is determined to be approximately 4.7 years.

Some managers are critical of payback analysis because it places all the emphasis on early costs and benefits and ignores the benefits received *after* the payback period. Even if the benefits for Project B in Year 6 soared as high as $500,000, the payback period for that project still is 4.7 years. In defense of payback analysis, the earlier cost and benefit predictions usually are more certain. In general, the further you extend your projections, the more unsure your forecast will be. Thus, payback analysis uses the most reliable of your cost and benefit estimates.

Payback analysis rarely is used to compare or rank projects because later benefits are ignored. You would never decide that Project A is better than Project B simply because the payback period for A is less than that for B; considering all the costs and all the benefits when comparing projects makes more sense.

Even with its drawbacks, payback analysis is a widely used tool. Many business organizations establish a minimum payback period for approved projects. If company policy requires a project to begin paying for itself within three years, then both projects in Figure 7 on the previous page are economically feasible, but neither project meets the three-year payback requirement.

Using a Spreadsheet to Compute Payback Analysis

You can use a spreadsheet to record and calculate accumulated costs and benefits, as shown in Figures 8a and 8b. The first step is to design the worksheet and label the rows and columns. After entering the cost and benefit data for each year, you can enter your formulas.

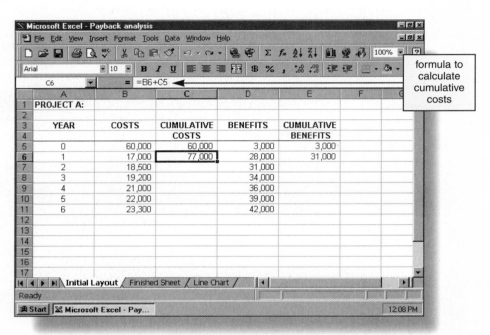

Figure 8a   A Microsoft Excel worksheet showing payback analysis data for Project A.

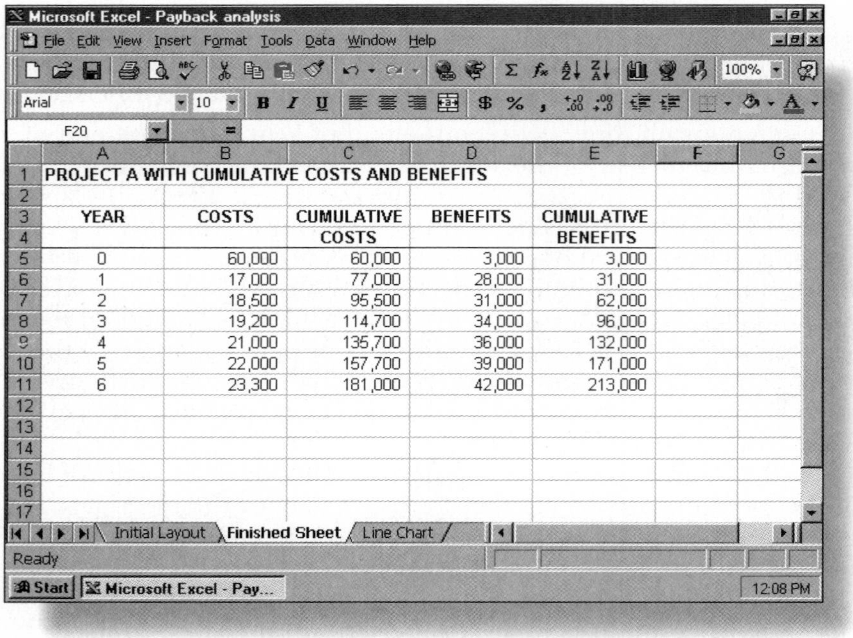

Figure 8b   The finished payback analysis worksheet in Microsoft Excel.

For payback analysis, you will need a formula to display cumulative totals, year by year. For example, the first year in the CUMULATIVE COSTS column is the same as Year 0 costs, so the formula in cell C5 is =B5. The cumulative cost total for the second year is Year 0 cumulative total + Year 1 costs, so the formula for cell C6 is =C5+B6, and so on. Figure 8a shows the initial layout and Figure 8b shows the finished worksheet.

After you verify that the spreadsheet operates properly, you can create a line chart that displays the cumulative costs and benefits. Figure 9 shows a Microsoft Excel chart, but any spreadsheet program can be used.

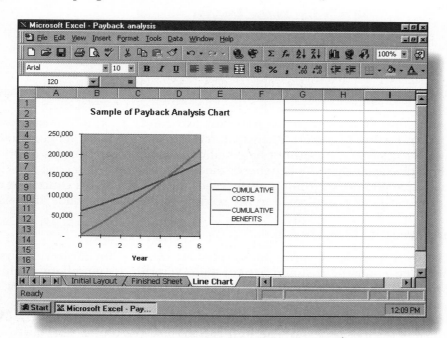

Figure 9 A Microsoft Excel chart showing cumulative costs and benefits.

To learn more about measuring **ROI**, visit Systems Analysis and Design Toolkit More on the Web.

www.scsite.com/ sad3e/chTK/

Return on Investment Analysis

Return on investment (**ROI**) is a percentage rate that measures profitability by comparing the total *net* benefits (the return) received from a project to the total costs (the investment) of the project. ROI is calculated as follows:

ROI = (total benefits - total costs) / total costs

Return on investment analysis considers costs and benefits over a longer time span than payback analysis. ROI calculations usually are based on total costs and benefits for a period of five to seven years. The tables shown in Figure 7 on page TK.17 include cost and benefit predictions for each of the two information systems during six years of operation. In Figure 10 on the next page, an ROI is calculated for each system. The ROI for Project A is 17.7% and the ROI for Project B is 33.3%.

In many organizations, projects must meet or exceed a minimum ROI. This minimum ROI can be an estimate of the return the organization would receive from investing its money in investment opportunities such as treasury bonds, or it can be a higher rate that the company requires for all new projects. If a company requires a minimum ROI of 15%, for example, then both Projects A and B would meet the criterion.

You also can use ROI for ranking projects. If Projects A and B represent two different proposed solutions for a single information systems project, then the solution represented by Project B is better than the Project A solution. If Projects A and B represent two different information systems projects, and if the organization has sufficient resources to pursue only one of the two projects, then Project B is the better choice.

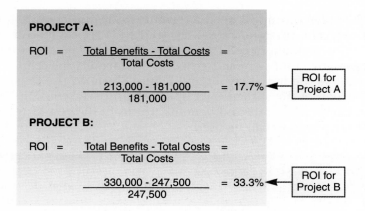

PROJECT A:

ROI =   Total Benefits - Total Costs   =
             Total Costs

             213,000 - 181,000   = 17.7%   ← ROI for Project A
             181,000

PROJECT B:

ROI =   Total Benefits - Total Costs   =
             Total Costs

             330,000 - 247,500   = 33.3%   ← ROI for Project B
             247,500

Figure 10   Return on investment analysis for Project A and Project B shown in Figure 7 on page TK.17.

Critics of return on investment analysis raise two points. First, ROI measures the overall rate of return for the total period, and annual return rates can vary considerably. Two projects with the same ROI might not be equally desirable if the benefits of one project occur significantly earlier than the benefits of the other project. The second criticism is that the ROI technique ignores the timing of the costs and benefits. This concept is called the time value of money, and is explained in the section on the present value analysis method.

Using a Spreadsheet to Compute ROI

You can use a spreadsheet program to calculate the ROI for Project A. First, set up the worksheet and enter the cost and benefit data. You can use cumulative columns (as you did in payback analysis) but you also will need two overall totals   one for costs and one for benefits, as shown in Figure 11.

The last step is to add a formula to calculate the ROI percentage rate, which is displayed in cell C15 in Figure 11. The ROI is total benefits minus total costs, divided by total costs. Therefore, the formula that displays the ROI percentage in cell C15 is =(D12-B12)/B12.

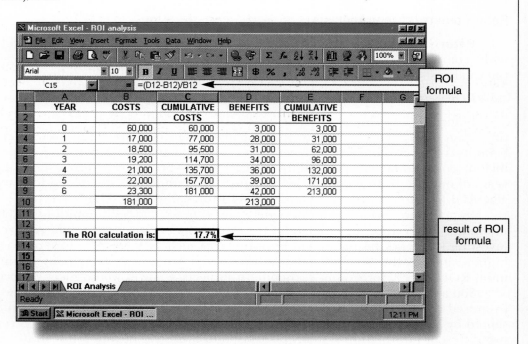

Figure 11   The worksheet for ROI analysis for Project A.

A major advantage of using a spreadsheet is if your data changes, you can modify your worksheet and calculate a new result instantly.

Present Value Analysis

A dollar you have today is worth more than a dollar you do not receive until one year from today. If you have the dollar now, you can invest it and it will grow in value. For example, would you rather have $100 right now or a year from now? The answer should be obvious. If you receive the $100 now, you might invest it in a mutual fund that has an annual return of 8 percent. One year from now, you will have $108 instead of $100.

Alternatively, you might start from a different point of view. Instead of asking, How much will my $100 be worth a year from now? you can ask, How much do I need to invest today, at 8 percent, in order to have $100 a year from now? This concept is known as the **time value of money**, and it is the basis of the technique called **present value analysis**.

The *present* **value** of a *future* dollar is the amount of money that, when invested today at a specified interest rate, grows to exactly one dollar at a certain point in the future. The specified interest rate is called the **discount rate**. In present value analysis, a company uses a discount rate that represents the rate of return if the money is put into relatively risk-free investments, such as bonds, instead of being invested in the project.

Most companies require a rate of return that is higher than the discount rate because of the degree of risk in any project compared to investing in a bond. Companies often reject projects that seem attractive because the risk is not worth the potential reward.

The present value (*PV*) of a dollar *n* years from now at a discount rate is calculated using the following formula:

$$PV = 1 / (1 + i)^n$$

Thus, the present value of $1 one year from now at 8% is:

$$PV = 1 / (1 + .08)^1 = \$0.926$$

Similarly, the present value of $1 five years from now at 12% is:

$$PV = 1 / (1 + .12)^5 = \$0.567$$

To help you perform present value analysis, adjustment factors for various interest rates and numbers of years are calculated and printed in tables called **present value tables**. Figure 12 shows a portion of a present value table, including values for 10 years at various discount rates. Many finance and accounting books contain comprehensive present value tables, or you can locate this information on the Internet, as shown in Figure 13 on the next page.

To learn more about the **Time Value of Money**, visit Systems Analysis and Design Toolkit More on the Web.

www.scsite.com/ sad3e/chTK/

Figure 12 Portion of a present value table showing adjustment factors for various time periods and discount rates. Values in the table are calculated using the formula shown in the text. Notice how the factors decrease as time and percentages increase.

PERIODS	6%	8%	10%	12%	14%
1	0.943	0.926	0.909	0.893	0.877
2	0.890	0.857	0.826	0.797	0.769
3	0.840	0.794	0.751	0.712	0.675
4	0.792	0.735	0.683	0.636	0.592
5	0.747	0.681	0.621	0.567	0.519
6	0.705	0.630	0.564	0.507	0.456
7	0.665	0.583	0.513	0.452	0.400
8	0.627	0.540	0.467	0.404	0.351
9	0.592	0.500	0.424	0.361	0.308
10	0.558	0.463	0.386	0.322	0.270

$PV = 1000 \times$
0.386
1000×0.386
386×1000
$= 386000$

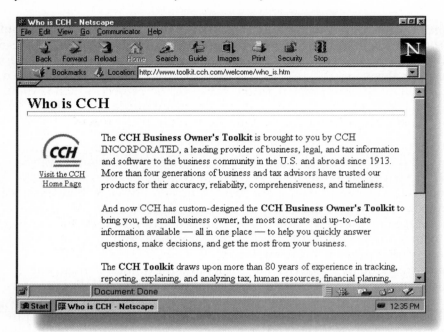

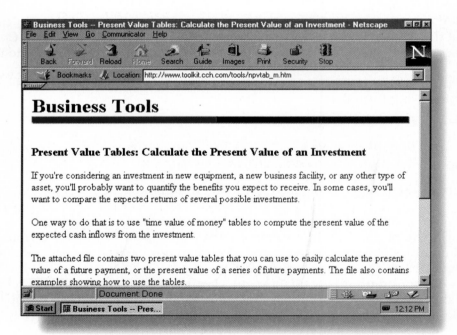

Figure 13   The CCH Web site provides a variety of information to the business community, including present value tables.

To use a present value table, you locate the value in the column with the appropriate discount rate and the row for the appropriate number of years. For example, to calculate the present value of $1 at 12% for five years, you look down the 12% column until you reach the row representing 5 years. The table value is 0.567, which is exactly the same value just calculated. To determine what the present value of $3,000 will be in five years with a discount rate of 12%, multiply the present value factor from the table by the dollar amount; that is, $PV = \$3,000 \times 0.567 = \$1,701$.

To perform present value analysis, you must *time-adjust* the cost and benefit figures. First, you multiply each of the projected benefits and costs by the proper present value factor, which depends on when the cost will be incurred or the benefit will be received. The second step is to sum all the time-adjusted benefits and the time-adjusted costs. Then, you calculate the **net present value** (**NPV**) of the project, which is the total present value of the benefits minus the total present value of the costs. Figure 14 shows the calculation of net present value for each of the two sample projects.

PROJECT A: **PRESENT VALUE ANALYSIS**

	Year 0	Year 1	Year 2	Year 3	Year 4	Year 5	Year 6	Total
Benefits:	3,000	28,000	31,000	34,000	36,000	39,000	42,000	
Present Value Factor (12%):	1.000	0.893	0.797	0.712	0.636	0.567	0.507	
Present Value:	3,000	25,004	24,707	24,208	22,896	22,113	21,294	143,222
Costs:	60,000	17,000	18,500	19,200	21,000	22,000	23,300	
Present Value Factor (12%):	1.000	0.893	0.797	0.712	0.636	0.567	0.507	
Present Value:	60,000	15,181	14,745	13,670	13,356	12,474	11,813	141,239
Net Present Value:							net present value of Project A ⟶	1,983

PROJECT B: **PRESENT VALUE ANALYSIS**

	Year 0	Year 1	Year 2	Year 3	Year 4	Year 5	Year 6	Total
Benefits:	——	6,000	26,000	54,000	70,000	82,000	92,000	
Present Value Factor (12%):	——	0.893	0.797	0.712	0.636	0.567	0.507	
Present Value:	——	5,358	20,722	38,448	44,520	46,494	46,644	202,186
Costs:	80,000	40,000	25,000	22,000	24,000	26,500	30,000	
Present Value Factor (12%):	1.000	0.893	0.797	0.712	0.636	0.567	0.507	
Present Value:	80,000	35,720	19,925	15,664	15,264	15,026	15,210	196,809
Net Present Value:							net present value of Project B ⟶	5,377

Figure 14   Present value analysis for Project A and Project B.

In theory, any project with a positive NPV is economically feasible because the project will produce a larger return than would be achieved by investing the same amount of money in a discount rate investment. Remember that risks are associated with any project, however, and management typically insists on a substantially higher return for high-risk projects. For example, both projects in Figure 14 on the previous page have positive net present values and appear economically worthwhile. Suppose, however, that you knew one of the projects had a 90 percent probability of achieving its goals, while the other project had only a 70 percent chance. To be attractive, the project with the higher risk would have to offer a corresponding higher reward.

Net present values also can be used to compare and rank projects. All things being equal, the project with the highest net present value is the best investment. Figure 14 on the previous page shows that Project B is a better investment than Project A because it has a higher net present value.

Present value analysis provides solutions to the shortcomings of payback analysis and return on investment analysis. Unlike payback analysis, present value analysis considers all the costs and benefits, and not just the earlier values. In addition, present value analysis takes into account the timing of costs and benefits, so their values can be adjusted by the discount rate that provides a common yardstick and recognizes the time value of money. Even so, companies often use all three methods to get more input for making decisions. Sometimes a project will score higher on one method of analysis and lower on another.

Using a Spreadsheet to Calculate Present Value

You can use a worksheet such as the one shown in Figure 15 to calculate the present value based on the data for Project A in Figure 14 on the previous page. You begin by entering the unadjusted cost and benefit values and the discount factors for each year as shown in Figure 14. Next, enter a formula to produce an adjusted value for each cost and benefit entry. To produce an adjusted value, you multiply the cost or benefit value times the discount factor. You can start with cell B8 by entering the formula =B6*B7. Because the factor is 1.000, the 3,000 amount remains unchanged.

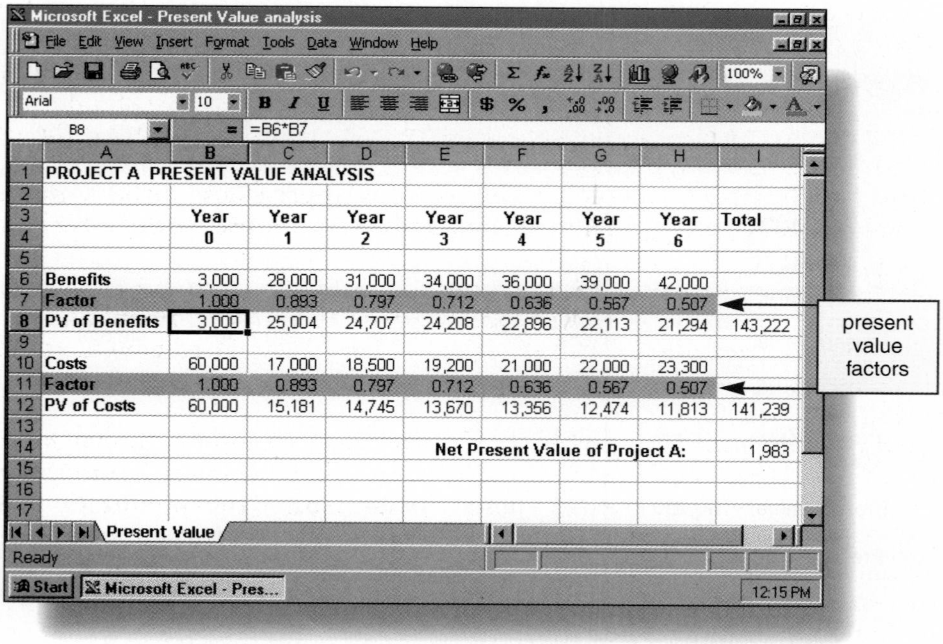

Figure 15   A Microsoft Excel worksheet can be used to calculate present value analysis.

Now, you can copy the formula from cell B8 to cells C8 through H8, and the adjusted values will display. You can total the adjusted benefits in cell I8 with the formula =SUM(B8:H8), and then use the same method for the cost figures. Your final step is to calculate the net present value in cell I14 by subtracting the adjusted costs in cell I12 from the adjusted benefits in cell I8.

One more way exists to use a worksheet in present value analysis. Most spreadsheet programs include a built-in present value function that calculates present value and other time-adjusted variable factors. The program inputs the formula, and then you input the investment amount, discount rate, and number of time periods.

SUMMARY

A s a systems analyst, you must be concerned with economic feasibility throughout the SDLC, and especially during the systems planning and systems analysis phases. A project is economically feasible if the anticipated benefits exceed the expected costs. When you review a project, you work with various feasibility and cost analysis tools.

You must classify project costs as either tangible or intangible, direct or indirect, fixed or variable, and developmental or operational. Tangible costs are those that have a specific dollar value, whereas intangible costs involve items that are difficult to measure in dollar terms, such as employee dissatisfaction. Direct costs can be associated with a particular information system, while indirect costs refer to overhead expenses that cannot be allocated to a specific project. Fixed costs remain the same regardless of activity levels, while variable costs are affected by the degree of system activity. Developmental costs are one-time systems development expenses, while operational costs continue during the systems operation and use phase.

Every company must decide how to charge or allocate information systems costs and the chargeback method. Common chargeback approaches are no charge, a fixed charge, a variable charge based on resource usage, or a variable change based on volume.

Some companies use a no charge approach because IS services benefit the overall organization. This method treats the IS group for accounting purposes as a cost center that offers services without charge. In contrast, if management imposes charges on other departments, the IS department is regarded as a profit center that sells services that would otherwise have to be purchased from outside the company.

You also must classify system benefits. Many benefit categories are similar to costs: tangible or intangible, fixed or variable, and direct or indirect. Benefits also can be classified as positive benefits that result in direct dollar savings or cost-avoidance benefits that allow the firm to avoid costs that would otherwise have been incurred.

Cost-benefit analysis involves three common approaches: payback analysis, return on investment analysis (ROI), and present value analysis. You can use spreadsheet programs to help you work with these tools.

Payback analysis determines the time it takes for a system to pay for itself, which is called the payback period. In payback analysis, you compare total development and operating costs to total benefits. The payback period is the point at which accumulated benefits equal accumulated costs. A disadvantage of this method is that payback analysis only analyzes costs and benefits incurred at the beginning of a system's useful life.

Return on investment analysis (ROI) measures a system by comparing total net benefits (the return) to total costs (the investment). The result is a percentage figure that represents a rate of return that the system offers as a potential investment. Many organizations set a minimum ROI that all projects must match or exceed, and use ROI to rank several projects. Although ROI provides additional information compared to payback analysis, ROI only expresses an overall average rate of return that might not be accurate for a given time period, and ROI does not recognize the time value of money.

Present value analysis adjusts the value of future costs and benefits costs to account for the time value of money. By measuring all future costs and benefits in current dollars, you can compare systems more accurately and consistently. Present value analysis uses mathematical factors that you can derive or look up in published tables. You also can use a spreadsheet function to calculate present value. Many companies use present value analysis to evaluate and rank projects.

Review Questions

1. What is economic feasibility? How do you know if a project is economically feasible?

2. How can you classify costs? Describe each cost classification and provide a typical example for each category.

3. What is a chargeback method? What are four common chargeback approaches?

4. How can you classify benefits? Describe each benefit classification and provide a typical example for each category.

5. Describe cost-benefit analysis, and identify the three main approaches systems analysts use.

6. What is payback analysis and what does it measure?

7. What is a payback period and what is the formula to calculate the payback period?

8. What is return on investment analysis (ROI) and what does it measure?

9. What is the formula to calculate ROI?

10. What is present value analysis and what does it measure?

11. What is the meaning of the phrase, *time value of money*?

12. Present value analysis can be a handy tool for the analyst in many situations. Suppose you are studying two hardware lease proposals, as shown in Figure 16. Lease Option 1 costs only $4,000 but requires that the money be paid up front. Option 2 costs $5,000, but the payments stretch out over a longer period. You performed a present value analysis using a 14% discount rate. What happens if you use an 8% rate? What if you use a 12% rate?

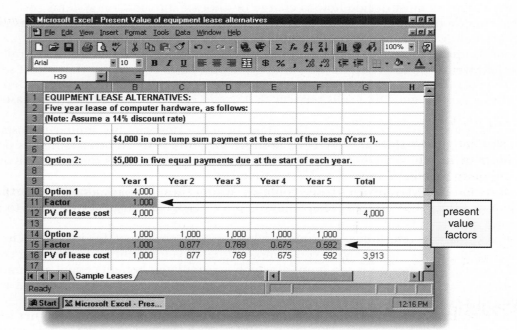

Figure 16   You can use a spreadsheet to evaluate two lease options by applying the present value factors in rows 11 and 15. Even though Option 2 requires the payment of $5,000, it is less expensive when present value is considered.

PART 3

The Systems Analyst's Toolkit

Project Management Tools

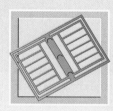

In Part Three, you will learn about project management tools that are important to the systems analyst.

OBJECTIVES

When you finish this section, you will be able to:

- Describe project management tools and how they are used
- Describe the steps used in project planning
- Define the methods used in project estimating
- Describe the different scheduling tools, including Gantt charts and PERT/CPM charts
- Calculate completion times, start dates, and end dates for a project
- Explain the tasks of project monitoring, control, and reporting
- Explain the steps involved in software change control
- Understand the reasons why projects sometimes fail

INTRODUCTION

I n this section, you will learn about project management, cost estimating, and change control for information systems projects. This section discusses planning, estimating, scheduling, monitoring, control, reporting, and the use of project management software. You will learn how to use Gantt charts and PERT/CPM to schedule and monitor projects and how to control and manage project changes.

PROJECT MANAGEMENT

 Project management is the process of defining, planning, organizing, leading, and controlling the development of an information system. Project management is important throughout the entire SDLC but is especially vital during systems implementation, which usually is the longest and most costly phase.

➡ For a comprehensive **Project Management** resource, visit Systems Analysis and Design Toolkit More on the Web.

www.scsite.com/ sad3e/chTK/

Project Management Overview

The goal of project management is to deliver an information system that is acceptable to users and is developed on time and within budget. The acceptability, deadline, and budget criteria *all* must be met for a project to be considered successful. To meet these requirements, you must manage the project carefully and effectively.

Every successful project must have a leader. The **project manager,** or **project leader**, usually is a senior systems analyst or an IS department manager if the project is large. An analyst or a programmer/analyst might manage smaller projects.

In addition to the project manager, most large projects also have a project coordinator. The **project coordinator** handles administrative responsibilities for the development team and negotiates with users who might have conflicting requirements or want changes that would require additional time or expense.

Management Functions

The basic **management functions** are planning, organizing, leading, and controlling. These activities apply to all types of managers, including IS project managers. A project manager's **planning** work includes identifying and planning project tasks and estimating completion times and costs. The **organizing** function consists of staffing, which includes selecting the project team and assigning specific tasks to team members. Organizing also requires structuring and scheduling the project work. **Leading**, or **directing**, involves guiding, supervising, and coordinating the team's workload. Finally, **controlling** activities include monitoring the progress of the project, evaluating results, and taking corrective action when necessary to stay on target.

PROJECT PLANNING

A project plan provides an overall framework for managing costs and schedules. Project planning takes place at the beginning and end of each SDLC phase to develop a plan and schedule for the phases that follow.

The planning process starts with a list of activities, or tasks. An **activity,** or **task,** is any work that has a beginning and an end, and requires the use of company resources including people, time, and/or money. Examples of activities include conducting a series of interviews, designing a report, selecting software, waiting for the delivery of equipment, or training users.

Activities are basic units of work that the project manager plans, monitors, and tracks, so tasks should be relatively small and manageable. For instance, if your project team needs to code five programs, you identify five separate tasks — one for each program — rather than one activity for all five programs.

In addition to activities, every project has events, or milestones. An **event,** or **milestone,** is described as a reference point that marks a major event. Events are used to monitor progress and manage the project. Every activity has two events: one represents the beginning of the task, and the other marks the end of the task. Figure 17 shows a plan for creating and analyzing a questionnaire, with specific activities and events.

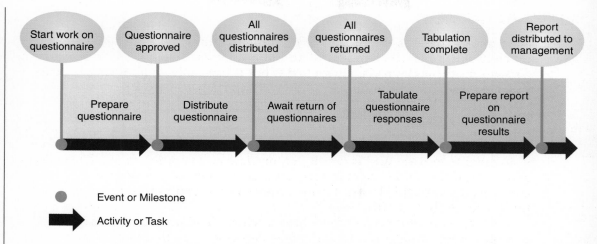

Figure 17   Using a questionnaire requires a series of activities and events to track the progress. The illustration shows the relationship between the activities and the events, or milestones, that mark the beginning and end of each task.

All events must be recognizable. Delivery of equipment, beginning the design of a report, obtaining user approval, completing user training, and completing the tabulation of returned questionnaires are good examples of recognizable events. Completing 50 percent of a program's testing would not be a good milestone, however, unless you could determine exactly when that event occurs.

Project managers must define all activities and events, with estimates of time and costs for each task. Then they stipulate the order of the tasks and develop a work schedule. The final step is to assign tasks to specific members of the project team. As the work is performed, the project manager leads and coordinates the team, monitors events, and reports on progress.

PROJECT ESTIMATING

D etermining precise time estimates for a project is not an easy task, because of the many factors a project manager must consider. One of the most important variables is the size of the project, because the amount of work does not relate directly to the size of the project. If one project is *twice* the size of another project, the larger project will take *more than twice* as many resources to develop. Why is this so?

For example, Figure 18 on the next page shows two projects. Project A has two development team members working on a system with three main programs and four end users. Project B has four people assigned to a system with six programs and eight end users. It appears that Project B is twice as large as Project A. Will Project B require twice as many resources as Project A?

Figure 19 on the next page shows all the possible interactions among the analysts. As you can see, only *one* interaction exists between the two analysts in Project A. Project B, however, has a four-member team, so as many as *six* different interactions can take place. Six times as many relationships can mean more delay, misunderstanding, and difficulty in coordinating tasks.

Also, look at the interfaces among programs, which was discussed in the systems analysis phase. Project A has three programs, so only *three* possible interfaces exist. In contrast, Project B has six programs, so it has *fifteen* possible interfaces, each with its own set of specifications, requirements, and potential problems. Finally, the analysts working on Project B know that it is more complex to satisfy twice as many users and to balance conflicting priorities.

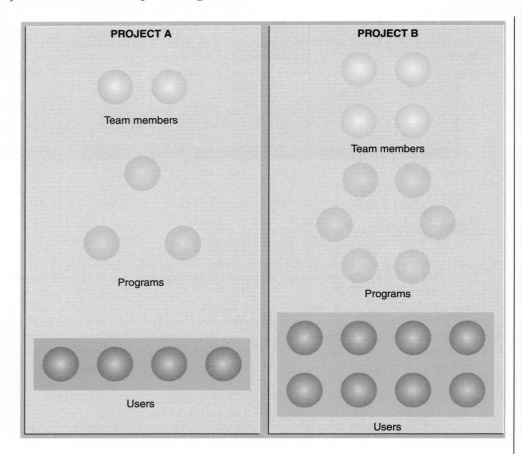

Figure 18   Project A has two team members, three programs, and four end users. Project B has twice as many team members, programs, and users. Is Project B twice as large as Project A?

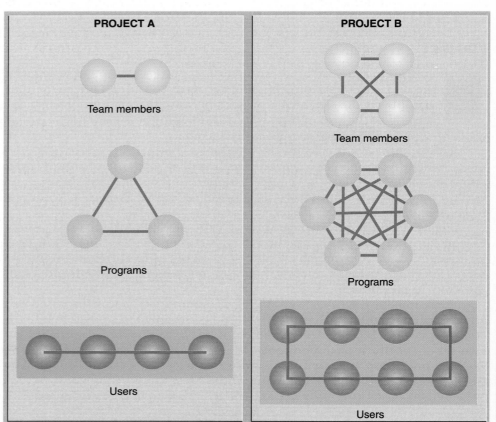

Figure 19   Now the relationships have been drawn. Notice that Project B has six team-member interactions, 15 possible program interfaces, and eight users to satisfy. Project B clearly is more than twice as large as Project A.

Figure 20 shows the relationship between project resources and project size. If doubling the project size requires exactly twice as many resources, then you would draw the dashed line to show a linear relationship. The solid line that shows the required resources, however, will increase much faster than the dashed line that represents project size.

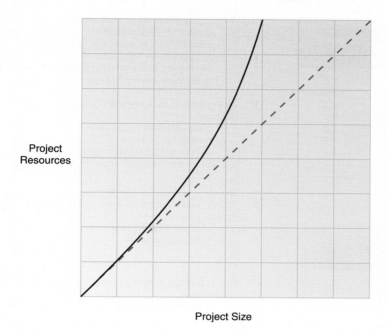

Project Resources

Project Size

Figure 20   As the size of a project grows, the resources needed to develop it will grow even faster.

The capabilities of project team members also affect time requirements. A less experienced analyst usually will need more time to complete a task than an experienced team member will. Other factors that can affect project time requirements include the attitudes of users, the degree of management support, and the priority of the project compared to other projects within the organization.

Time estimates usually are expressed in **person-days** that represent the amount of work that one person can complete in one day. This approach, however, can present some problems. For example, if it will take one person 20 days to perform a particular task, it might not be true that two people could complete the same task in 10 days or that 10 people could perform the task in two days.

Some tasks can be divided evenly so it is possible to use different combinations of time and people, up to a point. For instance, if it takes two person-days to install the cables for a new local area network, the task might be done by one person in two days, two people in one day, or four people in half a day. In most systems analysis tasks, however, time and people are not interchangeable. If one analyst needs two hours to interview a user, two analysts also will need two hours to do the same interview.

Because programming activities represent a significant part of the project, it is important to estimate the time required for these tasks. Project managers typically use three techniques to do this: the quantitative method, the experience method, and the constraint method.

Quantitative Method

The **quantitative method** uses tables and formulas to estimate the time required to develop a single program, as shown in Figure 21a on the next page. Using the quantitative method, the number and types of the files, the functions performed by the program, and the programmer's experience are assigned *weighting points* from the tables.

The weighting points then are combined and a general productivity factor is applied. The result is an estimate of the person-days required, as shown in Figure 21b.

(a)

TABLE 1: FILES AND THEIR CHARACTERISTICS	
File Type	Points
Sequential tape or disk file	0.5
Indexed or direct disk file	1.0
Database file	2.0
Printer report, one line per detail	0.5
Printer report, multiple lines per detail	1.0
Screen display, single screen	1.0
Screen display, multiple screens	3.0

(b)

TABLE 2: PROGRAM FUNCTIONS	
Program Function	Points
Validate	1.0
Complex calculations	1.0
Update files	2.0

(c)

TABLE 3: PROGRAMMER EXPERIENCE	
Position	Points
Programmer/analyst or senior programmer	0.5
Programmer	1.0
Programmer trainee	3.0

Task: Write, test, and document a program that will read and validate a sequential file of transaction records, update an indexed master file, and generate a master file update report and a report of transactions errors. The program will be developed by a programmer with two years of programming experience. Only 70 percent of the programmer's total available time will be spent productively working on the program.

1.   Using Table 1, determine the points based on the files used by the program.

Sequential transaction file	0.5
Indexed master file	1.0
Simple output update report	0.5
Simple output error report	0.5
Total:	2.5

2.   Using Table 2, determine the points based on the program's function.

Validate input transactions	1.0
Update master file	2.0
Total:	3.0

3.   Using Table 3, determine the points based on the programmer's experience.

Programmer position	1.0

4.   Calculate total program points by adding the points based on the files used (step 1) to the points based on the program's functions (step 2).

$$2.5 + 3.0 = 5.5$$

5.   Multiply the total program points (step 4) by the programmer's experience (step 3).

$$5.5 \times 1.0 = 5.5$$

6.   Determine the estimated person-days by dividing the result of step 5 by the productivity factor.

$$5.5/.70 = 7.8 \text{ person-days}$$

Figure 21   In the quantitative method, points are assigned to each program development step, as shown in Tables 1, 2, and 3. The project manager then uses these values to estimate the programming time that will be required.

The productivity factor recognizes that a programmer does not spend eight hours a day on project assignments. Meetings, project reviews, other interactions with people, training, computer unavailability and downtime, vacations, holidays, and sick days all contribute to a reduction in productive time. Figure 21b shows the introduction of an overall factor that adjusts productivity in a single step. A productivity factor of 70 percent for example, indicates that the project manager expects a programmer to be involved in actual productive programming work for an *average* of 5.6 hours per day.

Experience Method

With the **experience method**, the project manager develops project estimates based on the resources used for similar, previously developed information systems. The experience method works best for small- or medium-sized projects where the two systems are similar in size, basic content, and operating environment. In large systems with more variables, the estimates are less reliable.

You might not be able to use experience from projects that were developed in a different environment. For example, when you use a new database package to develop an application, you have no previous experience to measure in this environment. In this situation, you can design a prototype or pilot system to gain technical and cost estimating experience. A **pilot system** is a small system that is developed as a basis for understanding a new environment.

Constraint Method

With the **constraint method**, one or more resources (time, dollars, or personnel) are fixed. Given these limitations, the project manager must define the system requirements that can be achieved realistically within the required constraints. This approach is similar to the *what-if* analysis that was discussed in Chapter 12.

With the quantitative or experience methods, the requirements remain fixed and the analyst calculates the resources needed. In contrast, in the constraint method, one or more resources are fixed, and the analyst either must adjust the other resources or change the requirements themselves.

PROJECT SCHEDULING

I n **project scheduling**, the project manager must know the duration of each activity, the order in which the activities will be performed, the start and end times for each activity, and who will be assigned to each specific task.

Once the time for each activity is estimated, the project manager determines whether certain tasks are dependent on other activities. An activity is **dependent** if it cannot be started until one or more other tasks are completed. You cannot tabulate questionnaires, for example, until they have been developed, tested, approved, distributed, and returned. After the project manager identifies all the activity dependencies, he or she arranges the tasks in a logical sequence.

The next step is to set starting and ending times for each activity. An activity cannot start until all preceding activities on which it depends are completed. The ending time for an activity is its start time plus whatever time it takes to complete the task.

When scheduling a project, project managers must decide how they will assign people to the work. Assignments should not overload or under-utilize team members, and alternate periods of inactivity followed by intense effort can cause problems and should be avoided. Although scheduling can be a difficult task, a project manager must balance activity time estimates, sequences, and personnel assignments to achieve a workable schedule.

SCHEDULING TOOLS

 everal graphical planning aids can help a project manager in the scheduling process. We will examine two of these tools: Gantt charts and PERT/CPM charts.

Gantt Charts

Gantt charts were developed by Henry L. Gantt in 1917 as a production control technique and are still in common use. A **Gantt chart** is a horizontal bar chart that illustrates a schedule. In the Gantt chart shown in Figure 22 on the next page, the analyst displays time on the horizontal axis and arranges the activities vertically, from top to bottom, in the order of their start dates. The horizontal position of the bar shows the start and end of the activity, and the length of the bar indicates its duration.

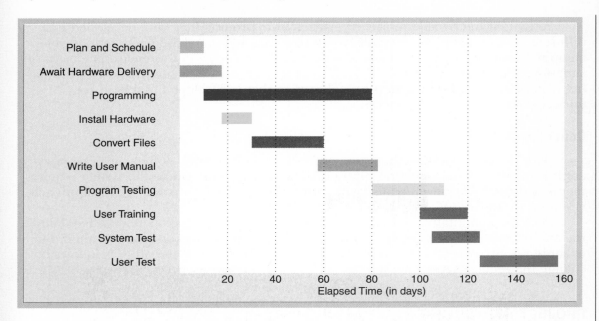

Figure 22   A Gantt chart for the implementation phase of a project. The chart shows 10 activities on the vertical axis and the elapsed time on the horizontal axis.

Medium-sized projects can have dozens of activities, and larger projects might have hundreds, or even thousands, of activities. A detailed Gantt chart for a very large project might be quite complex and hard to understand. To simplify the chart, the project manager can combine related activities into one task. Figure 22 shows a Gantt chart for systems development tasks. The activities labeled Programming, Write User Manual, and Program Testing actually are **activity groups**, where each activity represents several tasks. For larger projects, project managers can create multiple Gantt charts. A master chart displays the major activity groups and is followed by individual Gantt charts that show the tasks assigned to team members.

For future project phases, the time axis usually is shown as elapsed time from a zero point. For work currently in progress, the actual dates are shown on the horizontal axis.

A Gantt chart also can be used to track and report progress in several ways. First, bars can be fully or partly darkened to show completed activities, as shown in Figure 23a. Arrowheads can be used to indicate the completed portion of an activity, as shown in Figure 23b. Finally, progress can be shown by including a second bar under the schedule bar, as shown in Figure 23c.

In all cases, a vertical line indicates the current, or reporting, date. Notice that all three charts show how much of the activity has been completed, *not* whether the work is on schedule. In Figure 23c, for example, Activity 2 is about 80% complete, although 100% of the time allotted for the task has passed. Similarly, Activity 4 appears to be almost half done, although the activity has used about only 5% of the time allotted for the task.

Gantt charts often are used to report progress because they present a clear picture of project status, but they are not an ideal tool for project *control*. One problem with Gantt charts is that they do not show activity dependencies. You cannot determine from a Gantt chart the impact on the entire project caused by a single activity that falls behind schedule. Also, a Gantt chart does not show the number of hours or days required to complete an activity. The length of a bar indicates only the *time* span for completing an activity, not the number of people assigned or the person-days required. For these reasons, looking at a Gantt chart does not provide enough detail for effective project management.

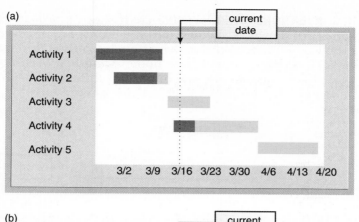

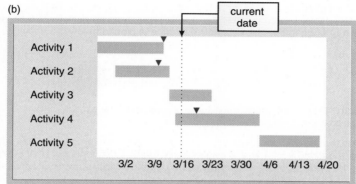

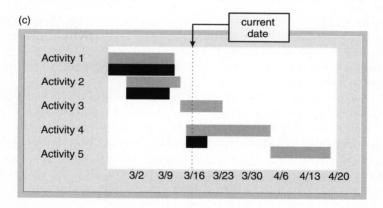

Figure 23   Three different ways to show the status of a project on a Gantt chart. In Figure 23a, the completed portion of each bar is shaded. In Figure 23b, a triangle or arrowhead, indicator is used. In Figure 23c, a second bar shows the completed work. All three methods show that Activity 1 is completed, Activity 2 is about 80% finished but behind schedule, Activity 3 has not yet started, Activity 4 is ahead of schedule, and Activity 5 has not yet begun.

PERT/CPM

The **Program Evaluation Review Technique** (**PERT**) was developed by the U.S. Navy in the 1950s to control the development of the Polaris submarine missile program. At approximately the same time, the **Critical Path Method** (**CPM**) was developed by private industry to meet similar project management needs. The important distinctions between the two methods have disappeared over time, and today the technique is called PERT, CPM, or PERT/CPM.

PERT/CPM CHARTING CONVENTIONS • A PERT/CPM chart shows a project as a network diagram. The activities are shown as **vectors,** and the events are displayed graphically as **nodes.** Figure 24a shows the event nodes drawn as circles, although rectangles also can be used. Activity **vectors,** or lines, connect one node to another. Vectors on a PERT/CPM chart are like bars on a Gantt chart, with one important difference — the length of the line has nothing to do with the duration of the activity it represents.

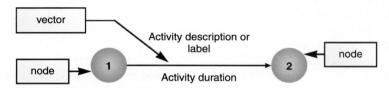

Figure 24a   In a PERT/CPM chart, a circle, or node, represents an event, or milestone, and is identified by a number. The vector line connecting the events represents an activity, or task, and is identified by a description or code letter. The estimated duration is placed below the activity.

Figure 24b   To show that one event depends on another, a dummy activity is used. The dummy activity is shown as a dashed vector line to illustrate that event 4 cannot occur until event 3 takes place. Because their only purpose is to show event dependencies, dummy activities do not have descriptions or durations.

Figure 24a shows two events connected by an activity vector. Each event is identified by a number — event 1 is the beginning of the activity, and event 2 marks the end.

For additional information on **PERT/CPM**, visit Systems Analysis and Design Toolkit More on the Web.

www.scsite.com/ sad3e/chTK/

Each activity is identified by a short description above the vector, or with a letter or code explained in a table. The estimated duration of the activity appears below the vector.

The activity connecting events 3 and 4 in Figure 24b is a **dummy activity**, which is shown by a dashed vector line. A dummy activity in a PERT/CPM chart indicates an **event dependency**, but does not require any resources or completion time. For example, the dummy activity connecting events 3 and 4 identifies that event 4 cannot take place until event 3 occurs.

When tasks must be completed in sequence, they are called **dependent,** or **serial,** activities. When activities can be completed at the same time, they are called **concurrent,** or **parallel,** activities. Figure 25a shows three dependent activities: A, B, and C. Notice that activity A must end before activity B can begin. Event 3, which marks the end of activity B, must occur before activity C can start.

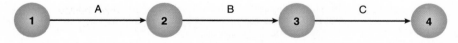

Figure 25a   Activities A, B, and C are sequential, or serial, tasks that must be completed in order. Activity A must be finished before activity B can start, and activity C cannot start until activity B is completed.

In Figure 25b, activities D and E are parallel activities that can be done at the same time, but the length of the two tasks may be different. Activity D could represent a two-week series of interviews, while activity E might show a one-day training session. Notice that activity F depends on D *and* E, and it cannot start until both D *and* E are completed. The dummy activity between events 6 and 7 connects activities D and E into a single path that leads to activity F, and shows that they both must be completed before F can begin.

Figure 26a shows a Gantt chart and Figure 26b illustrates a PERT/CPM chart. The Gantt chart includes 10 activities, some of which are groups of related activities. To keep the PERT/CPM chart simple, the same 10 activities are included. In an actual PERT/CPM chart, individual tasks are shown in more detail and all the activity dependencies are displayed.

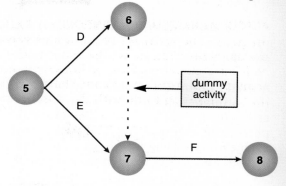

Figure 25b Activities D and E are parallel tasks that can be worked on at the same time. Both activities D and E must be finished, however, before activity F can begin. Therefore, it is necessary to show a dummy activity leading to event 7. Event 7, which marks the start of activity F, cannot begin until activities D and E are done.

(a)

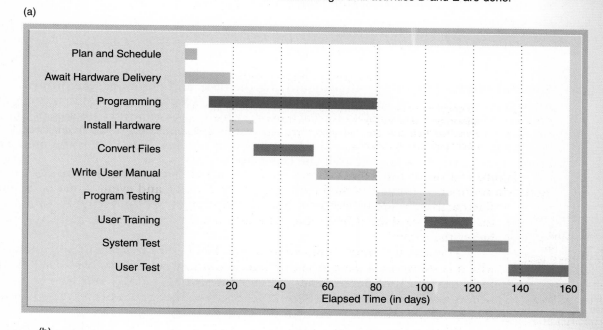

(b)

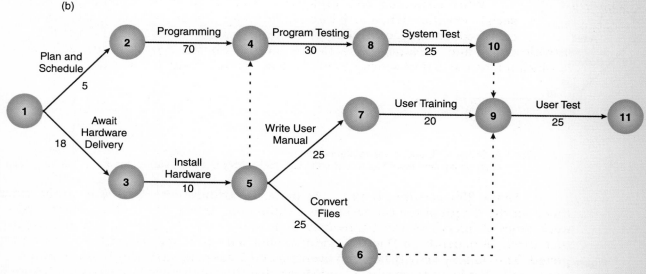

Figure 26 A Gantt chart and a PERT/CPM chart for the implementation phase of the same project shown in Figure 22 on page TK.34.

In addition to the 10 activities, the PERT/CPM chart shown in Figure 26b on the previous page includes 11 events, and three dummy activities are used to reconnect parallel paths.

ACTIVITY DURATION • Traditional PERT techniques use a weighted formula for calculating the estimated **duration** of each activity. The project manager first makes three time estimates for each activity: an optimistic estimate (O), a most likely estimate (M), and a pessimistic estimate (P). The manager then assigns a weight, or importance value to each estimate. The weight can vary, but a common approach is to use a ratio of $O = 1$, $M = 4$, and $P = 1$. The expected activity duration then is calculated as:

$$\frac{(O+4M+P)}{6}$$

For example, a project manager might estimate that a file-conversion activity could be completed in as few as 20 days or could take as many as 34 days, but most likely is to require 24 days. Using the formula, the expected activity duration is 25 days from the calculation:

$$\frac{(20+4*24+34)}{6} = 25$$

EARLIEST COMPLETION TIMES • After identifying the tasks and durations, the project manager determines the overall length of the project. The first step is to determine the **earliest completion time** (**ECT**) for each event, which is the *minimum* amount of time necessary to complete all the activities that precede the event, as shown in Figure 27. The number in the *left half* of each node is the event number. The ECT is the number entered in the *upper-right* section of the event node.

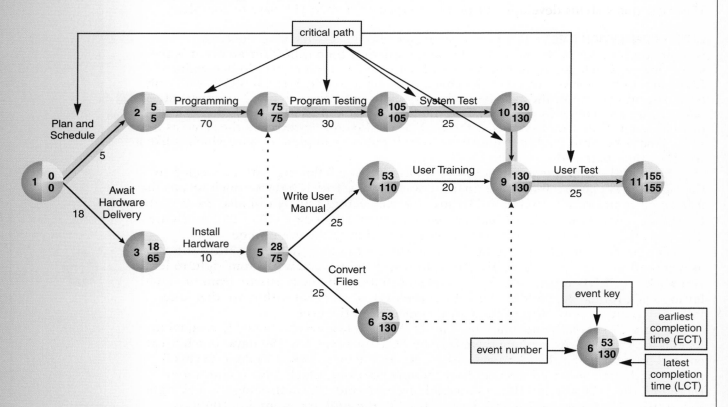

Figure 27   After doing the calculations, the PERT/CPM chart now shows the ECTs, LCTs, and the critical path.

You calculate earliest completion times by working from left to right across the chart. Event 1 always is given an ECT of zero days because no preceding events exist. The ECT for event 2 is five days, because the expected duration of the Plan and Schedule activity is five days. Similarly, the ECT for event 3 is 18 days.

To calculate the ECT for event 5, you take the ECT for the preceding event 3 and add 10 days, which is the duration of the Install Hardware activity. In these cases, the ECT for an event is determined by adding the duration of the immediately preceding activity to the ECT of the immediately preceding event.

How do you calculate the ECT for an event, such as event 4, that has more than one preceding event? Here you see a dummy activity leading into the event, showing that *both* events, 2 *and* 5, must be completed before event 4 can occur. This shows that the ECT for event 4 will be the *largest* of the earliest completion times for each path into the event. You could say that an event must await the completion of the *latest* event that precedes it. For example, if you cannot start a meeting until all four people arrive, then the meeting cannot begin until the last person arrives, although the other three already are present. Now, apply that concept to the PERT/CPM chart shown in Figure 26b on page TK.35.

As previously mentioned, two paths lead into event 4. One of the paths is 1-2-4, meaning event 1, followed by event 2, followed by event 4. The earliest completion time for this path is 75 days (5 + 70). The other path leading to event 4 is 1-3-5-4, where the dummy activity is shown. The earliest completion time for this path is 28 days (18 + 10 + 0). Because event 4 cannot occur until all preceding events have occurred, the ECT for event 4 is the largest of 75 and 28, which is 75 days. A general rule now can be stated: the ECT for any event is the *largest* of the paths leading into that event.

When you have determined ECTs for all the nodes in the PERT/CPM network, the ECT of the *last* node is the **expected project duration**. Because the ECT for event 11 is 155 days, this systems development phase is expected to take 155 days to complete.

LATEST COMPLETION TIMES • The project manager also must determine the latest completion time for each event. The **latest completion time (LCT)** for an event is the latest time at which the event can occur without delaying the project. To determine LCTs, you work *backward* through the chart, from right to left. Just like ECTs, with only one path into an event, the calculation is simple. To determine the LCT of an event, you *subtract* the last activity from the LCT of the following event, starting with the rightmost, or final, event. The first rule is that the LCT of the final event *always* is the same as its ECT. That is because the last event is the overall project completion date, which is like a specific target date with no room for slippage.

Look at the example of event 9, which has only one following path connected to the right. As explained above, the final event has an LCT of 155 days, which means that it must be completed by that time. Because the connecting activity will take 25 days, the latest that event 9 can occur *without delaying the project* is 130 days (155 - 25). As Figure 27 shows, the LCT is entered in the lower-right section of the event node.

The process for finding the LCT for an event with more than one path is the same as you used for determining ECTs, except for three points: you work from right to left, you work with LCTs rather than ECTs, and you subtract the next activity from the following LCT, rather than add it. Therefore, the LCT of an event with more than one following path is the *smallest* of the paths connected to the event.

Figure 27 shows the calculations. The LCT of the last event, event 11, is equal to its ECT of 155 days. As explained earlier, the LCT for event 9 is 130 days, which is calculated by subtracting the 25 days for the User Test activity from 155 days. Events 6 and 10 both are connected to event 9 by dummy activities, which have no duration; therefore, the LCT also is 130 days for both events 6 and 10. Continuing to work right to left, the LCT for event 7 is 110 days (130 - 20), the LCT for event 8 is 105 days (130 - 25), and the LCT for event 4 is 75 days (105 - 30).

What about the LCT for event 5? Event 5 connects to three other events (4, 6, and 7) so you must calculate all three to see which is the smallest. You would proceed as follows:

Event 4:   75 days (75 - 0)

Event 7:   105 days (130 - 25)

Event 6:   85 days (110 - 25)

Thus, the LCT for event 5 is 75 days, the *smallest* of 75, 85, and 105.

In Figure 27, each node contains three numbers. You already know that the number in the left half of a node is the event identification number, and the number in the upper-right section is the ECT for the event. The number in the lower-right is the LCT event.

The **slack time** for an event is the amount of time by which an event can be late without delaying the project. The slack time for an event is the difference between its LCT and ECT. You can see that the Convert Files activity could be completed as *early* as 53 days (ECT) and as *late* as 130 days (LCT). Therefore, the slack time is 77 days (130 - 53). That means that this event could be as many as 77 days behind schedule without delaying the project schedule or affecting the project completion date.

CRITICAL PATH • At least one complete path will exist through a PERT/CPM network for which every node has equal ECTs and LCTs. In Figure 27 on page TK.38, the ECTs and LCTs are equal for every event in the path 1-2-4-8-10-9-11. That path is called the critical path and has been highlighted in the figure. A **critical path** is a series of events and activities with no slack time. If any activity along the critical path falls behind schedule, the entire project schedule is similarly delayed. As the name implies, a critical path includes all activities that are vital to the project schedule. Project managers always must know what the critical path is, so they can monitor progress and make prompt decisions, if necessary, to keep the project on track.

Comparing Gantt Charts and PERT/CPM

One significant advantage of PERT/CPM charts is that, unlike Gantt charts, all individual activities and dependencies are shown. Most project managers find PERT/CPM charts very helpful for scheduling, monitoring, and controlling projects. A project manager would convert all ECTs and LCTs to actual dates by laying out the entire project on a calendar. Then, on any given day, the manager can compare what *should* be happening to what *is* taking place, and react accordingly.

PERT/CPM charts differ from Gantt charts in two respects. First, a PERT/CPM chart for even a small project can be rather complicated, and the degree of complexity increases significantly for larger projects. Secondly, the picture presented by a PERT/CPM chart is not as clear as a Gantt chart, which graphically displays the timing and duration of the activities.

PERT/CPM and Gantt charts are not mutually exclusive techniques. Project managers often use both methods. Neither Gantt charts nor PERT/CPM, however, handle the scheduling of personnel and the allocation of resources. To achieve efficient utilization of people, time, and company resources, you must use other tools and techniques.

PROJECT MONITORING, CONTROLLING, AND REPORTING

 project must be planned, organized, and scheduled before the work actually starts. After the project activities begin, the project manager concentrates on leading, directing, and controlling the project.

Project Monitoring and Control

The project manager must set standards and ensure that they are followed, keep track of the activities and progress of team members, compare actual progress to the project plan, and verify the completion of project milestones. To help ensure that quality standards are met, many project managers institute structured walkthroughs. A **structured walkthrough** is a review of a project team member's work by other members of the team. Generally, systems analysts review the work of other systems analysts, and programmers review the work of other programmers as a form of peer review. Structured walkthroughs should take place throughout the SDLC and are called **requirements reviews**, **design reviews**, **code reviews**, or **testing reviews**, depending on the phase in which they occur.

Setting a schedule can be a challenging task, but following it is even more difficult. Most projects run into at least some problems or delays. By monitoring and controlling the work, the project manager tries to anticipate problems, avoid them or minimize their impact, identify potential solutions, and select the best way to solve the problem.

The better the original plan, the easier it will be to control the project. If clear, verifiable milestones exist, it will be simple to determine if and when these targets are achieved. If enough milestones and frequent checkpoints exist, problems will be detected rapidly.

A project that is planned and scheduled with PERT/CPM techniques can be tracked and controlled using the same tools. As work continues, the project manager revises the network to record actual times for completed activities and revises times for tasks that are not yet finished. Project managers often spend most of their time tracking the activities along the critical path, because delays in these tasks have the greatest potential to delay or jeopardize the project. Other activities cannot be ignored, however. If some activity off the critical path takes too long, the slack time for that task will be exceeded. At that point, the activity actually becomes part of the critical path and any further delay will push back the overall project.

PROJECT REPORTING

Members of the project team regularly report their progress to the project manager, who in turn reports to management and users. The project manager first collects, verifies, organizes, and evaluates the information he or she receives from the team. Then the manager decides which information needs to be passed along, prepares a summary that can be understood easily, adds comments and explanations if needed, and submits it to management and users.

Project Status Meetings

Although team members constantly use e-mail to communicate, most project managers schedule regular status meetings with the entire project team. At these meetings, each team member updates the group and identifies any problems or delays. Although meetings can be time-consuming, most project managers believe it is worth the effort. The sessions give team members an opportunity to share information, discuss common problems, explain new techniques, and offer comments that can be extremely valuable to team members working on other areas of the project. These meetings also give the project manger an opportunity to update the entire group, seek input, and conduct brainstorming sessions.

Project Status Reports

A project manager must report regularly to his or her immediate supervisor, upper management, and to users. Although a progress report might be given verbally to an immediate supervisor, reports to management and users usually are written. Gantt charts often are included in progress reports to show project status graphically.

Deciding how to handle potential problems can be difficult. At what point should you inform management about the possibility of cost overruns, schedule delays, or technical problems? At one extreme is the overly cautious project manager who alerts management to every potential snag and every slight delay. The danger here is that the manager loses credibility over a period of time, and management might ignore potentially serious situations. At the other extreme is the project manager who tries to handle all situations single-handedly and does not alert management until a problem is serious. By the time management learns of the problem, little time might remain in which to react or come up with a solution.

A project manager's best course of action lies somewhere between the two extremes, but probably closer to the first. If you are unsure of the consequences, you should be cautious and warn management about the possibility of a problem. When you report the situation, you also should explain what you are doing to handle and monitor the problem. If you believe the situation is beyond your control, you might want to suggest possible actions that management can take to resolve the situation. Most managers recognize that problems do occur on most projects; it is better to alert management sooner rather than later.

PROJECT MANAGEMENT SOFTWARE

Project management software can assist you in project planning, estimating, scheduling, monitoring, and reporting. Powerful project management packages offer many features, including PERT/CPM, Gantt charts, resource scheduling, project calendars, cost tracking, and cost-benefit analysis. The analyst can select output in the form of printed reports, screen displays, or graphical plots.

Figure 28a shows a Gantt chart produced by Microsoft Project, a project management program. The display includes 12 systems planning tasks, beginning with a review of the systems request and ending with a review of Internet access delays. The display is similar to the Gantt chart in Figure 26a on page TK.35 that was developed manually, although some differences exist. Notice that Saturdays and Sundays are shown as shaded areas, and that arrows indicate task dependencies.

Using Microsoft Project, you also can produce a PERT/CPM chart, as shown in Figure 28b, which is based on the same information as the Gantt chart shown in Figure 28a. Notice the several differences in the computer-generated PERT/CPM chart compared to the chart that appears in Figure 27 on page TK.36. In traditional PERT/CPM charts, events are shown as nodes and activities are shown as vectors. Computer-generated PERT/CPM charts use a reverse style, showing activities as nodes, with vectors to connect the activities. The vectors also show task dependencies, so it is unnecessary to use dummy activities with dashed lines as in the traditional PERT/CPM method.

The activity nodes in Microsoft Project are rectangular instead of circular, which is typical of PERT/CPM charts produced by project management software packages. Each node contains the activity description, activity identification number, task duration, start date, and the end date. The critical path is indicated by a bold vector line and thicker borders that outline critical path activity nodes.

You learned that project schedules, activity estimates, and personnel assignments all are interrelated. Therefore, project planning is a dynamic task and involves constant change. One significant advantage of integrated interactive project management software is that it allows the project manager to adjust schedules, estimates, and resource assignments rapidly to develop a workable plan.

For links to **Project Management Software** vendors, visit Systems Analysis and Design Toolkit More on the Web.

www.scsite.com/ sad3e/chTK/

(a)

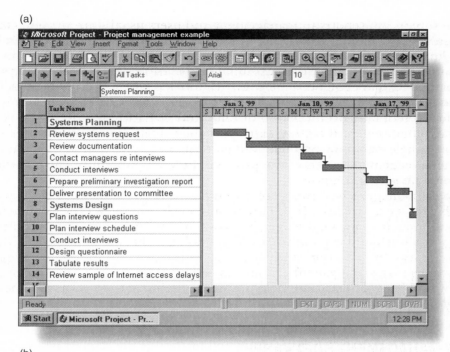

(b)

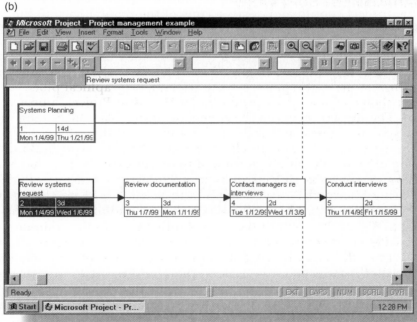

Figure 28   The Microsoft Project screen in Figure 28a shows an example of a systems development project in the form of a GANTT chart. The same information is displayed in Figure 28b in the form of a PERT/CPM chart.

SOFTWARE CHANGE CONTROL

Software change control is the process of managing and controlling changes requested *after* the system requirements document has been submitted and accepted. Software change control can be a real problem because the development process involves many compromises, and users are never entirely satisfied with the results. Changes to an information system's requirements are inevitable. The issue, therefore, is how to create an effective process for controlling changes that protects the overall project, but allows those changes that are necessary and desirable.

The project coordinator, rather than the project manager, has primary responsibility for change control because requests for change most often are initiated by someone outside the information systems department. There must be a specific process for handling requested changes. The process must be formal, but flexible enough to incorporate desired changes promptly with minimal impact to the overall project.

A procedure for processing requests for changes to an information system's requirements consists of four steps: complete a change request form, take initial action on the request, analyze the impact of the requested change, and determine the disposition of the requested change.

1. **Complete a change request form.** The person requesting the change completes a System Requirements Change Request form similar to the one shown in Figure 29. On the form, the requester describes and justifies the desired changes. The requester attaches helpful documents and pertinent information, such as new calculations, copies of government regulations, and memos from executives specifying new strategies and directions.

2. **Take initial action on the request.** The project coordinator completes a sequential control number and the date on the change request form, reviews the specific change, and then determines if the change should be deferred to a later date, rejected for specific reasons, or investigated further. If the request is deferred or rejected, the project coordinator sends a copy of the request back to the requester. If the change is to be investigated further, then the request is reviewed for impact by the project manager or a systems analyst.

3. **Analyze the impact of the requested change.** The project manager or a systems analyst must review the request and determine the impact of incorporating the change into the information system's requirements. Then, the manager or analyst prepares an impact analysis that describes the effect of the change on the information system's requirements and on costs and schedules. The analysis should address the impact of incorporating the change immediately versus incorporating the change after the currently configured information system has been implemented.

4. **Determine the disposition of the requested change.** Based on the impact analysis and the project coordinator's recommendation, the change might be accepted, deferred, or rejected. In each of these three cases, the project coordinator informs the requester of the action taken.

KEYS TO PROJECT SUCCESS

To be successful, an information system must satisfy business requirements, meet users' needs, stay within its budget, and be completed on time. What happens when these goals are not achieved?

The major objective of every system is to provide a solution to a business problem or opportunity. If the system fails to do this, then it is a failure — regardless of positive reaction from users, acceptable budget performance, or timely delivery.

When the final information system does not meet business requirements, the most likely causes include unidentified or unclear requirements, inadequately defined scope, imprecise targets, shortcuts or sloppy work during systems analysis, poor design choices, insufficient testing or inadequate testing procedures, and lack of appropriate change control. Systems also fail because of changes in the organization's culture, funding, or objectives. A system that falls short of business needs also produces problems for users, and reduces morale and productivity.

SYSTEM REQUIREMENTS CHANGE REQUEST

PRINT THE FOLLOWING INFORMATION:

NAME	
DEPARTMENT	JOB TITLE

DESCRIPTION OF CHANGE:

REASON FOR CHANGE:

ATTACH ADDITIONAL INFORMATION AND DOCUMENTS AS NEEDED:
CHECK THIS BOX IF ATTACHMENTS ARE INCLUDED: ☐

SIGNED _____ DATE _____

TO BE COMPLETED BY THE PROJECT COORDINATOR:

CONTROL NUMBER	DATE RECEIVED

IMPACT ANALYSIS:

Include an estimate of resources needed, with specific costs and timetables.

ACTION:

_____ ACCEPT

_____ DEFER UNTIL _____ (DATE)

_____ REJECT FOR THE FOLLOWING REASONS:

SIGNED _____ DATE _____

Figure 29   Sample of a Change Request form. Notice the Impact Analysis section. If a system has a great number of changes, what does that indicate?

Cost overruns typically result from unrealistic estimates that either were too optimistic or were based on incomplete definitions of work to be done, from poor monitoring of progress and inadequate reaction to early signs of problems, or from schedule delays due to unanticipated factors.

Overdue or late completion of projects can indicate a failure to recognize activity interdependencies, confusing effort with progress, poor monitoring and control of progress, personality conflicts among the team members, or turnover of project personnel.

The failure of an information system usually is due to a failure in project management. If the project manager fails to plan, staff, organize, supervise, communicate, motivate, evaluate, direct, and control properly, then the project is certain to fail. Even when factors outside the project manager's control contribute to the failure, the project manager is responsible if those factors were not recognized quickly and handled appropriately.

When the project manager first recognizes that a project is in trouble, behind schedule, or out of control, what options are available? In general, these are the four options: trimming the project requirements, adding to the project resources, delaying the project deadline, and improving the quality of the project management.

Sometimes, when a project experiences delays or cost overruns, the system still can be delivered on time and within budget if several less critical requirements are trimmed. The system can be delivered to satisfy the most necessary requirements, and additional features can be added later as a part of a maintenance or enhancement project.

If a project is in trouble because of a lack of resources or organizational support, management might be willing to give the project a higher priority for computer turn-around times, clerical support, end user attention, and management decisions. If more project work needs to be completed than people to do it, adding more people to the project team might help. Adding staff, however, will reduce the time necessary to complete the work only if the work to be done can be divided into separate tasks on which different people can work.

If the problem is that current team members lack experience or technical proficiency, you might obtain expert temporary help, such as consultants, contract programmers or analysts, or service bureau personnel. Adding staff might require time for training and orienting new people, however. At some point, adding more people to a project actually increases the time necessary to complete the project. Adding new staff also means adding costs, with the potential for going over the budgeted project costs.

The action most often taken when a project is behind schedule is to add more time to the schedule. Additional time is an alternative only if the original target date is not an absolute deadline that must be met and if extending the target date will not result in excessive costs.

When a project is in trouble for whatever reason, the project manager must try to get the project back under control and keep it under control.

SUMMARY

Project management is the process of defining, planning, organizing, leading, and controlling the development of an information system. Project management is important throughout the SDLC, but is especially vital during the implementation phase of a project. The primary objective of project management is to deliver a system that meets all requirements on time and within budget. Although the project manager can use a variety of software tools that make the job easier, he or she must have a clear understanding of project management concepts and techniques.

Project management begins with identifying and planning all specific activities or tasks. Projects also have events or milestones that provide major reference points to monitor progress. After identifying the tasks, project managers must develop a work schedule that assigns specific tasks to project team members.

Time estimates for tasks usually are made in person-days. A person-day represents the work that one person can accomplish in one day. Estimating the time for project activities is more difficult with larger systems. To develop estimates, project managers often use a quantitative method, an experience method, or a constraint method.

The quantitative method is based on the size and nature of the task, the experience of the programmer or analyst, and the productivity that can be expected. The experience method considers similar projects, where the systems are comparable in terms of size, basic content, and operating environment. The constraint method is used when one or more fixed resources exist, such as time, dollars, or personnel. Based on the constraints, the project manager must adjust specifications or use *what-if* analysis to calculate alternatives.

In project scheduling, the project manager develops a specific time for each activity, based on available resources and whether the task is dependent on other activities being accomplished earlier. The project manager can use graphical tools such as Gantt charts and PERT/CPM charts to assist in the scheduling process.

A Gantt chart is a horizontal bar chart that represents the project schedule, with time on the horizontal axis and tasks arranged vertically. It shows individual tasks and activity groups, which include several tasks. In a Gantt chart, the length of the bar indicates the duration of the tasks. Progress can be displayed, but Gantt charts do not show task dependency details of resource assignment.

A PERT/CPM chart shows the project as a network diagram, with activities shown as vectors and events displayed as nodes. Using a prescribed calculation method, the project manager uses a PERT/CPM charts to determine the overall duration of the project, and provide specific information for each activity, including the earliest completion time (ECT), the latest completion time (LCT). With this information, the manager can determine the critical path, which is the sequence of tasks that must be performed on time in order to meet the overall project deadline.

A project manager uses a variety of techniques to monitor, control, and report project efforts. These methods include structured walkthroughs, which are reviews of a team member's work by other team members. A project manager also keeps team members and others posted with regular reports and periodic meetings.

Software change control is concerned with change requests that arise after the system requirements document has been approved, and most companies establish a specific procedure for managing such requests. A typical change control procedure consists of four steps: completion of a change request form, initial determination, impact analysis, and final disposition.

In the end, every successful information system must support business requirements, satisfy users, stay within budget, and be available on time. Sound project management involves the same skills as any type of management. The project manager must be perceptive, analytical, well-organized, and a good communicator. If the project manager senses that the project is offtrack, he or she must take immediate steps to diagnose and solve the problem.

Review Questions

1. What is project management and what are its main objectives?

2. What is the relationship among activities (or tasks) and events (or milestones)?

3. If Project A has twice as many resources as Project B, will Project A be twice as complex as Project B? Why or why not?

4. In project estimating, describe the quantitative method, the experience method, and the constraint method.

5. What makes an activity dependent on another activity? What is the difference between dependent (or serial) and concurrent (or parallel) activities?

6. Describe the characteristics, advantages, and disadvantages of a Gantt chart.

7. Describe the characteristics, advantages, and disadvantages of a PERT/CPM chart.

8. What do the terms, best case, probable case, and worst case mean, and how does a project manager use these concepts to estimate activity duration?

9. How does a project manager calculate earliest completion time (ECT) and latest completion time (LCT) for the tasks in a project?

10. What is a critical path and why it important to project managers?

11. Name three examples of techniques used for project monitoring, controlling, and reporting.

12. What is software change control, and what are the four steps involved?

Index